Robert Maynard Hutchins
A Memoir

Also by Milton Mayer

Biodegradable Man
The Nature of the Beast
If Men Were Angels
The Art of the Impossible: A Study of the Czech Resistance
Man versus the State
Anatomy of Anti-Communism (with others)
What Can a Man Do?
Humanistic Education and Western Civilization (with others)
Revolution in Education (with Mortimer J. Adler)
The Tradition of Freedom (ed.)
Young Man in a Hurry: The Life of William Rainey Harper
They Thought They Were Free: The Germans, 1933–1945
Speak Truth to Power (with others)
Steps in the Dark (with John P. Howe)

Robert Maynard Hutchins
A Memoir

MILTON MAYER
Edited by John H. Hicks
Foreword by Studs Terkel

University of California Press

BERKELEY   LOS ANGELES   OXFORD

The publisher gratefully acknowledges the contribution provided by the General Endowment Fund of the Associates of the University of California Press.

University of California Press
Berkeley and Los Angeles, California

University of California Press, Ltd.
Oxford, England

Library of Congress Cataloging-in-Publication Data

Mayer, Milton Sanford, 1908–
    Robert Maynard Hutchins : a memoir / Milton Mayer; edited by John
H. Hicks; foreword by Studs Terkel.
        p.   cm.
    Includes bibliographical references and index.
    ISBN 0-520-07091-7 (alk. paper)
    1. Hutchins, Robert Maynard, 1899–   .   2. University of Chicago—
Presidents—Biography.   3. University of Chicago—History.
4. Center for the Study of Democratic Institutions—History.
I. Hicks, John H. (John Harland), 1919–   .   II. Title.
LD925 1929.M39   1993
378.773'11—dc20
                                                                    92-16512

Printed in the United States of America
9 8 7 6 5 4 3 2 1

The paper used in this publication meets the minimum requirements of
American National Standard for Information Sciences—Permanence
of Paper for Printed Library Materials, ANSI Z39.48-1984. ∞

To Ms. Baby—"My name is Jane"—*Mayer, without whom neither I, nor this book, nor the world would be.*

Contents

Illustrations follow page 276

Foreword

They were a couple of naturals, Robert Hutchins and Milton Mayer. It was preordained (if you are theologically inclined) that one would write a biography of the other. That it turns out to be something of a memoir, too, is no accident; both were "characters" in the deepest sense: they were inordinately possessed of character.

Their wit was acerbic and quicksilv'ry, but you can find that in any good cerebral comic. Their singularity lay in their vision: a world in which it would be easier for people to behave decently. A sane, enlightened society. What comes forth in these pages is an unconventional life story recounted by "the hired hand" (Mayer's self-description), irreverent, yet loving, and by its very nature, revelatory.

Robert Maynard Hutchins was cut from an archetypal American mold, a preacher's son with Calvin in his blood. Yet he was something else: a tragic hero out of the Greeks. Fatally flawed. It was not hubris that was his ultimate undoing, though his stiff-necked pride was, to put it mildly, overbearing. It was the epoch he lived through. The times were out of joint; he was out of sync.

We see in this work the Boy President (the youngest ever to head a world-renowned university) gradually change from Blake's golden youth bursting through the sun into a sudden, defeated old man. Yet his imprint on American education, thanks to his imagination, daring, and yes, stiff-neckedness, is indelible. He made learning an exciting adventure.

As for the biographer, he came out of the hard-boiled school of Chicago journalism. Yet he was not a cut-out from *The Front Page*. He was much closer to Tom Paine than to Hildy Johnson. He also was too stiff-necked to be a hireling. There are moments in this book when it's hard to tell where

Hutchins leaves off and Mayer begins. That was another of their common attributes: a respect for the American language.

As a street-car student at the University of Chicago in the early thirties, I was aware of the young chieftain, who turned the school's curriculum on its head, much to the dismay of respected faculty members. He had allies among them, but the turmoil that ensued lasted through the twenty-two years of his tenure. I found it exciting. "The purpose of higher education is to *unsettle* the minds of young men . . . to *inflame* their intellects." (Italics mine.) You see, he gave them due warning in his June 1929 convocation speech. The man of cool demeanor was passionate in some matters. There was no apathy on this campus.

Though noncompulsory attendance, no grades, a degree after two years, and Great Books courses stirred the campus pot, his staunch defense of academic freedom was the candle that lit the darkness. In 1935, when an elderly maverick professor, beloved by his students, was attacked by the witch-hunters for his "communistic" teachings and some trustees called for his head, a faculty member confronted Hutchins. "If the trustees fire Lovett, you'll receive the resignations of twenty full professors tomorrow morning." The president replied, "Oh, no, I won't. My successor will." That said it all.

A personal memory. Two years later, that old professor, Robert Morss Lovett, chaired an indignation rally in Chicago. It was a few days after the 1937 Memorial Day Massacre, during which Chicago cops shot and killed ten steel workers, who had attended a union picnic. Fifty-three years later, I'm still touched by the fire in the old man's voice: "Mooney is a killer!" It was his recurring refrain, his reference to the police captain who ordered the attack. It is good to know that his university's president would sooner have been sacked himself than sack this man.

L'affaire Lovett came off with Hutchins a laughing winner. It was the niece of a wealthy drugstore magnate who had accused the old man. That set off the hearings; an inquisition that turned into burlesque. Hutchins persuaded the magnate to fork over a half-million as a grant to the university. To save him further public embarrassment. Golden Boy was equally adept in raising money as he was in raising hell. The man of the Ideal, who warned students against practical men, was himself remarkably practical when it came down to the nitty-gritty, money.

He had no such luck fifteen years later. In 1950, with Hutchins heading the Fund for the Republic, the Cold War was at its most frigid, the Red scare at its most scary. The man, "the impudent spirit," was as intransigent as ever. He insisted that any member of the Communist Party had the right to teach in American schools, provided he was competent in his field and did not impose his views on his students. "I ought to have the courage to say he should be appointed without regard to his political associations. The popularity or unpopularity of a man's views shall not determine whether or not he may be a professor." Does he surrender his fundamental rights as an American citizen to think as he pleases once he becomes a teacher? Hutchins called on the Romans: "Let justice be done though the heavens fall."

And they fell, you bet. It was an avalanche. This one really asked for it, at a time when all practical men ran for cover. Every two-bit patriot, every journalistic pander, every hack congressman had open season on Robert Maynard Hutchins. Though he came off badly bruised and never quite recovered, the credo remained intact: "Let justice be done. . . ." Though his tall, frailing frame was bending, he was as stiff-necked as ever. His darkest hour may have been his most shining.

Prescience was another hallmark of the man. During his VE Day sermon, while still at the university, he warned: "We are on the verge of forgetting history. A bleak, torpid epoch may lie ahead." Yet when Enrico Fermi and his colleagues caused that nuclear chain reaction behind the abandoned stands of Stagg Field, he was enthusiastic, if somewhat hyperbolic: "This is history's greatest moment." Hiroshima changed his opinion quick as a nuclear flash. The remainder of his days were spent in large part challenging the myth of scientific secrecy and society's madness in the guise of "national security." He insisted, "War is the ultimate wickedness, the ultimate stupidity."

While on the subject of stupidity, Hutchins had shocked college alumni from sea to shining sea by abolishing football at the university. His reasoning was irrefutable: "It was possible to win twelve letters without learning to write one." Oh, RMH, where are you, now that we need you?

There is a tale told that may be apocryphal, though I wouldn't bet on it. Shortly after Hiroshima, while ruminating on Fermi and history's greatest moment, Hutchins is reputed to have said, "We should never have given up football."

Always, Robert Maynard Hutchins was against the grain. Had he been otherwise, had he played ball, had he gone along, as all ambitious ones do—and make no mistake, he was ambitious—he might eventually have become president of the United States. There was such talk in high circles in the thirties. His was the quandary of Jimmy Durante: Did you ever have the feeling you wanted to go and still have the feeling you wanted to stay?

I, for one, am glad he stayed at the university as long as he did. Consider this passage from his 1935 commencement address: "'Getting on' is the greatest American aspiration. The way to get on is to be safe, to be sound, to be agreeable, to be inoffensive, to have no views on important matters not sanctioned by the majority, by your superiors, or by your group. You are closer to the truth now than you will ever be again. Don't let practical men surrender your ideals. . . ." Damn, I missed that one. I was in the class of '34. Still, I glory in it, as I've discovered in this book by "the hired hand."

Studs Terkel

Acknowledgments

My debt to my friends is immense and unpayable. Here are the friends who each and several helped me write this book. Many of them are gone now, some of them long gone. I celebrate them here, the dead and the quick, and thank them for their loving labors, most especially John H. Hicks, lately of the University of Massachusetts (Amherst). Long a distinguished editor of the *Massachusetts Review*, John Hicks saw the manuscript in early progress and then undertook to help me see it through over a period of devoted years; a man whose (and whose wife's) exemplary conscientiousness is matched by his unflagging civility and by his positive genius as an editor.

Mortimer J. Adler; the late Frederick Lewis Allen; Harry S. Ashmore; Ivan von Auw; the late Stringfellow Barr; Sabrina Barton; Saul Bellow; the late Helen Benton; the late William Benton; Jean Friedberg Block; Elizabeth Mann Borgese; William Brandon; Clarissa Hutchins Bronson; the late Scott Buchanan; Catherine Carver; Henry Steele Commager; the late Winthrop Dakin; the late Esther Donnelly; James H. Douglas, Jr.; Patricia Douglas; the late Paul H. Douglas; the late Gordon Dupee; Clifton Fadiman; the late Clarence H. Faust; Andrew Fetler; W. H. Ferry; the late John Fischer; Noel B. Gerson; Ruth M. Grodzins; Ruth Hammen; Bobbie Harms; John D. Harms; Sydney J. Harris; Richard Haven; Robert Hemenway; Priscilla Gibson Hicks; the late Paul Hoffman; Hallock Hoffman; Jeanette Hopkins; the late John P. Howe; Francis Hutchins; Maude Phelps McVeigh Hutchins; the late Robert Maynard Hutchins; Vesta Hutchins; the late William Hutchins; Mrs. William Hutchins; the late Paul Jacobs; the late Joseph Jaffe; the late Wilbur Jerger; Amy Kass; Louise Kelley; Frank K. Kelly; the late Laura Bergquist Knebel; Herman Kogan; The late Philip LaFollette; Edward H. Levi; the late Sinclair Lewis; Donald McDonald; the late Archibald MacLeish; Robert C. McNamara; Dexter Masters; Bertha Tepper Mayer; the late Richard McKeon; the late W.C. Munnecke; the late William O'Meara; the late Max Otto; the late Robert Pollack; the late Edward Reed; Thomas C. Reeves; the late Arthur L.H. Rubin; the late Morris H. Rubin; the late Carl Sandburg; William P. Schenk; Joseph J. Schwab; Rosamund McGill Schwab; John Seeley; Stanley Sheinbaum; Leone Stein; Lloyd E. Stein; the late Rexford Guy Tugwell; Ralph W. Tyler; the late Mark Van Doren; Carl Friedrich von Weizsäcker; Phyllis Westberg; Harvey Wheeler; John Wilkinson; the late Thornton Wilder; the late Clara Winston; the late Richard Winston.

The generous assistance of the National Endowment for the Humanities facilitated the research and writing of this book.

An earlier version of the chapter entitled "The Red Room" appeared in *The Massachusetts Review* 16, no. 3 (Summer 1975): 520–50.

I wish also to thank the librarians at the Joseph Regenstein Library at the University of Chicago for their courtesies and their assistance.

For permitting me access to papers and records in the Hutchins archives at their respective institutions, I thank the president and trustees of the University of Chicago and of Oberlin College, and the officers of the Center for the Study of Democratic Institutions, Santa Barbara, California.

I express my gratitude as well to members of the Hutchins family for granting me interviews and other valuable assistance.

Carmel, California
March 1986

Introduction

Robert Maynard Hutchins (1899–1977): dean, Yale Law School (1928–29); president, University of Chicago (1930–1951); associate director, Ford Foundation (1951–54); president, Fund for the Republic (1954–77); chairman, board of editors, Encyclopaedia Britannica (1947–77); president, Center for Study of Democratic Institutions (1959–73, 1975–77); author of (inter alia) *No Friendly Voice, The Higher Learning in America, Education for Freedom, The Democratic Dilemma, The Conflict in Education, The University of Utopia, The Learning Society.*

Though it embodies all the relevant biographical materials, this is not an orthodox biography; the author appears passim in both professional and personal relation to the subject. (They were friends and associates for forty years.) Neither is it a linear account of educational reform—it is not a book "on" education—though this central aspect of Hutchins' career is dealt with as appropriate. It is, rather, a nearly-a-success story of the preacher's son, phenomenally bright, preternaturally handsome, who comes sauntering out of small-town Ohio ("Cleveland was forty miles away, but it might as well have been in China") to dazzle Yale with his insouciance (with two years off in between, "mastering all of the arts implied in the verb 'to soldier'"); rockets into the upper reaches of the American 1920s as the Boy President of a great university (he was inaugurated a month before the 1929 crash); and within five years is a figure of the first eminence both in educational innovation and in liberal politics. (At seventy-five he told a friend, "I should have died at thirty-five.")

Remorselessly driven by duty—though he thought he had sloughed off the atavistic Calvinism—he managed to keep himself so busy his life long that he never had time to confront his dilemmas or his disorders and disasters—surviving a brilliant, impossible marriage; manipulating a

1

thousand prima donnas; fighting those same prima donnas (in the end unsuccessfully) on administrative and educational policy; prying the liberal arts and his (and Aristotle's) iron metaphysics of the Rational Animal into the curriculum; making new enemies and attacking old ones; preparing and delivering a total of eleven hundred speeches (or eleven speeches eleven hundred times); teaching college freshmen the classics; getting rid of intercollegiate football; leaving Chicago (the country's oldest university president in point of service) for the new Ford Foundation ("We have a half-billion dollars and we're going to change the temper of the country in two years"—a childishly innocent prophecy; the country changed all right, for the McCarthyite worse); and, finally, running his would-be Athenian academy in Santa Barbara with his stable of fairly Great Minds shuffling (if not resolving) the Great Issues, and nobody paying much attention to it.

At Chicago he had knocked the spots off the adding-machine-cum-lockstep-cum-fun-and-frolic of the higher learning, establishing a new model for the country (and the world); parlayed the reading of the great books into a national industry and a commercial bonanza; insisted that "PhDs be doctors of philosophy"; and maneuvered his mendicant corporation through the Depression (and the freest of universities through the Red hunts). He turned down top New Deal jobs, the while finagling to get the topmost job—and kicking that prospect away by being an ardent isolationist before Pearl Harbor (immediately afterward becoming the prime contractor for the atomic bomb). He wrote, and spoke, not just brilliantly but radically for across-the-board social change (including world government, after Hiroshima): the establishment's antiestablishmentarian, for fifty years slopping water from both elegant shoulders as he wheedled the rich; and lived on to see most (not all) of his efforts undone or disappointed, his high hopes dilapidated, his dark-unto-ebon predictions materialized in the national plunge to illiteracy, consumerism, banality.

A cautionary tale of as good a man as a great man can be, and as lively a wit as a man, great or small, can be possessed of.

Beginning with his defense of Sacco and Vanzetti as a young instructor in the Yale Law School, he sallied forth again and again from the ivory tower (which he was sapping from the clerestory) to do brazen battle on the social front. But his influence rested, and rests, on his challenge to twentieth-century education—as vivid a challenge today (more so; more so) as it was when he first mounted it against the moral and intellectual relativists, the progressivists, and the electivists of the 1930s. President Clark Kerr of the University of California called him "the last of the giants."

Prologue: Hired Hand

I was desperate that April afternoon in 1937—not because I might lose my job with William Randolph Hearst's *Chicago American*, but because I might not. Covering Robert Maynard Hutchins' public performances for the *American*, I had seen him a half-dozen times since I'd interviewed him for the *Forum* magazine in 1933. True, the city editor had not let me cover the state legislature's investigation of the University of Chicago for subversive activities in 1935; I was assumed to be a partisan of the university and Chief was assumed to be a partisan of Charles R. Walgreen, the drugstore magnate and double-page advertiser whose niece had informed her uncle that her professors had been teaching her communism. I went to the "Walgreen" hearings anyway.

Some time later the city editor of the *American* threw me a University of Chicago handout: the commencement address to the class of 1935, by President Robert M. Hutchins. As the paper's University of Chicago specialist—except for the Walgreen affair—I had fifteen minutes in which to scan it and cut it down to a five-head story of three short-as-possible paragraphs. Instead of scanning it, I read it. And then I read it again. And then read it again and missed the deadline. It began:

> My experience and observation lead me to warn you that the greatest, the most insidious, the most paralyzing danger you will face is the danger of corruption. Time will corrupt you. Your friends, your wives or husbands, your business or professional associates will corrupt you; your social, political, and financial ambitions will corrupt you. The worst thing about life is that it is demoralizing.

It went on:

"Getting on" is the great American aspiration. The way to get on is to be safe, to be sound, to be agreeable, to be inoffensive, to have no views on important matters not sanctioned by the majority, by your superiors, or by your group. We are convinced that by knowing the right people, wearing the right clothes, saying the right things, holding the right opinions, and thinking the right thoughts, we shall all get on; we shall all get on to some motion-picture paradise, surrounded by fine cars, refreshing drinks, and admiring ladies. So persuasive is this picture that we find politicians during campaigns making every effort to avoid saying anything; we find important people condoning fraud and corruption in high places because it would be upsetting to attack it; and we find, I fear, that university presidents limit their utterances to platitudes. Timidity thus engendered turns into habit.

And it ended:

So I am worried about your morals. This University will not have done its whole duty to the nation if you give way before the current of contemporary life. Believe me, you are closer to the truth now than you will ever be again. Do not let "practical" men tell you that you should surrender your ideals because they are impractical. Do not be reconciled to dishonesty, indecency, and brutality because gentlemanly ways have been discovered of being dishonest, indecent, and brutal. As time passes, resist the corruption that comes with it. Take your stand now before time has corrupted you.[1]

Last call for salvation.

The deadline for the three-paragraph five-head passed and I was still sitting there in the city room with the handout in my hand. Not a word about the Rational Animal. (Hutchins was supposed to exemplify the Rational Animal and the Discipline of the Intellect.) Every word about what he had been saying all along was none of education's business, namely, morals. Where was the intellect—and what would it do for politicians, important people, and university presidents who took care to say nothing, who condoned fraud, who uttered platitudes? Apparently what was wanted in this life was not the capacity to reason but the capacity to resist rationalizing. Where was it to be got?

This might be interesting.

This might be so interesting that, still sitting there with that commencement address in my hand, still June 1935, I phoned the university for a copy of the speech Hutchins had given when the "Walgreen" headhunters tried to shut the place down for subversion a couple of months before. I had heard it on the radio, over NBC. The speech was entitled "What Is a University?" and as I recalled it, it was a reasoned defense of reasoning. It began with that rat-a-tat trademark.

> A university is a community of scholars. It is not a kindergarten; it is not a club; it is not a reform school; it is not a political party; it is not an agency of propaganda. A university is a community of scholars.

Reasonable enough. And then:

> Socrates used to say that the one thing he knew positively was that we were under the duty to inquire. Inquiry involves still, as it did with Socrates, the discussion of all important problems and of all points of view. You will even find Socrates discussing Communism in the *Republic* of Plato. The charge upon which Socrates was executed was the same that is now hurled at our own educators: he was accused of corrupting the youth. The scholars of America are attempting in their humble way to follow the profession of Socrates. Some people talk as if they would like to visit upon these scholars the same fate which Socrates suffered. Such people should be reminded that the Athenians missed Socrates when he was gone.

Still reasonable enough, but a rising undertone there. And then, at the end:

> In America we have had such confidence in democracy that we have been willing to support institutions of higher learning in which truth might be pursued and, when found, might be communicated to our people. We have not been afraid of the truth, or afraid to hope that it might emerge from the clash of opinion. The American people must decide whether they will longer tolerate the search for truth. If they will, the universities will endure and give light and leading to the nation. If they will not, we can blow out the light and fight it out in the dark; for when the voice of reason is silenced the rattle of machine guns begins.[2]

But this, when you read it, was not the voice of reason. This was an appeal to confidence and courage and hope and tolerance—none of which was one of Aristotle's intellectual virtues. This was a commitment, not to the process of inquiry but to the *duty* to inquire, not to the pursuit of truth but to the *will* to pursue it; a call and a challenge and a warning, a preachment, a prophecy. "Such people should be reminded that the Athenians missed Socrates when he was gone."

The Rational Animal was a missionary in academic drag. But it took me two more years of Hearst, ever further from the truth, to make my way to the altar rail.

When I entered the sanctuary sore-hearted that day in April of 1937—a lifetime ago and a world away—the missionary was reading the English pages of the Greek-English Loeb edition of Aristotle's *Metaphysics*. He always said afterward that I was lying when I said he had his feet on the desk. He had his feet, actually, *in* his desk, in the top left-hand drawer, which was otherwise empty. The top right-hand drawer was filled with oddities he found in the newspapers or that people, who were always giving him oddities, gave him, such as the announcement of the award somewhere of a doctorate of philosophy for a dissertation on the Bacteriological Content of the Cotton Undershirt or somewhere else of a course in Family Living (the last unit of which was How to Be Livable, Lovable, and Datable). In the center drawer he kept two small signs, which he displayed on appropriate occasions: "Don't Tell the President Things He Already Knows" and "We Wash Money."

He looked down on me and said, "The last time you favored me with a visitation"—if he had meant "visit," he would have said "visit"—"you were in better shape than you are now. You had been an Old Plan boy and, in consequence of your having been an Old Plan boy, you were unemployed. You may remember"—*he* remembered—"that on that occasion I despaired of anybody's ever being able to do anything for you. I was right, as usual. Look at you now. You are a hireling of Hearst. You ought to be ashamed. Are you ashamed?"

"Worse than ashamed," I said, "and that's what I've come to talk to you about."

He looked at his watch and said, "Professor Adler and I have to conduct a great books class in half an hour—this," holding up the *Metaphysics*, "is a great book—and Professor Adler will be here in twenty minutes to tell me what to think. So make it snappy, son." *Son.*

"I have come to be saved," I said.

"You have come to the right party," he said. "What do you want to be saved from?"

"Not 'what,'" I said, "'whom.'"

"Nobody ever needs saving from anybody else," he said. "Who do you mistakenly think threatens you besides Milton Mayer?"

"William Randolph Hearst," I said.

"Don't tell me you aren't happy working for Hearst," he said, "and besides, what has Hearst got to do with your being saved or lost?"

"How did you get saved from him?" I said.

"I didn't," he said. "Four years ago, when I was chairman of the Regional Labor Board I found for a CIO union and Hearst called me an accomplice of Communists and murderers. When he found he couldn't lick me, he tried to join me; he offered me a job. I turned it down and became an accomplice of Communists and murderers again. But you're wasting my time. What do you want me to do?"

"Save me."

"What will you do to be saved?"

"Anything."

"Anything?"

"Anything."

"How much is Hearst paying you?"

"Ninety. I'm the white-headed boy."

"I'll give you forty-five and you'll be the black-headed man."

"I can't live on that," I said.

"You didn't say you wanted to live," he said, "you said you wanted to be saved. You cannot be saved any cheaper."

Mousetrapped. "Your offer is irresistible," I said. "What can I do?"

"Get educated, like me," holding up the *Metaphysics* again. "I will introduce you to Professor Adler, who is educated, and he will introduce you to Aristotle, and you will learn that the cause of all ruin is ignorance, a condition which you exemplify by supposing that Hearst is the cause of your or anybody else's ruin. Hearst is not a cause but an effect—and a secondary effect at that. He is a secondary effect of ignorance. Wise up."

"How?"

"By reading the books, or even, like me, by buying them and intending to read them. I was ignorant, like you, until I became a university president with nothing to do but intend to read the books. Look at me now. You too can do this. You can't become a university president, because you're a Jew, and neither can you be buried in the university chapel, where I'm going to be buried if they kill me before they fire me. Now get out of here like a good fellow—or at any rate get out of here—and think it over."

Think it over, my foot.

"Bob"—this is Thornton Wilder—"has the habit of being right." He wasn't right the day he hired me at forty-five a week. He could have had me at twenty-two-fifty.

Part One

OBERLIN

1   The End of an Erea

January 17, 1899.

Fin de siècle, or, as it was translated from the French by Alderman Hinky Dink Kenna of Chicago's First Ward, the end of an erea.

On January 17, 1899, two remarkable boys were born to two modest families in Brooklyn, one on Herkimer Street (near the firehouse), one on Navy Street (near the corner of Sands and the entrance to the Navy Yard). Herkimer and Navy Streets were not all that far apart—nor were the two families all that widely separated economically. On Herkimer Street the family income was earned always by the father alone; on Navy, earned always by the father, the mother, and the children together. Herkimer was respectable "American" middle class; Navy was shanty-Irish, crowded hard by the new wave of Neapolitans and Sicilians. The two remarkable boys were born on different planets a few blocks apart.

Both families were pious—Brooklyn was pious—and both babies were baptized. The Caponi baby (the fourth of nine) was christened Alfonso by Father Garafalo at Santo Michele on the corner of Tillary and Lawrence, a block from Navy. The baby on Herkimer Street (the second of three) was christened Robert Maynard by his father, the Reverend William James Hutchins of the Bedford Presbyterian Church.

They were both destined, in their young prime, to emigrate to Chicago. The Lexington Hotel, headquarters of the Navy Street baby, on the corner of Michigan Avenue and Twenty-Second, was not all that far from the Herkimer Street baby's hangout at Fifty-Ninth and University. And in Chicago they were destined, each in his own way, to set that city, and with it the country and the world, on its ear. Each in his own way, they were destined to be immortalized among the great entrepreneurs of the new era, dreamers, both, of no small dreams, only big ones, each in his own way a classic triumph of the American Dream.

The two boys almost met, thirty-odd years later. In the terrible national paralysis of 1932 President Hutchins of the University of Chicago had taken on the direction of a local effort to raise ten million dollars—he raised eleven—for relief of the starving unemployed. The drive began with the solicitation of one hundred thousand dollars from each of ten leading citizens, and the tenth was yet to be found when Hutchins and the chairman of the Citizens' Committee discussed the situation. Hutchins: "I think I can get the tenth man, and I'd like to go to see him. He's rich, he's generous, and I doubt that he's been approached." Chairman: "Who is he?" Hutchins: "Al Capone." Chairman: "No—it's out of the question. We can't accept money from a criminal."[1]

(It was on that same occasion that the chairman of the Citizens' Committee had to get somewhere in a hurry and could not make a train connection in time. Hutchins suggested that he fly. "Young man," said the chairman, "if you had the responsibility of fourteen billion dollars of other people's money, *you* wouldn't fly." But it wasn't long afterward that the chairman, whose name was Samuel Insul., and whose Middle West Utilities empire had collapsed, found himself one step ahead of the sheriff, and fled, and flew, to Canada.)

2 The Way It Maybe Was

Robert was eight—his brothers twelve and four—when he discovered there were no Indians in Oberlin, Ohio. It was a great disappointment. He didn't want to fight Indians; he just wanted to see them. Instead, he saw what he later recalled as "the hottest, coldest, wettest, flattest part of the state of Ohio."[1] Oberlin College had been established by Congregational missionaries "who selected the most disagreeable part of Ohio they could find in order to be sure that they were not living in luxury."[2] It was a long, long way from the new era that was burgeoning even in Brooklyn. He had been a city boy for eight years, and now he found himself on a Puritan island of two thousand souls consecrated by its founders to "the total abolition of all forms of sin." Oberlin College was one of the oldest and most reputable in the west. In Congregational ecumenicity it welcomed the services of a distinguished Presbyterian preacher who had entered the ministry from the associated Oberlin Graduate School of Theology (where free-will "Oberlin Calvinism," embracing revivalism *and* abolitionism, had flourished in the 1830s, 40s, and 50s).

Now Will Hutchins was back there, with his wife and three boys, living in a faculty boarding house. After Yale (class of '92), he had begun his theological studies at the nonsectarian Union Seminary in New York and finished them at Oberlin. (His father, Robert Grosvenor Hutchins, had been graduated from the nonsectarian Williams College in 1862, when less than 1 percent of the male college-age population of the country got a higher education, and had then prepared for the ministry at Union and Andover Seminary in Massachusetts. Early in his preaching career he had been pastor of the Second Congregational Church in Oberlin and was later a trustee of the college.) For Robert's father, if not for Robert, Oberlin was more like home than Brooklyn was.

Oberlin was not only nonsectarian. It was the first college in the United States to admit women and Negroes. Even in 1907 there weren't many such, and the very few women who had gone beyond high school in the 1890s had attended women's colleges like Mount Holyoke—from which Anna Laura Murch had been graduated before her marriage to Will Hutchins. Her New England ancestors had been sea captains. (*Their* Scottish ancestry was attested by her given names.) They were an especially rugged, dogged breed. Her father had gone to sea at the age of eleven on a four-year voyage. She was intelligent and capable, a quiet woman who, however, had no great difficulty in keeping her three sons in order, and no difficulty at all in sharing her husband's life as a preacher and professor.

But for Will Hutchins, giving up preaching for the teaching of preaching was a considerable change. One of its attractions was an immediate jump in salary from eight hundred dollars a year to two thousand. On two thousand a year a professor could rent a good-size frame house on Elm Street. By the time the boys were ready for college their father's salary had risen to five thousand dollars—the maximum then paid a professor in the United States except in the universities. The boys all did odd jobs around town to earn money for college. With the family's installation at Mrs. Rawdon's faculty boarding house, Robert, at eight, found himself waiting table at lunch (called dinner)—and never dreamed that he shouldn't be. That summer he had a short-lived job as a printer's devil at the local press, which paid four dollars a week.

There were no rich or even "comfortable" families in Oberlin, Ohio. The students all had jobs, after school, weekends, summers, and the self-supporting student enjoyed an elevated social standing merely because he was self-supporting. (The college motto was "Learning and Labor.") The life of service would be the life of austerity. Everyone was plain, every pleasure plain. No one was hungry or ever would be. In Oberlin, economic insecurity, like economic splendor, was unknown. Parents took care of their children, and children, when their parents were old, took care of their parents.

After his sons were grown and gone, Will Hutchins left Oberlin for a hardy adventure—the presidency of little Berea College in Kentucky, a school for mountain boys that in those days lived from hand to mouth, and after his retirement from Berea he became president of the Danforth Foundation in St. Louis.

The Oberlin salary would not have moved Will Hutchins to leave the ministry for education. He was moved by something he called the Cause. His sons knew what the Cause was without his ever having had to explicate. The Cause was doing good, in the sense of leading men and women to the Christian life. He was not a fundamentalist, but what was known then as a "full Gospel" man, bent on influencing lives in the interest of service here below. Long afterward, a fellow president of a university complained to Robert Hutchins about an Oberlin graduate in his faculty. The man was excellent in his field, but he was always stirring up trouble about "public questions." Hutchins could have told the president that that's what he got for hiring an Oberlin graduate. "Public questions" were as much the essence of Oberlin as the abolition of all forms of sin. The college had been a station on the Underground Railroad, and in Robert's boyhood the campus still had two little red buildings crumbling away at the corners that had been used to house the fugitives on their way to Canada. The Martyrs' Arch memorialized the Oberlin graduates who as missionaries had been killed in the Boer War. Oberlin was beset by a sense of mission abroad and at home, and a professorship of preaching was as much a ministry as the ministry itself.

"At fourteen I was going to be a missionary,"[3] said Bob Hutchins afterward. "Every fourteen-year-old in Oberlin was going to be a missionary." Oberlin's sons and daughters thought of themselves as "going out," with the Gospel of Christ and the gospel of service, into missionary occupations. Fifteen years out of college, Robert Hutchins found that if one of his classmates was actually engaged in making money he was almost always apologetic about it and insistent upon telling his fellow alumni privately that his extracurricular life was devoted to civic betterment. Law was not an entirely respectable vocation—there was too much money-wrangling about it. But doctoring (even for women) was a high calling; *its* modest temporal rewards did not discountenance its high professions. Nursing was, of course, a particularly suitable career for an Oberlin woman, whether or not she became a missionary's (or a preacher's) wife. And a high proportion of female graduates went into the then limited field of "social work," in the city settlement houses or church welfare agencies.

But the Oberlin professor of preaching had no occasion to doubt that his sons would be either preachers (or missionaries, or both) or teachers in church-related schools. Two of Will Hutchins' three gratified his expectations. William, the eldest, became a master at the Presbyterian-founded Westminster School in Connecticut. Francis (always "Frank"), the youngest and most religious of the three, eventually succeeded his father as president of Berea College, after serving as director of Yale-in-China (where his father's evangelical contemporaries had cried, "A million a month are dying without God!"). But Robert—well, Robert turned out differently. He turned out to be dedicated to Christian service—if the expression may be used loosely to embrace the running of a university—but without ever being able to confess Christianity.

Not that his boyhood was any different from William's and Frank's, nor their home different from any other in Oberlin. The sense of obligation was bred in the bone; it did not weigh on them. It all went without saying. It went without saying, when Will Hutchins (watching the time for his first class) put his watch on the table at breakfast, with its Phi Beta Kappa key on the fob, that his three sons would one day have Phi Beta Kappa keys on *their* watch fobs. It went without saying that there was college chapel every day, and church twice on Sunday, and Christian Endeavor meeting Wednesday, and choir practice Friday evening. Oberlin had two choirs, and any student who could even try to sing was a member of one or the other.

The consequences of all this exposure to the Light and the Leading were considerable, especially for Robert Hutchins, who was never able to eradicate anything from his memory. His life long, his speeches were laced with allusions to Scripture—usually unattributed, because it would never occur to an old Oberlin boy that their source would not be recognized; as a college teacher he was amazed to encounter a senior who had never heard of Joshua. And he invariably found himself "singing, humming, or moaning third-rate hymns like 'Blessed Be the Tie That Binds,' while shaving, while waiting on the platform to make a speech or catch a train, or in other moments of abstraction or crisis."[4] On one occasion in later life he explained—though there were other explanations he found it harder to make—that the outward signs of inward grace that he endured in his boyhood made it "very hard for me to go to church now." (On yet another occasion he said that he had been unable to go to church for many years because of his father's sermons: "Every other preacher seems so vapid, insipid, vacuous, fatuous, inane, and empty that I cannot listen to him.")

It was not that the Oberlin young were unwholesomely religious or depressingly earnest. Rather, these observances, to which they were not always attentive, were among the centerpieces of their daily and hourly furnishings. "We had no radios, no automobiles, no movies, and no pulp magazines. We had to entertain ourselves. We could not, by turning a small knob or paying a small fee, get somebody else to do it for us. It never occurred to us that, unless we could go somewhere or do something, our lives were empty. We had nowhere to go and no way to get there."[5]

That wasn't quite the case. They had nowhere to go, but they did have a way to get there. Mr. Thomas W. Henderson's big red touring car— he had retired to Oberlin as vice-president of the Winton Motor Car

Company—was parked outside the Second Congregational Church every Thursday evening for prayer meeting. Cars (and houses) weren't locked in Oberlin, and Sophomore Hutchins and three classmates went joyriding in it. They were going to return it before church services were over, but it ran out of gas outside of town. The thieves pushed it off the road and walked home. The next day a $150 reward notice for the return of the stolen car was posted all over town. The scoundrels went to Mr. Henderson's house and confessed. Mr. Henderson called the mayor over and the mayor suggested the county jail in Elyria. The four penitents suggested that the irate Mr. Henderson join them in prayer then and there. He did so, and cooled off, and decided not to press charges. Sixty years later one of the culprits, recalling the event in the *Cleveland Plain Dealer*, said that as the shriven sinners were leaving the house, the "show-off" Hutchins began his fund-raising career by proposing (unsuccessfully) that the victim split the $150 reward money with them.[6]

Apart from stealing automobiles, "our recreations were limited to two: reading and physical exercise. The first meant reading anything you could lay your hands on. The second meant playing tennis." So the Oberlin boy acquired some knowledge of one good book—the Good Book—and the habit of reading. He had all the more time for reading because of what he later maintained was his intense aversion to physical exercise, masked by the alibi that he had no time for it. (He claimed to have inherited the aversion from his father.)

He was a tough, strong boy (as he would be a man), so strong and tough that he was a prime target of the Oberlin College upperclassmen in the free-for-all "initiation" of the freshmen, from which he emerged, still on his feet, so exhausted that his father succeeded in having the college put an end to hazing. And as president of his freshman class he scaled the impressively high college heating-plant chimney by night to adorn it with his class numerals: 1919.[7]

He was inordinately tall for his age, and at twelve he was captain of the freshman basketball team in high school. But that was just about his last appearance as an *athleticus*. He decided that he was going to get to be taller than anybody—he said afterward that it was the only decision of his life that he made stick—and sacrificed his every other activity to that determination. He added the extra cubit lying on his bed reading "and," said his brother William, "reading and reading" while ("according to me," said William) his brothers did the chores.[8] At fourteen Robert topped his father by an inch and stood six feet. ("My height," he said later, "has been of enormous advantage to me in the course of my public career. It has enabled me to change light bulbs that the ordinary man cannot reach.")

The children of Oberlin professors attended the four-year Oberlin Academy free. Bob Hutchins made a clean sweep of the academy's distinctions. In the 1915 yearbook there appeared the following item under the heading "An Intimate Interview": "Mr. Robert M. Hutchins, President of the Senior Class, stepped up to Mr. Robert M. Hutchins, President of the Athletic Association, who was walking down the hall accompanied by Mr. Robert M. Hutchins, Captain of the Debate Team, Mr. Robert M. Hutchins, Manager of the Football Team, Mr. Robert M. Hutchins, Manager of the Glee Club, Mr. Robert M. Hutchins of the Men's Council and the Tennis Team, and Mr. Robert M. Hutchins, the Commencement Orator. 'Hello, Bunch,' remarked the President, 'Where is Mr. Robert M. Hutchins, the Sporting Editor of the Annual?' 'Hello, President,' answered the Captain and the Manager and their friends, 'he's over at the Second Church Choir practice.' 'Much obliged, fellows,' returned the President. 'I just wanted to see him a moment about writing up the Class basketball for the last two years, when he has been Captain of the Team.'"

He made his first public address at fourteen, and after some eleven hundred subsequent platform appearances he was still, at seventy-five, uncomfortable as a "set" speaker. But he was a debater born. He would never stop arguing, and he started early. As a small boy he was amusing but saucy—or, as his aunt complained to his father, "smart," meaning smart-aleck, with a proclivity for breaking into the talk of his elders with an always relevant (but not always timely) observation that revealed the impatience of a quick intelligence quickly bored.[9] His sauciness was unabated in later life, but he had got it under urbane control. He appeared to be the most equable of men.

Whenever he was complimented on his graceful forbearance (and it was often) his reply, "My father always said that there is no excuse for bad manners" or "My mother always told me to be polite," suggested that his aunt's complaint had produced some effective remonstrance. But the quick impatience abode beneath the urbanity. He would wait his turn, and wait beyond his turn—and then let go with, more often than not, a question so ingenuously put that the colloquist did not know where or how he had been hit. He learned to suffer fools faultlessly, to listen (or appear to listen). But he never learned to suffer them gladly. The pedestrian Henry Luce (whose envy of him was a lifelong love-hate passion) called him a wisecracker. Alexander Woollcott and Harry Hopkins and Sinclair Lewis and Carl Sandburg and Aldous Huxley and Harold Ickes and Gertrude Stein (and Alice B. Toklas) thought that he was just great.

How he got that way, or was born that way, is not to be discovered in the family annals. His father, his mother, his brothers weren't like that.

He was never to lose that compulsive impudence of spirit that lifted him, again and again, when the personal (not the institutional) stakes were high enough, to an insistence on having his say, if necessary to the detriment of the Cause, a compulsion to upset his own apple cart. (One day at the height of his twenty years' war at the University of Chicago, his dean of humanities, Dick McKeon, when the two of them were walking to a meeting of the faculty senate, tried to argue him out of letting a critical issue come to the floor. "We haven't got the votes," said McKeon, "there's no point in going in there and getting licked." "Let's go in there and get licked," said Hutchins. And they did.)[10]

It didn't happen that way consistently, or even customarily; the life of the successful administrator is one of both shameful and shameless truckling. But it happened again and again. (What university president would have done anything but dodge when the McCarthyites crowded him into a corner and asked him if he would have a Communist on his faculty? But this one said, "Of course I would, if the competent colleagues regarded him as competent in his field and his social views did not affect his competence.")[11]

There is a behavior pattern that is adequately explained by masochism; or by parental influence; or by Hutchins—alternatively or in combination. Robert Hutchins' childhood was distorted—nourished, *he* said—by the stories of his ancestors' independence, ancestors who were "all of them stubborn and some of them vain. Their notion of success did not seem to involve material goods as much as it did holding onto their own convictions in the face of external pressure. I began to think at an early age that the ideal American was the perpendicular man."[12] The perpendicularity, if not the sauciness, was hereditary. When Robert was fourteen his father received for Christmas a portrait of a friend of his "who had amassed a great deal of money and power by concentrating on doing so, and who looked it. My father put the photograph on the piano and said, 'I will put this here to remind us of the things we are fighting against.' I have sometimes thought that if I were to write my autobiography I would call it *The Picture on the Piano.*"[13]

Nobody ever meant as much to Robert Hutchins as his father, and nothing his father ever said or did meant more than the statement he made when he put the photograph on the piano. Of all the things "we are fighting against," the earliest to which a fourteen-year-old's attention was directed was the deliberate amassing of a great deal of money.

It was an Oberlin assumption that a man might be rich or honorable, but hardly both. A Will Hutchins could accept a Teddy Roosevelt because the imperialist bully-boy (while he accepted their campaign contributions) crusaded against "the malefactors of great wealth"—among whom John D. Rockefeller's name led all the rest. Over a lifetime largely spent in convincing the malefactors of great wealth (including John D. Rockefeller, Jr.) that the things they represented were not bad things, and could be put to good uses, Robert Hutchins adverted again and again (in public as well as in private) to his father's words when the Christmas present was unwrapped on Elm Street. The picture on the piano never faded. "I still cherish the view"—this in his old age—"that the independent individual is the heart of society, that his independence is his most precious attribute, and that discussion is the essence of democracy. It is hard for me to concern myself with the material prosperity of my country or with that of the individuals who compose it, because I was brought up to believe that prosperity and power were secondary, perhaps even dangerous, goals."[14]

The man who admires independence per se is, of course, a sucker for all sorts of fanatics, as the word gets around at home and abroad that he will listen to you when nobody else will. A war veteran who rejected pacifism, President Hutchins of the University of Chicago sent a memorandum to a vice-president covering the appeal of a conscientious objector for a job: "Dear Pomp—see what you can do. I like these boys."

It was a coincidence, but no accident, that Oberlin was established the same year as the American Anti-Slavery Society, 1833. Issues burned at Oberlin, and home and school alike provided an atmosphere of continuous discussion of them. The mock political convention—Republican of course, in those parts—was traditional at Oberlin. The great extracurricular activity of the college was not intercollegiate athletics; physical fitness was encouraged, and whoever wanted to maintain it by playing football played football. (Thus Ohio State's preseason defeat of Oberlin, by 128-0, in Robert Hutchins' last year was no more exhilarating for the victors than it was desponding for the vanquished.) The great extracurricular activity at Oberlin was debating. Literary societies took the place of fraternities and sororities. "We were not merely free to talk about everything; we were required to. You were entitled to your own opinion but only if you were willing to submit it to examination and to change it if it could not survive rational scrutiny."[15]

The Congregational tradition called for congregational rule; the small college was operated by thirty-two faculty committees, an all-time record in the history of nonadministration, and the faculty encouraged the students to be no less congregational than they were themselves. There was a singular emphasis on "rational scrutiny"—singular in an institution with so strong a religious commitment, a commitment which passed from denominational to interdenominational and eventually to the nonsectarian character which, in spite of chapel and choir, set Oberlin apart from the "church colleges" that dotted Ohio. The president, in Hutchins' day, was Henry Churchill King, author of a half-dozen treatises on rational living. When President King had a cold he told the students that its cause was his failure to live rationally.[16]

Pleasures were to be weighed against pains, especially present pleasures against future pains, and dismissed accordingly. The pleasures of the mind alone were excepted from this procedure; they were *rational* pleasures. (But the pleasure of pride in the achievement of the pleasures of the mind was not to be condoned.) The students took this dedication seriously, but not so seriously that they did not have to be directed along the strait way of rationality. As the first American college to admit women, the Oberlin of Hutchins' day was still acutely sensitive to what was then called the boy-girl problem. Dancing was of course forbidden. Freshman girls were required to stay in their dormitories after 6:30 P.M., sophomores after 7:30, juniors after 8:30, and seniors after 10. An uncharitable cynic might have ascribed the popularity of book-learning and singing to the fact that dormitory curfew was suspended only for choir practice and library work.

Drinking was not against the rules because nobody even contemplated so unrational an indulgence. The ultimate nonrationality came to the male students in the form of tobacco—Hutchins wanted to smoke but was too timid to break the rule—and when the son of another professor was detected smoking he was summarily expelled and the community agreed that the only thing for that boy to do was to join the navy.[17]

If the life of Oberlin College in the early decades of the twentieth century was deadly, those who lived it didn't know it. It never occurred to them that there was any other way to live. "It was only many years afterward that a classmate of mine named Thornton Wilder drew my attention to the fact that our early environment had been highly unusual."[18]

In at least one respect it was not unusual. "I do not remember that I ever thought about being educated at all. I thought of getting through school. This, as I recall it, was a business of passing examinations and meeting requirements, all of which were meaningless to me but presumably had some meaning to those who had me in their power."[19] He had no doubt that the Latin and Greek he studied at Oberlin Academy were supposed to do him good, but he had no idea of what particular kind of good they were intended to do him. Since he had got into the habit of reading, he was perfectly willing to read anything anybody gave him. Apart from a few plays of Shakespeare, nobody gave him anything good to read until he was a sophomore in college, when he was allowed to examine the grammar and philology of Plato's *Apology* in a Greek course. And since he had

"had" an unusual amount of German, he was permitted to take a course on *Faust*. These were the only good books that anybody would give him to read until he was president of the University of Chicago long afterward and Mortimer Adler gave him all the good books to read at once.

"My father once happened to remark to me that he had never liked mathematics. Since I admired my father very much, it became a point of honor with me not to like mathematics either. I finally squeezed through Solid Geometry. But when at the age of sixteen, I entered college, I found that you could take either mathematics or Greek. (Of course, if you took Greek, you were allowed to drop Latin.) I did not hesitate a moment. Languages were pie for me. It would have been unfilial to take mathematics. I took advanced Greek, and have never seen a mathematics book since. I have been permitted to glory in the possession of an unmathematical mind."[20]

His scientific attainments were of the same order. (It did not take the scientists at the University of Chicago long to find this out and, having found it out, to convict him of being antiscientific when his only offenses were being nonscientific and more than ordinarily suspicious that scientific work taught nobody anything more than scientific work). He had got through a course in physics at Oberlin Academy with a high grade—but only because his father expected his sons to get through all their courses with high grades. (It was long afterward and, of course, at Yale that he first learned that it was respectable to pass a course with a "gentleman's C.")

One course in science was required by the college "because one course in everything, in everything, that is, but Greek *and* mathematics, was required by the College."[21] After he had blown up too many retorts in the Oberlin laboratory doing the Marsh test for arsenic, the chemistry professor was glad to give him a high grade and get rid of him. What he later remembered of college philosophy, prior to his becoming a philosophical university president, was that the text book in a ten weeks' course in the history of philosophy had green covers and pictures of Plato and Aristotle. "I learned later that the pictures were wholly imaginary representations of these writers. I have some reason now to believe that the content of the book bore the same relation to their doctrines."[22]

His formal education, then, when he left Oberlin at the end of his sophomore year, had given him no understanding of science, mathematics, or philosophy. It had added almost nothing to his knowledge of literature. He had some facility with language, but he was not long away from Oberlin before he found himself unable to read Latin or Greek except by guesswork. (He retained a mastery of German through the accident of being able to find nothing in English during his military service in Italy, but several books in German.) So, when he left Oberlin, he had, he said later, no idea of what he was doing or why.[23] College was a lot of courses. You toiled your way through those which were required and for the rest wandered around taking those that seemed most entertaining (or least boring). The days of the week and the hours of the day at which courses were offered were, he said, perhaps the most important factor in determining the Oberlin (like every other college's) student's course of study.

Not quite monstrosities, then, or juvenile monks and nuns, but college students. It was a time when college still had magic, largely because so few had the means to go, when colleges did not call themselves universities, and when college professors were teachers and college teaching a vocation. It was a time when a university had two or three thousand students. A college like Oberlin had a thousand, all of whom knew each other and nearly all of whom came from within a small, homogeneous area. The mark that college made—not the courses, but the college—was indelible, and the mark that Oberlin made peculiarly so.

Innocent sons of innocent fathers in an innocent time and place, preparing, or being prepared, without their thinking about it, to sally forth from its innocent fastness with no other purpose than to change the world or, more likely, innocently fail in trying. Was it really like that? "Of course not," said Hutchins fifty years afterward. "It wasn't like that because it couldn't have been. Nothing could have been. It was either a dream, or something like a dream. I suppose that everything that has happened since has been so bad that that's the way it seems it was."

He always said that he could not bear sentimentality—which he carefully distinguished from sentiment—and made the point in billing himself as the sentimental alumnus when he returned to Oberlin, fifteen years after he left it, to speak at Convocation in the college chapel. The sentimental alumnus—and he, he said, was the sentimental alumnus par excellence— sees his alma mater "through a rosy haze that gets thicker with the years. He wants to imagine that it is like what he thought it was like in his time. He sees a beautiful uniqueness about the period when he was in college. That period has not been equaled before or since. The sole object of the institution should be to return to those glorious days that produced him."[24]

He was the most sentimental, and therefore the most dangerous, of all alumni because his sentimentality was compounded by the emotions we all have when we think of home. "It is impossible for me to separate the streets of Oberlin, the trees, the buildings, the activities of the College, from my family and my family's friends who in those surroundings were a part of those activities. And since those were the most impressionable years of my life, those people seem to me much more real than you whom I see before me now, and far more gifted." A mirage, and "the inhabitants of that mirage move against a background that you will tell me has long since disappeared. Indeed, you will say that they may have, many of them, disappeared themselves. You may even hint that neither the place nor the people ever existed as I claim. This may be true for you, but not for me. For me there is no retiring age for faculty, nor any new appointments to it. For me the Class of 1919 never went to war and never graduated. This static, beautiful Oberlin wherein my friends and I are forever young and forever friends deprives me of the powers of reason and leaves me only the power of recollection."[25]

That was fifteen years after Oberlin. Fifty-five years after Oberlin "a classmate of mine named Thornton Wilder" said: "Bob was righter about Oberlin than you'll ever get him to say. It really was something like that. We were young and serene—imagine, young *and* serene. We didn't know what we were, but we knew where we were. Our inner life, so terribly hard for young people today, was untroubled in its essentials. Our fathers— Bob's was a notable case—were possessed of unassailable omniscience. They knew everything, and our mothers knew how to do everything. There were sorrows and some hardships, there were sickness and accidents and disappointments and bickering and dying and being born. But there was something that went on and on and carried us with it, into it, through it, out of it, and beyond."[26] Something like what Hutchins might have referred to as "a play called *Our Town*," in which "the strain's so bad that every sixteen hours everybody lies down and gets a rest."

3 Fallen Away

Innocent sons of innocent fathers...and grandfathers. Grandfather Robert Grosvenor Hutchins was preaching the Memorial Day sermon at the Second Congregational Church of Oberlin, and Bobby, age ten, went to the services with his father. (As best he could later remember, Billy, fourteen, and Frank, six, were not along.) Memorial Day was still a stirring occasion in 1909 in Oberlin. It memorialized the Civil War to abolish chattel slavery; and Oberlin people, some still alive, had played a great role in the abolition movement and the war.

At sixty-seven, Grandfather Hutchins was in his fervent prime. He had the voice, orotund, organistic, that the popular evangelist required. His son Will was a less spectacular preacher, a product of the new day of the "higher criticism" of Scripture, equal in faith to his father, superior in education, but decidedly inferior in what was already being referred to as Bible-banging. The differences between the two generations were highly visible, and Bobby at ten was aware of them. But Memorial Day was a stirring occasion, and Grandfather Hutchins was one of the great stirrers of the region round.

He was describing the way Abraham Lincoln, when confronted with a dilemma, would get down on his knees and pray to the Lord for guidance. Carried away with his parishioners—or further than his parishioners—the preacher sank to his knees in the pulpit and prayed for guidance in his dilemmas, just as the Martyred President had in *his*. Will Hutchins took his son Bobby by the hand and said something like, "Let's get out of here" (as Bobby would later recall it), and they got.[1]

Bobby, when he had long since become Robert Maynard, did not recall how badly he himself had been put off by his grandfather's performance, but he remembered how badly his father had been put off—and that was enough for him. The incident did not move him to commit himself to the Lord; it moved him to commit himself to public decorum. All his life he would find himself vaguely uncomfortable on the platform. He was to become the lowest-keyed of orators, the barest-boned of debaters, the driest of wits.

If his grandfather's bathos was already an anachronism in a college community at the beginning of the twentieth century, his father, for all his restraint, was nevertheless heir to the limitations that in the earlier genera-tion produced the bathos. There is no doubt that Will Hutchins was a fine preacher. "A great preacher," his son said, and his sermons "very good, beautiful." But his greatness as a preacher did not depend on the goodness of his sermons. "The reason that my father was a great preacher was sug-gested to me by my step-grandmother. She said the reason Will was a great preacher was that everybody could see when he preached that he was a good man."[2] One day the president of the University of Chicago would put his feet up on his desk and open Aristotle's *Rhetoric* (which he and Mor-timer Adler would be teaching in another twenty minutes), and for the first time read that the most potent of all means of persuasion is "the ethos of the speaker," and lay the book down and recall his step-grandmother's words about his father.

Will Hutchins personified the ethos of the speaker, and so (on his knees in the pulpit) did Grandfather. But there is a fine line between descant and cant. If Bobby Hutchins gagged at his grandfather's exaltation at the Second Congregational Church on Memorial Day in 1909, he would have gagged at his father's incantation a decade later, which won a five-thousand-dollar prize and publication in the *American Magazine*.[3] It had to have come from the author's heart. But it came from his mind in addition—the mind his son recalled as first rate.

The prize was established by the National Institute of Moral Instruc-tion, whose chairman, one Milton Fairchild, was "trying to place character education on the same plane with 'the three R's in the public schools.'"

The winning Code of Morals consisted (after a preamble) of ten laws. (The preamble read: "Boys and girls who are good Americans try to be-come strong and useful, that our country may become ever greater and better. Therefore they obey the laws of right living which the best Amer-icans have always obeyed.") Each law had its own preamble, which began, in all ten instances, with the phrase, "The Good American. . . ." The ten laws were the Law of Health, the Law of Self-Control, the Law of Self-Reliance, the Law of Reliability, the Law of Clean Play, the Law of Duty, the Law of Good Workmanship, the Law of Team-Work, the Law of Kindness, and the Law of Loyalty—and the last eighteen words of the essay (at a dollar and sixty-six cents a word) read, "He who obeys the Law of Loyalty obeys all of the other nine laws of the Good American."

Apart from the chauvinism—true, there was a war on—the Code consisted almost entirely of the unexceptional platitudes of the Boy Scout oath. And apart from a quick curtsy to independence ("I will not be afraid of being laughed at," "I will not be afraid of doing right when the crowd does wrong") and a still quicker curtsy to racial tolerance ("I will not think of myself above any other girl or boy just because I am of a different race or color or condition"), there was no least suggestion of the perpendicular man that Bobby Hutchins had been given to understand was the ideal American.

But he respected his father immensely, would always respect him, and would turn always to his father for counsel, even when the son was elderly and the father very old. The counsel was customarily moral, not intellectual. The only criticism the son was ever heard to have made, and this one off-handedly to a stranger, was that his father was "too sentimental" and "told too many stories."

But the son did not believe that morality could be inculcated by teaching (or, for that matter, by preaching). He never would believe it, and he would all his life inveigh against the claim that it could be, and against the concomitant claim that morality should have a place in the curriculum at any level.[4] That claim belonged to the age when admission to the priesthood was the object of higher education—an age that ended (some time between Grandfather Hutchins' day and his grandson's) when the importation of the university from Germany compelled the American college to accept a broader function than the preparation of ministers. There was now no faith left that morality could be instructed or that the Oberlin of 1832 could ever have achieved its goal of the total abolition of all forms of sin (or even the partial abolition of any of them). The parochial schools, Protestant, Catholic, or Jewish, still meant to make men good, but there was no evidence, hard or soft, that they did or could. It went without saying that the alumni of, say, Holy Cross were all very fine fellows. But it was not demonstrable that they were categorically finer than the alumni of, say, City College; as it should have been were there a necessary correlation between fineness and an academic program designed to impart, increase, or secure that commodity.

What Bobby, and later Robert, balked at was bathos—bathos disguised as "character education," bathos overt like his grandfather's Memorial Day sermon, bathos gussied up (had his filial piety not blinded him) as a five-thousand-dollar prize-winning Code of Morals in the *American Magazine*. There was a story told of his first predecessor at the University of Chicago who, one night in 1876, at the age of twenty, appeared at a Baptist prayer meeting in Granville, Ohio, and announced his conversion—a conversion which would one day cost Baptist John D. Rockefeller and his Baptist heirs $135 million. The young William Rainey Harper was said to have transported the prayer meeting by rising in his place and saying, "I want to be a Christian. I don't know what it is to be a Christian, but I know I am not a Christian and I want to be one." Certainly by the age of twenty his successor knew what it was to be a Christian— how could Will Hutchins' boy not know?—and knew that he wasn't one and didn't much want to be one. His aversion is not as readily datable as Harper's conversion. Was it at ten, when he heard his grandfather's sermon? At nineteen, when he read his father's Code of Morals (if he read it)? At twenty-one when, a junior at Yale, he was offered the pastorate of the Pilgrim Church of Terre Haute, Indiana, and, upon asking, and heeding, his father's advice, he found his father skeptical of his religious qualifications? In the crypto-autobiographical novel *Theophilus North*, his boyhood friend Wilder tells of his own determination to be a missionary (and a saint) between his twelfth and fourteenth years, and of his having ceased to believe in the existence of God at seventeen.[5]

There are ways, and still other ways, of looking at these things. Why didn't Will Hutchins' boy, who respected and revered his father, want to be a Christian? Why didn't he warm his father's heart by rising in his place and saying, "I don't know what it is to be a Christian, but I know I want to be one"? Because it would not have been the rational thing to do. The rational thing to do, if a boy respected and revered his father, was to find a rational basis for living the respectful and reverential life. Something had to give; in this case, God.

4   The Verb "to Soldier"

The United States entered the Great War on April 6, 1917. Universal con-scription of all able-bodied males between the ages of twenty-one and thirty was introduced almost immediately—the first time in American his-tory that draftees were not permitted to hire a substitute or buy exemption for cash. Six months later volunteering was discontinued, on the grounds that it was depleting the labor force without regard to the wartime needs of industry and agriculture. There is a military statistic that, in the light of these enactments, is unbelievable, but accurate: of the 4,500,000 men the armed forces raised in the Great War, 1,500,000 were volunteers. It was a great war in a way no such war would ever be again.

It never occurred to Bob Hutchins not to enlist, or to think of being conscripted as anything but a disgrace. But neither he nor any other college sophomore—with few exceptions—would have been drafted anyway. He had just passed his eighteenth birthday; almost none of his classmates were older than twenty. Of Oberlin's 500 male students, 232 (plus 22 women) left school for one branch or another of "the colors" in 1917. Nor did they run away from home to enlist. Their elders were glad to see them go, or at least readily resigned. And some of their elders went, too—younger in-structors, and even old: Professor William James Hutchins, father of three teenagers, left to serve with the YMCA in India.

If Bob Hutchins remembered Oberlin, Ohio, as a place so wonderful that it couldn't have been, and suspected his own memories of it, he had no least doubt that his recollection of 1917 was reliable: "President Wilson said we had to make the world safe for democracy. We didn't know what the world was, or what democracy might be outside of Oberlin (where we were already safe), but we believed President Wilson. He was a professor, like my father; he had to be honest. We believed everything. We believed everything we heard about the Huns, including the Belgian babies' hands. We believed that the Kaiser's mustache was ferocious. We believed that we were called to rescue civilization, and that we had to fight to rescue it. I don't recall anybody who wanted to serve from the depths of an over-stuffed chair in Washington; I have no difficulty at all in recalling such cases in the next war or the wars after that."

"Absolute" pacifism was unknown, unconsidered, and—outside the historic little peace churches like the Quakers, the Mennonites, the Brethren, and the Jehovah's Witnesses—unheard of. But there were some seven thousand "conchies," or conscientious objectors, the country over. They were exempted from military service—solely on the ground of religion—but the category is nowhere mentioned in the Oberlin president's annual reports during the war years.

To leap from the genteel shelter of Elm Street in Oberlin into the rugged realm of the genuine doughboy was a shocking experience for an eighteen-year-old sophomore fresh from choir practice, compulsory chapel, and Bible study. He discovered that there was a world far from Oberlin, Ohio. His two years in uniform taught him to roll cigarettes, to blow smoke rings, and to swear. (An occasional "hell" and "damn," pronounced under stress, adorned his vocabulary ever thereafter.) He learned, too, that the military arts are not liberal arts and that the manual of arms is not a Great Book.[1] With his aptitude for language, he couldn't help picking up a little French and a little more Italian. And when he happened upon a stray copy of Goethe, he tucked it into his kit and sharpened his German on it.

The cultural shock was tempered, on his side, if not on the army's, by the fact that section 587 of the US Army consisted entirely of Oberlin students organized as a unit of the Ambulance Service, a procedure that was common on college campuses where nice young men, though they may never have heard of conscientious objection, wanted to fight without hurting anybody. These were military units under military discipline, but they carried no weapons; in combat they were as likely to be hurt as were armed men. Certainly no one thought of the Ambulance Corps as dodgers.

Learning to smoke, blow smoke rings, and swear came hard. But it came because their morale was under constant attack from the day they shipped out—not to the Western Front, but to Eastern Pennsylvania. In early September they left Oberlin steeled for deadly combat. What they weren't steeled for was a deadly year converting the Allentown Fair Grounds into a camp for five thousand soldiers. They were housed in stalls and pens marked variously "Pigeons," "Horses," "Hogs," which they converted, slightly, for military use; and then in barracks, which they built.

(All these facilities were unheated, and the winter of '17 was famously cold.)[2] They dug all the ditches and did all the dirty work involved in transforming a jerry-built fairground into a jerry-built army camp. When they weren't digging, they were marching—thirty miles a day under full kit, including a tin can of water and two dry sandwiches. Looking back, Hutchins said that the thirty-mile marches had been required because "we were ambulance drivers; they got us into good walking condition so that if our cars ever broke down we could walk back."[3]

So morale sank in the mud of Allentown (and its thirty-mile environs). "As an alternative to suicide"—so he said—"I devoted myself to the mastery of all of the arts implied in the verb 'to soldier.'"[4] By way of deterioration recruits became slovenly, especially under cover of darkness when they could display their deterioration undetected. But Private Hutchins' resentment transcended caution.

One night when he was walking across the parade ground, a beautiful vision of a lieutenant crossed his path. The lieutenant had on a tailor-made hat, a tailor-made uniform, tailor-made shoes, tailor-made puttees, and a tailor-made mustache. Private Hutchins saluted him in a slovenly way, and the tailor-made lieutenant stopped him and demanded his name and serial number and the name of his commanding officer. Private Hutchins complied laconically, and the lieutenant said, "You go back and tell Captain Moore that you are not to walk across the parade ground with your blouse unbuttoned. And tell him that Lieutenant Adolphe Menjou told you so."[5] Private Hutchins thereafter walked around Hollywood (on the few later occasions that took him to that precinct) in the vain hope of crossing the path of the lieutenant again.

The deterioration and the mud were one impenetrable gumbo when, in March of 1918, section 587 was off to Italy, to remain there for a year. For the most part they saw no action, except at a distance. There were not many wounded and not many dead, and not much to do. If the world was being saved for democracy, it was being saved somewhere else. There was no romance and no heroism.

Then why did Private Hutchins get the Croce di Guerra?

"They gave everybody one."

"Let's see that Croce di Guerra."

"I lost it."

"Don't tell me that you got it for doing nothing."

"I won't try to tell you anything of the sort. I got it for heroism. Four of us were cut off from our base, and we decided we'd better stay where we were for a while. We got down to one can of cocoa, one-half can of sugar, and one can of salmon. The other boys were older than I, so they got the cocoa and sugar on the ground of seniority and I got the salmon and got jaundice and the Croce di Guerra for heroism."[6]

Like many another innocent, Private Hutchins returned from the wars neither madder nor wiser, but only less innocent. He had gone forth to save the world, and what he had done was learn how to get by, to soldier. He would ever after describe those two years as a mental and moral siesta.

There would never be another Great War. There would never be another in which hamburger steak would be rechristened liberty steak; another in which the troops would march down flower-strewn boulevards to the transports; another in which one million two hundred thousand young men, no one of whom had ever offended another, would spend a year killing one another (the whole million two hundred thousand of them) for possession and repossession and yet again repossession of a few hundred yards of desolated earth on the River Somme. One way or another each succeeding war would be greater than the one before, but there would never be another Great War.

Part Two

THE YALE MAN

5 The Yale Man

"Debating amounts to practically nothing here," the disconsolate William Benton, '21, wrote his mother back in Minnesota. "Very few take any interest in it. Only rubes are supposed even to go out for it."[1] Among the rubes who went out for it in the fall of 1919 was Robert Maynard Hutchins. The Hutchinses of Oberlin, Ohio, for all their New England lineage, and for all the Reverend William James Hutchins' having been Yale, '92, were nobodies at the Yale of the 1920s. Hutchins, '21, arrived at New Haven with no contacts and no sponsoring upperclassman except another nobody, Thornton Wilder—his Oberlin classmate who, having been demobilized early from the Coast Artillery, had come to New Haven in 1918 to enter the class of '20. But the best that Wilder had to offer was the Lizzie-Lit circle of the Elizabethan Club and the Yale Literary Magazine, where the fellows a fellow would get to know meant to become writers— men like Stephen Vincent Benet and Archibald MacLeish, or Walter Millis and Henry Luce.

They had to make it on their own, and they were likelier to make it, then and thereafter, than the gentlemen who had it made for them. They had to make it with what they had and with what they could do, not with what they were. Since most of them were self-supporting as well as bright and ambitious, they had as many outside jobs as they could rustle up, and had neither the time nor the money for social life or campus politics. They were Yale's Horatio Alger boys.

Hutchins, '21, was a war hero. But Yale was crawling with handsome war heroes in 1919. This one looked more heroic than most. As Benton recalled it, his classmates that fall were awed by his "physical splendor." He was "among the leaders of his class in academic standing. He had marked gifts as an orator," and "was clearly marked for 'success.'"[2] Lofty of mien and manner, but reserved, his reserve actually enhanced his acceptability among the gentlemen whose hallmarks were impassivity and ennui and who regarded the rubes as pushy.

This one was pushy, too, if by pushy is meant nothing more than ambitious. He was intellectually aggressive his life long, forever looking for a fight and forever finding it.

Looking back at their childhood and youth, Bill Hutchins felt that his younger brother was shy and sensitive at bottom and had developed "a manner, a shell, with which he tries to protect himself as he crusades for unpopular causes. This manner, commanding, urbane, nonchalant, sometimes forbidding,"[3] was what his boyhood friend Theodore Green (hearing him lecture after a separation of many years) called the hard mask he had clamped over his face. One of his undergraduate classmates remembered Hutchins as "stand-offish." Haughty?—No, not haughty. Arrogant?— You might think so on meeting him, but—no. Abrupt?—Not really. Sharp, clipped—you know what I mean?—but not abrupt. Taciturn?— Oh, no. Shy, then? Well, you wouldn't say shy—just stand-offish. At twenty he was already a rising master of the arm's-distance posture, easy, "informal," that characterized him ever after.

The young gentlemen he met at New Haven had not come to Yale to be saved; they had come to Yale because they were already saved. Not that they didn't have a Cause. Their Cause was not confined to Yale, but it wasn't Oberlin's. Their Cause was winning your "Y" in the Great Game of Life, and the Great Game of Life was the Money Game, or, more precisely, and more mystifying, the Still More Money Game. The aspiration of an extremely poor boy, as Hutchins was not, was intelligible; it was intelligible that Bill Benton, who had been an extremely poor boy, would write his mother that he was going to "earn all the money I can, and let everyone else go to the devil."[4] But why would very rich boys want to "get on," and on? They were born on. Private Hutchins had earned thirty dollars a month in the army, all of which, except for six dollars, was sent home to be invested in Liberty Bonds to help get him through college.

Like Benton, he wanted to earn all the money he could just then, to stay in college. He got a job in an ice cream spoon factory at sixty cents an hour. He swept floors, washed dishes, waited tables, sold clotheslines, kept books, lumberjacked, and during his two college summers, typed for Thornton Wilder's father on the New Haven paper and learned a little accounting there, and at last got to Cleveland (something he hadn't done at Oberlin) as assistant secretary of the local YMCA. In his second year on campus, as a senior, he did better. Alpha Delta Phi honored him with membership and an assistant stewardship (he had to join in order to get the job). He tutored at Rosenbaum's agency and then organized a cooperative agency of his own. The net result was a dissent from the peculiarly American myth that it is a good thing for a boy to work his way through college. It was the only opinion he ever had on education that he claimed to have come by on his own.

"I think I'm the first person in American history who ever said that working your way through college was an anti-educational program, that if you were going to college the thing to do was to beg, borrow, or steal the money and go to college and get an education."[5] He expatiated: "If we want to know whether work—by 'work' I mean here the expenditure of from one to eight or ten hours of a student's day as a dishwasher, janitor, groundskeeper, clerk, or housemaid—is good for a college student, we shall have to ask what a college is for. A college is a place to get an education. College education is the training of the young to think, to think straight, and to think for themselves. It is carried on for the immediate sake of the mind and for the ultimate sake of the character. If it were carried on for the ultimate sake of the mind, we might produce wise embezzlers or learned thieves. We are trying to produce men and women of good character. . . .

"One of the elements of good character is the habit of hard work. This brings us to dishwashing. Dishwashing is hard work with the hands. Studying is hard work with the head. Hard work with the hands may be exciting, healthful, boring, or painful. Hard work with the head is excruciating. In colleges which are actually engaged in education, studying is not only hard work, it is full-time work. As an ambitious boy I made the mistake of working my way through college. I worked as much as eight hours a day. I found that I had no energy left for study. And by energy I mean physical energy. Professor Einstein is as tired at night as you and I are, though his profession, unlike yours and mine, is strictly sedentary.

"The trouble with dishwashing as a habit is that it is preparation for a life of hard work at whatever the work turns out to be. If the work turns out to be safe-blowing, we'd prefer a sluggard to a hard worker. Good character involves something more than sweat and the habit of sweating; it involves the exercise of the mind on the distinction between good and bad and the application of that distinction to the problems that test character in later life. Study sweats a man and exercises his mind."[6]

The college curriculum—at Yale and elsewhere—did not demand much. The remedy was not to put the students to manual labor, but to reform the curriculum. The college student has four years to develop his mind and fortify his character for the fifty ahead. He can achieve both these ends at once by studying hard. "It is paradoxical that the student who loves learning so much that he is willing to slave for it must be deprived of some of the learning by the necessity of slaving."[7]

In 1940, when the president of the University of Chicago gave vent to these reflections, the American Youth Commission discovered that for every boy or girl who completed the first year of college there was a former high school classmate of equal promise and ability who was getting no further education. His education was over, not because he lacked intelligence, but because he lacked funds. "This single statistic is the answer to those who say, 'Ah, but there are scholarships.' I suppose it is generally agreed that this country needs all the brains it can lay its hands on. When we compel some of our best boys and girls to work their way through college, we assert that we do not need to develop our best brains to their fullest power. When we compel half of our best boys and girls to forego a college education if they fail to find an off-campus job, we assert that we do not need our best brains at all."[8]

Working six to eight hours a day did not prevent an ambitious student from graduating from college—"the college being what it was." What the college was was a mock-up, without moving parts, of a place to get an education—classrooms, courses, professors, students, playing fields, chapels, dining halls, dormitories, lawns, trees, and even a Fence. Hutchins, '21 cum laude, Phi Beta Kappa, did not get an education: "I graduated from college, which is not the same thing."[9]

At the end of the junior year he took the examinations for admission to the Yale Law School. Why? "Because I didn't know what else to do." Did he think he would be a lawyer? "I didn't think I'd be anything. I was afraid that with a Yale A.B. I'd be a prep school teacher all my life. I knew I couldn't be a banker or a businessman. Nobody at Oberlin would have understood it." Did he want to be a teacher? "I was afraid I'd be a teacher, so I suppose I didn't want to be. I suppose I should have obeyed that wholesome negative impulse and become a New York lawyer and been rich as well as happy. But my parents wouldn't have understood that, either."

That spring—after taking the law school admission exams—he was accosted in the library by Professor Charles E. Clark of the Yale Law School, who said: "I am impressed by your examination. Come in and see me." Insofar as anything changes a man's full-grown life, this changed his. He would still be a candidate for the AB but be permitted to do all his senior year's work in the law school, except for obeying a regulation "of obscure origin and purpose" which compelled every Yale College student working in the law school to take one two-hour course in the college. He enrolled for a two-hour course in American literature.

And that, too, changed his life. By his own testimony he had entered Yale illiterate, that is, unread. After a year he was still illiterate. What little he had read that year was textbooks. The reading of textbooks—he had found this out at Oberlin—was enough to persuade a student never to read anything again as long as he lived. But the course in American literature would require him to read some real books—or so he thought. What it required him to read was snippets from real books and then listen to the instructor talk about the whole book. But as often as not the instructor talked not about the book but about the author's life and times, which were presumed to explain the book and, of course, did not.

So it was that young Hutchins, '21 cum laude, Phi Beta Kappa, completed his college education without having read a good book—except for the three he had read before he came to Yale: the Bible, part 1 of *Faust*, and one dialogue of Plato. Nor did it appear that he would ever read any others, for the only books he read in law school were those from which the case method was taught. He discovered, as he said afterward, that "not more than two or three judges in the history of Anglo-American law have been great writers. One who is immersed long enough in the turgidities of some of the masters of the split infinitive who have graced the American bench may eventually come to write like them."[10] There was no attempt, either at Yale or anywhere else, to have the student learn anything about the intellectual history or the intellectual content of the law, or to connect it with ethics, politics, and economics.

"I see now," he said, when he had long since been a law school dean and was a university president, "that my formal education began in Law School. I do not mean to say that I knew then that I was getting an education. I am sure the professors did not know they were giving me one. They would have been shocked at such an insinuation. They thought they were teaching me law. They did not teach me any law. But they did something far more important: they introduced me to the liberal arts.

"It is sad but true"—he was saying this not at twenty-one, but at forty-one—"that the only place in an American university where the student is taught to read, write, and speak is the law school. The principal, if not the sole, merit of the case method of instruction is that the student is compelled to read accurately and carefully, to state accurately and carefully the meaning of what he has read, to criticize the reasoning of opposing cases, and to write very extended examinations in which the same standards of accuracy, care, and criticism are imposed. It is too bad that this experience is limited to very few students and that those few arrive at the stage where they may avail themselves of it only at about age twenty-two. It is unfortunate that the teachers have no training in the liberal arts as such. The whole thing is on a rough-and-ready basis, but it is grammar, rhetoric, and logic just the same, and a good deal better than none at all. One may regret, too, that the materials upon which these disciplines are employed are no more significant than they are. No case book is a great book."[11]

The process of learning how to read, write, and speak accurately, carefully, and critically, and the use of "significant materials" to facilitate the process, was to become the basis of the "Hutchins Plan" at Chicago and the Hutchins crusade everywhere. The necessary modifications were obvious: it would be made available to every college student—even to every senior high school student—and not just to law students; the teachers would be trained in the liberal arts and would know that it was the liberal arts they were teaching; and the teaching materials would be the masterpieces, old and new, of the mind and imagination of man, and not the judicial opinions of masters of the split infinitive. The Hutchins Plan would even, in time, under Dean Hutchins, change the Yale Law School and many another.

In his first year at Yale he met a girl named Maude Phelps McVeigh, the multifariously talented daughter of the editor of the New York *Sun*. They met at the home of Hutchins' one rich relative, a New York lawyer. She was almost as tall as he was, and more accomplished (in sculpture and drawing). They spoke the same sparkling language, hers a bit sharper even than his. Maude McVeigh was tough and imperious. They married—three months after he got his AB. The Hutchins ancestry produced able women and educated women. But they were not generally Career Women. They shared their husband's work and their husband's ministry. Maude McVeigh was an Eastern girl, of the sort that Yale '21 called classy. Her schooling was fashionable and her artistic talents were encouraged. She meant to have her own career—not her husband's—and she had it. If he was shy, or stand-offish, she was genuinely aloof. She wasn't meant to be a schoolteacher's wife. (Perhaps she wasn't meant to be anyone's wife.)

But in 1920 all that was up ahead somewhere and, naturally, unforeseen. In 1920 Bob Hutchins was still working his way through college. He couldn't afford most recreations, but there was one extracurricular activity he couldn't resist: he couldn't resist debating. "He could," as Bill Benton thought he remembered it, "fell an adversary with a single stroke of his ironic wit"[12]—but the stroke was toneless (and all the more effective for being so) and the wit bone-dry. His audience would never be sure that they should laugh, or even smile, and he wouldn't pause to let them.

The captain of the Yale debating team of 1920–21 was plainly a strong candidate for the 1921 DeForest Prize, awarded annually by the faculty to "that scholar of the Senior Class who shall write and pronounce an English oration in the best manner." The previous year's DeForest winner was Henry R. Luce, '20, the most vociferous anti-Bolshevik on the campus and one of the few who cared one way or another about such matters. Luce had emerged as a bidder for the prize in 1920 when he argued the case of the Russian Whites against the Reds before a sparsely attended meeting of the Yale Union. His theme—which would one day be the theme of Time, Inc.—was that if we did not intervene soon against "this radical group of Communists" in Russia, bolshevism would "undermine the civilization of the world." His audience indicated the attitude of the most advanced thinkers on the undergraduate campus by voting for his position 45 to 18.

Chosen, as a consequence, to deliver the DeForest Oration, Luce spoke about what he (and his publications) would one day call the American Century: "When we say 'America' today, we connote power. We hold the purse strings of the world. . . . America is power, and it sits astride the globe."

William James Hutchins had won the DeForest Prize in '92. So his son Robert had to win it in '21. In 1920 Harry Luce had offered America the world. In 1921 Bob Hutchins offered America Appalachia, which he characterized as the country's "back yard." His oration, entitled, "Our Contemporary Ancestors," was a straightforward exposition of the history and condition of the five million so-called hillbillies "isolated and forgotten, the mountaineers of the Southern Highlands." It was a solid report by a young man who, over the previous two years, had spent a profitable few holidays visiting the Reverend and Mrs. William James Hutchins in Berea, Kentucky.

"Our Contemporary Ancestors," in contrast with Luce's performance of the year before, seemed to be concerned not with the American challenge to the world but with the challenge to America of its own people. "Every man, woman, and child in three Highland counties was born in America, and in fifty-nine counties all but ten individuals were born in America. . . . In New York there is $2,600 worth of taxable property for every child of school age. In the mountains there is $248 worth." The ovation ended with an unpretentious appeal: "Give them the opportunities they crave, and we shall yet impart to these ancient Americans the ideals of today's America. We shall yet make the mountains 'a good place to be born in'; we shall emancipate five million people."

Hutchins was awarded the DeForest Prize in April 1921. Prizes awarded by the faculty cut no more ice with the undergraduate body than the captaincy of the debating team. What did was the selection by the senior class of its Class Day speaker in June. Hutchins was chosen. He had made the grade at Yale at last.

The Class Day speech was vintage Hutchins. In some seventeen hundred words—one of the shortest addresses he would ever make—it encapsulated in substance every Hutchins Plan that would ever be sprung.

"We have only forty-four hours more as undergraduates. Never again shall we be in a position collectively to estimate what Yale has done for us. Never again shall we be able collectively to determine what we can do for Yale. On manifold occasions in the past few years we have announced that we are for God, for Country, and for Yale. Appreciating in a vague way what it meant to support God and Country, and understanding that it was certainly the right thing to do, we have scarcely stopped to consider what constitutes being for Yale."

It was popularly supposed, he went on, that all a man had to do for Yale was to sit in its cheering section. He was moved to demur from the popular supposition. The class of '21 had entered Yale for many reasons, but probably the only one their relatives would assign was that they were to be educated there. What they had certainly done was make a few firm friends and many acquaintances. "More or less untrammeled by parental restraint, we have learned to be free without being wild and how to be self-reliant without being self-important."

According to the *Yale Daily News*, the purpose of college education was to fit a man better for his career in life. "If that definition is correct, we may say (may we not?) that we are educated men. For certainly we are better fitted for the careers we shall follow than we were four years ago. We shall most of us go into business, and in business the name of Yale carries far, opening avenues of social success that we otherwise could not travel. But if the *News'* definition is correct, is it worth while to come to college at all?" Success in business depends in the end on merit; wouldn't it be better, perhaps, to go immediately into business after prep school and get the technical training at once? And couldn't young men acquire the experience in meeting people and the social graces Yale gave them by afternoon and evening courses at some convenient country club? That would require less effort, time, and money, than their college courses had consumed.

Another definition of education might be in order. The incoming president of Yale, James Rowland Angell, had said that the purpose of college education was to inflame young men with ideas, to stimulate their intellects, to get them to think. "That is, instead of fitting a man better for his career in life, college should fit a man for a better career in life. Instead of sending its graduates out to become conventional American financial successes, which they would eventually be if they had never passed its doors, the college should develop men intellectually alive, awake to the needs of their time, eager to meet those needs, and acquainted with that most difficult exercise, thinking. Only such men may be called in any real sense 'educated.' Are we, by this standard, educated men?"

The most distressing feature of the eastern college, he went on, was the conformity which looked with disfavor and distrust upon the man who varied from the college type of thinking. "The most conservative places in the United States today are the universities. The religious and political dogmas inculcated at the paternal breakfast table we have either accepted whole or forgotten, without bringing the pressure of our own minds to bear upon them. And in this direction it can not be said that our professors have inspired us. As a member of a faculty has remarked, teachers and pupils seem individuals of different species, useful and well disposed toward one another, like a cow and a milkmaid; periodic contributions can pass between them, but not conversation."

It was true that college life merely reflected the national life. "If at colleges we have never tested what may be called the sweetness and glory of being rational animals, it is because America does not know nor highly esteem that sweetness and that glory. And we are products of America. But we are supposed to be the finest products of America . . . favored by four years of college. Can we vindicate our failure to bring forth leaders of American life by saying that we have brought forth accurate reflections of it? From the flat mediocrity, the crass commercialism, the narrow politics, the irreligion of commonplace affairs, the nation looks to the colleges, and especially to Yale, which was founded to train men for service in church and civil state. The nation looks to Yale for men who shall come up from the crowd." As about-to-be alumni, they were called to pledge their loyalty "to the high purpose of making Yale enkindle the minds of men as she has through centuries enkindled their hearts."[13]

James Rowland Angell was probably there that day; he had been made an honorary member of the class of '21. It would appear that he either heard the speech or read it, for when he summoned Alumnus Hutchins to New Haven two years later and offered him the secretaryship of the university, and Alumnus Hutchins asked him why, President Angell said; "Because you are the only member of your generation of Yale men who is interested in education";[14] to which Alumnus Hutchins replied, silently at the time, aloud ever afterward, "I didn't know that I was interested in education."

In the spring of 1921 Robert Maynard Hutchins made the ultimate grade at Yale. He was voted Most Likely to Succeed.

Why? Was it because the class of '21 was comfortably agreed that though he talked a fast game of nonconformity and coming up from the crowd, he would come around in time to the gentlemanly Episcopalian

Republicanism that led to the good banking houses or law firms? Or may it have been that the class perceived something that Benton, '21, perceived? "The rest," said Benton, "was mystery. . . . He looked at the world with ineffable sadness. Here was a young man clearly marked for 'success'—who conveyed a sense that his life must be one of atonement. For what? No one knew."[15] Hutchins himself, asked (in 1971) what he was ineffably sad about in 1921, said: "I was mourning my lost youth."

And he may have been. He—and Thornton Wilder—had been brought up in what Wilder once referred to as the late foam-rubber period of American Protestantism. Now he was exposed at last to the unsheltered life. A Yale man who would never be able to outgrow his innocence, he would never be able to leave Oberlin—or go back there. Reason enough for the sadness of the man who was now Most Likely to Succeed.

Doing what? "I didn't want to do anything special. I wanted to get a job and stay out of the tenement houses I saw around 125th Street when I took the train between New York and New Haven." "Was that your ideal then?" "Yes." "Your only ideal?" "The only one that mattered."[16]

6 A Fellow Has to Do Something

What Hutchins had been afraid of, namely, that his AB would land him in a prep school, probably for the rest of his life, is what came to pass. He had no intention of going into education, and no ground for doing so; he wasn't educated. Besides, it was a difficult occupation if you took it seriously, and Oberlin would not understand his not taking it seriously. "But a fellow had to do *something*"—and, in the fall of 1921, soon. The war boom had collapsed. Hard times were upon the land.

So he applied at all the prep schools. All the prep schools always wanted nice, clean young men from "a good school like Yale." It went without saying that he was a white Anglo-Saxon Protestant. A Phi Beta Kappa key didn't hurt, but it didn't help the way profile and politeness did. What should have helped was his having been voted—at Yale in the 1920s—Most Likely to Succeed. He should have been a cinch for a job at Hotchkiss or Groton, or Andover or Exeter. But 1921 was a buyer's market. He got a total of one offer, and grabbed it. It paid him two thousand dollars, plus what in Oberlin they call keep: housing, meals, and laundry for Mr. and Mrs. Robert M. Hutchins—she who had been Maude Phelps McVeigh. They had enough clothes and no need for a car or a house. The two thousand dollars was net.

It was also the funniest job he would ever have and the most educational. The Lake Placid–Florida School in upper New York—it moved to Florida each year for the winter—was "a semipenal institution for rich juvenile delinquents. The requirements were three. You had to be a boy. You had to have been fired out of three other schools. And your parents had to be willing to put up $3,000 (a scandalous amount then) for one last shot. The school's purpose was to get its graduates into college, no matter how. And we did. We got them all into college. They all flunked out at the end of the first semester, but we had done our part."[1]

The pupils ranged in age from twelve to twenty-one—the oldest a year younger than the new teacher of English and history. Keeping order in the classroom wasn't easy; one of the reasons many of the pupils were inmates of the Lake Placid–Florida School was that they had never been kept in order. There was no prohibition against the application of corporal means; there couldn't have been. When other forms of intimidation failed him, Hutchins threw erasers and threatened to throw a couple of dry cell batteries at them. When everything failed, as it often did, the English teacher lined his charges up against the classroom wall for a spell-down. If they hung their heads, he hit them on the head with a book; if they stood slumping, he kneed them in the stomach.

On such occasions as you managed to get and keep them in order, you had to try to get them into college. The way to do that was to get them by the College Board Examinations. The College Boards were pie if the teachers knew the tricks, and it was the moral duty of the teachers to know the tricks and apply them vigorously. One trick was spelling. The College Boards specified that if the examinee misspelled ten words on any examination, he failed the examination no matter what else he'd done on it. The trick was to train the pupils not to use words they couldn't spell. The result was a very limited vocabulary of monosyllabic words—but it was enough to meet the spelling requirement.

The history trick was a little harder. The teacher had to be careful not to confuse the pupils, so he did not allow them to read anything but the most compact textbook available. This was Muzzey's *American History*. (The College Boards assumed that there was no history that wasn't American.) Muzzey was 483 pages, and the teacher took his charges through it at the rate of 8 pages a day. They had to memorize who did what when, and the teacher had to discourage them from asking why. With Muzzey's names, dates, and places under their belts, they were almost ready for the College Boards, but the teacher had to make sure. So he got his hands on all the College Board Examinations beginning with 1909, the first year they were published, and correlated the history questions; then he drilled the answers into his class. What was required of them, in sum, was a prodigious, if short-term, memory and nothing else—especially nothing else.

Hutchins didn't learn any history, because history does not consist of names, dates, and places. But in teaching English he learned that there were rules of reading, writing, and speaking and that it was useful to know them. "I came to suspect, for the first time, that my teachers in school had had something in mind. I began to fall into the heresy that since the best way to learn something is to teach it, the only way to learn anything is to teach it. I am sure that in what is called the curriculum of the conventional school, college, or university the only people who are getting an education are the teachers. They work in more or less coherent, if narrow, fields, and they work in more or less intelligible ways. The student, on the other hand, works through a multifarious collection of disconnected courses in such a way that the realms of knowledge are likely to become less and less intelligible as he proceeds. In such an institution the only way to learn anything is to teach it. The difficulty with this procedure is that in the teacher's early years, at least, it is likely to make the education of his students even worse than it would have been otherwise."[2]

After his first year at Lake Placid it was clear that he wasn't going to be fired. The headmaster said, long afterward, that Hutchins had set high scholastic standards and had performed brilliantly. He had got his juvenile delinquents through the College Boards and had introduced an up to then unheard-of student activity, debating.[3] It seemed he was condemned to spend his life as a prep school teacher, and at Lake Placid at that. He thought that a year of it was as much as a man could stand, yet he stayed on. He wasn't interested in education and he wasn't educating anybody, but it was a living.

Getting to Utica meant getting the 3:41 A.M. train. When, half way through his second year at Lake Placid, he got a telegram from George Parmelee Day, the treasurer of Yale, asking him when and where they could meet, he said he would take the 3:41 train to Utica. Mr. Day confessed himself impressed by the young man's energy in doing so (and may have communicated his impression to President Angell).

In darkest Utica—at that hour—Mr. Day informed Hutchins that Yale was looking for a new secretary who would at the same time be an assistant to President Angell. He wanted to know if Hutchins was interested. Hutchins was. The pay would be higher (though it didn't include free laundry). He didn't know how he felt about going back to New Haven, except insofar as it meant going away from throwing erasers and reading Muzzey.

President Angell was the first non-Yale man to be president of Yale. His father had made the University of Michigan a distinguished institution. He himself, a psychologist under John Dewey, had become a professor at William Rainey Harper's University of Chicago and then head of its psychology department, dean of faculties, and acting president. Angell was not an aggressive administrator; he had, however, spotted the Hutchins of the Class Day speech.

Angell explained the job to him. The way Yale was organized under the president, there was a treasurer and comptroller on the financial side and the secretary, the actual administrative officer of the university, with a staff of some fifty persons under him. The secretary was in charge of publications and alumni and public relations. He was in charge of the secretarial staff. He was secretary of all administrative committees. And he was secretary of the corporation and of all its committees.

He was twenty-three years old.

He had drifted a long way.

7   A Blow on the Head

Hutchins became secretary of Yale on January 1, 1923, and on January 2 he received an invitation to speak to the Montclair, New Jersey, Alumni Association. He asked the secretary of the association what he wanted him to talk about. The secretary said he didn't care as long as what he said was vivid, sympathetic, and gutsy. Hutchins subsequently told his friends that he had spent the rest of his life trying to rise to the standards set by the Montclair alumni. During the two years in which (as he told his friends) he was doing oratorical work for Yale University, he delivered the customary talk about Yale as a glorious opportunity for young men of courage, brains, and ability, with its trained and devoted group of teachers, its great library, its monumental buildings, its twenty different sports. As a traveling salesman he had the advantage of appearing to be the product of the product he was pushing. He was—hadn't he dreamed of being one ten years before?—a missionary.

His one-night stands were never farther than a couple of hundred miles from home base; what would one day be the Boston-Washington corridor was where the alumni and the prep schools were clustered. Rising early and retiring late, always working and never doing anything else, neglecting his wife as he would later neglect his wife and children (and, of course, himself), he sandwiched his oratorical duties into his administrative job. The job was everything President Angell had said it was. It put him in a position to learn how a fairly large and expensive institution of higher learning was run and to see its operation as a whole. At twenty-four he was interning for a university presidency.

His interview with Angell had had an offhand quality which he himself would later display in hiring people. Something was said about a twenty-million-dollar endowment campaign, and the secretary of the university had to organize and manage it. It involved an analysis of the university's finances and the priority of its needs. It involved preparing and disseminating propaganda at a variety of levels, right up to the presentations to the foundations and the individual cultivating of the rich. This devolved on the president and the board members, but the secretary was called in on it, not merely because he was an able protagonist but because he represented to potential benefactors the kind of man they envisioned at the helm in the next generation.

His internship proceeded, not only in New Haven but, significantly, in Manhattan. The endowment campaign put him into contact with big money for the first time in his life. He would never be out of contact with it again. He discovered how the rich were located, how they were approached, how they were dealt with. This was what a university president would have to know. The endowment campaign was the capstone of his internship. He learned early that mass alumni giving is essential, but the money that counts is the big money, which does not proceed from speeches about young men of courage, brains, and ability. The young Hutchins who had lately swept floors at sixty cents an hour was now talking about hundreds of thousands, and about millions, of dollars. None of the dollars belonged to him, or ever would; no matter. The twenty million came in.

The Expense-Account Way of Life was a decade ahead. He didn't "have" an expense account; he was reimbursed for out-of-pocket expenditures in the line of duty, and he would always be as meticulous as he had been with his own sixty cents. But the comfortable reality would grow from a novelty to an unconsidered habit. Before he was thirty, he would no longer marvel to find himself in the most expensive hotels and restaurants, to find himself in the most exclusive clubs and doctors' and lawyers' offices and barbershops and haberdasheries, picking up the tab with a cursory affectation (if that much) of interest in its constituent items. He would never himself become a rich man. He would never become a sybarite. He would never become a fool. He would devote his attention and his energies to money and the moneyed—and snatch an hour early in the morning or late at night to do the things he thought a man should do, namely, thinking, writing, teaching, and arguing important issues. The things he thought a man should do he would do, the rest of his life, on the side.

Yale, which had robbed him of some of his innocence, was robbing him of more. He was still opposed to the idea of staying in education—"there was nothing I was more opposed to."[1] He didn't know why, except that educational institutions had so little to do with education and so much to do with the three deadly sins of triviality, amusement, and business. Rustling up rich donors for Yale, and the money to provide their amenities, dejected him. If he didn't want to be an educator, he certainly didn't want to be an educational administrator. Evidence shows that no sooner was he ensconced in his new job as secretary than he made a bee-line back to the law school and asked Dean Thomas W. Swan if he could resume his studies there out of hours. Swan agreed, and Professor Charles Clark—the man his entrance examination had impressed two years before—took him on as his assistant. "Being secretary of Yale didn't turn me around. It was Charlie Clark and the law school that began to turn me around. The law turned out to be completely fascinating."[2] Not because of the case method of teaching, which was employed in a superficial way; still less because of "the turgidities of some of the masters of the split infinitive" that served as teaching materials; least of all because of the trade-school purpose of the teaching. The law itself was fascinating, because it was an introduction to the liberal arts and the life of the mind.

He was graduated in June 1925, *magna cum laude*—nobody got a *summa*—which placed him at the head of his class and admitted him to the professional honor society, the Order of the Coif. Professor Clark was a perceptive man. He perceived in Hutchins both the mind and the missionary. He saw that "Oberlin" would never let the missionary engage in the practice of law (that is, the practice of money-making in the law). But he saw the gift for jurisprudence, the facility in penetrating the morass of fact, and the instinct for the issue of principle. He saw the educator beneath the disdain for a career in education.

Charlie Clark was perceptive. He was also the most influential member of the Yale Law School faculty.

Shortly before graduation a man who was to come to Yale that summer as a lecturer in public utilities law came down with appendicitis. The concatenation of this unhappy accident with the happy accident that the secretary of the university—"he's already on the payroll"—was just then graduating at the head of his law school class and did not want to practice law was an easy opening for Charlie Clark. The day after his graduation Hutchins was a lecturer in the Yale Law School.[3]

It took some fast footwork. The university required an advanced degree of every member of its faculty. There was no giving a doctorate—it would have had to be honorary, of course—to a man who had got out of law school the day before. And the matter was urgent. Dean Swan went to President Angell. The president agreed to Hutchins' part-time appointment on the condition that Hutchins remain on the job as secretary of the university. A master's degree was, technically, an advanced degree. So Robert Maynard Hutchins was immediately awarded a Master of Arts, the first of many honorary degrees conferred upon him in the course of his career. The two baccalaureates, AB and LB, were the only degrees he would ever "earn."

His qualifications for teaching public utilities law in the Yale Law School were exceptional. First, he did not want to be a teacher of anything (except insofar as teaching provided the teacher with the opportunity to learn). Second, he had never studied public utilities law (which he had to teach immediately). And third, he considered public utilities law a particularly unattractive subject. He was taken with the idea of law. He was not taken with its practice or the preparation of students for its practice.

Yale's was a how-to-do-it school; they all were. Its object was to teach the student "to make a noise like a lawyer . . . to memorize and manipulate the rules. This is what the School held itself out as doing. This is what the students expected. They were impatient with anything else, and they had the powerful support of the Bar."[4] "Anything else" was jurisprudence, the philosophy of law. (The best law schools offered an elective course in jurisprudence, generally in the last year; Yale's never attracted more than 10 percent of the graduating class. Hutchins was among the few who had taken it.)

He had already discovered that law schools prepared their charges by teaching that law was what the courts would do. "There were some progressives who thought that what the courts would do was principally determined by what the judges had for breakfast—what might be called digestive jurisprudence. But the more authoritative view was that the courts would do what they had done."[5] The study of precedent and prediction meant analyzing the opinions of the courts of last resort and confining your students to the cases and the statutes—the way Hutchins had confined his Lake Placid pupils to the reading that could get them past the College Boards. The case method had its uses. But the Yale catalogue informed the prospective student that *all* its courses were taught by that method. You might try to reconcile Justice White's opinion in the *American Tobacco* case with his opinion in the *Standard Oil* case. But if you couldn't—and you couldn't, without going to the principles behind the cases—you could go no further because there was no allusion to such principles in the record and no suggestion that such principles anywhere existed.

"We knew that it shouldn't be done that way, but there was nothing we could do about it. It had 'always' been done that way, and the bench and the bar consisted almost entirely of men who did it that way and expected it to go on being done that way. The last thing a justice was expected to ask was where justice lay; the possibility that it lay altogether outside the body of decisions that served as precedent was generally thought to be irrelevant, incompetent, and immaterial, and probably unpatriotic."[6] The greatest justices were those who were concerned with justice—but they were almost always in dissent, and their dissenting opinions did not constitute precedent until ten, or fifty, or a hundred years later the courts or the legislature adopted them.

It was almost forty years later that the ex-lecturer in the Yale Law School was the speaker at a dinner in honor of one of the great dissenting justices who had lived to see some of his lonely opinions accepted, Hugo L. Black. The ex-lecturer recalled his own days of teaching public utilities law.

"In *Smyth v. Ames* the Supreme Court had held—that was in 1898— that regulatory bodies could not constitutionally fix rates that did not give a fair return on the fair value of the property, and fair value came to mean cost of reproduction new less depreciation. My course was based on *Smyth v. Ames*. What a bonanza the rule of *Smyth v. Ames* turned out to be. Almost everybody, except the public, profited by it. When New York City began its rate case against the Edison Company, that corporation's expenditures for appraising, accounting, and legal fees were over $4,000,000. The New York Telephone's, in a similar case, were over $5,000,000. And in 1932 it appeared that the valuation of the American railroads, which had been going on for eighteen years, had cost $178,000,000.

"No sooner had Justice Black got on the Court than he attacked the rule of *Smyth v. Ames*. Perhaps little more could be expected of a man who as a Senator had announced that *stare decisis*—adherence to precedent—did not apply to the Constitution. We law school teachers took some comfort in the fact that his attack was a dissent. But such was the pertinacity and persuasiveness of the dissenter that by 1944 he had brought the majority around to his opinion, and *Smyth v. Ames* was overruled. Thus at one stroke Justice Black hit the utilities and the appraising, accounting, engineering, and legal professions a tremendous blow in the pocketbook— and repealed everything my students ever knew."[7]

The ex-lecturer shuddered "to think of those aging law students of mine, now fifty or sixty years old, wandering around the streets of New York trying to figure out what had happened. Did I lie to them? No, I don't think I lied to them consciously. What I did was to tell them what the law was, and, as of the date on which I told them, I think I was substantially correct. But as of the date on which they had to put it into practice I was overwhelmingly wrong. The reception accorded to the Warren Court was a perfect example of what I mean. The American bar as a whole could not understand the Warren Court because it couldn't understand the United States of America. There was no way in which my students could have come to understand the United States because we never mentioned it."[8]

His students were now living lives of perpetual dismay. They had been required to memorize *Smyth v. Ames* so that they could use it in any court in the land and cite it in objection to any evidence the other side presented. They had not been taught to *understand* the rule. That would have required a grasp, however primitive, of economics and politics—and they were studying, not economics and politics, but precedent and prediction. Hugo L. Black had been their ruin and the shame of their teachers.

"And what Justice Black did to me and my students he did to my colleagues of those days and their students. He assailed the rule, unquestioned since 1842, on the interpretation of state law by the Federal courts, and got it overturned in 1938. He inveigled the Court into upsetting an almost equally ancient tradition by holding that insurance was commerce. He seemed to suggest, in *Marsh v. Alabama*, decided in 1945, that corporations under certain circumstances might be subject, like governments, to the prohibitions of the Bill of Rights. In the Lovett case he renovated an almost forgotten piece of furniture, the bill of attainder, and turned it into a weapon with which he repulsed a rapacious majority in Congress.

"Nor is this all. If we explore the Black country, the world of Justice Black's dissenting opinions, we see that if we lived there we should be living in a different atmosphere. The protections accorded the accused in criminal cases would be extended. Aliens would be treated almost as well as citizens. The protection of the Fifth Amendment would be broadened. It would be regarded as guaranteeing the right to be silent; the waiver of the privilege would be more narrowly interpreted; and no governmental penalty of any kind could be inflicted on a witness availing himself of it. The immemorial rule permitting the trial of criminal contempts without a jury would be abolished. So would blue-ribbon juries. The rights of labor unions to picket peacefully and to engage in political activity would be widened. No test oaths of any sort would be permitted. Censorship, obscenity legislation, and group libel would be unconstitutional. A corporation would not be a person within the meaning of the Fourteenth Amendment, contrary to the rule ever since Roscoe Conkling, by carefully editing history, convinced the Court many years ago. The Federal government would be held to have completely preempted the field of repressing subversion. The House Un-American Activities Committee would be regarded as an un-American activity. The whole of the Bill of Rights would operate against the States. The doctrine that the necessities of the community must be balanced against the rights of the citizen, so that the citizen usually loses, would go out the window. Neither subway conductors nor applicants for admission to the Bar would be declared unreliable because they refused to answer questions about membership in the Communist Party."[9]

The lawyers in every field, like the *Smyth v. Ames* public-utility practitioners, would have to unmemorize everything they had memorized if they found themselves living in "the Black country." And so would their teachers—unless law schools should come to confess that the law is more than precedent and prediction, more, indeed, than law, and recognize it as the application of the principles of human life and of human society to the legal process—principles argued and understood, not memorized. And even then—unless the whole of education was changed from the bottom up—the law schools would find themselves having to go on teaching college graduates the things they could have begun learning at the age of six, or four; a student of law ought to be able to read and write before he begins his study of it.

But the law school was under the thumb of the bar, and its object all mundane was identical with that of Lake Placid: to get its uneducated students past the examinations. The students regarded themselves as receptacles into which the answers to the questions were to be poured and out of which, at the bar examination, they would be poured again. The depressed and dejected young lecturer walked into his first class meeting and asked if the students had any questions on the reading assignment for that day. None of them had. The lecturer said, "This is one of the most difficult aspects of this branch of the law. Questions will undoubtedly be asked about it on the bar examination. I congratulate you on not having any. Class dismissed." After that, some of the more ingenious of his students tried to think up questions to ask.

He was a great success that summer, and when a full-time lecturer resigned Charlie Clark saw no reason why Hutchins should not be put on full-time. Nor did his colleagues. Nor did the president or the board—as long as Hutchins continued his work as secretary of the university. It meant a wage raise—"he's on the payroll anyhow."

So he became a full-time lecturer three months after his graduation. One of his courses was Code Pleading, which nobody would care about in another twenty years (and which Justice Douglas would one day characterize as an example of "the sway that arid technicalities can acquire over the human mind"). His other course was Evidence. Hutchins was not interested in code pleading or evidence and, of course, had never studied them; his qualifications to teach them were identical with his qualifications to teach public utilities law. But Dean Swan and Professor Clark wanted to hang on to him; they thought he might do something some day.

While evidence didn't interest him, it bothered him as soon as he began to teach it, and the botheration gave rise to his philosophy of education as an undertaking that, whatever else it was, had to be general in character. The botheration proceeded from the same kind of question he had asked himself when he taught *Smyth v. Ames* without bringing in politics and economics. The test of the validity of evidence obviously lay outside the law, in the realms of psychology and logic—which neither he nor his students had ever studied (nor, with exceptions, had the bar or the bench). He couldn't understand what made the law of evidence go, separated as it was from nonlegal disciplines. There was the rule, for example, that the evidence of flight from the scene of a crime is admissible as tending to show guilt. After painful research the only foundation he could find for this rule was the statement he remembered having heard at his father's preprandial reading on Elm Street: "The wicked flee when no man pursueth, but the righteous are as bold as a lion." There was another rule that, in cases of homicide, the dying victim's statement, "Hutchins shot me," was admissible because the victim was about to meet his Maker and would not say a thing like that about Hutchins if it weren't true. And there was a related rule called Spontaneous Exclamation, under which an exception is made to the Hearsay Rule and utterances are admissible without direct or cross-examination if they were made immediately after any sudden shock, such as a blow on the head. This rule appeared to rest on the principle that a blow on the head prevents, momentarily but effectively, even the habitual liar from indulging in the exercise of his low habit.

These rules, and, indeed, the whole of the law of evidence, were ancient, honorable, and, supposedly, self-evident and incontrovertible. They were inferred from a long line of decisions made by a long line of judges about the way human beings behave. Since the rules were unchallenged, it was a fair assumption that the courts would always decide the way they always had. But the heretical question injected itself: Do people actually behave the way the rules say they do? If they didn't, the rules ought to be changed. (If they did, the rules ought to rest on a less sandy foundation than the decisions of men who, for the most part, were neither learned nor inquisitive.) Do the wicked really flee when no man pursueth? Are the righteous really as bold as a lion? Can you really startle a liar out of his disregard for the truth? Is the reliability of a dying victim's statement assured by his being about to meet his Maker?

The academic year 1926–27 was passing in the same wearying and wearisome way, the heretical questions unejected, when Robert Maynard

Hutchins suffered a blow on the head. He who had been given the rank of part-time lecturer the day after graduation, and the rank of full-time lecturer three months later, was appointed professor of law at Yale University beginning in September 1927. He was twenty-eight.

The lecturer is not a member of the faculty proper; he is not on the promotion track, or the tenure track, or the salary track. The lowest formal faculty rank is instructor. Somewhere between his third and sixth year of annual reappointment as instructor—he may, in the meanwhile, have been promoted to the rank of assistant professor—he comes up for tenure. If he gets tenure he becomes an assistant professor or associate professor at the same time. (As an associate professor he is regarded as a member of the senior faculty, but with no special prerogatives.) From five to ten years later he may be elevated to the top of the heap with a full professorship. Or he may not; some faculty members neither publish nor perish after they get their tenure and remain assistant or associate professors the rest of their lives. In the 1920s the measured rise through the ranks still took ten or fifteen (or even twenty) years; the exaltation in a professional school was especially slow.

At twenty-eight Professor Hutchins was old enough to have come to the settled conclusion that he was not going to get the answers to the heretical questions about the fleeing wicked, the righteous bold, the startled liar, and the dying victim. He was not going to get the answers or even ask the questions—not in the law school, nor, he realized, in Yale University as it was then organized and staffed. If the questions had been scientific questions he could properly have conducted laboratory experiments. But the questions were psychological and logical; even, for all anybody knew, moral; even theological. "I could not think about them, because I had no education. The psychologists and logicians I met could not think about them, because they had no education either. I could think about legal problems as legal. They could think about psychological or logical problems as psychological or logical. I didn't know how to think about psychological or logical problems as psychological or logical; they didn't know how to think about psychological or logical problems as legal."[10]

Hutchins went on being bothered by the law of evidence. The relevant literature, produced by the psychologists, the logicians, and the legalists, was prolific without being rich—or even, on close examination, relevant. But there was a young psychologician at Columbia who was actually examining the seven-volume bible of Professor Hutchins' specialty, *Wigmore on Evidence*.

Mortimer Adler and another young upstart at Columbia, Jerome Michael, were writing on the psychology of law, in the learned journals.

Hutchins corresponded with Adler and then sat himself down to write something serious about the law of evidence and the heretical questions it raised. Before he could write he had to find out something about psychology. But his efforts to communicate with his colleagues in the psychology department were fruitless until he happened upon a young instructor, by name Donald Slesinger. (He would later bring Slesinger to Chicago with him as his dean of social sciences.) The two of them undertook the preparation of heretical articles in the learned journals. The articles, like Adler's and Michael's, had no effect whatever on the course of legal study at Yale or Columbia or anywhere else.

Since he could not be both a professor and an administrative officer, Hutchins resigned as secretary of the university. Now he would have time to think about the law. But not for long.

In the spring of 1927 Calvin Coolidge appointed Dean Swan to "the Yale seat" on the United States Court of Appeals for the Second Circuit. The law school faculty, which had the prerogative of nominating its dean, was unable to agree on a successor. The faculty was hopelessly divided between the traditional case-and-rules method of teaching and the "realistic" movement that asked the kinds of questions that Hutchins did. The realists were the leading members of the faculty—Walter Wheeler Cook, Arthur L. Corbin, and, of course, Charles E. Clark—but they did not have the numerical or chronological muscle they needed to overturn the traditionalist faction. The stalemate indicated the one-year appointment of an acting dean. Nobody wanted the acting appointment, and nobody objected when Clark suggested Hutchins (even though Hutchins was thought of as a Clark man).

The one-year appointment was an interruption to the life of the mind—which had only just begun its struggle to come to birth. But it was only a temporary interruption. The acting dean was the youngest member of the faculty and therefore the likeliest to take on the administrative chores without the exercise of power. He had had some administrative experience as secretary of the university and was understood to have performed successfully in the dismal art of management. He could do no harm, and no good, and he could hold the place together until the struggle over the deanship was resolved. In his circumscribed role as gap filler, or walk-on, the suspicion of the traditionalists that he had nontraditional tendencies was of no consequence. He'd be out of the acting deanship in a year.

He was out in six months.

In the late fall of 1927 Charlie Clark struck again. An extraordinarily persuasive man, he had the respect even of those who disagreed with his "realist" principles. He addressed himself to the Greater Good of the law school and its neglect by the university and the corporation, both of them preoccupied with the development of Sheff—the Sheffield Scientific School—and the undergraduate college. Their persistent indifference was a mortal danger to the standing of the school. Harvard in particular was running away with legal teaching. What was wanted was a man who could reverse the process, who had worked with the university and the corporation and was friendly with them, who had influence in those two quarters where, when it came to getting the money to rescue the school, influence counted, a man who, moreover, would grow over the years and put the school back where it belonged: in a word, Hutchins.

By now the factions of the faculty recognized that the prospect was remote of their agreeing to fill the post with a man of eminence; every man of eminence who was otherwise acceptable was an established factionalist unacceptable to the other faction. Hutchins was scandalously young and had risen scandalously fast. He was not even a member of the Connecticut Bar and—imagine, the dean of the Yale Law School—would have to take the bar examination. His credentials were inconsequential—a couple of articles in the journals. And the burdens of the deanship were not likely to leave him the time to accumulate any more. On the other hand . . . on the other hand. . . . It would be a sensational appointment—and he did have the ear of the university and the corporation. And as dean, in the present stalemate, he would certainly be diffident about upsetting anybody's applecart. And the school could be sure he'd move on—if not in five years, surely in ten.

Move on where? And why "surely" in ten? The answer to the second question was obvious: At forty he would still be very young for the "Yale seat" on the U.S. Court of Appeals for the Second Circuit, the famous "CCA 2," but not impossibly so after ten years as dean. Dean—now Judge—Swan had succeeded Judge Henry Wade Rogers on CCA 2, and Rogers had been Swan's predecessor at Yale. (Hutchins' own successor as dean would be Charles Clark, and *he* later moved on to a brilliant career in the "Yale seat.")

Between his presidency of the United States and his appointment by President Harding to the Supreme Court, Chief Justice William Howard Taft had been professor of law at Yale. With men like Harding (and Coolidge, and Hoover) in the White House, the chief justice's influence with judicial appointments was (like the chief justice himself) immense. It wouldn't be easy for the diehard Taft (if he should still be around five or ten years hence) to propose the young scalawag who was already challenging the unchallengeable rules of evidence; still, the chief justice was the most loyal of Yalies and the most observant of any and all traditions.

Clark reported his maneuver to Hutchins. The young professor was ambitious to lead the life of the mind. He was equally ambitious to save himself from the stultifying routine of educational administration. But something had happened to him as he was being carried from crest to crest. He had become ambitious—period.

The ultimate ambition of the dean of a great law school was appointment to the federal appellate court. Its calibre was at least as high as the Supreme Court's because its appointments were usually freer of political considerations and public attention, and its decisions often ploughed significant new constitutional ground because its members were often more scholarly and independent. Judge Learned Hand of the Second Circuit was a great jurist; Chief Justice William Howard Taft of the Supreme Court was not. Still, a law school dean who went to CCA 2 in early middle life stood an actuarial chance of ascending to the highest court on one of those infrequent occasions when a man of independent eminence might be named without reference to his regional, denominational, or political or governmental background. A professor of law could be forgiven for dreaming of ending his days as one of the fabled few Great Dissenters like Oliver Wendell Holmes and Louis Brandeis, whose minority opinions would ring through the years and ultimately be accepted by their successors.

The deanship of the Yale Law School might be the long, long way around to the life of the mind, but the men who survived it might live the life of the mind and make that life an instrument for shaping the life of the law and the life of the country. On December 21, 1927, Yale University announced the appointment of Robert Maynard Hutchins as dean of the law school.

In another three weeks he would be twenty-nine years old.

8 Anyone over Thirty

The New York newspapers of December 22, 1927, announced on the front page the appointment of Robert M. Hutchins as dean of Yale Law School. The announcements did not report the date of his birth but only the date of his graduation from Yale College, 1921, leaving the alert reader to draw the untoward inference that he might be some twenty-seven years old. It was the last time, for a long time, that his precosity would not be overtly celebrated, stigmatized, or twitted.

A lifelong consequence attended his elevation to celebrity. While most of the associates in whose appointment (then and thereafter) he would have a hand would be men and women of his own age, the senior members of his faculty would many of them be his father's. His career as an administrator would associate him, day in and night out, with administrative superiors and then with directors, trustees, donors, and civil and political leaders—generally anywhere from thirty to forty, even fifty, years older than he. He would have to put up with the genteel condescension of associates who had the ultimate custody of the enterprises he directed and, as they came to care for him, the custody of his own frisky impulses. The habit of being young among the old would, in their presence, subdue him, and, in their presence and their absence, chafe him. He would have to wear the mask of solemnity. But he wasn't a solemn man.

Installed in February of 1928, he was immediately called upon from around the country for speeches about the Yale Law School, in particular what he intended to do about it. The first speech was at the Harvard Law Review dinner on April 2. For the most part his audience were his chronological peers, perhaps a year or two younger; the faculty were there on sufferance.

Here he was, making, he said, his first appearance at the school which loyalty alone forbade his calling the country's greatest; he would content himself with calling it the most venerable. And here he was, he said, neither a lawyer nor a teacher of law but a traveling salesman, adducing in support of that characterization the fact that he had taken the Connecticut bar examination only a few weeks before and had only just got past it.

As for the Yale Law School, everything it had done or was doing or was trying to do turned out to be a pale imitation, or a still paler variant, of what was done better at Harvard. Great Harvard did marvelously well with large classes utilizing the case method of study; inept Yale did so badly that way that it was reduced to trying to teach small classes by the situation method—the discussion of an unassigned situation which covered many cases. The irony was graceful and unmistakable: the case method in large classes was no good. And so it went; Yale tried to copy Harvard, but didn't know how to, and it had to resort to tinkering with the curriculum "in the denseness of our ignorance."

But he hadn't been sure how the audience would receive him. He *tried*—it was the last time in his speaking career that he did—to be funny. His opening disclaimer—the traveling-salesman, bar-exam patter—was pleasantly acceptable. And then on to an obviously apocryphal account of a visit to the Connecticut Asylum for the Insane "to talk to the inmates about the Yale Law School. Several of them later applied for admission and were accepted." He continued in this vein with the report that one of the inmates, in the course of his talk, rose in the back of the room and screamed, "I can't stand it any longer," and the warden said to the speaker, "That's the first sane moment she's had in twenty years."

Twenty years later John Gunther pondered Hutchins' "curious juvenile streak which makes him like to affront dull people and say things he doesn't really mean." But the Harvard Law Review audience wasn't dull and wasn't affronted. *Any* Harvard-Yale affair was expected to be a monkeyshine.

Once he had run through the patter, he said things he really meant, with transparent irony. But his opening remarks at the Harvard dinner were undeniably juvenile. And juvenility is no small shortcoming in a twenty-eight-year-old called upon to make noises like a law school dean. It wouldn't ever happen again.

On the occasion of his first national public performance, April 28, 1928, he was almost certainly the youngest man in the hall by twenty-five or thirty years. The toastmaster and president of the organization was old enough to be his grandfather. Besides being old, he was George Woodward Wickersham, who had been attorney general of the United States when Hutchins was ten—and a senior member of the New York law firm of Strong and Cadwalader when Hutchins was born. He was the Mr. Republican of his day, destined to crown his career a few years later with the Wickersham Commission's finding (in its studied report to President Hoover) that Prohibition was unenforceable but should be enforced.

The audience was crowded with the elite of the American bar. This was the sixth annual dinner of the American Law Institute (ALI), established to "clarify the uncertainties and simplify the complexities" of American law, and, in addition, "to promote those changes which will tend better to adapt the laws to the needs of life." The dinner address was the high point of the institute's meeting in Washington. The speaker was invariably a Supreme Court justice, an attorney general, a president of the American Bar Association, or the mellowed dean of one of *the* law schools. The address was invariably published, reprinted, excerpted, and cited in the professional journals and the schools.

Wickersham's presentation of the speaker is not recorded, but the speaker's response indicates its character. "I had some hope that your president would be the first toastmaster to introduce me without giving his audience a good laugh about my youth; never has hope been so rudely dashed. I had decided that if he said nothing about my age I should refer to him as the guardian of a beautiful flock. . . . Now I renounce him and all his generation." At this point the *ALI Proceedings* reports "[Laughter.]"[1]

The dean's speech was met, so the *Proceedings* tells us, with "prolonged applause." Hutchins moved to, and through, his theme without a trace of irony, much less juvenility. The institute, he said, had made significant progress in its commitment to the clarification and simplification of the rules of law. He was graceful, gracious, and pointed. It now confronted its second commitment, "to promote those changes which will tend better to adapt the law to the needs of life." He reduced the issue to two questions: Do the rules work? and, How do we find out? To the second question the long, hard, even endless road was the massive accumulation and correlation of facts by responsible investigators of the effects of similar and differing procedures in representative jurisdictions (including those of other countries). As of now (by way of several examples he cited) the separate states have "wobbled back and forth between the abolition and the restoration of capital punishment according to the presence or absence of crime waves. Here there is exact information which might guide legislation, but information compiled by people without sufficient standing to influence the lawmaker." In the absence of the facts in every fundamental field of law, learned men of bench and bar were condemned to differ radically in their interpretation and application of the rules because they had to rely on chance impressions or speculation, on "introspective certainties." "We pass judgment on the suggestions of courts, lawyers, and legislators largely through the exercise of those two dangerous synonyms: hunch and common sense."

Twenty years later—*ten* years later, *five* years later—the empiricist who called for the facts in 1928 would be under sustained attack by the whole body of empiricists as the man who despised facts and disparaged their collectors as "pebble-pickers" and "telephone-pole counters." In the vanguard of his critics would be the natural scientists and their sociological acolytes, deploring Hutchins' attachment to metaphysics—whatever that was—and the "prescientific" thinking of the Greeks and the medievals.

His insistence that he opposed, not fact-gathering but the faith that facts provided the basis of reasoning, would never overcome the hostility of the academic empiricists. They would be as hard-nosed as he, and their predispositions more popular than his. They would be as unacquainted with his legal papers and addresses as they were with the argument, a while before, between Hume and Kant. If they heard (which they wouldn't) that a speaker before the American Law Institute had said, "The history of science has been the history of the downfall of common-sense assumptions before the onslaught of scientific data,"[2] they would have agreed that the one man who could not possibly have made that statement was Robert M. Hutchins.

His colleagues in 1928 were better educated than his colleagues of twenty, ten, and five years later. For all the limitations of their training, they were men of the law, acquainted with the relationship, and the levels of relationship, between fact and principle. They comprehended his allusions to "the pitfalls that lie in the common-sense approach to law," without themselves falling into the pit of factuality unordered by the common sense of the race, common sense codified, however clumsily, in the statutes they used to make daily decisions involving specific observation and specific data. At professional issue was social action to be taken then and there, not mere accumulation and analysis.

The lawyers could accept Hutchins' answer to his second question, How do we find out if the rules work? But his answer to his first question was bound to come as uncomfortably to them as it would to any body of specialists: Do the rules work? When we have clarified and simplified the rules, then what? "Does the discovery of what a rule is always teach us whether it is accomplishing its object. . . how it is meeting the needs of life and the demands of society?" Can we improve the law by the study of law alone? "Our study may"—he graciously said "may"—"carry us into the social, economic, and political background of legal problems, raising questions about the family, about business practices, or about the organization of governments." There was some thought being given to this matter at Yale. But he left the horrendous implication in the after-dinner-cigar-laden air: If the law was ever to be improved to serve "the needs of life," lawyers would have to be psychologists, economists, political scientists, and masters of that branch of philosophy vaguely known as ethics.

He dropped his bombshell—or time-bomb—so gently that his audience had no defensive sense of being challenged, much less derided. His answer to his question, Do the rules work? was itself a diffident question: How can we find out unless we go beyond the law to the nature of man and society?—he was only wondering. Not a phrase, not a word that might jar his listeners; no suggestion that five years later he would be saying that professional men generally (including professors) were uneducated specialists. His low-key witness was sufficient unto the occasion.

His deanship established him. His salary was now ten thousand dollars—the counterpart of at least a hundred thousand a half-century afterward. It was within five thousand dollars of the highest income of any professor in America (always excepting the professors of medicine). What of his recollection long afterward that the driving force of his postgraduate life had been to make enough money to live and then, when he had done that, to continue to make enough money to live? Had he ever really been afraid that the Most Likely Yale Man to Succeed might find himself in the tenements? Or had "enough money to live" even then meant enough money to live the way so many Yale men were destined to? So much for the low ambition of an Oberlin boy—to make enough money to live.

But then there were those two negative ambitions that seemed to be honest. One was not to practice law—a fate that in every likelihood was now behind him. The other was not to be an educational administrator. That one caught up with him, for fair. But not—surely not—for the rest of a long life. In ten years, at the most, the Yale seat on the Second Circuit Court of Appeals would open up. He would be off the treadmill with a lifetime appointment. And beyond that, depending on the vagaries that might put an Al Smith or a Herbert Hoover in the White House, there was the Supreme Court. He would be a judge, and judges in the courts of last resort *made* law, as every mother's son knew. People paid lip service to the doctrine that legislators made it, but a "strict constructionist" like Hoover no less than a lax constructionist like FDR, would always do his damnedest to pack the Court with men of his own predilections.

Yale could be said in the 1920s to be one of the three most highly regarded law schools in the country. (The other two were Harvard and Columbia.) Dean Hutchins had just been through it as a student, had just done business with it as a junior administrator, and had just taught in it.

He thought that it wasn't a good law school (and that none of them was). He knew it wasn't. And he knew the reason why, as did a rambunctious minority of its faculty, which included some of its weightiest members.

The reason the law schools were bad law schools was, of course, their commitment to vocational training. Their purpose was to prepare young men to pass the bar examination and then to get a job. The traditionalist majority of the Yale faculty—and others—believed that the way to teach law was to teach a student how to draw up a will (which he could learn much faster in a law office), and to teach him the current rules of procedure (which could have been learned faster under supervision in court—and which, in any event, would be outdated by the time he was ready to apply them). The men in Constitutional Law, Contracts, Evidence, Criminal Law, Labor Law, Equity, Torts, each of them insulated from all the others, each perpetuating his insulation by bringing on his disciples through the ranks, took the rules as their subject matter and demonstrated the mechanical application of rules to cases. But the business of a university was understanding.

The catch was that the law school was not in the university, but only attached to it. This was true of all the professional schools. There was no contact among them, and no contact between the university and any of them. Hutchins and his supporters in the faculty—Cook, Corbin, Llewellyn (now at Columbia but teaching at Yale in the summer), and, of course, Clark, none of them yearlings—were not interested in feeding a yearly tribute of youth to Wall Street. They were interested in the improvement of the law as the architectonic component of political society. The improvement of the law required an understanding of it. The purpose of a university, and therefore of a law school in a university, was not to transmit knowledge—least of all transient knowledge—but to increase it.

Hutchins saw the law as "a dazzling panorama of the world showing what is happening to society and, in particular, what is happening to two basic American values, freedom and justice. To understand the law is to understand the stage of civilization mankind has reached and to develop some faint notion about how it might advance to a higher stage."[3] And years later: "The Founding Fathers meant us to learn. . . . The reliance on us to continue learning is evident in every line of the Constitution and in the brevity of the whole. The Constitution is to be interpreted as a charter of learning. . . . Learning is a rational process. Law is an ordinance of reason, directed to the common good. The process of deciding to make or not make a law, or the process of reaching a judicial conclusion, is to be criticized in terms of its conformity not to local or popular but to universal standards of reasonableness. If the Constitution is to teach us, and we are to learn under its instruction, the dialogue that goes on about its meaning must be about what is reasonable and unreasonable, right and wrong, just and unjust. The question is not what interests are at stake, not what are the mores of the community, not who has the power or who is the dominant group, but what is reasonable, right, and just. . . . Lawyers should understand that there is, or ought to be, a normative jurisprudence which prescribes something more than correct procedure. The lamentable state of legal education is one of the principal obstacles to our learning through the political community."[4]

And, what was more: "Conformity to the precise words of the laws and the Constitution is not enough. It is well to remember that Hitler was called Adolf Legalité. Everything he did, like everything that is being done in South Africa, was strictly according to law. Critics of President Eisenhower were correct in saying that his defense of the desegregation decision—*Brown v. Board of Education* in 1954—was ineffectual. He should have said not merely that the decision was the law of the land, but also that it was based on reason, right, and justice. . . . Law does not represent that minimum of morality necessary to hold the community together. It stands rather for such moral truth as the community has discovered that can and should be supported by the authority of the community. The conception of law as coercion, or the command of the sovereign, or the expression of power, or what the courts will do, leads to the conclusion that every effort should be made to avoid law and that it is proper to do anything that no sovereign, power, or court can compel you to abstain from doing."[5]

"Reason, right, and justice," "normative jurisprudence," "moral truth"—what had these to do with a law school? What had they to do with winning lawsuits? Fifty years later the after-Watergate analysts were trying to understand the gap between law and the lawyers. "The main evil involved," said the dean of the Ohio State University Law School, "is one which is prevalent throughout our legal system. Clients expect lawyers to do anything" to win their cases, and often lawyers "don't say no" to clients' demands for improper behavior.

Hutchins threw his weight behind the realists on his faculty, the men who taught that the business of the law school was to understand the law. Given the changing conditions of life and society and the diversity of statutes and judicial opinions, it was folly to arrive at decisions on the ground that (a) this is the way this kind of case has always been decided in this jurisdiction or (b) the weight of conflicting decisions seems to be on this side rather than that. Where Harvard's concentration on the case method of study had established it as the foremost legal plant in the land, a few members of the Columbia faculty, notably Underhill Moore, Karl Llewellyn, and a young instructor named William O. Douglas, had become interested in what was then called the functional approach and was later known as sociological jurisprudence. This cut across the classic disciplines and went after the facts to try to determine whether and how the rules were actually working. The functional approach got no encouragement from Columbia's president, Nicholas Murray Butler—quite the opposite. But Hutchins had already established a bridgehead between New Haven and Morningside Heights, where Adler and Michael in the Columbia psychology department were kicking up the interdisciplinary dust; and within a couple of months after his elevation to the deanship the two schools had two joint legal research projects going, one on the psychology of evidence and one on the family and the law. But the proposition that law had something to do with life and society, was both easier said *and* done than understood.

With thirty thousand new opinions handed down every year by the courts of last resort, and legislatures enacting eight thousand new statutes annually, the obsolescence of legal data was as torrentious as the data were oceanic. Leaders in the law schools spoke of extending the curriculum from three years to four. But that would be no solution, if the last fact the student swallowed whole on the last day of his four years of gorging would be so much roughage by the time he entered practice.

What was wanted, when the law had been clarified and simplified, was "the accumulation and interpretation of facts concerning the working of the then restated law." "Hunch and common sense" had to be replaced by "the scientific approach to the law through the painstaking collection of facts as to its practical results." Though he thought that the scientific approach "may carry us into the social, economic, and political background of legal problems," he did not suggest that that background was other than factual; he seemed to be suggesting (and nowhere suggested anything different) that he would pile the fact-crammed social sciences on top of the legal facts for accumulation and interpretation. Interpretation by what yardstick? Presumably workability; we want to find out whether and how the rules work. But what is workability? Expedition? Efficiency? Uniformity? Public acceptance? There was no suggestion that the question had occurred to him then.

How was the scientifically accumulated mass of materials to be judged, some to be discharged as irrelevant or trivial and the rest to be ordered in terms of their significance and utility (once we had decided what was significant and useful, and why)? Could legal research *or legal training* be undertaken—could the law, *any* law, be justified—without agreement as to the needs of life and the order of their urgency? How could the legal profession even begin to fulfill the obligation laid upon it by the American Law Institute, "to improve the law," without having first decided what improvement was?

The Hutchins of the Law Institute dinner in 1928, and the Hutchins who told the Connecticut Bar Association eight days earlier that "Our effort [at Yale], like that at Columbia, is focused on the facts,"[6] consistently talked law-school law (and the scientific approach to it) to the lawyers; his emphasis on reason, right, and justice, normative procedure, and moral truth seems only to have developed in the course of his year-and-a-half tenure as dean at Yale, from February 1928 to June 1929. He had been brought up on right and justice. His legal studies awakened his respect for reasoning. But he found that the data on which the statutes were based were confused and contradictory. Then he came to see that this confusion arose in part from the inadequacy of the data and in part from the isolation of the law from other humanistic and social disciplines. These were not remarkable discoveries. They were observations which other highly perceptive men had, like him, made on their own. They brought him together with men of the law—Charles Clark had been the first with whom he would undertake reforms of law and its teaching.

It wasn't until the end of his legal career that Hutchins seems fully to have comprehended the limitations of the functional, or scientific, approach to the law and the full significance of its scholarly isolation. Four years after he had left Yale, in "The Autobiography of an Ex–Law Student" (and ex–law dean), a speech delivered before the Association of American Law Schools, he said: "We must accumulate cases, facts, and data. But we must have a scheme into which to fit them. The law school that ignores the cases, the facts, or the social sciences will be a poor law school. The legal scholar who ignores these things will be a poor legal scholar. . . . [But] law is a body of principles and rules developed in the light of the rational sciences of ethics and politics. The aim of ethics and politics is the good life. The aim of the law is the same. Decisions of courts may be tested by their conformity to the rules of law. The rules may be tested by their conformity to the legal principles. . . . [But] the legal principles are derived from ethics and politics. The student and teacher should understand the principles of those sciences. Since they are concerned with ideas, they must read books that contain them. To assist in understanding them they should be trained in those intellectual techniques which have been developed to promote the comprehension and statement of principles. They will not ignore the cases, the facts, or the social sciences. At last they will understand them. They will be educated."[7]

They weren't educated by the Yale Law School, either before or during his tenure: "Our curriculum was anti-intellectual from beginning to end. It involved not a single idea, not a single great book, not a single contact with the tremendous intellectual heritage of the law. We did not even expect intellectual exercise. We discussed the logic of cases; but none of us knew any logic. We could not engage in intellectual exercises because we were not competent in the intellectual techniques which it requires."[8]

His experience at Yale carried him into principles of ethics and politics, whose aim is the good life. If the aim of law is the good life, so is the aim of education. The formation of a theory of how to learn and teach law turned out to be the formulation of how to learn and teach anything. The man of facts had become the man of ideas by discovering that ideas alone made the facts intelligible. By the time he got around to the formal presentation of the formula, his career and his formulation of the legal theory which turned out to be an educational theory were happily joined: in 1931, when he spoke on "The New Atlantis," the dean of a law school had become the president of a university.

Francis Bacon's *New Atlantis* in 1627 depicted a utopia in which men sought and got information—all the facts, all the discoveries and inventions their single-minded pursuit led to. Bacon maintained that his New Atlantis was a land of dreams to which we could never attain, a land too good to be true. "He was wrong. The New Atlantis did come true. We are living in it. We have more information, more means of getting more information, more means of distributing information, and more practical applications of the information we have than Francis Bacon in his wildest imaginings could have predicted." But "poverty, unemployment, crime, demoralization, and the race problems are with us still, and with us in new and discouraging shapes. Admitting that the more facts we have the better, we must confess that we do not know what to do with the facts we have. And yet this is Utopia."[9]

The American educational system now reflected the aspirations of the New Atlantis. So startling and beneficent had the discoveries of the natural sciences been, that everybody wanted to be scientific. But "science"—this from the fact-gathering enthusiast of "the scientific approach" of a few years before—"is not the collection of facts or the accumulation of data. A discipline does not become scientific merely because its professors have acquired a great deal of information. Facts do not arrange themselves. Facts do not solve problems. . . . We must learn to think about the facts we have, and train up others to think more widely and more intelligently than we. We who have achieved the Baconian ideal and more must confess that something is missing from Utopia. It is ideas. It is not through facts but through ideas that Utopia will be achieved. Insight, understanding, the appreciation of values, intelligence, ideas were not esteemed in the New Atlantis. We pay the penalty today. Leadership, direction, judgment critical and constructive, the ability to plan, to formulate policies, obtained no place in the New Atlantis. We seek and rarely find them now. . . . Upon the proper balance of fact and idea depends our eventual escape from the New Atlantis."[10]

He was talking about balance, and would go on talking about it the rest of his life. But the New Atlantis address confirmed the suspicion of most of the natural scientists and social scientists with whom he would be wrangling, sometimes furiously, during the twenty-one years of his university presidency and beyond. Some of his allies blamed his rhetoric; it was brilliant, but it was cryptic—a kind of shorthand: "The most practical education is the theoretical education" could too easily be taken to mean that he despised data and data-gathering and data-measuring. What did he mean by "ideas," "values," "insight"? What did he mean by "principles"? He might have made his lot easier by talking about hypothesis instead of theory, but that would have been a surrender to his opponents—a surrender, and a dodge. "Hypothesis" had been preempted by empirical science, but by principles Hutchins meant hypotheses that were not scientifically verifiable. Men might, and should, argue that the aim of ethics and politics was or wasn't the good life; but they could not prove their case by public-opinion polls or by counting the number of hospitals, churches, and saloons, or by citing Supreme Court opinions. In neither experiential nor experimental terms could the case be proved at all. The men who enunciated the *self-evident truths* of the Declaration of Independence—Lord North called them self-evident nonsense—did not argue for them on the basis of either historical or contemporary social conditions.

So the ardent advocate of the scientific approach to the law was, almost overnight, to be seen as the implacable enemy of science. He might say, again and again, that he was talking about emphasis and nothing but emphasis. No use; his deemphasis of the facts defined his position, and Mortimer Adler's outspoken contempt for the fact-centered social sciences didn't help. Hutchins brought Adler to Chicago. Adler was his closest ideological associate. And Adler was not restrained either by administrative responsibility or by having been brought up to be polite. Actually, the limitations of the scientific method, insofar as the scientific method relied on raw data, were incidental to the "Hutchins-Adler" doctrine (if it could be said to be *a* doctrine). But the rhetoric of the doctrinaires, on both sides, would focus intellectual, and particularly academic, passion on the incidental argument, and in the popular apprehension of the great squabble at Chicago it boiled down to facts versus ideas. In Hutchins' office at Chicago, and ever thereafter, would hang a *New Yorker* cartoon of James Thurber's, in which two barflies contemptuously contemplate a dejected third, sitting alone, and one of the two says to the other, "He doesn't know anything but facts."

All that was ahead, if only a year or two ahead; but it was incubating during that year-and-a-half of the deanship at Yale. The alternative to drowning in data was to try to understand law, not the laws, and to teach its understanding so that the practicing lawyer would be equipped intellectually to make sense of the data that would confront him. The understanding of the law was jurisprudence—the senior-year elective that almost nobody took at Yale (or anywhere else). Dean Hutchins and some of his realist colleagues, even while they pushed the "scientific approach," had crusaded for jurisprudence, for "the formulation of legal theory" on which the myriad materials of practice could be sorted. By the time he left Yale he was convinced that every law school should establish a department of jurisprudence. "Gradually its efforts would be reflected in the curriculum and studies of the law school. Gradually it would be discovered that its students were more successful at the bar and even in predicting what the courts would do than the progeny of the law school"[11]—twenty years later he challenged one of his disciples, Dean Edward H. Levi of the University of Chicago Law School, to establish such a department and compare its graduates' performance at the bar with those of the orthodox curriculum—"and gradually, very gradually, the law might become once more a learned profession."

"Jurisprudence," said Professor Lon Fuller, "is concerned with the nature of law, its purposes, the means (institutional and conceptual) necessary to effectuate those purposes, the limits of the law's efficacy, the relation of law to justice and morality, and the modes by which law changes and grows historically." Obviously the law, on the jurisprudential reading of it, could not be understood, much less improved, in isolation. Fuller's definition required the law's integration into every other humanistic and social discipline; it required an intellectual *community*. To understand the law was to understand the nature of reason, right, and justice; to understand the nature of reason, right, and justice was to understand the nature of man and society. Law was ultimately inseparable from the humanities, which went to the nature of man; from the social sciences, which went to the nature of society; and even from the natural sciences and medicine.

This was the meaning of the word *university*, which had lost its meaning in the departmental university. This was the *e pluribus unum* of learning and teaching which Hutchins would spend the rest of his life proclaiming and promoting, only to see the intellect increasingly fragmented in every field and the world of teaching and research shattered into smaller and smaller units. At Yale Dean Hutchins pushed legal research as far as he could into the social sciences, even into the natural sciences; his transcendent triumph was a grant of seven million dollars from the Rockefeller Foundation for the establishment, with his friend Milton Winternitz, the dean of the medical school, of an Institute of Human Relations for the interdisciplinary investigation of the criminal law. The institute opened with a bang, but it needed time to assemble a faculty and become the intellectual community that Hutchins would, again and again, try to assemble. He sought men and women (almost exclusively men, in those days) who had come to see, as he had, that the compartmentalization of thought and action was the clue to the most mature of all mature realizations: that everything is somehow connected with everything else and that general intelligence, the intelligence which the specialist scorned as dilettantism, was the only hope. After Hutchins' departure and the retirement of Winternitz, the institute was absorbed into the medical school and the law school left it. Still, in those eighteen months Hutchins and his associates at Yale and Columbia made some apparent—if only apparent—progress.

The reason they did not make more, and did not make stick the progress they made, was what a famous football coach would have called the viscous circle. On taking the deanship at Yale Hutchins sat down to try to figure out what he wanted to do with the curriculum. He had not sat very long before he realized that he could not do very much. The curriculum was in the hands of the faculty (where, one supposed, it belonged); the power of the dean, like (he would discover) the power of the president, was the power of persuasion and nothing else. The curriculum could not be changed until the men who had power were changed. But the more power they had, and the longer they had had the power, the less likely it was that they would change; trying to persuade them meant succeeding in annoying them, and that got nowhere. To do anything about the faculty meant doing something about the curriculum; but to do anything about the curriculum meant doing something about the faculty. This meant hiring; and hiring, unless new money could be found, meant firing. But under the tenure system, firing could not be done directly. It could be done indirectly, by persuasion and low connivance. The long life of lofty persuasion and low connivance had begun. In his *Go East, Young Man*, William O. Douglas writes: "Law faculties were encrusted with heavy-footed traditionalists. Hutchins worked hard to get rid of two such men"—Douglas names them—"who had come to Yale from Harvard by subtly indicating to Harvard that they wanted to return, implying that he would view such an event with sorrow. Sure enough, Harvard rose to the bait and made them offers which they accepted."[12]

On the whole the projects that got off the ground during the months of the Hutchins regime at Yale were sporadic and ad hoc. There wasn't time to get the grand design—the intellectual community—off the ground. Not that the new dean was languid; not at all. He plunged, as he always would, with the deceptive languor of a man who had all the time in the world. His manner was gelatinously academic, his activity frenzied. There was no earthly reason for a dean to be teaching, especially a dean who was tearing sedately around the country making speeches, raising money, and raiding other schools' faculties in an effort to move his own. Except the Lake Placid reason that the only way to learn is to teach. So he went on teaching Evidence, this time with a psychiatrist as his coinstructor. He discovered that to teach the blow-on-the-head exception to the hearsay rule required not only a lawyer and a psychologist, but a neurologist; and so his friendship with Winternitz developed. In addition, he discovered that Evidence could use a theologian in teaching the prospective lawyer how to object to all the evidence the adversary introduced.

Ninety days after he took office in January 1928, Hutchins was making another of those after-dinner speeches, this one at a club in Pelham, New York. After the speech a cozy group assembled in the locker room (where the bootleg liquor was served), and when Hutchins was put aboard the New Haven train very late that night he had a quick conversation with a man from Yakima, Washington, by name William O. Douglas, then in his first teaching post in the Columbia law faculty. (He had declined an offer from Harvard.) At ten in the morning-after-the-night-before Douglas was awakened by a phone call. It was Hutchins, who had summoned his faculty to a 9 A.M. meeting and got them to offer Douglas an associate professorship at Yale. Douglas said (in all innocence), "Where is Yale?" Hutchins told him, and Douglas came in September.[13]

The two men were made for each other—the polished Oberlinite and the unpolishable Yakimite. Douglas's teaching technique, by his own testimony, was "a rather hard-bitten approach, fashioned on the Socratic method. . . . I bore down hard. . . . I tended to treat the class as the lion tamer in the circus treats his wards. Soon the class was in protest, sending a committee to Dean Hutchins to have me fired." Hutchins called him in, and Douglas said that the students were "grandsons of very eminent and at times disreputable characters, and that as a result of the wealth of their ancestors they had been spoiled all their lives. I said I thought it was time they learned that when they stood before a court or a jury they would be judged by their perception and fidelity to the law, not by their ancestors." "Wonderful," said the dean. "It's fine with me if you fire me. I'm inclined to bear down even harder with the brats." "Wonderful," said the dean, "revolutionary and wonderful."[14]

They were the same age and they felt the same way about the law and what they were up against. Hutchins was an early retirer and an even earlier riser, but a fiery man like Douglas (or Felix Frankfurter of Harvard) could keep him awake until late. They sat talking about the profession into which they both appeared to be locked. "Finance was predatory"—this was Douglas—"and many men who managed it had predatory proclivities. Their lawyers took on the coloration of their clients and designed ways and means of accomplishing certain projects that should have been beyond the pale. . . . The great names in the law were, with few exceptions, attached to men who exploited the system. . . . Few had rendered public service, and those who did used that front merely to get more business." Teaching? "Why spend one's life teaching bright youngsters how to do things that should not be done?" A fellow might just as well go into practice "and use the new-found fitness for one's own benefit."[15]

The trustees of Yale University, many of them lawyers, might have been interested in these midnight conversations—to the point of excruciation. They may even have imagined them and shuddered. But they didn't hear them. Neither did the trustees of the University of Chicago. What the trustees of both institutions—and of all the others—did hear was that this man Hutchins of Yale was pulling off some front-page coups in money-raising among the predatory financiers, including a handsomely endowed Sterling Research Chair for investigation. Hutchins had the magic touch in that magic year on Wall Street. By the end of 1928 the Yale law faculty, which had numbered fifteen a decade earlier, had increased to thirty-two, including a sociologist, an economist, and a psychologist.

Brilliant, and always controversial, men began moving over to Yale, among them Walton Hamilton, a Brookings Institution economist who had never studied law. Hamilton joined Charlie Clark in the latter's pioneering investigation of civil procedure (an investigation that ended in 1938 with the new Federal Rules of Civil Procedure, drafted by Clark's committee for Congress and the Supreme Court). The premature death of another newcomer, Walter Nellis, cut off his brilliant work in the hot-potato field of civil rights and labor injunctions. Wesley Sturgis came, and so did Thurman Arnold, whose *Folklore of Capitalism* would make a public splash when the Wall Street bubble burst in 1929. Within a matter of months the Yale Law School came alive, with men from other schools, at home and abroad, coming in and out; men like the great nontraditionalist

Harold Laski of the London School of Economics and the great traditionalist Felix Frankfurter from Harvard. They gave lectures, conducted seminars, and helped frame cooperative research projects with institutions like the Connecticut Judicial Council and the U.S. Department of Commerce (and, of course, with Columbia). There were anthropologists among them, even philosophers. Those years that Hutchins had spent in the central administration—"doing oratorical work for Yale University"—while he studied law were paying off now: the foundation people knew him; President Angell was tolerant of the high jinks, especially since Hutchins was able to raise the money; and so were some of the weightier trustees and alumni who had got to know him during his service as secretary. Not every last one of them: William Howard Taft was heard to say that the boy would wreck the law school, and when they were introduced he said, "Well, young man, I suppose you teach your students that the judges are fools," evoking the sassiness to which, as on so many such occasions, the sassy young man was entitled: "No, Mr. Chief Justice, we let them find that out for themselves."

Little by little, if only little by little, the Yale Law School curriculum was being remade. An honors program—small groups of students working on special problems and individual research—had been introduced in 1926–27 when the student body numbered 422. The doubling of the size of the faculty meant it was possible to extend the honors program, first to admit the best second-year students, and then the best first-year students. The dean made the headlines with the announcement that Yale would henceforth limit its first-year enrollment in law to one hundred, and the announcement at once attracted the best applicants in the country. (In the midst of the fanfare nobody thought to ask what the present first-year enrollment had been: it had been 106). Enrollment was further reduced—to 328 in 1928–29 (Harvard's was 500 and growing)—by the abolition of the so-called Combined Course, to which seniors in the College were admitted (as Hutchins himself had been). With no noise at all, almost surreptitiously, women were admitted to the law school; the dean, in his reports, still referred to the student body as "men."

It was a period of frank experimentation, Dean Hutchins told a professional audience who asked him what was going on there. "We hope we shall not recklessly abandon anything that is good or embrace new ventures simply because they are new. But we do not much care whether all our experiments are successful. We shall be satisfied if other law schools can profit by them if only to the extent of avoiding our mistakes. After all, the great thing about a university is that it can afford to experiment: and I use the word afford not in its financial connotation but to remind us that a university is free to cultivate and exhibit independence of thought, the willingness to depart from tradition, the readiness to take a chance, if you will, that may come from the possession of a life that is nearly immortal."[16]

The frank experimentation included new tests for admission, tests that went beyond the usual requirement of a high undergraduate grade average. What followed from this innovation—other schools were working on it, especially as regards college admission—was a much more fundamental innovation. If the undergraduate grade average was to be only one of the conditions for admission to graduate school, why should the graduate school grade average be the only condition for a law school degree? Grading was the most unreliable of measures. The sum of the number of courses taken and passed, perhaps just barely passed, did not make a man a lawyer; the "gentleman's C" was too often given because the candidate for it (or his grandfather) was a gentleman. If a higher standard was to be demanded of applicants for admission, a higher standard should be demanded of applicants for graduation. At the end of his first semester as dean, Hutchins informed the law school alumni that "the adding machine method of obtaining the graduate degree has departed. We plan to admit to candidacy only men who can accomplish creditable research work, and to award them only for its accomplishment. With the problem of how to tell a man who can accomplish creditable research work and with the definition of creditable we are still struggling."[17] The adding-machine metaphor would become the operative symbol of this twenty-year crusade at Chicago to admit students at all levels whenever they were ready to enter college; at eighteen, or sixteen, or fourteen, or twelve; and to graduate them at forty, at twenty, or at fifteen—whenever they were able to demonstrate on general examinations, not that they had passed a required number of courses over a required number of years with a required accumulation of grade points, but that they had mastered the materials.

Forty years later Hutchins read an article in the current *Yale Law Journal* that reported legal education in ferment. It had been in ferment when he entered it fifty years before. "How can anything ferment for fifty years? There must be a process called pseudo-fermentation, in which gaseous bubbles rise constantly to the surface but the final, cheering, ambrosial draught is indefinitely postponed." The writer in the *Yale Law Journal* said that the heart of the trouble was vocationalism. "As long as we continue to see legal education as the acquisition of marketable skills, it will never cease to be anything more than a dreary task for a future payoff."

Hutchins was, according to Hutchins, a failure at Yale. He and his allies—the Douglases, the Clarks, the Corbins, the Hamiltons, the

Arnolds—wanted to shake the law school out of its how-to-do-it mold. They wanted to convert it into something like an intellectual community, with men from other disciplines. They failed because "the disciplines were even worse than the law." They failed because the bar, the bench, and the compartmentalized university were all organized to withstand all radical change.

But there had been vitality at the Yale Law School. The very few survivors from its faculty, forty years later, remembered it as exciting: "We were arguing about the aims and methods of education and trying to do something about them." Was there anything left of it forty years later? Hutchins thought that "its remains—and to some extent its spirit—are still to be seen." Douglas didn't think so: "The whole project gradually faded. The total effect of the Institute of Human Relations and of all our efforts was zero. . . . The same problems are being discussed today. . . . Yet almost nothing has been accomplished in all these years. . . . My years at Yale disillusioned me concerning the law as an instrument of power for the social good."[18] That, in 1974, was the disconsolate view of the longest-tenured member of the United States Supreme Court in its history, who had now joined the very small coterie of the Great Dissenters.

Hutchins wanted to take Douglas to Chicago with him in 1929; with his characteristic audacity he had persuaded the Chicago trustees to offer his friend the law school deanship at twenty-five thousand dollars—two-and-a-half times the top salary of a professor—saying that (as the nominee recalled it) "I was 'the most outstanding law professor' in the nation," a statement that (again, according to the nominee) "insulted many law professors who defected as friends of Hutchins." Douglas accepted, but never took the job. He stayed on at Yale, as Sterling Professor of Law, until President Roosevelt appointed him chairman of the Securities and Exchange Commission in 1934. In his autobiography Douglas lists in chronological order the six men who, in his words, shaped his life: Robert M. Hutchins, FDR, Ben Cohen, Jerome Frank, Louis Brandeis, and Hugo L. Black.[19]

The Yale Law School wasn't an intellectual community when Hutchins entered it as a college senior in 1920, or when he left it ten years later as its dean; and Yale University was less of an intellectual-community in 1930 (and still less in each succeeding decade) than it was in 1920. Would there ever be an intellectual community, with a common preparation among its members and a common body of principles, assumptions, "hypotheses," grown out of that sort of preparation (and perhaps out of other, deeper roots of the sort that made Oberlin a community without the intellectualism): with a common dedication, a common vocabulary and a common conversation; with a common comprehension that everything was somehow related to everything else and that nothing that touched men at the center existed in isolation? Would the law ever be a profession? Professing what? Would lawyers at last be educated men? And how would such a community producing such men ever be erected? And where? In a university?

The eight members of the United States Supreme Court—Justice Brewer did not participate—who heard the case of *Plessy v. Ferguson* in 1896 were all of them lawyers and university men. Seven of them found that racial segregation in interstate commerce was constitutional (providing that the separate facilities on the railroad train were equal). One member of the Court dissented: "The Constitution," said John Marshall Harlan, "is color blind."

Courts and justices came and went—lawyers, university men—for another fifty-eight years. In 1954 the Supreme Court unanimously reversed *Plessy* in *Brown v. Board of Education* and held that the Constitution is color-blind. What had John Marshall Harlan known—*known*—that his seven colleagues and their successors didn't? The Constitution? They all knew the Constitution, and the Equal Protection Clause of the Fourteenth Amendment was thirty years old when *Plessy* was decided. The law? Did Harlan know more law than his fellow lawyers and fellow university men of the high court? He had attended an undistinguished law school. Social data? Did Harlan have more social data available than his colleagues or their successors for fifty-eight years? It was as easy in 1896 as it was in 1954 to gather data that demonstrated that separate meant unequal.

What did John Marshall Harlan know that no Supreme Court would know for another half-century? Where, and how, had he learned it?

Reason, right, and justice; normative jurisprudence; moral truth—could they be acquired in a school? In a law school? In a university? Could they be acquired in an *intellectual* community?

Two-and-a-half millennia before Justice Harlan was taught and practiced law, the first recorded discussion of education opened with the question, "Can you tell me, Socrates, whether virtue is acquired by teaching or by practice—or in some other way?" Perhaps it would take another two-and-a-half millennia of frank experimentation, either of the sort that went on at the Yale Law School in the late 1920s or of some other sort. Two-and-a-half millennia; and on January 15, 1929, Robert Maynard Hutchins would be thirty years old.

Part Three

CHICAGO (1)

9 7:00 A.M.

The Association of American Law Schools met Christmas week of 1928 in Chicago. Its theme was Modern Movements in Legal Education. The centerpiece of the meeting was a symposium of the deans of Johns Hopkins, Columbia, and Yale. As the Yale dean walked to the platform he was stopped by a man twice his age, Frederick C. Woodward of the University of Chicago. The two had met before; Woodward had been dean of Chicago's law school until six months earlier, when President Max Mason had suddenly resigned and Woodward had agreed to serve as acting president of the university while the trustee-faculty search committee found a permanent replacement. Woodward was a blunt man. He said, "Hutchins, we are looking for a new president at Chicago, and your name has been suggested. Would you be willing to meet with a committee of the trustees?" Hutchins was a blunt man. He said, as he later recalled it, "I've got to make a speech. Don't be silly." After the symposium Woodward repeated the invitation, and Hutchins accepted it.[1]

At lunch with the Chicago trustees he spoke without regard to possible personal consequences; he did not believe that he was being seriously considered. The trustees asked him about the University of Chicago. He knew nothing about Chicago, but he thought he knew something about universities and what ought to be done about them. How would he strengthen a university? Well, he'd begin by paying full professors fifteen thousand dollars a year. (The country's top salary was then ten thousand.) What about "this academic freedom business"? asked the vice chairman of the university's board, the country's biggest printer. Hutchins thought the academic freedom business was good academic business. The printer, Thomas B. Donnelley, said that there was a professor in industrial relations at the university, Paul Douglas (later to become a U.S. senator), who "ought to be lined up against the wall and shot." Hutchins winced. There wasn't much he could do about his interrogator's stupidity, or his diction (in wanting to line up one man); but he could gratify his own impishness. "Why," he said, "do you think Professor Douglas ought to be lined up and shot?" Donnelley said, "Because he goes around saying he doesn't believe in the free enterprise system." There was silence around the table, and Hutchins said, "I'm a professor of the law of evidence, and I've just written an article in which I attack the Supreme Judicial Court of Massachusetts for the errors which I claim it made in the admission and exclusion of evidence in the case of Sacco and Vanzetti. Is it your opinion that I should be lined up and shot?" "Well, no," said Donnelley, "that's perfectly all right." "If a man is a professor of industrial relations," said Hutchins, "shouldn't he be allowed to go around expressing his opinion on industrial relations?" "I think he ought to be shot," said Donnelley.[2]

There was another wincer at the table, Harold Higgins Swift, the chairman of the board (a post he would hold for all but the last two years of the Hutchins tenure as president and chancellor). Harold Swift was a meat packer who might have been chosen by his college classmates Least Likely to Pack Meat. The third of the four sons of Gustavus Franklin Swift, who came from Massachusetts in 1875 to found the company which established Chicago as the world's hog butcher, Harold Swift was single-mindedly dedicated to the University of Chicago his life long, beginning with his graduation in 1907—one of the very few sons of the city's rich who did not go east to college then. He was a precise, meticulous bachelor of considerable cultivation in the arts; gentle, even prissy in bearing and manner; a man worried about the attitude of the local gentry to the university, but invariably coming down on the side of academic freedom when the gentry (including fellow trustees) were disturbed; an inordinately modest man, given to saying he "wanted one vote"—and abstaining from that when the academic body of the institution disagreed with him.

He relieved the uneasiness around the table after the lining up and shooting of Paul Douglas by asking the guest how he managed to get his several jobs done—deaning, teaching, writing, speaking, and money-raising. Hutchins said that he didn't get his jobs done, but he began each day manfully at 7 A.M. Swift wanted to know what time he got to the office, and Hutchins said that that was when he got to the office—7 A.M. The luncheon ended on that small-talk note, and the visitor caught the afternoon train back to New Haven. The morning following his return the telephone rang in the office of the Yale Law School at 7 A.M. and Hutchins picked it up. "This," said the caller, "is Harold Swift of Chicago. I wanted to thank you on behalf of our committee for the time you took to have lunch with us. It was enjoyable and constructive." Hutchins was mildly puzzled: Harold Swift was known as a man who, like John D. Rockefeller, thought twice before making a long-distance call to say what could just as easily be said on a penny postcard. The puzzlement ended when he learned later that Swift couldn't believe he got to the office at 7 A.M. and couldn't resist the wastrel temptation to find out.[3]

People are impressed by people who get up early, with the result, said Thorstein Veblen, that people who get up early are conceited in the morning and sleepy in the afternoon. "Consider the matter in Aristotelian fashion," said President Hutchins one morning at seven o'clock in his office. "Virtue is its own reward. But getting up early has rewarded me beyond the dreams of avarice. Therefore getting up early is not a virtue. It is a morally indifferent habit and I am a morally indifferent man. It had nothing to do with character. I get up early because I can't sleep late. My father and the army made me what I am today."

He wasn't a candidate in December, when Board Chairman Swift asked him what time he got to his office. He was still twenty-nine—he wouldn't be thirty until January. He couldn't believe that a great university, or even a not so great university, would hire so young a president; none ever had. The deanship of the Yale Law School had been a fluke attributable to a series of minor flukes beginning with the appendectomy of the lecturer in Public Utilities Law, and few (hard-headed philanthropists included) cared all that much what a law school did. But a university—. So he hadn't taken the Chicago matter seriously. He had done his best to put his worst foot forward, his Calvinistic best. One of his hosts long afterward recalled having had an *uneasy* impression of him. "Handsomest devil, never saw a man like him, before or since. Obviously brilliant and confident—or putting on a great show of confidence. But he certainly wasn't trying to sell himself. Either that or he was doing it with reverse English. Flip . . . supercilious . . .—and yet—he wasn't a showoff. He was serious, serious about education, about universities. . . . Puzzling. I suspected he thought he was more intelligent than we were. Well—he was."

He was invited back in February, and again in March. Now he knew they were serious. And now so was he. He wanted to be president of the University of Chicago. It had been established as a research institution, the only one of its kind that had not grown out of a college; it had been established only thirty-seven years before by a radical educator whose memory was still green, William Rainey Harper. Hutchins, as a consequence of his discovery of the ramifications of the law, had become interested in (of all things) education. No matter how far afield and into how many fields the law carried you, in the end it was essentially a procedural study and a procedural practice. Politics and economics and ethics and psychology and logic were substantive disciplines, but the law was a profession; a profession was practiced, and the substantive element of its practice was procedure. His men and his mentors at Yale—the Clarks, the Douglases—were lawyers interested in jurisprudence, but first of all, lawyers. The difference between his approach and theirs was radical. As he turned to general education, to the fields they thought were relevant (but no more than relevant) to the law, his outlook diverged from theirs. They would always be friends, closely associated in professional and public undertakings. But they would become critical of him, and he of them. Insofar as he was a lawyer, he was concerned with constitutional law, that is, with the polity and with law as an instrument of the polity.

Thus he had been drifting into education and away from professional training. He was still mildly horrified to think of himself as an administrator; but maybe what an administrator becoming interested in education was destined for was educational administration. There was his internship under President Angell and his experience as dean of the law school. His father was a college president. "I thought as a result of observing my father and Mr. Angell at work that all you needed to do was have a bright young man get hold of one of these institutions, and he could fix it up. I thought I was a bright young man. I thought I would not make their mistakes, and that all I had to do to develop an adequate educational program was the opposite of what was done at New Haven. That's how bright a young man I thought I was."[4]

In mid-April Harold Swift phoned him to ask when he could meet with the full board of trustees, most of whom he had met individually or in small groups. It was understood that the committee would present him to the board for election, and that he was willing to be presented. After lunch at the Chicago Club, attorney Laird Bell, then the youngest member of the board, and who would one day succeed Swift as chairman—asked Hutchins if he would care to join him for a few minutes in another room. The few minutes went on for a few hours, and "Laird and I, meeting for the first time, had very little to say to one another. It got to be embarrassing. I didn't know what was happening, but I could surmise (and so, of course, could Laird) that the 'enthusiastic unanimity' with which my appointment would be announced was being reached with mixed enthusiasm."[5] It was almost dark when the members of the committee came in and informed him that he had been elected and that the board hoped that he would accept. He did.

The announcement, on April 26, was made by Swift, who rejoiced at "the unanimous and enthusiastic choice" and explained that although

President-elect Hutchins was a comparatively young man, his experience in university administration was greater than that of either the university's first president, Mr. Harper, or Harvard's Eliot when they assumed office each at the age of thirty-five. The president-elect posed for pictures and told the press that the University of Chicago was "the greatest educational opportunity in the United States . . . because of its geographical location, because of its tradition of freedom and enterprise, the excellence of its faculty . . . an able and enthusiastic group of investigators and teachers engaged in inspiring and valuable effort. . . . I welcome the opportunity." (Ten years later he would be writing in a personal letter to his Chicago friend and colleague Professor William Fielding Ogburn: "The faculty is bad, and you and I know it.")

He was saying all the right things and none of the wrong ones. The youngest man ever chosen president of a university, he responded to his election like a sere and sober pontiff. Nothing flip, nothing supercilious. When he brought his wife to Chicago a month later for a two-day visit to the campus and a full-scale press appearance, the *Chicago-Daily News* found him "tall . . . at once keen and kindly, with a manner both suave and gentle." The *Tribune*'s feature writer, Philip Kinsley, had an ankle-deep in-depth interview: "Here is no revolutionist. . . . He has no idea of revolutionizing the University's work or even diverting it from its present channels. 'My largest opportunity,' he said, 'is in keeping the wheels of the University going as effectively as now.' He is not ready to announce any policies beyond these. 'I am in no position to talk about my educational program.'"

Did he have one? The *Tribune* man was not investigative; he recorded the young president's work at Yale "to establish a closer application of the social sciences to the law. He added to the law faculty professors of political economy and political science. Dean Winternitz was experimenting in the medical school with the application of the biological sciences, the closer relationship of psychiatry with medicine, for instance. It was finally decided to correlate these programs, and the plan of the Institute of Human Relations was launched. What happened at Yale, however is to be no criterion for the University of Chicago. It is important as showing the lines of his intellectual interest. He is a lawyer and an administrator who wishes to take advantage of scientific methods in aiding the human race."

The *Tribune* man had not been misled, but what he told his readers was misleading. "Closer application," "closer relationship," "experiment," "establish," "correlate"—the *record* sustained them all. The trouble was, is, and always will be, that the record isn't the record. In the world of intangibles—arts, politics, learning, love—the record may conceal the reality and, in any case, doesn't reveal it. The record revealed that Dean Hutchins got five and a half million dollars from the Sterling Trust for a new law school for Yale. The record did not reveal that Dean Hutchins wanted a great deal less than that sum for a new law school in the New Haven slums next to the medical school so that the two schools, cooperating in the Institute for Human Relations, could more easily work together. But the Sterling trustees wanted a Gothic memorial to Mr. Sterling in the center of the campus, and that's what they got—"a five-million-dollar bowling alley," said Hutchins later. "It set the work of the law school back ten years." So "what happened at Yale" was not what had actually happened at Yale: the failure to get the institute properly off the ground; the failure to change the law school's professional approach to the law; the failure of the social sciences and the scientific method to touch reason, right, and justice, or normative jurisprudence, or moral truth; the failure of Yale University to do anything about intellectual community.

Once Hutchins realized that he was likely to be offered the job at Chicago he had turned his attention to the possibility of "fixing up one of these institutions." He had spent more and more of his time exchanging letters with friends at Columbia—and discussing Chicago with his friends in New Haven. (Pondering Yale's equanimity at his going, Hutchins paraphrased Scripture: the guilty flee when none pursue; "I must have been guilty, because nobody pursued me.") The administrative organization could not be changed overnight. What could be done overnight was to bring Bill Douglas to take the deanship of the law school, Mortimer Adler and Dick McKeon from Columbia and Scott Buchanan to be professors of philosophy, and some of the young social scientists like Donald Slesinger from Yale, and they'd pick up where they left off.

Chicago, the university not less than the city, would surely be tickled to have Thornton Wilder, the author of *The Bridge of San Luis Rey*, in the English department. Chicago was a roomier institution than Yale; the money—it was 1929, wasn't it?—was rolling in at the rate of some twenty-seven million a year. Who could object to the new president's bringing in a few brilliant men with him to strengthen the faculty? It was, and would ever after remain, marvelous to think that even a daring young man, even one with a limited experience of universities, imagined that a faculty like Chicago's would not object strenuously to being strengthened by a high-handed president. In his exuberance he supposed that the president of a university could get men appointed—in fields other than his own—the way the dean of a law school had been able to bring new men into his own faculty. Not only would Adler be rejected by the philosophy department, Buchanan's appointment fall through, and Douglas turn him down, but Wilder would never be accepted by the English department except as a visiting lecturer.

Hutchins took office in July, and after a few days in Chicago—during which the reconstruction of the President's House was planned, to provide his wife with a studio for her sculpturing—the Hutchinses left for Europe. There was no tour; the Hutchinses made a beeline for Berlin, where Mrs. Hutchins wanted to arrange the bronze casting of some of her sculptures. (She specialized in heads.)

Toby Dakin—Winthrop Saltonstall Dakin—was a Princeton junior in 1929, majoring in German. He went to Berlin that summer too, and installed himself at the Pension Brunke in Potsdammerstrasse, the choice habitat of the better-paid American academics. He was surprised, the first evening he went down to dinner, to find the Hutchinses there. He knew who they were (and would one day marry Wilder's younger sister, Janet). The Pension Brunke was deluxe, as pensions go, but why (especially with prices as low as they were in Berlin) wouldn't the president of the University of Chicago be staying at the Adlon or the Bristol and availing himself of the privacy of a great hotel? The Brunke was a small place, and the guests ate at a common table. Hutchins was "a dazzling individual, and most amiable; he inquired about my studies and my plans and his interest was flattering." Mrs. Hutchins *looked* like a dazzling individual but she did no dazzling. She seemed to be completely preoccupied, sat silent through the meal, and as soon as coffee had been served she would catch her husband's eye and crook her finger; he would nod imperceptibly, close his conversation with his neighbors, and leave the dining room with his wife. That much Dakin remembered fifty years later; whether he wondered at the great man's subservience (or was it adoration?) he remembered not.[6]

The European holiday was the first of the many that Hutchins would have at his wife's sovereign suggestion. But he managed—the long, devious life—to hold it down to three weeks. He had to get back to work on his inaugural address. He would be especially closely scrutinized because of his nonage—a prima facie insult to the tradition of the office. He would have to be general and acceptable and appear to be specific and bold. The object was to have the attenders at the inauguration say to each other, as they left the chapel, "Impressive...very impressive.... You wouldn't think he was only thirty."

He had spoken at the chapel before, having, a few weeks after his election, been asked to deliver the convocation address to the class of '29. American education, he told the graduates, needed to be attacked, but not for the reasons that it was being attacked. It was being attacked for making young people immoral and godless, for upsetting and disturbing them (a complaint that "might be phrased alternatively to read that the universities were teaching bolshevism"). He was able to inform his listeners—as he should have been, having been a party to the episode—that "one of the greatest scholars in the country wrote a university president of a man who was about to be made a dean, 'I wish strenuously to advise you not to make this appointment. Mr. X is a man who will unsettle the minds of young men at a time when they are most in need of settling.'" His own view was exactly the opposite of the great scholar's: "The purpose of higher education is to unsettle the minds of young men, to widen their horizons, to inflame their intellects. And by this series of mixed metaphors I mean to assert that education is not to teach men facts, theories, or laws; it is not to reform them, or amuse them, or make them expert technicians in any field; it is to teach them to think, to think straight, if possible, but to think always for themselves."

"The picture of the professors of America undermining religion, communizing the sons of capitalists, and knocking the lares and penates off the shelf is far removed from reality. I once taught a class of college freshmen a course called Introduction to the Social Sciences. But there were many aspects of the social sciences to which I could not introduce them, because they would not let me. There was only one Democrat in the class, and he battled alone against the protective tariff, with a degree of success in exact proportion to his numerical strength. The question whether vast military and naval expenditures were necessary could hardly be raised because everybody knew that the United States was the greatest nation on earth and ought to keep other countries in a state of wholesome awe. Suggestions that there were some slight weaknesses in the party system in this country, or in our foreign policy since the War, or that there were a few words one could say for the labor unions, were repelled as unworthy of a college professor. The social and political dogmas inculcated at the paternal breakfast table these gentlemen had accepted whole, nor were they inclined to listen to the words of a professor as against the teachings of practical men."

In his own age—his youthful audience knew how recent *that* was—you went to college to get to know the fellows "who provided one another with the gayest amusements and the most profitable relationships, and who afterward formed a great brotherhood of men ready and willing to help out socially, politically, and financially those of their brethren who might be down on their luck, ostracized from their party, or out of a job . . . the open sesame into the company of people who matter." This, not bolshevism, or irreligion, or immorality, was what was wrong with education. The professor who wanted to indoctrinate his students hadn't a chance; they wouldn't listen to him, no matter what he said. Consider the case of the Harvard instructor who told his class, "The fool hath said in his heart there is no God"; the whole class wrote in their notebooks, "Professor X says there is no God."

"You may have heard that your generation is the hope of America. Mine used to be. If your generation makes no better use of its educational opportunities than mine there is little hope that the millennium will soon arrive or, if it does, that education will have been responsible for its coming."[7]

This was addressed not to an inaugural audience but to a graduating class. If any of his colleagues-to-be were disturbed by his irreverence, there was no indication of it that commencement day; whatever else Hutchins would turn out to be, he would be entertaining. And most of whatever else he would turn out to be would come out in his inaugural, scheduled for November 19; by then he would have been on campus for three months.

What came out at the inaugural was an unentertaining analysis of the University of Chicago, historically and contemporaneously, and its relationship to the problems of American education. It wasn't deadly, but it was dead serious, sober, and proper; the only dead proper paper he ever read. There was a hint—only one—that it had been prepared by a man who had an appetite for phraseology: "If the first faculty of the University of Chicago had met in a tent, this would still have been a great university."[8]

His intention was obvious. In every interview he was charged with being only thirty years old—what, the charge implied, could a fellow of thirty possibly know about running anything?—and his regretful rejoinder had been that his being thirty was something he couldn't do much about. In his inaugural address he decided to do something about it. The occasion would assemble the presidents of the country's leading colleges and universities, almost all of whom (the press pointed out the day after) were old enough to be his father and one of whom, the president of Berea, actually was. He would deliver a speech that would double his age in half an hour.

It didn't go on interminably, but it did go on. He addressed himself, one by one, to the certified problems, at every point supporting his analysis of them with well-researched references to the purpose and practice of his first predecessor, President William Rainey Harper. Whoever would read revolution into his proposals would have to read it into the founding father. Whoever would find this proposal or that insupportable would have to find Harper himself insupportable, and this no one at Chicago was disposed to do. If the university's fifth president was a revolutionist—as the *Tribune* had assured its readers he wasn't—he was the undevoured son of the first, a traditionalist in the sainted tradition which had scandalized education thirty-seven years before.

He called for higher pay for professors—Harper had doubled the salaries of his day—to keep "the best men" from going into business and the professions. (Uneasy with his own materialism at this point, and the materialism he was ascribing to "the best men," he pleaded "the characteristic American feeling that there must be some connection between compensation and ability. It is hopeless to try to combat that feeling. . . . This matter will never be settled until professorial salaries are such as to make scholarship respected in the United States.") He called for continued educational experimentation in the institution whose "principal tradition has been that of freedom" and whose value had been "to try out new ideas, undertake new ventures, to pioneer." Citing the university's historic interest in the city and its problems, he called for continued investigation of social issues to counteract the layman's complaint that research was "remote from reality" (a complaint that would one day be launched against his own college program based on the great books and the liberal arts). Praising the "admirable cooperative work" of the faculty, he called for "formulation of University programs rather than departmental or school policies. . . . We must regard the University as a whole," the "common enterprise" to which each member would contribute his special abilities. He jettisoned—just this once—his insistence that the true function of the professional schools was to improve the professions, and not to train practitioners; he declared his support for the university's dual obligation (as he called it) to do both, and its dual obligation in education to devise the best methods of preparing men and women for research and creative scholarship and for teaching. In view of the traditional focus of the PhD on research, the university which produced more college teachers than any other might well consider awarding a teaching degree equivalent to the PhD.

His tone was that of thoughtful moderation, his proposals couched in terms of "considerations," "study," and "examination." On only one point did he take a clearly defined position: "At times, members of the faculty have suggested that we withdraw from undergraduate work, or at least from the first two years of it. But we do not propose to abandon or dismember the Colleges." The argument from authority was decisive: at a time when most educators were chiefly concerned with undergraduate teaching, William Rainey Harper had insisted upon a university established for research—but also "having a college." The college was intended

to be primarily a laboratory for experimentation in education and the preparation of teachers. This it should remain. "The whole question of the
relation of the first two years of college to the high school on the one hand
and the senior college on the other is one of the most baffling [in educa-
tion]. Instead of withdrawing from this field we should vigorously carry
forward experiments in it." How vigorously he would later insist on
carrying forward the experiments—even unto awarding a degree at the
end of the second year—his colleagues who heard him that day did not
suspect. They were all in favor of vigorous experimentation's being proclaimed by incoming presidents. The new Laura Spellman Rockefeller
Chapel, towering over the Midway and the restrained Gothic of the rest of
the campus, represented the last of the great giver's personal benefactions
(thirty-five million dollars in all) to the university. ("He gives with both
hands," said Old Bob La Follette, "but he takes with many.") The massive
chapel had all the lineaments of a cathedral, and the occasion was a
cathedratic occasion.

It was the finest kind of a mid-October day—in mid-November—and
the longer shadows subdued the sunshine to the appropriate combination
of panoply and severity. The procession up the broad walk to the great
doors was democracy's closest approximation to a coronation. Among the
six hundred members of the academic procession that day on the Midway
were the delegates of three hundred colleges and universities—including
one hundred twelve presidents—marshaled in the order of the founding of
the institutions they represented.

The investiture itself was short. After the address, the welcomes on behalf of the sister institutions east, west, north, and south, and the award of
the doctorate of laws, *honoris causa*, to the president of Berea College, the
Mighty Wurlitzer, which had thundered the processional, thundered the
recessional, and the pageant receded in the order of the founding, from
1411, Saint Andrews, Sir Andrew Craigie to *1892, Chicago, President
Robert Maynard Hutchins.* "Impressive . . . very impressive," the president
of Yale University, James Rowland Angell, was heard to say. "A good
boy . . . he deserves everything he is getting."[9]

This, then, if his vagrant lot was to cast him into education, was
the ultimate rite of passage. Any list of the world's half-dozen great
universities—or America's quarter-dozen—had Chicago at or near the
top. And at the top of Chicago was the young man from Elm Street in
Oberlin. It was 1929, November.

10   Of Cawse It's Impawtant

A university president (like any other) who means to get anything done has got to get it done in his first term; five years, say. The presidency of a great university is a great pulpit. Charles W. Eliot of Harvard, Woodrow Wilson of Princeton, and Nicholas Murray Butler of Columbia all became national figures as university presidents; but none of them was anywhere near as widely known as young as Hutchins. He received a thousand speaking invitations a year and accepted a hundred—and appeared with increasing frequency in the slick magazines as well as the scholarly journals. There are immediate destinies for a man of such prepossessing and precocious parts.

His classmate, Bill Benton, remembered that the tenth reunion of Yale '21 speculated that Bob Hutchins would some day be the nation's president; and that was when he had only begun to make waves as President of Chicago. Five years later the waves would be breakers. Immediately after the Hundred Days of 1933, Roosevelt sent Harry Hopkins to Chicago to sound Hutchins out, and kept on sending emissaries. For the better part of eight years "Dear Mr. Roosevelt" was determined to get "Dear Bob" on the New Deal team, and Dear Bob was the only man he was ever determined to get that he never got. The emissaries kept coming to Chicago and going back to Washington with the same message that the persistently inquiring reporters got: "I am not interested in public life." Impossible; in Washington there is no such thing as a man who is not interested in public life. Impossible, too, that a man who was moldering in a Midwest monastery couldn't be had. The emissaries kept coming, among them (the boss was given to mixing his pitches) Roosevelt's "Mr. Wall Street," otherwise known as Sidney Weinberg of Goldman Sachs.

"Damn it all, Hutchins, it's impawtant."

"Isn't education impawtant, too, Mr. Weinberg?"

"Impawtant, of cawse it's impawtant, but it's been *ovahdone.*"

Of course education is important to a university president, including one who will resign a week later to become a vice president of Standard Oil at twice the salary. Stand him up in front of an audience (or a donor) (or a mirror) and he will say that civilization is a race between education and catastrophe. Hutchins said so too—without the banalities—and said it every time he stood up. The difficulty is to distinguish the straight men from the comics; you have to catch them off the platform, or, as Felix Frankfurter did Hutchins, on the platform of the Sixty-Third Street Station in Chicago, where the New York Central's New England States stopped on its way out to Boston and Cambridge. It was a dreadful stormy day in December of 1932, and the States (which Frankfurter was catching after a lecture in Chicago) was running forty minutes late. The amenities of the Sixty-Third Street Station being what they were, he and his host walked up and down the platform and talked.

Professor Frankfurter of the Harvard Law School was seventeen years older than Hutchins but they had been close friends since the young dean at Yale had assisted the great man in the fruitless futile defense of Sacco and Vanzetti in 1927. Frankfurter had wanted to be invited to Chicago for a lecture precisely at that most unlikely pre-Christmas time of the academic year. What he really wanted was to talk to Hutchins about Harvard's search for a new president. He knew that Hutchins didn't want the job, and he wanted Hutchins' advice. He got some of the advice in the Hutchins kitchen after the lecture, and some more of it on the Sixty-Third Street platform. When he got back to Cambridge he wrote his host asking him to put his advice in writing so that he could use it effectively.[1] Hutchins did:

"You gentlemen who are sitting in deep cushions in Harvard Clubs about the country have probably not heard that the condition of American education is now so critical that we are facing in the West and Middle West the practical extermination of higher learning as we have known it. Most of the higher learning in America is carried on in the state universities. The legislatures, one after another, are wrecking them. . . . At this juncture the system of public education higher and lower requires strong and vocal leadership as never before. This leadership must direct attention not merely to the financial crisis but also to the sweeping changes which must be made to adjust the educational system to the demands of the present day. This means that we must revise our methods, our organization, and our curriculum. In the good old days Harvard supplied educational ideas to the United States. There can be no doubt that the system's leadership resided in Cambridge. At the present time there is no evidence that Harvard is aware of the educational system or has anything to offer it. . . . I wish to see Harvard regain its position of leadership in educational thought and action. It should do so now when such leadership is more needed than at any period in our history. . . . The election as president of a nice Harvard man acceptable to nice Harvard men and consequently ignorant of American education and quite indifferent to its needs would be a fatal mistake for Harvard. There must be among your graduates, if you insist on electing one, a man who has knowledge of and ideas on the development of education in this country. I hope that you will satisfy yourselves that no such person exists before you become reconciled to the election of a safe, dull Bostonian, under whose leadership you will roll down the years in peace, quiet, and dishonor."[2]

Frankfurter replied: "Your extraordinarily persuasive analysis—that happy blend that you have of impudent cajolery and venerable wisdom—came the very morning of the day that I had a chance to put in an effective lick. . . . Really, your letter not only as an astute document but as an expression of faith makes me love you more than ever with wisdom as well as with affection. . . . The dominant experience I brought back from Chicago was that out there there was a President who really was passionate about education,—and education as the pursuit, systematically, of the richest and most sensitive experience of life."[3]

Apparently education was impawtant, and not, in Hutchins' view, overdone. He had no sooner got back to Chicago than he indicated his intention to overdo it, and less than a year after his installation, with no power other than persuasion, he had got the no-motion machinery of a great university to adopt the "Hutchins Plan." (The quotation marks here are significant.) The honeymooning faculty senate adopted his first proposal—presented on one side of one sheet of paper—in twelve minutes.[4] It revived the "junior division" of the college—the freshman and sophomore years—by assigning it the responsibility for the development and administration of a program of general education. "Revived" is the word; the junior division had been the spectacular invention of William Rainey Harper, the first president of the University of Chicago, in 1892. But at Chicago, no less than everywhere else, this segment of the university had been progressively orphaned by the phenomenal increases of scholarly specialization, in whose interest the graduate schools had all but absorbed the junior and senior years. Under the combined influences of specialization and the elective system, the education of a human being, without reference to his future occupation, had been nearly abandoned to the vocational interests of industry, commerce, and finance; to the whims of legislatures, parents, alumni, and benefactors; and to the vagrant heart's desire of the adolescent. ("This institution," Professor Philip Schuyler Allen told a Chicago class just before Hutchins' advent, "is becoming an intellectual whorehouse—I suppose that in mixed company I should say a brothel.—But I mean whorehouse. An intellectual whorehouse is a university which, like this one, permits its Home Economics Department to give a student credit for weaving a straw hat.")

It became a point of status—to avoid teaching in the first two years, which were ultimately delegated to what Hutchins called a "Coxey's army of graduate teaching assistants." This practice alone was an educational atrocity, and it was to be ever more atrocious as the state universities expanded and the colleges took to pretending to be universities. But it did not, then or thereafter, arouse any appreciable scandal in or out of education. Its victims were only students; its perpetrators were the scholars to whom the graduate teaching assistants would some day have to look for jobs; and the teaching assistants themselves (with an annual turnover of 50 percent) had no other way to earn a pittance to maintain their preparation for the PhD.

Sentiment overt and covert was strong at Chicago (and at other great graduate schools) for getting rid of the folderol of undergraduate education altogether. Just prior to Hutchins' advent, Dean Gordon Jennings Laing of Chicago's graduate school was saying that "not even in the best university is the graduate work on the scale and quality that would be possible if the institutions were entirely free from undergraduate entanglements." But Hutchins had no sooner hung up his fedora than he announced that he—he used the polite amorphism "we"—did not intend to abandon or dismember the college but to revive it: "A college is an institution devoted to the advancement of knowledge. A college in a university is an institution devoted to discovering what an education ought to be." The discovery, he let it be understood, would be made at Chicago and the college would be the laboratory.

The faculty senate, composed of the full professors, was unperturbed; it didn't care all that much about the college, one way or another. What should have perturbed it, but apparently didn't, was something else it subscribed to in those twelve minutes: perceptible, if only perceptible, breaching of the walls between the departments. They would retain their myriad identities, but they would be gathered into four basic divisions—the humanities, the biological sciences, the physical sciences, and the social sciences—charged with the development and direction of the programs at the junior/senior, graduate, and professional levels. The medical school, for instance—at Chicago, as everywhere, a splendidly isolated sanctum—would now be an integral part of the biological sciences division.

A university is an aggregation of separate sovereignties "connected," as

Hutchins put it, "by a common heating plant." The sovereignties are the departments. Proliferating as specialization proliferated, the departments were and are autonomous, each and severally pitted against the *universum* of the university. There was and is nothing to unify them except the demand of their own development—demand stimulated by the use of their work in practical applications. Forced to cooperate by the prospect of application, the natural science departments, still fighting each other for the research money that follows prestige, were yielding to interdisciplinary undertakings: in physics and chemistry; chemistry (and the biological sciences) and medicine; chemistry and geology; geology and physics; physics and astronomy; astronomy and meteorology; and all of them with mathematics. But where popular utility was less readily demonstrable, as in the social sciences, or indemonstrable, as in the humanities, there was, and still is, nothing to knock departmental heads together and every parochial reason to build walls ever higher.

The argument for the department was, and is, persuasive, at least in the natural sciences. Who except a microbiologist knows enough about microbiology to say what the department of microbiology needs, or whether its work is important, or whether, at budget time, its work is more important than, say, organic chemistry's or invertebrate zoology's? The more sophisticated the university, the more exalted the unintelligibility and the higher the walls around each departmental cosa nostra. And "areas" within a department were (and would be ever more so) almost as widely separated as the disciplines themselves.

Whoever would want to bring university out of diversity would have to mount an assault against those walls. There would seem to be one way— one very slow way—to do it. The professors of the next generation, if as senior high school and college students they had acquired a common stock of learning, and as graduate students and instructors continued to refine and rework that common stock irrespective of their special fields, could perhaps have something intelligible to say to one another and a common interest in going on saying it. But then the departments would have to be got out of collegiate education and subordinated even at the graduate level. But who was there to try to do it? Not an administrator with five years (at the most) to try to do anything, and with neither the general power nor the special credentials to get so much as a hearing.

A university president was not supposed to be a scholar and very rarely was; rarest of all the kind of scholar with whom scientists might communicate even elementarily—namely a scientist. The young president of the University of Chicago might be acknowledged to know a little something about law. But law was not a science, not even when it called itself jurisprudence. And here was a nonscientist who was so impudent as to claim to have all of the competence—fortunately he could not claim to have any of the power—to reorganize a great university when he *prided himself* (as he himself put it) on having a nonmathematical mind (though he would subject every student to the study of mathematics, as the purest form of reasoning).

The twelve-minute faculty meeting that adopted the "Hutchins Plan" of divisional organization may be seen in distant retrospect as the president's first sly feint at those impregnable repositories, the departments. Survivors of that occasion say variously that there was no opposition because the defenders of things as they were and always would be were unprepared and unorganized, or believed that the president knew better than to suppose he could do anything about the hallowed sovereignties and prerogatives. Or were they momentarily mesmerized? Besides, the divisional consolidation made epistemological and pedagogical sense (on paper) and was later adopted (on paper) by colleges and universities generally. (A sporadic flourish of "interdepartmental" or "interdisciplinary" courses continued to appear across the country, even in the supposedly "soft" studies, as a supposed concession to the imperative vagaries of the New Student of the 1960s. The orthodox departmentalist continued to pay no attention to them.)

The second battery of proposals, a few months later, bit deeper into the academic bedrock, but they were adopted almost as readily as the first.[5] The college teaching faculty was granted substantial autonomy;[6] and the country's first faculty awards for excellence in undergraduate teaching were established by the University of Chicago in 1930, when Hutchins got the endowment for them from broker Ernest Quantrell.

In another of the second set of "Hutchins Plan" reforms, the elective system was invaded by year-long general courses in the four divisional fields. The course-credit system was junked. A Chicago baccalaureate would no longer represent an accumulation of unrelated oddments, no sooner passed than past. Instead of being graduated on the basis of what he had known and forgotten, the candidate for a degree would take a series of comprehensive examinations on what he now knew; he would take them whenever he thought that he was ready to take them, and take them as often as he wanted to. The residence requirement was reduced to a year, and though most students continued to complete the undergraduate requirements in three or four years, some passed the comprehensive after two years (and in one historic case a graduate of an Italian liceo passed them immediately after his admission to the college). The examinations were to be administered by an independent board of examiners—putting an end to the time-dishonored system of studying the instructor instead of the subject. Compulsory class attendance was eliminated.[7] Freshmen were to be graded Satisfactory or Unsatisfactory—the pass/fail "innovation" of a generation later. Some of the effects were measurable as early as the close of the plan's first year of operation, in the spring of 1932. With the elimination of compulsory class attendance at Chicago, attendance actually rose that year by 1.3 percent. Freshman failures went down from 6 to 5 percent, and dropouts went down by 5 percent. Applications rose—this in the depression pit of 1932—and went on rising. By all the tests that could be applied, the entering students were markedly superior to their predecessors, and in the first year of the program thirty-nine freshmen presented themselves for examination in subjects they had studied by themselves, without the benefit of instruction. They all passed, and passed with an average higher than the general average of the class. The pursuit of knowledge had become an undergraduate activity.[8]

All of this was revolutionary, and Hutchins wanted all of it. But it wasn't Hutchins' revolution. Bits and pieces of it had been urged—and some of them instituted—at one time or another by Eliot and then Lowell at Harvard, by Harper and Dewey at Chicago, by Wilson at Princeton. But it had never been put together in a package, and most of the bits and pieces had fallen, or been swept, away by the competitive rah-rahism, "development" programs, and fragmentation of teaching and research in the 1920s. Most of the elements of the new program at Chicago had been proposed by a faculty committee which had been sitting (and sitting on it) for two years before Hutchins got there. Everybody everywhere knew that something fundamental had to be done. What doing it had waited on was somebody to say, "Let's do it now." The something that was done was a series of fundamental changes in structure. It did no more than brush against the bedeviling issues of deadly lectures and the lifeless content of traditional textbook curricula. The "Hutchins Plan" was not the Hutchins Plan.

But it was hailed at home and abroad as the first great educational reform of the century, and the young president as the century's first great educational reformer. In the midst of the general hubbub attending the reforms on the Midway nobody paid much attention to the great reformer's ominous animadversion: "We are now in a position to teach the wrong things in the right way."

What was the matter with him? Hadn't he got everything—well, almost everything—he wanted (or should have wanted)? The faculty as a whole had overridden the traditional uneasiness which some of the leading figures in the natural sciences and the professional schools voiced about deemphasizing specialization, which they wanted to emphasize as preparation for graduate work. The thirty-year-old president had cut a great swathe in a great hurry. He could move on any time, as move he must, and cut a great swathe in another great hurry somewhere else. And on, and on.

—Provided that he was ready to move on any time without having got any of the three things he really wanted. He wanted a "new" method of education. He wanted a "new" curriculum. And he wanted a genuine consolidation of research, a common set of principles which might establish an order and proportion of the goods of the mind just as there is an order and proportion of all other goods.

This last was the most scandalous of his three announced objectives (apart from his careful exacerbation of the anti-Catholicism of the academic adversaries by his use of the perfectly proper term "hierarchy" to indicate order and proportion). It was impossible for modern academics even in philosophy (or especially in philosophy) to accept his insistence that the "first principles" of "metaphysics," which would hierarchize all other disciplines, were to be determined by uncoerced consensus based on uncoerced investigation. How did he mean to investigate chimeras? *Whose* first principles? *What* metaphysics?

Hutchins said that the first business of scholarship was to recover the university from the confusion that constituted the chief glory of the higher learning. He denounced the happy anarchy that (in the name of academic freedom) held one subject matter to be as good as another. Naturally none of the anarchists really felt that way, or really approved of a budget that allocated as much money to what they regarded as frivolous projects as they themselves got for their own fundamental projects; but the freedom doctrine, if it protected the other fellow's frivolity, also protected their own fundamentalism; so they never complained outside the family. The family was the department, and little by little it came to be widely, and correctly, suspected that Hutchins' divisional organization at the university level and his general education program for the college were backdoor tricks to perpetrate the metaphysician's absolutism.

The fact that some academics thought that his objectives were something new—and resisted them for *that* reason—simply confirmed his conviction that educators were badly educated. The things he wanted were all of them very old.

He set the scientists against him by asserting that it was philosophy—specifically that crumbled cornerstone of philosophy which went (or had gone) by the name of metaphysics and professed itself the science of being—that put all other studies in their place and sent them about *her* sovereign business. He outraged the philosophers by insisting that the philosopher's work was not to teach philosophy—or philosophies—but to teach philosophizing. In the land where every man was king, every man must be a philosopher and not an alumnus who had swallowed, regurgitated, and forgotten lectures in other men's philosophies. There was no right way to teach the things that were not matters of rote; there was only a right way to learn, in which the teacher was an auxiliary to the process, the classic "midwife" of ideas that the student himself must bring to birth.

In coming to that position—by whatever magic one comes to a position in such matters—Hutchins had enrolled himself in the everlasting dispute over cognition. How do we learn, and how, if at all, is what we learn imparted by others? "Man learns," said Erasmus, "at the school of example, and will attend no other." Augustine wept: "The unlearned arise and take heaven by force, and here are we with all our learning, stuck fast in flesh and blood"; and then, weeping, heard the voice of an angel saying, "Take up and read, take up and read," and the Book fell open to Romans 13:13, and he had no need to read further. "They are wise to do evil," said the prophet, "but to do good they have no knowledge." "The triumph of my art," Socrates told Theaetetus, "is in thoroughly examining whether the thought which the mind of the young man is bringing to birth is a false idol or a noble and true spirit. Like the midwife, I myself am barren, and the reproach which is often made against me, that I ask questions of others and have not the wit to answer them myself, is very just; the reason is that the gods compel me to be a midwife but forbid me to bring forth. And therefore I am not myself at all wise, nor have I anything to show which is the invention or birth of my own soul, but those who converse with me profit. . . . It is quite clear that they never learned anything from me. The many fine discoveries to which they cling are of their own making." The twentieth-century progressives, with John Dewey at their head, maintained that we learn by doing and argued that the school should somehow prefigure the experience of "real life."

But Hutchins could not get the right way of teaching—even teaching the wrong things—introduced at Chicago. Nor would he ever, until a race of teachers would arise in the spirit of Socrates, asking pertinent questions in persistent dialogue instead of reciting answers, forcing disputation instead of information on their students, converting education from a process of absorbing to a process of challenge and counterchallenge. Some young instructors, marvelously uncorrupted by their own experience as students, could employ the Socratic method; some always had. But not often the old hats, whose attitudes dominated the colleges and the universities. Socrates was, of course, born, not made; and until the schools, at whatever level, would recognize that there is no other true teacher and hunt out this one and hire him away from taxi-driving, or half-soling, or a bench in the park, or a jail cell, or even a schoolhouse, even the wrong things would never be taught in the right way.

The things the misnamed "Hutchins Plan" went on teaching in the wrong (*not* the right) way were the wrong things. These courses could not be taught via the textbooks that went on dominating, or trying to dominate, education, books written (or pasted together) by academic hacks. The textbook publishers, corruptionists of school superintendents, school boards, state boards of education, were as rich as the schoolmarms (of both sexes) were poor. They could give a five-thousand-a-year professor five thousand dollars for a month's cut-and-paste job. His rank, on the title page, was secondary; what was primary was the name (by implication, the imprimatur) of the institution he was connected with.

With the rise of the one-semester or one-term "survey" courses for freshmen in the 1920s, the publishers had turned their attention to the assembly of teams to produce survey texts, which were just as pedantic. The most (and in some respect the only) impressive exception to this output was a series of Chicago faculty lectures in the university's one survey course, "The Nature of the World and Man," inaugurated in 1924. This introduction to the natural sciences became so popular that the university published it as a book, which colleges across the country had adopted long before Hutchins became president.

But the right things that Hutchins wanted taught the right way were neither lectures nor surveys. He wanted the Socratic method of discussion to draw the young into the great debates of the ages conducted by the great minds of the ages on the great issues of the ages. The great books would constitute the heart of a fixed curriculum to be taught to "everybody who can learn from books" in a four-year institution beginning with the junior year of high school, an institution open at public expense to every member of the rising generation, whether or not he or she meant to go on to university work. That curriculum would consist of the greatest books of the Western world and the arts of reading, writing, thinking, and speaking, together with mathematics, the best exemplar of the process of human reason. "If our hope has been to frame a curriculum which educes the elements of our common human nature, this program should realize our hope. If we wish to prepare the young for intelligent action, this course of study should assist us; for they will have learned what has been done in the past, and what the greatest men have thought. They will have learned how to think for themselves. If we wish to lay a basis for advanced study, that basis is provided. If we wish to secure true universities, we may look forward to them, because students and professors may acquire through this course of study a common stock of ideas and common methods of dealing with them."9

The reason that these objectives—and the curriculum that served them—were unlikely to be pursued at Chicago or anywhere else was that they were profoundly un-American. *And* un-German. But the German university was a scholarly institution concerned entirely with investigation and the training of investigators. It did not prepare its students for the practice of the professions but for the advancement of the professions, both in science and the humanities. Vocationalism (in every vocation but scholarship) was beneath it; beneath it, too, was everything that the American thought of as college life. The German (and European) elementary schooling was six years, after which the sheep, rigorously separated from the goats, went on to the four-year *Gymnasium* or—this was a twentieth-century development—to the science-oriented *Realgymnasium*. There they got their general education, which, after a total of ten years of schooling, was regarded as terminal. Most of them went into white-collar work, a relatively small minority to the technical institutes which produced professional practioners, and a very few to the university. There was no institution comparable to the American college on top of which, little by little, the PhDs from Leipzig superimposed little Leipzigs.

The result was the mélange of the American university. From the start it did not know what it was—a collegiate extension of general education, a center for research and scholarly training, or a gaggle of professional schools. And it never found out. The time came, with a rush, when American affluence sent a hundred (or a thousand) young people to "college" where European austerity sent one to the university.

The American founding fathers wanted to establish a popular form of government. Such government, even with a restricted franchise, had as its first requirement an educated citizenry. The American fervor for popular schooling, unknown anywhere else in the world, was such that by the turn of the twentieth century, education appeared to have become the state religion. But what was worshiped was not education. What was worshiped was the schoolhouse, which ultimately displaced the church as the national ground cover. What went on in the schoolhouse depended on what the public wanted, for (as Hutchins never wearied of quoting from Plato) what is honored in a country will be cultivated there. What was honored in modern America was the "practical"—the realizable return on the investment. Americans were the most practical people in history, and with good reason. They'd had to be. But their preoccupation with the practical—a national motto, "Do it," was coined by the Yippies a half-century later—diminished their interest in the theoretical to the vanishing point. Their founding fathers had been spectacularly practical theorists. But their latter-day heroes, right out of Horatio Alger, were nontheoretical, even antitheoretical, men. The only defensible object of schooling was, not thinking for oneself, but doing for oneself (and always for oneself).

Reality meant improving oneself, and improving oneself was a measurable matter of money. The disparagement of hereditary aristocracy in the euphoric name of egalitarianism disparaged only one kind of aristocracy; in a society where being born ahead was treason, the only way to be ahead was to get ahead. The privileged few who, in the 1930s, went to college were expected to get rich. Parents scraped and borrowed to send their children to college, not so that they would be better than they themselves were, but so that they would be better off. For the poor, education meant a better job—or, in times like the thirties, any kind of job—and was appraised accordingly. Job training, once the province of apprenticeship, with the rise of technology became vocational training in the schools; and vocational training, to gratify both its democratic practitioners and its democratic beneficiaries, became "vocational education" (and, a generation of gobbledegook later, "career education").

This wasn't education, but it was what the country honored and, in its schools, its colleges, and its professions, cultivated. What Hutchins wanted had once been called education—the preparation, of the few to whom it was open, for independent participation in the common life and the development of the individual's highest powers. It was now called liberal education, generally disparaged as at best useless and at worst elitist. Hutchins called it education for democracy, on the ground that the best education of the few, where the few governed, was the best education for all where all governed. It was the education he fought for for twenty years at Chicago and for twenty-five years afterward; fought for unsuccessfully, and ever more unsuccessfully as the national plunge to illiteracy proceeded and the American "kid" entered college with thirty thousand hours behind him of staring at thirty thousand electronically projected dots on a glass screen. Still, the end of Hutchins' tenure at Chicago saw the great books occupying as much as 25 percent of the syllabi of the general courses of the College, and the College faculty preponderantly staffed by men (preponderantly younger men) who used the method of instruction-by-inquiry, in which the teacher was only the midwife.

It is one thing (and no presidential thing) for a university president to think he knows what education ought to be. It is another and still less presidential thing to try to foist it on the great faculty of a great university. But the unpresidentialest thing of all is to show them how it is done. And this, in his honors course for (of all things) freshmen, Hutchins had the effrontery to do as soon as he became president and to go on doing year after year. In the History of Ideas course, 4 to 6 P.M. every Tuesday, with another impudent young pup cobadgering the forty honors students ranged around an immense seminar table, the president of the University of Chicago went ahead and taught in the way he said the professors ought to teach. And if that wasn't effrontery enough, his cobadgerer was the same Professor Adler who, that April day in 1937, was coming into Hutchins' office behind me to tell him (as Hutchins put it) what to think about Aristotle's *Metaphysics*.

11   Mert

In 1927—when as dean of the Yale Law School Hutchins was introducing such arcane subjects as economics, psychology, and even ethics, on the ground that it would not do a lawyer any durable harm to be an educated man or, in a pinch, to know right from wrong—a most unlikely author, a psychology instructor at Columbia, had written a paper criticizing the classic law school text, *Wigmore on Evidence*. Hutchins asked him to come to New Haven and talk. Mortimer J. Adler suggested a date two weeks ahead and spent the two weeks mastering (or appearing to have mastered) the whole body of the law of evidence.

At twenty-four—as at forty-four, sixty-four, and seventy-four—Mortimer Adler talked a blue streak. He did so at this meeting—after he recovered from the shock of realizing the young man in tennis ducks wasn't the dean's clerk, but the dean. Adler knew that Hutchins was only twenty-eight; but a law school dean of twenty-eight, when you're a psychology instructor four years younger, is bound to be a somber man, and Adler had got himself up as somberly as possible, black suit, black hat, for the occasion. Hutchins didn't break the ice, he crushed it. "Tell me everything you know," he said, gazing down at Adler, "about the law of evidence."[1] Evidence was Hutchins' own field, but Adler had come loaded.

The archives of that and subsequent meetings disclose that Adler told Hutchins, always at length and always at fever pitch, everything he knew, or thought he knew, or thought he might know, or thought that if he didn't know, nobody else did, about the law of evidence and everything else. And about everybody else. But Adler never recovered from his second shock, the realization that here was a grand master of the art of remoteness conveyed (conveyed; not covered) by badinage, an expert at fending off the personal question; sitting somehow apart from his every interlocutor in the peculiarly discountenancing kind of judgment that put the interlocutor off balance: moral judgment. The guilty sense of being seen through was such that the father-figure gap never closed, not even in this closest and longest of all Hutchins' close relationships: "What did Bob say? Did he say anything about me?"

He was Hutchins' antithesis and Hutchins' complement; ferociously didactic, belligerent, consumptive of codified learning, and productive of uncodified learning. He was unfunny, ungraceful, and unquiet. The easy arrogance that Hutchins exuded, Adler had to articulate. Everything was, or in two weeks became, his field; sufficiently so, at least, to confound (or appear to have confounded) the men who claimed the field for their hard-earned own. In the half-century that followed, everything that Hutchins needed to know in a hurry—it was always in a hurry—Adler found out and compiled, in a still greater hurry.

The schools around New York City saw a thousand straight-A boys a year like Mortimer Adler driven into whatever occupation they could pry themselves into, sometimes in two or three occupations successively and sometimes in three or four at once. The New York legend has enough documentation behind it to confirm the supposition that a Mortimer Adler at, say, sixteen was certain to make it big and uncertain only whether to make it big as a lawyer, a doctor, a producer (or a banker or broker, bucking the closed-door gentiles in Wall Street), a playwright, a professor, a wholesale liquor dealer, or a dialectical revolutionary.

Adler was married—uncomfortable for her family and ultimately too uncomfortable for her—to a handsome, high-minded, stony lady from a North Shore Chicago suburb. She may have meant to derogate him by calling him Mert—though it may have been Clifton Fadiman, who didn't mean to derogate him, who nicknamed him. (Fadiman was a student, along with Lionel Trilling and Whitaker Chambers, in the first class Adler taught at Columbia.) Nobody called him Mort. Gentiles, except for his wife, called him Mortimer. Hutchins, a gentile, called him Mortimer. I called him Mert: for Mert was what he was. The "little fellow," the "little metaphysician," overpowered everyone and intimidated no one. He sassed you, you sassed him back, and he sassed you back, and you sassed him back, and he never let go or let up; let him but fail to satisfy a persistent freshman and he would go home and bone up for a week and come back to demolish the freshman (unsurprisingly), or (surprisingly) to report that the freshman had demolished him. While he was growing on you—and grow he did, marvelously—you were growing on him. Mert was what he was.

He had no genius (and wanted none) for concealing his ungentle despite for his fellow academics. His psychology of education—which he said he got from Aristotle, and it must be in there somewhere—was that the edu-catee had first to be reduced from error to ignorance before knowledge could be imparted to him. When he spoke to his colleagues (which was seldom) or of them (which was often and in public), he snapped his jaws shut on a leg or an arm. His pugnacity was an astonishment and a splen-dor. There was no getting him to go easy or lay off, no headshake, nudge, or surreptitious shin-kick that he recognized as a signal to leave well enough alone; it wasn't well enough for Mert until his adversary was pinned to the mat. "He's so unpleasant," said a woman who had to work closely with him, "that it's a pleasure."

Some of us are born maddening; some achieve it; and some have it thrust upon them. Mert was a happy concatenation of all three blessings. On one immortal occasion—immortalized by, among others, Gertrude Stein—Hutchins invited Gertrude and Alice B. Toklas to dinner at the president's house at Chicago. Gertrude's version of her encounter with Mert (whom Hutchins had also invited with deviltry prepense) is recorded in her *Everybody's Autobiography*. It begins with her asking Hutchins what ideas are important and Hutchins' handing her a list of the books he and Adler were teaching in their honors course. She observes that none of them was originally written in English, and Hutchins (according to her) replies that there have been no ideas expressed in English. She replies that she gathers that in his view there are no ideas that are not sociological or governmental, and he says, "Well, are there?"

"Well yes I said. Government is the least interesting thing in human life, creation and the expression of that creation is a damn sight more interest-ing, yes I know and I began to get excited yes I know, naturally you are teachers and teaching is your occupation and naturally what you call ideas are easy to teach and so you are convinced that they are the only ideas but the real ideas are not the relation of human beings as groups but a human being to himself inside him and that is an idea that is more interesting than humanity in groups, after all the minute that there are a lot of them they do not do it for themselves but somebody does it for them and that is a darn sight less interesting. Then Adler began and I have forgotten what the detail of it was but we were saying violent things to each other and I was telling him that anybody could tell by looking at him that he was a man who would be singularly unsusceptible to ideas that are created within oneself that he would take to either inside or outside regulation but not to creation, and Hutchins was saying well if you can improve upon what we are doing I challenge you to do it take our class next week and I said of course I will and then Adler said something and I was standing next to him and violently telling him and everybody was excited and the maid came and said Madame the police. Adler went a little white and we all stopped and then burst out laughing. Fanny Butcher had arranged that Alice Toklas and I should go off that evening in the homicidal squad and they had come and there they were waiting. Well we said good-night and we went off with the policemen."²

All of Gertrude Stein's versions are unauthorized versions—as she herself would have been quick to say. There is another unauthorized, but widely attested, version (by the other dinner guests) of her "standing next to him and violently telling him and everybody was excited." This version has it that the violence was beyond telling, with the excited poet hitting the excited prosist on the head with her fist (she was taller enough than he to do it) and saying, "Young man, you like to win arguments. I won't argue with you any more. You fail to hold my attention."

New York hones the hide and the tongue. In high school, with a copy boy's job on the old *Sun*, Adler broke into print writing editorials at seven dollars a column and went on building his library, gorging himself on books that weren't assigned in courses, books like John Stuart Mill's autobiography (and arguing with the author in the margin). When he learned that Mill had read Plato before he was ten, Mert, at fifteen, "felt like a savage." He got a seven-dollar advance from the *Sun* and bought the *Republic*, read it, argued with it in the margin, and was off on one of his careers. He discovered that he was a philosopher like Socrates, a Jewish gadfly sent to sting the high priests and pretenders.

Plato led him to Aristotle, whose relentless logic suited Mert right down to where Aristotle stood: the ground. Plato was the first philosopher—but Aristotle arguing with Plato made of philosophy the queen of sciences. Between them they divided Western philosophy into the two schools that contended for the Middle Ages, the Augustinian, with its Platonic perturbations, and the Thomistic, which swelled into the twenty-one volumes of the *Summa Theologica*—which as a high school boy Adler bought one by one as he accumulated the money. Mortimer J. Adler did not know whether or not he believed in God; he once said that he had all of the reason and none of the faith. But he became one of the twentieth century's half-dozen most distinguished disciples of the greatest of all of Aristotle's commentators, Thomas Aquinas—*Saint* Thomas Aquinas, the Angelic Doctor of the Roman Catholic Church, who asked of men only that they reason with him about the body of faith (which could not be maintained if it contradicted reason, God being the author of both).

Disputation, as it had been Aquinas's business, and before him Aristotle's, was Mert's; a Talmudic terrier if ever there was one. By the time he met Hutchins he was a Thomist, and a Thomist in the best of standing he remained for twenty years, until (of course) he challenged every one of the Holy Doctor's five proofs of the existence of God (part 1, question 2, article 3, "Whether God Exists?"). His best of standing, while he maintained it, was confined to the circle of Catholic philosophers identified with the liberalization of the social views of the Church following Leo XIII's "labor" encyclical *Rerum novarum* at the turn of the century. In time Adler came to be known as the foremost American Thomist and—with Jacques Maritain and Etienne Gilson of France, who became his friends—one of the world's foremost exponents of the doctrine.

Until Adler—and, alas, Hutchins—Thomism in the 1940s had a serious constituency only in the more advanced Catholic schools. In the secular (and nominally Protestant) institutions, "neo-Thomist" and "neo-Thomism" came to be devil words, with Mert as the devil. The "alas, Hutchins" was inevitable, as was Beardsley Ruml's gag that "a Thomist is somebody who's in favor of Hutchins." Here was a Presbyterian president of a Baptist institution—nobody cared about *that* little discrepancy any more—promoting Catholicism among the bright Jewish boys and girls who crowded into one of the few great private schools that had set no quiet quota on undergraduate admissions.

No questions agitated more back-room (and front-room) frenzy during the Twenty Years' War at Chicago than whether Hutchins was Mortimer Adler's Mortimer Snerd. His enemies were enjoyably divided on the issue: Hutchins was either a fool or a rogue, have it your own way. His admirers had much the harder time of it: since he could not be a rogue, he must be a fool, unless (1) Adler and Aristotle and Aquinas were all misrepresented by the opposition or (2) Adler and Aristotle and Aquinas were right. That they were all misrepresented was hard to believe, what with Adler's lectures "demonstrating" the existence of God and the immortality of the soul. (His demonstrations, based on timeless reasoning from timeless "common sense" assumptions, or self-evident truths, validated only by common experience, fascinated those devotees of the theoretical, the bright students—a phenomenon all the more maddening to their academic, and nonacademic, elders, who associated demonstration with the laboratory.)

The second option, that Adler, Aristotle, and Aquinas were right, was not much more palatable. How could men be right who had lived before the dawn of empirical science, who (in Aristotle's case) accepted slavery and (in Aquinas's) monarchy and the inquisition of suspected heretics? How could a twentieth-century apologist for such men be right? Down the years, some of these friendly acquaintances of Hutchins came to know Adler well and to understand and respect him (*and* Aristotle *and* Aquinas).

A few came to know him still better and to like him immensely. (In good company outside the academic bullring he was delightful.) But very, very few of them could ever bring themselves to believe that, on balance— a balance that always included public relations—Adler's influence on Hutchins was anything but unfortunate.

It wasn't. One of the reasons it wasn't anything but unfortunate, was that Poor Bob had never had it so good as when he had to carry extra weight, like a fast jockey. Milton Mayer—that glib radical—was a millstone around his neck, but Mortimer Adler was a windmill. Mayer probably wrote his speeches for him, *but Adler probably thought his thoughts for him.* If it hadn't been for Adler, Hutchins would not have tried to wreck the higher learning and turn the university into a seminary. Didn't he admit that he hadn't read a book before he met Adler? Where but from Adler could he have got his retrogressive ideas; his preoccupation with the Great Books, so-called; his denigration of science and scientific method; his Greco-Christian patter about *virtues* and *vices* and a curriculum derived from the medieval *trivium* of grammar, rhetoric, and logic; his inflammatory *metaphysics*; his "science of first principles"? True, he had been brought up in a Presbyterian minister's home—but, my God, he *had* been in the army and he *had* been at Yale, and he *had* run a law school that staffed the junior partners' offices on Wall Street. Where could he have picked up those dusty answers if not from Adler?

His friends and his enemies were all of them wrong. It was Adler all right who brought him to the Great Books (or rather, the Great Books to him). It was Adler all right who got him started on Aristotle and Aquinas. It was Adler who dug up the citations Hutchins wanted and deluged him with innumerable, interminable memoranda. The metaphysical scheme— and much of its vocabulary—was Adler's. But the educational scheme was Hutchins' before he knew Adler, and so was the educational philosophy. He had not articulated them in the terms he used after his life with Adler began, but he had articulated them in the curriculum he introduced at Yale, in the method of instruction he called for, and in his unrelenting effort (insofar as the law school could reach) to integrate the scholarly disciplines. Adler wasn't that much interested in educational structure. The "Hutchins Plan" wasn't Hutchins', but the Hutchins Plan certainly wasn't Adler's.

But it was easier for Hutchins' friends and for Hutchins' enemies to blame Adler than to blame Hutchins. Hutchins would not disclaim Adler. Why should he? On the theoretical level he was righter than he was wrong—and righter than his red-eyed critics; the twentieth century was the first to discard the thought of the Greeks (or the faith of the Christians), the first to cut itself off from its own roots. On the practical level Mert may have been wrong in his indifference to the personal and social agonies of his time, but not a bit wronger than the traditional (and still characteristic) scholars who buried themselves in parochial investigations far less significant than Adler's.

At least Adler was not likely to be accused of writing Hutchins' speeches; he wrote far too badly for that. His language was bare *and* turgid ("Dear Mortimer: Thanks for the statement about the Honors course. I shall translate it into English and have it inserted into the catalogue. Ever yours, Bob"). But his mind was an Aristotelian laser. As a public lecturer, raising those exotic questions of his—Is Man Different from the Animals? Does God Exist? Is the Soul Immortal?—he wowed the women's clubs and the temple forums; nobody in twentieth-century America except Adler thought that such questions (lifted, along with the answers, from Aristotle, Aquinas, and Plato, respectively) were questions anymore. His cockiness aroused the frenzy of the few who came to his lectures loaded for him—or who thought they were. Once, in the question period after a lecture, a woman asked him if he could have made an equally strong argument for the opposite position. "That," said Mert, "is the first sensible question of the evening. The answer is, Yes."

Adler had no interest whatever in what was going on around him. It wasn't that he was unworldly; far, far from it. He was unconcerned. Hutchins lived in the present, for all his real or affected affinity for the desiccate past and his vehemence against "presentism." Whatever else Hutchins was, he was a modern man, a practical man, an American man. He was up to his ears in the affairs of his secular time and place, and he dealt with them in secular style. Adler did not participate in community life at any level, on or off campus. As a Jew, a New Yorker, an intelligent man, and an educated man, he was a visceral liberal of sorts who would vote (if he bothered to vote) for, say, the New Deal. But his habitual impatience rose to outright intolerance of the social activism of his associates. He dismissed them as sentimentalists and emotionalists and disturbers of his peace.

He did not care who wrote his country's laws. He dealt not with the laws, but with law, and not with his country's laws, but with any country's law anywhere any time, and with what nobody else gave a hoot about: the nature of law. His world was abstract and his meat was abstraction, and abstraction was always and everywhere the same. Except for his refusal to be programmed, he was the first-born of the first generation of computers. If you could have got him to sit still while you pushed a few facts down him, you could have got an immediate printout with which there was no arguing. He could, and did, deal with democracy in the abstract, capitalism in the abstract, war in the abstract, world government in the abstract, man in the abstract, and God (how else?) in the abstract—with no documentation at all from a world in which these doctrines were embedded in the cracking and crackling concrete of life.

Warm among friends, hot among adversaries, Mert was, in fact, the absent-hearted professor. With Americans passionately divided on the issue of U.S. "intervention" versus "isolation" prior to Pearl Harbor, Hutchins was one of the earliest and most sonorous anti-interventionists on the left. Adler was silent until he was pressed for his view—pressed by Hutchins-Adler watchers who were pretty sure in advance that they'd get just what they got: ADLER AGAINST HUTCHINS ON WAR. The statement did not reflect any unusual intellectual pretension or consideration; Adler was for war for the reasons that intelligent, educated New York Jews were for it, and the reasons were not unsentimental or unemotional. Having said his piece, he returned to thirteenth-century crises and did not, in the furious years that followed, say another or display any interest in discussing his further views (if he had any) with any of his associates (including Hutchins) who had taken the opposite position. He had no time for transitory matters.

This, then, was what Hutchins, for whom read Adler, and his dead classics came down to: the reimposition of medieval authoritarianism, absolutism, hair-splitting; medieval *Catholicism.* You had only to catch a glimpse on those Gothic walks, where the heirs of Galileo trod, of the little convoys of pale priests and fluttering nuns on their way to visit his and Hutchins' Great Books class, and the case was clear: Adler was a secret convert, "the worst kind." (He would not descend, of course, to deny the canard.) And Hutchins—Hutchins just *sat there.*

Mert's colleagues had no access to his charms. He did not so much as go through the formality of joining the faculty club. He lived and worked as far away from campus as he could—just off Lake Shore Drive—in a two-story apartment. His lifelong marketplace moonlighting, all of it legal and some of it respectable, included lecturing to women's clubs for a platform agency which took him out on the road for a month a year. It included consultantships to anybody or anything: for Bamberger's department store he developed the theory that electric toasters and bobby pins evolve like new biological species—an admirer there called him the Drygoods Darwin—and in Hollywood he prepared the annual whitewash of the movie industry that appeared under the name of the tame watchdog Will Hays. In 1927, when he went to see Hutchins, he was holding down two teaching jobs at Columbia and one at CCNY—besides lecturing at the

People's Institute of New York and teaching a Great Books course in a church basement. His income was eleven thousand dollars at a time when an endowed professorship paid its eminent occupant ten thousand.

He was fanatically fastidious. His working materials had to be of the most lavish order and always in order. Every book in his own library was classified and catalogued, and none was ever lent. His pipes were sent out to be cleaned, and he screamed when he saw me pull a dirty pipe-cleaner out of my jacket pocket. What made Sammy run made Mert dust the seat of a chair before he sat down.

As intellectually excited as he was intellectually exciting, frisky, frenetic, and forever a-bubble with notions and nostrums, dancing around, jumping up and down, hollering his head off, and swinging from the chandelier, Mert was a one-man infestation of the ivory tower, a bulldozer in the academic grove. He was lovable in a hundred ways and hatable, if you didn't love him, in a hundred and one, even if it was only for his being a Jew of the kind that reminded learned gentiles that there are worse things than a genteel anti-Semitism. But one of the ingredients of every one of the hundred and one ways in which he was hated was envy. Consciously or unconsciously, the pedants wished they had half his head, half his gusto, and half the aplomb that takes a man through stop signs while the traffic cop, staring after him, takes off his cap, scratches his head, and says, "Well, I am damned."

What they should have envied him was half his industry. Many men like their work, but Mert *liked working*. He maintained an iron schedule and was never diverted from it—except by work. He made notes while he read, he made notes while he shaved and while he ate, and he probably made notes while he slept. (I know that he made notes when he dreamed and recorded them when he awoke.) He made notes when he talked and on the rare occasions (except in debate) when he listened. Of course he blew up, and blew up his home, somewhere along the dangerous age that runs from nine to ninety, but he regrouped his one-man forces a year or so later; and in his seventies, and into his eighties, he maintained a schedule that would kill a mechanical rabbit. In the Twenty Years' War at the University of Chicago one Mortimer J. Adler—and there was only one—was worth a battalion of self-respecting professors.

This, then, was Mert, chock-a-block with St. Thomas *and* St. Anselm *and* St. Ambrose *and* St. Bonaventura, and cheek by jowl with his pale priests and fluttering nuns (whose very vestments drove the academic "Protestants" wild), with Hutchins for an imprimatur and the Great Books for an imprint. He had got into the great books by way of John Erskine at Columbia. Erskine established a general honors course at Columbia using the discussion method of teaching the great books. (He never used that expression.) Among his students there, or later in the adult program at New York's People's Institute, were Adler, Clifton Fadiman (who became the *New Yorker's* book reviewer), Richard McKeon (who went on to translate Aristotle), and Scott Buchanan. As a Rhodes scholar at Oxford, Buchanan, a disciple of Amherst's Alexander Meiklejohn, met another Great Bookie, Stringfellow Barr, who came home to teach ancient history at the University of Virginia and edit the *Virginia Quarterly.*

This was the Adler coterie—they were all thirty or under—that found in Hutchins their own propensity for liberal education combined with the muscle and the pulpit which Chicago provided. Outside the academy Fadiman kept close contact with them, as did a phenomenal character named Arthur L.H. Rubin (who lived with the Adlers for several years on Chicago's Gold Coast), an all-sorts man of independent means who had served as union-management arbitrator for the New York clothing industry. In time many others were, and remained, marginally involved, such as Thornton Wilder, who had grown up with Hutchins, and Mark Van Doren of Columbia. But Adler, McKeon, Buchanan, and Barr were to become (and ever to remain) Hutchins' general staff in the crusade for the revival of the humanist tradition, "the great conversation."

12   The Blue Sky

By the time that Hutchins was invited to take the presidency of Chicago there was no surprise in his airy suggestion that Mortimer Adler come on along with him. And no surprise in Adler's acceptance. (Columbia's psychology department wouldn't hold Adler very long anyway—or try to.) The deluge of Adlerian memoranda ("I have a grand idea for you. It's a little wild, but has a real kick.") became a cascade of schemes to abolish courses, credits, grades, textbooks, lectures—and why not (this seriously) professors somehow? Older and wiser (if not smarter) at twenty-eight, seasoned by administration of a law school, Hutchins knew that it was not going to be like that—but hadn't they for two years now talked about how it might be like that if there was ever to be a real university?

Each of them, sizing up the other in New Haven, suspected that the other, like himself, got his exercise swimming upstream. Each suspected that the other would go places. Each suspected, after their first few meetings, that they would go together.

It was like Hutchins to say "Come on along," and like Adler to say, "And do what?" Hutchins thought they ought to teach the Great Books together; in that way he'd get to read them. Adler wanted to know where they ought to teach them. Hutchins thought they ought to teach them all over the campus. Adler wanted to know to whom. Hutchins thought to freshmen, who hadn't had a chance to be ruined by professors. Adler thought there'd be trouble. Hutchins was sure there would be.

The trouble they had in mind, and they certainly had trouble in mind, would begin when they started teaching. A new university president has more pressing, not to say more useful, things to do than teach—and teach *freshmen*, and teach the *Great Books*, and teach them with another Johnny-come-lately as his coinstructor. The trouble would, they supposed, begin the first day they met their freshmen, when the president of the university opened the honors course by saying, "It will come as a surprise to you to learn on the highest authority in this educational institution that the purpose of an educational institution is education."

Hutchins and Adler understood each other, though they spoke different languages—or, more precisely, the same language in different tones of voice, Adler undeceptively shrill and insistent, Hutchins deceptively bland and sedate. The radically different styles of the reasoning man and the reasonable man would ever afterward astonish their students (and not only their students). Adler told them what dialectic was and reached for the blackboard; Hutchins tilted back in his chair, quizzed them dialectically, and now and again turned to his fellow votary of dialectics to thank him for his enlightening lecture. (The students giggled, and Adler, who wasn't foolish, looked foolish.) They were two radically different kinds of men. But they possessed one kind of mind, and were of one mind about education.

What neither of the two seemed to have realized when the tall one said to the short one, "Come on along," was that the trouble would begin when Mortimer J. Adler had to be appointed to the faculty of a great university. To the extent that Adler was unidentified when he came along, he was suspect. To the extent that he was identified, he was more suspect still. The psychologists at Columbia told their Chicago colleagues that Adler might be a philosopher, but they doubted it. The philosophers said that he might be a psychologist, but they doubted it. He was, all agreed, an ebullient young man; objectionably so.

The honeymoon that saw Hutchins get almost everything he wanted (or should have wanted) saw him, in the Adler case, get one furious, first-first-class beating. It wouldn't have been much of a beating for another, less truculent administrator. After all, it was a single appointment, and a junior appointment at that. But it was the most important appointment, the most important beating, and the most important association of his career.

When Adler came on along, early in 1930, Hutchins had not yet unleashed his assault on departmentalism. But there could have been no doubt around the campus that he would, if he meant to do anything at all about the higher learning. The department—any department—was the enemy. The enemy's general staff were the senior members of the department, and the senior members of the department were the great specialists. Adler wasn't great when Hutchins invited him to come along, or (at twenty-four) senior. He wasn't a specialist; he was a strident enemy of specialization. He was the original Professor of the Blue Sky.

But there was no Department of the Blue Sky, and Adler had to be appointed to a department. Statutorily the president made all the appointments to the faculty—or, rather, forwarded them to the board of trustees, which made them. The way it went (and goes) was something else entirely. The board had all the nominal power, but nobody, including the board, thought that the board had any academic competence. In practice the department brought the appointment to the president (who had no competence in that or any field) and the president "recommended" the appointment to the board; the president was the messenger boy.

A messenger boy with a message of his own is an autocrat begging for a broken head. Hutchins went begging for twenty years. He should have "known better." He didn't, and he never would. In the winter of 1943— he'd been president for thirteen years—Igor Stravinsky and Jacques Maritain came to Chicago at the same time, to lecture for the Committee on Social Thought, an interdepartmental beachhead which Hutchins had established with private funds. The three had lunch with economist John U. Nef, a solid Hutchins man, who presided over the committee. As they rose from lunch, Hutchins invited both visitors to join the faculty of the University of Chicago. Stravinsky was unable to consider the invitation, but Maritain was interested. The Frenchman was the leading living Thomist and one of the world's leading living philosophers. A convert to Catholicism, he had broken with the church leadership by supporting the Spanish Loyalists in 1936, and now, with France occupied by the Nazis, he was stranded in America.

Nef, in his memoirs, tells us that three times in the next few years Hutchins tried to get Maritain appointed in the philosophy department. The department blocked the appointment each time—even when Hutchins offered to put Maritain on the committee's private payroll. There are two accounts, both of them doubtless correct, of what happened. In Nef's, Hutchins sent "emissaries" (probably Nef) to the department chairman, who said, "Maritain is not a good philosopher." Emissaries: "Is there a good philosopher in the Department?" Chairman: "No—but we know what a good philosopher is."[1] The other account has Hutchins pressing one of the department's logical positivists (whose own appointment Hutchins had urged) with the need to balance the dominant pragmatism of the department. Logical positivist: "Maritain is a propagandist." Hutchins: "You're all propagandists."

The appointment was never made. Maritain continued to lecture a few days a year in the committee as a visiting professor—the department's acquiescence wasn't required for such status—until 1958. He finally accepted a permanent post in another (and better) philosophy department—Princeton's. Jacques Maritain was no young Johnny-come-lately like the Mortimer Adler of 1930; he was, in 1943, and earlier, a man of the first eminence in European scholarship.

When, on the other hand, Hutchins himself presumed to stand pat against a departmental recommendation, the few friends he had closed ranks against his presumption. The history department chairman, William E. Dodd—later Roosevelt's heroic ambassador to Berlin—had been one of the trustee-faculty committee that had chosen Hutchins as president. On one occasion in the early 1930s, he came in to inform the president that the department wanted to have a certain man appointed in ancient history. "It's my impression," said Hutchins, "that he isn't very good." "He's one of the most respected men in his field," said Dodd. "I know that," said Hutchins, "but *I* don't respect him. But I'm willing to be converted. Let me talk to him." The candidate came to Chicago and, to his surprise, found himself discussing Roman history with the president, who wasn't an historian. After he left, Hutchins said to Dodd, "I'm sorry, but I think he's no good. He's worse than I thought he was before I met him. If the department insists, I'll forward its recommendation to the board with the strongest possible objection attached to it."[2] The department withdrew its recommendation, and the relations between the heroic chairman and the stand-pat president were never again quite the same; very far from it. The two had liked each other, the old historical revisionist (of the Civil War) who admired President Woodrow Wilson of Princeton and the young revisionist of education who studied Wilson's futile attempts to do something sensible about the American university. Dodd had introduced Carl Sandburg to Hutchins, and these two, too, had taken a shine to one another. Dodd had been far from unhappy when Hutchins invited Sandburg to lecture at the university—in the university, but not in the history department. For Dodd was a stern departmentalist, a product of the departmentalist supremacy at Leipzig. In 1936 he was called home from the U.S. embassy in Berlin for critical consultation on the Nazi threat, and came back to Chicago to meet with his colleagues and their graduate students. "From what they say," he wrote in his diary, "the University's merging of history into the social science as a minor subject is most discouraging. They lament the failure of the University to give American history in a large comprehensive way, and add that they can not get sufficient knowledge except upon their own initiative and with library work. This is Hutchins' system. I have long feared his scheme of limiting departments and avoiding departmental selection of professors would greatly injure this institution. Nothing is more important than eminent professors developing their subjects in their own way, first being sure the professors are worthy of appointment. I am distressed at the University of Chicago.

Sometimes I wish I might again bring pressure to bear here."[3] Two years later, when Hitler found him persona non grata in Berlin, he came back to the university and did bring all the pressure to bear that he could.

The complication in the Adler case was that Adler seemed not to conform to any acceptable department type. He belonged (if at all) in the Blue Sky, and all the nonphilosophers in all the nonphilosophy departments always agree that the repository of the Blue Sky is the philosophy department. And that was where the trouble was going to be.

A philosophy department of ten men would like as not have ten mutually unintelligible schools in it. The exception would be the department headed by a man who, in the patient, persistent exercise of seniority had weeded out every school but his own and weeded in his acolytes—an understandable proclivity. The two most notable such cases were Chicago and Columbia. In both institutions the philosophy departments were implacably Deweyite—and, since John Dewey was preeminently a philosopher of education, so were Chicago's School of Education and Columbia's Teachers' College.

Dewey was no more a philosopher than Adler was, or Goethe, or Jefferson, or Emerson, or Russell. Adler was (or was to become) a commentator on systematic philosophy and an elaborator of it. Dewey was a learned critic of it; a highly original thinker (as neither Adler nor Hutchins was) in the tradition of the educational reformers of early twentieth-century Germany. To call him (still less Adler, least of all Hutchins) a philosopher was only a commonplace courtesy; even at the painstaking hands of brilliant disciples, "Deweyism" defied systematization. What John Dewey was was a psychologist of learning who believed that the principles of growth—the central term of his doctrine—had been discovered by modern psychology in its experimental form. "Change," "process," "experience" were all. There was no real dichotomy between science and philosophy except as to subject matter, no nonscientific method of obtaining knowledge, no immutable knowledge, no immutability, no fixed natural or moral (much less divine) law, no *species aeterna*. "Everything," said Socrates of the Deweys of his time, "is a charming flux." The contemporary child learned in and from contemporary society: "The school is not a preparation for life," said Dewey. "It is life itself." It is the life the child is living in the place that he lives that interests him, not the life of a past he didn't know and couldn't relate to himself. Education had to be child-centered, interest-centered, activity-centered. John Dewey was the nearest thing to a philosopher that a nonphilosophical America had produced in the twentieth century. When Hutchins began his career, Dewey was the most influential educator of his time.

To the extent that Dewey was a philosopher, he was above all else a philosopher of science as (he said) "the organ of general social progress." He saw the hope of the world in the refinement of the arts of precise measurement, controlled experimentation, and the conscientious collection and confrontation of the facts. He saw the social sciences coming into their own as true sciences, producing findings as irresistible in their application to human life and human society as the mathematician's are to engineering. It went without saying—though he said it—that he was irreligious, incapable (like the consecrated scientist) of recognizing that the validity of his own method, his own materials, his own objectives rested squarely on faith in those indemonstrable assumptions that Hutchins and Adler (like Aristotle before them) insisted on calling first principles or, as one ardent Dewey disciple called them, "the ultimate trivialities."

In the early 1920s, as the most eminent of the Columbia faculty Dewey characteristically attended the meetings of the student philosophy club, and at one meeting one of his students was delivering a paper on philosophy and religion. Professor Dewey's face warmed as the intense, insistent young man warmed to this theme, finally quoting a passage from Dewey himself and saying, "There is certainly nothing of the love of God in this utterance." Dewey blew up. He got to his feet, said "Nobody is going to tell *me* how to love God," and walked out.[4]

The outrageous young man, Mortimer J. Adler by name, then began harassing the outraged sage with very long letters arguing that later Dewey lectures contradicted earlier Dewey lectures. Dewey, generous, tolerant, responsive, read the letters aloud in class for a while, and then (as Adler tells it) summoned this jump-up member of the rising generation to his office and suggested that he lay off; which, of course, Adler didn't. Picture the preposterous confrontation: *the* American philosopher, in his towering midsixties, with a Praetorian guard of loving disciples and a swirl of reverent students at his hem—and an unloving, irreverent upstart in his early twenties tearing into him with that merciless kind of picayune analysis that Dewey considered the root of sterile scholarship. It was precisely that kind of analysis, demanding the definition of terms and then the definition of the terms used in the definition, that "Deweyism" was incapable of standing up to.

Adler was a one-man category. That he should turn up at Chicago—and with Hutchins as what Dewey must have regarded as his mouthpiece—added a peculiarly sensitive injury to the insult. For Chicago (like Columbia) was Dewey country.

To be a non-Deweyite at Chicago was one thing; to be an anti-Deweyite an unthinkable another, above all in the philosophy department, whose two senior members, George Herbert Mead and James Hayden Tufts, both of them friends and contemporaries of the master, rotated the departmental chairmanship between them. Mead had great distinction as a pragmatist. (Tufts was memorable for a jaw that made Don Quixote look chinless.) Their junior faculty was predominantly Deweyite, and Chicago at the apex of Deweyism was generally regarded as one of the country's strongpoints in philosophy. That it was so regarded was itself a commentary on the condition of the discipline in America. The department was weak in every area except pragmatism, and spectacularly weak in the Greek and scholastic traditions, which underlay all of Western thought prior to the work of Charles Sanders Peirce and William James at the end of the nineteenth century—and the thinking of the two great pragmatists (unlike that of their followers) by no means represented a clean break with ancient and medieval Europe.

Hutchins knew that this was the kind of philosophy department he was going to have. What he didn't know was that he was not going to have it. The record of the disaster has to be pieced together from a few letters, a few memoranda, and a few fading recollections. On June 27, 1929, four months before he was even inaugurated, he got a letter from Adler informing him that Scott Buchanan and Richard McKeon had both refused the philosophy chairmanship at Cornell because they preferred to join Hutchins at Chicago; it is clear that Hutchins was (or thought he was) handing out jobs like a politician between election day and inauguration day. He was either magnificently presumptuous or magnificently innocent, and his experience at Yale militates against his having been innocent.

So far as any record indicates, he had not at this point discussed any of these men with the philosophy department. It didn't take anything more than a philosophical tyro to recognize that the department was incestuous. To legitimate it meant to strengthen the classic areas. Adler already had some small status as a medievalist. Buchanan and McKeon were "Greeks."

Hutchins' lifelong fight for general education was directed against the provincialism of what he called the uneducated specialist. He could have traded all his multifarious crusades for this one—and just possibly have been more effective in the end than he was. His uneducated specialist was Aristotle's natural slave, born and bred to serve a purpose that was not his own. He was, still is, and always will be, in and out of education, something much more pernicious than the popular hyperbole suggests—the man who knows more and more about less and less until he knows everything about nothing at all.

The elective system encouraged ever more premature specialization in collegiate, even in subcollegiate, education. For young men and women bent on an academic career, the earlier a student got started up the ladder the better—and one ladder rather than just any. It meant the narrowing of perspective not to one field but to one area in that field, and to one school (that is, one man) in that area. And in 1930 Chicago's "Deweyite" philosophy department was a characteristic case in point. Adler was previsioned at Chicago—letters going back and forth between the Midway and Morningside Heights—as a Thomist (or, by way of further denigration, if that should be possible, a neo-Thomist). That took care of Adler, however roundly he was criticized in bona fide Thomistic circles as a dilettante and however headily he might take issue with the angelic holy doctor of the Church on points of the highest order (including the cornerstone "five proofs" of God's existence).

That noble jurist, Felix Frankfurter, for all his European training, repeatedly, and heavy handedly, twitted Hutchins about his "Tomism," his "Tomist institution," and his "Tomist belief in universals." Hutchins just as repeatedly (and with no success whatever) tried to convince Frankfurter that it took more than teaching St. Thomas to make a man a Thomist, just as it took more than delivering milk to make a man a cow. On one playful occasion, while Frankfurter was still at Harvard, Hutchins wrote him, "I want very much to have you go on the Supreme Court. For that reason I should take the time to explain to you the difference between the Platonic and Thomistic views of universals. I can not have one of my friends exhibiting his ignorance in the law courts. Unfortunately, I am so occupied just now in trying to make my students understand this point that I can not undertake your education in addition. I shall have to content myself with pointing out that 'Thomist' is spelled with an 'h'."[5]

The western end of the Midway–Morningside Heights correspondence did not elicit anything much about Buchanan apart from the fact that, like Adler, he was suspiciously involved in the great books and had been teaching them evenings to unsuspecting immigrants at Everett Dean Martin's People's Institute in New York. His specialty seemed to be logic, but logic of the fossilized, (i.e., prepositivist) sort. McKeon, like the other members of the Hutchins consortium, was under thirty; but he had already published on Aristotle. (His edition of Aristotle's basic works appeared a decade later and remains a scholarly landmark.) Thirty-five years later he recalled his amazement at being classed as an "Aristotelian": "In the first place, my interpretation of Aristotle does not agree with what is commonly held, on the authority of recent scholars, to be Aristotelian doctrines and errors. I have never troubled to point out these differences because the name 'Aristotelian' is used not to describe a person or a position but to be unkind, and if I was to be charged with guilt by association, I could not do better than be associated with 'the Master of Them That Know.'"[6]

It was six wild and wooly months before Hutchins (now installed as president) replied to Adler's June 1929 letter in which it was clear that Adler, Buchanan, and McKeon were to come to Chicago. On December 4, Hutchins informed Adler that Buchanan would teach logic, McKeon medieval philosophy, and Adler "the geometrics of the soul," but it would be a year before the Holy Trinity (as Hutchins put it) would be operative, the stock market (and with it the university's budget) having collapsed between Dear Mortimer's letter and Dear Bob's reply. The appointments of Buchanan and McKeon would have to wait until 1931; but Adler was to come on as soon as he could for the academic year 1930–31.

Buchanan was an associate professor at Virginia when Hutchins told him—just like that—to "come along." He went to the president to tell him of the offer, and the president, in an effort to keep him, went immediately to the board and got Buchanan a promotion to full professor. A few weeks later Buchanan, hearing from Hutchins (just like that, again) that there was no money for the Chicago appointment that year, had to tell the president that he wanted to stay. The president, of course, who had no previous suspicion of Buchanan's apparent duplicity, now had no choice but to conclude that the Chicago invitation had been a fake on Buchanan's part (with or without the connivance of Hutchins), designed to obtain the Virginia promotion.

Forty years afterward Dr. Irene Tufts Mead, daughter of Professor Tufts and daughter-in-law of Professor Mead, was sure that Hutchins had simply informed the department of 1930 that Adler and McKeon were to join it (she did not recall Buchanan's having been involved); and there was no one, after forty years, to gainsay her recollection. Mead and Tufts, she said, were "incensed" and the whole department "felt depreciated."[7]

Shortly after confirming his invitation to Adler, Hutchins asked the department to have lunch with him and Adler in a private dining room at the faculty's Quadrangle Club. Adler showed up in amiable (if amiably contemptuous) form, and Hutchins amiably introduced him around the table.

The weather, the depression, and the low quality of the lunch having been taken care of, the philosophers turned, as usual, not to philosophy, but to courses. The department was giving an introductory course "covering" the field. When Adler asked what field, he was told "Philosophy." His ears and his hair went up, his jaw began jutting: one course *covering* philosophy. Whether it was Adler or Hutchins who asked the inevitable question is unrecorded, but instantly asked it was by one or the other of them:

What were the students reading for the course? Nor is the identity of the answerer known, but answered the question was: Will Durant's *Story of Philosophy*.

Silence; Hutchins drumming inaudibly on the table, Adler swelling as he reddened. He always seemed to stammer when he was enraged, and he stammered: "But—but—but that's a very bad book." He was right, of course, and somebody around the table besides him and Hutchins must have known he was right; maybe everybody. Durant was prefabricated pop, directed at the mass market. It "explained" philosophy—all philosophy—to people who wanted (or thought they wanted) all philosophy explained to them. Philosophy—the Queen of the Sciences. A *university*. And not just a university, but *Chicago*. Adler would have been a little (but only a little) less horrified if the students had been given a standard textbook instead of the original writings of the philosophers themselves. But Durant—.

After Adler finished his outraged stammer there may be supposed to have been an outraged silence on the part of the entire party of the second part. And then the philosophy hit the fan. One thing led—as it would, logic being a province of philosophy—to another. The man who challenged Dewey, and then (as Dewey himself would have done) challenged Durant, was denounced as an *Aristotelian*. The luncheon did not end on the ostensibly amiable note on which it began. What Hutchins must have suspected, he now knew, and so did Adler. There would be a finish fight and it would determine the course, perhaps of Adler's career, certainly of Hutchins'.

To lose his first fight would be a premonitory scandal; if he could not do anything with the philosophy department, what would he be able to do with the departments in which he himself could not pretend to any competence whatever? He was, after all, a lawyer; he knew that his power under the university's statutes was the power of persuasion—nothing more. If he was ever going to get anything done, he had to win this one. If he lost it, he might as well resign—or resign himself to being a messenger boy. He had been in office six months.

If Hutchins was arrogant and grim, Adler was arrogant and manic. He wouldn't fight the stupid bastards—them and their Durant—and wouldn't take the job if they offered it to him. Hutchins corrected him: he wouldn't have to fight, but he would have to take the job. And it would be offered to him. Hutchins knew he could pull it off.

He thought he knew.

He went to the department with a proposal. An outside committee of philosophers would be invited to evaluate the department—member by member—to determine its qualifications vis-à-vis Adler's. The proposal did not even get as far as the method by which the committee would be selected—an issue on which no agreement would be likely. The department spurned the proposal and exploded. Tufts, who had reached the retirement age but could have been invited to stay on a year-to-year basis, retired. Mead, with an offer from Columbia, decided to resign. (He died the same year.) Two of the three younger members of the department quit and got jobs at other schools. The department was not merely wrecked; it as good as disappeared.

Hutchins was beaten. Badly beaten. He knew better than to go back to what was left of the department and push the appointment, and Adler, still sure that he'd be coming to Chicago anyway, didn't want him to try. The law school was more amenable. It was a solid professional drill-ground of the kind Hutchins had found (but hadn't left behind him) at Yale. It prepared good students for good bar examinations and good law offices, and its faculty, including the senior members, had no special adherence to doctrine. Chicago's recognized Yale's as a law school of its own rank and the ex-dean of Yale as a member of its own fraternity and an able administrator. There was no objection—not at the time, at least—when Hutchins recommended Adler's appointment, not as associate professor of philosophy, but as associate professor of law.[8]

For twenty years thereafter Adler, when he wasn't teaching the Great Books honors course with Hutchins, came hurtling across town (and through all the stop lights) to the law school to teach, naturally, The Philosophy of Law, The Nature of Law, Law and the Nature of Man—in one word, philosophy. With no more than a minor assist from Adler, Hutchins transformed Chicago's Law School; its emphasis shifted from the training of lawyers to the education of jurists, much as the first universities educated theologians and left the preparation of preachers to the seminaries. Hutchins (like Adler) was a Natural Law man, and the curriculum, as it was generalized, was strengthened in that area. But the subsequent appointments testified to Hutchins' insistence that what he wanted was not to "pack" the faculty but to make it more representative of conflicting viewpoints than faculties in the nature of things tended to be.

Philosophers—that is, professors of philosophy—across the country joined Dewey in deploring the Hutchins-Adler *attentat*. A Harvard man was reported (by Tufts) to have said that the sacrifice of a philosophy department was a high price to pay for the education of a president. But there was no report of the matter in the learned, much less in the unlearned, press; and no open outcry on the Chicago campus or anywhere else. The *affaire* was Hutchins' sorriest hour. It could have been used—

and, had it occurred a few years later, would have been—as a bomb under him. But this was the beginning of his tenure. The surviving memoranda—even those written by members of the philosophy department—uniformly suggest that the reasons for not making the issue public were on the whole lofty. The least lofty of the sentiments: nobody in one of the world's scientific centers cared what happened to the philosophy department *or* the law school. If there is one thing that is supposed to do a university less good than trouble, it is the disclosure of trouble. Hutchins was new and (as the then chairman of the board of trustees said several years later) didn't know the ropes. He had made a power grab and had failed, and he wouldn't be likely to try it again—a view that discloses a charming combination of naiveté and optimism. Perhaps he had some sort of right to have his man at hand; and, after all, Adler was an academic and did have rank at Columbia.

Of course Hutchins wanted to "pack" the faculty, just as Roosevelt wanted to "pack" the Court—but not quite. The political reformer saw no way to break into the classic circle of self-perpetuation short of breaking the circle; so too the educational reformer. But the political reformer wanted his own programs supported. The educational reformer wanted to introduce diversification into a stultified and stultifying system. In so far as Hutchins' own views were unrepresented—as they were in the philosophy department, and not only there—he would appear to be trying to do what the political reformer tries to do. But the record pretty well sustains Hutchins' insistence that what he wanted was a broad representation regardless of his own persuasion. There were only four "Hutchins men" among the more than five hundred appointments during the first ten years of his presidency; and of those four—Adler, McKeon, Buchanan, and Barr—only two, Adler and McKeon, remained, and only one, McKeon (who made it into a reconstructed philosophy department in 1934 and subsequently became dean of the humanities division), was appointed as a full professor. Of the eleven holders of distinguished-service professorships elevated to that Olympus during Hutchins' first decade, nine were scientists, one an educationalist opposed to Hutchins, and one, McKeon, a "Hutchins man." When Ralph Waldo Tyler of Ohio State was offered the chairmanship of Chicago's Board of Examinations—he later became dean of the social sciences division—he asked Hutchins, "Are you sure I'm the man you're looking for? I'm what they call a Progressive Educator and you're what they call something else altogether," and Hutchins said, "I know what you are, and I know what I am, and I want you here."

But the memory of the Adler debacle died a long, hard death; indeed, it never died. It was maintained by the recognition on the part of friends and enemies alike that Hutchins did want to exercise power the statutes didn't give him in order to get men he respected into the institution—and men he respected were likely, given the prevailing imbalance, to be men of his own views. He was a lawyer, given, like some lawyers, to legality. For twenty years he tried to get the statutes changed to give him the kind of power a parliamentary ministry has, subject to dismissal on a vote of no confidence—or, alternatively, to strip the office he held of all power and retain the president as merely the chairman, or presiding officer, of the faculty. He never succeeded.

But neither did he fail completely; such men seldom do. Within a year of the Adler appointment the separate college faculty had been established, and within a year of that victory the faculty senate abrogated the requirement that all members of the college faculty be members of departmental faculties in the four upper divisions of the university. The dean of the college was empowered to recommend to the president appointments to the college faculty without departmental status. It was a Chicago first and a Hutchins triumph. Now, by virtue of his power to appoint deans—a power the faculty could override only by open rebellion—he could in effect appoint professors in the college. In the divisions he was careful to appoint deans of unexceptionable credentials, as witness Tyler in the social sciences. His appointment of his friend Beardsley Ruml, Tyler's predecessor, raised eyebrows among the natural scientists; but they did not much more care what happened in the social sciences division than they cared what happened in the philosophy department or the law school. Among the social scientists there was some objection to the lusty activist—it was "B" Ruml who later invented the pay-as-you-go system of withholding income taxes—but here Hutchins had his way on the assumption that Ruml would soon move on; and he did, after a couple of years: to the board chairmanship of Macy's. (Hutchins, who enjoyed his company and his brashness, wistfully announced that Ruml had leaped from the ivory tower into the bargain basement; Mrs. Hutchins topped that one by observing that "B" had exchanged ideas for notions.)

All that the reformer had to do now, with his separate college faculty, was to be patient and live long enough, and he would get the college he wanted. He despised patience as a high-grade way of doing nothing. He would, however, live a very long time. Long enough to realize that he would never get the college he wanted.

13 The End of Everything

Hutchins was chosen president of the University of Chicago because, he said, "it was 1929." It was, more precisely, the spring of 1929, and everybody agreed that America was poised for takeoff into the wild blue-chip yonder. President Coolidge announced ex cathedra that prosperity was permanent—a prosperity built upon the rock of the participatory democracy in which four million common capitalists were buying stock on margin. What was wanted that spring, was a clean-cut, energetic young man who would go downtown and get the money.

He was inaugurated in the fall, on the third Wednesday following Black Thursday. In the intervening three weeks between that Thursday in October and that Wednesday in November there had occurred the End of Everything—or, more exactly, the Beginning of the End. It would go on, and on, and on for another ten years.

Not excepting the company towns like Detroit, Chicago was struck harder and faster by the stock market crash than any other center. Two local factors were devastating. One of them was Samuel Insull, a real tiger, but a paper titan. Insull's Middle West Utilities was the 1920s antecedent of the go-go conglomerate of forty years later. Nothing had ever been bought so widely or hit such day-by-day highs—and then day-by-day lows, pulling the city, rich and poor, up, and then down, with it. The other devastating factor was real estate. Like Florida and southern California, Chicago, with its unbounded expanse outside the loop of the downtown "L," was empty-lot-crazy. (In time the downtown banks and department stores went to the wall, too.) Real estate speculation (especially in second mortgages) was almost as pervasive as Insull stock. The Michigan Avenue skyline was dominated by the mortgage banking house tower of S.W. Strauss and Company and its electric sign, "Never a Loss to Any Investor in 99 years." (In the course of the 100th year all the investors lost everything.)

Chicago money was new and adventurous, but for those very reasons sensitive. It had no cushion like eastern money's, nothing to fall back on when margins were called, no ancient holding deep down in the sock. There were twenty-five thousand suicides in the United States in 1930, and Chicago's led all the rest. An additional twenty-five thousand deaths that year were pronounced "accidental." Two-thirds of the suicides were incontestably assignable to "financial difficulties"; suicide increased 10 percent among blue-collar and 20 percent among white-collar policy holders—apart from the "accidental" deaths, which were predominantly white collar. Within two years after Black Thursday the life insurance companies had paid out some three hundred million dollars on suicides.

The university president who went downtown to get the money might or might not find the prospect in, or in business, or in being. Within the course of three months three Chicagoans on Hutchins' "A" list got off the list the hard way. One was a banker, one a merchant, and one a financier who dabbled in science. The banker plunged from a window seat in his seventh-floor apartment, the merchant from a ninth-floor bathroom. The financier plunged from the roof of a ten-story garage he owned.

A sorry state for a privately endowed university in a city which never did know what it needed a university for. Benefactions plunged faster than bankers, merchants, and financiers. Half of the Chicago alumni were school teachers, and half the country's school teachers were out of work, or not getting paid, or getting paid late, or getting paid in script. Teachers and their supporters set up a cry for federal aid; traditionalists said that federal aid would mean federal control. Hutchins called for federal aid to save the nation's public schools. He took to the public prints to press the doctrine that federal aid did not necessarily mean federal control. It did not mean government control in England; why need it do so here? The public schools had to be saved to save democracy. But he repudiated such aid for private schools.

As Chicagoans, the university's trustees were not disposed to be fiscally conservative; as trustees, they were. The diversified portfolio's rock-bottom return was a modest, unsinkable 4.3 percent. But the rock bottom dropped out. They discovered to their horror that, like all trustees, they had not been conserving the institution's assets but gambling with them, speculating where they thought they had been investing. As the panic proceeded into 1930, 1931, 1932, money, any kind of money, from any source and for any purpose, dried up.

Hutchins had come to Chicago guilty of the worst offense in the businessman's lexicon: he had never had to meet a payroll. But he was innocent of the businessman's characteristic faith: he believed that there were more important things than making money, keeping money, or even spending money; things that had to be done no matter what.

The trustees knew better than to suppose that he could operate a quarter-billion-dollar corporation. These ivory-tower types knew how to expand, but they did not know how to retrench. If the faculty had to keep him in line on education, the board had to keep him in line on money—or try. (They never succeeded; in his twenty years at Chicago, including the Depression decade, he never ran a deficit of less than a million dollars.) He had a few real supporters, among them the most public-spirited man in town, Julius Rosenwald of Sears Roebuck and Company. Rosenwald was the man he could go to for the anonymous ten (or hundred) thousand to match a gift or repair the plumbing or the scholarship fund. It was Rosenwald who provided him with a general rule of administration which he had never heard put that way before: when you're stuck with a lemon, make lemonade out of it. The year 1930 was the juiciest lemon a university (or any other) president could be stuck with.

It is doubtful that Hutchins was familiar with J.M. Keynes's two-volume *Treatise on Money*, published the year the money ran out: 1930. Keynes, whose economics was crudely characterized as "spending the country rich," was another who had never had to meet a payroll. (Franklin Roosevelt was another.)

By the time Hutchins had framed his institutional economics, in, of all things, a speech to the YMCA in 1933—as an alumnus who had worked for the "Y" on a summer holiday in Cleveland—he was a rabid Keynesian in practice. To the YMCA the president of the University of Chicago spoke as follows:

"If we can determine analytically the function of the YMCA, subsidiary problems will settle themselves; we can test the performance of the organization and suggest its future. And in the first place, I should observe that the Young Men's Christian Association is not a business. It is not an investment trust or a bank or a hotel company. Its investments, its property, its hotels can be justified only as assisting it to carry out its main function—whatever that may prove to be. Consequently, emphasis on the business aspects of the organization is a false emphasis. Laymen, and particularly those who become members of boards of trustees, quite naturally think in terms of the tangible assets of the organization. It is not surprising that sometimes they seem to regard these things and the preservation of these things as the sole object of the institution. It is the perpetual task of professional leadership to direct the mind of the public and of boards of trustees to the real function for which such institutions were established. This problem is particularly serious now [since the crash of '29]. Professional leadership must demonstrate to lay boards that what is 'sound' finance in business may not be sound in philanthropic activities.

" . . . The temptation is strong to think only of the property, not of the purposes it was accumulated to serve. . . . The YMCA should stop worrying about its budget and think about its program. If the program is a good one, support for it will be forthcoming. If the program is bad or non-existent, the properties are useless anyway. . . . A professional leader who is compelled to think first about money and second about professional ideals is not likely to make a strong fight for those ideals when they come in conflict with vested interests. Particularly is this true if he may be removed for expressions or activities which may run counter to the views of the ruling class."[1]

For "YMCA" read University of Chicago. For "professional leadership" read Hutchins. For "boards of trustees" read the board of trustees of the university. For "the ruling class" read the benefactors and potential benefactors of the university.

As Chicago's productive endowment became daily less productive and new money daily more improbable to come by, trustee institutions were peculiarly affected. The Chicago trustees knew nothing about the enterprise they held in trust. Some of them were moderately well educated, or rather, schooled. Some of them were (among other things) unschooled, like the industrialist who, attacking the faculty for permitting Earl Browder to speak on campus, said: "I know the faculty of the University of Chicago. They are not strong and virulent men." Some trustees were unintelligent. Hutchins reported one conversation to his old friend Raymond Fosdick of the Rockefeller Foundation: "A trustee of the University of Chicago said to me 'There is no use in worrying about the intellects of these young people. God gave them their intellect and there is nothing you can do about them. All you can do is to have them meet other nice young people under auspices of nice older people and give them a good time.' I said 'What's the difference between running a university and running a country club?' He said, 'None.' " Some of them were intelligent but uninformed. A few of them were intelligent, informed, and enlightened. And a few of them were unintelligent, uninformed, and benighted.

The vice-chairman of the board who told Hutchins that Professor Paul Douglas, the liberal economist (and later U.S. senator), should be "lined up and shot," and the head of the Gas Company—an Insull errand boy—

resigned from the board when Hutchins declined to fire Douglas and the board declined to fire Hutchins for his disinclination to fire Douglas.

Then there was Sewell Avery of Montgomery Ward and Company, immortalized by being carried out of his office by U.S. marshals when he refused to negotiate with his employees under the National Labor Relations Act. (As late as 1948 Avery, back in his office, threatened to have the same Professor Douglas arrested if Douglas, in his successful campaign for the U.S. Senate, appeared in the neighborhood of the mail order plant.)

Hutchins pondered Julius Rosenwald's advice to convert the lemon into lemonade. The question was how. "My education as an administrator," he remembered afterward, "began in 1931 when I opened Aristotle's *Ethics* for the first time and read, 'In practical matters the end is the first principle.' I was shocked to realize that in the ten years I had been in universities I had never seriously asked myself what they were for. I had taken them for granted, had assumed that the aims they proclaimed were valid, and had attempted to administer them in terms of those aims. About the only idea I had of the University of Chicago when I went there was that it was great. The Depression seemed to postpone any immediate hope of making it greater in ways that I understood: I could not expect to make it richer; it was more likely that I would take it into bankruptcy. What was a great university, anyway?"[2]

The only defensible role for the university—a role that no other institution would or could fulfill—was that of a center of independent thought and criticism. If the university abandoned its distinctive function and rolled along with the vicissitudes of its time and place, it had no claim on public tolerance, much less public support. But to resist the pressures, maintain the independence of the institution, and reconstruct it the better to serve its distinguishing role, seemed to be an unlikely undertaking in the best of seasons.

And these were the worst of seasons. But they provided an occasion that the best did not: "We were able to do things on financial grounds that would have been regarded as impossible in prosperous times.

"If you encounter a depression of the severity of the one we encountered, and that lasts as long as that one, you've got to do one of two things. You've either got to say that you'll cut the whole thing percentage-wise across the board, cut 20% if your income goes off 20%, or you've got to say, 'Now we're up against it. Now we have to ask ourselves what things we value and what things we don't, what things we value more and what things we value less.' This required us, whether we wanted to or not, to think about the *kind* of institution we had on our hands.

"We took the second course. We said, for example, 'We're not going to cut faculty salaries unless we absolutely have to'—a decision that required the prior decision that faculty salaries are more important than cleaning up the gymnasium or mowing the lawns. Once the University was embarked on this line, the Depression required it to define itself, reorient itself, reorganize itself, to think about everything once more, to try to act intelligently in the light of its resources. If we had taken the other line and cut everything across the board, we could have gone through the Depression just as thoughtlessly as we went through periods of prosperity. I don't recommend Depression, but it would be a good thing to try to establish its moral equivalent, so that a university would have to act as if there were one, or as if there were going to be one, all the time."[3]

It was the counterpart of Thomas Jefferson's recommendation of periodic revolution—or Hutchins' recommendation (to Westbrook Pegler) that universities ought to be torn down every generation and established all over again.

His genius lay in the application of the first principle to the vicissitudes of the academic hour. If there was no money to be got by doing the right thing *or* the wrong thing, a man might just as well try to do the right thing and pursue the policy of incantative financing. The trustees would have to be persuaded that he was fiscally sound, or at least that he was not fiscally berserk. Here the Depression was a godsend. Many of the conservative rich, having discovered that they had not been conservative and were no longer rich, were open (as they would not have been six months before) to suggestion. Under the now prevailing conditions—conditions which prevailed ever more painfully as the 1930s proceeded—they were disposed to release fiduciary control to the administrator and see if he could do anything. They saw that he could.

As the "Hutchins Plan" was implemented in 1931 and 1932, three hundred courses were dropped from the curriculum, and nobody missed them. It was clear to the faculty that the transcendent problem was survival—the university's and their own. There were no jobs to be had. Whoever was dissatisfied with being told that he would no longer be teaching his favorite course, knew that he was not as dissatisfied as he would be on the breadline. Young men and women could be got for coffee and buns, and Hutchins scoured the countryside for them; and the age level of the faculty dropped perceptibly while, by virtue of that same fact, Hutchins' strength in the faculty rose. The plan, which boasted of the small tutorial sections it introduced, did not make any public noise about the concomitant introduction of lecture sessions in which as many as six hundred of the one thousand freshmen were herded into an auditorium to listen to a great man tell them all about it. The big lecture sessions were not only concomitant, they were compensatory, financing the tutorial program with no increase in staff. Not a peep out of the faculty old boys who might have complained (but didn't, because most of them preferred lecturing anyway) that the lecture was the very antithesis of what Hutchins said he wanted. Not a peep—naturally—out of the trustees. The students, always more serious at Chicago than they were at most places, had become still more serious as the Depression deepened; most of them would learn, even in packed auditoriums.

But it would take more than fewer courses and larger classes to meet the continuing crisis. The University of Chicago had never been a place that professors left readily, and the faculty was heavily loaded with men and women who had been around long enough to acquire the very expensive status of lifetime tenure. But tenure is no protection to a professor when financial conditions are critical. His job can be abolished, his department can be abolished, his division can be abolished—and he with them. There were at least a few occasions, during the early 1930s, none of them on public record, on which a trustee made such a tentative suggestion. As an administrator Hutchins had no tenure. Though he favored such scandalously "socialistic" schemes as a national system of unemployment and medical insurance—and old age pensions—he had seen too many tenured professors of thirty-five or forty drawing a permanent pension in the form of a full salary. But faculty job security was an essential ingredient of the university as a center of independent thought and criticism. It is said that his rejoinder to the proposal of invading tenure was short: "It is out of the question," so clearly enunciated that the proposal was never pressed further.

Salary cuts were something else. In the 1930s there was not a commercial enterprise (and scarcely a noncommercial enterprise) which survived without slashing wages and salaries again and again. Here he made a modest counterproposal to the board. Except in the medical schools, where men with private practices could not be got part-time at less than $18,000, Chicago was paying a top faculty salary of $10,000—$2,000 to $5,000 less than competing institutions in the East. The Chicago minimum was a shameful $3,500. "We have always said," Hutchins reminded the board, 'that the faculty *was* the University. We have always said that the function of the administration was to minister to the needs of the faculty. Let us see if we can make it through by cutting administrative salaries on a progressive percentage basis." This would be painful for the highest-paid administrators and excruciating for the lowest paid. But the faculty should be the last to suffer, and indeed, this was the time to hire, at every level, first-class men and women whose salaries had been reduced at other institutions. The morale of the faculty—which was voiceless in such matters—would be greatly buoyed. The morale of the administrative officers was secondary. Hutchins did not need to point out to the board, or to the faculty, that his own $20,000 would, on the progressive basis he proposed, be hit the hardest. (He proposed that he take a 25 percent reduction; the board agreed to 20 percent. The salary of the chancellor of the University of Pittsburgh, for comparison, had been cut from $35,000 to $31,000.)

On financial grounds alone, he proposed a consolidation of the university's seventy-two budgets into twelve, to make the business of the university more manageable. What it did, besides making it more manageable, was to make it more manageable by him. The process, highly esteemed in the Depression and ever thereafter, was called streamlining. It reduced bureaucratic shuffling all the way down (and up) the line and facilitated intelligent allocation of dwindling funds. Its appeal to the trustees was irresistible. (In a letter to the board chairman, Harold Swift, who raised the question of merging some investments, Hutchins wrote, "I am in favor... of merging everything that we can possibly merge.")[4]

The combined terror and euphoria—the latter the result of the salary policy—temporarily distracted the attention of the faculty from the implications of the budget consolidation. It could have been seen, but only by unglazed eyes, as a great grab for executive power at the expense of the professors who *were* the university. The twelve new budgets were those of the divisions and the professional schools, a few of whose deans (but only a few, so early in the administration) were more or less sympathetic to the educational views of the man whose influence over their appointment, while it was far from absolute, was much more significant than his influence over appointments to the faculty.

But it took still more—more than combining budgets, cutting courses, packing classes, and sweating salaries—to keep the university afloat during the years in which personable young men who could sell anybody anything were going begging and nobody could sell anybody anything. Casting about, with the lemon/lemonade metaphor always in mind, Hutchins discovered one of the university's operations that was losing a lot of money—an operation he would have been delighted to lay the axe to even if it had been making money. The lemon, hot potato, or nettle, was big-time football.

14   The Unkindest Cut

The once unbeatable Maroons had, by the early 1930s, achieved in football a grip on the Big Ten basement from which there was no prospect of their being dislodged. Scores were of basketball dimensions, and the weekly gate did not cover the cost of liniment—at Chicago the largest single item of athletic expense.

There was no mystery about this melancholy state of muscular affairs. Thirty—even twenty—years earlier Chicago had been a large university; in the course of the 1920s it had become a small one. It still had two thousand male undergraduates. (California had 7,500. Even Harvard had 3,700.) An ever increasing proportion of its students were transfers— young men who moved to Chicago for strictly scholarly reasons. The proportion of self-supporting students had increased steadily. The proportion of street-car students, with no interest in athletics, had increased steadily. And Chicago had—and was proud to have—no School of Physical Education as a shelter for broad-shouldered collegians who could not have remained collegians in any other department. (As early as the 1930s it was estimated that 50 percent of the Big Ten varsity players were phys-ed majors.)

It was possible—of course it was Hutchins who said it—to win twelve letters without learning how to write one. This was the inevitable consequence of the almost universal practice of subsidizing players through the generosity of football alumni; there was no point in buying high school stars on the hoof if they had to be able to read and write by the time they become eligible at the end of their freshman year in college. Big-time football corrupted the higher learning academically and financially.

Everybody everywhere knew it. Everybody everywhere mumbled it, including a Carnegie Foundation study. "The trouble with football," said

Hutchins right out in public, "is the money that is in it"—or was supposed to be in it. Football, like crime, didn't pay; the president of Oberlin College had just made a study of football costs in twenty-two typical colleges and learned that twenty of them lost money. Coaches' salaries ran as high as twenty-five thousand dollars, in an era when the salaries of full professors averaged five thousand. One university, which paid its president eight thousand a year in 1930, could not get the coach it wanted for less than fifteen thousand to maintain his dignity. Equipment, advertising, travel (including Pullman trains with accommodations for the sports writers) were enormously expensive. The construction of ever bigger stadiums was back-breaking.

Big-time football was supposed to attract more students, but every additional student cost the institution money—even including the privately endowed institutions, colleges and universities with high tuition fees. These last were in a position to resist the pressure to enlarge their enrollment; they did not want more but better students. Big-time football was supposed to bring in gifts too—another myth based on the hallucination that the kind of people who admired football would admire a university like Chicago if only it had a winning team. (There was a companion hallucination that a great team would make a university that wasn't great look like a great university.) Harvard, Yale, and Chicago led the list of the country's universities in terms of donations and bequests during the 1920s and 30s, and Williams, Wesleyan, and Bowdoin led the list of colleges—all of them with notably inconsequential, and some of them with positively bad, football teams.

Chicago's outlay was, by comparison with its sister schools in the Big Ten, minuscule. It did not buy players under or over the table. Its stadium (one of two in the Western Conference that wasn't mortgaged) was one of the country's lesser arenas. Its head coach had a modest salary, and it did not schedule cross-country games. Even so it was losing money on football—it was lucky to sell 5,700 of its 57,000 seats—and there was a depression.

But there was nothing to be done about it.

The reason why nothing could be done about it was the Grand Old Man. The Old Man was Chicago's oldest—and only indigenous—collegiate tradition except for the campus carillon rendition of the Alma Mater at 10:06 every night because the Old Man wanted his players to start for bed at 10:00 and to get there when the Alma Mater was finished at 10:06:45. The most reverent moment of the year was the moment at the Interfraternity Sing when the old grads of Psi Upsilon marched down the steps to the fountain in Hutchison Court with the Old Man at their head.

If ever there was a granite figure that bespoke the granite virtues, it was his.

In 1892 William Rainey Harper, like most of his predecessors and successors among university presidents, denounced "the spectacular entertainment of enormous crowds of people." The difference between Harper and his predecessors and successors (prior to Hutchins) was that he thought he could do something about it. The new University of Chicago would provide a playing field for games—if there were students who wanted to play them. (Harper had never had any time for them, himself.) As his director of athletics, head coach, and captain of the football team, he hired a stern young man who had been a Bible student of his at Yale. Amos Alonzo Stagg was appointed as an associate professor (at $2,500 a year) with lifetime tenure—the first (and very probably the last) such appointment in history. His job would never depend upon his winning games. But he won them; in his heyday, all of them. As a stern middle-aged, and then old, man he continued to believe in the literalism of the Bible and the amateurism of sports. If (as untrackable rumor had it) some of his latter-day players were slipped a little something—even so much as priority in getting campus jobs—he never knew it. If their fraternity brothers selected their courses (with professors who liked football) and wrote their papers for them, if, in a word, they were intellectually needy, he never recognized it; apart from coaching football, he was not intellectually affluent himself.

The Old Man was sacred, sacred to a relatively small but ardent segment of the alumni, sacred to some of the old professors who had come with him in 1892, sacred to some of the trustees who, in their time, had had their picture taken on the Yale Fence, sacred to the students, who had nothing else to hold sacred, sacred to the local barbers and their customers, sacred, above all, to the local sports writers who, with the Cubs and the White Sox where they were, had nothing much else to write about. The first Marshall Field had given Harper a great tract adjoining the original campus for the student games that Harper spoke of. It was called, of course, Marshall Field, but it had long since become Stagg Field. The Old Man was untouchable—and so, therefore, was football.

Hutchins, who did not like to sit and watch anything, especially gladiators, attended the home games in his carefully battered and beer-stained football fedora, on the theory, it may be assumed, that it was good for a man to do the things he did not want to do. He was not violently opposed to exercise; to have been violently opposed would itself have been more exercise than he was impelled to. He was opposed to both violence and exercise.

He could not see why people had to hit, kick, or throw things around, why they could not keep in condition by getting up early, going to work, going home, going to work again, and going to bed; and eating and drinking enough to keep going. If other, and especially younger, people were so underworked and overfed that they thought they needed to disport themselves, he had no objection to letting them go somewhere and do it. Like Harper, he could not imagine where they got the time for it and held himself responsible, as an educator, for their having time on their hands.

Athleticism—the perversion of athletics to commercialism—he abominated. Most of all he abominated the myths that were fabricated to justify it. Far from its being good for the minds and morals of the students, it was not even good for their health. It injured—even killed—some of them in the name of that false morality which held that nothing is as important as winning, and it developed in some of them the "athlete's heart" that would kill them prematurely. It did not habituate them to the games that they could play in later life. It did not even provide college students with exercise, if exercise was what they wanted or needed. Chicago had six thousand students, three thousand of them undergraduates, two thousand of them males. Athleticism did nothing for the females except get them excited (a bad thing in a woman) and it exercised, or overexercised, eleven of the two thousand undergraduate males.

The local sports writers, football alumni, football professors, football trustees, football students, and football barbers, yes, and the Old Man himself, still coaching in his seventies, all suspected Hutchins from the first—and they were right. He assured and reassured them, via the sports writers, that football would always be an integral part of the Chicago program. They didn't believe him—but they were wrong. They should have asked him, "Intercollegiate or intramural?" and they didn't. But you can't fool the sports writers. That sixth sense they all had kept them from being reassured by his reassurances. It told them that he was some kind of an intellectual; and intellectuals, as everybody knows, think that they are too intellectual for athletics. The sports writers took note of his backhand jabs. They took note when he said that a university is not a body-building institute. They took note when he said that the country needed brains almost as much as it did brawn. They took note when he told the YMCA that "the American public is overexercised and overbathed. The great resources of the YMCA should not be directed primarily at aggravating this great evil."[1] They took note when he cited the Big Ten rules against subsidization. They took note when he embellished the proposal of the student editor—a Hutchins Plan boy—that instead of buying football players, the colleges should buy race horses: "Alumni could show their devotion by giving their stables to alma mater. For the time being, Yale would be 'way out in front, for both Mr. Jock Whitney and Mr. Cornelius Vanderbilt Whitney graduated there. But by a judicious distribution of honorary degrees horse fanciers who never went to college might be induced to come to the assistance of institutions which had not attracted students who had become prosperous enough to indulge in the sport of kings. Chicago could, for instance, confer the doctorate of letters upon that prominent turfman, Alderman Bathhouse John Coughlin, and persuade The Bath to change the color of his silks from green to maroon. The alumni could place their money on Chicago across the board. The students could cheer. Most important of all, the horses would not have to pass examinations." And they took note when Hutchins told the unsubsidized Chicago eleven, before it went down to yet another 86-0 defeat, "Your strength is as the strength of ten because your hearts are pure."

They took note. And so did the Grand Old Man, whose squads grew fewer and smaller year after year and whose unbroken record of unbeaten seasons, season after season, was now an unbroken record of beatings.

It took almost ten years—nine, to be exact. The trustees were skittish. The university had a big-domed reputation, maybe too much so for its own good. Its public relations ranged from nonexistent (except for the regular announcement of Nobel Prize winners and such) to positively poor. Football was a drag—and it cost money—but maybe it had to be kept for public relations purposes. Besides, it sort of sustained internal morale, didn't it? The trustee who wanted to know was Albert Lasker, the advertising mogul who had once owned the Chicago Cubs and in sports matters was generally deferred to by most of the board members. According to his biographer, Lasker said to Hutchins, after many a board meeting on the subject, "Football is what unifies a university—what will take its place?" And Hutchins said, "Education."² This (says the biographer) brought Lasker around, in 1937, and Hutchins' hand in the board was strengthened—and still further strengthened when trustee John Nuveen, a stockbroker weekdays (and a churchgoer Sundays) came to the settled conclusion that the subsidization of college athletes was positively immoral, and probably irreligious.

A year later the canny suspicions of all the sports writers were materialized when Hutchins turned sports writer. Proponent and practitioner of impatience, he had spent almost a decade talking it over (and over and over) with trustees, donors, faculty, students, and barbers. He had gone again and again to the sports writers and the football alumni beseeching their arguments for the retention of big-time football not by Notre Dame but by the University of Chicago. They had none that made sense in terms of a center of independent thought and criticism. His presidential colleagues in the state universities explained that their budgets depended directly on football because it was the one activity of the institution that the legislators understood. None of them was willing, on the record, to reveal that darkest secret of the academic underworld, the cost of their stadiums, in spite of the plea of the American Association of University Professors that it be made public. All of them said that somebody ought to do something.

Somebody did something, but not until somebody else did something else. The somebody else was the Grand Old Man himself. The 1936 season was the Maroons' worst to date. At its close Hutchins and Stagg conferred—something they had never done before. Like many college graduates, these two graduates of Yale did not have much in common. At the close of the conference Stagg announced that after forty-four years as Chicago's coach he was leaving. Not retiring—leaving. It was a very bad day for the university in the local papers. It was a very bad day for Hutchins on the campus and off. It might not be his fault that the university could not play good football—though his sniping hadn't done any good—but it was certainly his fault that the Old Man was being let out. Another head coach was dutifully hired; Amos Alonzo Stagg took off into the sunset, and in his nineties was still coaching football at a small college in California. He lived to be a hundred, and if Hutchins had lived to be a hundred he would never have overcome the bitterness of the lovers of things-as-they-had-been, a bitterness aggravated by the sports writers and their full-page recapitulations of "the great days of Chicago"; when, some years later, President Truman recalled General MacArthur from Korea, one long-memoried Chicagoan recalled the similar awful agony that had accompanied the retirement of the Grand Old Man at Chicago. The football fans did not need to ask the question, but they asked it: could there be any doubt any longer that the Boy President meant to dismantle the university?

The Maroons had a worse season in 1937 than they had had in 1936, and a worse season in 1938 than in 1937. It was at the close of the 1938 season that Hutchins turned sports writer and blew the whistle across the country. "Gate Receipts and Glory" appeared in the *Saturday Evening Post.*[3] It began:

"The football season is about to release the nation's colleges to the pursuit of education, more or less. Soon the last nickel will be rung up at the gate, the last halfback will receive his check, and the last alumnus will try to pay off those bets he can recall. Most of the students have cheered themselves into insensibility long since.

"This has been going on for almost fifty years. It is called 'overemphasis on athletics,' and everybody deplores it. It has been the subject of scores of reports, all of them shocking. It has been held to be crass professionalism, all the more shameful because it masquerades as higher education. But nobody has done anything about it. Why? I think it is because nobody wants to. Nobody wants, or dares, to defy the public, dishearten the students, or deprive alma mater of the loyalty of the alumni. Most emphatically of all, nobody wants to give up the gate receipts. Every code of amateurism ever written has failed for this reason. . . .

"Athleticism is not athletics or physical education but sports promotion, and it is carried on for the monetary profit of the colleges through the entertainment of the public. . . ."

The sports writer—Robert M. Hutchins—then proceeded to an analysis of the cause of the symptoms:

"The apologists for athleticism have created a collection of myths to convince the public that biceps are a substitute for brains. Athletics, we are told, produces well-rounded men, filled with the spirit of free play. Athletics is good for the health of the players; it is also good for the morals of the spectators. Leadership in sports means leadership in life. Athletes are red-blooded Americans, and athletic colleges are bulwarks against Communism. Gate receipts are used to build laboratories and to pay for those sports which can't pay for themselves. Football is purely a supplement to study. And without a winning team a college can not hope to attract the students or the gifts which its work requires.

"These myths have a certain air of plausibility. They are widely accepted. But they are myths, designed, consciously or unconsciously, to conceal the color of money and to surround a financial enterprise with the rosy glow of Health, Manhood, Public Spirit, and Education."

Armed to the teeth with the vital statistics, he proceeded to strip the myths, one by one, of their plausibility, and to go on from the cause and the symptoms to the cure:

"We must reform ourselves. How?

"The committees which have studied the subject—and their name is legion—have suggested stricter eligibility rules, reduction of training periods, elimination of recruiting and subsidizing, easier schedules, limitation of each student's participation to one sport, and abandonment of the double scholastic standards for athletes. . . . These reforms will never achieve reform. They may serve to offset athleticism at those few institutions which are already trying to be colleges instead of football teams. But it is too much to hope that they will affect the colleges and universities at large.

"Since money is the cause of athleticism, the cure is to take the money out of athletics. This can be done only in defiance of the students, the alumni, the public, and, in many cases, the colleges themselves. . . . The task of taking the money out of athletics must be undertaken by those institutions which are leaders, institutions which can afford the loss of prestige and popularity involved. I suggest that a group of colleges and of universities composed, say, of Amherst, Williams, Dartmouth, Harvard, Yale, Chicago, Michigan, Stanford, and California agree to take the following steps, to take them in unison and to take them at once:

"1. Reduce admission to ten cents. This will cover the handling costs. For years prominent educators, all the way from Harper, of Chicago, to Butler, at Columbia, have insisted that college athletics should be supported from endowment like any other educational activity. Colleges should support athletics out of their budgets, or get out of athletics, or get out of education.

"2. Give the director of athletics and the major coaches some kind of academic tenure, so that their jobs depend on their ability as instructors and their character as men and not on the gates they draw.

"While these two steps are being taken, it might be well, for the sake of once more putting students instead of athletes on the college playing fields, to try to stimulate the urge to play for fun and health, instead of the urge to win at any cost. There are two ways to do this, and many colleges and universities are trying both with considerable satisfaction to their students:

"1. Broaden the base of athletic participation, so that all students, graduate and undergraduate, big fellows and little fellows, can play. The development of intramural athletics, which costs less than the maintenance of present programs, is a step in this direction. The English system of selecting a varsity from the intramural teams toward the end of the season and then playing a limited number of intercollegiate games suggests itself at this point.

"2. Emphasize games which students will play in later life, when they need recreation and physical fitness as much as in college. Such sports are tennis, handball, skating, swimming, softball, bowling, rackets, golf, and touch football. Few college graduates are able to use football, baseball, or basketball, except as topics of conversation.

"I think that after the steps I have suggested have been taken by the colleges and universities I have named, the rest of the country's educational institutions will not long be able to ignore their example. Nor will the public, once the break has been made, attempt for long to prevent reform. The public, in the last analysis, pays for the colleges and the univer-

sities. It wants something for its money. It has been taught to accept football. It can, I am confident, be taught to accept education.

"The public will not like ten-cent football, because ten-cent football will
not be great football. The task of the colleges and the universities, then, is
to show the country a substitute for athleticism. That substitute is light
and learning. The colleges and universities which taught the country football, can teach the country that the effort to discover truth, to transmit the
wisdom of the race, and to preserve civilization is exciting and perhaps
important too."

Going public did it. It didn't do it anywhere else—there was no Hutchins at the colleges and universities he listed—but it did it at Chicago. The
row, at Chicago, was out in the open at last—and high time. It took exactly one more year of pushing, hard now, in the board of trustees—this
time in the face of a student poll overwhelmingly for football and "legitimate subsidization."

At the end of December 1939, the Chicago board decided in a series of
special meetings to get out of intercollegiate football and develop an elaborate program of intramural football—the answer Hutchins would have
given down the years if his fellow sports writers, when he told them that
football would always be an integral part of the Chicago program, had
thought to ask him, "What kind of football?" The announcement, made
during the Christmas student holiday, was published on the front pages,
not of the sports sections but of the news sections, across the country. As
soon as the students got back, Hutchins called a special convocation, in
which he said he hoped it was not necessary to tell them that a university
was an educational institution, that "education is primarily concerned
with the training of the mind, and athletics and social life, though they
may contribute to education, are not the heart of it and can not be permitted to interfere with it. All questions of management are questions of
emphasis. Even so variegated an institution as a department store, which
may teach skiing or distribute Christmas baskets, must be tested at the last
by its success as a department store. An educational institution can do one
thing uniquely: it can educate. It is by its success in performing this one
function that it must be judged. The object of the University of Chicago,
therefore, is to help you get the finest education that its resources and
intelligence can supply. It is your responsibility to make the most of your
opportunities, to cooperate with the University in the achievement of its
aims—and to go forth and preach the gospel."[4]

It was by all odds the most spectacular and most durable educational
reform of Hutchins' whole career. The irony, a Hutchins kind of irony,

was that it was not an educational reform at all but merely the elimination of one obstacle to education.

The abolition of football did not save all that much money—not at Chicago—and it didn't save it until the worst of the Depression was past. In the first years after Hutchins' departure from Chicago and the succession of a "community oriented" president, there was talk of reviving intercollegiate football on the Midway, but it would never be done. The empty stands at Stagg Field looked blindly down on students playing the intramural games that William Rainey Harper and every other educator thought were good for students. Underneath the abandoned stands, on December 2, 1942, at 3:25 P.M., Enrico Fermi told a young physicist to go ahead and pull a cadmium rod out of a metal "pile"—and the Atomic Age began. And then the stands were torn down, and the Regenstein Library was erected where they'd stood.

In a sense, nobody would ever forgive Hutchins football—nobody, including the opponents of football. He had done what the opponents thought ought to be done—and the proponents agreed could not be done. The proponents were righter than they were wrong: nobody who was anybody followed Chicago's example, and big-time football went from more to more at the colleges and universities Hutchins had named (and at all the others), its progress unimpeded by the popular rise of avowed professionalism. (In 1982 Texas A & M University agreed to pay its head coach $275,000 a year.)

15   The Red Room

"We do just what the Old Man orders," said Charley Wheeler.[1] "One week he orders a campaign against rats. The next week he orders a campaign against dope peddlers. Pretty soon he's going to campaign against college professors. It's all the bunk, but orders are orders." Wheeler, a Chicago *Herald-Examiner* reporter, was speaking to Assistant Professor Frederick Schuman of the University of Chicago, in Schuman's office. (The professor had arranged to have a colleague present to corroborate the conversation.) The Old Man was W.R. Hearst, the owner of the *Examiner* and forty-one other metropolitan newspapers. The date: December 18, 1934.

"Pretty soon he's going to campaign against college professors."

Two months later, Hearst unleashed his editorial hordes against the Red professors. In the *Examiner* of February 24, 1935, under the headline, HOPE LIES IN SOVIET, U. OF C. TEACHER SAYS, Schuman was grossly misquoted; and an editorial in the same edition of all the Hearst papers condemned some of the country's foremost educators as "advisors to Moscow...authorized disseminators of Communist propaganda in the U.S. who deliberately and designedly mislead our fine young people and bring them up to be disloyal to our American ideals and institutions and stupidly to favor the brutal and bloody tyranny of Soviet Russia."

The new Hearst crusade, like so many before it, was highly, not to say totally, imaginative. With the Great Crash, America had lost its bearings. A bewildered country, angry at being bewildered, was angrily determined to discover the traitors; for traitors there had to be, or it couldn't have happened at all. Roosevelt put the finger on the rich—it wasn't hard to do—and the poor and near-poor were his. But the poor and near-poor were the natural Hearst constituency, and this constituency mistrusted intellectuals; and professors were intellectuals.

Hearst could not hope to hold his natural constituency with agonized editorials about "confiscatory taxes" that "soaked the thrifty." His constituency hadn't been able to be thrifty, and it was unemployment, not taxes, that they found confiscatory. What Hearst had ordered his editors to call the Raw Deal was crawling with professors—Red professors, corrupting the young and selling out the country to the Bolsheviks. The way to destroy the Raw Deal was to convince the Hearst readers (still one out of every four families in the country) that Roosevelt was a tool of the academic devils.

The crusade was imaginative, but it was desperate too. The Hearst empire was bleeding to death; gross revenue was down from $113,000,000 to $40,000,000. Half his newspapers were now losing money—none more than the Chicago *Herald-Examiner*. And FDR had moved in with higher taxes on corporation and upper-bracket incomes. Reading his cabinet a draft of his 1935 tax message to Congress, the president looked up at one point, grinning, and said, "That's for Hearst." The Lord of San Simeon had always been able to lump all his publications together for tax purposes, to offset his winners with his losers. No more.

Early in 1935 the Red Terror approached a crescendo in every Hearst town that had a university. Hearst reporters disguised as students enrolled in classes and then exposed the seditious utterances of the instructors. The Syracuse *Journal* carried a typical "news" headline: DRIVE ALL RADICAL PROFESSORS AND STUDENTS FROM THE UNIVERSITIES. California, Pittsburgh, Washington, along with Columbia, Harvard, NYU, and Howard, all came under sustained barrage. But the *crème de la Kremlin* was the University of Chicago.

The universities all had Red professors, but only one had a Red president. By 1935 Hutchins was one of Hearst's *bêtes rouges*. In addition, he had outraged "the Chief" personally. As chairman of the Chicago Regional Labor Board he had found for a CIO union, and the Hearst papers denounced him as an accomplice of Communists and murderers. Hutchins went right ahead calling the shots as he saw them, and Hearst, finding that he couldn't lick him, tried to join him; he offered him a job as a Hearst publisher. Hutchins turned it down and became an accomplice of Communists and murderers again. At the Tribune Tower in Chicago he occupied an even more distinguished niche: on the orders of the "Morning Colonel," R. R. McCormick, the *Tribune* never used his name, referring, when it had to, only to "the president of the University of Chicago."

The Hearst *American* divided the Chicago P.M. market with the *News*, which had fallen into the hands of the "Evening Colonel," Frank Knox (a former Hearst executive). The recently established tabloid *Times*, the only

New Deal paper in town, was a very poor third. The morning field was as good as monopolized by the unscrupulously reactionary *Tribune*. Its feeble competition was the lurid *Herald-Examiner*—the sickest kitten in the whole Hearst litter.

There was strong medicine handy in the San Simeon pharmacopoeia, in the person of Victor Watson. Watson's ultimate suicide fortified the frothing legend that he was crazy; people who came into his office at mealtimes and found him cutting his steak with his copy-shears certainly thought he was. Victor Watson was Hearst's peripatetic fomenter. A man who would start anything and stop at nothing, he enjoyed the prerogative of putting the chief's mouth where his money was. (It was Watson whose forgery of documents designed to provoke an American invasion of Mexico in 1927 moved Senator George W. Norris to characterize the Hearst newspapers as "the sewer system of American journalism.")

Hearst sent Watson to Chicago to do what it would take to save the *Examiner*. What it would take was a Red scare to end all Red scares. The whole country was inflammable in the early 1930s, but Chicago was something special. It was a Roosevelt town—in some small measure because of the graveyard vote produced by the Democratic machine, whose boss, Mayor Edward J. Kelly, was the creature of the Republican Colonel McCormick, and whose next-in-line, State's Attorney Tom Courtney, was the creature of the Republican Colonel Knox. (You had to hold on to your hat in Chicago politics.)

In the early spring of 1935 Miss Lucille Norton of Seattle was an eighteen-year-old University of Chicago freshman who lived with her uncle. At dinnertime she was given to regaling him with her adventures on campus. The professors were teaching her free trade and free love—it was not always clear which, or whether there was a difference. They were teaching her communism out of Communist textbooks. They were teaching her. . . . Years afterward her uncle voiced the tardy suspicion that she had been having him on, as an escape from the boredom of the avuncular table . . . but that was years afterward.

Miss Norton's uncle may not have been one of the most scintillating men in Chicago, but he was one of the most influential. One of the reasons that he was influential was that he was the city's biggest newspaper advertiser, whose double-page spreads meant life or death to a staggering sheet like the *Examiner*. If ever there was a druggist—not a pharmacist, a druggist—it was Charles R. Walgreen, the owner (according to *Who's Who*) of five hundred drugstores in thirty-nine cities. He had attended a small-town business college, apprenticed himself to a pharmacist, and gone on from there to invent the drugstore which *also* sold drugs and which specialized in garish edibles at its long lunch counter. (At the height of the Walgreen Affair the university's dour publicity man, Bill Morgenstern, heaved a sigh and said, "To think that the higher learning in America is at the mercy of the man who thought up tuna-fish marble cake.")

Apart from his membership in the Sons of the American Revolution, Walgreen's civic record was pretty close to blank. But he had performed one philanthropic act of cataclysmic consequence. He had given a scholarship to the University of Chicago—on the shameless condition that he be allowed to name the recipient. The university lived to regret (and right soon) its shameless acquiescence to the shameless condition: the recipient was Walgreen's niece, Miss Norton.

On April 10, 1935, while Victor Watson sat in his office at the *Examiner* carving his steak with his shears, Charles R. Walgreen notified President Hutchins by letter (with copies to the university's trustees) that he was withdrawing his niece from the University of Chicago. "I am," he wrote, "unwilling to have her absorb the Communist influences to which she is so insidiously exposed." Hutchins replied immediately, asking for evidence. Walgreen's reply was a demand for an open meeting of the trustees—to be attended by the press. Hutchins replied that the university would "ignore your vague and unsupported charges until it receives the evidence it has asked for."

Out from behind his five hundred drug counters in thirty-nine cities Charles R. Walgreen was, and ever after remained, a guileless man, much too guileless to do what he did unguided. He had a guide, and a guileful guide. On April 20 the *New York Times* reported from Chicago that "the brew had been simmering for some time . . . and some of the legislators were itching for an investigation. . . . One widely current report has it that the local link of a national chain of newspapers has been diligently heaping fagots under the pot."

The morning after Miss Norton's withdrawal, the *Examiner* had a front-page exclusive on it. Walgreen announced, according to the *Examiner*, that he had "plenty of ammunition" to support his charges. "When it comes to Communism and advocating violence in overthrowing the government of our country," he was quoted as saying, "I am dead set against it." The *Examiner* was able to report—exclusively—from the state capitol at Springfield that Senator Charles W. Baker (Rep., Davis Junction) would that same day introduce a motion to withhold funds to state-subsidized educational institutions found guilty, on investigation, of teaching subversive doctrines *and to deny tax exemption to private institutions found similarly guilty.*

Senator Baker had been introducing his motion for years, with Hearst support. This time it went through with a whoop and a holler and the almost unanimous support of the rural Republicans who had controlled the legislature for a century by refusing to redistrict the state in favor of the metropolitan Democrats. Denial of tax exemption would close an institution like the University of Chicago. The end of the privately endowed university's independence was at hand. The yahoos were at the gates. A few senators opposed the action, including James J. Barbour, who called it "a damned fool resolution that would make another Tennessee out of Illinois." Barbour was named to the investigating committee along with another Chicago Democrat and three downstate Republicans.

Druggist Walgreen was a front for the political forces that, by 1935, were grimly mobilized for a last-ditch stand against the New Deal. Communism was the bogey; the real objective was the cornucopia of social legislation. If the "Roosevelt Revolution" was not turned back in the 1936 presidential election, it never would be. The "Walgreen" case was the *Examiner*'s baby, but the Hearst *American* (of course), the *News*, and the *Tribune* had to string along—had to and wanted to. Had to, because Walgreen was *their* biggest advertiser too. Wanted to, because they were all hell-bent on destroying That Man. The shaky little afternoon tabloid *Times* had to string along too. But it didn't want to and, under the intrepid management of its publisher, Emory Thomason, and its editor, Richard Finnegan, it didn't. Walgreen withdrew his advertising from the *Times*—a mortal blow—and the paper was later picked up by Marshall Field to be merged with his morning *Sun*.

Hutchins was at odds with most of his trustees regarding the limits of academic freedom. In 1931 he told the American Association of University Professors, "Four times in two years, Chicago interests have raised with me the propriety of private or public utterances of members of our staff. We have got to make ourselves clear. The only question that can properly be raised about a professor with the institution to which he belongs is his competence in his field. His private life, his political views, his social attitudes, his economic doctrine—these are not the concern of his university."[2] Even the enlightened and devoted chairman of the board, Harold H. Swift, was disturbed by Hutchins' uncompromising position. He gently reminded "Robert" that in the past the university had fired faculty members for immorality. Robert did not argue the point, but just as gently let it be known that as long as he was president no professor would be fired for anything but incompetence. It was obvious that the Walgreen charges would involve the activities of faculty members outside the classroom and off the campus. The issue of the professor's rights as citizen would have to be joined.

A majority of the board members—including Chairman Swift—recognized the real issue in the matter of the druggist's niece. The real issue was the destruction of the free university, beginning with the freest of them all. Sharply divided over Hutchins' educational reforms, his faculty were solid in their admiration of his defense of academic freedom. The students adored him as a stand-up guy, and when the Walgreen case broke, the Big Men on Campus (including the captains of all the varsity teams) drafted an open letter accusing the accusers.

There was no doubt, as the date of the Walgreen hearings approached, that Victor Watson was performing a masterful orchestration, with his steak shears as baton. In day-by-day front-page revelations, the *Examiner* leaked the substance of "Walgreen's" case, and it was no secret that the paper was providing the senate committee staff with its documentary evidence. Then the *Tribune* announced that attorney Joseph B. Fleming would represent Mr. Walgreen at the hearings. Colonel McCormick had decided to muscle into the act in a big way: Fleming was the *Tribune*'s lawyer.

The day after Walgreen first made his charges, Watson stuck in his steak shears and pulled out a plum. On April 12, 1935, there was a nationwide antiwar "strike" on the campuses. The movement had been growing for more than a year among students with no Communist leanings, the winds having carried the pacifist "Oxford oath" across the Atlantic from Britain. The morning after the strike all the Hearst papers carried a *Herald-Examiner* photo of an unidentified group in the university of Chicago contingent carrying a banner reading YOUNG COMMUNISTS. "According to persons who assert they know," said the *New York Times* carefully, "the banner was furnished by an outside interested agency that wanted a picture that would sustain the charge of rife sedition." Victor Watson sat in his office, with his *au jus* shears in his hand.

The *Examiner* was able to inform its readers that the prosecution's star witness in the Walgreen hearings would be Mrs. Elizabeth Dilling. Mrs. Dilling, self-styled super-expert patriot, was director of the Patriotic Research Bureau of Chicago and author of *The Red Network*. This celebrated who's who of the Communist conspiracy included Chief Justice Charles Evans Hughes, Senator Robert A. Taft, Chairman Glenn Frank of the Republican Party Policy Committee, President William Green of the AFL, *and* the National Council of Churches, the National Catholic Welfare Conference, and the YWCA. But the most dangerous man alive—in Mrs. Dilling's book—was Professor Robert Morss Lovett of the University of Chicago, known to the Chicago *Tribune* as "a pacifist, bolshevik, communist, and pale pink radical" (though the *New York Times* could not think of "any act in his life inconsistent with the purest patriotism," and President Eliot of Harvard once said, "Lovett is a man by whose character Harvard is willing to be judged").

The prospect of Mrs. Dilling and Professor Lovett as contending protagonists was enough to pack the Red Room—it was actually called the Red Room—of the old LaSalle Hotel. But there was a third personage involved, who would pack any hall in America. The hearings opened when Robert Hutchins, tall, inordinately handsome, inordinately commanding, walked into the Red Room, bent over a roundish, smallish, balding figure seated at the complainant's table and said amiably, "Mr. Walgreen, this is going to cost you half a million dollars." The druggist blinked up at Hutchins and was still blinking when the chairman of the committee read the senate resolution which authorized the investigation and introduced counsel—Joseph B. Fleming for Mr. Walgreen and Laird Bell and James H. Douglas, Jr., for the university. Still blinking, the complainant was called to the stand.

His niece, he said, had expressed no decided views on social questions until she entered the University of Chicago. Then "her thoughts as disclosed by her conversation centered on Communism and its various tendencies." In her social science course she was required to read "the *Communism* [sic] *Manifesto* by Karl Marx and F. Engels . . . and it was during this period that she told me that the family as an institution was disappearing. I asked her where she got that idea and she said, 'At school.' . . . I became somewhat bewildered. . . . It becomes a serious matter when a professor upon being asked, 'What do you think of free love?' replies, 'I believe in free love for myself.' "

He told her, he testified, that she was getting to be a Communist, and she replied, "I am not the only one—there are a lot more on the campus."

"Don't you realize that this means bloodshed?"

"Yes, but how did we get our independence—wasn't it by revolution?"

"Well, Lucille, are they really teaching you these things over at the University?"

"No, I don't think they are teaching it to us."

"Are they advocating these things?"

"No, not exactly."

"Well, where do you get all these radical ideas?"

"Well, we have a lot of reading on Communism."

"More than on our own government?"

"Oh, yes, much more." Even in her English course, said Uncle Charles in conclusion, Lucille was required to read a section of a Communist book called *The New Russian Primer*.

Q (by the committee). What professor was it that required that the Karl Marx *Manifesto* be carefully read? *A.* It is listed in the syllabus. It is Professor Gideon. *Q.* G-i-d-e-o-n, is that right? *A.* I think so. *Q.* Is he the man that puts the Bibles in our hotel rooms? *A.* I think it is his father—the old fashioned kind. *Q.* Who is this professor that is advocating free love? *A.* Well, it is Professor Schuman. *Q.* A five-year plan—that was set out in *The New Russian Primer*, was it? *A.* Yes. . . . *Q.* And we have a better plan? *A.* I think so. . . . *Q.* Well, I do too. Hoover thought so too. I don't know who else thinks so, besides us three. *A.* I do not keep very close to the political situation. . . .

The blinking druggist stepped down and Board Chairman Swift of the university took the stand. This top-drawer representative of Chicago's butcher-baker gentry affirmed his conviction that there was no Communist teaching at Chicago, that no faculty member was a Communist, and that no faculty member advocated violent overthrow of the government or tried to instill such ideas in the minds of students. He went on to recite a long litany of indices that ranked Chicago just behind, just even with, or just ahead of Harvard as the most eminent university in America. He welcomed this opportunity. . . .

Hutchins took the stand, all six feet three inches of him, and presented the committee with the catalogue of the university's 3,492 courses taught by 901 instructors. He had examined the complete outlines of the 161 undergraduate courses in social, political, and economic problems and found nothing subversive in them. "The University," he went on, "would not permit the indoctrination of students or the use of the classroom as a center of propaganda. On the other hand, the professor is not disfranchised when he takes an academic post; he may think, live, worship, and vote as he pleases. Under the laws of Illinois it is illegal to advocate the overthrow of the government by violence. (304 Ill. 23.) Anybody who thinks that any of our faculty are doing so should inform the State's Attorney of Cook County."

All of this was delivered in the Boy President's characteristically wooden manner. But now his voice rose a shade. "The members of the faculty of the University of Chicago are law-abiding, patriotic citizens. On their behalf I repudiate the charges against them." And then, half-turning to face Charles R. Walgreen, he concluded extemporaneously, "Those who have made these charges are either ignorant, malicious, deluded, or misinformed," and sat down.

The next witness was Charles E. Merriam, chairman of the Department of Political Science, a member of President Hoover's National Committee on Recent Social Trends, and a member of President Roosevelt's National

Resources Board. Merriam had been a member of a distinguished faculty for thirty-five years and was now its most distinguished member. Famous for his imperturbability and his easy slouch, he was a tower of rage as he assaulted "the persons" who were assaulting *his* university. "I charge them, wittingly or unwittingly, with attacking one of the strongest forces for the stabilization and maintenance of our civilization. I charge them with grand larceny of human reputation and achievement. . . .

"If there is unrest in this land, and there is, and if many men in their bitterness and discontent reach out blindly in a feverish struggle to find a way out, then we must seek out the causes of discontent and cure them; otherwise the anguish and the bitterness will grow greater. . . . Only madness moves those who in the name of American liberty try to suppress thought on how that liberty may be preserved." There was silence as Charley Merriam, neither raging nor slouching now, but bent like a very old man, fumbled his way back to his seat at the counsel table.

The university concluded its case in chief by calling Mrs. Edith Foster Flint, the professor of English in charge of the college course that used a passage from *The New Russian Primer*. The committee was favored with a lecture in the elementary procedure of confronting college students with critical materials drawn from every field of knowledge and opinion and requiring a comparative analysis of them. The lordly Mrs. Flint was not in the habit of being interrogated, and, when nobody presumed to interrogate her now, she stepped lordlily down.

The chairman of the committee was in the process of adjourning the hearing for a week when the prelude to the fun began. A man in a U.S. Army uniform—he had been a soldier, but no longer was—stood up in the back of the room and said, "In the name of the American Legion, may I say a few words?" The chairman said, "We will be glad to hear from you. Will you come back here at another time and. . . ." The ex-soldier interrupted him: "Here is the Red meeting of Professor Robert Lovett, the Commission they had in the city of Chicago. . . . That is for three hours May Day a Red Flag floats over the University of Chicago. Three hours May Day. . . . Professor Lovett was connected with that convention. . . . In the name of the American Legion, Disabled Veterans of the American Legion, Disabled Veterans of the World War, and the Veterans of the World War. . . ."

June rolled away with week-to-week recesses in the Red Room, attributed by a Hearst blabbermouth to Victor Watson's order to keep the thing going as long as there was pay dirt in it. The original scenario, or game plan, did not call for Miss Norton's appearance, lest she cave in under cross-examination by her corrupters. But a communications breakdown occurred (reportedly between the Hearst Building and the Tribune

Tower), and one of the committee members, Senator John W. Fribley (Rep., Pana) said that he would like to have Miss Norton produced. She was produced a week later. She read a statement in a very small voice. At the University of Chicago she had "gained the feeling, through readings and contacts, that Communism would be an excellent form of government, despite the fact that its installation would undoubtedly necessitate a revolution. . . .

"Through reading and lectures we were told repeatedly that the family is disintegrating. This was emphasized by Professor Schuman's remark, 'I believe in religion for some people, and free love for myself,' at a symposium at which I was present. It never occurred to me that Professor Schuman might be insincere." *Sen. Barbour* (who had opposed the investigation): Did the students break out in laughter after Professor Schuman made that remark? *A.* (Pause.) I think there was some laughter. . . . *Q.* Did the remark indoctrinate you? *A.* (Long pause.) No.

A committee member asked her if she still believed in communism. Again a long pause, a small voice: "No." Nobody asked her how she had become detoxified in the sixty days that followed her removal from the university. There was no cross-examination by her now frustrated corrupters.

Assistant Professor Schuman took the stand, a very sharp young man whose book, *The Nazi Dictatorship*, was already a minor classic. Married; two children, both legitimate. He said his name had once been misused in support of the Communist candidate for president in 1932—he had voted for Roosevelt—and confessed to having attended a banquet for the Communist candidate for vice-president (a Negro). The banquet was sponsored by the Chicago *Defender*, a Negro Republican newspaper, at a time when he, Schuman, was making a study of the Negro in American politics.

Before he could be asked about his advocacy of free love his place was taken by Associate Professor Harry A. Gideonse. Gideonse advised the honorable committee that neither he nor his father distributed the Gideon Bible, and that he was responsible for the freshman social science course which included the *Communist Manifesto*—and Herbert Hoover's *American Individualism*. He invited Mr. Walgreen and the committee to cross-examine him. When they declined he informed them that he had participated in the symposium—not a class—in which a silly student had interrupted the discussion to ask if the panel believed in free love. "Perhaps Professor Schuman should have said, 'I am going to be funny,' before he spoke."

Attorney Fleming then presented a mass of documentary evidence, including (in addition to the *Manifesto*) announcements of radical meetings in the student *Daily Maroon* and several items of current Communist-front propaganda, some of which bore the names of Schuman and Lovett. While he was reading the committee an exposition of Party doctrine by William Z. Foster, Professor Merriam asked for permission to make a point of order: Oughtn't the Red Room to be cleared of students while Mr. Fleming was reading these materials? No response from Attorney Fleming.

The end was in sight. One last session would do it; one last spectacular session, presenting Mrs. Dilling for the patriots and Professor Lovett for the corrupters. The great day came. The senate committee sat at one end of the Red Room at a long trestle table on a temporary dais. At a table on one side of the room, sat Hutchins and Board Chairman Swift, flanked by attorneys Bell and Douglas (both of them trustees of the university). Facing them, at a table on the other side of the room, sat Charles R. Walgreen. On one side of him sat Attorney Fleming. On his other side, in a red dress, sat an attractive, indeed, arresting woman, who *didn't* blink. Directly behind her, whispering to her, sat a large, beefy man of reddest countenance. These two counselors were Victor Watson's friends at court.

The beefy man was Harry A. Jung, founder, president, and chairman of the American Vigilant Intelligence Federation. His counselee, the druggist's counselor, was Mrs. Elizabeth Dilling.

Mrs. Dilling had hold of a very good thing. Her *Red Network* (dedicated to Harry A. Jung), an alphabetical list of traitors in reference-work form, was a staple of American Legion posts across the land, and of police departments (including New York's and Chicago's), sheriffs' offices, and Klan, Bund, and Save-the-Constitution societies. Its authenticity was attested by the *Army and Navy Register*, the American Coalition of Patriotic Societies, and the chairman of the National Americanism Commission of the American Legion. It was cited regularly as expert testimony at state legislative and congressional hearings. Now with Walgreen, Hearst, and the *Tribune* behind her, Mrs. Dilling's time had come.

She leaped to her feet before the last syllable of her name had been sounded and explained that she had to talk fast because she had too much to tell the committee in so little time. There was no previous record of her ever having been interrupted—but she was interrupted this time, by Senator Barbour, the committee's opposition member. She had run through half the Chicago faculty, including Hutchins as a sponsor of the Soviet-American Institute, "of which Jane Addams was a sponsor," when Senator Barbour seized the chairman's gavel and brought it down hard on the echoing trestle table. The explosion stopped the witness long enough for Barbour to say: "Do you want an hour or two to run down the memory of Jane Addams?"

"I can give you an hour or two on her record," said Mrs. Dilling, "but Eleanor Roosevelt's is worse, and Professor Robert Lovett's is the worst of them all"—and she immediately started in on Justice Brandeis, "one of the biggest contributors to this filthy, lousy little college [Commonwealth College] down in Arkansas"—and immediately went on to Board Chairman Swift of the University of Chicago: "There's a cream-puff type that would get its throat cut. Some rich men play with chorus girls, others with booze, and others with Communism. Mr. Swift wouldn't have a nickel left—he wouldn't have that pretty suit he's wearing—if the ideas he's playing with had their way."

While Mr. Swift looked somberly down at the vest of his pretty suit, and even Walgreen and his lawyer looked down at theirs, the witness lit into "the notorious, Communist-aiding American Civil Liberties Union. . . . Smoke-screening with incessant cries for 'free speech,' 'free press,' and 'free assembly,' the Civil Liberties Union by means of legal battles all over the country, and tons of well-financed propaganda, fights to keep the way open for Communists to agitate revolutionary theory that leads to revolutionary practice and the destruction of all freedom and the American Constitution. The University of Chicago not only retains a president and teachers with Communist affiliations, but also allows them to sponsor Red meetings on the campus." A reporter for the New Deal Chicago *Times* concluded his account of Mrs. Dilling's testimony with; "[*All* punctuation added]"—but a sober-sided man on the copy desk struck it out.

After two hours of this farrago the chairman of the committee hit the exploding table with his gavel—it was well past his lunchtime—and asked if there was any cross-examination of the witness. Attorney Bell for the university looked up from the contemplation of *his* vest and shook his head sadly. At the rear of the room a tumult began. It seemed that a spectator had turned to the man next to him and whispered, "Is that Mrs. Dillinger?"—Mr. Dillinger having passed away a year earlier in front of the Biograph Theatre—and for his impertinence the spectator received a punch in the nose from his neighbor, who turned out to be Mrs. Dilling's husband Albert, whose sole known occupation was to hold up Communist posters at his wife's meetings while she told the audience, "You don't know the Red Harlot, the Red Beast, and the signs of the times that are coming. Albert and I have been in Russia. The food makes you sick at your stomach. It did me. It really did. I don't care what anybody says. We saw Lenin. He's God in Russia. Pickled in alcohol under glass. A little sandy-whiskered thing. I thought to myself—pooh, you don't amount to much."

The Red Room was still reeling from the testimony of the lady muckraker when the name of Harry A. Jung was called. The beefy, red-faced man who had sat behind Walgreen and Mrs. Dilling from the start of the hearings took the stand. The founder, president, and chairman of the American Vigilant Intelligence Federation was unknown to some of the people in the room—but not to Attorney Fleming, who, it will be remembered, was not only Mr. Walgreen's lawyer but Colonel McCormick's: Jung's American Vigilant Intelligence Federation had long enjoyed rent-free hospitality in the colonel's Tribune Tower.

Once a professional labor spy, Jung was now a tinhorn fascist of no real consequence; his specialty was the distribution of the Jewish-plot forgery known as *The Protocols of the Elders of Zion*. He began his testimony by reading the names of Chicago faculty members who belonged to Communist organizations like the ACLU. When he got to the name of Professor T. V. Smith, Senator Barbour said, "Is that our colleague from the Fifth Senatorial District of Illinois?" When Jung said it was, Barbour said, "Who called this man to testify?" Nobody knew and nobody ever found out. "I call for adjournment," said Senator Barbour, and the committee rose. As the room emptied Jung was still in the witness chair, testifying to the empty dais.

The case against the university had collapsed—almost. Walgreen—that is, Victor Watson—had one last hope of extracting a diamond from the dung. There was a letter—a genuine letter, not a forgery—that had passed from Watson to the senate committee. It had been written a decade earlier to a Russian refugee who had asked, and got, the help of an American man of letters in publishing a book exposing Soviet corruption. When the book flopped, the refugee accused the man of letters of having sabotaged it in behalf of the Soviet government. The man of letters courteously—always courteously—replied, in a scribbled note of consolation, that he himself "did not care whether the book reflects on the Russian government or the United States government or any other—all in my opinion being rotten. Sincerely yours, Robert Morss Lovett." (The scribble was introduced by the senate committee as its Exhibit 19 in the Walgreen hearings, and the committee, in its final report, said that "if all the exhibits offered in evidence against Professor Lovett were disregarded except Exhibit 19, proof of his disloyal conduct is conclusive.")

If Watson lost everything else and nailed Lovett, the chief would be satisfied. More then satisfied. "I have never understood how I first offended Hearst," Lovett once told a friend. "It is true that I called him Public Enemy Number One, but everybody else had a list of public enemies, so I thought that I should have one of my own."

Mrs. Dilling's most dangerous man alive shambled into the Red Room with his tattered old briefcase under his arm—the handle had fallen off in the early 1920s—his high, wispy (where it wasn't barren) old dome shining in the June sunlight. He was stout and slow, with a head like Hearst's (nothing so leonine, of course), and his suit was as shapeless as he. Two or three students got up from their seats and escorted him to the witness chair. Obviously a broken old man—a shame to have to dismember him.

What the dismemberers didn't know was that they were up against a man whose false façade of genteel senility had long since earned him the sobriquet of the Buster Keaton of the Saints. The deceptive thing about Bob Lovett was his air of bewildered innocence, coupled with the ineffable politeness of the Boston Brahmin he was. The deceit had been penetrated by his mother when he was very young: he asked her why he should remember the Ten Commandments for the dollar *she* gave him, when his aunt had given him *ten* dollars for remembering not to pick his nose. The politeness persisted unfailingly into his dotage: testifying against him on a charge of riot, a policeman told the court, "And when I went to put him in the wagon, the old gentleman there, he held the door for me."

The old gentleman's official status was itself deceptive: professor of English at the University of Chicago since 1893. Hundreds of thousands of school children had struggled through "Moody and Lovett," the *History of English Literature* he had written in 1916 with William Vaughn Moody. At Chicago, with a year off to edit the *Dial*, and a decade as literary editor of the *New Republic*, he had launched more young writers than any man before or since—beginning with Frank Norris, Malcolm Cowley, Lewis Mumford, Edmund Wilson, Howard Mumford Jones, and Carl Van Vechten. Recently there had been a crazy wild Irish kid who talked big and did nothing, who came into Lovett's office on campus one day and threw a short story on the desk and turned to go. Lovett pushed him into a chair and held him there while he read the story. Then he said, "Do you know what we're going to do, Jimmy? We're going to stretch this into a novel." The story was *Studs Lonigan*.

But there was another Lovett outside the classroom and the editorial office, of whom his adorers said that wherever there was trouble, there was Lovett. (His deplorers said that wherever there was Lovett, there was trouble.) He was an inveterate recidivist. He had been brought to bar a couple of dozen times in the course of a lifetime of un-American activities. He had gone bail for Communists, Nazis, anarchists, pacifists, and black and white rioters. Cofounder (with Roger Baldwin) of the American Civil Liberties Union, he had sat for days on end in police courts all over the country. Discovered thus sitting one day by one of his academic colleagues, he explained, "I am fixing the court with my eye in an effort to intimidate it into a carriage of justice." His historic defense of the IWWs before Judge Landis in Chicago may have contributed to their conviction by a jury of professing Christians: "There is a ritual of violence and a ritual of Christianity," Lovett testified on that occasion, "to which the sub-scribers, in both cases, pay lip service without in the least intending to put them into practice." (Two years after the Walgreen affair the broken old man shambled into the General Motors plant at Flint, Michigan, at the height of the great sit-down strike. Holding his five shares of GM stock over his head, he informed the grinning strikers that "my manage-ment is mistreating my workers and I am here as one of the owners of the corporation to tell my workers that I am behind them.")

He'd been chairman of the Sacco-Vanzetti League and the Committee for the Relief of Russian Women and Children, president of the Friends of Freedom for India and the socialist League for Industrial Democracy, and was now vice-president of the American League against War and Fascism—and a member of any and every organization that asked him. The FBI found his name on *four hundred* letterheads, only four of which could be safely said to be free of the taint of communism—the Pulitzer Prize Committee, the National Institute of Arts and Letters, the Harvard Club of New York, and the American Red Cross. If the Communists were fighting the Mooney and Scottsboro cases to provoke the class struggle, Lovett was fighting the same cases to rectify injustice; if they were using him for their purposes, he was using them for his. "I have never been as afraid of liberals going Communist," he once said, "as I have of their pull-ing out of liberal organizations when the Communists, with their disci-pline, their persistence, and their eagerness, threatened to seize control." Persons who valued their good names above trash had a hard time under-standing Robert Morss Lovett.

He sat in the witness chair in the Red Room and undid his crumbling briefcase. "I have here," he said, nobody having asked him what he had there, "the lectures I deliver to my classes in seventeenth-century literature at the University of Chicago. I should like to read them aloud on this occasion. I am unable to find anything subversive in them, but there may be something of the sort, and I should like to have expert opinion in the matter." This time the senators blinked. What was this? His piles of lecture notes in front of him, the most dangerous man on earth sat there a picture of disingenuous aplomb.

The first to recover was Mr. Walgreen's lawyer, Mr. Fleming. He asked the witness if he approved of "the slacker oath against our country." Lovett pushed his lecture notes aside and said, "If you refer to the so-called Oxford Oath not to bear arms, I regard it as the individual equivalent of the Kellogg-Briand Pact of 1925 by which the United States gave up war as an instrument of national policy. Congress is not authorized to declare war, because the Kellogg-Briand Pact is equally law with the Constitution of the United States." The senators stared as they heard this thirty-second classroom lecture in political science. The first of them to recover wanted to know what Professor Lovett would do if Germany declared war and his grandchildren were asked to go. Lovett said, "I should do exactly as I did in the case of my son, who was killed at Belleau Wood. I should tell them nothing. I should not attempt to decide for another individual."

The senators stared some more, until Mr. Fleming asked the witness whether he was the author of the letter which had passed from Mr. Watson of the *Examiner* to the senate committee—the letter that asserted that all governments are rotten. The witness said that indeed he was, and he wished to refer the committee to that morning's edition of the Chicago *Tribune*, which carried a front-page cartoon in which a figure labeled "world dictators" is driving "poor old world" along a road marked "back to the dark ages," while overhead burst bombs labeled "Fascism," "Communism," "Nazism," and "New Dealism." The witness understood the cartoon to mean that the present government of the United States was rotten, but perhaps somebody—and he looked around the room until his bewildered gaze fell upon Mr. Fleming—could enlighten him to the contrary. This time the *Tribune*'s (and Mr. Walgreen's) lawyer stared at the red plush drapes that had been pulled to block out the lowering sunlight of late afternoon.

It was getting on for the committee's suppertime. The witness sat there expectantly, still prepared to read his seventeenth-century English literature lectures. The chairman proposed adjournment *sine die*, and nobody objected.

The Walgreen hearings had petered out. But not the Walgreen affair. On June 26 the senate committee issued its report—the only report ever issued in consequence of the resolution to investigate "Communism in state-supported and tax-exempt institutions in Illinois." Senator Baker, the author of the resolution, dissented, finding the University of Chicago "entirely partisan and pro-Communistic," but three of the other four committee members called his dissent "a bid for publicity in three of the metropolitan newspapers in Chicago. It is not based on evidence offered at the committee's hearings."

The majority report, signed by four of the five members, acquitted the university of subversive teaching or indoctrination: "All oral testimony offered by Mr. Walgreen does not prove the charges against the University of Chicago, even if his witnesses were uncontradicted." But Assistant Professor Schuman should be censured for his reckless associations, and "Fair consideration of all the evidence compels a conclusion that Professor Robert Morss Lovett has pursued an unpatriotic course of conduct for many years. Exhibits offered in evidence disclosing Professor Lovett's activities in Communistic or unpatriotic organizations and his association with Communist speakers, regardless of their reputation, prove that Professor Lovett cannot be an asset to any forward looking institution."

But the two Chicagoans on the committee, both Democrats, felt constrained to rinse their hands before the doddering heretic was handed over by the holy office of Victor Watson to the secular arm of the university: "We cannot fail to express our feeling that the outside activities and some of the extra-campus associations of Professor Lovett are not conducive to effective or helpful service on his part as a member of the faculty of the University of Chicago, and that in view of his long service and scholastic achievements in the field of English literature, he is deserving of honorary retirement, with usual and suitable provisions for emeritus professors. It is in no unfriendly spirit that we express the belief that his long years of study and authorship and a family affliction incident to the World War may have weakened his judgment."

What could a forward looking university do about a faculty member unhinged by long years of study and authorship? Lovett, like all full professors, and unlike the young Schuman, had lifetime tenure. His unpatriotic course of conduct had taken place off the university's premises and therefore (according to Hutchins) entirely outside the university's responsibility or jurisdiction.

For a week the wolves howled in concert under Victor Watson's copyshears baton. The chief wanted Lovett's skin nailed to the wall. Not a word was heard from the forward-looking university. Not a word was said about a special meeting of the Board of Trustees requested by Hutchins. And then the *Examiner* burst forth with its triumphant front-page streamer: U. OF C. TO LET LOVETT GO. Watson had carried the day for the chief. The chief had carried the cause for the country. The Raw Deal—and the pacifist, Bolshevik, Communist, pale pink radical professors—had been depth-bombed out of the water. The ship of state was once more on course.

"Under pressure of the demand for his ouster," the *Examiner* reported in twelve-point bold, "the University of Chicago has decided to drop Professor Robert Morss Lovett from its faculty, according to authoritative sources." At the end of the sensational story, in eight-point lightface, was the kicker: "The University administration contemplates retiring him on Christmas Day. At that time Professor Lovett will be eligible for a pension." (With forty-two years of service Lovett had been eligible for a pension for a long time, but it was true that he would reach the compulsory retirement age of sixty-five on December 25, 1935.)

When Hutchins reached his office the morning of the *Examiner*'s bombshell, he found Professor James Weber Linn waiting for him. As usual, a burning cigarette stub, less than an inch long, hung from "Teddy" Linn's lips—a miracle that had transfixed generations of Chicago undergraduates waiting for him either to swallow it or go up in smoke. Standing in the doorway to block the president's entrance Linn said, "Hutchins"—he had never before called him anything but Bob—"if the trustees fire Lovett you'll receive the resignations of twenty full professors tomorrow morning." "Oh no, I won't," said Hutchins, "my successor will."

That afternoon a statement was delivered to the downtown papers for immediate release. It was signed by Robert M. Hutchins, and it announced that in view of the distinction conferred upon the University of Chicago by Professor Robert Morss Lovett's scholarship and teaching, and his unfaltering capacity to continue his work, the Board of Trustees had waived the compulsory retirement age of sixty-five in this one instance and persuaded Professor Lovett to remain on the faculty.

After the university's reappointment of Lovett, Hutchins received a letter which began, "Dear Bob," and ended, "You must have had a vile time with that inquisition. I sometimes think that Hearst has done more harm to the cause of democracy and civilization in America than any three other contemporaries put together. Always sincerely, Franklin D. Roosevelt."[3]

With the ignominious collapse of the "Walgreen" case—and of the chief's great crusade against the country's Red professors—the guileless druggist should have retired to his five hundred drug stores in thirty-nine cities. But he didn't. On June 8, a week before the hearings ended, Harold L. Ickes wrote in his wonderful Washington diary: "Merriam came in to see me this afternoon. Walgreen has been making distinct overtures to him and Merriam thinks he is pretty sick of the whole business."[4]

Hutchins had a flaring nostril for money, and a backhand genius for prying it loose. "*Mr. Walgreen, this is going to cost you half a million dollars.*" The druggist had gone to Merriam even before the hearings ended and said, "Nobody out there will talk to me."—five hundred drug stores in thirty-nine cities, and "nobody out there will talk to me." Now the senate committee, which was supposed to have been his stooge, had dismissed his charges as hearsay and failed to retire Lovett (or even to censure Schuman). He betook himself to Merriam again, confessed the distress which nothing on his prescription shelf would palliate, and said,

"What can I do about Hutchins?" Merriam replied, "I don't know... I don't know. You've hurt his feelings pretty badly."

A couple of months after Walgreen learned that he had hurt Hutchins' feelings pretty badly, Physics Professor Henry Gordon Gale bumped into the president on the campus. "I know we had to stand behind Lovett," said Gale, "but he's cost the university millions in gifts." "Oh, I don't know, Henry," said Hutchins, "this last time around he brought us in about four million dollars."

At the conclusion of the Walgreen hearings the Rockefeller Foundation, without referring to the matter, had made an unrestricted gift to the university of three million dollars "for general excellence." A letter with a "token check" of ten thousand dollars had been received, together with an offer of "whatever service for which you may wish to call on me," from a resident of far-off Long Island, one Marshall Field III (whose grandfather had given the new university the acreage that was later known as Stagg Field). Another ten thousand dollars, followed almost immediately by $250,000 more, came in with a letter to Hutchins from the five children of the founder of Sears Roebuck and Company:

"We are impressed by your liberal and courageous stand in behalf of academic freedom. . . . The Rosenwald Family Association has not, as yet, received its bequest under the will of Mr. Julius Rosenwald. We are unable, therefore, to express our confidence in your administration as we should like to do. It is our present intention to make the University of Chicago one of three principal beneficiaries as soon as we are in a position to do so."

All of that did not add up to a firm four million. What added up to it was the meeting of Hutchins and Charles R. Walgreen. Hutchins gave the occasion all he had, turning the insouciant screw until the victim came up with a blushing bid of $250,000. Hutchins was overwhelmed—but he did not see how the university could do what it wanted to do on $250,000. It wanted to establish the Charles R. Walgreen Foundation for the Study of American Institutions. How much would it cost to establish the Charles R. Walgreen Foundation for the Study of American Institutions? It would cost—let me see, now—approximately $550,000. Hutchins walked out with the $550,000 (and Charles R. Walgreen) in his pocket.

But it was something of a two-way ride. The $550,000 had no effect whatever on the curriculum of the University of Chicago, but it had a considerable effect on the digestion of the university's president. For the next two years, until Walgreen's death, Hutchins had lunch with the druggist in the druggist's office on an average of once a week. The druggist asked for, and got, a great deal of administrative advice on the management of his five hundred drugstores in thirty-nine cities, and the president got, without asking for it, the occasional opportunity to advise the druggist on a new variant of tuna-fish marble cake about to be introduced at the Walgreen lunch counters.

A year or so after it was all over, Hutchins made a speech which he sent on to his friend Walgreen. In the speech he said; "There would not be much point in sending young people to college if they were not going to learn something they did not know before. Parents who are not willing to have their children enter the world of ideas should keep them at home."[5] A couple of days later Walgreen phoned to tell his friend Hutchins how much he had enjoyed the speech. There was something else—he had something new for the Walgreen lunch counters that he'd like Hutchins to try. If Hutchins didn't mind, he'd send his chauffeur over with a sample of it right away.

Hutchins said he didn't mind, hung up the phone, took a pill out of his desk drawer, and waited.

16 Cease-fire

Hutchins never did get the college he wanted or (unlike simpler men) understand why he didn't. Why wasn't it self-evident to advocates of the elective system that children couldn't possibly know what it was they would need to know in later life? Why wasn't it self-evident that liberal education was the best preparation (to the extent that education *was* preparation) for the vagaries and vicissitudes that commence with commencement? That specialized study (and, at a low level, vocational training) was no preparation at all for those vagaries and vicissitudes? That technology would continue to reduce and eliminate the crafts and skills which vocational training imparted? That a man, no matter what his occupation, needed more to know how to live (and die) than how to make a living? Why wasn't it self-evident that a self-governing people could not hope to perpetuate self-government without the development of their powers to comprehend, analyze, and judge the social issues that turned on their understanding of the nature of man and society?

He didn't understand. He never would.

But he would never be closer to getting what he wanted than he was by the spring of 1937. The reasons he was close were wholly extraneous to the merits of his case. In those seven years of financial collapse following the crash of 1929 he had performed the financial wonders that saved the university. In those seven years of anti-intellectual assault on education by the yahoos he had stood and fought for academic freedom and, more than any other front-fighter in America, beaten back the superpatriots who were bent on destroying the independence of the universities generally, and his own in particular.

After the reforms—the "Hutchins Plan" so-called—that had been got through the faculty senate in his first year-and-a-half in office, his stock went down as his faculty opposition consolidated. There was a succession of reports that he was quitting—for a New Deal job, usually—and a continuum of rumors that conservative trustees (and they were almost all of them conservative) were under pressure from their rich friends downtown, or their poor friends on the faculty, to get him out. Little by little the reports and the rumors subsided. He would certainly go on, one of these days, to those higher things to which, if ever a man was destined, he was. But by 1937 it was acknowledged, uptown and down, that, for all his educational idiocies, he had been heroic against the financial bears and the political boa constrictors. His early offenses—above all, the *affaire* Mert—had been neither forgiven nor forgotten. They were, however, soft-pedaled for the nonce in a kind of second honeymoon.

Half honeymoon and half standoff.

The Hutchins batting average on *structural* reform—"teaching the wrong things the right way"—was close to .500. Won: The faculty senate accepted his proposal to give the college jurisdiction over the last two years of the University High School. Lost: The trustees, "accepting" the proposal, rejected the integration of the eleventh and twelfth grades in the first two years of the College as a four-year unit, which Hutchins (and many other educators) wanted as a segment of a "six-four-four" system to replace the eight years of elementary school followed by four years of high school and four years of college.[1]

As for teaching the right things, he appeared (but only appeared) to have carried the day when, on March 9, 1937, the senate adopted a uniform four-year college curriculum which all but eliminated electives on the "Hutchins" principle that (as the senate worded it) "the end of general education can be achieved best by helping students to master the leading ideas and significant facts in the principle fields of knowledge, with a view to the development of intelligent action." The program provided a mélange of fifteen courses (ranging from a year to three years each) in the four great general fields of study. It would run parallel with the two-year program of the college, already adopted, and was thought of as ultimately serving students who would enter it (primarily from the University High School) at the end of the tenth grade.

But—it would utilize course syllabi, which instead of being constructed around the great books, merely included some readings from them. Three times in those years the faculty of the college, "Hutchins' own," denied him his all-out great book curriculum. His batting average on content, in spite of the spectacular new curriculum: .500 at best. As to method, though the small class size in the new four-year program conduced to discussion, nothing fundamental was done to get rid of the soporific lecture—nor indeed could it be done, there or anywhere, then or any time, except by the slow infusion, over years, of Socratic young men and women (a) possessed of and (b) devoted to general education. The Hutchins batting average on method: perhaps .500—mostly by extrapolation from the actuarial table.

Not bad. Not too bad. But not too good. His two-front war for academic money and academic freedom had got him a reprieve—nothing more. In ten years of depression, before the federal government contracts began, the Chicago take from Hutchins' fund-raising would exceed every university's in America except Harvard's and Yale's. Eventually, over the twenty-year span of his administration, Hutchins would bring in ninety-three million dollars. On the second front he had, in the midthirties, saved Chicago, and perhaps American universities generally, from a more formidable disaster than depression. He saved their freedom of intellectual and political inquiry from the Un-Americanist witch-hunters; more precisely, from the potentates of business and industry who promoted the hunts and maintained the huntsmen.

The faculty opposition was charmed by his fund-raising and his freedom fight, but it was not charmed out of its educational principles. As of 1937 his heroics off the campus had simply deferred the counterattack. Within a year the opposition would find its feet; in 1938 the faculty senate voted for a "review" of the presidency—true, it was never completed—and a year after that he suffered a portentous setback when the biological sciences division refused any longer to accept the comprehensive examination as a substitute for the course credit system. But that would not be until 1939, when his position was fortified by the secret government negotiations which established the "Metallurgical Project" (and ultimately the achievement of the self-sustaining nuclear chain reaction).

In 1929 Chicago's eminence rested, as it always had, on research, especially in the physical sciences. Some of Hutchins' colleagues (and some of his readers) would accuse him, during the whole of his career, of indifference to empirical research, hostility to the natural sciences, preoccupation with humanistic education at the collegiate level, and a special contempt for Deweyism. Apart from the fact that nine of the eleven men elevated to distinguished-service professorships during the first decade of his administration were natural scientists (and one a Deweyite educationalist), he more than maintained the university's eminence attested by the Hughes Report of 1924—five years before his advent—which ranked Chicago first in more departments than any other American university.

It was specialization that determined a university's rank: the university with the greatest number of great men was the greatest university, and the university with the greatest number of great men in a given field had the greatest department in the field. The University of Chicago of 1929 was great because it was a geographical locus, and nothing more, of specialists working in isolation or with one or two similarly specialized colleagues and a half-dozen specialized students, while the undergraduates nibbled around the collegiate smorgasbord. It was this Chicago that Hutchins tried to transform from a locus into a center, from a congeries into a community, from a *diversum* into a *universum*. What he succeeded in doing was to alter (no more than that) undergraduate teaching and the undergraduate curriculum while doing his duty, as a man of duty does. His duty was to find and reward the specialists who would make Chicago a second Harvard—or a first. But the alteration of undergraduate teaching, and the undergraduate teaching staff for whom he obtained autonomy within the institution, was more than superficial. Caught up in the hot bidding for big money and big men, especially in science and medicine, he pushed what money he could get his hands on into the development of the Hutchins Plan. In the dark night of the 1930s, Hutchins would tell the unsalable prospect why he should buy Chicago: "It's not a very good university—it's only the best there is."

After the first five years of his assault on the overemphasis of science and specialization, Chicago led the country in the number of its Nobel Prize winners in science; and according to the authoritative *American Men of Science*, which indicates by a star the names of scientists distinguished in their respective fields, Chicago had the greatest number of starred scientists in proportion to its faculty of any university in the country—and was second only to Harvard in total number. A *Fortune* study in 1939 concluded: "When you come to equate endowment and income figures with scholarship, a reasonable case could be made out that Chicago gets more B.T.U.'s of teaching and research energy per dollar than any other U.S. university, even including Harvard." And when Hutchins resigned, in 1950, one out of every fifteen men listed in *American Men of Science* was a Chicago product, one out of every eleven in *Leaders of Education*, one out of every ten in the *Directory of American Scholars*.

The fact is that most of Hutchins' opponents in the faculty and on the board were, and always would be, ambivalent about him. None—at least none of the faculty—was ever found who wanted to see him go. What was wanted was to bring him into line, or get him back into line, and keep him there. Not a chance. Their miscalculation was as extravagant as his own that he would ever get the college (or the university) that he wanted. The lawyer was careful always to proceed constitutionally, but there is no constitution so perforate as the gentlemanly statutes of a university. Ralph Tyler, whom Hutchins hired as University Examiner in spite of Tyler's insistence that he was a progressive educator, suggested that the statutes be examined closely to see if they inhibited the establishment of degree-granting committees by the divisions, without departmental involvement in appointments. The lawyer, after close examination, reported back that there was no inhibition. The result was the proliferation of such novel dodges under the aegis of the social sciences and humanities divisions, where Hutchins' strength lay, and whose deans, Robert Redfield (and later Tyler) and Richard McKeon, were Hutchins supporters. Indeed, they enabled the conglomerator to appoint men who already were, or in time would be, eminent as non-Hutchins and anti-Hutchins men: men like Edward Shils, David Riesman, Rexford Tugwell, and Bruno Bettelheim (the first three rejected by the sociology department). By the time Tyler retired as dean of the social sciences there were eight such committees (the precise number of bypassed departments) in the division. Two of the committees—Human Development and Social Thought—achieved durable eminence. The latter, under the chairmanship of a close Hutchins associate, the economist John U. Nef, included one of the most distinguished anti-Hutchins crusaders, the laissez-faire economist Frank Knight, and ultimately provided a home for the young Deweyite turned novelist, Saul Bellow.

The committee stratagem, legitimate as it was, contributed considerably to the head of steam that was building in the faculty boiler. It was a trick. It was one way of Hutchins' getting what he wanted if he couldn't get it another, and his enemies were unmollified by the character of the appointments that indicated (or should have indicated) that what he wanted was fresh air in the institution. What vented some of the steam was the appointments themselves—but were they only window dressing, to be removed in due season?—and the fact that they were confined to the social sciences, the least respectable area of the university. The social science departments were outraged, of course, but nobody cared that much; and in addition to Ralph Tyler, Hutchins had some of the biggest guns of those departments more or less with him, including Robert Redfield in sociology and the frisky heavyweight Charles Merriam in political science. It went without saying that the trickster knew better than to try the independent committee in the natural sciences, where the real firepower was concentrated and where Hutchins was well advised (futilely, in the event) not to tread.

But there was one committee that was not in the social sciences but in the humanities—the locus of the philosophy department—a committee generically different from all the others except for the president's power of appointment to it. That one, the nonteaching, non-degree-granting Committee on the Liberal Arts, was a Hutchins baby staffed entirely with Hutchins babies and independently financed by Hutchins' friends. Its operation came close to blowing the lid off during the one year it functioned at the top of one of the twin towers of Harper Library. There, under those unvisited eaves, was where the conspiracy against the higher learning was hatching. Its personnel was unabashed evidence, even unto its staff director, the same dollar-a-year Arthur L. H. Rubin who shared his old friend Adler's duplex on the Gold Coast and had, wanted, and needed no academic credentials.

Hutchins told the story, in, as usual, capsule, to the Columbia Oral History Project thirty years afterward: "I thought that liberal education was in a fair state of collapse. . . . It happened that McKeon, Adler, Buchanan, and Barr were all interested in this question, and I thought it would be interesting to see what they could work out. This was regarded, of course, as a threat to the University faculty. I was bringing in these outsiders"—Adler was already there, but still an "outsider"—"who were in some way going to carry away the University, invade the prerogatives of the faculty. It caused a great deal of excitement, but as far as I know it did no harm." "Did they come up with any recommendations?" "They never had time, because the St. John's opportunity opened, and Barr and Buchanan went there. McKeon then became a regular member of the faculty. Adler was already a member of the faculty."[2]

Buchanan, writing in the *Amherst Graduate's Quarterly* only a year after the occasion, was a bit more vivid: "The University saw red, and they almost burned our books so that we couldn't read. Our presence made. . . [the] Dean of the Humanities a great deal of trouble. It was a great relief for everybody but the donors of the money for this project when St. John's College called the members of the Liberal Arts Committee to put its program into operation."[3] The year of the liberal arts committee—1936–37—was more furious than the Adler year had been, not only because the Adler business was more narrowly confined (and arose at the beginning of the Hutchins regime) but because it aroused otherwise apathetic elements in the faculty (*and* the board) who wanted nothing so much as a rest from perpetual revolution; they had approved the great *structural* reform of the four-year-college program and they did not see why they should be pushed in the direction of considering *content*.

And it was content, and, essentially, nothing but content, that interested Hutchins. Announcing the liberal arts committee's creation he had said: "In view of the state into which . . . [some] disciplines have fallen, the vocational attitudes of most students, and the . . . hostility of many professors, it is doubtful whether . . . [the liberal arts] can be adapted to contemporary conditions. The difficulties of framing a general education without some resort to them, however, justify the attempt." The agitation over the Committee on the Liberal Arts, financed outside the university's budget and engaging the efforts of men who were not widely thought to be otherwise useful, is marvelous to reflect on in these days of the multi-mega-university in which immense academic engines flourish undisturbed in the special interest of commercial and industrial enterprises and international warfare. Why *shouldn't* Chicago have housed as high-minded an undertaking as the liberal arts committee? The answer could only have been, and was, nothing but a nameless terror: What is he going to do to us next?

Overnight it blew over. St. John's College in Annapolis, one of the oldest institutions of higher education in America, was on the rocks. Admirers of Hutchins got it for coffee and buns and asked him to make it the college he wanted. He should have—perhaps. He would have been putting his life where his mouth was. But Chicago was a nonpareil pulpit and St. John's none at all. And Chicago was a great university, St. John's was a bankrupt college. And Chicago was a going institution, St. John's a hard try from scratch. And Chicago, where the president had no power, was a powerful place in which to be a powerless president; St. John's was the boondocks. It would have been a stupendous gesture—a Hutchins kind of gesture. But...but what? Buchanan (who could have persuaded him if anyone could) remembered his last-ditch try on a train to Annapolis to meet with the board: "Why not? We don't need much money, and we can do what we want to do." "A general has a row of medals across his chest, and the row of medals distinguishes him from being nothing. The University of Chicago is my row of medals. Without them I'm nothing." So he said no. He accepted the chairmanship of the St. John's board, and Barr and Buchanan tossed a coin to determine which of them would be president and which of them dean. (Barr lost and took the presidency.)

Thus Hutchins' college—or something like it; not quite—came into being, the only college in America with a completely fixed curriculum: four years of language, four years of mathematics, four years of science, and four years of great books. The whole faculty (with the modest title of tutor, the *teachers* being the great minds of the ages) would have to teach all four years of the "greats," from Homer and Aeschylus and Archimedes and Ptolemy to Jefferson and Marx and Freud and Russell.

St. John's made a modest splash, largely because of its association with Hutchins. Forty years later, with a second campus at Santa Fe, New Mexico, it continued to make a modest splash. It was still the only college of its kind in the world, still the kind of college Hutchins generally envisioned, where some six hundred students on the two campuses were getting a straight-out liberal education. Barr and Buchanan opened the school in the fall of 1937 with an overdue mortgage of $350,000 on the property. Walter Lippman paid it a state visit and ventured to predict that men would some day say that St. John's was the seedbed of the American Renaissance.

A modest splash in the educational world—and an immodest sigh of relief at Chicago. Hutchins had moved his circus and his clowns out of town and that would be that. There was no resentment over his role at Annapolis. He had his plaything now and could be expected to do his real job where his real job was and, like a busy man with a mistress, divert himself on an occasional evening off. There would be no American Renaissance outside the great universities—outside the greatest of them— and a jerk-water college would be the seedbed of another footnote in the history of the higher learning. The terror of the Committee on the Liberal Arts dissipated. In the spring of 1937 the Chicago board and faculty, each in its own way, each by its own measure, took stock of Robert Maynard Hutchins and found him (now that he'd got his shenanigans out of his system, or at least out of sight) pretty good. And, of course, in some non-academic respects, pretty great.

Part Four

THE NATURE OF THE BEAST

17   Like a President Should

The Chicago of the 1930s was something Hutchins had never known or imagined ever having to know. It was rough, with a rough, tough elite that managed men, not (as New York, Boston, Philadelphia did) money; a pig-and-pig-iron elite up from nowhere fast and a dozen First Families (i.e., second generation) of bankers and lawyers. The old, *old* families (i.e., third generation), the Palmers, Fields, Pullmans, Ogdens, Wentworths, had gone to New York or London. (All five of Julius Rosenwald's children left Chicago.) Chicago's was an operating, not an investing, aristocracy, "democratic" with the drawback of democracy: the highest denominator wasn't that much higher than the lowest, and the values, the tastes, and the manner were according. The Chicago rich were as hard-driven as the Chicago poor.

Even the University Club on Michigan Avenue—a considerable cut beneath the Chicago Club down the street—accepted some university men and not others. It went without saying that no Negro, let him have a string of degrees as long as your arm, would ever pass through its portals. And it went without saying—until Rabbi Emil G. Hirsch said it—that no Jew would. On the occasion of a civic committee luncheon Rabbi Hirsch was in the club's dining room, whose walls were hung with the shields of the country's universities. The luncheoners were looking at the shields, most of whose mottoes were in Latin but one of which was in a strange calligraphy. Somebody asked the learned rabbi if he knew what the language was, and he said it was Hebrew. "And what does it say?" said someone politely. "It says," said Rabbi Hirsch, "We don't take Jews."

It would be downright hyperbolic, but, still, suggestive, to say that there is an absolute correlation between a university's eminence and its ability to pay its faculty—but it would be as downright hyperbolic to say that there is a downright dichotomy. Chicago was a very expensive university. It was a very expensive university because it did proportionately more graduate work and more research than any other university in America. (Its astronomy department had as many professors as students.) Compared to the national average, Chicago's salaries were high and, if the faculty level was to be maintained, had to go higher.

A university president, then as now, was supposed to go downtown and get the money. (The money, in those days, was downtown, not in Washington.) Most of the money would build stadiums, administration buildings, dormitories, and laboratories, in that order (and, in those days, chapels). What was needed, of course, was general purpose funds to repair the heating plant, shovel the snow, provide more scholarships, and raise the starvation wages of junior faculty; but there is no immortality in such mortal odds and ends. (In the decade preceding Hutchins' appointment, less than one-sixth of what Chicago received in benefactions was unrestricted, and the percentage was falling steadily. Vice-president (and pal) Munnecke: "I've got to see you about the coal contract"—a $500,000 item. President Hutchins: "Don't bother me. I've got to convince an assistant professor that he doesn't want to be an associate professor."

He was not a jolly good fellow. He never slapped a back, or guffawed. He never played golf. He never told an off- or on-color story to break the ice. He could kill a cocktail conversation by entering the room or (having done his painful duty) by leaving it, or ignite a dinner table at forty feet—if he could be got to the dinner table. (On one of the few occasions when he was, shortly after he became president, he was introduced to the handsome wife of a colleague named Wright and said, "I would rather be Wright than president.") He could be got to the luncheon table at the Chicago Club downtown, and he was, almost every day for twenty years; but at 5:00 P.M. the door of his office shut behind him and at 5:05 the door of his house shut behind him and, unless he had an evening lecture, he did not emerge until six the next morning. His tall wife was seen walking her Great Dane—never her small daughters—in the daytime, but at night the only lights in the president's house were upstairs. He never spoke of his domestic difficulties, only raising an eyebrow when an intimate asked how things were at home—and thus it was known that the difficulties were chronic and acute. But he exploited them to decline social invitations or, at the last moment, break them without an explanation.

Though the Crash had so shattered the rich that they had lost their faith in the sales pitch and would not buy the hard sell or the soft sell, they fell so hard for the antisell that by the time the War Deal (not the New Deal) got the country "going" again, circa 1940, Hutchins had talked them out of more than fifty million dollars. Nobody who went by the book ever understood how he did it. He did it by being sassy.

It wasn't tempered to the time or the place; it was the quintessence of the man, wherever, whenever, however. In the washroom of the Chicago Faculty Club, a colleague at the next basin says to Professor of Philosophy Charles Hartshorn, "Are you still working on God?" and a voice from the gentleman's stalls is heard: "He ought to let God work on him."

The fractious donor of $25,000 who was told that "anybody who gives us less than $50,000 is not allowed to open his head," was, as Hutchins knew he'd be, tickled; he doubled his money (and still wasn't allowed to open his head). When a promotional brochure called "Great Men" went out, with studio photographs, on opposing pages, of the donor of each $250,000 chair and the incumbent of the chair, Hutchins got a note from a jocular prospect: "If I give you $250,000, will it make me Great?"—"Give us the $250,000 and it will make you feel Great." Old money, too, east of Chicago, needed different kinds of nursing. You could tell Ray Fosdick, the President of the Rockefeller Foundation, that the money he was sitting on was burning a hole in his soul, but you couldn't talk that way to John D., Jr., whose money it was.

There was a fine irony in Hutchins' grandee courtesy, the irony of the one-way window. Its object must not get the point; if he does he takes his money elsewhere. The trick is to offend without being offensive. The man would never know that he had been had on, any more than the questioner who, having asked an unintelligent question which was in fact an oration and not a question at all, would be asked if he would be so kind as to repeat the question. The self-compounding insult rebuffs its object for a fool and then rebuffs him properly for not knowing he's a fool. To be a fool is nothing much; to suspect, vaguely or sharply, that one is being made a fool of is something considerable.

Sometimes early in life, and oftentimes later, a man is simply too tired and testy to suffer fools at all, much less gladly; so tired that the artful shaft emerges artless. Fortunate the man who in such circumstances lets go at a friend. Having to perform at a testimonial dinner, and in pain, Hutchins winced to hear his friend Bill Benton, owner of the Encyclopaedia Britannica, say, "Bob Hutchins has been a lucky man—the luckiest man in the world." Pulling himself painfully to his feet, the chairman of Britannica's editorial board said, "I am the second luckiest man in the world. The first is the previous speaker—he has never had to work for Bill Benton."

Somewhere down the line he had acquired the perfectly preposterous aplomb that can get away with it at home or abroad.

He was meeting Harvey Wheeler at the Waldorf Men's Bar—there were men's bars then, in the 1950s. Robert M. Hutchins was accustomed to being patient with the rich; that was what he had always been paid for. But the staff at the Waldorf were not the rich, and Hutchins was impatient. He kept beckoning to the waiters as they went hurrying past his table, but none of them stopped. Then he turned his chair around and beckoned to the waiters' captain. The captain didn't, or wouldn't, meet his eye. He turned his chair back to the table and picked up the silver with both hands and threw it over his shoulder. The captain and all the lower ranks came running to the table, and he placidly placed his order. "It never fails," he said to Wheeler.

Abroad he was required to preside over a banquet in London celebrating the bicentennial of Encyclopaedia Britannica. There were too many speeches and they were all too long. It got to be past his bedtime and he was very tired, but the prime minister and the lord mayor were there, and there was nothing to do about it; nothing, that is, that anyone but Hutchins could think of. When he could bear it no longer and concluded that the other guests shouldn't bear it any longer, whether or not they could, he rose and lifted his glass and said, "The Queen." The ritual toast always ended the evening in England, but it had never before, in such company, and so prematurely, been called for by an American.

Precisely what it is—the art of getting away with it—is hard to say, and how it is come by harder still. It goes by a variety of names—"presence," say. It has nothing to do with popularity. It neither seeks nor finds a following. It is not an entertainer's, a politician's, or an athlete's projection of himself. Its authority doesn't soar and plummet with its office or its victories or defeats; it is immanent and independent of the circumstances. "I think," said Archibald MacLeish, and he said it thoughtfully, "that I never knew another man like him." It began (but only began) with the towering figure, the figure that in any room, at any table, was the cynosure.

He had to be conscious of always being watched. A hard thing to carry, and probably unbearable without an immense substructure of vanity. What I could see was the man who led a small group of friends into the Biltmore dining room, found the table reserved too close to other tables for his liking, said to the maître d', "We'll take that one," indicating a corner table reserved for another party, and led his party to it and seated them. What I could see was the man who walked into a florist's on his wedding anniversary, selected a plant, rejected the clerk's offer to wrap it, and picked it up and walked out with it. (Clerk to manager: "That man just walked out with that plant." Manager: "That's all right. That's Dr. Hutchins.")

Arch. And what is the way to be arch? He and I hove into Palm Springs one evening to attend a rich woman's soiree. The purpose of the soiree was to enable him to make a genteel pitch for money for the Great Books Foundation. The big money. He thought it would be nice if I went along. The rich woman's place was California Trianon, and the rich woman's friends were all there to meet the great man. A maid opened the door, with the hostess behind her. "Ah, Reverend Hutchings"—so help me—"how nice of you to come." "I want you," said the Reverend Hutchings, "to meet my friend, Rabbi Meyers." The hostess would never know; only the Reverend Hutchings and Rabbi Meyers would know. That is the way to be arch.

For all his having been brought up to be polite, the patrician made could not quite repress the unconscious insolence of the (amused and, to his aficionados, amusing) monosyllabic answer to the foolish question in the question period after a lecture, the abrupt departure from the platform when he had had enough of it, the interjected "I'm sorry, but it's past my bedtime" at a dinner party. The hauteur was drawn from a world that revolved around him everywhere: a peremptory manner with servants, speaking in front of them as if they weren't there, as if they would never repeat what they'd overheard (or as if it wouldn't matter if they did). But subalterns—secretaries, assistants, and always students—were charmed.

The non-hail-fellow met at the subtle distance that kept you from taking more time than you needed. The distance still conveyed itself when people who were prepared to be awed were put at their ease by a pleasantry and still remained uneasy. It was all very engaging; it wasn't all to the good. Distance breeds distance, and deference deprives the deferred-to. The distance was not engendered by any indication to his associates that he was above them. It was engendered by their taking themselves to be beneath him. He didn't fend off argument, rebuke, or admonition; he just didn't get it, and he didn't get it when he needed it. The little placard he pulled out of his desk drawer, only in the presence of friends—Don't Tell the President Things He Already Knows—would have done him some good if it had read: What Is It That Keeps You from Telling the President the Things He Ought to Know? Engaging, when an appointee went sour and he said, "And I appointed him, I appointed them all"; less engaging, but more useful if, before the appointment, he had found a way to be told the things he needed to know.

Somebody might have told him that the reason the Socratic dialogue at the center in Santa Barbara wasn't Socratic (or even dialogic) was that, unlike the gadfly of Athens, he simply sat there at the head of the table and let his associates ride their hobby-horses, and never gadflew at anybody.

He was beset by age and illness and responsibilities, yes. He was tired. And he was Bob; and Bob, even when he asked to be told, didn't know how to ask. So nobody ever told him. And if anyone had? Then he'd have pulled out the placard: Don't Tell the President Things He Already Knows, and everybody would have had a good laugh. When Hutchins was seventy-five, one of the rising stars in the academic firmament joined the group at the center in Santa Barbara. Asked how his conversations with Hutchins went, the rising star said, "Every time I say something, I have the feeling he already knows it." "How can that be? You've got an original mind." "He knows all the original stuff, too."

In the whole course of his speaking and writing career he appears to have relied on specialist friends for substantial specialized help in only two or three instances. His Aquinas Lecture at Marquette University in 1949, "St. Thomas and the World State," though the style of the paper was unmistakably Hutchins', must have been as much Adler's work as his own; it was a philosophically radical statement that had to undergo the close (and in some cases hostile) scrutiny of Catholic scholars, and Hutchins certainly hadn't the ready command of the whole of the Aquinas corpus necessary to the presentation.

In an *Atlantic Monthly* article in 1936 he interrupted his controversy with John Dewey to take philosophical issue with Alfred North Whitehead.[1] Hutchins drafted his article and sent it on to Richard McKeon to make sure "that I have been fair to Whitehead." McKeon suggested several serious emendations, and Hutchins, having adopted them, acknowledged his indebtedness in his monkeyshine manner: "Your article has gone to the *Atlantic*. It is a much better article than the one I sent you. It is so much better that I am afraid my friends, to say nothing of my enemies, will recognize that it is ghost-written. There are a couple of pages of frank plagiarism; the rest is plagiarized, but not so frankly. I have striven to protect myself by omitting your brightest remarks. This leads to a certain incoherence and lack of continuity which will remind my readers of my original works."[2]

He knew his philosophical limitations, and he knew that he would never have the opportunity to overcome them. He understood Whitehead. He understood Aquinas. But he could not be sure that his understanding of them was foolproof against their professional interpreters and commentators. He had to seem to know more than he possibly could have known. He did what generalists commonly do, in and out of scholarship: he asked collegial specialists to advise him and check his work, leaving him open to attack only by rabid partisans.

The only Hutchins offspring of obviously illegitimate paternity was legitimated by respectable practice. In his lectures after Hiroshima he invariably advanced the thesis that science is international; nearly all of the men who made the bomb in America were eminent before they came to America; scientific secrecy is a myth; the USSR and other countries will have the bomb within a few years.[3] He supported his thesis with a detailed delineation of the scientific considerations bearing on foreign policy, and offered a recital that simply could not have been prepared by a busy layman: "The hypothesis of a violent splitting of the uranium nucleus, based on the work of Hahn and Strassman in Germany, was independently proposed and verified at the same time by Frisch in Copenhagen and Joliot in Paris. The suggestion that plutonium would be a suitable explosive for an atomic bomb was made independently at the same time by Turner in America, Cockcroft in England, and von Halban in France."[4]

He did not have an original mind. His originality lay in the kind of mind he had: deft, epitomic, telegraphic. He was born able to do what he said a general education (which he hadn't got) should enable a man to do: operate in any field. How well such a man is able to operate is something else again. He is skating on thin ice, and the thinner the ice the faster he has to skate. The lesson Hutchins learned teaching evidence at Yale—that everything is related to everything else—determined his intellectual attitude for the rest of his life.

"Bob's singular gift," said Richard McKeon, "is what the Greeks—in Greek, of course—called wit. It hasn't anything to do with being witty in our sense. It means what we call 'getting the idea.'" Again and again, in his writings, in his speeches, and in conference, he would ask, "What are we trying to do?" His instinct for the important cut through the incidental and the conditional, through the immediate and the immaterial, to the heart of the matter. "In apprehension," said a Shakespearean of him, "how like an X ray." He was first and last an apprehender.

Lucidity is the mark of the best of lawyers. But it is not the lawyer's lucidity that asserts that "modern medicine has done almost as much to lengthen life as modern physics has done to shorten it." Mere lucidity isn't the mark of a lawyer eulogizing another lawyer by saying, "Laird Bell said that he always agreed with the last man he talked to. This was not true, as I often found out when I was the last man."

We all write, and some of us write well, but there are individuals whose voices are inimitably their own. They alone are writers. Hutchins was a writer. His writing was undeviating and undeviable. His ideal was Aristotle's definition of art as that from which nothing can be taken and to which nothing can be added. But lucid writing does not have to be wooden: "When we remember that only a little more than 1500 years ago the ancestors of most of us, many of them painted blue, were roaming the trackless forests of Transalpine Gaul, despised by the civilized citizens of Rome and Antioch, interested, in the intervals of rapine, only in deep drinking and high gaming, savage, barbarous, cruel, and illiterate, we may reflect with awe and expectation on the potentialities of our race."[5]

It is hard to be terse and charming. It is not impossible:

"Dear Central Administration: By God I am. Sincerely yours."

"Dear Pomp: I'll be sure to do it. Ever yours."

"Dear Willie: No, if you will spell accommodations with two m's. Sincerely yours."

"Dear Reuben: l. No. Ever yours."

"Dear Flash: I do. Sincerely yours."[6]

Once in a while he lost his hold on concision and waxed garrulous: To Felix Frankfurter (in 1933): "I understand that you are to be Attorney General. I hope that this is not the case. You are the person who tells Attorneys General what to do; why should you bother to do it yourself? You are my candidate for any vacancy that may occur in the Holy Trinity; if none occurs, you should stay in legal scholarship." To Chairman William O. Douglas of the Securities and Exchange Commission, who wanted to know what he should talk about at the University of Chicago: "How about, 'My Ten Years at Yale with Robert Maynard Hutchins'?" To Adlai Stevenson, who had heard that Hutchins was going to take the presidency of Harvard: "All reports that I am going to be president of another university originate in this one." To Dean Edward H. Levi of the University of Chicago Law School: "This fellow D—— is a dope. I suppose he represents the vanguard of our profession." And to publisher Henry R. Luce of *Time*, who wrote him that "my paper did not convey seriously enough my admiration for you": "I shall pass your letter on to my heirs so that they can see you for my obituary."[7]

To Milton Mayer: "Dear (in the sense of expensive) Mr. M. Will you take less? How much less?" "It's o.k. Your every word is a pearl." "Come along. There is a cross for everyone, and you are the cross for me."

He seemed never to have understood how the simple declarative sentence—his great gift to educational discourse—could be misunderstood. And it wasn't. It was mis-taken. His lucidity was refreshing in the peculiarly obscurantist world of the higher learning. No one else had it. It read beautifully; it never palled. But it cut—"cut" is the word—two ways. He knew he was riling up the animals by calling them rational and insisting that "the purpose of education is to make rational animals more perfectly rational"; driven to irrationality, they took him to be saying that the adjective, instead of modifying the noun, defined it and excluded the emotions. (He called them by their outmoded name from antiquity, "the passions.") He riled the animals up by his employment of archaic terms like "the virtues" and his hope that "the University of Chicago can make a civilization in the Twentieth Century as the University of Paris molded the civilization of the Middle Age"—as if the medieval (i.e., Catholic) university could be a model for anything but prescientific authoritarianism, as if diversity, and not unity, were not the glory of the modern university, as if there were such a thing as metaphysics. He riled them up by saying that "every great change in American education has been secured over the dead bodies of countless professors," by saying that "the function of the American college is adolescent-sitting," by saying that "American education is anti-intellectual."

He didn't have to say these things or to say them the way he said them. But he plainly calculated that the animals could not be brought out of their year-round hibernation with anything less than a little riling. His rhetoric was inflammatory, and outrageous. It was not designed to make friends, but to influence people. The enemies it made would, most of them, have been enemies whatever the rhetoric. He was attacking American education, which needed to be attacked precisely on the grounds he attacked it. The end of the 1960s confirmed all of his direct jeremiads and produced the frantic discovery, in the mid 1970s, that there simply had to be a restoration of the general education—the "basic studies"—for which he had fought for fifty years.

His prose owed almost nothing to the time and place he lived in. (When his opponents in education called him a nineteenth-century man, he defended himself by saying, "I am an eighteenth-century man.") Though he was all too well acquainted with the jargons of the social sciences, he never used them except in mockery. (Arguing with a friendly dean about a sociologist he wanted to get rid of: "One more peep out of you and I'll extrapolate you out the window.")

He rarely employed the contemporary idiom, never the contemporary vernacular or the perennial cliché. (He could no more say than be "visibly shaken.") As the culture degenerated, and the mother tongue with it, the country was swept by suddenly epidemic expressions, banal or pretentious (or both), like "have a nice day" or "at this point in time." Among friends he was given to saying "ain't," "don't" (as in "he don't"), "got" (for "have"), and "he writes pretty good"—affectations of the literate. But in writing and in formal discussion he never used an expression with a limited life expectancy.

He may or may not have written for the ages, but he wrote in them, shunning every first and last linguistic atrocity that popped up in the popular -eses—sociologese, psychologese, technologese, legalese, bureau-cratese, and Pentagonese—meant to mark the user as a specialist and to give him authority. From his hand, or (as far as anyone recalls) his lips, Hutchins never let escape words or phrases like *interface, finalize*, or *input*; never *-wise* as a suffix, except in "likewise" and "otherwise"; never *behavior modification, conflict resolution*, or any other such.

We all have to fool around to divert ourselves. He did it deriding the rhetorical fatuities of others. It would have been cruel if the others had been unlettered, making unlettered mistakes, but he picked on boys his own size who, though they certainly resented the punishment, could hardly cry foul. They, too, were men of words, none of them wordier than President Nicholas Murray Butler of Columbia, the great platitudinist of stand-pat Republicanism. The polite way for one university president to call another foolish is to rib him in passing: "The identification of freedom with lack of discipline is, in the somewhat lurid language of Mr. Butler of Columbia, the 'rabbit theory' of education, according to which, he says, 'any infant is encouraged to roam about an enclosed field, nibbling here and there at whatever root or flower or weed may, for the moment, attract his attention or tempt his appetite.' Mr. Butler adds, varying the figure slightly, 'Those who call this type of schoolwork progressive reveal themselves as afloat on a sea of inexperience without chart or compass or even rudder.' Obviously we should not look to rudderless rabbits to lead us through the mazes of the modern world."[8]

And his victims were almost invariably highly placed persons who could properly be held accountable for their absurdities. A professor at Yale was given anonymous credit for "the chiropractic approach to litera-ture" when he told his students that a work of art could be measured by the thrill it sent down your spine. The president of the United States was invariably cited as the source of the most excessive imaginable enthusiasm: "I am for it one thousand percent, as Mr. Roosevelt would say."

When at a press conference President Kennedy was asked whether in his crusade against racial discrimination he was going to attack state laws prohibiting racial intermarriage, he answered: "Well, I, the law would, if there was a marriage of the kind you described, I would assume that, and if any legal action was taken against the party then I, they would have a relief, it would seem to me, in the courts, and it would be carried, I pre-sume, to the higher courts depending on the judgment, so that the laws themselves would be affected by the ultimate decision of the Supreme Court. So that I think that there are legal remedies for any abuses in this field now available." Careful reading convinced Hutchins that "what he meant was, 'I don't have to attack the laws against miscegenation, because the courts will hold them unconstitutional.' At least I think that's what he meant. And I hope his prophecy comes true."9

The man who calls general attention to the bumbles of others has to be bumble-proof himself. Once—and it need only be once—he lays himself open to the same sort of genteel savaging, his game is up. As an intellectual addressing himself to intellectual issues before an audience which acknowledged intellectuality alone, Hutchins was foreclosed the possibility of overt preaching. But he had sprung from a line of preachers. The faculty of the University of Chicago was not in the least surprised when he told them that "we are called to a moral, spiritual, and intellectual revolution." They detected the Calvinist man in this juvenile patriarch. They had the secular distaste for the summons to salvation, and the scientific resistance to being hurried into anything. His aphoristic moralizing, cloaked in cool litany, was the ultimate condescension. There was no mistaking that black-and-white approach, and no bearing it by men whose own calling was peculiarly committed to seeing shades of gray. There was no mistaking the over-simplification of matters whose complexities had consumed generations and ages of research. There was the moralist for you, flaunting the selected superficialities that a man might get away with in the pulpit on a Sunday morning—but not in a university weekdays. The most offensive thing about the superficialities—in or out of the pulpit—was their employment as the answers to the most fundamental of questions. The weekday moralist would not, of course, address his congregation as "my children"—but he would think of them as children, and recalcitrant children at that.

He wouldn't have had to sit at *their* feet and drink in *their* wisdom. It would have been enough if he had associated with them or found a way to indicate that he only wished he were able to keep their company. But he didn't. He seemed to hold himself aloof and his colleagues at a distance. He hid himself assiduously and disclosed himself warily.

"People say," said Archibald MacLeish, "that Bob never had an intimate friend, that he was too formal—too bashful, at bottom—for intimacy. There was a time when I'd have said it myself and, you know, I never really knew him well. But I'd see him after a long separation and he'd suddenly recall something I'd said in passing a year or two earlier, and I'd realize that we really were intimate in the sense of a meaningful relationship."

It would seem that meaningful relationships between persons whose business is words would involve a great many words. Not so. The intimacy of meaningfulness does not depend very much on either separation or contact. There was a middle period of a few years, after he left Chicago westbound to the Ford Foundation in 1950, when I didn't see him for six months at a time. An occasional one-liner, dictated: "Mr. M: I am a great admirer of your work. Are you doing any? Sincerely yours, Mr. H." (Underneath the handwritten "Mr. H," "Robert Maynard Hutchins" is typed, and the "Maynard" is crossed out by hand and replaced by "Mayer.") And when he left the Ford Foundation in 1952 and took over the Fund for the Republic to fight McCarthyism I don't suppose I saw him ten times in five years. I was working long stretches in central Europe. "Mr. H: Why don't you come to the Alps?—Mr. M." "Mr. M: The mountain comes to Mohammed.—Mr. H." However brisk or infrequent your exchanges with him, they picked up where they had left off as if the interval between them had been an hour or a day instead of a year or a decade.

Stripped of all decor, of all salutations and complimentary closes, of all circumbendibus ambiguous efflorescence and—in a word—of necessity to *sound out* the other man, communication can be close to instantaneous. You pass in the hall and one of you says, "Is Jones any good?" and the other says, "No." Or, "Can you talk to the freshmen Wednesday at ten o'clock?" and the other says, "Yes, for ten minutes." Or, "Do you know anything about Augustine's brother?" and the other says, "I'll let you know tomorrow." Or (head in his door): "There were these two Irishmen . . ." (and head out—a half-minute by the clock). On the way home from his office (*his* head in the door): "Wanna walk?"—three minutes by the clock, and no standing around outside his house where a faculty member will buttonhole him. At five of twelve: "Wanna ride downtown?"—twenty minutes by the clock, eighteen to read something he'd hand you, and two to speak your piece about it. Conversations were all snatches that never began or ended, only resumed. All possible assumptions mutually assumed, a relationship maintained by intermittent rapid fire.

Most of his academic colleagues were easygoing men who liked to sit around and talk. They were not characteristically glib. His dry playfulness did not really amuse them; it had what could be taken for a touch of amiable contempt. Of course he wasn't disagreeable, but of course he wasn't agreeable. When he lectured the medical men on Galen—whom they hadn't read and didn't need to read—and told them "where Galen does not agree with me, I shall suppress the fact, in the hope that you will not be aware of it,"[10] they knew he was having them on. They resented his know-it-all the more because they recognized that he really knew some of it.

"The facts," in his rhetoric, was code for what most of his colleagues were concerned with most of the time. He was telling them that their learning and their teaching were devoted to triviality, except in so far as they illuminated theories which themselves did not arise from fact-gathering.

"Vatt," said the great physiologist Anton Carlson, who wasn't above exaggerating his Swedish accent, "iss de effidence?"

His trouble—that is, the trouble he got into—arose from his intuitive grasp. He didn't need the fact. He would seize one from out of the welter of the world and cite it as sufficient support for the principle he was arguing. The fact is that the casually introduced fact was not intended to support the principle, but simply to illustrate it. All the worse. His airiness was an assault on the very idea of scholarship; he was arguing (if it could be said to be arguing) from the indemonstrables that nobody knew and the undemonstrated that nobody had proved. He was arguing from "common sense" and "common knowledge," which it was scholarship's business to explode as common error. When he said, "The experience of the race indicates. . . ." or, "As every fairly mature infant knows. . ." he was deprecating the only principle that scientific investigation maintained, the principle that the experience of the race and the knowledge that every fairly mature infant drew from it were, unless they were documented, so much folk-myth.

A little generosity, a little more interrogative and little less declarative—a little give and a little take, a little you-know-and-I-know à la FDR, a quip instead of a dig, and—who knows where a man might not go (or have gone)? And be what when he got there? And have been what when he started?

18   The Bad Man Trick

I suppose it is possible, however unlikely, for a man who insists that he's bad to be as bad as he insists he is. Hutchins hyperbolized his badness—but he didn't invent it. He was a bad man by the token that all men are bad, but more to the point is his lifelong pursuit of a calling that required and rewarded bad things, day in and day out, that good might come of it.

So it was the job, not the man, that was wicked, and the wickedness of the man was nothing worse than vanity. Not so; it was the man, and vanity was the least of his vices. "A university president should spend his time on education and scholarship. Actually he spends his time like other business executives and is judged like them by his balance sheet and his public relations." "He has to try to find people who are better than he is and get the credit for what they do. . . . So act—the neo-Kantian Categorical Imperative which guided my life—to gain the maximum of credit with a minimum of work."[1] "All college presidents are liars. If they weren't they couldn't be college presidents. They lie because their lives must in the nature of things be a series of compromises." "A lifetime"—he was characterizing his own—"devoted to money-raising." "Everyone should take a look at the way I behaved, and do the opposite."[2] "I have a bad character and therefore a good reputation." "If I am so great as you say, why haven't I been able to stop smoking?"[3]

"Without listing the full panoply of my vices, I may refer to the one most pertinent here, which was vanity."[4] On many another occasion he proclaimed himself variously a model of indolence, disorganization, negligence, impatience, stubbornness, and impetuosity.

"Do you have any redeeming features?" "I refer you to Shakespeare: 'What a man hath his tailor made him.'"[5] "Bill Benton knew you longer and better than anyone but Thornton Wilder, and he once said, 'Bob's difficulty is that he's so enormously critical of himself and not critical enough of others, so he's overly generous with his friends and associates and puts all the blame on himself if anything goes wrong.'" "Bill is an overly generous man."

Hutchins did not enjoy being somebody else's scapegoat. What he enjoyed was being his own. Having the trick down pat meant not merely claiming to be a bad man but being able to prove it. Whoever agreed with him that he was a bad man—I never knew anyone who did—was finessed as he recited the litany of his selective sins. Whoever disagreed with him smiled. Whoever disagreed with him and watched him in action smiled and admired. The Bad Man Trick is a good trick. And there is nobody to the trick better born than a resurfaced Presbyterian.

And the reforms he undertook at Chicago? "We didn't know enough to know that you weren't supposed to do those things."[6] Forty years later his competence as president of the Center for Democratic Institutions was just as deplorable: "I have to learn more than anybody else around here because my associates have spent their lives in the intensive study of basic disciplines. One characteristic of a lifetime of administration is that you become excessively superficial. You have to make a lot of decisions very rapidly on the basis of totally inadequate knowledge; I made most of my decisions at the University of Chicago on the basis of snap impressions. How could I deal intelligently with a professor of archaeology, or of astronomy, or of anthropology—subjects I'd never studied? I had to do it on the basis of my judgment of the man not on my knowledge of the discipline. The notion that a university president is in some way a learned man is absurd. You may—I say 'may'—become an experienced man in judging men. But you never learn anything."[7]

There is nothing harder on the character than fifty years or so of continuous wear and tear. The frustration and the fury never flared and never diminished. It was steady, it was persistent, it was cumulative. Its genesis was not the blockheadedness of the professors, which he ridiculed in public. It was not his domestic misery which, without confessing it, he let be known to an ever widening circle of whisperers. Its genesis was his calling itself. He was an educator, but education was not his calling. He was an administrator, but administration was not his calling. His calling was mendicancy.

His calling compelled him to caginess in his every relationship. He had to be armed with the secret lowdown on everyone with whom he had to do (or had to want to do) business. His files were crammed with dossiers, and his head with gossip that was more revealing than the dossiers. He had to know just how much this man had to give (no matter what the man himself said) and how he gave it and why he gave it and how he was most effectively approached; what his (and his wife's) fancies and phobias were, what was to be spoken of and what not. He had to know—he knew that Epstein, Eckstein, Smith, Jones, and Robinson were rich—that whoever called Epstein Epstein (rather than Epsteen) would never get another appointment with Epstein; that Eckstein hit the ceiling if anybody called him Ecksteen; that Smith did not like Jews (no matter how they pronounced their names); that Jones knew, from personal experience, that Negroes were ineducable; and that Mrs. Robinson on one martini would address Hutchins' friend Cardinal Mundelein as the Whore of Babylon.

This was what money-raising meant. And what being the chief executive of a great corporation meant wasn't all that different. With few exceptions the faculty members needed more money, or thought they needed more money, or thought they deserved more money—in a word, wanted more money. Was it or wasn't it true that Professor A had inherited money, or that Professor B's wife had money, or that Professor C had made a killing in real estate? Was Professor E worth the money he was getting now, and was it worth more to keep him? Was Professor F's recommendation from his department head based on their being bridge partners, or on Professor F's appreciation of the head's own research, or on the head's spite against Professor G (who along with Professor F was a candidate for the available wage raise)?

How could all this day-in-and-night-out finagling, dissembling, and lying—"All college presidents are liars"—be other than morally debilitating, the more so since all of it was both honorable and honored? It was the expected and respectable essence of his calling.

His lot was the dreary lot of the used car lot, except that he could not even deliver the junker. He could not promise that the product would ever be produced. He was a salesman of the farthest vistas, and in order to sell them he had to oversell them. Money, and money alone, was Hutchins' nexus with nearly all of the people with whom he spent nearly all of his time outside his office (and most of the time within it). He called them his friends, dedicated his books to them, delivered funeral orations over them, and, always polite, perhaps because they might cough up still more, perhaps because he had come to be comfortable with them, he continued his vapid association with them even after he had got their money.

The walking consequence of such a career, pursued from the occupational cradle to the grave, was, besides a frustrated and furious man, a great compromiser who made uncompromising noises of a crafted character; an immensely secretive man who, speaking openly, sharply, and memorably of trade secrets in general, was careful to tell no tales out of school or in it; a narrator of his own corruption (and that delightfully narrated) with never a clue to the identity of his corruptors or his reasons for abiding the process; a querulous establishmentarian, true, in the pinches, to the canons of the establishment he served as gadfly.

He could not have been a trial lawyer; manners, and not just morals, were involved, and his manners were inadequate to the pretense (and pretensions) of the courtroom. Temperamentally impelled to controversy and its provocation, he was temperamentally repelled by ad hominem conflict. His was the most civil of façades. His disputatious posture simply crumbled in the face of acrimony. For almost twenty years he was engaged in torrid debate with the notably irascible John Dewey—on paper; he persistently rejected his friends' suggestion that he challenge his adversary to a face to face exchange. He would not, if he could help it, have it out with a peer across the desk, and I never knew him to reprimand a subordinate. There were people in the direct line of his administrative duty who needed to be admonished, dressed down, or, in extremis, fired; he would dodge the first two treatments—"It doesn't do any good"—and almost invariably find a way to administer the third in writing. (Or dodge *it*, too. He once hired a needy fellow on my recommendation, one of what he called my cripples. When he informed me, a few weeks later, that the fellow was no good, I suggested that he give him a second telephone, a second secretary, and a bigger desk. He did as I suggested, and a few weeks later informed me that the fellow was still no good. But the fellow stayed on, and, unless he became a university president, I suppose he's still there. True, true—academe is, or then and there was, a little like that anyway.)

In his manipulation of the rich, his antiemotionalism served him similarly as a salubrious check on his impulse to honest indignation. Men who had money believed in the things he didn't believe in and disbelieved in. Once in a while the tension was too much for him and he let go with the passion of Oberlin. Attacking materialism as the ruin of education—this in a 1941 lecture—he plunged into an Oberlinesque polemic on the institution of property itself: "Since the earth was given to man and not to individual men, since man is a social animal with social responsibilities, one who acquires property beyond the needs of himself and his family must dedicate it to social purposes."[8] The lecture was delivered at Louisiana State University—well out of earshot of LaSalle Street. But it was subsequently published and duly distributed in book form to the University of Chicago's trustees. One of them, the financier Frank McNair, chairman of the finance committee, read the remark and said, meaning "president" when he said "university": "If that is the kind of university we have, I don't want to be connected with it."

So Hutchins wasn't as bad as he said he was. In his time and (more particularly) place, he was peerless. No university president and no college president ever put his job in jeopardy as sharply and persistently as he did on issues that do not force themselves on a professional educator.

None ever spoke the way the thirty-three-year-old president of the University of Chicago spoke to the Young Democratic Clubs on June 27, 1932, a few days before the Democratic Convention in Chicago. His address opened with what may mildly be called a two-fisted denunciation of the Republican administration's "history of inaction, bias, and misrepresentation of the last four years." Its fiscal policy was simple: "Soak the poor." And now, in the depths of the depression, while workingmen and their families starved, it lay "recumbent on a featherbed of pious hopes," preaching "salvation by incantation." But was the Democratic Party, the traditional party of the people, any better? "The Democratic effort has been to convince erstwhile contributors to Republican campaign funds that the Democrats are just as safe as the Republicans, and perhaps a little safer. 'You need not worry,' Democratic leaders seem to have said. 'We have no ideas. We have no plans that will disturb you. We are just as conservative as the Republicans. In fact we aim to be indistinguishable from them.'" What was wanted was a "truly democratic program stated in unmistakable terms," a program that would call for tariff reduction, government regulation ("if necessary, government ownership") of monopolies natural and unnatural, immensely increased inheritance and income taxes (corporate and personal), government reform of banking ("if necessary elimination of private profit from banking"), farm allotments, unemployment and old age insurance, and a program of public works.[9] His denunciation of Hooverism was so passionate and his proposals for a Democratic program so rabid—remember, this was 1932—that they were front-page news the country over. Nor did he ever temper any of them afterward.

So, too, in terms of war and peace, in terms of racial and religious restrictions on economic and social opportunity, in terms of civil liberties, civil rights, and intellectual and artistic freedom, no eminent figure of his time and place had a batting average to compare with his. For all his highwire caginess in the timing and wording of most of his public statements, he left no one in doubt of his position on the sovereign issues of the day.

True, the higher learning was an easy league to look good in and even be good in. Had he quit the academic grove for the bare-knuckle business of politics—had he become the chief administrative officer of the United States, as it once appeared that he would—his principle of subordination might have compelled him to choose between resignation and, say, the deportation of fellow Americans into concentration camps because of their "Japanese blood," or the atom bombing of an undefended city, or the attempt to assassinate a foreign head of state. Under those unhappy circumstances the principle might have been put to harder test, and courage have come costlier.

Bedeviled with so many urgent and monotonous demands on his everyday, he always had the excuse that he had no time to think. Back along about, oh, 1948, I sauntered into the president's office on a flimsy pretext and, having got the pretext out of the way, I said, "You know what you ought to do? You ought to take a year off." "And do what? Solve my personal problems?" He always referred to his domestic problems as his personal problems. "No," I said, "you should take a year off to sit and think. Aren't you in favor of thinking?" "I am in favor of thinking, but I never do it. If I accepted your advice I might find myself thinking about why I'm not a socialist, a pacifist, and a Christian. And that's what I don't want to do most." "You are," I said, "a man who never wearies of saying that 'nothing less than a moral, intellectual, and spiritual revolution can save mankind.'" "I am weary of saying it," he said, "but I admit I say it. I am too busy to do it." A quarter-century afterward I sauntered into his office in Santa Barbara, and reminded him what he'd said a quarter century before. "I was too busy then," he said, "and now I'm too busy and too old."[10]

Beneath the humility he enjoyed professing was the arrogance of the Michelangelo who says, "I'm just a dauber." But beneath the arrogance in this case was an oppressive sense of his unworthiness. Accepted by everyone else, he could not accept himself. Contemptuous of others' high evaluation of him, he could not but have a contemptuous opinion of their capacity to evaluate. Ashamed of his contemptuousness, he spent his life listening politely, with fixed attention, to their inferior evaluations and their inferior insights and their inferior alibis. It takes a Calvinist to be despicable, but any fool of an atheist can be unworthy.

What Hutchins knew, he didn't know by virtue of intelligence. He was a lover not of wisdom, but of goodness; and not a possessor of it (any more than the philosopher is a possessor of wisdom, but only a lover of it). But the love of the good is itself a good, and the possessor of that love is to that extent a good man. The Bad Man Trick was a matter of manners, the Bad Man a man of morals.

He could always have quit doing what he was doing and do something else that was (or might be) less demoralizing. At Chicago the trustees understood that his resignation was on the table on more than one occasion, but on the table it remained for twenty-one years; the trustees who knew him best calculated, rightly, that it was a bargaining chip he was likelier to display than to play. There were a dozen occasions when he might have resigned on principle, having failed to get his way. There was one occasion when he offered to—of that later—and another when he actually did (from, of all places, the board of the New York Stock Exchange).

In 1938 the president of the New York Stock Exchange, by name Richard Whitney, was sent to prison, and the exchange went through the motions of reform. Public hostility drove it to a demonstration of public fervor and it elected three public trustees, one of them President Hutchins of the University of Chicago. But it was common knowledge on the Street that Whitney had been an errand boy for J.P. Morgan and Company. "The Morgan interests," Harold Ickes wrote in his diary, "kept him there"—at the exchange—"apparently as long as he could serve them. Meanwhile, taking advantage of the depression, the Morgan people have extended their financial domination. Ordered to put a stop to the underwriting business of their bank, they have organized a separate company which is doing even more business than was done by the bank itself along this line. They control a number of banks in addition to their own as well as insurance companies and manufacturing concerns." Cyrus Eaton of Cleveland, the financial titan who supported Franklin Roosevelt, told Ickes that the appointment of Hutchins to the board of the exchange was "a good time to put the house of Morgan where it belongs, using the Richard Whitney incident as a lever."[11]

Eaton was a trustee of the University of Chicago and, like Ickes, a friend of Hutchins. The next time Hutchins saw Roosevelt, who was trying to persuade him to take the chairmanship of the Securities and Exchange Commission, he said to the president, "Why don't you go after J.P. Morgan and Company?" (The president "turned green," Hutchins recalled afterward.) "The undisputed testimony," Hutchins told Roosevelt, "shows that there were two members of the [Morgan] firm who knew all about [Whitney's depredations]. . . . I don't want to prejudge the case, but I think that the connection ought to be investigated in view of the fact that you're stamping all over these minor crooks who have turned up."[12] Roosevelt didn't act, and Hutchins brought the issue to a meeting of the board of the exchange. The vote to investigate Morgan was defeated thirty-five to one, and the dissenting public member resigned on principle—with no loss of job or salary, and a great afflatus of reputation as a man of shining integrity. Roosevelt summoned him to Warm Springs and offered him the SEC again, and, when Hutchins turned it down again, the president said, "It would have been a wonderful joke on the New York Stock Exchange."[13]

(On October 10, 1975—thirty-seven years later—the *New York Times* said, "Some of Wall Street's leading forces have started accepting the inevitability of reform [of the exchange]." But "the by-play over reform proposals has the earmarks of a diversionary or delaying maneuver.")

"Noble moments come and go," said Professor Carl Hermann of Marburg University after the Second World War. "It was a noble moment when I said I would not take the oath of loyalty to Hitler, but after thinking what it would mean to my political effectiveness if I stayed where I was, and, of course, to my family and my work, I went back the next day and took the oath. It was one of my ordinary days, as the day before had not been."

It may have been a noble moment when Hutchins offered to quit on principle and nobody picked up the offer. It was one of those fine fall evenings in Chicago, the wind cutting right through the bone, and we were standing on North Michigan Avenue, Hutchins, my wife, and I, outside one of his clubs, where he had taken us to dinner. We were preparing to go our separate ways, we to the South Side, he to the downtown hotel where he was hiding. He was hiding because he had recently walked out of the President's House and did not want to talk to his wife or to reporters about his wife (then or ever thereafter).

He had just completed a year's leave of absence from his job—a leave taken with the intention or, rather, illusion, of figuring out what to do about his domestic life. He had not figured it out, and he should not have been surprised that he hadn't. His Presbyterian objection to his situation at home was not, of course, that he had suffered—only that it had kept him from doing his work. (Though he told a friend, long afterward, "I worked in order to keep my mind off my domestic problems, so I ought to have been thankful—or ought I?") During his year's leave he had let his pal Bill Benton, publisher of the Chicago-based Encylopaedia Britannica, pay him twenty-five thousand dollars as chairman of its board of editors. Now he was back in the President's Office—and out of the President's House.

It was 1948, a fine fall evening.

The boss had got me an assistant professorship two or three years before, and while he was on leave I was due to come up for tenure. His vice-regents sent one of their factotums to see me first before he came back on the job. It was strongly suggested to me that I shift myself to something called the Great Books Foundation, a nationwide program of adult education that had grown up out of the Hutchins-Adler great books project at the university. The suggestion was almost plausible. I had been connected with the program both locally and nationally. The program needed me. The job had a title and a substantial wage raise. That I would be losing the prospect of tenure at the university wasn't mentioned. Only passing reference was made to the fact that my not having a college degree would not be an obstacle in the new situation. I wasn't too proud to fight; I was just too tired. And so the president's Hired Hand was euchred out of the university.

The wind had been howling up North Michigan Avenue. Now it was shrieking. Time to buck it and go. "By the way," said the homeless president, "about the job business. You know who's been after you on the board, and you know that my associates were simply hatchet men. Not that *they* like you. Say the word, and I'll put my resignation on the table."

And he would have. He would do whatever he had to do.

A magnificent offer.

"Don't be crazy," I said.

It wasn't a magnificent offer at all. He knew that I would say, "Don't be crazy."

The Bad Man.

19   Something for Poor Bob

When people worried about the selection of a thirty-year-old for the presidency of a university (of *that* university), Professor Gordon Jennings Laing said, "Don't worry—he'll age ten years in his first six months in office." He was, at thirty, mind you, a case of that tedium vitae for which the Stoics prescribed suicide.

If the weariness was real, the reality had simply caught up with the protective pretense. At thirty he displayed the ennui that a Yale man in those days learned to display at twenty. (But at sixty he seemed to be not a bit less tired of it all, and at seventy and seventy-five not a bit more.) He seemed to be as tired as a man could be, and he seemed to be that way all the time. Once when I was bedded down in the university clinic he came to see me, electrifying the staff which, prior to his visit, had left me to die, and asked me what I pretended to be suffering from. I said lassitude, and he said, "I've suffered from lassitude all my life. My mother's first words the first time she saw me were, 'My, what a lassitudinous baby.'"

When he said, looking back on his life, that his treatment of his family and his friends had been utter and unforgivable neglect, his only excuse was that he had never had time to think about anything except what he had to do in the next half-hour: "I have never been less than three months behind in my work in my life."[1] He neglected his family and his friends, and he neglected to let a shining hour pass unexploited, to fritter away a sunset or an evening, to chew the undirected fat, to goof off. He did not dislike children—those rational animals *in posse* (and sometimes *in actu*); he simply didn't *like* them. When I asked him about the uproarious young of the 1960s, some of whose antics, and all of whose rights, he defended on every public occasion, he said, "They bore me." His family's care, like his job's, was his duty—perhaps the more painful of the two. But a lover of pain would choose the more painful course. The trouble with the more painful course was that it would have meant taking time off to do what he had to do with all his time on—deal with people, and with even more difficult people than his job entailed.

Those were primitive times, when a campus could be traversed on foot in a quarter of an hour, and there were no college (much less high school) parking lots. There was no such thing in a university as an administration with a hierarchy of divisions and subdivisions. There was only the office of the president, with a couple of vice-presidents who were not vice-presidents *for* anything. There was no department of public relations but, across the hall from the president's office, a two-room suite with Bill Morgenstern, the man who always wrote the handouts, at a desk, and two or three miscellaneous persons at other desks. There was one letterhead for everybody in administration, right down to the bottom of the totem pole: Office of the President.

So insatiable for punishment was this president of this university, that he saw everybody who wanted to see him. (That's how he first saw me.) He saw them all. It wasn't necessary to listen to them, nor, indeed, possible to say anything to them, but it was necessary to reckon with forty minutes apiece from the time they came in and began talking until, still talking, they had been got out with an assist at the elbow.

Poor Bob.

What I could do, not for him, but for my forty-five dollars a week, was to see the Cranks who came to see him and would not stop coming. The Cranks were a separate category from the cranks. The latter were the professors who had a right to see him and who had to be seen again and yet again. They were cranky and inconsolably so, painful and debilitating to see; but they could not be fobbed off. The Cranks, on the other hand, though they were persistent, asserted no right, only a persistent longing. They were not painful or debilitating, merely time-consuming. They were never cranky.

They were Medical Cranks, Dietary Cranks, Exercise Cranks, and Deep-Breathing Cranks; Jesus Cranks, Anti-Jesus Cranks, Psychic and Physic Cranks, Engineering and Automotive Cranks, and Astronomical, Astrological, and Gastronomical Cranks; Educational and Antieducational Cranks, Government (but usually Antigovernment) Cranks, and Anticommunist (but more likely Communist) Cranks; and a great swarm of unclassifiables Hutchins brought down on himself by proclaiming metaphysics the highest science. Since nobody knew then, or knows now, what metaphysics is or does or where to get it or put it, the Cranks who could not otherwise classify themselves did so as Metaphysicians. (In time, just off the campus, there was a sign in a first-floor apartment window giving the name of the Crank and under the name: Licensed Metaphysician.) But the most plexiform, plethoric, proliferate, and pluvial of them all, exceeding all the rest in combination, were the Money Cranks.

They had all of them a total of seven characteristics in common. (1) They had each of them discovered the Way—like the young of a couple of generations later who told each other, "This is It, man." (2) Nobody else had discovered it. (3) They were indefatigable. (4) They had nothing else to do but disseminate the good news. (5) They carried the good news in bulging, bottomless briefcases of dessicate imitation leather. (6) Their only hope—and at once their highest—was to see somebody in the only institution on earth committed to the open-minded search for truth. This somebody was, of course, a professor, it mattered not of what, or the president. (7) As they were being got out, they all variably promised to return the next day with further proof (never argument or evidence, always proof) and they invariably kept their promise. In one historic case the president said, "Keep him away from me or you're fired." I said, "How do I do it?" "Hand him over to Robinson, you sap." Robinson was the faculty member who most often insisted on his right to see the president and saw him the longest each time he exercised his right.

The worst of it was that every fiftieth (or hundredth) Crank made some sense—I *thought*—but there was nobody in the place or in the world with both the competence to know it and the time to spend. One old gentleman had long white hair and a long white mustache and an immense chart that—already talking—he thumbtacked to your wall. As long as it was on the wall he would go on talking; the only way you could end the interview was to take it down yourself. It was a money chart. He was a Money Crank. He was irrepressible, inveterate, and, of course, unintelligible. I told him, grasping him by the elbow, that time was running out on the money question and there was not a moment more to waste on a man like me, who, for all my honors, was a mere disciple of Professor Robinson. "I've already seen him," said the Money Crank, "and he sent me to President Hutchins."

On any one day ten to twenty of his colleagues wanted to see him urgently for five minutes (which always turned out to be twenty or forty). All of them highly trained and perennially practiced in the trade of inexhaustible loquacity. If he didn't see them all, they would be offended each and separately, and each and separately broadcast the offense. But instead of staying away offended they would demand to see him the next day.

For twenty years—twenty-one—he attempted to do something about a university, and, more, about universities. (And for fifty years, embracing those twenty-one, he attempted to promote the general welfare of his country.) A university is by definition (a definition he tried and failed to obliterate) a participatory anarchy composed, again by definition, of people whose pleasure it is, and who (instead of sticking to their business) make it their business to talk all the time, and who cannot understand one another because they all speak mutually unintelligible languages. Hutchins' determination to convert the anarchy into a responsible republic was enough to unstring him, and it did.

What little he did get done—he was supposed to be revolutionizing the higher learning—he did not get done right, because there was no time to do it right. And if there had been, he wouldn't have got it done because he was trying to get everything else in the world done at the same time.

Here, then, was one of those perceptive compulsives who all his life had to try to be administrator, agitator, presider, jurist, politician, businessman, financier, finagler, teacher, learner, philosopher, political scientist, preacher, reader, writer, editor, speaker, lecturer (some thirteen hundred formal engagements), peacemonger, warmonger, humanist, humanitarian, civil libertarian, civil rightsist, and receiver of an unabating cascade of visiting policemen, FBI men, visiting CIA men, pitchmen, con men, rich men (and many more visiting poor men), schoolmen, statesmen, holy men, and visiting Englishmen—many of whom would drown in their sorrows or take their money, their children, or their scholarship somewhere else, or denounce him to the rest of their kind if he did not give them those five— that is, forty—minutes of attentive concern.

All his life all these things at the same time; but as Moran said to Mack, when Mack said that the doctor told him to take one pill three times a day, you can't do that. Perceptive—but not that perceptive—and compulsive, he tried.

If a capitalist is what Jacques Maritain said he is: a man who has no time, this was capitalism's finest flower. Occasionally he drooped out loud at the end of the day's multifarious occupations: "I am so busy being sorry for myself that I haven't any time to be sorry for anybody else." A lie; he was, in addition to his other compulsive careers, a steady sympathizer. But his usual entendre was triple; he bespoke one's sympathy without ever speaking, with an appeal that was slyly mute, mutely transmitting the cry for help that never crosses a great man's lips. All his associates knew that his foreign and domestic concerns were more than a man could be imagined bearing, and his closest associates knew that his most intimate domestic concerns were alone enough to do a man down.

His airiness conveyed his exhaustion of spirit ever so effectively, as if to say, "See how manfully I go on performing when I wish I could drop," and the effect on his friends was uniform: "Poor Bob."

Say that it was at least partly part of the act; but the act, too, is the man. It was the real Hutchins who stood up—and stood up under it all. Such men are unusual, even exceptional, but they are not rare; not in the twentieth century. They are energetic men of enormous aptitude, natural opportunists (in a nonpejorative sense of the term). Such a man is not tragic and may, indeed, be comic; the whirling dervish is good for a smile. Hutchins, if he had a kick coming at the end of the multifarious day's work, had no one to kick but himself.

But such a man, in his perennial condition and situation, has a singular advantage over other men bent their life long over their lifetime job. Such a man's friends all want to do things for him. But what could they do?

He had friends who could give him ideas and friends who could give him money, but the only thing I could have given him was time. By staying out of trouble—trouble into which his office would draw him—I could have saved him one (or a hundred) of those half-hours he needed. I didn't. I gave him trouble, and by sitting still he encouraged me to give him more trouble, and I never failed him. If I'd only sated his appetite for trouble without devouring his time I'd have done him no harm. But the trouble I gave him took time disproportionate to the satisfaction he got from the trouble. Town and gown knew me for bad news. Mortimer Adler was a heavier cross than I for Poor Bob to tote through the academic jungle; but there was no denying his usefulness in Poor Bob's misguided terms. There was denying mine.

Adler offended only professors, and the public did not mind seeing professors offended. I offended the public. I was bad publicity. My magazine pieces were all controversial, and they were not confined to controverting remote desperadoes in Moscow, Berlin, or Washington; my specialty was right there at home, in Chicago, where the University of Chicago had to live or die. I threw rocks at the people who could wound or kill it, at City Hall and LaSalle Street and the wondrous ways of the North Shore rich with the property tax, the zoning laws, and the safety and sanitary regulations in the factories and slums they owned (and the restrictive covenants that held the Blacks at bay).

On one such controversial occasion Hutchins had a suggestion. Innocent of the fact that my older brother had just got a publicity contract to promote the City of Chicago, I had concurrently published an article in *Harper's* entitled "Chicago—Time for Another Fire."[2] (U. OF C. ASSISTANT DENOUNCES CHICAGO—WANTS IT BURNED DOWN.) *Commerce*, put out by the Chicago Association of Commerce, ran an editorial lament which I sent in for Hutchins to see. Under the heading, "Two Brothers," the editor mused on the marvel that these two scions of a fine Chicago family could be so radically and, in the case of the younger scion, deplorably different. "The younger," said the editor, "does his best to tear down everything that the older builds up." I got the editorial back with a comment: "Mr. M: You two boys ought to go into business as Mayer & Mayer, Builders and Wreckers. Mr. H." The only Controversial Man who would have a Controversial Hired Hand was one who believed in controversy.

Down the years with the controversial hired hand, Hutchins, wherever he was and whatever he was doing, was set upon by letters and by callers (singly and in delegation and deputation), by alumni, and by faculty, all of them irate, plus donors and trustees, all of them regretful, all of them demanding (never asking) to know just what Mayer did around the place. The Hutchins archives (I got to see them years later) include a great stack of letters all of which read more or less like one of them dealing with a controversial attack I had made on the "adjusting" Jew:[3] "Dear Fred,"— Fred being a donor of a $250,000 distinguished-service professorship—"I did not read Milton Mayer's article before it was published, but if I had I would have approved it. Ever yours, Bob." Ever whose Bob?

I knew that his incoming mail under ordinary circumstances had to be carried in a box car. I knew that he wrote his own answers to everything but form letters. I knew that he would rather fight, preferably on every front at once, than eat. But never a word of adjuration, or abjuration. He never asked me to answer an irate letter or receive an irate caller. Poor Bob, always poorer in the rich man's poverty of time.

What could I do for Bob?

One day he phoned and asked me if I could spare a few minutes of *my* time to talk to him. Streak across the hall and in the door. "Sit down." "*Sit down?*" "Sit down. Sit down while I tell you that my wife admires your wife, specifically your wife's head."

"How nice for them both."

"Sit down and don't interrupt me. My wife is a sculptor, or, as you would probably say, sculptress. A very good sculptor. She would like to do your wife's head in bronze. If your wife is agreeable, it would take a dozen sittings. If you are agreeable, it would cost you seven hundred fifty dollars—my wife is a very good sculptor—and you would get to keep the head, both the original and the representation."

It was a good thing I was sitting down, or I'd have fallen down. I was trying to support my wife and baby on forty-five dollars a week. I said, "OK," in a faraway tone. "That's peachy," he said. "Now get out of here, and thank you *very* much." I must have felt my way along the corridor office to the chair in front of my desk. I must have sat in the chair in front of my desk saying either "*Seven hundred and fifty* dollars" or "Seven hundred and fifty *dollars.*" I must have said to him subsequently that I wondered if I could pay ten dollars a week, and he must have said, "That will be peachy."

I'd done something for Bob. He must have felt bad, shilling for his talented wife's talented hobby; and I appreciated his exposing his ridiculous situation to me. But *seven hundred and fifty dollars.* Hadn't I done something for Bob, though.

I hadn't.

The head was done and delivered, and it is in the family still. Hutchins said never a word more about it—ever. But a couple of months later he phoned again to bespeak a few minutes of my time and handed me a sheaf of his speeches on education. "*The Saturday Evening Post,*" he said, "wants to cut and paste this stuff together for a series of articles on American education. I said I had a good man to do the job at forty-five dollars a week and they said fine. Do you want to do it?" I said I did, and I did it. It was a breeze; his writing came apart in smooth, sharp, cohesive segments. A couple of months later I got his personal check for $1,250 with a note: "Mr. M: I got $2,500 from the *Post.* Since you did all the work, you get half the proceeds. Stop bothering me. Mr. H." Net profit on one bronze head (with gold patina): $500.

On Pearl Harbor Day his quixotic friend Luce of Time, Inc., called him in Chicago to ask how much he thought I would have to be paid to hop it to Washington and do a piece for *Life* on the capital city in shock. Hutchins said, knowing that I would push a peanut east of Suez for fifteen hundred dollars, "It is my impression that Mr. Mayer does not go east of Gary for less than fifteen hundred dollars." Thus he stole for me more than once, and more than twice, but never from any institution in which he held a fiduciary position. One day at the University of Chicago I went in to his office to tell him that I had an offer from another university. He said, "Why are you telling me this?" "In order," I said, "to use it as a lever on you to get a raise." "You will be hoist," he said, "with your own lever. You are getting more gold now than a good man can bear and carry. Don't you want to be a good man?"

The years passed, and then the decades, and I stood on a platform in St. Louis, Missouri, having delivered myself of a Milton Maynard Hutchins lecture, and the usual handshakers came to the front to shake the hand of the lecturer (who had to get down on his knees to reach them). They melted away until, hanging back, there was only an old couple who came haltingly forward. "Mr. Mayer," said the old man, "you don't know us, but we know you. We are William and Anna Hutchins. We wanted to thank you for everything you have done for Bob."

All the doing that had been done he had done for me. I promised myself—and him—when I said yes to that forty-five dollars a week that I would stick with him until death did us part or his money ran out, whichever should occur first. And I kept my promise.

Part Five

ONWARD AS TO WAR

20 Onward As to War

With something approaching acclaim, President Franklin D. Roosevelt was nominated for a third term by the Democratic convention in Chicago the night of July 17, 1940. There remained only his decision as to his running mate. That same morning Robert Maynard Hutchins phoned his friend Harold Ickes—in town for the convention—and asked to see him. "To my surprise," the secretary of the interior wrote in his diary that night, "he suggested that either he or I ought to be nominated for Vice-President. He had come from the Chicago Club where he had been talking the matter over with a group of friends and apparently something in the way of a boom had been started for him. I laughingly told him that Jane"—Mrs. Ickes—"was managing my own campaign for Vice-President and I agreed with him that either one of us would make the kind of candidate the situation required. I had not thought of Hutchins in connection with the Vice-Presidency and I did not think that at any stage he was available because he had no record in public life, and the booms of others, who had a considerable following in the Democratic party, had gone too far. However, I was bound to say to Jane, and to admit to myself, that Hutchins makes an ideal candidate. He is highly intelligent, speaks well, is young and highly personable. I could think of nothing better than having Hutchins trail Willkie"—the Republican presidential nominee—"around the country. . . .

"What Hutchins really had come to see me about was to enlist my support for his own candidacy. When he discovered what had been running in our minds, he offered to do anything he could in my support. I told him that I would be perfectly satisfied if he were nominated and, in the end, we agreed to team up. He volunteered to have some of his friends send telegrams to the President in my behalf and, personally, he sent one to [presidential intimate] Tom Corcoran, although that could not do any possible good. He volunteered once or twice to telegraph directly to the President, but I asked him not to do that. It was on this same day that I sent the following telegram to the President:

Chicago, July 18, 1940

PERSONAL
STRAIGHT MESSAGE
The President
The White House
Washington, D.C.

I doubt whether anyone is happier over the action of the convention last night than I and my warmest regards and congratulations go to you. I do not know whether you have considered the advisability of selecting as Vice-Presidential candidate a man like Robert M. Hutchins. He is well located geographically, is a liberal and one of the most facile and forceful speakers in the country. It might appeal to the imagination of the people to give them a new and attractive person like Hutchins and I know of no one better able to take care of himself in a free-for-all fight with Willkie. I am inclined to think that he would be the strongest man we could name. May I say also that if Hutchins does not appeal to you, I would feel honored to be considered as your running mate. . . . However, you know better than I whether I am available and I need not tell you that, whatever your decision may be, the fact that you are the head of the ticket is all that is necessary to assure it of my loyal support.

Harold I. Ickes

"I sincerely believed what I said in this telegram about Hutchins. I also believed that I had some availability." The next morning—the day of the vice-presidential nomination—Ickes had several visitors, among them Hutchins, who "again offered to telegraph the President. I said that it was too late and I showed him a copy of the telegram that I had sent the afternoon before." Just then a call came through to Ickes from "Pa" Watson, the president's secretary in Washington. Watson said that "considering the farm vote, the labor vote, and the foreign situation, the President thought Henry Wallace would make the strongest candidate." "Obviously, this was the President's indirect reply to my telegram of the afternoon before in which I had suggested either Hutchins or myself for the Vice-Presidency. He didn't like to turn me down himself, but something had to be said to me. This was the only communication, direct or indirect, that I had from the White House during my days in Chicago."[1]

So much for Hutchins' haughty I-am-not-interested-in-public-life. He wasn't interested in public life—except at the top. Often elected and never a candidate, this once he abandoned his above-it-all posture and made a lunge at the brass ring in clumsy competition with the seasoned lungers of American party politics. His one-day campaign was not generally known—none of the "group of friends" at the Chicago Club ever spoke up—until the Ickes diaries were published in 1954.

What was known, of course, was that admirers of his had here and there been touting him for the presidency since 1936 (when columnist Dorothy Thompson proposed him against Landon *and* Roosevelt).[2] Yale men William Benton and Thornton Wilder were confident that he would one day occupy the White House to the greater glory of Yale.[3] Harvard man Walter Lippmann (to whom Hutchins offered a professorship) admired him ever more fervently. *New Yorker* critic Alexander Woollcott, taking a long, easy look in the Roosevelt spring of 1940, publicly "nominated" him for president in 1944.[4] (FDR was a third-term shoo-in, and it was unthinkable that he would run a fourth time.)

The Hutchins boosters in 1940 included two very different men of very different tastes, backgrounds, and interests, with this much in common: social worker Harry Hopkins (Roosevelt's secretary of commerce, confidant and agent) and Nobel Prize–winning novelist Sinclair Lewis (the one-time husband of booster Dorothy Thompson) were both of them political outsiders, long, lean, sardonic men whose irrepressibly independent views of men and affairs made both of them a great gallery of friends and enemies. Neither of them had the savvy of a political pro, and Lewis had none of the external restraints that Hopkins had in Washington. In the early spring of 1940 the wild and wooly novelist visited Chicago and after two or three agreeable meetings with Hutchins informed his Chicago acquaintances that he was going to go to Washington and push his new friend for the vice-presidency. Bill Benton, who also envisioned Hutchins as FDR's successor, heard of Lewis's scheme and reacted prophylactically. Knowing Washington, Benton knew that Lewis would do more harm than good "wandering around town on any such mission." He asked Lewis to let him go along, and Lewis agreed. "We talked to many of the leading intellectuals in Washington," Benton recalled later. "I suppose most of them were too incredulous to let us know how incredulous they were. The conversation I most vividly remember was the one with Supreme Court Justice William O. Douglas. He said to me flatly, 'Your friend Hutchins could have had the vice-presidential nomination of the Democratic party for the asking, if he had accepted the chairmanship of the Securities and Exchange Commission when Roosevelt offered it to him at the time I resigned the chairmanship to go onto the Supreme Court. But by turning it down, he forfeited his chance.'

"There may have been a great deal to this," Benton went on, "but that was not the end of the matter. Later, while the 1940 Democratic Convention was getting under way at Chicago, Harry Hopkins called on Hutchins at his home on the University of Chicago campus. The oldest Hutchins child, Franja, was then about fifteen. She opened the door of her home, peered up, saw Hopkins standing there and said to him: 'Who are you and what do you want?' Hopkins replied: 'I am Harry Hopkins and I have come to offer your father the vice-presidential nomination of the Democratic party.' Hopkins and Hutchins were on the telephone that night with Roosevelt. What was said? I don't know. But there must have been something in the wind concerning the vice-presidency, since important elements at the 1940 Democratic Convention were uneasy and resentful about the nomination going to Henry Wallace."⁵

Hopkins, like Ickes, was a radical reformer. Neither man (nor, for that matter, Henry A. Wallace) would have been likely to be in any president's cabinet except Franklin Roosevelt's. They came to dislike each other intensely early in the New Deal days, since they found themselves treading on one another's territorial toes, Ickes as head of the Public Works Administration, Hopkins as head of the Works Progress Administration. But they both saw in Hutchins a kindred outsider spirit who had the makings (as neither of them had) of a spectacular figure on the national scene. Each was moved by a passionate desire to see the New Deal perpetuated after Roosevelt's time; each saw in the younger Hutchins the promise for the future.

Like the "group of friends at the Chicago Club" the morning Hutchins called on Ickes, none of the three participants in the telephone conversation between Hutchins' house and the White House ever spoke publicly about it—except that one of them must have told Benton that it took place. One thing that neither Hopkins nor Roosevelt—nor Ickes—seems to have known was that Hutchins wouldn't have done at all. Not at all. Not in July of 1940.

By July of 1940, the real war had begun; the Germans invaded Norway and Denmark on April 9, France and the Low Countries a month later; the British were driven from Dunkirk in early June; Italy attacked a collapsing France (and inspired Roosevelt's "stab in the back" speech) on June 10, and Paris fell on June 12. Taking office as prime minister the day the Blitzkrieg struck at France, Winston Churchill promised his countrymen "blood, toil, tears, and sweat," but the day Great Britain's 335,000-man expeditionary force evacuated Dunkirk he promised them something more, something that was widely overlooked in his great "we shall fight on the beaches" oration: "And even if, which I do not for a moment believe, this Island or a large part of it were subjugated and starving, then our Empire beyond the seas, armed and guarded by the British Fleet, would carry on the struggle until, in God's good time, the New World, with all its power and might, steps forth to the rescue and liberation of the old."

Without congressional sanction Roosevelt at once replied, in a public address, that "in our American unity . . . we will extend to the opponents of force the material resources of this nation." As it was Churchill's first direct appeal for American aid, so it was Roosevelt's first formal offer of it.

Ickes and Hopkins in Washington were over their ears in the national and international crises of the day. Boosting Hutchins for the vice-presidential nomination, they were both of them guilty (or, more precisely, innocent) of having paid no attention to his recent antics out there in the Chicago wilderness. Had they done so, or taken the time to talk to him, they would have discovered why he wouldn't have done at all. For Hutchins opposed American intervention in the war in Europe and had made his opposition known publicly as early as June of 1940—a month before the Democratic convention. In a commencement address, under the title, "What Shall We Defend?" he amplified the view he had been expressing informally, that the outcome of the war, whoever won, would be a disaster for democracy.[6] The address made modest national headlines, though it could not, obviously, have come to the attention of Ickes or Hopkins. They both supported the president's pro-allied program to the hilt, and they both knew him well enough to know that he would have no truck with anyone who opposed it. In the succeeding months Franklin Roosevelt would push ever more stridently for "all measures short of war," and Robert Hutchins would pull ever more strenuously in the other direction. "Dear Bob" and "Dear Mr. President" would never again, after the 1940 convention, see each other or communicate directly or indirectly.

On September 7, 1939, six days after the German invasion of Poland, Hutchins wrote his friend John U. Nef, the Chicago economist, "The war has got me down. I wish I could think either that it would be short or that we could stay out of it. I think it will be long, and that though we could stay out of it, we are not likely to. I remember 1914 with horror and 1917 with something worse. I don't see that after the war is over, though Hitler will be gone, the actions of the French and English governments will be any more enlightened than they were after the last war." Two years later, in one of his antiwar speeches: "Before 1917 the country had serious problems. The war settled none of them and produced some new ones we had never dreamed of. From 1919 to 1929 we paid no attention to these problems, or anything else, except the price of stocks. From 1929 to 1939 we thought of nothing but these problems. We applied a whole pharmacopaeia of desperate remedies. . . . But there was little fundamental improvement. . . . This, then, is the spectacle of a country with appalling problems, many of them resulting from the last war, about to plunge into another in the hope of ending its troubles that way. In the life of individuals this method of solving problems is known as suicide."[7]

In 1937 President Roosevelt's "quarantine the aggressors" speech—directed against the Japanese attack on China—aroused no great interest in the country. The rise of Nazism and its successive atrocities, including its 1938 annexation of Austria and occupation of the Czech Sudetenland, likewise left Americans unmoved; even after the beginning of the war in Europe a mere 8.9 percent were willing to supply England, France, and Poland while refusing matériel to Germany. (37.5 percent were willing to sell matériel of all sorts to all comers, 30 percent wanted nothing whatever to do with any warring country, and only 14.7 percent were willing to go to war if the allies should be losing.)

Many of the country's most influential Jews, proud of being assimilated to the secular American life, were shy of supporting their coreligionists in Germany, fearful of intensifying anti-Semitism by being politically conspicuous and supporting unpopular, or even merely controversial, causes. In 1939 a Jewish donor asked Hutchins to try to persuade Felix Frankfurter not to accept Roosevelt's appointment of him to the Supreme Court. Hutchins demurred, saying that such intercession would be improper and, besides, Professor Frankfurter would be a great justice. "I know this," said the donor, "but every time a Jew is appointed to a high post it feeds the fires of anti-Semitism."

There were Jews of that sort before Hitler, one of them one of the wealthiest men in America. "Let me," said Hutchins ten or twenty years after the event, "tell you about him so that you will understand how I became anti-Semitic. I was already anti-Gentile, but I didn't know I was anti-Semitic until the evening of December 31, 1932, at a New Year's Eve party I had to attend because it was given by a man who was reported, erroneously, to have some money left, and the University of Chicago needed money. In order to stay awake past my bedtime, I engaged one of our trustees in a conversation. *He* had money left, he was generous, and, what was more to the point, he was a leader of the Jewish community—a pushover for purposes of the conversation. I told him that for $250,000 I could make the University of Chicago the greatest university in history in ninety days. He said he thought that the money could be found—I always liked that 'found'—but how did I propose to bring the miracle to pass? I told him that I was a great student of modern European history and that President von Hindenburg could not avoid appointing Hitler chancellor of

Germany for more than another sixty days. (I turned out to be optimistic by thirty.) All I would need, if I could get started right away, would be another thirty days after that to hire every Jewish scholar in Germany— and get them for coffee and buns. The leader of the Jewish community said, 'Oh,' and then he said, 'Bob, there is a lot of anti-Semitism in this country, and it's growing. The trouble is that there are too many Jews here now.' In the succeeding years before the war the University had to go into the open market and share the emigrés with the other leading institutions around the world."

A few weeks after the invasion of Poland in 1939 Harry Hopkins wrote his brother, "I believe that we can really keep out of it. Fortunately there is no great sentiment in this country for getting into it, although I think almost everyone wants to see England and France win."[8]

But the beginnings of the bitter division of the country between "isolation" and "intervention" were already detectable. Chester Bowles in New York, although he repudiated the idea of American isolation from the world, was among those who were already doing what they could to dampen the incipient war fever. On June 25, two weeks after the fall of France, his one-time advertising partner Benton wrote Hutchins from New York: "Chet Bowles is so steamed up over this problem of aid to the Allies that he'd like to see you take to the radio this week, go on record, address a speech either to the world . . . or to Winston Churchill announcing that millions of Americans are against any form of intervention whatsoever. . . . Chet and I privately agree that if England can and does hold out for one year, the U.S. will drift into this war. There isn't any leadership on the horizon to keep us out of it. Are we reflecting the hysteria to which we are exposed here in the East?"

But what about the "group of friends" assembled in his behalf at the Chicago Club the morning of the vice-presidential nomination? Surely they knew where Roosevelt stood and, after the 1940 commencement address (and just as surely some of them before it), where Hutchins stood. He may have appeared, at first blush, to have been only incidentally interested in the cosmic calamity of Europe. But there was no mistaking his attitude toward his country's involvement. "What Shall We Defend?" Democracy, said Roosevelt. Hardly, said Hutchins; reciting the painful injustices of American society, he argued that we were not prepared to defend democracy: "Precisely here lies our unpreparedness against the only enemy we may have to face. Such principles as we have are not different enough from Hitler's to make us very rugged in defending ours in preference to his. Moreover, we are not united and clear about such principles as we have. We are losing our moral principles. But the vestiges of them remain to bother us and to interfere with a thoroughgoing commitment to immoral principles. Hence we are like confused, divided, ineffective Hitlers. In a contest between Hitler and people who are wondering why they shouldn't be Hitlers the finished product is bound to win."9 (Stylish prose, that; and, perhaps, a little slick.)

In November of 1940 Mr. Roosevelt was reelected by another colossal landslide, which he took to be something between an acceptance and an endorsement of his pro-allied position. By 1941 the country was sharply divided between the miscalled interventionists and the similarly miscalled isolationists. Each of the two camps was in fact a mélange of divided camps.

The interventionists, so called, included not only the Anglophilic socialites and intellectuals of the east coast (and elsewhere) but the admirers everywhere of the political, cultural, and economic institutions of England; east (and later west) coast residents farsightedly fearful of a victorious Axis attack on the western hemisphere; nearly all the country's Jews and their sympathizers; saber-rattling militarists; international financiers and industrialists with British ties; certainly tens of millions of disinterested freedom lovers and enemies of tyranny who believed that all "measures," "steps," and "aid short of war" to the democratic countries was a realistic program and not a catchphrase or a morally dubious scheme to help the victim up to (and only up to) the point where the helper might get hurt.

The "isolationists" were an even more heterogeneous crew, consisting of the country's few (but disproportionately noisy) Communists prior to Hitler's attack on the Soviet Union; the few (but likewise disproportionately noisy) doctrinaire pacifists both secular and religious; a considerable and influential number of Anglophobic enemies of empire and imperialism in the best American spirit; a tremendously influential assortment of across-the-board xenophobics like William Randolph Hearst; a considerable (but, under the circumstances, decreasingly influential) body of conservative, but anti-Nazi, admirers of Germany; some anti-British Irish; a handful (only a handful this time around) of descendants of German and Italian immigrants, actual immigration having come to a substantial halt in the early 1920s; a few secret Nazi agents; a more than embarrassing motley of "native-American" fascist, racist, and anti-Semitic elements overtly or covertly enthusiastic about Nazism; and tens of millions of genuinely neutralist Americans of purest patriotism who wanted no part of what Jefferson called "the broils of Europe," together with many liberal internationalists like Hutchins who all too clearly recalled the failure of the First World War to make the world safe for democracy and saw war, not Germany or Nazism but war itself, as the scourge of liberty.

If "isolation" meant simply staying out of war, and no more than that, there was no doubt that most of the "interventionists" were, logically or illogically, isolationists right up to Pearl Harbor. And if "intervention" meant nothing more bellicose than material aid to the Allies there was no doubt that most of the "isolationists" were interventionists. But the opposition of the American people to actual military involvement, more than 85 percent at the beginning of the war, never fell below 70 percent prior to Pearl Harbor, right through the Roosevelt success in obtaining from Congress piecemeal repeal of the U.S. Neutrality Act and its arms embargo provisions, the leasing of overage destroyers to Britain, the arming of U.S. merchant ships, the adoption of peacetime conscription, and the decisive passage of Lend-Lease in March of 1941. (Even congressional resistance to the president was stiffening before Pearl Harbor. In August the House passed the draft-extension bill by a single vote, and in November more congressmen voted against neutrality revision than had voted against Lend-Lease in March.)

Thus the isolationist amalgam, though it contained more disparate, and even malodorous, elements than the interventionist, was much more representative of the country. Its spearhead organization was the America First Committee, which was never able to rid itself of its "pro-Nazi" tailcoaters and its reactionary image, though its membership included many distinguished libertarians such as Oswald Garrison Villard of *The Nation*, Amos Pinchot of Pennsylvania, the economist John T. Flynn, and Vice-president William Benton of the University of Chicago, Hutchins' Yale classmate and friend. (Benton's formidable schoolmarm mother, who had homesteaded in the northwest, roundly disapproved of her son's isolationism and told him so: "There is nothing creditable in failing to give the last full measure of devotion to your country when her life is at stake. . . . You have put yourself in a very ugly position because of the America First connection. . . . I fear it is a case of Old Dog Tray getting into bad company. I shall always consider Robert Hutchins responsible for that.")[10]

So it went, as the frenzy mounted and the lines were more sharply drawn with each day's dire reports from across the sea. In his diary entry of April 12, 1941, Interior Secretary Ickes wrote of a visit from his and Hutchins' old friend Charles E. Merriam. (A prominent Roosevelt advisor, Merriam was a moderate interventionist.) "I asked him," Ickes wrote, "if he could explain Bob Hutchins' late speeches. They have sounded to me like those of an appeaser. . . . Merriam and I found that our view with respect to Hutchins coincided. We think that his very just resentment over the manner in which the Administration has treated him, plus political ambition, has led him to take the stand that he has. However, on the other side, Hutchins has jeopardized the endowment drive [of the University of Chicago] next fall. Merriam thought that he was looking for a large sum of money from Marshall Field, and Field is distinctly on the other side. . . . The Rockefellers are also against him on this issue."[11]

So Ickes and Merriam could believe that so low a consideration as political ambition or personal grudge was enough to determine the position of the otherwise admirable Hutchins on the issue of war and peace. The "however, on the other side" gave them away, with their recognition that this politically ambitious cynic in his willingness to jeopardize the endowment drive he headed, was prepared to sacrifice his career to principle. (In 1941 John Gunther, in his notes for *Inside U.S.A.* recorded his impression that Hutchins might be the isolationists' candidate for president in 1944.)[12]

Hutchins was widely identified with the America First Committee, although he never spoke under its, or anybody's, auspices. (Forty years later a contemporary inquired if it was true that he had appeared on a platform with the tinhorn fascist Gerald L. K. Smith. He hadn't.) He not only did not become an America Firster, he made a repeated point of his not having done so: "I am not an isolationist. I have not joined the America First Committee. I should like to join a Committee for Humanity First."

Some of his close friends and colleagues were either members or advisors and consultants of America First, among them Wisconsin's liberal Senator Robert M. La Follette, Jr. (and his brother, Governor Phil La Follette), Columbia Law School Professor Philip K. Jessup, the Reverend Harry Emerson Fosdick, and Hutchins' most implacable academic enemy on his own campus, the physiologist Anton Julius Carlson. ("It was the only time in our lives that Professor Carlson and I ever agreed about anything.") Hutchins' 1932 candidate for president, Norman Thomas, though he himself headed the Socialist-pacifist-oriented Keep America Out of War Congress, spoke at America First meetings, as did President Henry Noble McCracken of Vassar. The organization boasted such mutually hostile personages as former president Herbert Hoover and United Mine Workers President John L. Lewis. And such eminently credentialed liberals as Harry Elmer Barnes, Charles A. Beard, and Stuart Chase figured prominently in the campaign against the Roosevelt approach to war, in direct or indirect association with the committee.

Hutchins was an ardent internationalist; proclaiming his affinity for an imaginary Humanity First Committee, he said, "If the United States can serve humanity it should do so, no matter what the cost in blood and treasure." (He had long been a tireless campaigner against separatism within the university structure. "Isolation," he said in a 1936 lecture, "is bad for everybody.") Not only were he and his kind of "isolationists" *anti*-isolationist (in contrast with xenophobics), they were very far from being neutral. One of the earliest supporters of Bundles for Britain, Hutchins was one of the most forthright advocates of unlimited American rearmament for defense: the Wilsonianism of 1916 all over again—"He Kept Us Out of War" *plus* "Preparedness." Hutchins: "Will Hitler attack us? Not if we are prepared." Again and again he prefaced his assertion that he was against military intervention by saying flatly, "I am for aid to Britain."

With the Battle of Britain in the winter of 1940–41 and the indiscriminate bombing of London and other cities, men and women like Hutchins recognized that a new kind of war had come into being. With the heavy bomber come into its stupendous own, and then the long-range rocket and missile, the whole world was a battlefield, every city, town, village, factory, farm, shop, school, hospital, prison, cemetery, church, home—and every civilian, of any age or condition, a potential victim. It was not Hiroshima that brought this great new fact home—except in degree. It was London, Rotterdam, Coventry, Hamburg, Dresden. It was the eye clinic in the open city of Marburg/Lahn, nearly all of its bandaged patients sightless, squarely hit by an aerial bomb that missed the railroad yard. A new kind of warfare, by definition consummate in the mass of pain it inflicted. And—although the airplane had invented it, and every nation would fight it from now on, its prime objective the shattering of urban industrial morale—it happened to have been launched by Adolf Hitler.

Hutchins' position, like that of the other antiwar liberals and radicals, ultimately was untenable. He wanted Nazi Germany to lose and he wanted England to win. He was for aid to Britain. How much aid? And for how long? Should a man who wanted England to win and Germany to lose and who favored aid to England draw a line at, say, arming the vessels carrying that aid, at turning over to the destined recipient destroyers to convoy that aid, at extending that aid from socks to guns and planes and, ultimately, troops? How could an advocate of aid to England say, "This far, and no further?" But Hutchins made a repeated point—without being asked—of stating that he was not a pacifist.

So the nonpacifist objector had to argue, unpersuasively—and Hutchins did—that America would be worse off if it went in and won than if it stayed out; that Nazi Germany, having conquered Europe, and in time (with its allies) Asia and Africa, could not successfully attack the United

States. He had to argue—and did—that the United States would lose its values, its very form of government, if it fought. ("Our form of government will not survive participation in this war and our ideals will be unrecognizable by the time we have gone through the conflict.") He had to argue—and did—that the peace that would follow our victorious war would be a bad peace. ("Our practice of life and government is not enough better to justify the hope that after we have won the war for democracy we can write a democratic peace.") He would be tempted to argue—as Hutchins was, and as Hutchins did—that this war was Armageddon and that American neutrality was what Armageddon demanded. ("If we plunge into war we shall deprive the world of its last hope. We shall rob mankind of its last chance.")

The America First Committee was predominantly conservative, with a liberal strain reflecting its origin in a group of antiwar Yale undergraduates led by R. Douglas Stuart and Kingman Brewster, Jr. (The latter would one day be president of Yale and U.S. ambassador to Great Britain.) Its chairman was a moderate conservative, Robert E. Wood of Sears, Roebuck and Company. Wood was a general—"my favorite general," Hutchins called him—but a general long since retired whose military expertise was not persuasive against that of the active military leaders supporting the president.

Though its position was supported by the great majority of the American people, America First was never able to shake the stigma attached to it by the acceptance of extreme, and even unsavory, rightists and rabble rousers. In the academic, literary, and journalistic circles of the eastern seaboard, the committee suffered a steady and steadily mounting succession of attacks as—the classic obloquy of the times—appeasers. The liberals among its leaders kept begging Hutchins to join it, with a view to his becoming its national chairman. Hutchins continued to resist, though he wrote his friend Professor Philip Jessup of Columbia, in the spring of 1941, "I now wonder if I was right in not joining America First. Although I do not like some of them, like Henry Ford, I know absolutely nothing against General Wood or Douglas Stuart, the director. On the contrary, I admire them both. . . . The reason why I am drifting toward America First is that it is the only group that is working with real effect on the problem."[13]

It was in this same letter that he made what seems to have been the strangest judgment of his life. "I recently spent an evening with Lindbergh," he wrote Jessup. "I regard him as the most misrepresented and maligned individual I have ever known. Perhaps I'm blind, but I can see nothing wrong with him whatever." Like all men, Lindbergh did have something wrong with him. Several things. He was Hutchins' "uneducated specialist" par excellence, who combined ignorance, political naiveté, and a legendary reputation, to a degree that came close to saddling his idolatrous countrymen with a Man on Horseback.

Lindbergh's five national radio addresses before Pearl Harbor, and his twelve packed platform speeches, identified him as the leader of the antiwar forces. Certainly President Roosevelt was afraid of him. With a view to clipping his wings or, alternatively, grounding him altogether, the always realistic, or cynical, Roosevelt let it be known, through a third party, that there was to be a new branch of the military, a separate air force parallel with the army and the navy, with its own cabinet secretary; the post was Lindbergh's if he would go along with the president's foreign policy. Lindbergh declined the carefully concealed—but well authenticated—offer, and the president then authorized an investigation of the unbending flyer's income tax returns (a low scheme which blew up in its contriver's face when Lindbergh called a press conference and revealed that to make sure that he was making no error of calculation prejudicial to the IRS he had always added 10 percent to his tax payments).

Anne Morrow Lindbergh tried in vain to dissuade her husband from making the public statement that ended his prewar influence: "The three most important groups which have been pressing this country toward war are the British, the Jewish, and the Roosevelt administration." This—and more of the same—in a speech in Des Moines on September 11, 1941. The meeting was sponsored by America First (whose officials never saw any of Lindbergh's speeches in advance), and the national reaction effectively collapsed the committee's effectiveness at a time when the national debate had reached crisis heat and the allied fortunes of war were at their nadir. "It would be difficult," says Professor Wayne S. Cole in his *America First: the Battle Against Intervention, 1940–41*, "to exaggerate the magnitude of the explosion which was set off by this speech. . . . Undoubtedly much of this uproar was due to genuine disapproval of Lindbergh's key statement regarding the Jews. Many may have denounced the speech publicly to protect themselves from any possible charge of anti-Semitism. But there can be no doubt that interventionists exploited this incident."[14] Isolationists on the whole said nothing—what could they say?—while interventionists danced in the streets. "The voice is the voice of Lindbergh," said the *San Francisco Chronicle*, not untypically, "but the words are the words of Hitler." Mr. Roosevelt said—and needed to say—nothing.

Hutchins had all along resisted the pleas of his friends in America First to join them. "You could almost make us respectable," Chester Bowles wrote.[15] But Hutchins did not feel that he could avoid taking a position on the Lindbergh imbroglio. In the Hutchins manner, he made no statement—and simply resigned (along with Oswald Garrison Villard of *The Nation*) publicly from the Committee against Intolerance when that organization of highly respected liberals attacked the fallen hero of the Des Moines speech as anti-Semitic. Although he greatly admired—and envied?—Lindbergh's unassailable independence and dogged disdain of censure, his extravagant esteem of the extremely limited technician remained, and remains, unsearchable. There is no record of the two or three talks the two men had in the months before Pearl Harbor, but thirty-five years after Des Moines Hutchins told a historian that the four persons he had worked with in developing his own position on the war were Benton, Bowles, Mayer—and Lindbergh. To the same careful interviewer, he said, still lamely after thirty-five years, that Lindbergh's statement "was not a timely remark."[16]

Hutchins' attitude toward the headstrong hero had the avuncular quality of a teacher who is taken with the pigheaded persistence of a backward pupil. The two men maintained an intermittent correspondence for five or ten years after the war. Their letters were long (an unusual thing for Hutchins); and Lindbergh's, which he typed himself, were filled with positively pre-elementary questions. Hutchins patiently, painstakingly, and on the same wide-eyed level, argued with him, as often as not with tongue in cheek: "I am much encouraged by your suggestion that the important thing is the clarification of issues through discussion. I have come to this conclusion myself, even to the extent of deciding that this is the chief purpose of a university."[17]

Hutchins, who professed disinterest in public office and quietly sought the highest one in 1940, was in all probability counted out as "unavailable" rather than politically obnoxious to the interventionist president who was choosing his running mate. For all of Ickes' and Hopkins' efforts, there is no hard evidence that Roosevelt—whose offers of high posts he had declined—gave Hutchins any consideration for the vice-presidential nomination.

The Supreme Court was, or may have been (or might have been), something else. Roosevelt filled the famous Cardozo and Brandeis vacancies with professors at Harvard and Yale, Felix Frankfurter in 1938 and William O. Douglas in 1939, both of them close friends and admirers of Hutchins.

When the conservative Justice McReynolds and the moderate Chief Justice Hughes retired in 1941, Hutchins' by then vociferous opposition to Roosevelt's foreign policy precluded his appointment had it otherwise been contemplated. As the former dean of the Yale Law School, and as a university president, he would have been acceptable "to the country." (Justice Harlan Fiske Stone, onetime dean of the Columbia Law School, was moved up into Hughes's seat.) He had supported Roosevelt's New Deal legislation and his foredoomed effort to reform, or "pack," the conservative Supreme Court. (He was a "loose" constructionist of a Constitution which was written before the modern corporate and technological world had come into being.) Five years earlier Robert Maynard Hutchins had had nowhere to go but up to the presidency or the chief justiceship; by 1941 he had nowhere to go.

There was no compelling reason why he shouldn't stay where he was. Though a probable majority of his senior faculty objected to his educational vagaries, and a faculty poll by the student newspaper in mid-1941 went two to one in favor of Roosevelt's "all aid short of war," there was no movement overt or covert to censure or get rid of Chicago's rapidly aging president on the basis of his antiwar activity. A few days before his June 1940 convocation address, "What Shall We Defend?" a campus mass meeting to arouse pro-allied sentiment presented some of his weightiest faculty members as interventionists (including Adler, who attacked the irrelevant issue of pacifism for its bad "moral thinking"); the somewhat fewer weighty colleagues who took Hutchins' position were much less loudly heard from. But Chicago was—in part because of its location—less inflammable than some of its sister institutions on the east and west coasts, and there was no personal break between Hutchins and any of his war-issue critics.

As for his trustees—Hutchins said they were "self-denying"—they were worried, as they had been ever since he'd taken office. The university's fiftieth anniversary celebration was taking place in the fall of 1941, and the celebration was the occasion (or vice versa) of the most ambitious endowment campaign in the institution's history. As Merriam and Ickes had already observed, some of the heaviest prospective donors, especially in the east, were interventionists. Middle western attitudes were divided, as Hutchins believed his board was. But isolationism was respectable in the Chicagoland of the reactionary, isolationist *Tribune*; still, accustomed though they were to having to be self-denying as far as their rambunctious president was concerned, Chicago's trustees were men (always men) of caution and reserve who deplored public controversy and, indeed, any but flattering public notice. They did not know what their president's unusual activity on the national front would do to the fund-raising effort. But they knew better than to remonstrate with him, with one exception. Trustee Clarence B. Randall of the Inland Steel Corporation—it would have been worse than impolite to observe that Inland Steel was a "Jewish" concern—

was an active interventionist, and in a sharp letter to Hutchins took him to task for using the pulpit of the university chapel to deliver an antiwar lecture in the spring of 1941. "The chapel," wrote Randall, "is not a suitable forum for the discussion of controversial questions."[18] Though Hutchins may have been on questionable ground—he had said (to a friend), "You can get away with murder under the sign of the cross"—he reminded Randall that president Angell of Yale had devoted his baccalaureate sermons to attacks on the New Deal, and added, "If a subject is important, it is likely to be controversial. I see no reason why university presidents should have to limit their chapel addresses to trivial topics."[19]

On the whole, the self-denying board held its uneasy peace and abode uncomfortably in the hope that rich and poor donors would not be turned away by Hutchins' unfortunate conduct. They weren't. John D. Rockefeller, Jr., of the interventionist Rockefellers, was the principal speaker at the culminating banquet of the fiftieth anniversary celebration. The endowment drive went over the top, and Hutchins was able to address the gathered alumni in late September 1941 in a self-congratulatory, as well as congratulatory, frame of mind, speaking of the university in his most graceful mode—and between the lines getting a word in on salvation through war.

There are two—at least two—ways of explaining the exceptional absence of anger at Hutchins' antiwar stand on the part of faculty, trustees, donors, and alumni. It may have been that the interventionists among them were admiring of him as an educator and administrator, were congenial to his social views, taken with him personally, and could forgive him (or at least tolerate) his extracurricular crusade as an isolationist. The perhaps likelier explanation was that they sensed that when the chips were down—whatever that might mean—he would go along with them and with the country. Why otherwise would he keep saying, "I am not a pacifist?" Why otherwise would he call for military preparedness? He was known to his admirers as a safe man at bottom, a team player, for all his academic high jinks, and even to his detractors as a constitutionalist, a rules player. He had signaled his dependability in a number of ways. In 1940 a defense council was formed to provide for the impact on the university's organization and finances and to plan with the government the war tasks it could do. "As a result of this planning," the university's publicity office announced at the same time, "many scientific projects designed by the government were under way long before war was declared." In some quarters it was known officially, in others unofficially, that Chicago administrators and faculty representatives had been dispatched to Washington in 1941 to engage government officials in considering the kinds of projects the university would be best suited to undertake; on one such mission, Vice-president Benton returned from the capital to report (more significantly than he could have known) that the government's scientific advisers were convinced that Chicago's progress in nuclear physics was uniquely advanced and its personnel in that area uniquely qualified. Ten days before Pearl Harbor, President Hutchins announced that the university's status in the natural sciences put it in a position of leadership in defense work.

More visibly significant was the Institute of Military Studies, established on the campus in October 1940 by Arthur L. H. Rubin, the all-round New Yorker of independent wealth who lived with the Mortimer Adlers and served as executive secretary of Hutchins' controversial Committee on the Liberal Arts at the university. The non-credit-course military institute was open to faculty, students, and the general (male, of course) public. Privately equipped, its students, many of them gray, many more of them portly, drilled with wooden guns and used pickup trucks as tanks. The five-dollar registration fee paid for a specially designed military cap. With volunteer civilians as instructors, the institute offered instruction in drill, manual of arms, elementary rifle marksmanship, elementary tactics and tactical exercise, mapping, bayonet and hand grenade drill, and other fundamentals. Its counterpart had appeared around the country during the preparedness campaign of 1915–16; and the professional military, now as then, had no use for it or interest in it. But before it was disbanded in 1942 it had "trained" some four thousand high-spirited, if otherwise unserviceable, enrollees. It was precisely the kind of vocationalism that Hutchins deplored as a hokey imitation of the real thing (and in this case an emotional jag). He took an especially dim view of its ecstatic leaders, Rubin (who went to the War Department after Pearl Harbor) and the economist and one-time pacifist Paul H. Douglas (who at fifty became a marine when war was declared, was wounded in the Pacific, and returned to become a Chicago alderman and ultimately an eminently liberal U.S. senator from Illinois). But the Institute for Military Studies had the formal support of the central administration of the university, and the head of the central administration was a one-man army opposing war.

This nonpacifist, propreparedness isolationist should certainly have lost friends among the extreme interventionists. But he didn't. His closest friend, over a lifetime, was Thornton Wilder. A biographer of Wilder says that the friendship really ended in 1941: "[Wilder] regarded Hitler as a virtual incarnation of the devil. . . . [He] saw Western civilization at bay, the barbarian at the gates. . . . He was terribly dismayed when on January 23, 1941, Robert Hutchins made a nationally broadcast address advocating American neutrality and warning his countryman against involvement in the European conflict. . . . Thus Wilder's adulation of Hutchins, at the end of a quarter century, fizzled out at this moment when Hutchins dug his political grave. . . . After January 1941, Wilder would speak privately about Hutchins, with a baleful shake of his head, as a man who, out of some kind of self-indulgence, had failed to fulfill his great potential."[20]

In 1974—thirty-three years after his "adulation of Hutchins fizzled out"—I had the opportunity to speak with Wilder, whom I'd known at Chicago. He spoke "privately" with the same adulation with which he had been writing letters in the intervening years. The two men had maintained their close correspondence but hadn't seen each other in ten years or more. Wilder had really withdrawn from circulation. But now Hutchins was ill, and Wilder complained that he "couldn't get Bob to complain." I said that I hoped he would be able to get to California some time to see Bob, and Wilder said, "I don't have to *look* at Bob to see him. I *see* him all the time."

He didn't get to look at Bob again. On December 7, 1975, Thornton Wilder was dead. A year before he died, his last book appeared, *Theophilus North*. It was the closest Wilder would come to writing an autobiography. It was dedicated to Robert Maynard Hutchins, who spoke at his memorial service at Yale and said: "For sixty years he was my teacher. His pedagogical methods were irresistible. They were deep personal concern and laughter. When I was ill or suffering from any misfortune, the letters were faster and funnier, but the lessons were not missing. . . . He was the best of teachers . . . the kindest of friends."[21]

If Wilder was the closest friend of his youth, Laird Bell of Chicago was perhaps the closest friend of his middle life—and his lawyer, and, as chairman of the Chicago board of trustees, his boss. Bell was not only a member of the city's leading law firm, he was a formidable figure in the corporate world (for example, chairman of the board of Weyerhaeuser Lumber Company and, for example, an overseer of Harvard). He was also, in 1940 and 1941, the head of the Chicago chapter of the Committee to Defend America by Aiding the Allies—the city's foremost interventionist, as Hutchins was its foremost noninterventionist. A decade after this confrontation Board Chairman Bell announced the anonymous endowment of the Robert Maynard Hutchins Distinguished Service Professorship at the university; a decade later Robert Maynard Hutchins, called back to the university to preside over the dedication of the Laird Bell Quadrangle, revealed that the anonymous donor of the Hutchins professorship had been Laird Bell.

But Bell was an even-tempered man and Wilder was an affectionate man; and Harold Ickes was neither. The Old Curmudgeon was a ravening anti-isolationist and a boiling supporter of all aid short of war. He supported Roosevelt worshipfully and, in his conversation with his friend Professor Merriam, voiced his deep disappointment in Hutchins' policy of "appeasement"; as a Chicago alumnus he had been a great admirer of Hutchins the civil libertarian and defender of academic freedom. But the last time the two men saw each other was the occasion they conspired at the Democratic convention of 1940 to advance one another's candidacy for the vice-presidential nomination. And then, on December 26, 1950, the former warmonger wrote to the former appeaser:

> Dear Bob,
>
> I have seen by the newspapers that you are about to resign from the University . . . and that you will be going to Pasadena to work for the Ford Foundation. I am glad that this important foundation is to have the benefit of your services, but I regret that Chicago will lose you. We need such leadership in this country today as you have been supplying. . . . Jane and I would love it if we could see you before you move west. . . .

And the appeaser replied to the warmonger:

> Dear Harold:
>
> . . . You have always been very generous to me and this occasion is no exception. I think of you and Jane often and only wish that our paths could manage to cross once in a while. . . . Do give my love to Jane. If I come to Washington, I will not fail to see you.

What these friends, who remained friends, had in common was that they were all gentiles. It could not have been expected that the Jews in his circle—trustees and donors among them—would forgive and forget all that easily. But they did. In a few cases he and they were lost to each other for the duration, but only in a few. And even in those few cases the separation was more in sorrow than in anger. None of his Jewish friends for a moment identified Hutchins with the right-wing extremists—and outright fascists—who cluttered around the isolationist movement. Jews had always been greatly drawn to him—and he to them. (I once asked him why it was that some of his best friends were rich and influential Jews. "Because," he said, "I feel sorry for oppressed people.") His university appointments and associations were disproportionately Jewish. His intimacy with Felix Frankfurter went back to his Yale days. There was one exception—a costly one—to this continuity of Jewish friendships.

John Gunther tells the story in his biography of Albert Lasker, the multimillionaire advertising man and University of Chicago board member. "Hutchins, like Lasker, was vigorous, enlivening, and original. The two men took to one another at once, and spent a dozen years in warm association. . . . Hutchins had the habit of getting up every morning at 5:30 A.M., and he liked to go to bed early at night. Sleep was, however, difficult for him if Lasker was in a conversational mood, because the older man would call him at all hours of the night, posing innumerable questions and soliciting advice. . . . 'Should Edward'—Lasker's collegiate son—'have polo ponies?' Hutchins replied, 'Certainly' and rang off. . . .[22]

"In the spring of 1942 Lasker resigned from the board of trustees of the University of Chicago. There were two reasons for this severance, which caused him much pain. First, he had turned full-wheel on international affairs [and] became . . . an ardent interventionist . . . even though this meant an irrevocable break with some of his oldest acquaintances, like Robert E. Wood of Sears Roebuck and Colonel McCormick of the *Chicago Tribune.* . . .

"All this, naturally, served to bring him into conflict with Hutchins [who] held views which Lasker, a whole-hogger if ever there was one, could not countenance, and Albert felt so deeply that Hutchins was wrong that he considered that he had no recourse but to resign his trusteeship at the University.

"However, there was a second issue. The spark which set off the explosion was something else. In March 1942, the *Saturday Evening Post* published an article called 'The Case Against the Jew' by Milton Mayer, a part-time employee of the University who was one of Hutchins' best friends. Mayer had done good work for the University. But his *Post* article (with which the University was not involved in any way) made Lasker angry, because he thought it was anti-Semitic—although Mayer was, of course, a Jew—and would give succor to anti-Semites everywhere at a time when Jews the world over were suffering the most painful, dangerous persecution in their history. Certainly Mayer's article, whatever it said, came out at a most unpropitious moment. What angered Lasker particularly was the title."[23]

Lasker demanded that Hutchins fire Mayer. Hutchins said he didn't see how he could do that, since Mayer was a half-time employee of the university and the article had apparently been written on the other half of his time. Lasker decided to leave the board. Hutchins tried his best to make him change his mind, but Lasker refused and resigned as a trustee on June 11, 1942. In his letter of resignation, which was nine pages long, Lasker wrote: "When a trustee differs from the president of a university, the trustee should resign." "I thought the sentence would end the other way," said Hutchins afterward.

Then Lasker went after the *Post.* He summoned its chief executives to

New York: they came running. He threatened to withdraw all Lord and Thomas advertising from the magazine, forced it to print a retraction and an apology, and forced it to agree never to print Mayer again and to have a leading Jew write a rebuttal. (Failing to interest a leading Jew in the assignment, the *Post* settled for Wendell Willkie.)

Lasker was reported to be one of the ten richest men in America. He was not only exorbitantly rich, and lavish, and generous, he was exorbitantly philanthropic; he had given the University of Chicago immense amounts of money, beginning with a million dollars in 1928 for medical research; and this was even before Hutchins became president.

The financial loss to the university as a result of the break was simply incalculable. Lasker's eccentric distribution of his largesse, had Hutchins held on to him, might well have focused on the university. Hutchins neither held on to him nor did he come hurriedly—unlike the *Post* executives—when the outraged Croesus summoned him and ordered him to fire Mayer. Hutchins had the sole responsibility for Lasker's cutoff of the university; the author of the *Post* article, though he did fill-in teaching in the Hutchins-Adler Great Books courses, was covered by neither tenure nor contract; Hutchins could have fired him on the instant. He could have—but didn't. The buck stopped there. He scaped no goats, stalked no horses, hoisted no lightning rods or weather vanes. He exaggerated a little when he said (as he often did) that the life of a university president consisted entirely of shameful compromise.

Hutchins and Lasker saw each other less and less as the years went on. On one occasion, some years after the war, the two old friends found themselves seated next to one another at a dinner party. The now elderly Lasker turned to Hutchins and said, "Do you remember an article about Jews in the *Saturday Evening Post* during the war?" "Vaguely," said Hutchins. "You know," said Lasker, "my son-in-law gave it to me to read the other day. It wasn't a bad article. But the title was unfortunate." "Wasn't it," said Hutchins.

Lasker had been fanatical, as, in their separate fashions, had been Ickes and Wilder. It was almost impossible for Jews not to be fanatical and only a little less so for liberals and humanitarians. Fanaticism had been the order—or disorder—of the day. In the spring of 1940 Hutchins' old friend Alexander Woollcott "shook his finger in my face and said, 'The day after France falls, Hitler will be at the Panama Canal.'" Interventionism was a passionate cause, sweeping people with it in the name of humanity; anti-interventionism was essentially a bloodless affair, calling people to consider distant causes and still more distant consequences. In his running correspondence with Thornton Wilder, Hutchins wrote, after his January 23,

1941, speech, "America and the War": "I made it because I thought Mr. Roosevelt and a lot of my other friends were getting awfully light-hearted and even irresponsible about going into battle. . . . I got mad, too, about Mr. Roosevelt's message to Congress, where he appropriated all the idealism of the world for what the *Chicago Tribune* calls the War Party."[24]

In mid-1941 Hutchins wrote his friend Cyrus McCormick: "If Mr. Roosevelt had never talked about the Four Freedoms, I probably should never have said anything about the war. I can understand going to war. I can understand going to war to protect yourself; I cannot understand war as a missionary enterprise, particularly when the missionary hasn't very much of a faith and isn't very sure of what he has."

The Roosevelt rhetoric simply was (as Hutchins so often said when friends suggested a phrase or an anecdote for his speeches) too rich for his blood. It wasn't reasonable. It wasn't rational. The rational animal had no choice but to reject it and attack it—rationally.

And attack it he did. Mr. Roosevelt had told the country that the war was being fought for "a world founded on freedom of speech, freedom of worship, freedom from want, and freedom from fear." America had been called upon to support the moral order and "the supremacy of human rights everywhere." Did we (Hutchins wanted to know) have freedom of speech and worship here? "We have freedom to say what everybody else is saying and freedom of worship if we do not take our religion too seriously. But teachers who do not conform to the established canons of social thought lose their jobs. People who are called 'radicals' have mysterious difficulties in renting halls. Labor organizers sometimes get beaten up and ridden out of town on a rail." What were we to say of freedom from want and freedom from fear? "Think of these things and then think of the sharecroppers, the Okies, the Negroes, the slumdwellers, downtrodden and oppressed for gain. . . . They hardly know they are living in a moral order or in a democracy where justice and human rights are supreme. . . .

"As for democracy, we know that millions of men and women are disenfranchised in this country because of their race, color, or condition of economic servitude. . . . The aims of a democratic community are moral. United by devotion to law, equality, and justice, the democratic community works together for the happiness of all its citizens. I leave to you the decision whether we have yet achieved a democratic community in the United States."

The country had made "some notable advances in the long march toward justice, freedom, and democracy" and was far ahead of most of the world. "But we Americans have only the faintest glimmering of what war is like. This war, if we enter it, will make the last one look like a stroll in the park. . . . For a generation, perhaps for a hundred years, we shall not be able to struggle back to where we were. In fact the changes that total war will bring may mean that we shall never be able to struggle back. Education will cease. Its place will be taken by vocational and military training. The effort to establish a democratic community will stop. We shall think no more of justice, the moral order, and the supremacy of human rights. We shall have hope no longer."[25]

So the sable litany proceeded, laced freely with unanswerable facts and extravagant predictions. "If the United States is to proceed through total war to total victory over totalitarian states, it will have to become totalitarian, too." "If we enter this war, we shall lose what we have of the four freedoms."

His tactics were scary, but they weren't scare tactics. The hyperbole everywhere rose measurably after Congress on March 8, 1941, passed the crucial Lend-Lease Act, Resolution 1776 by Senate and House majorities of 60-31 and 317-71 respectively, and the country was committed to all-out aid—with no more "short of war" provisos—while the Gallup poll showed 83 percent of the American people against entering the war, a higher percentage than a year earlier. (On the other hand, a majority said they favored aiding Britain at the risk of war.)

Hutchins, too, wanted to "aid Britain, and stay out of the war" (and never did confront the implicit contradiction in those two policies). He, too, wanted the country to defend itself, to "bend every energy to the construction of an adequate navy and air force and the training of an adequate army . . . adequate for defense against any power or combination of powers"[26] (and never did confront the implicit contradiction of that surrender to the policy of the armed-to-the-teeth garrison state and the simultaneous pursuit of the four freedoms at home to achieve "total victory over poverty, disease, ignorance, and injustice"—*and* at the same time "make this country a refuge for those who will not live without liberty").

This was America's destiny, to show the world "a nation which understands, values, and practices the four freedoms." This was America's destiny, to create a civilization "in which people will not suffer so much that they will trade their liberties for the pitiful security which the tyrant offers. The war to create this civilization is our war. We must take advantage of every day we have left to build a democracy which will command the faith of our people, and, which, by the light of our example, will restore the democratic faith to the people of the world. America has been called the arsenal of democracy. It has been called the larder of democracy. Let us make it the home of democracy."[27]

He was an uncommon scold calling upon his countrymen to bend their every energy to pursue the rapidly receding objectives of the New Deal. He was pleading with them not to run away from their destiny because it was a hard one. The country had not begun to solve its problems, and he somehow seemed to suggest his hopelessness that—war or no war—it would. A strong pessimistic strain ran through his exhortatory discourse.

He had been pessimistic at Yale in 1921. He would be as much of a pessimist forty years later when as the speaker at a dinner in honor of Justice Hugo L. Black in 1961 he said, "Only if we can tear ourselves loose from our prejudices, from our ideology, from slogans, only if we can take a fresh look at the world and exercise the same kind of intelligence, character, and inventiveness that the Founding Fathers showed can we hope to revive, reconstruct, and preserve the political community."[28]

In the decades between those two occasions he had not become any sunnier. In the decades between those two occasions he had often quoted William the Silent—or Charles the Bold, he could never remember which—as having said, "It is not necessary to hope in order to undertake, nor to succeed in order to persevere."

The emotionalism from which Hutchins recoiled was sweeping everything before it. In his post-Lend-Lease address in March—delivered as a university chapel sermon but broadcast nationwide—he used the title, "The Proposition Is Peace," borrowing the expression from Edmund Burke's address against war with the American colonies: "Judging of what you are by what you ought to be, I persuaded myself that you would not reject a reasonable proposition because it had nothing but its reason to recommend it. . . . The proposition is peace." And so Hutchins reasoned in a time of mounting frenzy, throwing himself against most of his fellow academics, his fellow humanitarians, his fellow writers and speakers. "Mr. Roosevelt tells us we are to save the 'democracies.' The democracies are, presumably, England, China, Greece, and possibly Turkey. Turkey is a dictatorship. Greece is a dictatorship. China is a dictatorship. As to England, in 1928 Mr. Anthony Eden, now Foreign Secretary, speaking in behalf of a bill extending the suffrage, felt it necessary to say to the House of Commons, 'We have not got democratic government in this country today; we never have had it and I venture to suggest to honorable Members opposite that we never shall have it.' There can be no doubt that the people of this country prefer the government of Britain to the governments of its allies or its enemies. . . . But we cannot use the word democracy to describe every country that is or may be at war with the Axis. If Russia is attacked by Germany"—as it was a few months later—"will she be welcomed into the choir of the democracies?"

The proposition had nothing but reason to recommend it, and the rational animal, addressing himself to rational animals, could not restrain his penchant for the reasoned ironic. If the British, the Chinese, and the Greeks were indeed our allies, "it is immoral for us to let them die for us while we sit safely at home. We should have been in the war from the start. We should fight now." Mr. Roosevelt had said, "We believe that any nationality, no matter how small, has the inherent right to its own nationhood." Did this statement imply the restoration of prewar boundaries in Austria, Czechoslovakia, Memel, Danzig, Poland, France, China, and Rumania? Was this undertaking to be worldwide? If so, how were we to induce Russia to restore the prewar boundaries of Estonia, Latvia, Lithuania, Finland, and Poland? And what were we to do about the countries which were victims of aggression before 1939? Was everybody who stole anything before that date to keep it, and everybody who stole anything after it to give it up? What were we to do about Hong Kong, the Malay States, the Dutch East Indies, French Indo-China, Africa, and, above all, India? Besides his commitment to national self-determination Mr. Roosevelt had made only one statement on the course the country was to pursue after the war: "There never has been, there isn't now, and there never will be any race of people fit to serve as masters over their fellowmen." If that was so, how could a postwar America tolerate "the mastery of the whites over their yellow, brown, and black fellow-men throughout the world?" "The British propose to defeat the Axis. What they propose to do then they do not say. They have repeatedly refused to say"—this with reference to India's unabating struggle for independence. "If we go to war, what are we going to war for?"[29]

As he had listened closely to Lindbergh and found a modicum of sense in the aviator's position—and said so—so he insisted, almost alone among the antiwar speakers, in giving his gallant due, in full measure, to the isolationist's devil: "I have supported Mr. Roosevelt since he first went to the White House. I have never questioned his integrity or his good will. But under the pressure of great responsibilities, in the heat of controversy, in the international game of bluff, the President's speeches and recommendations are committing us to obligations abroad which we cannot perform. The effort to perform them will prevent the achievement of the aims for which the President stands at home. . . . With the President's desire to see freedom of speech, freedom of worship, freedom from want, and freedom from fear flourish everywhere we must all agree. Millions of Americans have supported the President because they felt that he wanted to achieve these four freedoms for America. Others"—dealing the fat cat interventionists a rational blow—"who now long to carry these blessings to the rest of the world, were not conspicuous on the firing line when Mr. Roosevelt called them, eight years ago, to do battle for the four freedoms at home."[30]

Rationality demanded a fair shake for the racist Lindbergh, for the bellicose Roosevelt, *and* for the execrable villain of the entire piece. Knowing that no rational animal could call him an admirer of Adolf Hitler, but that many an irrationalized animal would, the frigid crusader against his own country's consuming materialism recalled that the Nazi leader had written in *Mein Kampf* that Greece would be remembered for its philosophy, Rome for its law, medieval Europe for its cathedrals, and the modern world for its department stores. "Hitler was right"—this in a nationwide broadcast in 1941—"in holding before the German people an ideal higher than comfort. He knew he could not give them that. He offered them instead a vision of national grandeur and 'racial' supremacy. These are false gods. Since they are false, they will fail in the end. But Hitler was half right. He was right in what he condemned, and wrong in what he offered in its place . . . a new order based on slavery and degradation."[31]

Hitler was half right. It was the wrong time and the wrong place— America in 1941, and a broadcast of the regular Sunday morning sermon in the university chapel at that. It was the wrong time and the wrong place to say that Hitler was half right or so much as an iota right. It was the rational animal's refusal to stoop to exploitation of the hatred of the Nazi leader. But the rational animal doggedly clung to his reasoning, and, as the national frenzy mounted, Hutchins of Chicago stood ever more clearly for a less and less frequently displayed evenhandedness. At the end of November 1941, Hutchins told Mayer that he was thinking of writing an article for the conservative, antiwar *Saturday Evening Post* entitled, "Where Hitler Is Right."

Rationality might carry a man just that far in an irrational world—and destroy him. Millions of magazine readers might, and at that point likely would, react with extreme excitement to that kind of headline and not bother to read the article, concluding that such an article, whatever its actual import, would give aid and comfort to the forces of the enemy of mankind in America and elsewhere. "Where Hitler Is Right," indeed.

The article was never written. Pearl Harbor put an end to all that and more. It put an end to the crystal-ball expertise on all sides. Everything that had been said—in the preceding two years and almost everything had been said, one way or another—was now put to the test, including Robert Maynard Hutchins' remarkably bald predictions of the consequences of the country's going to war and winning it—"the United States will have to become totalitarian"—"the sacrifice of millions of our youth"—"we shall have hope no longer."

On balance, his blackly pessimistic, and largely unqualified, predictions turned out to be altogether wrong or overdrawn. "Suppose that by some miracle we were to defeat the totalitarian powers without becoming one ourselves, would we be prepared, even then, to write a just and durable peace? We don't know what to do with ourselves. What shall we do with the Germans, Italians, and Japanese? What shall we do with the British and the Chinese? Are we to fight them to make them see things our way? What shall we do with Czechoslovakia, Poland, Latvia, Estonia, Lithuania, France, Luxembourg, Denmark, Norway, Belgium, Holland, Rumania, Yugoslavia, and Greece? Are we to restore the status quo which contributed to this war and simply hope that it will work next time? Until we know what to do with ourselves we can hardly venture to set the whole world right."

He was right—but who wasn't?—in asserting almost gleefully after the Germans turned on Russia that "alliance between Great Britain and Russia makes it clear that this is a war and not a crusade. Great Britain can not expect Russian tyranny to cooperate in the establishment of the four freedoms." But none of the most abysmal horrors he foretold was consummated with the restoration of the peace—or in the next half-century. Very far from it. True, the four freedoms could not be said to have flourished anywhere in the postwar decades (except in the one limited respect, in a few societies, of increased opportunity for minorities and women). One of President Roosevelt's asserted war aims was realized (without respect to American influence): for better or for worse, national self-determination spread through Africa and southern Asia. But freedom of speech and worship were circumscribed; want continued unabated; and fear grew pandemic as the nuclear destruction of the habitable planet loomed ever larger. Still, the antiwar campaigners of 1941 would be hard put fifty years later—though the book was not yet closed—to contend that the program of the New Deal at home was dead and buried. It fell failing after the war (just as Truman's Fair Deal and Johnson's Great Society would in large measure succumb successively to Korea and Vietnam), but the America of the 1980s was not an America that could be said to "have hope no longer."

Hutchins' extravagant polemics, wildly wide of the mark as they proved to be, were no further from the eventual reality than the ecstasies of his opponents. Neither a just nor a durable peace was written. Injustice extended its sway through eastern Europe and simply changed hands in

Africa and southeast Asia as the victorious and defeated powers alike lost their empires; and five years after Mr. Truman proclaimed, in the wake of Hiroshima, that "there must never be another war," the United States was at war in Korea. Neither the isolationists nor the interventionists proved to have a monopoly on being dead wrong within a decade of their prognostications.

How could the rational animal have gone so far out on a limb? How could he have let himself descend to so irrational a level? In one sense it was characteristic of him to speak with overweening certitude. He had been doing it most of his life. But most of his life he had known what he was talking about, and a great deal more than most of his opponents, on the subject to which he addressed himself, namely, education.

But in 1941 he was making cathedratic pronouncements on the life-and-death issue of world war in which his competence was derived from his genius for quick apprehension of the unfamiliar. His public activity during those months—no other college or university president appeared anywhere nearly as prominently in the great debate—was decidedly uncharacteristic of the man who had been the most conscientious and self-confined of educational administrators and had, what was more, achieved a considerable national reputation as a pleader for the evenhanded dialogue of inquiring minds.

There may have been two good explanations, if not justifications, for his having gone to such rhetorical extremes on the war issue. First, he had taken a lonely position. Hutchins had distanced himself completely from organized support. Not only did he dissociate himself, as he said in an early address, from "all Nazis, Fascists, Communists, and appeasers"; he dissociated himself from the true-blue isolationists, "from those who want us to stay out of war to save our own skins and our own property." He was, on the contrary, a true-blue interventionist opposing war: "National selfishness should not determine national policy." He stood alone, in the antiwar position least likely to draw or hold the interest of a substantial following. It was a position that might well push a man to overstatement.

But there was, perhaps, a better explanation than that for the recklessness that so clearly contradicted the close reasoning with which he habitually confronted his opponents in academic controversy. Beneath the frigid isolationist was the passionate moralist. Behind the thinking man's façade was the true believer not in rightness but in righteousness, who saw himself fighting the eternal rearguard action against the forces of evil and the false prophets of sweet deceits like the four freedoms. The glories of war—and of the peace that would follow it—were simply too rich for his blood. He had been brought up, he once said, on the Old Testament prophets. His favorite castigation was Jeremiah's, who said that his people were "wise to do evil, but to do good they have no knowledge."

Neither did the eminent intellectual call his countrymen to an intellectual revolution but rather, again and again, in season and out, to a "moral, intellectual, and spiritual revolution." He took occasion more than once in the great debate to crib Jacques Maritain's solemn maxim, "If we would change the face of the earth, we must first change our own hearts." Robert Maynard Hutchins called his countrymen to "build a new moral order for America...a new conception of security...a new conception of sacrifice."

It would pass, as peace would pass and war would overcome; he would be a university president again, doing what a university president does. But for a few months of his life he was a missionary, the whole world his mission.

21   A War Plant

A month after Pearl Harbor, Hutchins addressed his faculty and board: "When war has been declared," he said, "long-run activities must be sacrificed to the short-run activity of winning the war. Education and research, as we have understood them at the University of Chicago, are long-run activities. We have stood for liberal education and pure research. What the country must have now is vocational training and applied research. What the country must have we must try to supply."[1]

But what the country "must have" was precisely what the prewar Hutchins didn't want to supply. For ten years he had been saying that education was the utilization of the liberal arts to inculcate independent thinking. Now he said, straight-faced, "Since we know what teaching is and how to teach what to whom, we can exercise our ingenuity in planning training courses which might not occur to persons less sophisticated than ourselves. Our special knowledge makes us directly useful in the effort to win the war."[2]

Thirty days after the country went to war—or, rather, war went to the country—he was able to report that there were sixteen military training programs of various kinds on the campus. A month later his office proudly announced that "all indications are that the University's service in this war will be even more striking than the notable part it played in World War I." Government contracts had already been signed for a million dollars' worth of research projects ("highly confidential") involving more than two hundred investigators, and still others had been launched by the university itself. Almost 3,500 persons, most of them special students, were enrolled in military courses in such subjects as meteorology, map reading, military medical hygiene, military optics, elementary gliding, mechanics, electronics, production supervision, nursing supervision, and German. Vacation and holidays had been shortened; instruction was increased to fifty-nine hours a week and from forty-four to forty-eight weeks a year; and a split-week course schedule had been arranged, enabling students to take on jobs three or four days out of seven.

And one of Hutchins' most long-stymied reforms was at last adopted. The BA degree—to be dubbed Bastard of Arts by its detractors—would now be awarded after two years of college to represent the completion of general education assumed to have been begun after the sophomore year of high school, either in the four-year "Hutchins" College of the university or, in the case of a student who completed two years of the standard high school, in the last two years of the university's traditional college program (which was maintained vestigially, amid some confusion, alongside the "Hutchins" College with a capital C).

What he dreamed of, and would never see, was a six-four-four plan of general education the country over. He had been calling for it since 1931 (and in 1938 the Educational Policies Commission of the National Education Association had endorsed it). The subsequent proliferation of two-year junior colleges produced the commonly adopted six-three-three-two system by splitting the high school into two three-year units of junior and senior high; but the final two-year unit floated in midair, essentially two more years of high school or a weak imitation of the first two years of the state university. (At the University of California in Berkeley 60 percent of the undergraduate enrollees entered in the third year from junior colleges.) Failing a rationalization on the system all the way down the line, Hutchins was now asking his faculty for the equivalent of an eight-two-four plan (with the last two elementary grades knocked off for pupils of the University of Chicago Laboratory School). With the country at war, he was suddenly persuasive: "We have waste because of the 8-4-4 plan of elementary, secondary, and collegiate education. We have waste because students without qualifications for independent intellectual work are allowed to continue beyond the end of the sophomore year. We have waste because the program of graduate instruction does not take into account a fact patent on the surface of our professional life: a course of study which aims to produce both good scholars and good college teachers ends by producing neither. This is an educational system which the country can no longer afford"[3]—a system which he had been saying for years that the country could not afford. But now there was a war on—there had been for thirty days, when he addressed the faculty—and the reformer was fighting for one more reform under the guise of wartime necessity and wartime economy. What assured its approval was the fact that it would enable the student to get his degree before he was called up for military service at twenty.

The new degree, Hutchins said, would have meaning. It would mean a general education. It would "assist out of the educational system at the end of the sophomore year students who have no business to go on. It would make it possible for the Divisions to organize intelligible courses of study covering years and leading to the master's degree. It would enable the professional schools to begin their work with the beginning of the junior year. It would put a quietus on the ambitions of the junior colleges of the country, all of which are now anxious to achieve a mistaken notion of respectability by becoming four-year colleges of liberal arts."[4] He pointed out that it was a system that could be installed at Chicago at once, because the college already admitted high school juniors.

While he was at it—calling for a program that, wartime or peacetime, was close to impossible for any intelligent educator to oppose—he tossed a much tougher proposal, peacetime or wartime, into the faculty hopper. He told his audience that two PhD degrees were wanted—one to signify preparation for research and the other to signify preparation for college teaching. But this would, he was afraid, require "a change of heart before attempting the mechanical change" that he had urged from time to time in the past. Without the change of heart the two PhD degrees "might simply give us two bad courses of study instead of one." He would not get the change of heart he called for. His proposal to touch the hallowed doctorate would be lost—as he doubtless supposed it would be—in the hurried hurrah with which the Bastard of Arts was approved by the senate.

The relocation of the BA was a major triumph for Hutchins, reminiscent of the honeymoon days of the early 1930s. (It was an illusory triumph in the long run; the faculty revoked it in 1954, after he had resigned.) In the thirties he had got what he wanted because of the Depression emergency. Now he got what he wanted because of the war emergency. The measure was presented to the Senate Committee on University Policy at 4:00 on a Friday afternoon; by 5:30 it (and three other measures) had been voted on favorably and transmitted to the full senate, where it was adopted on a sixty-three to forty-three vote.

Less than three months later, on April 9, 1942, a motion to rescind the action was introduced on the senate floor. The meeting was one of the most heavily attended in the body's history; and Hutchins, presiding, was aware, as the discussion proceeded, that the new "two-year degree" was in danger. He appeared to be detached, the very model of a nonpartisan presiding officer, and at no point allowed himself to be drawn into the discussion. And then one of his enemies, Professor George K. K. Link, in botany, made the mistake of asking that the vote on the issue be by ballot instead of by voice—obviously implying that there were senators who did not want to defy the president openly. Link's proposal was accepted, and the vote was fifty-eight to rescind the action and fifty-seven to sustain it.

This was, in effect, a vote of no confidence. The two-year college had the support of the leading members of the Department of Education and other social scientists, including the heavyweight professors William E. Dodd in history and Charles E. Merriam in political science, much of the humanities division, and representatives of the professional schools; but the hard core of the natural sciences opposed it. What saved it, that crucial day in April, was a shabby trick played by Robert M. Hutchins, who knew (as he knew so many odd things) his Robert's Rules of Order. The presiding officer had no voice ordinarily—that is, in a viva voce decision—but when a measure was balloted he had a vote. With the tally of fifty-eight to fifty-seven in favor of rescinding, Hutchins cast his vote to sustain, and on the resulting tie the motion was lost.

The trick was not only shabby; it was, in the short, no less than the long, term ineffectual. It simply hardened the opposition to him and worried his friends in the faculty and on the board. It would have been better, he said afterward, had he accepted the immediate defeat and lobbied patiently to have it reversed later on.[5] But he had run out of patience. The debonair presiding officer was, when he coolly cast the deciding vote to retain the new degree, an outraged partisan who saw his fifteen years' labor coming undone.

The adoption of the two-year degree three months earlier had evoked only casual notice, and general approval, outside the educational establishment as a sensible step in connection with conscription. Inside the establishment the "cut-rate degree" was massively deplored. It was deplored by, inter alia, the Association of American Colleges, the National Association of State Universities, and the North Central Association of Colleges and Secondary Schools. The NCA supposedly held the power of academic life and death in the central states through its system of accreditation of institutions. It first threatened to disaccredit the University of Chicago, but softened its attitude (after the university ignored the threat) to approval of the arrangement as a five-year "experimental" program. (It never again mentioned the matter.)

"This," said Hutchins, "is the first time that the full-dress assemblages of principalities and powers have publicly, officially, and formally deplored the University's conduct. It marks an all-time high in educational deploring. The University must have done something very bad indeed."

"What the University has done is to announce that it will make it possible for students to get a liberal education by the end of the sophomore year and that it will award at that point, in recognition of their efforts, the degree traditionally associated with liberal education, namely, the Bachelor of Arts.

"Why is this bad? Offhand, it would appear highly desirable. Nobody has ever complained that college students work too hard. On the contrary. . . . It has often been asserted on very high authority that the American educational system prolongs adolescence far beyond the point at which young people in other countries are turned out of education to assume adult responsibilities. In other countries this age is eighteen or nineteen; here the first honorable stopping-place is at twenty-two. . . . Apparently the time is available in the educational system to complete liberal education at the age of twenty; and, if it can be done, there seem to be great advantages in doing it.

"The war emphasizes these advantages. The conscription age is twenty. If the members of the American community are to get a liberal education, which is the education every free citizen of a free community ought to have, they must get it by the time they are twenty years old. . . .

"[The BA] is the recognition accorded a person who has passed through an eight-year elementary school, a four-year high school, and a four-year college. These institutions are regarded as fixed and immutable, to be eternally crowned by the bachelor's degree. What goes on in them is not important. The degree does not stand for education; it stands for a certain number of years in an educational institution, and this is not the same thing. . . .

"If, then, the bachelor's degree has no meaning, why is the action of the University of Chicago, which is an attempt to give it meaning, so bad? The answer is that the degree is the symbol of the status quo. It is the symbol of the eight-year elementary school, the four-year high school, and the four-year college. It is the only thing that holds this system together. If you take away the degree, this system must fall apart—or reorganize. The degree has operated like a protective tariff in favor of this system. If it can be awarded at the end of the sophomore year, then those committed to this system must face the educational problems they have been able to dodge. They must figure out what they are doing at each level and why. They must change the habits of their lives. Such suggestions are disconcerting. . . . What the academic potentates want to do is to keep things as they are. . . . With the world in dissolution the status quo can not be maintained. But even if it could be, we should not attempt it. We should welcome the opportunity which the war has given us to rectify the American educational system."[6]

"I shall be glad," Hutchins wrote the president of one of the deploring organizations, "to have graduating seniors in the institutions of the Southern Association [of Colleges and Secondary Schools] try the examinations that will be given for the bachelor's degree at the University of Chicago."[7] During the new BA's first few years in effect, undergraduate enrollment dropped; many graduate schools (and Chicago's own natural sciences division) refused to recognize the "two-year degree." The deploring and the boycott both subsided, in time, and three years after the adoption of the new degree Hutchins informed the British Association of University Professors that studies by the Chicago Board of Examinations "have demonstrated that students completing the College do as good or better work than graduates of any program of undergraduate study in the country."

"We are signing more government contracts every day," he wrote his friend Professor Malcolm Sharp of the law school.[8] "You wouldn't," he wrote the retired Egyptologist Charles Breasted, "know the old place. We are simply running a big war industry here."[9] He appeared before the neighborhood draft board on behalf of junior administrative officers to ask that they be placed in category 2-A, "indispensable war workers." Program piled on program, in spectroscopy, high-frequency radio, signaling, surveying, and, of course, physics and chemistry. More and more of the campus was commandeered as civilian enrollment of men fell steadily. In August of 1942 the university announced that its facilities were largely being employed for direct war purposes; the navy was using part or all of twelve buildings on the campus, including the men's and women's gymnasiums and the men's dormitories. The air force was training cadets in the field house and glider pilots in the stadium. And—*mirabile dictu*—the university's Charles R. Walgreen Foundation for the Study of American Institutions was giving a series of pep-rally public lectures on democracy and the democratic system.

President Conant of Harvard, a pre-Pearl-Harbor interventionist, said that it was the responsibility of the universities in wartime to guard carefully "the eternal verities." Never again—he was referring to the First World War—would Harvard be allowed to become merely an armed camp because of global conditions. But an armed camp was what Harvard and every other university became in a marvelous hurry. Tuition income everywhere (as much as 80 percent of the revenue of state universities) plummeted with enrollment; in January 1943, Hutchins wrote that he expected no students at Chicago after July except those sent by the government, and in the fall of that year the entire Harvard Graduate School was down to two hundred students. The story was the same across the country.

In 1941 the U.S. Army was staging maneuvers with wooden guns; in 1942 the United States, including Harvard, including Chicago, was the armed camp Conant hoped it wouldn't be, fueling the fires of war all over the earth; exactly six months after the "destruction" of their Pacific Fleet the Americans turned the course of the war in the Battle of Midway. At the beginning of 1944 Hutchins informed the faculty that that year "the income and expenditures of the University of Chicago will be the largest of any university in the world."[10]

At the outset of the conversation the ex-isolationist told the faculty, "We are now engaged in total war. Total war may mean the total extinction, for the time being, at least, of the characteristic functions of the University. I say this as flatly and crudely as I can, not because I expect it to happen but because it seems to me essential that we understand that the setting of our work has completely changed. We are now an instrumentality of total war."[11] Like Lucky Strike green, Chicago maroon had gone to the front.

In telling Malcolm Sharp that he expected only government students to be entering the university in July of 1943, Hutchins said: "The Army program for the eighteen-nineteen-year-olds looks worse and worse. But we have no right to expect that the Army would be interested in education."[12] What then of his fine talk of the university's knowing "what teaching is and how to teach what to whom"? Had he really supposed that the university's knowledge of the liberal arts and the Socratic seminar was what would be wanted? He had been a soldier and had read *Faust* in a pup tent on the Italian front; but it wasn't reading *Faust* in a pup tent on the Italian front that had won that war or any other.

The University's million-dollar-a-year deficits—in a budget of ten million or so—had been ascribable entirely to pure research, the chief glory of a great institution of higher learning. The financial outlook, before Pearl Harbor, had not been rosy; year after year gifts to income, instead of to endowment, had kept the Gothic doors open. Every great university, even the oldest and most heavily endowed, was always in the same case: where was the money to come from to finance the kinds of investigation that only a university would undertake, investigation that might or might not yield results, or yield them in one year or a hundred, or yield them in such form as to have consequences adaptable to the concrete problems of life and society? "If it had not been for the Rockefeller, Carnegie, and Harkness fortunes," said Hutchins retrospectively, "there would have been no such thing as research in American universities [prior to 1939]. A.P. Sloan, chairman of General Motors, told me that all useful inventions came out of the shop: there was no point in supporting basic research. What was true of industry was even truer of government. Government saw no point in research; and the universities never thought of asking its support. If a president or professor had thought of doing so, he would have been restrained by the trustees or regents, who would have been horrified by such a socialistic idea. This war will be won in the laboratories."[13] It would be won in the laboratories, all right; specifically in the laboratories of the University of Chicago on December 2, 1942—though the manner of its winning would not be made known to the world until August 6, 1945, at Hiroshima.

That historic research that culminated in the University of Chicago laboratories was certainly pure research. But it would never have been subsidized by the government had it not promised earth-shaking consequences of a practical order. What ordinarily distinguished the work of the university scientist was its divorce—irresponsibly?—from the end purpose to which it might ultimately be put by others. Hutchins, and he alone, could follow the gleam wherever it might lead, with the "value-free" detachment that the philosopher deplored—the philosopher preoccupied with the ends and the means appropriate to the ends. The commercial or governmental scientist's research was, in itself, just as pure; it might be a dozen, or a hundred, steps removed from application; the researcher might not even know what the application was intended to be; but he knew that he would not be maintained if there were no purpose beyond his own. The purpose he served was somebody else's; the purpose of the university scientist was his own: knowledge for the sake of knowing. There was no such thing in his lexicon as failure—there were discarded hypotheses, tried and found wanting, on the road to knowledge. He was not trying to produce something. The institution which employed him was not trying to produce something. In this sense most of the work being done in the university laboratories after Pearl Harbor was not, strictly, university work.

Thirty days after Pearl Harbor, 50 percent of all the research going forward in the natural sciences at Chicago—up to 80 percent in some departments—was war research specifically designed and supported as such by the federal government. A year later that percentage "in some departments" (physics, certainly) was put at 90 percent. Even as he committed the institution to the whole hog war effort, the educational revolutionary who had done his best to keep his country out of war concluded his January 1942 address to the faculty on a cautionary note that recalled what now seemed to be a bygone Hutchins, or at least a shelved one, to an audience that had never before heard him (and would never again hear him) throw himself and his university into the service of total war:

"Our basic function, intellectual leadership, remains the same. Another has been superimposed upon it which will make it hard, perhaps impossible, to carry on our basic function. . . . Victory can not save civilization. It can merely prevent its destruction by one spectacular method. To formulate, to clarify, to vitalize the ideals which should animate mankind, this task . . . is the incredibly heavy burden which rests, even in total war, upon the universities. If they can not carry it, nobody else will; for nobody else can. If it can not be carried, civilization can not be saved."[14]

Lots the country cared, in 1942, about the incredibly heavy burden to formulate, to clarify, to vitalize the ideals which should animate mankind. It was no time for bemoaning the condition of civilization, at least not of American civilization. There was a war on.

In 1942, five thousand soldiers and sailors, in civilian clothes, took the place of the nine hundred male students who had already left, and more than 60 percent of all the Spring graduates went one way or another to war. Now there was no extracurricular activity to be seen. "The war program," a memo to the alumni said, "demonstrates the University's capacity to serve the nation in a new way."

But President Hutchins, commander in chief of the university's new way of serving, was dissatisfied with the way it was going. "My objection to what the Army is doing," he wrote a friend, "is that it does not seem to me to be good military training." He took to the pages of the *Saturday Evening Post*, under the title, "Blueprint for Wartime Education," to attack what he called the chaos and to suggest the Hutchins Plan, as the *Post* called it, for bringing order out of it. The Hutchins Plan had six major proposals, none of them thereafter adopted in full. ("The war," he said afterward, "lasted only three years longer. That was not time enough for the Army to get moving.") "If," he wrote, summarizing his proposals, "we have a comprehensive plan under the War Manpower Commission, if we prohibit volunteering and competitive recruitment and lower the conscription age to 18, if we select the young people to be educated in terms of the contribution they can make to victory, with a two-year liberal arts course before determining aptitudes for special training, if we pay them, so we can be sure that intelligence and not money gets them into college, then we can supply the leaders we need. . . . I am proposing that the higher learning should be reformed"—getting a lick in as the bombs burst in the air—"to do what we have always said it did—train the minds of the leaders of our country."[15]

The overnight transformation of the university involved the transformation of its faculty. The new men and women—nearly all men—on the campus were almost all of them unidentifiable, and nobody bothered to think of them in terms of academic rank; they were all but nameless government types sent to Chicago to run training programs. But there was one area in which that was not the case at all, and that was physics (and to some extent chemistry).

The new men in physics had been coming in since 1939, indeed since Hitlerism drove some of them out of Germany as refugees. They were famous, a fistful of Nobel Prize winners among them. Some of them were at the university regularly now, some from time to time. They had names like Urey, Franck, Teller, Oppenheimer, Wigner, Rabi, Bethe, Lawrence, Seaborg. Nobel Prize winner Arthur H. Compton, the head of the physics department, was reported to be in charge of the super-hush-hush "Metallurgical Project." Hearing of the Compton project, Mortimer Adler, whose forte was metaphysics, not physics, and who didn't know an atom from an atomizer, said to a friend, "Do you suppose he's split the atom?" (The splitting of the atom nucleus, atomic fission, had been achieved in 1934 by Fermi in Italy and by the Joliot-Curies in France.) The general nature of Compton's recent work was known; around the peacetime faculty-club luncheon tables he had airily predicted that the day would come when a transatlantic liner would cross the ocean for a dime.

The great men of physics and chemistry were not seen much, on or off the campus; they seemed to be much busier than even conscientious research men usually were; and they seemed to be traveling a great deal (no one knew where). They joined in luncheon small talk at the club—very small talk.

They were, on the whole, amiable but uncommunicative, even regarding trivial matters, as if they were afraid that they might say something that might lead to an embarrassing question from someone at the table, a commonplace question like, "Did you ever meet Professor So-and-So in Denmark?" During all of the war years I frequently sat with one or more of them at one of the large round tables at the club—they did not ordinarily segregate themselves at lunch—and I did not ever hear any of them say anything that might lead to a discussion of anything more sensitive than the weather. (I never heard the expression "atomic bomb.")

There was one exception to the reserved (not grim, simply reserved) presence of these giants; a short, rotund Hungarian of whom nothing at all seemed to be known outside the closed world of physics. As I was living at the club at the time and so was he, we often talked at breakfast or in the club residence corridors. I was properly circumspect, to avoid prying; but he displayed an interest in me and my work (as he did in everyone's) that flowered after the war in a personal friendship and an exchange of manuscripts. (One of the hundred-and-one things he did well was writing pixieish short stories. Another was making imperishable observations *à la hongroise*. At the time of the Berlin air lift after the war he said, "We should notify the Russians that if they take one more aggressive step we'll blow ourselves up.") Unlike most, if not all, of his colleagues in and out of science, he dressed very expensively and fastidiously and still managed to look like a bag of laundry. He abhorred manual labor; and long before it was generally known, I was (so to say) privy to the fact that he refused to flush the toilet in his room.

Day after day I had breakfast with the father of the atomic age—not of this or that device that shook the world, but of the discovery that turned it upside down. This little hanka-stanka of a man was Leo Szilard, known very fondly to Hutchins as Leo the Lizard. He and Hutchins enjoyed an immense degree of mutual confidence both during and after the war, and he, along with Enrico Fermi, played a central role in the postwar establishment of the three nuclear institutes on the campus.

On August 2, 1939, Albert Einstein signed a letter to President Roosevelt that began, "Some recent work by E. Fermi and L. Szilard, which has been communicated to me in manuscript, leads me to expect that the element uranium may be turned into a new and important source of energy in the immediate future. . . . It may become possible to set up nuclear chain reactions in a large mass of uranium. . . . This new phenomenon would also lead to the construction of bombs, and it is conceivable—though much less certain—that extremely powerful bombs of a new type may thus be constructed." The letter had been drafted by Szilard after the material for it had been presented to Einstein (who had no expertise in nuclear physics) by Szilard and Edward Teller, the subsequent "father of the H-bomb." It was in response to the Einstein letter that the "Manhattan Engineering District" and the "Metallurgical Laboratory"— code names for the atomic bomb project—were established a few months later.

Szilard was a mystery man among the mystery men when he came to Chicago with Fermi from Columbia at the outset of the Metallurgical Project. He was a bachelor of obviously independent means who accepted important research appointments in Europe and America without salary. At St. Bartholomew's Hospital in London he had discovered what is known as the Szilard-Chalmers effect, the basis of so-called "hot-atom" chemistry, and with Einstein he had developed a liquid-metal pumping system. All his scientific patents he turned over to the British and U.S. governments.

The total scientific cosmopolitan, he was all over the world lot in nuclear studies. Well before the war his knowledge that the production of a nuclear explosive would require great quantities of uranium combined with his knowledge of Einstein's friendship with the Belgian royal family to produce a letter to the Belgian Queen Elizabeth, which effectively urged that government to keep the Belgian Congo's uranium out of German hands. At the very outset of the Metallurgical Project Szilard crusaded for absolute secrecy, long before anyone in the American government understood what the odds were. That secrecy was recognized after the war as a major factor in preventing the German scientists from constructing an atomic pile. An exotic genius, Szilard, as the French critic Jacques Monod said, "knew that meaningful ideas are more important than any ego." It was Szilard, said Teller long afterward, "who prodded us into working on atomic energy." The paternity of the nuclear age was, of course, multiple; the godfathers were the two theorists of modern science, Einstein with his general theory of relativity and Max Planck with his quantum mechanics. The fathers were a dozen men and women in Europe and America who had one man as a referent in common: Leo Szilard.

22 Unhappy Warrior

This was the company into which Hutchins was thrown (or had thrown himself) for the duration—the "generals" of Washington (many of them civilians but all of them happy warriors) and the sententious scientists. The business that brought them together was the kind of investigation in which Hutchins had no interest or competence. Apart from the people in the laboratories, he alone had been told what the project really was and what progress was being made on it; and what even he knew, he knew on a strictly need-to-know basis. He had gone to his deans with the government's proposal that Chicago take it on, and then to his trustees, and he had had to ask both groups to take him, and the proposal, almost entirely on faith.

He was permitted to tell them only that the project had to do with the possible discovery of the technique for manufacturing a new kind of weapon which, if it could be built, might alone win the war; that there was no limit to the demands which might be made upon the university by the government (and the army) in connection with the investigation; that it was an unbelievably expensive kind of investigation that had to be conducted on a half-dozen different fronts all at once because of the war urgency; and that the urgency was critical because it was possible that the Germans were trying to produce the same weapon. He was not allowed to mention uranium, from which it was supposed that the explosive material would have to be extracted by an ás yet unknown process; he knew (because Szilard knew) that one of the first things the Germans had done when they took over Czechoslovakia in 1938 was stop the export of uranium from one of the world's few major deposits there.

He was asked (by one of his trustees) if there was the possibility of physical danger to the university "or the city." He said he would have to

250

find out about that, and several weeks later reported that he had been told that such danger appeared to be unlikely but could not be excluded. One of his deans—McKeon, of humanities—recalled many years later that Hutchins' reply to the question whether any other institution had been approached by the government was that Harvard had turned it down for fear it might fail and that Columbia had rejected it for other reasons. (The implication in the case of Columbia was either that it might be physically dangerous or that the great scientific strength on Morningside Heights lay in other areas than that of the project). No source other than McKeon is to be found for the Harvard/Columbia story in any of the literature of the project or of the institutions involved or their heads. Hutchins was free to say that one of the reasons Chicago was asked to undertake the project was its location in the country's interior.

Informed only in bare outline, prohibited from sharing even that degree of information, and precluded from asking questions of the scientists, he occupied a peculiarly lonely position—all the lonelier for a so recently vehement opponent of war and a long-time critic of what he called scientism, the Deweyite faith that man's problems were soluble in the laboratory. It was a lonely post and an unentertaining one, running a vast congeries of barracks, drill grounds, job programs, and secret laboratories. He was the maintenance man, or custodian, of a half-billion-dollar multipurpose housing project with which he had no integral connection. The man who a few months earlier addressed the country so eloquently on the proposition, "The Proposition Is Peace," was now administering an establishment dedicated to the proposition that the proposition was war.

He saw less and less of his friends, more and more of people he had nothing in common with except the endless making of endless administrative arrangements. The Office of the President was now the Central Administration, falling all over itself with vice-presidents who were capable of doing all the donkey work and passing it on to him in the final, contractual stages. He was able to depend on them, but they were not his friends, and one or two of them were less friendly than that. The notable exception was W. C. Munnecke, Wilbur, Will, or Willie, a friend and neighbor of the Mortimer Adlers and a singularly gifted and literate businessman. Hutchins had kidnapped him from the vice-presidency of Marshall Field and Company, and he served as liaison between the administration and the echelons of the Metallurgical Project, including the "generals" (some in Washington, some on the campus) and the scientists. Munnecke knew the names of all the people involved, visited the various sites and laboratories at Argonne and Oak Ridge—and remembered having to convince the General Accounting Office that a bill for one ton of heavy water at

$250,000 was OK to pass for payment ("That's what the Canadians were charging for the stuff"). He was over his ears in procurement and budgeting, and, along with Szilard, he was the one person directly connected with the secret project whose company Hutchins enjoyed.[1]

Dutifully and despondently Hutchins went about the business that so radically distinguished the culture of the mechanic, including the mechanical wizard, from the culture of the philosopher. One of the traditional taunts of his academic enemies had been, "The philosopher has no laboratory." The philosopher had laboratories enough now, but they were not conducting philosophical research. Even the despondent, dutiful philosopher could not sustain himself on that sort of diet. He was bound to break loose, one way or another; many ways, likely.

Many ways. One Sunday in April of 1942 he preached in the university chapel (still filled, that first spring of the war, with the kind of student, the Chicago student, who would soon vanish for the duration). His sermon was a kind of cry—and not a war cry: "I am not so naive as to assume that the American people can become good overnight, or that if they try and fail they will lose the war and lose the peace. The question is rather what are the ideals that we set before us and how sincere and serious is the effort we make to achieve them.

". . . [The American people] do not need to be told that war calls for equality of sacrifice and that neither capital nor labor can be allowed to extract profit from a process which is sending thousands of men to their deaths. They do not need to be told that racial and religious discrimination in the Army, Navy, and war industries is undemocratic. They do not need to be told that rural slums and urban slums are undemocratic or that the condition of those on public relief is as undemocratic as it was before the war. They do need to be told that it is undemocratic to arrange the distribution of educational opportunity so that the child in the poor State gets little compared with the child in the rich State, the child of a poor family gets little compared with the child of a rich family, and the negro child gets little compared with the white. . . .

"We can try to establish the good society here and now." *Here and now*, with a world war on. "The effort is not expensive." As if any effort that wasn't the war effort would be seen to be inexpensive. "It will not divert the country from its military endeavors." As if anything that wasn't military wouldn't divert the country from its military endeavors. "Unless we make it, our military endeavors will fail." In the event, the effort wasn't made, and the military endeavors succeeded. "We are accustomed to the doctrine that mere defensive military operations can not win a war. It is just as true that mere defensive social, economic, and political operations, mere defense of the status quo, will lose a war." But the war would be won for the status quo. "It will also lose the peace. And international organization, without a change of heart, would be the greatest prize of greed and ambition, and hence the most alarming portent of universal destruction, that the world has ever seen." This was three years before anyone thought of the United Nations. "We need a new order for America. If we do not provide it, Hitler will." We didn't provide it, and neither did Hitler. Men who do not want to live like beasts must make up their minds to live like men." But there was a war on.

He spoke, that Sunday, to a sympathetic audience of his own students, Chicago students, Hutchins students. But the audience outside had disappeared. His sermon was neither broadcast nor printed.[2]

That summer, the first summer of the war, was the liveliest in the history of the Chicago campus. Chicago's quarter system had always included an abbreviated session in the midwestern heat under loungelike conditions with classes under the trees and something like an idyllic tempo. Most faculty and most students were traditionally away; most administrators, too, including, invariably, the chief administrator. Hutchins did not know what it was to have a holiday. He had no hobbies and no interests unrelated to his work. But he could get work done out of the office that he couldn't in it. And he was pretty forcibly urged by his wife to get away for the two summer months or so with her, their small girls relegated to the care of a none too satisfactory nanny. The two of them worked—Maude Hutchins was writing novels—and took long walks with Mrs. Hutchins' very expensive Great Dane. Ordinarily they went east, taking a seashore house in his ancestral Connecticut. There they lived in isolation.

There, in Connecticut, in spite of the fact that the summer quarter of 1942 was the university's busiest since its establishment, he made the most of his isolation by working on a project every day and into the night. But it was not a war project. It was an elaborate exercise in orthodox scholarship, such as he had not done since Yale and would never take time to do again—a two-part treatise on the political philosophy of Edmund Burke, complete with a hundred or so footnotes citing both eighteenth-century and modern sources and commentaries in English, French, and American letters. The two parts were published as "The Theory of Oligarchy," in the Maritain celebratory volume of *The Thomist* in January 1943, and "The Theory of the State," in *The Review of Politics* for April of 1943). They traced Burke's flamboyant inconsistencies and self-contradictions, from his egalitarian support of natural rights as anterior to the state, in the case of the American colonies, to the blackest sort of reactionary defense of the prerevolutionary monarchy of absolutist France. The two essays together constituted a serious and substantial contribution to American revolutionary theory and its derivation from Locke.

Here, then, was the chief executive officer of a $150,000,000 war plant (with a sudden annual budget twice that) turning out assembly-line glider pilots, meteorologists, atomic bombs—running the operation by remote control, telephone, telegraph, scribbled notes, through a network of hastily installed vice-presidents, and devoting himself to a close analysis of an eighteenth-century Englishman. What emerges from this historical juxtaposition is the recognition that the chief executive was so little enamored of the assembly line he operated that he would do anything else at all, preferably something that was two centuries and an ocean distant, to get away from it for a bit.

It was a solid job, the unmistakably substantial work of a constitutional lawyer catapulted, at a most paradoxical season, into constitutional history and constitutional philosophy. But if it hadn't been Burke it would have been—and soon it was—something else.

The Burke project was his own idea—unlike most of the things he turned up doing. He sounded as if he was pulling the Bad Man trick when he observed (as he often did) that the enterprises he directed were all thrust on him by his friends. His modesty exaggerated the fact, but not entirely. Anybody who wanted to get anything done that needed forthright leadership in the cultural arena came to Hutchins with it; he was known as a fearless (even a reckless) innovator.

It was not only the cranks with a dozen bad ideas who forced themselves on him; his associates with a good idea found him a pushover for it. It was Bill Benton who broached the university's acceptance of the Encyclopaedia Britannica and put up the necessary $100,000 to transfer the ownership of the ancient and honorable enterprise from Sears Roebuck. The deal was consummated the day after pearl Harbor at a luncheon Benton arranged with the Sears board chairman, Robert E. Wood; and it was Benton who reorganized the business and ran it—with Hutchins in and out as chairman of its editorial board. It was Benton who conceived the fifty-four-volume Britannica set of the Great Books of the Western World, Mortimer Adler who conceived the best-selling Syntopicon as a two-volume topical index to the set—with Hutchins in and out as editor-in-chief. It was the philosophical economist John U. Nef who concocted the Committee on Social Thought as an independent graduate body within the university; Bruno Bettelheim, whom Hutchins brought from Germany, who directed the university's Orthogenic School; Antonio Borgese, the great Italian émigré journalist whom Hutchins brought to Chicago, who propagated the Committee to Frame a World Constitution—with Hutchins as chairman—and Rexford Guy Tugwell who later on thought of drafting a new American Constitution under the aegis of Hutchins' Center for the Study of Democratic Institutions. It was Barr and Buchanan whose idea it was to establish St. John's College—with Hutchins as head of the board of trustees. What all of these men (and others who came to him with other schemes) had in common was the friendship of a powerfully placed man who recognized a lively notion and a lively need and was willing to assume the leadership and responsibility to carry it out. Nominally he administered a university; by choice he engaged his intellect and his energies in taking it apart and putting it back together. But neither his nominal nor his chosen activities exhausted his ranging intellect and his vagrant energies. His fervent admirer Borgese saw in him a born *condottiere*, a kind of intellectual mercenary chief.

So it was that in December 1942 at an Encyclopaedia Britannica board meeting, Henry Luce, Hutchins' old friend from Yale, sent him a note reading, "How do I find out about freedom of the press and what my obligations are?" Luce's mind had evidently wandered from the business of the meeting, and Hutchins, whose mind may have wandered in still other directions, replied, "I don't know." Luce then sent him another note reading, "Why don't we set up a commission on freedom of the press and find out what it is?" The two men talked when the meeting adjourned, and the outcome was a $200,000 grant from Luce's Time, Inc., to the university, under whose financial auspices the Commission on Freedom of the Press was established as an independent entity. The commission held seventeen two- or three-day meetings between 1944 (there was still a war on) and 1946, and in 1947 issued its report, "A Free and Responsible Press."

The report was the original exploding cigar. Its burden was that the periodical press—primarily newspapers, but incidentally magazines, movies, and radio—failed miserably to discharge its moral obligation to the community, more often than not reflecting the views of its owners and advertisers in the treatment of news, and pandering to the lowest tastes of the readers who had to depend on it for the understanding of the great issues that confronted them in a democratic society. The press as a whole was outraged by the report, and Luce himself was unhappy with it (especially, perhaps, with its criticism of the kind of journalism his publications, among others, represented).

Hutchins had long jousted with elements of the press, having taken on Hearst in the earliest days of his Chicago presidency when that mad magnate attacked the public schools, and having later conducted a public feud with Colonel Robert R. McCormick's antediluvian *Chicago Tribune* during the early years of the New Deal. (McCormick forgave Hutchins when the latter shared his own anti-interventionism before Pearl Harbor, but found him a dangerous Red again and resumed the feud upon the release of the Press Commission's report.) Although Hutchins enjoyed cordial personal relations with several newspapermen, including Barry Bingham, the publisher of the *Louisville Courier-Journal*, he had playfully assaulted the daily papers for years. As early as 1930 he told the American Society of Newspaper Editors, "In spite of the frightful lies you have printed about me I still believe everything you print about other people." He informed his audience on that occasion that in his new post he hoped to be able to introduce education into the educational institutions of the country so that "in the long run we may be able to produce a generation that will demand better things of you."[3] Addressing that same society after the publication of the Press Commission's report, he said, "All over the country you attacked the Report. I hope you will read it some time. But for fear you won't, I shall quote a passage from it that will give you the main idea: 'If modern society requires great agencies of mass communication, if these concentrations become so powerful that they are a threat to democracy, if democracy can not solve the problem simply by breaking them up—then those agencies must control themselves or be controlled by government. If they are controlled by government, we lose our chief safeguard against totalitarianism—and at the same time take a long step toward it.' "[4]

He reserved his loving barbs for the National Conference of Editorial Writers: "My words today were written to the music of that moving American folk-song, 'I'm Bringing You a Big Bouquet of Roses, One for Each Time You Broke My Heart.' Since some of you said that you could not grasp the Report of the Commission on Freedom of the Press because my style was dark and dense, I shall try to tell you what I think of you in words both few and short. In words both few and short, you are guilty of inveteracy and recidivism. . . . I think you are teachers. I did not say you were good teachers. . . . The American people should be eagerly looking to the press for guidance. I do not need to tell you that they are not doing so. . . . The reason the people who buy your newspapers do not take your advice is that they do not believe what you say. . . . They may buy the papers to find out what happened to Dagwood, or who won the fifth race at Santa Anita, or what is on sale at Gimbel's. They read the editorials, if at all, for amusement; they do not read them for instruction. Yet I think you are teachers. If you are to have pupils, you must establish public confidence in yourselves."[5]

The execration of the commission's report was not universal; among those who praised it were the *New York Times* and the *Herald-Tribune* (and the *Herald-Tribune*'s Walter Lippmann). Even though Luce's *Time* magazine thought that "for the time and money and the caliber of the men, it was a disappointing report," his *Fortune* magazine, which printed the report, found it "important, balanced, meaty, difficult," and found that its obscurities and overcondensations were "inexcusable."[6] But the publishers as a whole, with Colonel McCormick in the van, had difficulty understanding its warning of government control as warning and not advocacy. (One newspaper captioned its editorial, "Professors Blindly Try to Curb Press by Regulations to End All Our Liberties.")[7] What the report advocated, as one device for staving off the totalitarianism of government control, was the establishment of an independent council to appraise and report on the performance of the press on a continuing basis. The commission said, "Some agency which reflects the ambitions of the American people for its press should exist for the purpose of comparing the accomplishments of the press with the aspirations which the people have for it."

This was the crux of the press's horror at the report. Addressing the same society whose panjandrums he had attacked in 1930, Hutchins accused it of putting itself in a class with the Eleusinian mysteries and insisting that it could criticize everybody else without anybody being allowed to criticize it. There was—and continued to be—so little criticism of the press in America that the report, in spite of the denunciation, soon became a fixture in journalistic studies the country over, and remained one. Its status in academic work consisted precisely in the fact that its members were not special pleaders. Their reputation for objectivity could hardly have been higher.

Although the commission had interviewed no end of practitioners of the profession and studied no end of professional documents in the course of its conscientious labors, the press lords and their executive hirelings appeared to be cruelly stung by the fact that the commissioners were not journalists. The president of the American Society of Newspaper Editors found them "left-wingers" inexperienced in the trade; the *Chicago Tribune* found them "totalitarian thinkers" who wanted "to stop effective criticism of New Deal Socialism, the one-world doctrine, and internationalism," and devoted column after front-page column to the Red connections of every one of them—and of Luce and William Benton (who had made a supplementary grant of fifteen thousand dollars to the commission on behalf of the Encyclopaedia Britannica).

Hutchins had taken the commission chairmanship when Judge Learned Hand declined it. The other members (whom Hutchins appointed) were Professor of Law Zechariah Chafee of Harvard, Professor of Economics

John M. Clark of Columbia, General Counsel of the Pennsylvania Railroad (and Professor of Law at Pennsylvania) John Dickinson, Emeritus Professor of Philosophy William E. Hocking of Harvard, Professor of Law Harold D. Lasswell of Yale, former Assistant Secretary of State Archibald MacLeish, Emeritus Professor of Political Science Charles E. Merriam of Chicago, Professor of Ethics and Philosophy of Religion Reinhold Niebuhr of Union Theological Seminary, Professor of Anthropology Robert Redfield of Chicago, Chairman Beardsley Ruml of the Federal Reserve Bank of New York, Professor of History Arthur M. Schlesinger of Harvard, and President George N. Shuster of Hunter College. The commission's foreign advisers were equally distinguished and intrepid: General Manager John Grierson of the Canadian Wartime Information Board, former Chinese Ambassador to the United States Hu Shih, President Jacques Maritain of the Free French School for Advanced Studies (and later French ambassador to the Vatican), and the German Professor of Philosophy Kurt Rietzler of the New School for Social Research.

The membership of the commission reflected both an aptitude and a strong disposition on Hutchins' part to use his own eminence and persuasive powers to round up blue-ribbon types as working members of his enterprises. There was nothing nominal in the service he had in mind, in the Press Commission, or in subsequent undertakings of an ad hoc character. He was completely conscious of his influence and completely comfortable about exploiting it to obtain the labors, let alone the signatures, of distinguished men and women (nearly always men). For both personal and professional reasons he was a hard man to say No to, and his reputation for discrimination was itself persuasive in enlisting glittering cooperation in his ventures. Scornful as he was of the ordinary gimmickry of public relations, in this one respect he was the PR man's dream; the people he brought with him guaranteed significant attention to his projects. There would come a time, long afterward, when he would find it difficult, and at the last impossible, to enlist the great men he sought to materialize his vision of an unaffiliated body of academicians engaged in continuous discussion of the great issues—a time when he no longer occupied the bully pulpit at Chicago.

23 The Good News of Damnation

The atomic age did not begin with a bang. It began with a nod by Professor Enrico Fermi. The nod, that afternoon of December 2, 1942, was the signal for pulling a cadmium rod out of a metal "pile" constructed in a former squash racquet court under the abandoned football stands in Stagg Field at the University of Chicago, initiating the self-sustaining nuclear chain reaction that the world's physicists had been desperately trying to achieve. The occasion—and the spot—was suitably memorialized three years later by a self-congratulatory plaque.

The university's publicity man, Bill Morgenstern, wanted the plaque to say something like "For Better or for Worse," or "For Good or Ill"—his memorandum is lost—but he was overruled. The release of atomic energy was the marvel of marvels. It would change the world more profoundly than anything since the capture of electricity. It had to be forever celebrated in bronze, with the university's great seal bearing the motto, *Crescat Scientia, Vita Excolatur*, Let Knowledge Grow, That Life May Be Enriched. An innocent invocation. In that converted squash court knowledge had grown, and human life would be enriched by it in Hiroshima on August 6, 1945.

"This is the biggest thing in history," said Robert Maynard Hutchins in a note to a friend. And it had been managed by Hutchins, under whose aegis some $400 million of government money had been spent pell-mell in the search for the secret. He it was who took on the task at the government's request, who hired the great scientists domestic and foreign. He turned the university's facilities over to them, having persuaded his board of trustees to go along with an important piece of "war work." He signed all the contracts (*one* of which, the operation of the plutonium works at Oak Ridge, Tennessee, doubled the university's budget).

He was the boss, nominally. His boss was the big boss in the White House who exercised his authority as follows: "This weapon is to be used against Japan between now and August 10. I have told the Secretary of War, Mr. Stimson, to use it so that military objectives and soldiers and sailors are the target and not women and children. He and I are in accord. The target will be a purely military one and we will issue a warning statement."[1]

They were all nominal bosses. The biggest thing in history was too big for Harry Truman. It was too big for Winston Churchill, who said, the day the bomb was exploded, "This revelation of the secrets of nature, long mercifully withheld from men, should arouse the most solemn reflections in the mind and conscience of every human being capable of comprehension." And of course it was too big for the scientists whom Hutchins had hired—and, of course, for Hutchins, who secretly masterminded the secret effort of the "Chicago group" to persuade Mr. Truman not to use the bomb they had invented, not even against the *purely military target* Mr. Truman had ordered.

It was too big for them all. But as of August 6—and again on August 9, when the second bomb exploded over Nagasaki—the American people were so exhilarated with their country's possession of the ultimate firepower that very few of them were worried lest it prove to be their master instead of their servant and one day, not too far distant, set them to digging holes in the ground to hide from it. On August 12, six days after Hiroshima, Robert Maynard Hutchins deplored its use as "unnecessary" and said that the United States, in using it, had lost its moral prestige. But he thought that the mushroom cloud might, however improbably, have a silver lining: "Leon Bloy, the French philosopher, referred to the good news of damnation doubtless on the theory that none of us would be Christians if we were not afraid of perpetual hell-fire. It may be that the atomic bomb is the good news of damnation, that it may frighten us into that Christian character and those righteous actions and those positive political steps necessary to the creation of a world society, not a thousand or five hundred years hence, but now."[2]

There was one man who did not seem to see the silver lining. When Albert Einstein, the godfather of the bomb, heard that it had been exploded he said one word: "Weh!" (which in German means, "Woe!").[3]

By VE Day, May 7, 1945, with "the biggest thing in history" still three months ahead, its prime contractor was validating his prewar claim that he would like to join, not the America First Committee but a committee for Humanity First. Immediately after Germany's surrender in May he preached a sermon of thanksgiving and prayer in the university chapel.

The devastation of Hiroshima was as yet unimaginable. "We can only imagine," he told his congregation, "the devastation that has been wrought in Europe.

"We come now to the real test of our professional ideals, for the sake of which we claimed to enter the war. We did so, we said, not to save our own skins, but to make possible a peaceful, just, humane society, which should embrace all the peoples of the earth. If that is what we want, we must now sacrifice, not our lives, but our goods to save millions of our fellow-men from starvation. . . . There are already some indications that we shall be less willing to sacrifice our goods than we have been our lives (or at least the lives of our soldiers and sailors). Educated people now come to the test of their education. Every educated person knows enough about human nature to know that war is brutalizing and that propaganda should be received with skepticism. . . . At this juncture we can afford to remember what Edmund Burke said of us: 'I do not know the method of drawing up an indictment against a whole people.'

"We can not support the thesis that because German leaders acted illegally, therefore they should be treated illegally. . . . We should remember that one of the points which Job urged in his own favor when seeking relief from his own misfortunes was that he did not rejoice when his enemy fell.

"We are now on the verge of forgetting history, and forgetting common sense as well. . . . To feed German citizens one-third of what the American soldier gets, to reduce Germany to a subsistence level; to make Germany a pastoral country; to split Germany into little states . . . [these] most inhuman proposals are brought forward. . . . The peace of the world depends upon the restoration of the German and Japanese people. The wildest atrocity stories can not alter the simple truths that all men are human, that no men are beasts, that all men are the children of God. . . . If we are going to have one good world, the Germans and the Japanese will somehow have to be incorporated into it."⁴

But he was already doubtful that there was going to be "one good world." The United Nations charter was taking shape at the conference in San Francisco, excluding Germany and Japan, reposing actual governance in the Security Council composed of the great powers, and preserving national sovereignty by means of the single-vote veto in the Security Council and the rejection of the organization's authority over the internal affairs of the member states. The charter—basically the same as the ill-fated League of Nations covenant—gave Hutchins the occasion to fire the opening gun in what would come to be an unremitting crusade for world government.⁵

"You can not at one and the same time join a world organization and stay out of it. You can not have all the advantages of membership in a world organization and none of the disadvantages. You can not have all the attributes of sovereignty and give up some of them. . . . You can't, for example, have an effective world court if you are going to insist that the court can't judge your country without its consent [as the United States insisted]. You can't have an effective world organization if the organization can act only when it is unanimous [as the charter provided for the Security Council]. This . . . misleads people into thinking that they can rely on the world organization when actually the world is as disorganized as ever.

"Equally pernicious is the doctrine that all right lies with the big powers and that their security and spheres of influence are the primary concern of the world. This is the surest foundation for the next war. . . . We can not pretend to have a world society unless all the members of it are equally subject to law and unless the society is founded on justice, not to our allies alone, but also to our defeated enemies. An unjust peace and an unjust world organization make the next war inevitable."[6]

A month after Germany's surrender he spoke on the "new realism" at the university's June 15 convocation and told his audience that Hitler had conquered the United States: "The words peace, justice, cooperation, community, and charity have fallen out of our vocabulary. . . . The new realism suggests that the one powerful nation in the world which claimed to hate machiavellianism and repudiated the doctrine that military superiority implied moral superiority must now embrace these theories or be accused of being 'soft.' A nation which fought two wars to end war must now, in the hour of victory, plan to have the greatest navy in the world; it must have perpetual conscription; and it must get all the island bases it can lay its hands on." He attacked the emerging Nuremberg doctrine which would soon put the German leaders on trial by a tribunal of the victorious allies:

"Hitler's conquest of America proceeds apace as we succumb to the idea that social and political problems can be most effectively solved with the aid of a firing squad. What [the German leaders] did to deserve punishment at the hands of human judges must have been illegal at the time it was done. If the judgment is to command the respect of Americans it must be shown that the act was one which a patriotic American would not have committed if he had been a patriotic German. . . . We must remember the ancient doctrine that no man is a good judge in his own cause. And it would do us no harm to apply the maxim of equity that one must come into court with clean hands."

The German people were certainly guilty, he said, of one crime: indifference. "If any nation can be found which is not guilty of this crime, then it is qualified to judge the German people for their indifference to the crimes committed by Germans against Germans. As for ourselves, it is not unfair to say that the American people, except for a few million of them, are guilty of indifference in the face of race prejudice, economic exploitation, political corruption, and the degradation of oppressed minorities."

He concluded the convocation address by taking a premonitory view of the long-term relations between the two great allies so recently united in the bloody and victorious struggle, the Soviet Union and the United States. "To state the thing in its lowest terms, in terms of money and power, which the new realists claim are the only terms there are, our political and economic interests require a prosperous Germany and Japan. Our interests may, in the light of current readjustments of power in Europe and Asia, require a strong Germany and Japan. But we can not trade with those who have nothing to exchange. And we can not be sure that our present allies will always be our friends and that we shall not some time need the help of our present enemies."[7]

All this with Hiroshima still to come. In the euphoric spring of 1945 the new realism was sweeping everything before it. Americans who spoke in Hutchins' unpalatable fashion were few. With the USSR in partial ruin and twenty million of its people dead, the only great nation left on earth supported the tough policies of the Truman administration. The whole United States was still a war plant, operating at its productive peak. It was no time for an American—above all, an American who had led the pre–Pearl Harbor forces of isolation—to talk like Cassandra. Cassandra may have been right, but she wasn't popular. In the nationwide flush of victory and the nearly universal cry for punishment and vengeance, the Hutchins audience was small.

And Hiroshima was still to come, to crown the United States in its unchallenged and unchallengeable mastery of the world: the new colossus. But Hiroshima would alter Hutchins' status radically. Overnight he would appear as the man who had stage-managed the mastery of the ultimate force, "the biggest thing in history." The pre–Pearl Harbor nay-sayer would be redeemed.

His audience would grow correspondingly. But he wouldn't be speaking for the scientists ideologically, most of whom, then as always, seem to have no pronounced social views—or none that differed from those of the community at large. In his August 12, 1945, appearance on the university's Round-Table of the Air over NBC—six days after Hiroshima, three days after Nagasaki—having denounced the use of the bomb as militarily unnecessary, he renewed his old assault on the status quo at home and abroad (especially at home) and struck up for a new world: "If the government has succeeded in creating a notable curse with two billion dollars and the concentrated effort of thousands of scientists over four or five years, why could we [not ask that] the government devote the same money and effort to the elimination of some [of] the already existing curses such as cancer, influenza, venereal disease, unemployment at home, or starvation abroad? . . . If we are going to have a society which knows what to do with these constant surprises from the physical scientists, we are going to have to have an entirely different level of general intelligence from the one which we have been used to. . . ."

"Up to last Monday"—the day of Hiroshima—"I must confess that I did not have much hope for the world state. I believed that no moral basis for it existed and that we had no world conscience and no sense of world community sufficient to keep a world state together. But the alternatives now seem clear. One is world suicide; another is agreement among sovereign states to refrain from using the bomb. This will not be effective. The only hope, therefore, of abolishing war is through the monopoly of atomic force by a world organization."[8]

Thus the good news of damnation for those who were willing to hear it. Its audience did not appear to include the victorious nations. The United States for the moment dominated the world by virtue of its monopoly of atomic force, and had no disposition to make that force available to others, least of all to the Russians. The "world organization" was in place, already stigmatized as a talking club, with the sovereign victors each and severally retaining their rights of independent action. The scientists basked in their new, above-it-all grandeur; but sixty-five of them at Chicago, under the whip of Leo Szilard, and with the secret connivance of Hutchins, had spent the weeks before Hiroshima trying desperately to persuade Mr. Truman not to use the bomb except in a harmless demonstration which would convince the Japanese of the hopelessness of further resistance.

After the successful Trinity test in July, Szilard drafted a petition to President Truman, asking him not to order the bomb dropped. It was urged, inter alia, on both long- and short-term moral grounds, that the Japanese were not Nazis and should not be subjected to the massacre proportions of a weapon that might have seemed more appropriate to use against Germany. "A nation which sets the precedent of using these newly liberated forces of nature for the purpose of destruction may have to bear the responsibility of opening the door to an era of devastation on an unimaginable scale." At Los Alamos, where production of the bomb was almost complete, the two leading scientists, Edward Teller and Robert Oppenheimer, though they would later split when the latter vainly opposed the development of the "super" hydrogen bomb, agreed that the petition should not be circulated there, and it wasn't; and the Oak Ridge plutonium works scientists in Tennessee followed suit. Szilard and his Chicago colleagues—and not all of them—stood alone.[9]

The Chicago group never succeeded in getting as far as Mr. Truman with their petition. With Szilard leading their forces, they were finally able to meet with Secretary of State Jimmy Byrnes, who complained, rightly, that this Szilard was trying to tell him what to do in the highest matter of national policy.[10] What Szilard told him was not to drop the atomic bomb on Japan, and Byrnes replied (so Szilard reported to Hutchins), "Congress would never understand how you could appropriate and spend two billion dollars and have nothing to show for it." Szilard said, "Well, why don't you get an uninhabited island and drop the bomb there and invite the Japanese to watch?" And Byrnes replied, "It might not go off."

Germany was out of the war. The Americans would have only two bombs ready at Los Alamos. The government and its advisers (including its scientific advisers) were afraid that the demonstration might prove to be a dud and that, even if the bomb should be exploded successfully, the Japanese might not believe that there were more in the American arsenal. (Announcing the Hiroshima explosion on August 6, President Truman said *both* that "there must never be another war" *and* that the United States would go on atomic-bombing Japanese cities until there was an unconditional surrender.) There was another high matter of national policy which was purely political: with the cold war already in its early stages and the Americans aware that the Russians intended to attack Japan from the east and get in on the kill, the actual use of the bomb against Japan would intimidate our glorious ally the Soviet Union, which was already overspreading eastern (and threatening central and southern) Europe.

Though the Chicago group of sixty-five included some of the foremost nuclear physicists there, it was unable to obtain the support of such men as Fermi and Compton, to whom most of their senior and junior colleagues deferred in the matter. Japan, almost entirely blockaded and its cities largely burned out, was known to have made no headway in atomic research and was attempting, through the USSR, to arrange surrender negotiations; but the Japanese would probably go on fighting in face of conventional weapon superiority rather than surrender unconditionally. For this reason alone the American public would doubtless have voted for the decision which bade fair to save hundreds of thousands of American (and Japanese) lives in an infantry invasion of the home islands.

The war-wearied masses of mankind were willing to accept peace—that is, the Japanese surrender—at any price and rest their come-easy-go-easy confidence for the future in the United Nations. Within five years of its creation, and within five years of Mr. Truman's proclamation that there must never be another war, Mr. Truman himself (only later getting the approval of a helpless Congress) brought the United States into another war, this time in Korea, as a "UN police force," though the two opposing sides both had the active support of UN members and were both entitled (if either was) to wave the already tattered UN flag. After Hiroshima and Nagasaki some physicists, including some who had approved of the use of the bomb, began to chafe under the onus of being used as magnificently remunerated stooges for government policy in general and military policy in particular. Hutchins said bluntly that now that the war was over the University of Chicago would not do any more classified research; he was, nevertheless, insistent on the continued government control of atomic power rather than see it fall into the hands of the few great industrial organizations with resources sufficient to exploit it.[11]

The two-billion-dollar bomb project, together with the other government-subsidized war research and training programs, had already changed the character of scientific research in the universities. Before the war, research was a private, poorly paid occupation, almost a hobby of individual professors and groups of professors.

But now, even in Washington, there were men who, at the very outset of the war, thought it possible that the war would (as Hutchins put it) be won in the laboratories. With the success of the bomb the government spigot was opened wide and the flow of money into the universities was increased enormously. Recalling the years immediately after Hiroshima, the microbiologist Ernest Borek of the University of Colorado Medical Center, said: "In addition to grants, emoluments began to come our way. The profession of research, which had been highly selective, became easily accessible. Graduate education was subsidized, post-doctoral fellowships became plentiful. . . . Career development awards [paid] a young scientist's salary for five years. . . . The so-called lifetime professorships [conferred] freedom from teaching . . . for a whole career."

At the same time the atmosphere of the university changed, in the social sciences. (Only the humanities escaped the governmental embrace, retreating ever further into the recesses of the campus.) "Since one [had to] publish to get grants," Professor Borek said, "and promotion in many institutions [hinged] on the size of the grants, publication and grants rather than discovery became the goals of the laboratory. . . . As large grants for medical research became available, entrepreneurial ability in some cases was added to scientific ability in securing funds, laboratories, and research associates. . . . The researcher became an employer."[12]

The government's wartime largesse had not come free of charge. "The one thing we know with certainty about the universities of the West, and particularly the American universities, is that they are very useful in the manufacture of armaments," said Hutchins after the war. "I think you could say that what happened during the war, when the scientists showed they could blow up the world, was the real beginning of the now general conviction that the road to power, and perhaps to prosperity, resides in these great enterprises that were formerly intellectual and are now the tools of government policy.

"Institutions are supported to solve problems selected by the government and to train men and women selected by the government, in fields and by methods prescribed by the government, using a staff assembled in terms of requirements laid down by the government." So he spilled the patriotic beans and gave voice to the warning that "a government which has once discovered that universities can be used to solve immediate problems is likely to intensify the practice as its problems grow more serious."[13]

A generation afterward the prediction had materialized in every university, and especially in what were known as the high-status private institutions. (But the scientific research work of a few state schools like the University of California at Berkeley was also dominated by government funding.) Revisiting his alma mater in 1967, John Gunther found that the University of Chicago, apart from the $85-million-a-year government support of the Argonne National Laboratory established by the university in connection with wartime research, had federal contracts representing almost one-third of its entire expenditure and more than one-half of its research funds. The then president of the institution, George W. Beadle, was bemoaning "the greater and greater salary differentials between scientists, mathematicians, and engineers on the one hand and social scientists on the other. . . . Almost all major universities in this country have succumbed to the temptation [of federal handouts for science]."[14]

If there was no reasonable alternative but to continue the monopoly of atomic power in the hands of the government, the scientists almost uniformly wanted to see the control transferred from the military to a civilian agency. The military opposed the transfer, and one of the opening guns in the struggle was fired when Hutchins, who of course supported civilian control, set up a four-day Atomic Energy Control Conference at the university for September 19–22, 1945. The agenda included discussion of the consequences of the bomb under national sovereignty; international control; and scientific secrecy in the event of an arms race. The conference was attended by many of the luminaries of the nuclear and social sciences. (Albert Einstein could not attend, but he wrote Hutchins that there would be bigger and "better" wars as long as nations clung to "unrestricted sovereignty." The role of intellectuals, he said, was to make it clear that the problem was a political and not a scientific one, and to make it clear that war preparations, including all kinds of military secrecy, must be abolished.)

But even though the proceedings were to be secret, "the generals" didn't like the idea. Two days before it was scheduled to open, Hutchins received a flat *Verbot* from the general-of-generals in Washington, L. R. Groves, who had directed the entire "Manhattan Engineering District," so-called, covering all aspects of the bomb research and production. "Frankly," General Groves wrote, "I am worried about the grave security hazards. . . . Experience has taught us that it is impossible to control such an affair. . . . The situation is made even worse by the well-known fact that the War Department still has a secret contract with the University of Chicago. . . . The President of the United States has directed all government executive agencies that all vital information pertaining to the Manhattan Project remain secret. . . . Not only is information harmful but misinformation and speculation . . . is certain to be most damaging to the security and best interests of the United States."[15]

The war had been over more than a month, and the old Hutchins was emerging from his red-white-and-blue wrappings. He flatly rejected the general's order: "As we informed your office on the campus some days ago, this conference is to be private. None of its discussions will be open to the public or the press. There are no plans for releasing any of its conclusions. The conference will deal only with matters of common knowledge. . . . I shall be glad to read your letter to the conference if you wish me to do so."[16]

As far as the record shows, the general did not reply. None of the proceedings reached the public; but it was known that the issue of civilian versus military control, and the attendance of Secretary of Commerce Henry A. Wallace, a partisan of civilian (*and* international) control, reinforced the distress of the generals generally, who supported the May-Johnson bill in the Senate to leave the further development of atomic energy in the hands of the military. The struggle was a bitter and protracted one before the Senate Special Committee on Atomic Energy, which finally came down on the side of a civilian commission with the continuance of government regulation and licensing of atomic energy production and development. The Senate committee's deliberations were edified, on January 25, 1946, by the round-table testimony, on behalf of the McMahon bill for civilian control, of a gaggle of eminent scientists presented by President Hutchins of the University of Chicago. Hutchins told the senators, in rejoinder to the argument that control should be left with the generals because of the possibility of another war, that "we had better start the war this morning because only this morning can we be sure of having supremacy in atomic bombs."[17] Hutchins' role in support of the embattled McMahon bill was considerable. He spoke for it across the country. Following the September 1945 off-the-record conference at Chicago, he organized an even more formidable meeting along the same stern lines in New York. He was clearly the voice of the scientific community mobilized behind the civilian campaign.

And he spoke as one having authority again. For he was once more the ringmaster—this time publicly—of an immense undertaking in the atomic energy field. When the bomb was exploded at Hiroshima there was no understanding of the possible application of atomic energy to peacetime use; the country, apart from the scientists, knew nothing at all, and, aside from the development of the bomb, the scientists were not much further ahead than they were in the midthirties. Three days later—the day that Nagasaki was destroyed—Hutchins called a press conference and announced the academic coup that immediately put Chicago in the forefront of nuclear research: the university's creation of institutes of nuclear studies, of metals, and of radiobiology and biophysics. "The purpose is to advance knowledge. . . . We expect these and other institutes will continue in the great tradition of scientific research."[18]

With the achievement of the chain reaction in late 1942, the great coterie of physicists, chemists, and mathematicians Hutchins had gathered in Chicago completed their fundamental work. They continued to be heavily involved in the subsequent work on plutonium—the hunt for the atomic trigger—but the focus of the Manhattan Project gradually shifted to the plutonium plant at Oak Ridge, Tennessee, under Chicago direction, and then to Los Alamos, New Mexico, where many of the top men and women were centered in the production of the bomb itself. With the two explosions and the Japanese surrender, the two-billion-dollar project came to a sudden end. The search for peacetime applications of the new force was next, and the leading research institutions were certain to engage in a mad scramble to attract the services of the scientists who had worked on the bomb. Hutchins anticipated the scramble in the last weeks of the war.

With the imminent departure from Chicago of the men and women who had gathered from all over the world to conduct the Metallurgical Project, he announced a twelve-million-dollar atomic research project a few days after Hiroshima. The great cyclotron and other costly gadgets of the wartime investigation were available, along with a conglomeration of eighty-five senior and a hundred junior scientists. Most of them decided to stay, and others came on. "While Chicago's best humanists of a decade ago have been lost to Harvard, Princeton, and the West Coast universities," one of them wrote (somewhat hyperbolically), "the cream of Columbia's nuclear research staff . . . is now at Chicago. . . . In pursuit of the Virgin (or at least the queen of the medieval disciplines, metaphysics), Mr. Rockefeller's university has wound up with the Dynamo. . . . In the quest of the Absolute, it discovered the Absolute Weapon."[19]

There was money, and not just military victory, in the Promethean release of the marvel of all the ages. While Nagasaki was still burning, the whilom metaphysician revealed that he had inveigled ten giant industrial combines into an exclusive twelve-million-dollar "atomic club"; companies like Standard Oil, U.S. Steel, Aluminum Corporation of America, and Westinghouse Electric paid fifty thousand dollars a year apiece to share in the research results of the University of Chicago's new institutes.

But that would be when there was no longer a war on, after the government had given up its support of nuclear research (until the Cold War reintroduced it). Among the fattest cats of the corporate world, the crusader for the university as the last hope of civilization would find a new answer to the question, "Where does the money come from?" to sustain the pure research that constituted the chief glory of the higher learning. In peacetime it would come henceforth from industry and business, in hot or cold wartime from the government.

Corporate money was highly suspect, more so than government money. Hutchins had tried to interest Henry Ford (to whom he was taken by their mutual friend Lindbergh) in supporting the three new institutes. "I should, of course," he wrote Lindbergh, "much prefer to have the Ford Foundation make the initial contribution because I do not like to have our work so closely tied up with and dependent upon industry."[20] But the Ford Foundation was still, in 1945, closely held, and Henry Ford, at eighty-three, was not interested in radical new undertakings. Nor were the other great philanthropies. But the corporations were willing to speculate. In his announcement of the three institutes Hutchins told the press that "the important thing is to get this work done under a university and not under the auspices of either industry or government. . . . The important thing is not the Bomb, although that has its own tragic significance, but that for the first time atomic energy has been released in controllable form. . . . It must be considered in its social and biological phases, and studied by physicists and chemists, all under university scrutiny. It is important that the workers shall not commit themselves to the study of its applications, which would be commercial, or to its military uses, which would be the government's motive, but be free to devote themselves entirely to basic scientific work.

The only place where they would have complete freedom to pursue their problems is in the university."[21]

The new institutes at Chicago were a bargain-basement deal for the corporate mammoths. They and their payroll scientists didn't know beans about the revolutionary procedures that produced the bomb; all they knew was that they were revolutionary and would have a profound effect on industrial processes. The Chicago institutes were the ground floor, and they got in on it for peanuts. Their fifty thousand dollars a year gave them first call on the work of a team of the world's greatest atomic scientists. On the side of the university—and the scientists—the arrangement was equally salubrious. The scientists were now free to do whatever they wanted to. They knew Hutchins and they knew he would protect them (should such protection be necessary) from the philanthropic sharks. The clustering of the most advanced atomic study at Chicago overtly distressed Vannevar Bush, director of the wartime Office of Scientific Research and Development, who mistakenly supposed that (as Hutchins put it) Chicago "was buying up all the leading scientists of the country by paying them exorbitant salaries." The corporate peanuts that fed the institutes provided modest professorial pittances (fifteen thousand dollars a year each for the physicist Fermi and the chemist Urey, the two Nobel Prize winners in the group—who, like Hutchins, turned over all outside earnings to the university).

There was no doubt that Hutchins had got the jump on the rest of the academic world. While the other universities were awaiting the end of the war to set their course in atomic studies, he had been spectacularly forehanded in rounding up the men and women for his institutes. As a consequence he now enjoyed the national respectability he had lost as an isolationist, regained as the prime contractor in the search for the bomb, and had already, immediately after Hiroshima, begun to throw away with his radical pronouncements that were anathema to Washington. The country's scientists were unsympathetic with his ideological position—or would have been, had they noticed it—but they were profoundly impressed by the establishment of the postwar institutes. Now he spoke for them—particularly as regards military control—and the pooh-bahs of the federal establishment knew that he did. "If a poll were taken among American scientists," said the *Saturday Review of Literature* some two years later, "as to which single person is contributing most today to the advancement of science in America, it is at least a fair bet that the winner would not be a scientist but [Robert M.] Hutchins."

24 The Guilty Flee
Where None Pursue

The creation of the nuclear institutes put period to the perennial charge by the most obdurate of his collegial enemies that Hutchins was unduly interested in teaching and unduly uninterested in research. It also put period—mistakenly—to the perennial charge that he was antiscientific.

He really was antiscientific, in two critical senses. For twenty-five years he had paid lip service to science and the indispensability of its study for the comprehension of the modern world. For twenty-five years he had strengthened the sciences in his Chicago appointments, repeatedly giving the lie (not that his enemies paid any attention to that) to the complaint that he was wedded to a prescientific view of man and the world. But for those same twenty-five years he had deprecated the utility of science in confrontation with the problems of human life, its vaunted "value-free" character: "Men do not get their purposes from science. Science has no purpose of its own."[1]

After Hiroshima he insisted, again and again, that the urgent question was "not how to make atomic energy, but what to do with it. Can we control it? Can we control ourselves in the use of it? To these questions science offers no answer. . . . Science can not give us the character, the intelligence, and the nobility which we may need to learn how to get along with other nations, to sink our own will-to-power in a world organization, to share our goods with suffering humanity everywhere. Science can not change the hearts of men, and yet it seems fairly clear that unless the hearts of men can be changed the scientific knowledge men have gained will at last destroy them."

Why, then, did he take the initiative to establish the institutes the instant the war was over? His motivation was various. First, because the challenge lay there, and no other academic leader had seen that immediate

272

action on a large and imaginative scale would crystallize America's un-rivaled position in nuclear studies and centralize them in one institution. It was a typically Hutchins action. True, his bent was antiscientific, certainly nonscientific; he deplored not only the moral purposelessness of science and the materialistic idolatry it stimulated, but also its commonplace servi-tude to technological adaptation for commercial profit and the pursuit of national power while the humanistic studies languished. Now, more than ever, those studies he had so long fought for at Chicago were put in the shade; the country's foremost protagonist of the liberal arts was now the head of the country's foremost center of non-liberal-arts research and teaching.

Like so many scientists and nonscientists, the country over and the world around, he saw, or thought he saw, the staggering possibilities of the use of the new power for peacetime purposes, phenomenally cheap energy. It would not be unleashed to destroy cities but to build them, lifting the burdens of life from mankind's shoulders as steam and electricity had only begun to do.

"New industries, new communities, more leisure, better health and longer life—these are among the blessings which atomic energy puts with-in our grasp. It can mean a higher standard of living for all the world." But, in the same speech: "We need, not a National Science Research Foundation, but a National Education Foundation. . . . The great task is to educate, to educate now, and to educate everybody now. If we can restrain the warmongers"—this a few months after the *end* of the war—"if we can avoid blundering into war with Soviet Russia . . . the job is not impossible. We must educate the peoples of the earth to be citizens of one world. It is one world, or none at all." On the one hand, the new world of atomic energy; on the other, the old world of war.[2]

One burden that atomic energy didn't lift was the burden of guilt that lay on Robert Maynard Hutchins, the man who had opposed the war and, in some hyperbolic sense, had won it. In his Round Table broadcast, six days after Hiroshima—three days after Nagasaki—he said: "This is the kind of weapon, I believe, which should be used, if at all, only as a last resort in self-defense. At the time this bomb was dropped the American authorities knew that Russia was going to enter the war. It was said that Japan was blockaded and that its cities were burned out. All the evidence points to the fact that the use of this bomb was unnecessary."—It had not yet come to light that the Japanese government had put out feelers through neutral governments to try to arrange a surrender that would spare the emperor.—"Therefore, the United States has lost its moral prestige."[3]

And Hutchins felt that he had lost his. Thirty-five years later his daughter, Clarissa Hutchins Bronson, a Boston lawyer, recalled his being challenged in the question period following a lecture at Harvard in 1960: "You oppose nuclear weapons, but you served as President of the university that discovered the way to make the atomic bomb. How do you square these two facts?" Hutchins: "I have never before made a public statement on this point." The hall was dead silent, said Clarissa Hutchins. "My administrative connection with the undertaking you speak of illustrates the dire necessity of scientific training as the essence of a liberal education. I was a scientific illiterate, and yet I was the presiding officer of an institution whose greatest energies were concentrated on a crucial scientific project—crucial for my country and for the world. That such a man should be a university president is, or ought to be, unthinkable."

An artless dodge, intimating as it did that he would have done differently had he had scientific training. With his paternal gift for the Scriptures, he had once said of one of his academic opponents, "The guilty flee where none pursue." Of the hundreds of scientists—roughly a thousand—who participated in the development of the bomb, only the sixty-five at Chicago who tried to persuade the government not to use it showed any sign of having wanted to "do differently," and they only after the mortal damage of its production had been done. For all his prediction of the peacetime wonders that would flow from installations like the three nuclear institutes, Hutchins was scared stiff on behalf of a benumbed and incredulous world; scared, however, of the moral jeopardy in which he had helped place it.

Prior to Pearl Harbor his opposition to American involvement in the war, like that of so many "isolationists" on the left, had been widely taken for pacifism. In his speeches his condemnation of the war extended by easy inference to all war. I had once asked him why, when he left Oberlin at the end of his sophomore year in 1917, he enlisted in the ambulance corps instead of the infantry. He said it was because he didn't want to kill anybody. I asked him why he didn't want to kill anybody, and he said it was because he was a pacifist. I asked him why he was a pacifist, and he said, "I don't know." On August 6, 1945, the atomic bomb killed everybody around, and the man who undertook to administer its invention, and discharged his undertaking with apocalyptic success, was Robert Maynard Hutchins.

In my old age, and in his still older, I asked him why he had undertaken that interesting assignment. "For the worst of all possible reasons," he said. "I believed it couldn't be done. I didn't think they could pull it off." I said, "By 'they' you mean the physicists?" "Yes."

Mayer: Are you saying that you were some kind of a physicist?

Hutchins: No, I'm saying that I was some kind of a university president. The point is that the chief executive officer of an institution is at all times faced with the question whether he can morally continue to occupy the position. The time I came closest to resigning was when the board of trustees indicated that it didn't intend to do anything about Negro segregation on the South Side of Chicago because the university had the whole neighborhood tied up in restrictive covenants. I regarded restrictive covenants as immoral and unconstitutional.

Mayer: You "came close" to resigning.

Hutchins: The Supreme Court happened along, just then, and decided that I was right about the unconstitutionality—it didn't go into the nonjuridical question of immorality. . . . So I could have resigned when the atomic bomb proposal was made, or I could have done what I could to carry out the wishes of the university. The fact that I was opposed to the war did not mean that the university was. There is a difference between the opinions that a man holds and his operations as the chief administrative officer of an institution.

Mayer: I recall that at the end of Plato's *Phaedrus* Socrates offers up a prayer that "the outward and inward man be at one."

Hutchins: That's a fine idea.

In 1941 "the generals" came to Hutchins to ask if the University of Chicago would accept the responsibility for a project in nuclear physics intended to produce a weapon of a sort, and of a magnitude, never before known. Why—the question wasn't asked—Hutchins, whose ardent antiinterventionism was regarded in some quarters as just short of treason? The Manhattan Engineering District—its code name—ultimately involved more than a thousand scientists and engineers and a total of seventy-two universities, research institutes, industrial corporations, and hospitals, in addition to the government. As prime contractor for the "Metallurgical Project," the University of Chicago assumed prime responsibility for the whole operation, and Hutchins was the only nonscientist outside the government who knew what it was all about. If the question, Why Hutchins, of all people? wasn't asked, neither was the answer given. The answer would have had to be that his polemics against war, and against this war, need not be taken seriously. A safe man, who would always do his duty as "the generals" saw it; as safe a man as they could ask for.

Hutchins: We didn't anticipate what happened. When it happened we did everything we could do to prevent the bomb from being dropped.

Mayer: What you're explaining is that it was impossible to foresee what would happen. But prior to Pearl Harbor you foresaw the evils that would follow if this country went to war, even though we should win. Couldn't you have foreseen what would happen if this country were to develop a bigger and better bomb? You say you tried to prevent the bomb from being dropped after it was constructed.

Hutchins: So I did. . . . At the outset of the Metallurgical Project we had something like twenty-five great physicists on the campus—from all over—and they were spending about fifty million dollars. By the time we knew that the thing was probably going to succeed, we had a commitment to these men that was inescapable. I could have resigned. But it would have been as though I had said, "I'll let you come here on the theory that you won't succeed," and then, when success loomed, I had said, "I'm awfully sorry now that you're going to succeed, and I'm going to withdraw."

Mayer: I think *you* care . . . that you've been against an awful lot of things that cause war, but when war comes and the bugle blows, it's Hutchins in the front line.

Hutchins: That's right.

Mayer: With that prospect before you, would you do the same thing again?

Hutchins: No.

Mayer: Why not?

Hutchins: Because I'm brighter now. . . . You get bright too late. There are all kinds of things that I would have done and would not have done if I had been as bright as I am now.

Robert Maynard Hutchins. Courtesy Mortimer J. Adler.

Robert Hutchins at Oberlin College. Courtesy Oberlin College Archives.

Father: William James Hutchins.
Courtesy Oberlin College Archives.

Mother: Anna Murch Hutchins.
Courtesy Oberlin College Archives.

Grandfather: The Reverend Robert
Grosvenor Hutchins. Courtesy Oberlin
College Archives.

Associate Professor William O.
Douglas, Yale Law School. Courtesy
Yale University Archives.

Professor Charles E. Clark, Yale Law
School. Courtesy Yale University
Archives.

Robert Maynard Hutchins, Dean, Yale Law School.
Courtesy Yale University Archives.

Robert Maynard Hutchins, newly appointed President of the University of Chicago, with acting President Frederick C. Woodward. Reprinted with permission from the *Chicago Sun-Times*.

Maude McVeigh Hutchins and President Robert M. Hutchins. Courtesy University of Chicago Archives.

Robert Hutchins at University Round-Table of the Air, a forum for adult education, NBC broadcast, 1944. Courtesy University of Chicago Archives.

Chancellor Robert Hutchins in football uniform with Mrs. Hector
Coates, Quadrangle Club Revels ("You're in the Styx, Professor"), 1949.
Courtesy Wide World Photos/Associated Press.

Mortimer J. Adler. Collection of Ruth Hammen.

Vesta Orlick Hutchins and Chancellor Robert M. Hutchins. Reprinted with permission from the *Chicago Sun-Times*.

Milton Mayer at Carmel, California, 1979. Courtesy *Monterey Peninsula Herald*.

Milton Mayer, Jane Mayer, and Robert M. Hutchins. Collection of Mrs. Jane Mayer.

25   One World or None

Less than a week after Hiroshima, Hutchins had gone on NBC to sound his clarion call for world government as mankind's one hope with the horrendous opening of the atomic age.[1] The call evoked a great response among the kind of people who listened to that kind of radio program—the country at large was celebrating the end of the hot war (and would soon be celebrating the beginning of the cold one). But two close friends lunching at the Quadrangle Club the next day were moved to something more than a mere affirmation of the clarion call. The two were Dean Richard McKeon and G. A. Borgese.

Giuseppe Antonio Borgese was a passionate, popeyed man of darkest Italian visage and fiery glare. The man himself jutted, not just his features. He was possessed of a firecracker vocabulary, grammar, and syntax; an extravagant master of the language he adopted when he emigrated to America in 1931. ("According to me" meant "in my opinion," and Mortimer Adler credited him with the invention of the past imperative, "Oh, Dick, do not have said that.") He joined the Chicago faculty, his field Italian literature, in 1936; and in 1937 he published the first of his books to be written in English, *Goliath: The March of Fascism*. He was thirty years older than his equally brilliant (but much less explosive) wife, Elizabeth, the daughter of Thomas Mann. ("Elisabetina, *cara mia*, be ruled by me.") As monumentally learned as he was literately original, he had a character to match his temper; a leading critic and historian in his native country, he was one of the few professors who refused to take the Fascist loyalty oath and paid the penalty of losing his livelihood.

After Hiroshima the war would end, in a day or two. But there was, among men like Borgese and McKeon, no conviction that the victory would save civilization. The glorious professions of the glorious allies would turn to ashes with the hostility between the two great survivors among them. The United States and the USSR had been anti-Communist and anticapitalist long before (and far more relentlessly than) they had been anti-Fascist and anti-Nazi.

Meanwhile the bomb certainly must be calling the race to the construction, not merely of a better world, but of a different one. Wendell Willkie, the 1940 Republican presidential nominee, in 1943 popularized the expression "one world" with his book by that title, but his recognition did not extend to the bottom-line issue of national sovereignty. Now, with Hiroshima, Hutchins (and many others) would be giving the expression a more fearful twist: "one world—or none." Whoever monopolized atomic energy would rule the world as long as that monopoly lasted; but when that monopoly ended, as it must, its possession in the hands of sovereign antagonists like the United States and the Soviet Union would certainly presage a murderous armaments race "with the world full of atomic bombs," as Hutchins put it. Almost certainly a war, by design or accident, would put an end to civilization and, possibly, to human society.

Borgese and McKeon decided, at lunch, that August 7, that what must be embarked upon at once, in response to Hutchins' call—embarked on, of course, by Hutchins—was a scholarly investigation to see if a plan could be devised for world government. The international control of atomic energy would require nothing less. All agreements to limit armaments had always been wrecked on the rock of national sovereignty. All. There was nothing new about world government as a concept; it went back to ancient times, and forward to, among others, William Penn's *Essay Towards the Present and Future Peace of Europe* at the end of the seventeenth century, and Immanuel Kant's *Perpetual Peace* at the end of the eighteenth. But no one had attempted to develop a constitutional basis for such a government, for such a state; nothing much had ever been done besides the proposal of an international (basically European) organization to arbitrate international disputes. Nor had anything ever been done along those lines to contemplate the international monopoly of the power to destroy the earth. Could a bullet-proof *constitutional* basis be found for actually organizing the world?—instead of ending world wars with a supposed organization like the League of Nations or the United Nations, which preserved the fatal independence of action that left no real judge, no real legislature, and no real police force or sheriff to resolve disputes as disputes had always been resolved within each independent state. Like the League's covenant, the UN charter was better than nothing: "We should," said Hutchins, "do everything we can to strengthen the United Nations, making it clear that we have accepted the obligation, by joining this organization, not to use the atomic bomb without the consent of other nations. Since the United Nations is an organization of sovereign states, with the power in the hands of a few large ones, we should recognize that it can not prevent the next war, that it can not be the world state which the survival of mankind demands, and that drastic constitutional revisions will be required before it can even be regarded as a serious step in this direction. Nevertheless, it is all we have."[2] The charter was to be revised every ten years. (It hasn't been.)

Borgese and McKeon went to Hutchins, who agreed to organize a study group and raise the money for its undertaking to frame a world constitution. The committee was in place within a month. It consisted of, from the Chicago faculty (besides Borgese, McKeon, Hutchins, and Mortimer Adler), Dean Robert Redfield of Social Sciences, Dean Wilbur Katz of the law school, and Roosevelt adviser Rexford Guy Tugwell, who was coming to Chicago as an economics professor from the governorship of Puerto Rico; Erich Kahler of Princeton, Charles McIlwain of Harvard, Albert Guérard of Stanford, Harold A. Innis of the University of Toronto, and Stringfellow Barr. ("Winkie" Barr and Scott Buchanan had just resigned as president and dean of St. John's and established the Foundation for World Government with a half-million-dollar bequest for the purpose; they provided half of the more than two hundred thousand dollars the Hutchins Committee managed to spend). Dean James Landis of the Harvard Law School, W. E. Hocking of Harvard, Beardsley Ruml of the Federal Reserve Board, and Reinhold Niebuhr of the Union Theological Seminary participated in some aspects of the work; but, like McKeon, who disagreed radically with the ultra-"maximalist" Borgese, they withheld their signatures from the committee's 1946 *Preliminary Draft of a World Constitution.* The *Draft* was followed—after two years of highly, and sometimes shrilly, argumentative meetings and hearings, some 150 position papers, and a quarterly journal, *Common Cause* (edited by Borgese)—by an elaboration of its findings in book form, *A Proposition to History.* Borgese completed his *Foundations of the World Republic* before his death in 1952.[3]

Like the report of the Hutchins Committee on Freedom of the Press, the *Preliminary Draft* generated a modicum of abuse. The still isolationist— and nationalist—*Chicago Tribune* said that Hutchins took his daydreams seriously. "He must elaborate them, write them out, debate the details in the atmosphere of secrecy dear to the juvenile heart. . . . It is said that he is conscience stricken over the achievement of his own faculties in the development of the atomic bomb. . . . The scheme is patently silly." The *Preliminary Draft* received more than a modicum of closely interested attention in intellectual circles, and the movement gained momentum both in America and abroad, especially in England. There a respectable number of MPs joined in support of a convention proposed for Geneva in 1950 to lay the foundations for a world parliament.

For a few years world "federalism"—in which the member nations would retain much of their sovereignty—had some small vogue among the American gentry, and its spokesmen were respectfully received. But even these "minimalists" failed to catch on in a large way anywhere, and the "maximalists" of the Hutchins stripe had almost no popular audience.

Variously splintered both on the maximalist/minimalist front and on a whole caboodle of procedural issues, the movement achieved neither coherence nor sufficient cohesion to present a clearly intelligible program to the public; nor did it ever permeate the public below the elitist levels of scholarship and liberal political activism. American mass leadership was uninterested, and the country's statesmen were as inattentive as the general public. The case for world community, world government, world law, was self-evident in the atomic age, and would ever after remain so; but until the Russians exploded their bomb in 1949, Americans were satisfied with the momentary fact that the atomic age was the American atomic age. Ignorant of the scientific and technological capability of the Russians, the American congressman no less than his constituent refused to heed the predictions of Hutchins and the scientists that the USSR would have the bomb within a few years, and when the Soviet explosion did take place it was quite generally believed that the "secret" had been stolen and that Allied (for which read American) genius would at once outstrip the Communists and nullify their possession of that first—already outmoded—bomb.

When the Hutchins Committee issued its *Preliminary Draft of a World Constitution*, the Berlin air lift was at its height, intensifying the Cold War sentiment of the Americans, with its concomitant nationalist resurgence, while the collapse of the European allies' imperial power all over the world was bringing forth a great succession of new nations, many of them almost wholly illiterate and all of them consumed with the fervor of their newly achieved national sovereignty. When the draft was issued, Prime Minister Nehru of India and Wellington Koo, the Chinese ambassador to the United States, joined Hutchins in a Round-Table of the Air discussion of "The Problem of World Government," and Nehru admitted that India's triple preoccupation with its economic distress, its division into two separate nations, and, above all, its newly won national independence from Great Britain promised the poorest of all possible receptions to the idea. Ambassador Koo had to say the same for China, which was torn by civil war and was on the verge of falling to nationalist Communism.[4]

It was the worst of all times, albeit the most necessitous, to talk to the peoples of the world about a better world, much less a different world altogether. The Americans were disturbed by the prospect of war with the USSR and the sudden emergence of McCarthyism and the witch hunts at home. The Truman loyal-security program reinvigorated the prewar House Committee on Un-American Activities and the Senate internal security program. Americans were mesmerized by what they perceived as the double threat—internal and external—to their lives, their fortunes, and their sacred honor. Whatever illusions they may have had at the war's end were dissipated. The world had—once more, and with sixty million lives consumed—not been made safe for democracy. It had not even been made safe.

But Hutchins and his committeemen were not downhearted, nor had they reason to be. People had at least heard about world government, world community, the world state, as their forebears had not, "and though we know that states do not make communities," said Hutchins when the committee began its work, "we should not forget that there is an interaction between political organization and political ideals. The Constitution of the United States has educated our people to believe in the Constitution of the United States. We had a community, when the Constitution was adopted, far more homogeneous and unified than the world today. Even then it took a bloody civil war to make the country finally one. But since there is an interaction between political institutions and political ideals, we should seek to frame and get adopted the constitution of a world state, in the hope that the discussion leading to its institution and its existence thereafter will promote the formation of the community which can be its only durable foundation."5

It was another straw to be grasped, at a time when there was nothing but straws to hand. Hutchins had always held firmly to the ancient adage that the law is a teacher. The adage did not promise that the lesson of the law would be learned, or learned soon. The lesson of world law, which might teach people to accept it, as the U.S. Constitution had taught people to accept the U.S. Constitution, might not be learned for five years or ten or a hundred; and Hutchins and his younger colleagues would live to see, a generation afterward, the nations of the one world further divided. Nationalism and nationalist alliances would be rampant, the world "full of atomic bombs," and world government and world community no longer spoken of anywhere.

26 "We're Only Scientists"

Bernie Loomer was no ordinary dean, still less an ordinary dean of a divinity school. But the divinity school at Chicago was no ordinary divinity school. It was another Hutchins amalgam, composed of the several denominational schools that clustered around the university. It was, and was so called, the Federated Theological Faculty. And as each grizzled old professor of New or Old Testament or Church history retired, he was being replaced by, generally, a younger, friskier person. Bernie Loomer, a Hutchins appointee, just five years out of graduate school, was one of those young and frisky theologians and was subject, as he himself put it, to harebrained ideas.

He had one one day in the late summer of 1947, while most of his federated faculty were still away for the summer. Thirty-two years later he told about it in the *University of Chicago Magazine*; in spite of the considerable number of persons ultimately involved in it, it had never been told about before. "Suppose, I theorized, that the University of Chicago had a monopoly or near monopoly of atomic scientists." He didn't know, he said, if this were the case. "And suppose, further, that these scientists were to form a solid community of mutual support dedicated to the purpose of making the most creative use of their unique position. And suppose, finally, that these scientists, with the help of many other members of the university, were to stipulate to the United States government certain conditions that must be realized if they were to continue in atomic research."[1]

The world's case, in 1947, was critical, as Loomer saw it. Maybe nothing could be done to utilize atomic power for the benefit of humanity. But "for the first time in western history academicians held the balance of political power—if only for a time. . . . What if they were to exercise their power in constructive or even revolutionary ways?" The harebrained dean didn't think he knew exactly what he was talking about or what he might propose. He thought he had a tiger by the tail—or vice versa. He called his predecessor as dean, Ernest "Pomp" Colwell. Colwell said, as a divine might properly say, "Good Lord" and, adding that such matters were beyond his depth, suggested that his youthful successor call the chancellor of the university. Loomer delayed—he did not want to hear Hutchins tell him he was ridiculous—"but I finally screwed up my courage and called him."

"Hutchins listened to my proposition without interruption. But when I had finished speaking there was no response at all. The silence continued for many seconds. . . . I asked him if he was still on the line. He finally said that he was. After another long pause he asked if I knew what he was doing. In response to my reply in the negative, he said: 'I'm kicking myself for not having thought of this idea myself.'" He said he had to go out of town and asked his caller to get in touch with some of the atomic scientists, especially Szilard.

Loomer was amazed at Hutchins' response: "His ready comprehension was not what amazed me. . . . But what really astonished me was his immediate willingness to explore the idea and to do so as the chief administrative officer of the University. . . . Even now I would have great difficulty in naming another person, comparably situated, who would have made such a reply or taken a similar action."[2]

Pondering the proposition in the next few days, Dean Loomer decided that he should go to the faculty of the university, and only then to the scientists; the scheme, even in its inchoate form, was one which would immediately involve the university as a whole. By way of preparing the way to lay the matter before the faculty he sent his own faculty, the divinity school, the draft of a proposed memorandum to the chancellor. The memorandum suggested conditions—including the calling of a world constitutional convention by the United States—under which the atomic scientists would be willing to continue to work. "It was recognized, of course," said Loomer, "that the strength of the proposal derived from the strategic role of the atomic scientists of the university, and from their willingness both to cooperate with the scheme and to conduct a sit-down strike if the stipulated conditions (whatever they turned out to be) were not met."

Out of the conversations both without and within the divinity faculty, several problems emerged. First, the university was legally the board of trustees; would their approval have to be got? Second, could the university as such be expected, in violation of the American (but not of the European) tradition, to take a political position? Third, could one department of a university (or the university as a whole) attempt in any way to interfere with the freedom of another department (or of its individual members) to conduct what research they wanted to? And fourth, on what grounds could a university make demands on a government anyway? On this last point Economics Professor Paul H. Douglas, a former pacifist turned Marine officer, Cold War proponent, and later U.S. Senator, buttonholed Loomer vehemently; when Loomer asked on what principles the proposition could be said to be unacceptable, Douglas replied, "Never mind the principles. A university just can't make demands on the government."[3]

Loomer felt, then and thereafter, that Hutchins' willingness to explore the proposal in part reflected his distress at the ever wider gap between the sciences and the humanities—C.P. Snow's "two cultures." Loomer: "I believe that he viewed the proposal as a way of taking a concrete step in the direction of redeeming what had become a fairly bleak scene."

With the onset of the fall quarter, the divinity faculty met to consider the proposal, and after prolonged discussion the dean was authorized to draft a resolution to the chancellor. Seventeen members of the faculty eventually signed it; eleven, several of whom had specific rather than general objections, declined to. The resolution began with a series of whereases: the real possibility that further research in atomic energy could be used to create more destructive military weapons as well as to serve peaceful purposes; the moral ambiguity of the university in engaging in this kind of research; the preeminent position of the university in this field and its consequent strategic political role; the threat of atomic energy to civilization under the present political organization of national states; the inadequacy of the United Nations to control these destructive forces; and the resultant need for a world government. The resolution then asserted that the university could discharge its moral responsibility and continue its research in atomic energy only under conditions such as the three following, which should be presented to the United States government: (1) that the U.S. government immediately call a world constitutional convention for the purpose of establishing a world government; (2) that the Marshall Plan be extended to any nation which would attend the convention; (3) that upon the adoption of the world constitution the United States would surrender its knowledge of the atomic bomb to the world government.

The three conditions were presented to the chancellor as tentative or suggestive, and the theologians were well aware (as Loomer put it) of "the idealistic, utopian, and possibly flamboyant" qualities of the proposal. Had it been made public it would certainly have been dismissed by the statesmen and bureaucrats as both naive and presumptuous, let alone idealistic, utopian, and flamboyant. But its signers did not choose to be more circumspect; the course of their discussion had made it clear that they felt that the world crisis was such as to demand radical measures of the sort they put forth.

The resolution was sent to Hutchins, who called two informal meetings of his deans to consider it. The divisions represented were divinity, physical science, biological science, social science, humanities, library, business, social service, law, and the Hutchins college. Hutchins, presiding, said almost nothing; every one of these men and women had been appointed by him in the course of his long administration. The tone of the meeting was uniformly negative, primarily on the ground that it was impermissible, and not just inappropriate, for a university or any other institution to make such demands and, in effect, by virtue of its strategic position, hold the country hostage to a proposition that envisaged a fundamental alteration of the fundamental law and organization of the national society. (There were not many asides, but one of the deans said that if the government rejected the conditions the scientists would lose their jobs because they had not been trained to do anything else.) There was no mistaking the deans' sentiment, and the resolution was obviously dead.

Then Hutchins, who hadn't spoken, rose and said, according to Loomer, "You don't understand, do you? You really don't understand. You will recall that when I first came here I suggested that the motto of the University should be Walt Whitman's 'Solitary, singing in the West, I strike up for a New World.' I now propose that the motto of the University should be, 'No Cross, No Crown.'" And he sat down, and the meeting, and with it the proposal, came to a quiet end.

But Loomer was able to add a postscript: "A short time later I met Will Munnecke, vice president of the University. He told me that, in view of the atomic energy proposal, I might be interested in the meeting he had just attended which involved Hutchins and David Lilienthal, the first chairman of the Atomic Energy Commission. The meeting was devoted to financial arrangements between the University and the Commission. Munnecke reported that after the business matters had been attended to, Lilienthal asked Hutchins to give him a few more minutes because he had another problem to discuss. Munnecke's account, again as closely as I can come to recapturing his words, went like this: Lilienthal said, 'I desperately need to talk to somebody. I preside over a commission that deals with the greatest physical power known to man. We make decisions that affect the whole planet. But we do not know what we are doing. . . . Do you know where I can go for help?' Hutchins replied that he didn't. Then he added: 'You might try the Divinity School of the University of Chicago. They seem to be worrying about this more than some of the rest of us.' "[4]

At the first of the two meetings called by Hutchins to discuss the Loomer resolution, one of the sorely troubled deans, balking, like the others, at making demands on the government, compared the proposal to "a threat by coal miners to let the country freeze to death by refusing to mine coal unless their demands are granted." Something over a year earlier that same parallel was introduced in a discussion in Santa Fe, New Mexico. It was April of 1946, and the debate over transferring control of atomic energy from the military to a civilian commission was at its height. A journalist, who was nationally active on behalf of civilian control, had met two young physicists from the giant atomic bomb development plant at nearby Los Alamos. The physicists asked if he would advise them and some of their colleagues on what they might do to campaign for civilian control. It was arranged that four of the Los Alamos physicists would come down from the hill for a discussion.

The four scientists were all under forty, and they represented themselves as speaking for a clear majority of their colleagues. Many of them had written individual letters to their congressmen and senators, and a few to the White House, urging the passage of the embattled McMahon bill for civilian control. But they were distressed by most of the acknowledgments they'd got. The generals, riding high after winning the war, were determined to remain in the saddle, and appeared to be impervious to the civilian challenge.

When asked how many atomic physicists there were in the country, the four of them agreed upon an estimate of two thousand to twenty-five hundred.

"You've got the making of a nice little closed shop," observed the journalist. "You have a couple of thousand of highly intelligent men and women, probably a majority of them one way or another already in touch with each other. You've got a house organ, and a powerful one, in the Bulletin of the Atomic Scientists reaching, would you say, a majority again?" They nodded. "Then, you're all set. You organize as fast as you can and demand of Congress that control be taken from the military, and you tell Congress that if your demand isn't met you'll strike."

"Strike?" said one.

"Strike," said the journalist. "Your union will constitute a natural monopoly, and there's no way to wreck it."

"Union?" asked another.

"Union," said the journalist. "Just like the miners. John L. Lewis said,

'You can't mine coal with bayonets.' Or produce atomic energy. You're in better shape than the miners, even. There's no substitute for your know-how, and nobody outside the union has it."

There was a silence, and then one of the physicists who hadn't said anything spoke: "Wait a minute," he said. "We're only scientists."

Scott Buchanan had already written, after Hiroshima, that "the heaviest responsibility of the scientist may be to refuse to make himself useful," and when the German physicists, including von Weizsäcker, quit nuclear research, Hutchins spoke of "the professional ideal. . . adopted by many individual scientists who have declined to lend themselves to commercial or political plans of which they disapproved." In an off-the-cuff remark a few years later—a remark that was picked up by the *Chronicle of Higher Education*—a plainer-spoken Hutchins looked back in anger and said, "On the whole, professors are worse than other people, and scientists are worse than other professors."

Antonio Borgese on hearing the Santa Fe story said, "When the Fascismo came to Italy, we said that the universities would be the last to surrender. They were the first."

Part Six

CHICAGO (2)

27　The Great Books Industry

His disappointing encounters with adult legislators led Hutchins to a new emphasis on a theme he had largely ignored in his fight to reform college teaching and university research: "This pedagogical principle that subjects requiring experience can be learned only by the experienced, leads to the conclusion that the most important branch of education is the education of adults. We sometimes seem to think of education as something like the measles, mumps, chicken-pox, or whooping-cough: having had it once, one need not, indeed one can not, have it again.

"To say that humans should learn only in childhood would mean that they were human only in childhood. And it would mean that they were unfit to be citizens of a republic." Republican citizenship required the *continual* exercise of the citizen's intelligence to achieve and extend justice, peace, freedom, and order; "the ideal republic is the republic of learning, the utopia by which all actual republics are measured."[1]

Education is not a matter for children: "Apart from mathematics, metaphysics, logic, astronomy, and similar theoretical subjects, it is clear that comprehension comes only with experience. A learned Greek"—the learned Greek was Aristotle—"remarked that young men should not listen to lectures on moral philosophy, and he was right. Moral philosophy, history, politics, economics, and literature can convey their full meaning only in maturity. When I taught *Macbeth* to boys in a preparatory school, it was a blood-and-thunder story, a good one, and well worth teaching, but a blood-and-thunder story still. *Macbeth* can mean what it meant to Shakespeare only when the reader has had sufficient experience, vicarious or otherwise, of marriage and ambition to understand the issues and their implications.

"A boy may be a brilliant mathematician or musician and I have known several astronomers who were contributing to the international journals at the age of thirteen. But I never knew a child of that age who had much that was useful to say about the ends of human life, the purposes of organized society, and the means of reconciling freedom and order. It is subjects like these about which we are most confused and about which we must obtain some clarification if our civilization is to survive."[2]

To the extent that it faithfully reflected the education of adolescents, adult education in the United States—in contrast, say, with the adult Folk School system of Denmark—was essentially a vocational program. It assumed that the student would work under the geographical and technical conditions under which he or she has studied: "Vocational agricultural training is given to students in the Dustbowl, who race for Chicago the moment they are through school. Mechanical training is given on obsolescent machines in Chicago to students who find themselves confronted with entirely different ones when they get a job."[3] The place to train hands for industry was in industry, as the wartime training of airplane mechanics demonstrated; the aircraft companies produced better mechanics in an intensive few weeks than the schools could produce in years.

The curse of vocationalism in adult education followed from the vocationalism which had overspread the universities because of the difficulty of interesting young people in what were known as "academic subjects": "The whole apparatus of football, fraternities, and fun is a means by which education is made palatable to those who have no business in it."[4] But every boy and girl had a business to have as much true education as he or she could absorb, without regard to financial capability—education interestingly offered through the employment of great books instead of textbooks, and discussion instead of lectures.

"The fact is that the best practical education is the most theoretical one. This is probably the first time in human history in which change on every front is so rapid that what one generation has learned of practical affairs in the realm of politics, industry, business, and technology is of little value to the next. What the father has learned of the facts of life is almost useless to his son. It is principles, and everlastingly principles, not data, not facts, not helpful hints, but principles which the rising generation requires if it is to find its way through the mazes of tomorrow"[5]—and the application of principle to the facts of life if the risen generation was to find its way through the mazes of today.

Where it wasn't vocational, adult education in the extension divisions of the urban colleges and universities in the first third of the twentieth century was almost entirely remedial or recreational. It taught arts and crafts for leisure time or retirement, or it provided training in fields like language for immigrants or for natives who had been deprived of childhood schooling. But there was another, almost forgotten tradition in adult education characterized by the old Chautauqua movement and a scattering of public forums that dealt with the liberal studies. One of these, in the 1920s, was the People's Institute of New York under Everett Dean Martin, where series after series of free lectures were offered to an audience interested in nonvocational self-improvement. One of the lecturers—who were paid a pittance—was young Mortimer Adler of the Columbia University psychology department.

In 1926 Martin, prodded by Adler, Scott Buchanan, and other of his lecturers, obtained a two-year grant from the Carnegie Corporation to introduce great books discussion groups around the city, staffed by rising young Columbians like Clifton Fadiman, Jacques Barzun, Richard McKeon, Mark Van Doren, and Whitaker Chambers (of later Alger Hiss case fame and infamy). These relative youngsters—two of them serving as coleaders of each discussion group—were all products of John Erskine's general honors course at Columbia, in which, instead of textbooks, the course materials were the classics.

The People's Institute experiment was a success, but there was no further funding for it. Ten years and more later, Adler and Hutchins, teaching the great books as a freshman honors course at Chicago, were moved to set up such courses for adults at the university's extension division downtown. The courses, taught by young members of the faculty, were not particularly popular in competition with the traditional evening school subjects. Then Adler concocted the scheme of establishing discussion groups around Chicago, much in the People's Institute manner of fifteen years before. The Chicago Public Library offered the use of its branches. The problem was to find a large enough number of group leaders, and Adler suggested to the university's dean of extension that the university train laymen to lead groups. Since the Socratic method involved the asking, not the answering, of questions and forbade lecturing, intelligent laymen might be ably trained to do the job and perhaps do it better than professional academics habituated to being experts and venting their expertise in lectures.

The effort, undertaken in 1944, was an immediate success. Other library systems, first in the Middle West and then all over the country, came into the program, and the University of Chicago found itself sending out extension faculty instructors to conduct training programs for lay leaders whose burgeoning groups met not only in libraries but in churches, factories, service and veterans' organizations, and in schoolrooms in the evening.

The burgeoning program was beset by two difficulties. Public libraries could not lay their hands on enough copies of say, Dante, Plato, or Gibbon, to supply a group of twenty-five or thirty at the same time. Other agencies and institutions that sponsored groups were even harder pressed. Besides, the sponsors of the program urged group members to buy, rather than borrow, the books, since it was a Hutchins-Adler dogma that a book well read (and reread) was a book well marked. For the purpose of group discussion it was important that the participants all had the same translation of a given text and, if possible, the same edition for page referral in the course of discussion. Bookstores, like libraries, did not stock enough such copies of a required book to meet the simultaneous demand of twenty-five or thirty customers—or, as was often the case when there were several groups in the same community, for fifty, seventy-five, or a hundred copies.

That wasn't all. Lists of readings had to be developed for second-, third- and fourth-year groups—ultimately through ten years—plus readings for high school and junior high school programs. And the university extension division was soon over its ears in administering a nationwide undertaking. But it wasn't until the war ended that the Great Books Foundation was established as an independent entity with Hutchins as board chairman. At this point Lynn A. Williams, Jr., came into the picture. Trained as a lawyer and an engineer, Williams was an ostensibly roughneck industrial executive with a passion for the liberal education of adults without regard to their previous schooling. As vice-president of the Stewart Warner Corporation, running its Indianapolis plant, he solicited the university's assistance in setting up a great books program for his workers on company time, with Adler and another Chicago faculty man coming to Indianapolis to conduct the discussions.

The Chicago people, Hutchins included, were at once taken with Williams and his wrong-side-of-the-tracks façade. (Item: "You want to give the competition a pasting? You hire their best salesman, send him to Maine, and fire him." Item: "Don't can the guy who's no good; can the guy who hired him.") Hutchins offered Williams the presidency of the Great Books Foundation—and later the vice-presidency of the university—and Williams quit industry and became an academic.

In the last months of the war and the first postwar years the nationwide great books discussion program took off like a modest wildfire. The six- or eight-session training of volunteer leaders was almost invariably successful, with laymen on the whole readily mastering the art of intellectual inquisition. With group members required to argue from the books themselves in conjunction with their own common sense and common experience, and the one-upmanship of the better schooled thus excluded, groups soon came to consist of a remarkably broad social mixture. Men and women who had never before mingled socially discovered that mingling intellectually was a lively introduction; the corridor hummed during the coffee-break in the middle of the two-hour sessions, and groups often regaled themselves with end-of-the-year social gatherings. The program, holding its participants from year to year, went far to confirm an old Hutchins thesis: persons of the most limited backgrounds and commonplace occupations were as susceptible to an exciting kind of self-education as their more liberally educated fellow citizens.

In the course of a long, prophetic lifetime Hutchins made two prophecies that the late Fiorello La Guardia would call beauts. In 1920 two of his undergraduate friends at Yale came to him with the mock-up, or dummy, of a projected weekly magazine; he told them it would never go and advised them to forget it. (The two friends were Henry R. Luce and Briton Hadden, and they did not forget it; the projected weekly was *Time*.) The second of the two beauts is dated 1947, when Hutchins was chairman of the board of the newly established Great Books Foundation. In the last years of the 1940s the great books program for adults acquired strong momentum across the country. Seeing it as a tool to help pry the whole of American education away from vocationalism and "presentism," Hutchins and Adler flogged it (as the term would be a generation later) with an immense amount of hype (as the term would be yet another generation later). Articles appeared not only in the highbrows but in publications like *Life*. Public demonstration discussions were mounted in major cities. Hutchins and Adler packed three thousand people into Chicago's Orchestra Hall for a panel session on Plato's *Apology*, and the city's semiliterate mayor proclaimed a Great Books Week. Carried away by the hoopla, Hutchins prophesied that fifteen million people would be involved in the great book program within five years.

He was wrong by something like 14,957,000. The movement peaked in the flush of the first postwar years to a maximum of some 43,000 enrollees in some three hundred communities—a not inconsiderable achievement. Then it leveled off, perhaps coincidentally with the onset of McCarthyist anti-intellectualism in the 1950s. It never recovered its sensational early steam, and Hutchins and Adler drifted away from it. Thirty years later it was still in business nationwide (and Lynn Williams was its board chairman). It was still the nearest thing the country had to liberal education for adults.

With the university out from under the administration of the program after 1947, money to support the independent Great Books Foundation had to be come by elsewhere. Paul Mellon's Old Dominion Fund kicked in. So, later, did the short-lived Fund for Adult Education (a Ford Foundation subsidiary set up by Hutchins after he had left the university for its associate directorship).

But the necessity to obtain the books in quantity provided the solution of the financial problem. The foundation published the paperback sets of eight or ten readings for each year's program and sold them at a modest profit to the participants. (There was no tuition fee; the lay leaders were unpaid; and the meeting places were provided without cost. The book profits, plus continued grants, also supported the travel and salaries of two or three leader trainers and an office staff.)

Supplying cheap paperback reprints to the community in the libraries and churches was one thing; supplying them to the Fat Men was another. The Fat Men were—or was—the brain child of Vice-president Will Munnecke, late of Marshall Field's. In the spring of 1943—oh yes, there was a world war on—Munnecke bethought himself of a little scheme on which he sounded out a few of the trustees and other Chicago nabobs with whom he was on good terms socially. The response was gratifying, and he went to Hutchins with the proposal that there be an invitation-only great books group of leading (i.e., financially corpulent or fat) Chicagoans and their wives to meet once a month at the posh University Club downtown, with Hutchins and Adler as its coleaders and Milton Mayer as water boy. And so the class continued, with a necessarily changing constituency, for thirty years. (Adler was delighted, when Hutchins left the university, to go on conducting the class solo, and uninterruptably, in violation of the ironclad tradition of two leaders for each group. He subsequently set up his own Men's group in San Francisco, and another one as an "executives' seminar" at the Aspen Institute for Humanistic Studies. A similar elite class was organized, with Adler and Mayer as its leaders, in Indianapolis, and it was as a member of this group that Lynn Williams moved into the great books circle.)

As "the generals" took more and more of his time and energies, Hutchins was ever harder pressed to pay attention to the things he cared about and the things he had to do at the university. He cared about the great books program, made speeches about it, and took part, with Adler (and occasionally Mayer), in public demonstration discussions of sure-fire items, like the Declaration of Independence and the Communist Manifesto in combination, in well-filled auditoriums across the country. But he had to leave the administrative work to Adler and the people at the extension division. Adler, with no generals on his back, was eager to jump into the expanding program and serve as its powerhouse.

Hutchins tried hard to show up for the Fat Men's class, for obvious reasons. It included a few of his influential friends among the one-third of his board who joined it. None of his most obdurate enemies on the board took part, though they were invited to. And apart from trustees it included some donors to the university and a few influential lawyers. The atmosphere of the meetings was saucy and refreshing, with the Gold Coast elite submitting themselves to friendly inquisition on the sorts of political, economic, religious, and, to some extent, the personal phobia and mania that were rarely mentioned, much less argued, in their respectable circles. Had the meetings not been closed to the press, Colonel McCormick's *Chicago Tribune* could have reported some subversive discussion, with supposedly nice people (the town's very nicest) batting Marx, free love, atheism, and even the Republican Party around. The Hutchins badinage was a mite restrained among the rich, but it still provided an unfailing entertainment, and some real enlightenment. The Fat Men's was a good class, and a tactically useful one.

But the finding of the books for it was something special. The gentry were not given to scrabbling in the second-hand bookstores: they were given to getting what they wanted new and to getting it when they wanted it. This meant the Chicago bookstores turning up thirty-five or forty copies of a bit of Plotinus, Hume, or Faraday in a hurry. (Adler's reading list for this special group was independent of the list for the regular program.)

The book problem soon seemed to be insoluble. But there was one Fat Man who specialized in solving the insoluble, at, if possible, a profit and, if possible, a colossal profit. This was William Burnett Benton—who had shortened his name to William B. to save time, and then to plain William to save still more time—the Hutchins classmate from Yale who served as on-and-off vice-president of the University of Chicago and as publisher and one-third owner (he had given the university the other two-thirds) of the Encyclopaedia Britannica. Benton suggested to Hutchins and Adler that the Britannica publish a great set of the Great Books.

28   Ad Man

Of the publishing of book sets—including that perennial money-maker, Eliot's Five-Foot Shelf—there was no end.

The Britannica, since Benton had taken it over from Sears right after Pearl Harbor, by the middle of 1943 was beginning to produce what would soon be fabulous profits. Benton was looking for new ventures, primarily in publishing, and picked up Compton's *Picture Encyclopaedia* and the dictionary-rich Merriam-Webster Company. But the publishing business wasn't big enough to hold him. He staked his friend Bill Joyce to five thousand dollars on the latter's bet that shoes could be made in Los Angeles, and wound up partners of the five-million-dollars-a-year Joyce Shoe Company. He had considerable taste in art and left a significant collection of American paintings, having launched Reginald Marsh. As a young ad man he invented one musical abomination, the singing commercial on radio; as a seasoned entrepreneur he got in (and out, at an immense profit) on the founding of the "musical wallpaper" of Muzak. (Introducing him on an informal occasion, Hutchins said that he ought to apologize for the things he'd invented.) He persuaded his boss at the Lord and Thomas advertising agency—the same Albert D. Lasker of the University of Chicago board—to propose to Pepsodent that they sponsor the local Amos 'n' Andy show on NBC. Ten years later he persuaded Alfred P. Sloan of General Motors to subsidize the University of Chicago Round-Table of the Air, and the two programs became the most widely heard of all radio shows in entertainment and in education.

Not everything was dross. As board chairman of Britannica he took the EB into the new field of educational films in the 1940s, buying Erpi Classroom Films from Western Electric and merging it with Eastman Kodak's Classroom Films Division (which Eastman gave him, just as Sears gave

298

him the Britannica, reaping a greater tax advantage by giving away rather than selling the operation). He expected to operate Encyclopaedia Britannica Films, Inc., in the red for several years, but the Benton touch betrayed him. Within a few years it was bringing $300,000 a year to the university and more than $100,000 to Benton.

As vice-president at Chicago he used his position to put himself on the Round-Table on such diverse subjects as censorship, cartels, aviation, American-British relations, the common man, and the conditions of peace, achieving an instant quasi mastery of all such grand subjects, and carrying that mastery into the Truman administration as assistant secretary of state, where he concocted the Voice of America propaganda broadcasts to Communist Europe. And he was statesman enough, on appointment by his old partner, Governor Chester Bowles, to serve two years in the U.S. Senate from Connecticut and there rise alone, in 1951, to propose the expulsion of Senator Joseph McCarthy.

Like all senators he never quit being "Senator" though he was defeated, by the McCarthy forces in Connecticut, for election in 1952. A decade later he was the first American ambassador to UNESCO in Paris. He had been one of the largest contributors to John F. Kennedy's presidential campaign and had let it be known, unavailingly, that he was available for the plum appointment to the Court of St. James. (He was fond of saying that American foreign-service people should speak the language of the country in which they were stationed; and he spoke an overflowing brand of English.) The United Nations Educational, Scientific, and Cultural Organization was not then (or thereafter) a very significant international agency, and the appointment to it was largely honorific, involving three or four brief transatlantic trips a year.

When he died, a friend of his was talking about him with Maude Hutchins. The friend said, "I hear that Bill died in his sleep." "If he'd been awake," said Mrs. Hutchins, "he wouldn't have died." He respected time more than he respected anything else (including persons), and his pursuit of it was relentless. He would say, "I think I'll sleep for twenty minutes"— and sleep for twenty minutes. Shortly after he joined Hutchins at Chicago, he heard of two time-savers and went after them pell-mell. Physiologist Nathaniel Kleitman was reported to be conducting experiments in the hope of cutting two hours out of the normal night's sleep. "Think of it," said Benton, hurrying over to Kleitman's laboratory, "two hours. Two hours that I'm throwing away."

One day Hutchins walked into Benton's office while he was dictating a letter to his mother, beginning, "Dear Mother. Colon. How are you. Question mark." Hutchins said, "How are *you*, question mark?" Benton wanted to know all about everything, provided he could find out about it in a short memorandum right away. He never stirred, or sat, without his dictaphone, rarely turned it off, and still more rarely *wrote* anything. One of the first American businessmen to fly regularly between Chicago and New York, he was never quite able to make up his mind on the time-saving advantages of the plane trip. A classic picture had him seated in the barber's chair on the Twentieth Century Limited, with a drink and his dictaphone in one hand, a manicurist working on the other, and an assistant sitting on a stool next to him taking notes.

When Hutchins, hearing of his resignation from Benton and Bowles, offered him the Chicago vice-presidency to beef up the university's public relations, Benton dictated a whole book for the delectation of the trustees, suggesting (among other things) that the university change its name so that it would not be taken for a public institution. Hutchins had the book distributed to the trustees, most of whom professed amazement at Benton's quick acquisition of knowledge about the institution. But one of them, the arch-conservative Sewell Avery, board chairman of Montgomery Ward and Company, "made a series of speeches of the usual type," as Hutchins wrote Benton, "from which I was able, by hard work, to gather that Mr. Avery thought the University was Red and that our public relations could not be improved by anybody until the administration had cleaned out the radicals. Mr. Swift"—the chairman of the board—"took a very strong line in reply to Mr. Avery with the result that Mr. Avery said that if the University was not Red your appointment was a fine idea."[1] Benton spent six months a year at the university for ten years, eventually leaving for the State Department.

He was not a frenetic man externally. He simply kept going all the time and kept everyone else going, in a steady frenzy. He was not a commanding figure, but he spent his life commanding and getting away with it, crudely, even brutally, but not ruthlessly. He exploited everyone he dealt with, intellectually, physically, and emotionally, but not financially. Secretaries were kept on half the night transcribing Benton memoranda and letters from his dictaphone tapes. If it meant leaving their families or admirers in the lurch, they and their families and admirers were all so handsomely compensated for the overtime that they didn't complain. (His personal assistant, John Howe, a Chicago boy, was once asked, when the pressure was especially intense in the office, if his boss had thought of hiring an additional "girl" to help out. "Bill doesn't hire a girl," Howe explained, "he hires a girl to hire a girl.")

"Bill," a longtime colleague explained, "thinks he's got 'muscle.' What he's got is money." He was not an inherently powerful person, simply a brazen and insistent one who was very rich and hired very bright people all over the world who could not resist his lavish offers. "Ideas," he was given to saying, "are a dime a dozen." The men who had the ideas, and whose ideas Benton bought, were more expensive. ("I'd be crazy if I let Bob Hutchins out of my sight for sixty days at a time. Every idea he's ever had has made me a fortune.") His biographer tells how he hired Governor Adlai Stevenson—who, after his unsuccessful presidential campaigns, was going to resign as US Ambassador to the United Nations—to return to the private practice of law to get rid of some of his debts. Benton's enthusiastic biographer offers what must have been Benton's reconstruction of his proposal to his distinguished friend and traveling companion:

"You're too old to fuss with clients and their minor problems," Benton is quoted as saying. "I'll give you $100,000 a year and a $100,000 a year expense account if you will work for Britannica."

"Well," said Stevenson, "what would I do?"

"You would be the greatest 'working ornament' Britannica ever had," said Benton. "You could contribute greatly to our developing educational programs, and help expand our film company into a broad-based educational company . . . inspire our young executives and salesmen . . . help us expand into a world-wide publishing and educational force. . . . Your association with the company could arouse the interest of all countries in the new educational technologies—teaching machines, the new mathematics, the use of films, and audio-visual materials. And you'd still have time to play your key role as a world figure—because I wouldn't dare hope to take even 40% of your time."[2]

Benton, or his money, was in the habit of being irresistible to men like Stevenson. After Stevenson's death and Hubert Humphrey's unsuccessful run for the presidency, he hired the latter as a consultant at $75,000 a year. He contributed large sums to the Stevenson and Humphrey campaigns and in 1968 baldly asked each of his board members to contribute $10,000 to candidate Humphrey: all but two complied. Stevenson and Humphrey were dime-a-dozen idea men par excellence, and their ideas stemmed from their own and Benton's Middle West populist backgrounds. (He was on close terms with Senator Bob and Governor Phil La Follette of Wisconsin). Like Benton, these were all men who never surrendered their primitive prairie radicalism. They were New Dealers before the New Deal, during the New Deal, and after the New Deal. They were all more mannerly than he was and at most levels much more intelligent—and they all needed money all their lives. His relations with such men were always symbiotic. They didn't lose, and he won.

He was the ultimate salesman, and in the Britannica (and later in the

Britannica's Great Books set) he had the ultimate item. Britannica (and the Great Books) advertised extensively, primarily through direct mail. It had no sales offices and was not stocked by bookstores; nor was its purchase arrangement ever advertised or given over the phone. It had a dozen or more prices, depending on the binding and the installment agreement. Its sole sales object was to get its salesman into the prospective customer's living room and have him deliver his pitch.

The quality of the Britannica had never again reached the peak of its famous 1911 edition; and, declining after the First World War, it went into a still steeper, steady decline under Benton, whose view (of which he himself was perhaps only half-conscious) was that what was between the covers of anything wasn't as important as the technique of selling the covers. Slashing the cost of everything but sales promotion, the new publisher reduced editorial correction and updating from edition to edition to the point where the shoddiness of the product inspired a serious critic to publish a book-length chapter-and-verse indictment of the dreadful inadequacies of the new and improved Britannica.[3] Benton ignored the attack and stepped up the sales tempo.

The heart of the whole worldwide enterprise was the collection office in Chicago. ("The Encyclopaedia Britannica lives off installment buying," said Benton. "This is our whole business.") Soon after becoming Britannica's publisher, he inaugurated an annual matching companion volume to the set at $12.50, called *The Britannica Book of the Year*. By the time the *Great Books of the Western World* was published, ten years later, that little $12.50 item had produced such an immense profit that he had Mortimer Adler devise another $12.50 companion item, called *The Great Ideas Today*, to be sold to the installment purchasers of *Great Books*— and this one was also a small gold mine. Benton's explanation for the two ventures was that people who are making installment payments will go on making them until somebody tells them to stop; they might as well have an additional $12.50 tacked on to their regular notice.

The Britannica's selling methods and promotional practices were sufficiently notorious to have played a role (according to Hutchins) in the refusal of the trustees to put up the working capital and accept the EB as a direct gift from Sears Roebuck to the university. Some fifteen years after Benton took over its publication, the Federal Trade Commission ordered it to cease and desist from "deceptive acts in recruiting sales personnel, in gaining entry to the consumer's home, in selling its encyclopaedias, other books and related services, and in collecting debts."[4] (Benton's biographer doesn't mention this sensational fact of corporate life.) A professor at the University of Colorado was interested in buying the fifty-four-volume set of the great books and wrote to the company to ask the price. The reply was a foot-in-the-door great books salesman who delivered an oration on the educational advantages of reading the books and the social advantages of merely owning them. The professor tried to interrupt and say that he was acquainted with the advantages of reading books and had written simply to ask the price of the set; to no avail. In a fury, after he got the man out of the house, and still had not learned the price of the set, he wrote Benton and got a polite reply from a Benton assistant to the effect that this sales method, including the oration, had proved to be effective and the company did not allow its salesmen to depart from it.

Benton's suggestion, that the problem of getting the great books for the Fat Men's class be solved by publication of a set of them, fell on deaf ears here and there; but there were two ears that weren't deaf to it: Mortimer Adler's. Benton and Adler were—as Hutchins said admiringly—made for each other. The two men were consummate promoters of hot products—Palmolive soap and Thomism respectively. Their association grew closer as the association of both of them with Hutchins grew gradually somewhat more distant, and when Hutchins retired as the highly paid chairman of the Britannica editorial board, Adler, who had meanwhile negotiated a lifetime contract with Benton, succeeded him.

In the spring of 1943 Benton and Adler came to Hutchins with their project for the Great Books of the Western World. Hutchins was a bit bearish. There was a war on, in 1943, and nobody knew when, or, indeed, how, it would end. There might not be a ready market available—among other things—or even paper for the printing of what Benton and Adler between them envisaged as a stupendous aggregation of the noblest of all the works of the Western intellect, in every field, from Homer to Freud. (Works of the Orient were arbitrarily excluded.)

Besides, Hutchins was, as usual, to be the front man for the venture, its editor-in-chief; and he didn't see how he could conscientiously commit any of his own time to an undertaking of the scope that Benton and Adler proposed. No problem; Adler would be associate editor and fill in for Bob where it was necessary. It turned out to be necessary everywhere. The advisory board, which selected the books for the set—ultimately 443 works of seventy-four authors—was chosen by Hutchins. It consisted of Barr, Buchanan, Erskine, Mark Van Doren, Alexander Meiklejohn, Dean Clarence H. Faust (Hutchins' dean of the college), and the biologist Joseph J. Schwab (one of the younger Chicago scientists who supported Hutchins). The selection of the works took a couple of dozen weekend meetings over a two-year period and no end of reading and correspondence by the advisers. Hutchins, missing most of the meetings, which were then chaired by Adler, manfully tried to read (or read in, at his usual phenomenal speed) the most earnestly disputed works. One-fourth of the authors included were mathematicians or natural scientists, and almost another fourth social scientists (including the great historians). The remaining authors were divided among the writers of imaginative literature and philosophers and theologians. The last four centuries were represented by fewer than one-sixth of the authors, and only Melville, William James, and the authors of the Federalist Papers were Americans. (With the possible exception of St. Augustine, there was no non-Caucasian author, and the list was 100 percent male.)

Apart from the enormous ballyhoo that attended its publication in 1952, the set was attacked, with varying degrees of justification, by those modernists who believed that the world began last Thursday; by the cultural jingoists, who believed it began in America; by the small cliques (in those days) of admirers of oriental, female, and Negro writings; and by the partisans of those great writers who were excluded, such as Cicero, Calvin, Nietzsche, Leibniz, Mark Twain, and the Brontës.

It was a classic undertaking, nine years in publication, all told, and the triumph of a vision as immense in literary and educational as it was in commercial terms. Apart from the special-interest carping, it was met with approbation. Gilbert Highet in the *New York Times* hailed it as "a noble monument to the power of the human mind." It was, in addition, a monument to the powers of William Benton and Mortimer Adler as promoters, perhaps more especially of Benton, who recognized the genius of Adler in proposing, and concocting, the two-volume Syntopicon that went with the set.

At the outset of the giant venture Benton demanded something that would appear more readable to the prospective buyer. Adler went into intense meditation and came up with an idea index that would guide the reader to the most significant passages of all the authors on any one topic and thereby realize the buyer's fondest dream.

The Syntopicon—Adler coined the term, "a collection of topics"—was to cost $60,000 and take two years to complete. It cost $1 million and took eight years. (Wars—with Germany, Japan, Korea—came and went.) Renting a large greystone residence across the Midway from the campus, Adler assembled a staff of fifty very bright young men and women (including the then unknown Saul Bellow), plus seventy-five clerical helpers, with a monthly payroll of $26,000. They read through 443 great books—plus the Bible, which was not included in the set but which was indexed. Indexed was every substantial reference to Adler's list of 102 great ideas, beginning with Angel and ending with World, and the three thousand topics under those 102 ideas; all in all, some 900,000 decisions to include or exclude passages were made, with Adler, who dropped most of his teaching and lecturing operations, whipping his small horde along in the bowels of Index House in much the same manner as Benton peptalking his Britannica salesmen. ("Aristotle and Aquinas are doing fine, but Kant, Descartes, and Plotinus must catch up. . . . Under Topic 2b, I find only three references to Aristotle and three to Locke. This can not be at all. Something has got to be done about this. . . . We can not rest on such a random collection with such a major topic. I am sure I am right. Don't give in.")

The Syntopicon was not an easy compilation to fault; its two-volume massiveness was superficially awesome, and serious scholars were not likely to check the references. It gave the lie to the canard that Hutchins and Adler had long since decided that there were only one hundred great books, and there was no serious ground for arguing that great ideas had been ruthlessly excluded (or included) among the 102. There had ultimately to be a degree of arbitrariness in their selection, but each of them was preceded by a lengthy essay, ostensibly by Adler, which associated them with other ideas; and there was an additional "inventory" of some 1,800 terms, comprising all the ordinarily imaginable subjects of nontechnical discourse and relating each of them to the appropriate reference section under one or another of the 102 capital-*I* Ideas. However, there was much that was academically arguable about the Syntopicon enterprise. Its very grandiosity was comical, and it certainly would have been subject, had they looked into it, to the choleric contempt of the scholars on the other side of the Midway.

During the nine years' gestation of the project as a whole, Benton found himself occupied with no end of other large-scale operations. He served as vice-chairman—Paul Hoffman was chairman—of the wartime Committee for Economic Development organized by the Department of Commerce to propagandize the nation's postwar business needs and opportunities in the changeover period to civilian production and distribution; and he was on the road more than he was off it. He paid no attention to the progress of the Great Books undertaking. Hutchins, too, immersed in the university's war program, was largely inactive in the project, except for persuading Paul Mellon of the Pittsburg Mellons to have his Old Dominion Foundation make a $250,000 grant to buy sixteen hundred sets for public libraries. A begging letter written by Adler and signed by Hutchins and Adler produced five hundred subscriptions of $500 each for a special set of the fifty-four volumes in an expensive almost-leather binding.

The whole job, including the financing *and* the sales promotion, wound up in Adler's hands. When Benton's Britannica executives balked at going on indefinitely with the $26,000 monthly payroll at Index House, Adler ripped around the country to raise the money, brazenly, and successfully, bearding such storied figures as William Paley, Marshall Field, Conrad Hilton, Chicago Board Chairman Harold H. Swift, and, less successfully, H. L. Hunt of Texas (who asked Board Chairman Wood of Sears if Adler was a Communist, since Marx was among the authors in the set).

The *Syntopicon* was finished at last, its staggering staff disbanded and Index House abandoned, and the *Great Books of the Western World* was unveiled at a Founders' Edition dinner—for the five hundred individuals who had put up $500 each for the special set—on April 15, 1952, at, of course, the Waldorf Astoria with, inter alia, a covey of Vanderbilts and Rockefellers in attendance.

In the quarter-century after its publication the Great Books set sold something like a million copies, hitting an early peak of 49,000 in a single year. For two or three years it actually outsold the Britannica itself. But costs skyrocketed in the 1970s, and the profit on the venture evaporated—but not before no end of people got rich.

As residual beneficiary of two-thirds of the Britannica, Inc., stock in shameless exchange for the use of its imprimatur, the University of Chicago got enormously rich. Between 1943 and 1980 it received almost $60 million in royalties; and William Benton, the first recipient of Chicago's William Benton Medal (which he inspired) became a bigger benefactor of the institution than the founding father, John D. Rockefeller (who was not so busy that he had to drop his middle initial). Enriched, too, if insufficiently, was the corporate philosopher and genius of the enterprise, Mortimer J. Adler, who spent a million of the EB's total investment of $2.5 million in the great books of the Western world. Adler afterward testified with a touch of melancholy to his own genuflective experience at the noble monument, or trough:

"At one point, it looked as if the work I did on the set and the *Syntopicon* might reap a reward that would take care of my family and me in the years ahead. Bill Benton, in a moment of enthusiasm and generosity, talked about a royalty payment, which, if it had been no more than 1% of sales price, might have added up to a small fortune in the last twenty-five years. I reminded him, on several occasions, of what he said, only to learn the difference between a passing remark and a serious promise. Nine years of work on the set and the *Syntopicon* turned out in the end to be what it was at the beginning—a labor of love."[5]

Love's labor, of course, was lost on the editor-in-chief, Robert Maynard Hutchins (who always turned over all his outside earnings to the University of Chicago). His contributions to the enterprise were sporadic and incidental, Adler standing in for him at every point. As it was actually published, the fifty-four-volume set included a slim volume 1, entitled *The Great Conversation*, an introductory essay by Robert Maynard Hutchins. It included no end of cut-and-paste-up passages from Hutchins' earlier writings, but it was obviously the work of a much more prosaic hand than his, perhaps the only occasion in his prolific career in which his name was signed to another's work. He had no time. While his associates pondered the profitable publication of the wisdom of the ages, he was running a war plant. And there was a war on, which he did his level best to help prosecute in spite of the wisdom of the ages that suggested that war and wisdom were not won by the same sort of study. "It is not," he said at the outset of the war, "the responsibility of the armed forces to give a liberal education. The test of any training program operated by the Army and Navy is whether it fits a man to fight, not whether it fits him to be free."[6]

29 "Eat, Shirley"

Before the first year of the war was out, Hutchins realized that he had to quit teaching the honors course for freshmen, which he had been teaching with Mortimer Adler for ten years. He would never again have a close association with the young—never again come as close to having a good time. It wasn't that he thought the young were the hope of the world. He thought they were brands to be snatched from the burning. On those rare occasions when he had seen them outside the classroom—he once addressed a campus meeting for the purpose, he said, of "dispelling the rumor that I do not exist"—he was rejuvenated.

Convocation 1942, with five hundred students receiving their diplomas—bachelor, master, doctor—from the hand of the president in Rockefeller Chapel. The name of Wilbur Jerger is called, and Jerger, in uniform, comes forward to receive his law degree. One of the most argumentative of Hutchins' students, graduate and undergraduate, he reached for the outstretched parchment. But the president holds on to it. "Gimme that," says Jerger, tugging away. "What for?" says Hutchins. "You won't need it where you're going." "Gimme," says Jerger, "I earned it." "You did?" says Hutchins, and lets go of it. Jerger falls back and hits the national flag, which teeters on its pediment. The chapel roars. Forty years later Jerger recalled it, as did all who were there that day. Just as Attorney Clarissa Hutchins Bronson remembered her law school graduation at the University of California at Davis and the opening words of the commencement orator: "I have journeyed here from my jasmine-scented bower in Santa Barbara because I wanted to talk to my daughter when she could not interrupt me."

Year after year he gave the departing graduates an unrousing send-off with his ice-cold charisma, just as year after year he gave the entering

308

freshmen an unhearty welcome: "Let me direct your attention to a fact which may have escaped your notice: this is an educational institution." And after the graduate and undergraduate deans had sounded off on the subject of "these hallowed quadrangles," he rose before the bemused freshmen and said, "I hope you will not disgrace these hallowed quadrangles," and sat down.

A bright freshman in his honors course who at one moment was warmed by his magnetism would, at the next, be frozen stiff when Hutchins said, "You have favored us with a stirring oration. Would you mind telling us what it means? . . . But don't let me intimidate you, Mr. Smith."

Students were in some sense unawed by his combination of Olympian loftiness and postadolescent sass. He kidded the things they kidded and mocked the things they mocked. "If we should ask you in the final examination in this course whether you would rather have Aristotle's *Politics* or the Boy Scout Manual on a desert island, which would you say you would rather have and why would you say you would rather have the *Politics*?" He scorned what they scorned, and honored what they honored, intent on sending them forth (he was quoting Woodrow Wilson) "as unlike their fathers as possible."

Talking neither up nor down to them, what he tried to teach them was to be seriously disputatious, exemplifying the characteristic word and deed. A dean—not a Hutchins appointee—ordered a splinter-party Communist group off campus during one of the Red hunts across the country, on the technical ground that it did not meet the university's minimum membership requirement; Hutchins arbitrarily reinstated the group. He looked at the world the way the best of the young looked at it: normatively, "judgmentally." His nonchalance transparently covered a passionate concern with personal and social agonies. The young knew it, felt it, and they knew that this university was an involved man.

"It is literally true," said Bob Bork, '48, who became U.S. Solicitor General, "that in the dormitories, with bull sessions all the time, I can't remember a single session about girls or sex or sports. There was a lot of girl-chasing and drinking, of course, but the talk was serious. In the student body people were terribly serious about ideas. They may make some difference in later life—how quickly you sell out your ideas. Exposure to that life tends to make you more resistant to other people when you think their ideas aren't as good as yours."[1]

"The atmosphere on campus"—this is University of Illinois Professor Bernard R. Kogan, of the Chicago class of '41—"was feverish. Students debated Plato versus Aristotle, Stalin versus Trotsky, Freud versus Jung endlessly and heatedly. Hutchins and his ideas, too, were argued at length and freely. Expression was untrammeled, and this freedom, too, was part of the Hutchins plan in its largest sense."

The idea of stirring students to life brought to the campus, for short or long stints, a steady succession of credentialed and uncredentialed visitors such as Sinclair Lewis, Artur Schnabel, Thomas Mann, Thornton Wilder, Alexander Woollcott, Carl Sandburg, Socialist Norman Thomas, Communist Earl Browder. Always casting about for exciting teachings, Hutchins brought G. A. Borgese from Italy, Bruno Bettelheim from Germany, exiled president Eduard Benes from Czechoslovakia. He tried to get President Conant to leave Harvard and take over the natural sciences at Chicago. He held Gertrude Stein to her promise to return to the university and take on the freshman honors class: "And then I went to take over their class with them. So we all sat around a long table and. . . I began to talk and they not Hutchins and Adler but the others began to talk and pretty soon we were all talking about epic poetry and what it was it was exciting we found out a good deal some of it I used in one of the four lectures I wrote for the course I came back to give them. . . . Well we all came out and they liked it and I liked it and Hutchins said to me as he and I were walking, you did make them all talk more than we can make them and a number of them talked who never talked before and it was very nice of him to say it. . . and then I said you see why they talk to me is that I do not know the answer, you say you do not know but you do know if you did not know the answer you could not spend your life in teaching but I really do not know, I really do not, I do not even know whether there is a question let alone having an answer for a question. To me when a thing is really interesting it is when there is no question and no answer, if there is then already the subject is not interesting and it is so, that is the reason that anything for which there is a solution is not interesting, that is the trouble with governments and Utopias and teaching, the things not that can be learnt but that can be taught are not interesting. Well anyway we went away."[2]

That was the idea, all over the campus and even in a few graduate areas such as the law school. The *Daily Maroon* must have been the only student newspaper in the country in which the curriculum was debated on the front page day after day. Associate Professor James Redfield (BA '54) recalled twenty years afterward: "The only time I ever took part in a student demonstration was on behalf of the College curriculum. That was the sort of thing we demonstrated about in those days at Chicago. For the first time in my life, I had actually come alive."

For several years a student group maintained an "Aquinas House," whose central preoccupation was the intellectual reconciliation of St.

Thomas Aquinas with Karl Marx. (This largely Catholic undertaking probably sparked the jocular canard that Chicago was "a Baptist institution where Marxist professors taught Catholic philosophy to Jewish students.") Chicago was a big-city "street-car school" for half of its students, and under Hutchins it had the instant and persistent reputation for religious (and racial) tolerance. The entrance requirements were stiff; the scholastic average of the entering freshmen was above 90. Most of the undergraduates were non-"collegiate." They were overwhelmingly with Hutchins in his campaign to get rid of big-time-big-money football. Some 65 percent had part-time jobs on or off campus. They weren't grinds. What they were was excited.

Shirley Shapiro was a street-car kid, whose West Side ghetto parents had scraped to send her to college to get the education they had never got. Mama and Papa Shapiro were Old Country Jews, who sighed more than they spoke. But their Shirley was full of beans, and on her way home after the Hutchins-Adler freshman honors class on Tuesday afternoons she would be so engrossed (and exalted) in revolving the four causes of things (first, formal, efficient, final), the divisibility of sovereignty (one world or none), or the nature of the passions (the rock covets the center of the earth), that she sometimes forgot to change street cars. She would eventually come bounding up the stairs to the little apartment above the Shapiro tailor shop, to share her fresh-paint perceptions with her parents. They had invariably finished supper by the time she got home, but they were still at the table waiting for her. She kissed her father—her mother, hearing her on the stairs, had gone to the kitchen to reheat the soup—and began talking a blue streak. Her mother brought the soup, and Shirley kissed her as she bent over and went right on talking. "And what," one of her friends asked her, "did *they* say?" "All they ever said," said Shirley, "was 'Eat, Shirley.'"

"The whole business about education in a university," said Hutchins a quarter-century afterward, "can be summed up in a question: Has the institution any vitality? Is anything going on? Is there anything exciting about it? Young people understand. They know whether or not a teacher is simply earning a salary. They know whether he is trying to win the Nobel Prize or trying to contribute to their education. At Chicago the students did have the impression that we were trying to do something about their education, and that a big fight about a fundamental issue was underway.

"This awareness spread throughout the whole place. Everybody was involved in it, even the lowliest freshman. I think the reason for some recent difficulties in higher education"—this was at the time of the student turmoil at the end of the 1960s—"is that the students feel that though they may be the basis for legislative appropriations, or the basis of tuition fees, the place does not exist for them and the administration and the trustees don't care about doing anything for them. I don't think the attitude of the students at the University of Chicago had anything to do with me. It was simply that there was no other place in the United States at that time where you could get the same kind of educational experience."[3]

The young faculty determined the content of the course sequences. "Since the large staffs"—of the collegiate divisions—"brought together persons of diverse backgrounds and trainings," Professor Daniel Bell of Columbia wrote in *The Reforming of General Education*, "the courses, as I can testify from personal experience, were extraordinary intellectual adventures for the teaching staff; and perhaps this was its prize, if unintended, virtue, for what a teacher finds exciting he can communicate best to his students. Whether in the end the courses had the intellectual unity or theoretical clarity claimed for them is moot."[4]

The intellectual adventure, for teachers and students alike, was supposedly on ice for the duration of the World War. But Hutchins chaffed increasingly after giving up the freshman honors course. Temperamentally he needed another kind of war than the one the country was fighting. In early 1944 there was one event that placed him at the head of a charge that led to victory. He won the Battle of Fifty-seventh Street.

The battle took place at the Quadrangle Club, the Georgian edifice on the campus that served as a faculty association—and wasn't one. It enjoyed free rent and utilities from the university, but it was independently incorporated and as many as a quarter of its members were non-university-connected gentlemen (most of them alumni) of the neighborhood. (Some years before, the Illinois Board of Tax Appeals had rejected its claim to tax exemption as a profssional, rather than a social, organization.) Half the faculty—and most of the senior professors—had lunch there regularly. Faculty and nonfaculty members used the three tennis courts, the periodical library, and the billiard and card rooms. Its private dining rooms served faculty committees for meetings at lunch or otherwise. The club was a stroll from their offices. All in all a most agreeable place.

In 1943 a tall young man named Gordon Dupee, who had been head waiter at the club, resigned that post to take a job in the university radio office. Dupee was not in uniform. He had a heart condition he'd tried unsuccessfully to conceal from his draft board; he was a conscientious objector to war and had wanted to be so classified. His pacifism was known on the campus and among the faculty. That wasn't all that was held against him at the club. As a student employee he wasn't expected to be subservient, but he was expected to be a bit deferential. And Dupee— you couldn't put a finger on it—somehow wasn't. Instead, his manner had been stiff and distant enough to be annoying. Now, as a newly hired university staff member, he was eligible for membership in the club. He applied, and he was blackballed.

The word of the Dupee blackball spread inexorably in the club and on the campus. Among the younger members—more rarely among the older—were sympathizers here and there with conscientious objection or, at least, with its being covered by the principle of academic freedom. Among the older members, and not just here and there, Dupee's dim view of the war in progress was a reminder of Hutchins' dim view of the world war in prospect. It was, to be sure, a social club, but it was also a faculty club, and the only faculty club in the university. But the membership as a whole hadn't known that the club was possessed of a blackball process. It was generally assumed that any faculty or staff member who applied was categorically accepted. Not so, it seemed.

Dupee's application for membership had been presented by Acting Dean Ralph W. Tyler of the Social Science Division and Professor Stephen N. Corey of Education. His name had been duly posted for two weeks on the club bulletin board and then acted upon by the membership committee. It came out later that the vote had been five to one against him. A delegation of a half-dozen members waited on Hutchins to ask him what should be done about the Quadrangle Club. He indicated that their visit was not entirely unexpected. He had, he said, written Professor Tom Peete Cross, the club president, asking him if Dupee had been blackballed because he was a pacifist, and Professor Cross had replied that it was for "purely personal reasons." Further, Hutchins wrote Cross, he had just been notified by the grapevine that the club had instituted the blackball only three years before, when a Hutchins faculty appointee, a Negro professor of education named Allison Davis, had applied for membership and then withdrawn his application. He had also, he went on, just been notified that Physics Professor Henry Gordon Gale had some time back requested the removal of a chair from the club because the distinguished Indian astronomer Chandrasekar had sat in it. He had further, he said, just been notified that the Quadrangle Club did not admit women. Under the circumstances just come to light, he thought, he said, that honorable men could do no less than fight and win, or, alternatively, fight, lose, and resign.

"I am a member of the Quadrangle Club because it is convenient for my colleagues and me to meet there to transact university business. I did not join on principle, and I shall not resign on principle. If, however, any of my colleagues resign on principle, and I can not, therefore meet them at the club on university business, I shall have to ask that they meet me elsewhere. Do I make myself clear?"

They thought he did. They asked him how many of his colleagues would have to resign before he would decline to enter the club. He was able to refer them to the eighteenth chapter of the Book of Genesis (where the Lord agreed to spare Sodom if as few as ten righteous men should be found in it).

The half-dozen righteous members then mobilized an opposition and demanded a meeting of the membership to review the by-laws. Three hundred of the five hundred members attended a closed meeting on the evening of June 11, 1945, and the discussion was genteelly acrimonious. The effective blackball of the Negro professor was answered by the bland assertion that the gentleman in question had withdrawn his application. The exclusion of women—there had always been many on the faculty— went unchallenged. The nature of the "purely personal reasons" was ruled out of order. A leading history professor said that the opposition ringleader was a friend of Hutchins in the habit of taking two desserts from the buffet table at lunch. But the burden of the defense was that the club was social in nature and the sole judge of its membership. The by-laws were upheld by a vote reported to have been 182 to 85.

The Chicago *Sun* quoted unnamed faculty members as saying that the whole affair "was confused by the injection of feelings for and against President Robert M. Hutchins." Neither at the June meeting nor later was the "Hutchins issue" ever given voice. But the *Sun* had reported correctly.

Ten righteous men (half non–university connected) at once resigned, and the next day Hutchins excused himself from a committee meeting at the club because some of his colleagues were not members; the meeting, and every subsequent meeting of the sort, was transferred to the nearest hotel, and guests could reach it from the campus only by rounding up transportation. (Hutchins attended in a chauffeur-driven livery car.) The drop of water was eroding the stone. But it was only a drop of water. The flood came not from the ten righteous colleagues, but from the students who admired the president who would not enter the club.

The day after the membership meeting the seventeen student employees of the club went on strike against what they called "discrimination against certain members of the faculty on the basis of race, sex, or political convictions." They called a student mass meeting and invited the club's officers to attend. (None did.) The meeting was advised of the results of the previous evening's events—the closed proceedings having been thoroughly disclosed by the strikers who had been on duty. Then they set up a picket line in front of the club, with fifty students carrying signs like, "Look Who Writes Our Textbooks." Hutchins rode by the picket line in his liveried limousine, and did not deign to turn his head to notice it.

Three months later a faculty group announced the organization of a new club "for educational and professional purposes, to enable every member of the University to join, regardless of his financial ability and regardless of color, religion, race, or opinion." It would be called the Faculty Club and would apply to the university administration for support. No word from the university administration, and the liveried limousine continued to drive by, followed by faculty committee members who wished to meet with the president. Three months still later, another membership meeting of the Quadrangle Club was called, to liberalize its admission policy to admit members by a majority vote of the club's council (the membership committee which had rejected Dupee). The blackball process was thus amended, but retained. The club's status as a social organization, judging the admissibility of its members, was reasserted. Still no word from the university administration.

But fewer and fewer faculty members went to the club, even among those who hadn't resigned. And one by one there were more resignations. And student help was progressively harder to get.

In March of 1946 a new set of officers of the beleaguered Quadrangle Club waited on Hutchins. The club, they informed him, was in some difficulty. He expressed his regret. Would the university administration consider helping it financially? Hutchins thought that it would be glad to and he referred them to Vice-president W. C. Munnecke. Mr. Munnecke took the matter under advisement for five minutes, then informed the club that the university would be happy to assume its financial responsibilities providing that membership was open to all faculty and staff members on a scale of dues within the means of the lowest paid member of the university.

It was the Quadrangle Club's Canossa, and it had come about through the connivance of president and students against resistant members of the faculty. The striking students had known they had the support of the president, who never turned his head to look upon them as he whisked by their picket line. It had been Hutchins' way of enjoying himself, impudently associated once more, if only episodically, with the impudent young.

With the Quadrangle Club incident, all the freshmen he had taught—and all those he hadn't—had another chapter to add to the Hutchins legend. It didn't take many myths to make a mythological creature of him. Any least encounter was enough.

One afternoon he was en route home—in the block along Harper Library between the president's office and the president's house—and a small group of students made way for him on the sidewalk, falling silent and covertly looking at him as he approached. As he went by them he said, without looking at them, "Tip your hat when the president passes." By the following day the story had fanned out across the campus, and it continued to be told for many a day and many a decade.

Many a year—and a decade or two—afterward, novelist Noel Gerson was having lunch at "21" in New York, and there was the idol of his undergraduate youth at Chicago. "He was standing at the bar with a couple of other guys, and he was looking and behaving like a normal human being, not like the great Greek god I had imagined him to be. That was the first inkling I ever had that he was other than an enormous figure. Many people came in and out and totally ignored him, to my astonishment and consternation."

The students he brought to life kept him alive, and after he decided that he had to quit teaching, with some possible premonition that he would never teach the young again, the Battle of Fifty-seventh Street briefly restored him. But only briefly. He once said that he could not think of a time during his Chicago presidency when he wasn't frustrated and furious. After Pearl Harbor he would confine his energies to the deadly and deadening business of the war. He kept his word for six miserable months, and his enemies smugly assumed that he would let things—and them—be, until it was over over there. But as the war went on, and as he thought he saw his gloomiest prophecies materializing and the prospective victory turning to ashes even before it was won; as the war went on and his administrative duties had less and less to do with the liberal arts, and more and more to do with the martial; as the war went on and he had less and less to do with fitting the rising generation to be free and more and more to do with fitting them to fight, he grew ever more furious.

30   Disturbing the War

In 1938, Hutchins had roundly deplored the University of Chicago's chaotic and ineffective administrative organization and suggested that he should be president in fact as well as in name. Under the statutes of the university the president had neither power nor responsibility. Nobody had. There was nobody at Chicago (or anywhere else) charged with asking, "What are we trying to do?"

His introduction of the question of power and responsibility had followed a 1938 vote of seventy-six members of the two-hundred-man university senate, who decided, forty-two to thirty-four, to investigate a complaint by the regional Association of University Professors that Hutchins and his deans had too much control over appointments, promotions, and salaries. They asked the investigatee to head the investigating committee, and nothing more was heard of it. But one of them was quoted anonymously at the time as saying that a large majority of the faculty "believe he has an insatiable lust for power."[1]

The issue of presidential power had been simmering on the back burner since then, though he let it be known now and again that it was still on his mind. But it was clear with the country at war that nothing so radical, in terms of the university's long-run activities, would be brought forward. Nor was it—until in mid-July 1942 he prepared a sixteen-page memorandum to the board of trustees—not to the faculty, to the board. The memorandum proposed a revision of the university's constitution, something which "has never been done, here or elsewhere."[2]

All he wanted to do was turn the organization of the institution upside down. After twelve years of bucking the faculty line, gaining a yard or two here, losing a yard or two there, he was attempting an end-run. The constitution of the university was the board's province. He condescended—

317

statutorily he needn't have—to suggest that the board send his proposal to the faculty senate and ask the senate to appoint a committee to advise with a committee of the board concerning it. (The board did so; the senate appointed its committee; and two years later he was constrained to observe that nothing had been done.)

Formally the proposal was couched in alternative forms. The structure of the modern university—Chicago included—was "confused and ineffective" as a consequence of its being modeled (with only minor changes) on the small college of the previous century. "If democratic government requires responsibility, then university government is undemocratic, for no academic individual is responsible for his acts as part of that government. . . . According to the [Chicago] Constitution the faculty controls educational policy. . . . But the President may refuse to appoint or promote members of the faculty"—and determine the range and diversity of the institution's activities in terms of its financial condition.

Thus the faculty "is for all practical purposes without a remedy against the use of these presidential powers to create an educational situation of which, if given a chance to vote, they would never approve. Though they participate at Chicago in the selection of a president, they can do very little about him after he is in office." On the other hand, "the powers of the faculty over education mean that nobody can be held responsible for education. The authority of the faculty is such that the President can not be held responsible. In no event could the faculty be. The members of a department could not be discharged because their judgment with regard to appointments proved to be bad or because their preoccupation with duties relating to part of a program led them to resist suggestions for the improvement of the program as a whole."

Could something fundamental be done? Could the University of Chicago be made orderly *and* democratic? Hutchins thought it could be—in one of two ways. Plan I (as it came to be known) involved "the abandonment of responsibility and efficiency as criteria of university government. We should simply say that these notions are inapplicable to the kind of thing a university is. We should hold that there are other values more important to a university and that these emerge in proportion as the community of scholars which is the university manages its affairs. On this theory all matters affecting the institution, its expenditures, its public relations, its plant, as well as its educational and scientific program, would be under the direction of the faculty." Under this plan the president would be the chairman of the faculty, simply a presiding officer who would also represent the institution at public events, like the rector of a German university, who serves for one year, exercises no power, has no educational function, and enjoys the improbable designation of *Magnifizenz*. (But the German and other European universities so operated are ultimately answerable to a government ministry.)

Hutchins went on advocating Plan I as an alternative—"preferable to that under which we are now operating"—in the ensuing two years of controversy. But he was disingenuous in doing so. Not only was it not like him temperamentally or philosophically to countenance such a "democratic" structure; it was not like the faculty of a university, Chicago or any other, to want to undertake the role Plan I assigned to it. Hutchins as much as cut it down in his memorandum to the board: "Nor are the background, training, and duties of American professors such as to give much hope that they could manage the affairs of a great institution in the interest of the institution as a whole. For the most part they are selected because they are or are expected to become experts in their special fields. Their first duty is to become as great experts in their fields as possible. The votes of great experts in special fields do not necessarily add up to the best judgment on the policies of the institution as a whole."

He was not being derogatory here, except, perhaps, by implication, the implication being (as he said elsewhere in the memorandum) that "the President is the only educational officer whose sole duty is to the University as a whole, rather than to a department or a division. The great size of the University and the increasingly narrow lines of specialization in scholarship make it almost impossible for a professor to know all that is going on in his division, or in the University, or even, in some cases, in his own department."

This consideration led him to his Plan II, after his dismissal of Plan I because of the "fatal objections" he delineated (though he would continue to insist that it was a viable alternative). Plan II—*this* was Hutchins—was "a simple plan of administrative responsibility. This would mean that as long as the President had the confidence of the University Senate and the Board of Trustees he would be authorized to decide issues of educational policy. In addition to participating in his election the Senate would at any time be able to raise the question of confidence, and could, if it felt strongly enough, force the removal of the President.

"The President would be unable to proceed without the advice of the Senate and without that of a reorganized Senate Committee on University Policy. But when he had listened"—or, his opponents would say, pretended to listen—"to their advice, he would be required to decide, and take the consequences. The consequences might be an appeal from a small fraction of the Senate to the Board of Trustees to request the resignation of the President; the compulsory resignation of the President, which might or might not be accepted by the Board; or the compulsory removal of the President. Since through inertia or timidity the faculty might not avail itself of any of these methods of showing its lack of confidence in the President, the President should be elected for a seven-year term." (The term of the chief executive of many European countries.)

"These changes would give the faculty protection against the President, protection which it does not now have. They would ensure the fullest expression of faculty opinion on all matters affecting the University. They would make the President responsible to the faculty and responsible in fact, as well as in theory, to the Board of Trustees. On the other hand, they would give a president who had the confidence of the faculty an opportunity to do something."

An opportunity to do something. To do "something" that Robert Maynard Hutchins had not up to then been able to do because of the checks on him by a majority of his faculty, or by an activist minority unopposed by a majority, or by a majority of the board, which legally owned the university and over which he had only the power of persuasion. In the closing pages of his memorandum he argued (and believed he had overcome) the objections that might be raised—including the unlikely objection in the current situation of the University of Chicago that the president would be sedulous to avoid antagonizing anybody or doing anything lest he fail of reelection at the end of seven years. The memorandum closed with the assertion that if Plan II—or, presumably, Plan I—were to be adopted, he would present his resignation, and the resignation of his deans, so that officers might be chosen in conformity with the new regulations.

What did he want? He wanted immense power—and immense responsibility to balance it. But the worst culmination of his assumption of the responsibility would be his mere dismissal, while the worst culmination of his assumption of the power might be a cunning and unconscionable succession of administrative actions which might injure, or even destroy, the university before the machinery to get rid of him was rolling. Or at least so his opponents might envision, and his opponents had had twelve years to come by the apprehension that he would, had he his way, make changes of a much more radical character than he had succeeded up to then in introducing. Way back there somewhere, when he had first got his college, he had said—and his enemies had long memories—"We are now able to teach the wrong things the right way." It was the *right things* his faculty had up to then forestalled.

A much milder man, or a forceful man without a program of his own, might have got some support in his faculty for his Plan II and some considerable support among the businessmen on his board who knew what it was to assume responsibility, and its risks, along with power and its opportunity. Or Hutchins himself, when he was still relatively fresh on the scene and the opposition to him had not yet been hardened. But not Hutchins in 1942, and not Hutchins thereafter. And he could hardly help knowing it; he was an excruciating realist. What he sought was a cross between benevolent despotism and responsible autocracy, a parliamentary prime ministry as far as the vote of confidence was concerned, but without the restraints of the party a prime minister leads. He would have no party. He would stand alone. The board—where his power of persuasion was considerable—might refuse to accept his resignation, as the monarch sometimes does under ministerial governments. One of his friends said that he wanted to be a Benedictine abbot, serving with the advice, but not the consent, of the monks.

There wasn't a prayer of his getting what he asked. And he was bright enough to know it. And so was his board, including Laird Bell, who was probably the strongest man on the board and was not only Hutchins' strongest supporter but his personal attorney. Bell responded to the Hutchins memo as chairman of the board's Committee on Instruction and Research, but his response was (as was his wont) informal.

> How would it work with a Chancellor Day—or whoever that Syracuse die-hard was?
>
> Will you . . . get and hold . . . [faculty of the] highest calibre if they do not enjoy at least a measure of autonomy in their departments and schools?
>
> Would faculties think they had much chance of getting you to accept the resignation of one of your own appointed deans?
>
> Won't faculties believe . . . that the Board will back you up unless there is a sure-enough scandal?
>
> Won't you stir up AAUP and radicals?
>
> Any less radical way than one which suggests you want "dictatorial" powers?
>
> I confess to a weakness for a not too definite blueprint of authority, and to checks and balances, God save the mark! You have in the end got, from the Board, most of what you went after.
>
> All judgments on education and educators seem to me to be subjective. Is it the kind of field for a one-man judgment?

You have in the end got . . . most of what you went after. For which read variously: You aren't going to get this, or, You aren't going to get any more. It was the sharpest official rebuke Hutchins would ever receive, and he received it from a friend. If Bell was unsympathetic to Plan II—Plan I was not even discussed—the board as a whole would certainly be unsympathetic. But Bell knew and the board knew that Hutchins was incapable of letting go. The man saw his administrative career as one of shameful compromise. In order to get things taught "the right way," he had yielded on having "the wrong things" taught; the liberal arts and the great books actually played a minor role in the undergraduate program. He had got the divisional organization and the autonomous college he wanted, but the university in its anarchical essentials was unaffected. Under cover of the war emergency he had got the "two-year" bachelor's degree (which would probably be revoked when the war was over). He had won a few skirmishes, such as the withdrawal from intercollegiate football and the severance of the Rush Medical School from the university and the incorporation of the university's own medical school into the new Division of the Biological Sciences. But twelve years had passed and he had been fought to a standstill on the central front: the exemplary reconstruction of the higher learning. He had, perhaps, meant to rest on his spear after Pearl Harbor and play the genteel role of an administrator of things as they were—or, now, as the wartime government wanted them. But it hadn't worked. He once said that he had the impression that his ancestors had been, on the whole, stubborn men and women. So, on the whole, was their descendant.

The Hutchins memorandum (of July 18, 1942) was marked Confidential. But it wasn't; board members had close friends in the faculty, and even an extremely able man like Bell, the busiest of lawyers, was unlikely to have undertaken to indite his response to Hutchins without considerable briefing from faculty friends. Certain senior members of the faculty were known to have the habit of going to board members with one or another aspect of "the Hutchins issue." While some of them had some effect, the habit had (as it always does) a tendency to backfire, too; university board members were generally administrators in their own fields of endeavor, and they preferred dealing with an able administrator rather than with professors. The Hutchins memorandum was followed by six months of board silence. At the end of December, the board sent a letter to the faculty senate, embodying the Hutchins alternatives and proposing a senate committee to discuss them with Bell's Committee on Instruction and Research.

The senate committee was appointed, consisting, of course, of senior professors, since only men and women of full professorial rank were senate members. That anything decisive would emerge from such quarters was itself most unlikely, in view of the fact that one of Hutchins' Plan II recommendations was that the size of the senate be radically reduced in the name of efficiency and its membership opened on a proportional basis to all ranks of the faculty. (His major strength, remember, was in the lower ranks). The two committees met jointly on several occasions but made no apparent headway.

On March 10, 1943, Hutchins made his last stab, submitting to the board of trustees a memorandum—this one was not marked Confidential—painstakingly restating his proposals and dismissing Plan I as "requiring no elaboration." Moving immediately to Plan II he said, "I am not personally involved in the matter. We are here concerned with the proper administrative structure for a great university rather than with the amount of power Mr. Hutchins should have. The university should organize itself in the best possible manner and then seek for the individual who would be the best executive under that form of organization."

He went on, his passion concealed by his benign posture, to present an argument that was nothing less than tricky and transparently so: "The present organization of the University has broken down and is leading to a Presidential dictatorship."—The wolf crying, "Wolf, wolf."—"The President, without consulting the faculty, and often without consulting the Board, is deciding important educational issues himself because the speed and secrecy required make consultation impossible. I do not believe that this situation will be materially altered at the end of the war. The government will use the universities during the period of reconstruction as it has been using them since the emergency began. . . . The present president of the University is full of good will; but I think that no individual, however benevolent, should be permitted to decide crucial educational questions without such checks and safeguards as are proposed in Plan II." (The decisions which required "speed and secrecy" were, of course, war decisions which were either unrelated to crucial educational questions or were by definition temporary.)

Plan II hadn't a prayer. The well into which it sank appeared, as the months passed, to be bottomless. By the beginning of 1944, fattened by a steady diet of frustration and fury, he was ready to set his blunted spear aside and try his hand at throwing thunderbolts.

31   The Cannon

In Victor Hugo's novel *Ninety-Three* a cannon breaks loose on the gun
deck of a French corvette under full sail, becoming "suddenly some inde-
scribably supernatural beast...a monster...[that] rolls with the rolling,
pitches with the pitching, goes, comes, pauses, seems to meditate, resumes
its course, rushes from end to end along the ship like an arrow, circles
about, springs aside, evades, roars, breaks, kills, exterminates.... In what
way can one attack it? You can make a mastiff hear reason, astonish a bull,
fascinate a boa, frighten a tiger, soften a lion; there is no resource with that
monster, a cannon let loose. It continued its work of destroying the ship."[1]
("We know our responsibilities as trustees," Board Chairman Harold H.
Swift of the University of Chicago wrote in a form letter to complaining
alumni in 1944. "We are working hard for the University, and we are
working constantly for its continued advancement. I don't believe we will
wreck it—nor let it be wrecked.... I am not sure that there is much I can
say to you which will seem convincing. For the most part people either like
Mr. Hutchins' educational philosophy, or they don't.... I know Mr.
Hutchins pretty well. While he has strong opinions, I believe his desire is to
make the strongest possible university in every field, and I see no evidence
that he is sacrificing any division of the University.")
    The quick winter evening of January 12, 1944, came in with a beatific
glitter over the South Shore Country Club. The occasion was the university's annual gala, for which the club's grand ballroom was always rented:
the trustees' dinner to the faculties. The preprandial bar at the club was
laden with the best free drinks. The main course was the finest steak that
money (*or* ration coupons) could buy. Board Chairman Harold H. Swift
always presided at the trustees' dinner and always introduced the speaker
of the evening, who was always the president. The faculty always ap-

plauded roundly when the president was introduced; it did not always applaud so roundly at the conclusion of his remarks, which were sometimes disturbing. It was, indeed, his wont to use the great dinner as a staging area for one or two awful assaults, on the ground, presumably, that his audience would not be able, when he moved the assault to the faculty senate chamber, to claim that they were taken by Draconian surprise.

There was nothing untoward to be anticipated this evening. The campus war plant was running smoothly and, as far as anyone could make out, successfully on every front. Whatever Hutchins would say, he would say it with that delicious laconic wit. And there was no real reason for any slashing, on this glittering evening when Hutchins would surely be entertaining.

And so he was, for the whole of five minutes. Observing that this was his fifteenth appearance at this annual festivity and comparing himself to the champion flagpole sitter whose distinction lay not in what he had done but in his having done it so long. Then he jollied them some more at, as usual, his own expense: "The fact is that as a university president proceeds up to and beyond the fifteenth year mark, his loss of knowledge, accompanied by the loss of health, hair, teeth, appetite, character, figure, and friends, becomes nothing short of sensational. Tonight, after fifteen years, I have only one point, and a very little one, to make."[2]

And then he suddenly stopped jollying:

"My little point is that nothing has been done here in the last fifteen years. . . . We have been engaged in pushing over pushovers. And since some of them have been large, as well as old, their collapse has caused a good deal of noise. . . . We abandon the most archaic and irrelevant of academic irrelevancies, intercollegiate football, and congratulate ourselves on having slain the giant. The giant was dead on his feet before we pushed him over. Although nobody has ventured to say a good word for the credit, or adding machine, system of education in fifty years, we like to think that we pioneered when we made certain gestures toward overthrowing it. The excesses of the departmental system having been unanimously condemned for a generation, we did something about them in the reorganization of 1930, with a flourish out of all proportion as to what we did. Since we had contended that academic freedom was indispensable to the existence of a university, we can not take much pride in the fact that we defended it when it was under attack in 1935." As to the most recent "stirring action of ours," the award of the bachelor's degree at the end of the conventional sophomore year, it had been advocated by one of his predecessors thirty years before.

Whence, then, the University of Chicago's great reputation for pioneering on the frontiers of education and research? It was due chiefly to the terrible state of American education. "A turtle, if it is in motion at all, will seem to whizz by a stationary object; and if the stationary object ceases to be stationary and starts slowly sagging downhill, the turtle will appear to be climbing at a terrific rate. The difference between us and the rest of American education does not lie in our intelligence, courage, and originality. It is simply a slight difference in tradition. The tradition elsewhere is to agree that something ought to be done, but that nothing can be. The tradition here is to agree that if the consensus of all literate men and women through the ages is that something ought to be done, perhaps we ought to try to do something about it."

But that something had not been enough. The credit, or "adding machine," system still prevailed in many of the university's divisions and schools; only the college and the social sciences division had got rid of it entirely. So, too, the course system, which was interwoven with the credit system. Reading lists, a tutorial system, and general examinations "constitute the only defensible educational combination. . . . The passion for courses, like the passion for textbooks, rests on the assumption that you can not educate in an American educational institution. . . . We are told that [the young] can not learn anything outside the classroom, especially not from good books. . . . Of the pushovers that still obstruct us, I hope that the course system, and the adding machine system dependent on it, will be among the first to fall."

The preprandial and prandial delights had given way to the same old scolding, the same old belittling, the same old taunting, and the same old demands. After fifteen years of watching him intently, his audience was still underestimating the intensity of his frustration and his fury. After fifteen years of a wild and woolly tenure, he was unwilling merely to add insult to injury; he was bent on adding injury to injury. He had just begun to fight.

"We are still entangled in the farce of academic rank. It performs no function except to guarantee a certain constant measure of division and disappointment·in the faculty. Tenure means nothing. New members of the faculty are guaranteed permanent tenure after ten years of service. Salary means something. Of salaries I shall speak in a moment. Rank means nothing except trouble. We should get rid of it."

The proposal to abolish rank was staggering. Everybody was to appear to be the equal of everybody else. The only instantly visible distinction among scholars was to be junked. It was—it was—it was—socialism, that's what it was. Some sort of socialism. In the great university where everyone was a Doctor, everyone was called Mister and no one was called (or called himself) Professor. But everyone knew who was a professor—and by that exclusionary fact, a member of the faculty senate. The titles were writ small, but indelibly. (And what about the president?—Did you hear him say anything about doing away with *that* title?)

Of salaries I shall speak in a moment. Now the glow of the evening was wholly dissipated. Rank—and salaries—were important. The professorial diners were sitting up. (And so were the trustees.) They all knew that the wisecracker had once been quoted as saying, "A businessman may have ideals, but a professor will do anything for money."

Now the phrases came measured: "As academic rank divides the academic community, so does our tendency to regard that professor as most successful who has the greatest number of paying interests outside the university. The members of the faculty should be put on a full-time basis; they should be paid decent salaries; and they should be free to engage in outside activities they like. To make sure that the ones they like are the ones that are good for them, they should be required to turn over all their outside earnings to the University. (Here at longest last the face of tyranny was unveiled: *To make sure that the ones they like are the ones that are good for them, they should be required. . . .*)

"We should promote the sense of community within the University by reconsidering the whole salary question. The only basis of compensation in a true community is need. The academic community should carefully select its members. When a man has been admitted to it, he should be paid enough to live as a professor should live." (And who would say how "a professor should live"? Plainer and plainer, the face of tyranny displayed.)

"This would mean that a young man with three children would have a larger living allowance than a departmental chairman with none. Under the present system the members of the faculty who get any money get it when they need it least and starve and cripple themselves and their scholarly development because they get nothing to live on when they need it most.

"These things are obvious and are all on the pushover level."

The only basis of compensation in a true community is need. ("Neither was there any among them that lacked: for as many as were possessors of lands or houses sold them, and brought the prices of the things that were sold, and laid them down at the apostles' feet: and distribution was made unto every man according as he had need." Acts 5:34–35.)

Bolshevism.

The president went on talking for another ten or fifteen minutes, but his hearers had been stunned into inattention. He brought up the issue of organization again, saying (again) that all that had to be done ("it is time we did something") was to elect a short-term president, require him to ask the faculty's advice, and compel him to decide and take the consequences. To his now inattentive listeners, the decisions that would be made by this president would come down to socialism and bolshevism.

And to what all else? "A university president is a political leader without patronage and without a party. He should have neither. He should be the responsible officer of a high-tension democracy."

A *high-tension* democracy.

"An academic community is not an end in itself. Neither is academic democracy. They are both in their turn preliminary steps."

To what?

"They are means to the accomplishment of the purpose of the University."

And the purpose of the University?

"And the purpose of the University is nothing less than to procure a moral, intellectual, and spiritual revolution throughout the world. . . . The whole scale of values by which our society lives must be reversed if any society is to endure. We want a democratic academic community because we know that if we have one we can multiply the power which the University can bring upon the character, the mind, and the spirit of men. Among the kinds of institution called to this crusade the specific task of the university is the development, release, and direction of intellectual power. . . . The total resources of the University must be focused on the problem of raising the intellectual level of the society which it serves."

The whole scale of values . . . multiply the power . . . the spirit of men . . . this crusade . . . the total resources. . . . A cannon let loose. . . .

"We have the only rationally organized college in the United States. . . . Since it is the only one which can do it, it is under a duty to reform, or rather to introduce, liberal education in this country. This requires the members of its faculty to figure out what a liberal education is, to get one themselves, and then reveal it to the world."

Get one themselves.

"If we are to show the way to liberal education for all, we shall have to get ready to educate the teachers who are to undertake this task. We may have to found a new organization for this purpose. At that time we shall have to reconsider our advanced degrees and think once more whether we ought not to award the PhD to those who have prepared themselves to teach through a new Institute of Liberal Studies."

Intermittently since his inaugural address fifteen years before, he had called for the award of separate PhDs for research and teaching. He had never before called for a new organization.

"It all comes to this. The University of Chicago has greater opportunities and greater obligations than any university in history, even greater than those which fell to the lot of the University of Paris seven hundred years ago. It is perhaps too much to hope that as the University of Paris moulded the civilization of the Middle Age, the University of Chicago can make a civilization in the Twentieth Century. But it can try."

The faculty that was going to lose its rank and its competitive wages was aghast. The board members scattered among them at the dinner tables in the ballroom were aghast at the prospect of introducing socialism and bolshevism into what was, after all, legally their property and their responsibility. The ballroom sat silent, mesmerized by the human cannon run amok among them.

"I must confess"—he drew a breath—"I must confess that I have never liked the motto of the University—Crescat Scientia Vita Excolatur. Let Knowledge Grow That Life May Be Enriched. In the first place, it seems incongruous and affected for those rugged and unsophisticated pioneers of the Nineties to think up a Latin slogan for their raw, new university. In the second place, 'enriched' is ambiguous. I do not like the materialistic interpretation to which it is open. Therefore I suggest a new motto for the University, one which will express its spirit and its purpose as it sallies forth to battle in the revolution that must come if men are to live together in peace. The new motto I suggest for the University is a line from Walt Whitman. It is this: 'Solitary, singing in the West, I strike up for a new world.'"

He sat down, as obviously unshaken as Hugo's cannon was. The applause was perhaps the least deafening he had ever received. But there was one segment of the audience which could not restrain itself completely. It was composed of "the young men with three children," the instructors at the very bottom of the totem pole to whose ears the proposal of full-time service with compensation on the basis of need sounded sweet indeed. ("They'll breed like rabbits," said Dean William Taliaferro of the biological sciences division.)

32　Brooks Brothers Bolshevik

As the faculty and trustees poured out of the grand ballroom of the South Shore Country Club that evening of January 12, 1944, they were sharply aware that the only thing their president had said that he hadn't said many times before was that "the only measure of compensation in a true community is need." He had caught them all—friends and enemies—off base. For fifteen years he had talked education and nothing but education (except when he had taken to the microphone in 1941 to talk war and peace). Of an unforeseeable sudden he had thrown moral and social philosophy at them.

The moralist demanded the application of the moral principle of social justice to a capitalist institution in a capitalist country. He could not have taken the University of Chicago to be the true community of which he spoke; it must have been that he intended to make it one. But it wasn't his university, and he had no statutory voice in the economic basis on which it operated. That was the sole prerogative of the trustees, who, if they were not capitalists in principle, were nothing. The Hutchins proposal, that storied evening, was some sort of bolshevism. His offhand projection of a family allowance combined with abolition of rank suggested that the faculty members of a great university, from the most renowned to the most obscure and unpromising, might all be paid the same salary by a board no one of whom would dream of running his own business that way.

It wouldn't work, of course; when did bolshevism ever work, and why wouldn't it succeed, in this case, in simply driving the best professors away and deter the best professors in other universities from coming to Chicago? ("I don't believe we will wreck it—nor let it be wrecked.") Who, if he had a chance to go elsewhere, would stay, besides the incompetent, the half-competent, the nonproductive, and a few young idealists who were more interested in utopianism than they were in their work? Who would want to come? Again, the same sort of utopian and the same sort of none too promising men and women who would exert all their energies to get taken on and achieve tenure with nothing further in view than being sustained in the Life of Professor Reilly their lives long.

Plainly, Hutchins had at last flown from the rock-hard reality of human nature and human society. There were some men and women—certainly in a university—who wanted other things more than they wanted money. But where were the men and women to be found who didn't want money, too, and not just enough money to keep them alive at a level determined by Robert M. Hutchins or his subalterns? Where were the men and women who didn't want a new car or a bigger house even though the old car and the old house were, however unsatisfactorily, still serviceable? And where was the governance of such a society that didn't come down, in the end, to arbitrary and capricious tyranny?

What *was* the man up to?

Interviewed by Donald McDonald for the Columbia University Oral History Project twenty-five years after the event, he dated the final faculty onslaught on him from that speech. He insisted (perhaps disingenuously) that he was actually surprised when his socialist proposal "struck terror in the hearts of many members of the faculty." The terrified were, of course, the old. They stood only to lose, the great men who in the largest sense make or break a university. Again, they saw Hutchins appealing against them to the lowly young.

The greatest of the great men had access to one or another of the trustees socially. They went to their friends on the board and "appealed to them not to listen to me any more. They did not suggest that I retire or resign, but they thought it would be nice if the Board were less attentive."[1] The Hutchins proposal was double-barreled. It would focus the whole attention of the professors on their proper work, and it would achieve something he had been trying to get from the board for several years past: a salary increase for the lower ranks of the faculty. (In the interest of disarming opposition in the higher ranks he had asked the board for an overall 25 percent increase.) It was appropriate, and inevitable, that the president of a corporation ask his board for wage raises for the employees who had no one else to represent them. But a wage raise, however steep, would not threaten the principle of differential compensation as long as it was proposed on a percentage basis. That wasn't bolshevism. This was.

He had, to be sure, been making radical noises, off and on, all his life and making them in public. As long ago as his speech to the Young Democrats in 1932 he had urged social legislation more radical than FDR's and had indicated his support for the Socialist presidential candidate Norman Thomas.[2] Again and again down the succeeding years he had emerged to fire a fine salvo at the ship of state laden with its inequities and iniquities. But he had never left the high-minded road of generality and got down to cases. He had never carried responsibility for the social order into his own back yard.

Neither his enemies nor his friends supposed he ever would. He was, after all, the chief executive of a great corporation and, as such, a man whose genteel sybaritism was so deeply ingrained as to be unconscious. What about *his* need and *his* family allowance? True, he had cut his own salary exemplarily during the Depression and had always turned his outside earnings over to the university (a practice he hadn't advertised); but who was to decide, and on what basis, how much *he* needed to support *his* three children, his wife, her studio and the family's summer sojourns on the Connecticut shore or in Europe? Or the servants at the university president's house? How could he set up a scheme that would level gross differentials in compensation and do away with the invidiousness on which the money-making world turned? In the first place, he seemed to be talking (and later said that he was) about *earned* income. Now professors A and B had gone about as far as they would go in biology and history respectively, and they drew down, it was understood, low wages at their already attained ultimate level of associate professor. But they lived lavishly in large houses, when leading professors were living in unpretentious apartments. A and B had married money. What kind of family allowance was A or B to get to maintain three children? What about professors C and D, who were themselves heirs? The earnings of such men were the least part of their income. At a faculty meeting on the subject someone asked what Hutchins would be expected to do with the money if he won a Nobel Prize of (at that time) $46,000. "Keep it," said Hutchins airily—as if such an exception wouldn't invalidate the whole scheme. The likely abuses were endless.

Reflecting long afterward on the immediate effect of that historic speech of his, Hutchins acknowledged that his hearers that evening could well have felt themselves threatened by a proposal as casually and cryptically presented as that one. Would a department head with no dependents actually be cut, and an instructor of no particular promise doubled in salary to support his three children—or more to support his six? But these were the least of the scandals that threatened the very fabric of the institution.

Hutchins had already broken the back of the scandal of scandals: medicine. The scheme in America was the affiliation of an independent medical school with a university, in Chicago's case the Rush Medical School, whose wealthy men in white treated many of the university's wealthy trustees and donors. Hutchins mounted a crusade to establish a new medical school integrated into the university's biological sciences division and succeeded, over the years, in persuading his board to accept this proposal over the agonized protest of the free-enterprising Rush faculty and the medical profession generally.[3]

The new medical school proved to be the most durable and exemplary of Hutchins' achievements, elevating Chicago to the forefront of medical research. But in economic terms the adoption of a full-salaried contract, eliminating private practice, constituted an outrageous invasion of the sacred and sacrificial halls of medical care. It was denounced by the doctors as the most arrant sort of socialism. Its opponents, said Hutchins afterwards, "were sagacious enough to foresee what eventually happened. They foresaw the ultimate abolition of their own school because of the establishment of the new one." The medical establishment never forgave him, and the University of Chicago doubtless lost the financial support of many who took their family physician's advice regarding benefactions.

But the practice of medicine was only the most egregious form of outside earnings that diverted faculty members from their research and teaching. The scandal lay in the academic moonlighting in the private sector. It was a perquisite of the academic trade if you happened to be in a field where your services might enrich a business or industrial firm—a biologist moonlighting for a pharmaceutical firm, a geologist for an oil company, a physicist or chemist for a steel or chemical combine. Consider the professors who wrote textbooks for the great textbook houses, walking away with colossal royalties. Department for department, the most prolific offenders were in the business school (called commerce and administration at Chicago). But the practice turned up everywhere.

Socialism—"in one country," at that—was ridiculous. It wouldn't work. It never had.

But the capitalist board of the University of Chicago adopted the full-time contract reform. In a letter to alumni who wrote in to ask about it, Board Chairman Swift said that the prevailing opinion of the trustees was at first unfavorable, but subsequent consideration turned the board around. He cited, in particular, the fact that all fourteen of the deans and all eight of the senior administrative officers supported it. What Swift did not advert to was the faculty opposition to it. Because it wasn't an educational issue but an administrative matter having to do with financing alone, the trustees saw no reason to listen too closely to the muttering of senior professors, many of whom saw their financial prerogatives jeopardized.

In the event, their prerogatives weren't jeopardized by the proposal as it came to the trustees (and as they adopted it). It was not compulsory to come into the scheme except for instructors after their four-year probationary terms, when they were advanced to assistant professorship or dropped. The plan was voluntary for faculty members with the rank of assistant professor and above. It wasn't, in a word, the imposition of all-out socialism but, rather, its imposition on the lowly and an invitation to the exalted. As for the abolition of rank, Chairman Swift told the alumni that it was in the exploratory state and would not be hastily undertaken. "My guess," he wrote, "is that it will not be done." He was right. It wasn't.

Swift had not, he said, expected as many as fifty applicants for full-time service. He was amazed to find that 115 had applied and been accepted. (Several had been rejected, "these being people who had few outside contacts and who probably thought a permanent increase in salary might be affected thereby.") The idea, he went on, was to take into the plan "many of the younger and most capable men and pay them enough to live comfortably so that outside money-grabbing will not be necessary." If, on the other hand, the professor who came into the plan felt that his outside activities were valuable to his professional development or to the university, there was no objection to his continuing them as long as the money went to the university. "The idea is not so much an attempt to control the individuals, but rather to control conditions so that they can give their chief time and attention to the things they want to do, and so that they will not need to deviate from them for the sake of making a living."

Because the term "socialism," in one form or another, had been widely used in the press in connection with the proposal, conservative alumni had come to the board in considerable number to express their concern. The board chairman assured them that the program was experimental, and that careful observation would be made of all aspects of it, including "whether desirable persons from other institutions hesitate to come to us."

The experiment was a middling success; in the course of a very few years a great majority of the lowest ranking faculty came into the plan, validating, in the view of the older men, their suspicion that the plan was one more Hutchins device for pitting the younger faculty members against the older. Even some people in the higher ranks came into it, and there was no indication, in the ensuing years, that able young men and women hesitated to join the Chicago faculty as instructors because they would be faced, four years later, with entering the program if they were to be retained.

But it did not change the character of the University of Chicago or catch on elsewhere. The higher learning in America remained a free-for-all bastion of free enterprise, and as the moonlighting proliferated both in availability and reward, and as both the cost and the conception of living went up in the succeeding decades, more and more college and university professors found themselves drawn to money on the side and away from the modest wages they had once been paid for having chosen the life of the mind. So the salaries of professors went up competitively, and nothing more was heard about need as the only basis for compensation in the true community or, for the matter of that, about the true community.

Hutchins' socialism—or bolshevism—in one part of one country was done away with after he left the university, seven years after it was initiated. It was a famous victory—but more famous than it was victorious. And it was the last one of any consequence he was to have as a university president.

One sunny Santa Barbara day, thirty years or so afterward, I sauntered into his office and reminded him of that icy Chicago evening in January of 1944, when he had proposed that members of the University of Chicago faculty be put on a full-time basis and be required to turn over all their outside earnings to the university. "The only basis for compensation in a true community is need." How much of an aberration (if it was one) was his assertion? If that proposal wasn't some sort of socialism, what was it? But he had lived like a capitalist all his life. I told him that before either of us lived any longer I wanted to know his view of the free enterprise system in the abstract. "Tell me why what you were trying to do was in essence different from socialism as the proper organization of society as a whole."

"What I was trying to do was to organize and operate the best university I could. . . . The specific measure that you refer to had nothing to do with my ideas of social, political, and economic matters in general."

"Tell me about your ideas of social, political, and economic matters in general."

"Well, I have a very strong belief in justice, and I have a very strong feeling that the present economic, social, and political order in the United States is unjust."

"Why is it unjust?"

"It is unjust because men are unjust, and because the institutions we have created are unjust, and because the procedures that we follow are unjust. . . . You may say there is no hope as long as we have the economic, social, and political structure we have now. And this is a serious question."

"Have you a serious answer?"

"My serious answer is that in my lifetime I have seen a tremendous amount of improvement in some respects and a tremendous amount of failure in many others. In some ways we were worse off. . . and in some ways. . . better. And I'm unable to decide whether if we had a major revolution we would be any better off than we are likely to be if we kept working away at trying to obtain justice, if it can be obtained under the present system. For example, the Fourteenth Amendment. . . . And there are various other things. . . . As long as we have tremendous concentrations of private power we are not going to have the kind of country we ought to have."

"But the fact is that the Constitution doesn't say anything about the economic order. Is justice possible under capitalism?"

"I don't know. It is necessary everywhere. But not inevitable under any system. I think that the possibilities of obtaining justice under our system are far from exhausted. At the same time we can not assume that injustice will ever be completely wiped out as long as men remain in their fallen condition. And I take their fallen condition to be congenital. The object, then, is to try to make whatever system you have as just as you can."

"Is there anything *inherently* just or unjust in capitalism or socialism?"

"Well, I would doubt it. I think there are some very serious questions raised by Marx's theory of surplus value.[4] I may say that I don't like the words 'socialism' and 'capitalism' because I don't know what they mean and I don't know how you would identify any existing state. Is Russia a socialist state? Is the United States capitalist? From some points of view Yes, and from some points of view No. . . . The question is, what can be done under given circumstances with given people at a given time? I merely say that ours is not a system that one could describe as altogether a free enterprise system, nor is it a socialist system however one defines socialism. We should take the United States as it is—forget whether it's capitalist or socialist—and say what's good and bad about it, what can be done about what's bad, what can be done to confirm what's good, and how you try to make it a better system. . . . I don't believe that I could recommend any existing economic system as it stands."

And so it went. He said nothing that would scandalize the rich beyond their bearing; he was an eccentric one of theirs, but still one of theirs. The establishment's antiestablishmentarian. If it wasn't the system that made the difference, if it was the men; and if the men were in a fallen condition, and the condition was congenital; then how could the men be expected to improve the system? How could congenitally unjust men be expected to "keep working away at trying to obtain justice"?

The vicious circle was obvious to him. In the pinches, the lover of grand abstractions about the true community abandoned the abstraction for reification.

33   Showdown

The convulsion precipitated by Hutchins' speech at the trustees' dinner in January 1944 did not subside in a day or two, or a week or two, or a month or two. It mounted in ungloved intensity during the whole of what was, after all, a year in which people might well have had more cataclysmic things to think about. To read that year's record of the Battle of the Midway—the Chicago Midway—with its increasingly impolite exchange of charges and countercharges, is to lose track (as the contending parties themselves appeared to have lost track) of the rising climax in Europe, Asia, and Africa of history's most stupendous and devastating conflagration.

The rank and salary proposals of the trustees' dinner speech certainly struck bellicosity, if not terror, in the hearts of the faculty opposition, but neither proposal was so much as mentioned during the controversy the speech engendered. The struggle turned on the loftier points the speaker had made with reference to the structure of the university, the character of the degrees it offered, and the power of the president. None of these issues was new. Maybe it was the long weariness and tension of the war, maybe it was a widespread feeling that the campus had simply had enough of the president's cannonading. In any case, the speech served to consolidate the camps of the enemy—camps, not camp, for there were all sorts of reasons why people loved or hated the man.

"Loved" and "hated" were, in general, much too strong to be said. As he himself observed in retrospect, there was no indication, not even when the opposing forces were most ferociously engaged, that there was a substantial movement in the faculty to get rid of him. Few colleagues disliked him unqualifiedly. A colleague who deplored his medievalism applauded his uncompromising fight for academic freedom; a colleague who resented

337

his prewar isolationism admired his ardor as a war plant manager; a colleague who disliked his deprecation of science lauded his scientific appointments; a colleague who disliked his philosophy of teaching liked the higher student standards his administration had achieved. What his consolidated opponents wanted to do—were at last determined to do—in 1944 was to stop him.

And stop him they did.

The twenty-year Battle of the Midway ended when the board, in response to the gathered clamor of his enemies, was at last forced to step in a year after the trustees' dinner speech and put an end to the finish fight by making a Solomonic award to the two sides. The award was an actual defeat for the perpetual revolutionary, a defeat that effectively ended his campaign to transform the institution into an exemplary university. But the board's decision was framed in evenhanded terms.

It could not have been otherwise. The contending forces were too evenly divided. By January 1944 Hutchins seemed to see that a showdown could no longer be deferred. Some sort of united front was said to be in the making, with a committee of senior professors at its head. The time had come for the Stop Hutchins movement to take on a formal character.

He decided to carry the fight to the enemy, and a month after his January speech he broke his restricted speaking schedule to accept a local invitation from the Northwestern University chapter of the American Association of University Professors. Attacking "the colossal frivolity" of higher education in America, he added that "the existing higher educational structure of the country could be closed without affecting liberal education in any way." He elaborated on his full-time service proposal of a month before, saying, in that connection, that a university was a "consecrated community," in which all distinctions of faculty rank should be abolished as inimical to comradeship and cooperation. The president should have full responsibility for generating the program of the university. He should be the responsible executive of a high-tension democracy. He should be fired "if he starts to go to the dogs."[1]

This elaboration of his January proposals was put forward as the recipe not for one university, but for all. He was issuing a nationwide indictment and making a nationwide demand. He was calling for reorganization and reconstitution—and "consecration"—everywhere in the land. This was news, formidable news even at the height of the world war. The press picked it up nationally and the Chicago papers gave it front-page billing. He had done what he did with his *Saturday Evening Post* series five years earlier: he had gone to the country at large, using a shotgun attack on his own constituency. If anything, the offense in the use of such a technique was greater, since he lumped his own institution with all the rest. Faculty members were interviewed extensively; and the respected *Chicago Daily News* began its column-and-a-half story by its leading reporter, with the headline: U. OF C. FACULTY IN UPROAR—Fear Recent Proposals to "Communize" Staff Are Power Grab.

"There is a large measure of both mystification and suspicion on the University of Chicago campus. Few faculty members below the rank of dean profess fully to understand their president's motives and objectives. Others profess to see in them implications that they find profoundly disturbing. . . . Dr. Hutchins, they assert, is a master of alluring generality; but when one attempts to pin him down to a definition, he invokes the Roosevelt technique and turns the query aside with a wise-crack. . . . These terms—'a consecrated community,' 'the basis of need,' 'high tension democracy,' 'authority commensurate with responsibility,' 'a very short term,'—are susceptible to varying interpretations. They may mean much or they may mean little. Some faculty members feel that they add up to something approximating the pattern that Sinclair Lewis had in mind when he wrote *It Can't Happen Here.* Some, recalling Huey Long's seizure of Louisiana State University, profess to see a danger of the University of Chicago coming under absolute control of a man whom they regard as no less ambitious than Huey and far abler and more subtle."[2]

The Hutchins rhetoric had at last hit the fan. The rhetoric had been exasperating people for fifteen years—people who didn't adore him and didn't like his sass. He reveled—no mistaking it—in riling up the animals by kidding them; but the kidding had an edge to it. Of course he didn't mean that "*the faculty isn't much good*, but the President and the students are wonderful"—or did he, maybe? Of course he didn't mean that "business men may have ideals, but *a professor will do anything for money*"— or did he, maybe? Older professors weren't used to being talked to that way, certainly not by a university president. They didn't—couldn't— cotton to his leprechaun humor. It had a touch of scorn in it; it had arrogance, it had contempt. His opponents didn't hate him; but they resented the purposively elfin terms in which he offered his views as deeply as they resented the views themselves.

The muted conversations in the Quadrangle Club dining room and corridors culminated a few weeks after the trustees' dinner speech in the formation of a spearhead group of six senior scholars, of considerably riper years than Hutchins', representing, among them, the social sciences, the natural sciences, and the humanities. They were designated by one of their number "the Burghers of Calais" (after the fourteenth-century incident, portrayed by Rodin, in which six citizens of the besieged city offered their lives to the English king in a petition for clemency toward the rest). In the first of their "letters" to Hutchins—the whole exchange was public— they said they had become "aware of a deep and widespread feeling of alarm concerning the present and future course of affairs in the University."

"Toward the close of your speech of January 12 you state that 'the purpose of the University is nothing less than to procure a moral, spiritual, and intellectual revolution throughout the world' and you refer later to 'the crusade to which we are called' and 'the revolution which must come if men are to live together in peace,' a revolution which you say must involve 'a reversal of the whole scale of values by which our society lives.'" It seemed to the burghers that these words implied a conception of the university which conflicted basically with the function of "advancing knowledge by freely determined research and teaching...[demanding] some kind of common institutional adherence to a particular analysis of what is wrong with the world and hence to a particular hierarchy of moral and intellectual values."

They were all the more seriously concerned, they said, because of his suggestions that the PhD "might well be so redefined as to make it a degree primarily for the teachers you think are needed to discover and introduce liberal education for all," that the PhD thus redefined be awarded through a new Institute of Liberal Studies, and that the university be reorganized to provide for electing the president for a very short term, requiring him to ask the faculty's advice ("but not its consent") and to make decisions and take the consequences. This last proposal, linked with the suggestion that the senate be reduced in size and made elective by and from all members of the faculty, seemed to the six burghers to have "profound implications for the intellectual as well as political future of the University as a free republic of scholars and teachers."[3]

Hutchins replied, a few days later, that he did not plan to impose a program upon the university, first because he didn't want to, and second, because he couldn't do it if he did. But "I have long since made it plain that I do not regard 'the advancement of knowledge by freely determined research and teaching' as an adequate statement of the purposes of the University." He had given his reasons, he said, as long ago as 1936 in *The Higher Learning in America*. As for the proposed creation of a new Institute of Liberal Studies, the creation of such an institute lay wholly within the prerogatives of the trustees, to whom he could have gone any time during the past fifteen years to propose the foundation of any new department, institute, or school without reference to the faculty. With regard to presidential powers, he had recommended to the board that the senate be asked to elect a committee to advise the board on his suggestions that the president should become either chairman of the faculty or a responsible executive.[4]

Two weeks later the six burghers replied, saying that they were "unable to see how such a revolutionary crusade" as Hutchins appeared to have in mind "could become effective without committing the University, as an institution, to a particular doctrine." They continued to be disturbed, they said, by his announcement of a unifying mission for the university "which could so easily be incompatible with our essential function of advancing knowledge by responsible research and teaching unhampered by any official ideology or philosophical dogma." If, as they inferred, he meant to use his present powers, and such further powers as the trustees might give him, to promote the series of changes he had outlined, they thought the faculty should know it.[5]

He answered them a week later, repeating that he had no plan to impose his personal views on the institution: "If the University is ever committed to a particular doctrine, it will be because the faculty has agreed upon it." The faculty would be consulted, as it had been in the past, on any measures to be taken toward the realization of a general educational plan; but, he added, many of their colleagues felt that the senate, its membership confined to the full professors, did not fairly represent the faculty. His suggestion for reorganizing the administration—either to drop the president and have a chairman of the faculty, or to make the president a responsible executive—"would increase the participation of the faculty in the formation and execution of educational policy."[6]

The controversy was getting nowhere, and bad temper, less and less effectively veiled, continued to rise on both sides. The exchange of letters ended with Hutchins' of March 25, but the campus continued to seethe. The burghers were unmollified, and the insouciant king (to whom they were not surrendering the keys to the city) had conceded nothing and offered them an unsatisfactory sort of bland, indeed, amiable reassurance that they had nothing to worry about. Deciding on open warfare, they asked for a meeting of the university senate—which had not met for more than a year. The meeting was held on May 22, with uniformed police barring the doors and windows and admitting senators by special pass. It was attended by some 135 of the 195 senators, a monstrous turnout. The three-hour meeting, from which the press was excluded, was reported via the grapevine to have been stormy; but Vice-president Will Munnecke, who was present ex officio, recalled thirty years later that Hutchins conducted it "without any visible show of emotion or anything more than passing interest." The principal item on the agenda—the only item of consequence—was a "memorial" to the board of trustees setting forth the grievances of the opposition.

The 120 signers of the memorial were close to two-thirds of the university's senators, including the overwhelming preponderance of the natural scientists. Hutchins was proposing an elected presidency, with the president removable by a senate vote of no confidence; he had not got the presidency he suggested, but he had already got the vote of no confidence (by, to be sure, a senate representing a small minority of the faculty). A noncommittal statement issued by the senate after the meeting recorded the fact that there had been a proposal tabled to reorganize the senate to include associate and assistant professors. There was, of course, no knowing how such a body would have voted; but its age would have averaged some fifteen years younger.

The senate vote to adopt the memorial was reported to have been 94 to 42. It is doubtful if the 42 nays were all pro-Hutchins men; some of them may simply have objected to the adversarial procedure. With some statistical confusion between the signers, an additional thirty or thirty-five anti-Hutchins senators didn't sign because they didn't like "trouble." On balance, there may not have been more than thirty or forty of the university's 195 full professors who were actually Hutchins supporters. In any case the fifteen years' war had reached its climax. His enemies had gone over his head to address their case directly to the men who constituted the legal university, and to address them on such matters as administrative reorganization and the creation of the new Institute of Liberal Studies, which were strictly board business, in which the board might be expected to consult the faculty—but not the faculty to lay a case before the board.

The men who prepared and lobbied the memorial in the senate were attentive to Hutchins' strength in the board. Their language was as temperate as their injury permitted. Though they may have felt otherwise, they insisted that they "could not believe that the President would not attend to the friendly advice, on matters of educational principle and policy, of the men upon whom he must rely for the execution of his plan, or that he would be reluctant to reveal his purposes in detail to those who would be called upon to fulfill them. . . . The Senate, recognizing the authority and responsibility of the Board of Trustees and believing that the Board would share its concern at the difficulties the University now faces if it were fully cognizant of them, appeals to the Board for its active assistance, with the President and the Faculty, in developing a comprehensive plan which . . . would explicitly safeguard those basic principles . . . without which . . . the University cannot continue great or free." But the memorialists—speaking as the senate—were sticking to their guns, requesting that the university "not be committed to any 'purpose' which would tend to subordinate . . . the free choice of principles and methods of research or teaching, to any particular formulation of moral, social philosophical, or scientific values."[7]

Accepting the memorial, the trustees noted that the president "has no intention of committing the University to any particular philosophy."[8] Chairman Swift added an expression of the board's confidence in Hutchins and a recognition of "the educational achievements of the University during the fifteen years of his leadership"; with what might be read as a gently ominous overtone, the chairman added that the board "expects him to continue to administer the affairs of the University in accordance with the existing Constitution and Statutes, until they are changed."[9] Asked about the memorial, Hutchins observed that the organization of the university, "which is neither efficient nor democratic, has been under study since January 1943, by a committee of the Board and a Committee of the Senate. . . . It is the duty of the president of a university to formulate and state his conception of the purposes of the institution. Nobody has to agree with the president's statements. The imposition of a particular doctrine would be a violation of the perfect academic freedom which the administration of the University of Chicago has always guaranteed."[10]

Everybody was publicly polite, but the strain was visible in all three parties—now that the board was fully involved—to the dispute. A majority of the board, some of whom certainly did not see what the shouting was all about, was disposed to support Hutchins both on the educational and the administrative issues. The first did not appear to be all that critical, and his position on the second reflected the mental set of most of the trustees. But here were the full professors of the university—all the greats, with a handful of exceptions—putting the board's feet to the fire. While the horrors that aroused the memorialists may not in themselves have aroused many members of the board, a majority of trustees (so informal polls indicated) had always found the Hutchins rhetoric much too high-flown; there was in all probability not one of them who saw the need of a moral, spiritual, and intellectual revolution in the world, or of a new purpose for the university whose faculty members had been following the gleam (or the dozens or hundreds of vagrant gleams) contentedly until the young president had come charging along.

There did not appear, after the submission of the memorial, any way in which Hutchins' and the senate's terms could really be accommodated, any way in which Hutchins could accept the "free choice of principles and methods of research or teaching," any way in which the senate could accept the university as a revolutionary crusader. What the board would have to do—if it could—was fudge the issue. And Hutchins appeared to be convinced that it would. He was now in a frame of mind that the board had not seen before, not once in those fifteen years they'd known him.

The board had had the senate memorial before it for less than a week when Hutchins handed Swift a memorandum enigmatically headed, "Personal Aspects," with the request, so Swift informed the appropriate board members, that it be distributed to the members of the board committee that had been meeting, on and off, with a senate committee for the past year and a half to consider Hutchins' proposals. The memorandum read:

> Omitting minor absurdities, like the claim that I did not call a Senate meeting and declined to consult the faculty, and passing over the systematic campaign of character assassination which has been carried on in the Quadrangle Club for the last four months [since his trustees' dinner speech of January] the principal charges are:
>
> 1. That I am seeking to impose a particular philosophy upon the University.
>   a. I have denied this in writing.
>   b. The record shows I mean it.
>   c. It is my duty to have and state a purpose for the University.
> 2. That I am threatening academic freedom.
>   a. No university president has done more for it.
> 3. That I am seeking a dictatorship.
>   a. From the beginning I have stated that I would resign if the theory of organization upon which I was elected were changed.
>   b. Neither of the two plans I have proposed resembles a dictatorship in the slightest degree.
> 4. That I am exceeding my powers.
>   a. Everything I have done has been approved by the Board, or the Senate, or both.
> 5. That I have sacrificed research to teaching.
>   a. Research has never been as well supported as it has during my administration and is nowhere as well supported as at the University of Chicago.[11]

One of Hutchins' characteristically wry remarks, which his friends ascribed to his supposedly unhappy domestic situation, was, "I'm so busy feeling sorry for myself that I haven't time to feel sorry for anybody else." In his memorandum to the board committee he was feeling so sorry for himself that he wrote in an angrily uncharacteristic way. He had never accused his opponents of offenses ranging from minor absurdities to character assassination. (He could scarcely have been imagined using the latter expression on his own behalf.) He defended himself by a combination of flat denial—"Not guilty"—and unsupported declarations which, unsupported, sounded like braggadocio. The claims that he made in items 2 and 5 were classics of overstatement by a man who was justly famous for classic and consistent understatement. After fifteen years of being urbane, Robert Maynard Hutchins was reduced to a crude outburst. He had often said he was "frustrated and furious"; at last he plainly was.

The memorandum called for no reply and received none. But the frustrated and furious president asked for the opportunity—in spite of the press of war work—to address the faculty and students of the truncated summer quarter on the subject of the organization and purpose of the university. The date of the convocation was put at July 20—sixty days away. The address was a very long one, its tone one of carefully modulated anger, but anger still. It began, "During recent discussions. . . I have had to remain silent. But in view of the misconceptions of my position scattered abroad during these discussions it now seems desirable, as well as proper, for me to try to state what my position is."

He went on to a Hutchinsesque apology to his audience, lightly concealing its bellicosity under a matter-of-fact cloak: "I am afraid that I shall be saying nothing that is new. But I have to admit that I have not for many years said anything in that category." He then proceeded to a full-scale review of each of his proposals and the faculty charges they inspired. On a hot summer's day, relieved by the shadowed cool of the university chapel, and before an audience of his own choosing on his and their own grounds, he was obviously speaking for the purpose of making a record. He could only have supposed that, if he replied in painstaking detail to everything that had been said against his proposals and his actions, the enemy would come penitently forward and respond to the altar call. But the address was as solidly packed as it was energetic, as elegant as it was precise. It turned out to be his last hard try. The date of that last hard try, July 20, 1944, was seven whole years before he resigned from the university.

Ignoring the possibility, indeed, the likelihood, given the sweltering weather, that his audience might grow restless, he plunged ahead, taking up the issues point by point and presenting their analysis and his own case. By way of supporting the board's power to establish new institutes, schools, and departments without reference to the faculty, he reminded his hearers that there were developments in education "now universally regarded as desirable [which] could not have taken place if the professors whose particular interests were involved had had the decisive voice as to whether these developments should have been started"—a polite way of saying (as he had once said) that the great achievements in American education had been made over the dead bodies of countless professors. He referred in passing to the Chicago board's elimination of the Rush Medical School in favor of the salaried faculty integrated with the university's division of biological sciences.

Then he rolled up his sleeves and went solemnly, patiently, and thoroughly to work on the issue that most persistently galled both him and his opponents. "I have lately heard"—he had been hearing it for fifteen years—"that I am seeking to impose a particular philosophy on the University. This is in a sense a highly complimentary suggestion, because it implies that I have a philosophy. I suppose everybody has a philosophy, in a way. We are all metaphysicians"—he couldn't resist it—"whether we know it or not and whether we like it or not. For we all act all the time on certain basic assumptions in regard to the nature of the world and of man. To say that freely determined teaching and research are the object of the University is to state a philosophy for the University. To say that no other philosophy is possible is to seek to impose it on the University.

". . . I could plausibly say that the particular philosophy which the majority of the senior members of the faculty share has therefore been imposed by them upon the University.

"I do not say that this is so. I say that it is much more nearly so than the charge that I am seeking to impose my philosophy. If I have not in fifteen years succeeded in moving the established philosophy an inch, it would seem likely that I am not trying to move it, but am merely endeavoring to prevent the established philosophy from being imposed on me, on those members of the faculty who may agree with me, and on all new appointees. . . .

"Is the call for a moral, spiritual, and intellectual revolution throughout the world the statement of a particular doctrine? I should call it the statement of a very general doctrine indeed. Wherever I have said this I have been attacking materialism, the view that wealth and power are the aim of human life and human organization. Since almost every philosophy and every religion take the same position, this hardly seems the statement of a particular doctrine. This general doctrine should, moreover, be very popular in a university, for men who regard wealth and power as the aim of life seldom select a university as the field for their ambition. . . .

"I suppose that a university could be unified through the imposition of an official dogma. I repudiated that method long ago. The university must find a way to be an agent of harmony and unification without suppressing the vagrant intellect or violating the claims of freedom. The way to do this is through a common training and a common purpose. A university becomes an understood diversity through a common training by virtue of which the members of the community may at last make themselves intelligible to one another. . . .

"The university cannot fashion the intellect of the modern world if it proclaims that the fundamental disorder of the modern world is indifferent to it as a university. . . . To fashion the intellect of the modern world is to raise insistently the great issues and to press urgently for answers to them. It is to hold before the people of the world a vision of what the world might be. To argue that this is no concern of a university and even that it is contrary to its purpose is to reject responsibility for the decisions which must be made as to the use of the knowledge and power accumulated by a university.

"To say let us gain knowledge and power and our ends will take care of themselves is not to fashion the intellect of the modern world, but to submit to it, for this is what the modern world is saying. Here the university abandons the task of intellectual leadership and mirrors, symbolizes, and justifies the great reversal of ends and means which is the underlying disorder of our society. And it does so at a time when all we have to do is to look around us to see that the growth of knowledge and power gives us no hint as to how to use them; for the world has reached at one and the same moment the zenith of its information, technology, and power over nature, and the nadir of its moral and political life. . . .

"In the moral, intellectual, and spiritual conflict which I foresee the university may take whichever side it pleases. It may endorse the scale of values by which our society lives; or it may join in the effort to reverse them. The only thing it can not do, as it seems to me, is to stand apart from the conflict on the theory that its function places it above it. This is to doom the University to sterility. It is to renounce the task of intellectual leadership. It is to deny at a great crisis in history our responsibility to mankind."[12]

He had said at the opening of his address that he would be glad to answer questions. There were none. There were none because his hearers either accepted what he said—this segment of the audience might include most of the students present and some of the younger faculty—or rejected it. The older men and women could not help but reject it. They could not help but reject the view that the university had the obligation to fashion the intellect of the world or place itself in the vanguard of a moral, intellectual, and spiritual revolution. They did not, indeed, see what was meant by "the university" in this unified, purposive, *consecrated* sense at all. The university—any university—was not a community. It was an aggregation of men and women whose only object was (as the Six Burghers of Calais said) freely determined teaching and research. Beyond this airy objective, which did not unite its myriad votaries housed in the same quadrangles, it had, and could have, in their view, no other. The practitioners of freely determined teaching and research in those quadrangles did not know one another; likely a majority did not even know one another by sight. How could *the university* take "whichever side in pleases" in the moral, intellectual, and spiritual contest for the world? There was, in that sense, no such thing as *the university*.

He could not have been sanguine about the effect of that address; it contained nothing that was new except a great many flourishes of sculptured elegance. But there it was—all of it. It was indeed his hardest try. It was indeed his last one. He had spoken for a solid hour. He had spoken for the record. But as far as effectiveness was concerned, after five, ten, or fifteen years of the same thing, he had spoken to the wind. The University of Chicago, to the extent that there was a University of Chicago, was neither going to endorse the scale of values by which our society lives nor join in the effort to reverse them. What it was going to do, then and thereafter, like every other free university, was exactly what he said it couldn't do; stand apart from the conflict.

34   Denouement

It went (as it had always gone) without saying that his resignation was on the table. ("The administrator must be in a perpetual mood of resignation, by which I do not mean mournful acceptance of the universe. I mean he must be perpetually prepared to get out.")[1] His board knew it, and he knew it. Hutchins spelled it out when he first submitted his two alternative proposals for presidential powers; should either of them be accepted, the administrative officers of the university would resign in a body, so that the new role of the president could be implemented de novo. He, at least, took the offer seriously; and in the next few months, while the board and senate committees met regularly in response to the senate memorial, he considered quitting in any case. He had gone all out in his speech of July 20, 1944; there was nothing more he could do; he was palpably tired of perpetual pushing. He had often discussed resigning and discussed it over a period of years. He had discussed it with a few of his friends—and with his father (who was, as usual, worried about his impetuosity and urged him to wait and see what the board did).

On December 1, 1944, he sent a note to Chairman Laird Bell of the Board Committee on Instruction and Research. "I can not emphasize too strongly," he wrote (somewhat prayerfully), "the effect on the faculty of a definite, clear-cut decision by the Board. The faculty should not be asked; it should be told. It has leaked out"—the leak proved to be inaccurate, its inaccuracy indicating that Hutchins and the senate were both left in the dark on the state of the board's sentiments—"that the Board has decided to have a small, representative Senate. The bitterest members of the opposition are now busily engaged in formulating its constitution. They are Adjusting themselves to their Environment!"[2] He was being blithe,

349

complete with an exclamation mark. It wasn't too much like him. Was he whistling in the dark?

Whether or not he was whistling, he was in the dark. The board, as of the date of that note, had already completed its work and made its decisions. They were announced three days later by Chairman Swift, in the form of six points:

1. The University Senate will be broadened to include associate and assistant professors who have been on the campus for at least three years. This will mean that the roster will be increased from 195 full professors now comprising the Senate to a total of 350.
2. A council of forty members will be elected to act on educational issues which will meet at least quarterly.
3. An executive committee of seven will be elected which will be continuously in touch with the president.
4. The council will take affirmative action on educational matters and has the right to disapprove of proposals of the presidents, but the president can veto the council's action. In case of a stalemate, the decision will be up to the Board of Trustees.
5. The president may recommend faculty appointments to the Board without the approval of department heads.
6. The Board can create or discontinue departments and divisions at its own discretion.

So Hutchins would get his more democratic senate, but it would be even more cumbersome than it had been, with its membership almost doubled. The council and executive committee might—or might not, if they reached a stalemate—facilitate decision-making, without the president's having new powers. Point 5 was a modest Hutchins victory, actually a reaffirmation of traditional procedure. Point 6 simply confirmed the university's established practice.

The new program was presented as a device to "establish a better exchange of ideas and information than present procedures permit." It provided clarification, but provided it at a much lower level than Hutchins had sought. The real differences between the president and the opposition were simply ignored. No choice was made between his alternative proposals of the presidency as a faculty chairmanship, on the one hand, and as the responsible repository of power on the other. No mention was made of his repeated and insistent call for a moral, intellectual, and spiritual revolution with the university in its vanguard. This call underlay his educational reforms, and he had been making it with increasing emphasis ever since he had come to the university. Ignoring it, the trustees were in effect saying that they regarded it as unworthy of notice. They were slapping him down and handing the opposition its validation.

True, he had moved the board to make decisions in areas such boards had always avoided; the senate had raised educational issues that college and university governors were unaccustomed to, and this body of governors faced at least the secondary, if not the primary, issues. Ordinarily the solemn custodians of conservatism, the Chicago board had issued (said the *Chicago Daily News*) a "declaration against the old fogeyism which had been the badge of trusteehood for two hundred years." It wasn't all that aggressive, but there was a real sense in which, where nobody traditionally ran a university, Hutchins had forced somebody to make a few gestures in running this one; and the faculty had, going with him to the board, awakened the board to responsibilities that were traditionally considered the professors'—or nobody's—prerogatives.

The University of Chicago would never again be quite the institution it had been before his advent. But its resemblance to the institution he wanted would be very slightly increased. He had fought hard for fifteen years and more, and had now been beaten. He had got his college at the very outset of his administration, and perhaps a fourth of all the courses offered at all levels bore his stamp, however lightly, as regards content and method. (Their twin hallmarks were the Socratic discussion format and the use of original writings instead of textbooks.) In the twelfth year of his administration he had got the award of the bachelor's degree at the end of the sophomore year of the college (a scheme that would be rescinded when he left the university). But the place was fundamentally the same, for all his fulmination, all his unrelenting effort at home and abroad. The divisional organization had not diminished the power and independence of the departments. The old anarchy abode. There wasn't—nor would there be—any community of scholars, at Chicago or anywhere else.

How much did the fact that the protagonist was Hutchins—that rarest of presidential birds—have to do with his failure to effect any fundamental and durable change in the character of the University of Chicago and of the higher learning in America?[3] Probably very little. Probably nothing at all. He had neither the temper nor the posture of the classic reformer, alternately glowering, shouting, threatening, pleading. He came through as a phenomenally frisky man of phenomenal lineaments who endeared himself in the first instance to men who themselves were frisky, who found friskiness (and lineaments) attractive. But he came through, too, as a thoroughly serious man who meant—underneath the friskiness—what he said, who did his homework and stuck by his guns. His opponents nearly all respected him or in time came to. But after fifteen or twenty years they were not to be dazzled by his splendor (including the splendor of his rhetoric) or, alternatively, repelled. It is impossible to go on being astonishing, outrageous, or enchanting to people you have to higgle and haggle and huckster with again and again, year in, year out. The charm and the annoyance both wore off, giving way to considered support or considered resistance.

His opponents came to understand him, by and large; to understand that he was not a bundle of whimsical contradictions and elevating or denigrating wisecracks, but a man with direction who wanted a change (however radical) of emphasis, not of educational principle. He was arguing about method, content, structure, not about the purpose or meaning of education. Again and again he insisted: "We are discussing a question of emphasis. . . . If you are running a steel company, you may run railroads and coal mines. You may have an extensive plant and an investment portfolio to look after. Yet your principal business is manufacturing and distributing steel." Again and again he insisted that he was not insisting on a particular method, structure, or body of materials, as long as the student mastered the liberal arts and the great tradition. "If he can do it by going fishing and taking the general examinations whenever he is ready to, that's just peachy." Again and again he insisted that he was arguing only that "there are other means of obtaining knowledge than scientific experimentation." But his academic listeners would not listen to his insistence that he was not insisting, and his depreciation of the mythology of science kept persuading them that he would consign empirical investigation to the playpen, along with the pragmatic achievements with which it had changed the face of the world. His insistence that he was not antiscientific, antiquarian, medieval, dogmatic, reactionary, and authoritarian was invariably couched in such provocative terms that his enemies could get away with scouting his claim that the issue was only an issue of emphasis.

He was an unyielding absolutist, not on method, material, or structure, but on one point: that there were such things as changeless, universal values—"courage, justice, temperance, these are still the virtues"—whose investigation commanded the adherence of a university committed, as a university must be, to the moral, intellectual, and spiritual renewal of society. And his opponents drew from this uncompromising absolutism an across-the-board adherence to everything they rejected. In the climactic debate of 1944 the redoubtable Quincy Wright wrote that "the values for which universities stand are so long run and so general that they can not be stated except in terms of process and methods. Truth itself is a process which can not be circumscribed in a formula or imagined in a Utopia.

Recognition of the limitations of all truths, of the fallibility of all formulations, of the relativity of all values is the characteristic which distinguishes a living civilization."[4] This comforting view of a world in flux, with every opinion as well entitled to adherence as every other, and all of them teetering, invariably included, as it did in Wright's case, a snide or condescending lip service to undefined, indefinable, and ephemeral values—or at least to the term. Chancellor Harry Woodburn Chase of the University of New York firmly asserted that "we need a keener sense of values. All knowledge is not of the same worth"—and at once leaped to the pleasant, popular highland of infirmity: "But again, values vary with individuals and with environment. By what universally valid criteria can we judge?"[5]—By none that Chancellor Chase went on to suggest; he rested his case right there.

So deaf to the Hutchins claim of emphasis was—and remained—John Dewey that at the age of eighty-five, in the same climactic summer of 1944, he wrote in *Fortune* magazine that "we are familiar with [Hutchins' view] from early childhood. It is a conventionally established part of a large portion of our training in family and Sunday school. Nevertheless, it is the expression of a provincial and conventional point of view, of a culture that is pre-scientific in the sense that science bears today." The problem of making "this and that definite factory and field operation . . . contribute to the educative release and growth of human capacities, as well as to production of a large and reasonably cheap supply of material goods . . . is one that, by its own terms, can be dealt with only by the continuous application of the scientific method of experimental observation and test"[6]—as if Hutchins had been saying or suggesting that factory and field operations be submitted to Aristotle or Aquinas for explication or validation. In the last venerable months of his life Dewey was still (in the phrase of Sean O'Casey) " 'arpin' on me dotter," and Hutchins was supposedly still condemning the rising generation to the provincial, conventional, and prescientific horrors of family and Sunday school.

Emphasis was what Hutchins was talking about, but the magnitude and complexity of the emphasis were too much for most of his colleagues. It came down to the thought-through substitution of one set of profound predilections—nothing more than predilections—for another. Most academics were not all that interested in thinking through predilections or in asking themselves what was scientific and what was prescientific. For teachers generally, at whatever level, being a teacher is a grinding occupation that wants a steady man or woman of the incurious sort. Hutchins was a stirrer-up of people who had no great interest in being stirred or in stirring, most of whom began the school year just sufficiently refreshed and ended it very tired, and had no great zest for an unrelenting succession of challenges. Being a teacher is a hard living, and a living that is not generally highly enough paid to free the practitioner from the financial problems that nag most people and divert them their life long from the contemplation of the verities. As it does to most people, the teacher's personal life usually means a great deal more to him than his job. His job, if he teaches in a university, is first of all research; and if he is susceptible to being excited by his job, it is his research that excites him. The routine of teaching and the grip of research pretty much exhaust his professional energies. The faculty at Chicago—like the faculty of any solidly established institution—could not and would not be kept at the incessant ready to do something about Education with a capital *E*, except for that minority (mostly the younger and least influential of them) who felt themselves called to crusade with the Boy President. By 1944, at forty-five, he had pretty well run out of boyishness.

Looking back at it all, Hutchins would insist that he might have done much better than he did at Chicago, that, with patience (which he ridiculed in the first years of his administration) he might, he thought, have done a great deal more to achieve a consensus—"that unfortunate word"— instead of relying on getting a mere majority, "which I constantly got and constantly relied on. This is not the spirit of an intellectual community, to proceed by majority votes, particularly by narrow votes, to say nothing of proceeding by tie votes."[7]

"I think that one has to say, on the other side, that the kind of patience that is required is almost superhuman. You have very little effective power. That is, you can't tell anybody to do anything. You can't threaten anybody, if only for the practical reason that in a university environment that would be a boomerang. If it became known that I threatened a professor, it would have had catastrophic results. By the same token, you can't reward anybody. That is, you can't reward anybody for being in sympathy with you. You can reward him within the limits of your budget and the approval of your board and the concurrence of his department, for his distinction in his field. But if I left a faculty meeting and recommended an increase in salary of a man who had done something to put through a program that I was interested in, this also would have been a dreadful boomerang. . . . [A university president] must rely entirely, therefore, on his powers of persuasion.

"Well, if you set out to try to persuade the same people over and over and over again, year after year, the charm of your personality, and even the fluency of your words, is likely to diminish. And this was another reason, of course, that I finally resigned. I felt that somebody else could come in and give the place a new and certainly a different impetus. I simply felt that I was losing what a university president who takes his position seriously has to have, namely, the power, the endurance constantly to keep at the job of persuading people."[8]

The power, the endurance—and the appetite. He tried, half-heartedly, to display the appetite to persuade. He recalled what seemed to him, years later, to have been an infinity of what he called hand-holding sessions. "You see one man after another. You talk to groups, you talk to anybody you can get hold of because you . . . have no power. . . . If anybody were to ask me how to run a university, I would—at least as far as the board and the public were concerned; this may not be necessary with the faculty—I would reply with one five-letter word: LUNCH. You've got to keep on having lunch with people. You get indigestion in the process, but you can sometimes do better missionary work under these circumstances than any other."[9]

Might he have been able to do more, or to do things more durably, if he had had more lunches, if his rhetoric had been less combustible, if his patience had been less easily exhausted, if he had made even more compromises than he claimed he did? Probably not; "the problem of time is insoluble."—This in 1945, while he was still on the job.—"The administrator should never do anything he does not have to do, because the things he will have to do are so numerous that he can not possibly have time to do them. He should never do today what he can put off till tomorrow. He should never do anything he can get anybody to do for him. He should have the largest number of good associates he can find; for they may be able to substitute for him. But he should be under no illusions here. The better his associates are, the more things they will think of for him to do."[10]

Ten years later, with Chicago five years behind him, he asserted his conviction that "the existing structure [of the university generally] is impossible. . . . Administration by persuasion and agreement, which is the only kind that brings lasting results, can not be conducted in the vast chaos of the American university. If I had it to do over again I might have begun in 1929 with a proposal more basic than any I ever advanced. I should have proposed the reorganization of the University of Chicago along the lines of Oxford and Cambridge. The University should have been reconstituted into a federation of colleges, each representing among its students and teachers the major fields of learning. These colleges should have begun their work with the junior year, resting on the foundation of the College of the University, which terminated its work at the end of the sophomore year. That college was intended to be the equivalent of the humanistic gymnasium or the lycee or the British public school. The change could have meant that basic liberal education would have been followed by compulsory communication with the representatives of disciplines other than one's own throughout the whole educational process, and, in the case of teachers, throughout their lives. Such colleges, with 250 students and 25 faculty members, would be of manageable size. Each one could have an administrative officer who could be expected to lead the way to improvements both numerous and lasting. The University as a whole should not have a permanent, full-time head. The ceremonial, representative functions of the university president could be performed, as at Oxford and Cambridge, by a temporary official."[11]

There was the pipe dream of all Hutchins pipe dreams for you. In the light of his failure to get the modest changes he fought for at Chicago for twenty years, it is not difficult to imagine what would have happened—and what would have happened to him—had he made any such totally radical proposal as this for the dismemberment of the university and its reconstitution as a collection of small colleges with "compulsory communication with the representatives of disciplines other than one's own throughout the whole educational process, and, in the case of teachers, throughout their lives." What would have happened to so mad a proposal would have been its instant and outraged dismissal along with the fiery resignation, within a few months of its being made, of its mad proponent. He would have made a point, but a point of no wide or durable interest; and not one of the things he did achieve over those two decades (in however inadequate and evanescent a form) would have come to pass or have even reached any considerable nationwide or worldwide attention.

They did. They came to be known, and imitated, in most of the nation's universities and many of its colleges, peripherally, to be sure, and transitorily, to be surer. They were argued all through the higher learning, not only in America but in Europe and in Asia. The name of Hutchins was universally heard, and some comprehension of his position expressed at every level of education over that twenty-year period. And it would remain the one name—after Dewey's—to be known at every level of education in the decades that followed. Fifty years after he came to Chicago, the collapse of the whole schooling process, elementary, secondary, and collegiate, aroused a great clamor to return—as if they had ever been there—to "basics," and in the 1980s there were still, in every university, faculty members and faculty movements tracing their heredity to Hutchins. And there were no end of teachers everywhere who, though they might only know his name, were his disciples via that animate heredity.

He maintained privately, and broadly implied in public, that he had failed as an educator. Of course he had failed. He had failed to change

American education for the better. So had everybody else. American education had changed, all right, but it had changed for the worse. So had a great many other things in the general demoralization and disintegration of the social order. The presidents, premiers, and packagers all failed of their ambitions, President Hutchins among them. Sinners innocent of some sins, including some cardinal sins, but guilty of the cardinal sin of pride. Bob Hutchins had read *Faust* (in German) in a pup tent on the Italian front in 1918. In the introduction to *Faust* he had read that the Lord asked Mephistopheles how His favorite creature on earth was getting along, and the Devil replied, "*Der Mensch bleibt Mensch*"—"He's still the same old man."

35 Denouement (2): Maude

They were as unlike as two peas in a closely examined pod. Their likenesses were obvious: she was almost as tall as he was; the way they carried themselves and their sense of dress stamped them as forerunners of what would one day be the beautiful people. Arch, casual, immensely self-possessed, immensely inattentive to the passing scene (*they* were the passing scene), they were both of them offhand in the way they handled money, having the air of two people who had never known what it was not to have money, though both of them had grown up without much of it; he the son of a parson professor who reared a family on two thousand dollars or so a year. (Her family, Phelpses, McVeighs, were genteel New Yorkers, her father a well-paid editor of the *Sun*.)

He must have got his toploftiness about money at Yale, where, without a bean, pushing a broom, waiting table, tutoring, he had made his name and fame among the best-padded young men in the land. Somewhere, somehow he had learned to pick up the check without ostentation or a quaver, to the manner born. All his life he sent back letters on the stationery of the George V in Paris, the Hassler in Rome, Claridge's in London, and Excelsiors and Grands all over the world without, plainly, ever supposing that anybody anywhere would say, "What does he do for money?" Possessed of the small-time bourgeois trait of being utterly closemouthed about his finances, he nevertheless let it be known among his close friends that he was in debt down the years, down all the years. He was forty when, damping down a friend's suggestion that he let his name be put forward for the United States presidency, he wrote, "But I could use the salary." He was seventy-five when President Edward Levi asked him to return to Chicago to deliver a series of lectures, and he said, "On what?" "On your reflections," said Levi. Hutchins: "I have never reflected on anything except how to pay my debts." And, again at seventy-five, he said to a friend, "I have always declined to write my autobiography. But if somebody would want to help me pay my debts by advancing $50,000, I'd do it." (The friend asked around; nobody would.)

"I never made any money," he said. He didn't have to. He was able to turn over to the university all the money he got from his lectures and books and still survive in style on his $25,000 wages (more or less), until he jumped to $35,000 at the Ford Foundation in 1950. He was able to survive in style in part because of the expense-account life he led from his early twenties on—remember, he was a law school dean at twenty-eight—and in part because the rich were always thrusting things on him, from summer houses to cars to, in Benton's case, great amounts of money for limited services to the Britannica operations. Still he was always heavily in debt, living not so much sumptuously as carelessly, the unselfconscious sybarite going blocks out of his busy way to buy himself a single pair of socks at Sulka's. Once, if only once, he revealed a passing self-consciousness: in his syndicated weekly column in the *Los Angeles Times* he wrote, in 1963, "Never in history has it been so easy for one group in a community to go through life without any awareness of the existence of others. Highways, trains, and airplanes take me quickly around or over sights that might shock my sensibilities or move my heart to compassion. I can travel from my agreeable home to my pleasant office and on to luxury restaurants and hotels serene in the assurance that I will meet nobody, not even a waiter, who looks much worse off than I."

The unselfconscious sybarite was an unselfconscious snob. Once Paul Jacobs and he were late for an appointment in New York and they couldn't get a cab. Jacobs suggested that they take the subway, and Hutchins said, "I never use public transportation in New York."[1] And once, when he had a 12:30 luncheon date downtown in Chicago, and I was going to ride with him in the livery car that carried him around, and the car didn't show up, I suggested that if he hotfooted it to the Illinois Central suburban station he could catch an express that would land him at the Chicago Club in time, and he said, "I have never ridden the IC, and I never will."

On at least one occasion his unselfconscious snobbery played a mean trick on him. A New Yorker of his acquaintance was going to be in Chicago briefly between trains en route home from California. Hutchins was anxious to talk to him and they made a date at the university. But Hutchins was also going to New York that day, and it was agreed that they would travel together and continue their talk. The New Yorker would be boarding the train in downtown Chicago, Hutchins at the outgoing Englewood stop near the university. Hutchins duly boarded the extra-fare Twentieth Century Limited (which he always rode) at Englewood, but he couldn't find the New Yorker. The reason he couldn't, he learned later, was that by "the train," the New Yorker meant the slower, regular-fare Commodore Vanderbilt on the same line. The New Yorker was John D. Rockefeller, Jr.

Hutchins could not plead, and did not attempt to, that he had no competence in personal finances—that his mind was on higher things. His mind for the last fifty and more years of his life was on lower things a great deal of the time. As an administrator, first at the Yale Law School, then successively at Chicago, the Ford Foundation, the Fund for the Republic, and the center in Santa Barbara, he knew who got how much money and why, and spent a great deal of his time listening to people who wanted more and deciding whether they should get it. He knew all the Eleusinian mysteries of a thousand families' finances (or what was presented to him as family finances). Men who would talk freely about their religion, their politics, and their sex lives could not be got to talk about how much money they made or had or spent—except by the boss to whom they were applying for a raise on the ground, always, of need. He knew all about poor-mouthing and had to indulge in it himself when, on extremely rare occasion, he went to his boards of trustees to get a raise for himself; extremely rare because his to-the-manner-born manner moved him to an apparent indifference to the sordid concerns of the workaday world.

It was an expensive life, partly because he lived it that customized way, partly because, as the big money earner, he was always a generous donor to members of his family near and far, including the three daughters he'd had (and regretfully said he'd had) too little time for. Plagued by his self-proclaimed neglect of his children—the claim was an honest one—he tried more than a little naively to compensate for the neglect by his financial generosity to them. Between Maude's work and her demand on his attention and his own work and weariness, their daughters were nearly always left to the mercies of nannies. They were not happy children, and the lives of the two oldest reflected childhood distresses. They were all three very bright. The oldest, Frances ("Franja") was thrice married, the last time to an orthodox Jew whose religion she adopted; she and her husband both died of cancer in early middle life. The second, Joanna Blessing ("Jo-Jo"), lived alone in Berkeley pretty well alienated from the family. Only the youngest, Clarissa, married to a Brandeis University faculty member, and herself an effective public-service lawyer in Cambridge, both stood up to her parents and fulfilled the hopeful role of the academic's child. But even bold and perceptive Clarissa, who said she regarded Hutchins as "a great guy rather than a great man," had grown up in relative isolation from her art-centered mother and her job-centered father. In 1965 an outfit called the National Father's Day Committee designated him Father of the Year (an honor awarded to Spiro Agnew in 1972), and he said it must have been to present the world with the world's most horrible example. The son of a strong father and a docile mother, brought up with two brothers, he had no early training in dealing with women and was never able to come to terms with them, whatever their proximity, whatever their age or his. He was infinitely polite, infinitely careful to see to it that they were appointed to posts and recognized in discussion, and infinitely capable of masking what may well have been a deep-seated scorn of their not unusual demand for special recognition as a sex. His attention, and attentiveness, to them was meticulous and faultless; it was clear, to those who knew him well, that it was not the attention or attentiveness given recognized equals. Incapable of recognizing their due, and of giving it because it was their due, he gave to them in the futile spirit of largesse.

It didn't work, not with women who wanted their due as due them. It didn't work, above all, with Maude Hutchins. He tried to buy her satisfaction for twenty-seven years, and had finally to acknowledge failure— without being able to acknowledge his failure as the consequence of his trying, for want of another way, to buy her satisfaction by buying her the things that money bought. Maude Hutchins was as rare a bird as he was; rarer. Her talents were several, each of them considerable, all of them aesthetic. She was, purposively, illiterate on social issues (including education) and as indifferent as she was illiterate, likely because of her resentment of him, just as likely because of her intense preoccupation with her variform artistic enterprises. She was a fine sculptor, a very good pen and pencil artist, and a hurry-up novelist (or novellaist) of parts. (Her published fiction was all of it embarrassingly racy, both for him and for the 1930s and 40s. Her *Diary of Love*[2] was characterized by the Chicago police censors as "purple.") But she was much more than her aesthetic capacities. Much, much more.

If he was imperial, she was imperious; imperious and impervious to what (and who) went on around her, as he never was. Hers was a nose-in-the-air posture which he, whatever his inclination, was foreclosed from maintaining consistently by virtue of his job. The two of them were born to trouble with one another as the sparks of their intercourse flew sideways. Their fiercely competitive—and exhausting—wit was singular to each of them; his saucy, hers caustic. (As when told Ruml was quitting the social sciences for Macy's: "Exchanging ideas for notions, eh?" or encountering one of her husband's friends after many years: "You're as ugly as ever.") Their public conversation was diamond-cut-diamond, their tête-à-tête imaginably acrid behind the forbidden doors of the president's house on the campus.

Those doors closed behind him at five minutes past five every weekday; and the man who had a hard day at the office every day, and before the day at the office a stretch of writing between 6 and 8 A.M., was under the imperious duty to be entertaining. He did not succeed very well or very often. He wanted to read, or work, for an hour after drinks and dinner and before his preferred bedtime of nine-thirty (better yet, nine). It wasn't vouchsafed him (as it isn't many men) to do so. He spent thirty years angrily yielding. At six in the evening, even six-thirty, he might phone one of three or four intimates in the neighborhood and ask him to come over—*without his wife*—for a lap dinner. A shameful command performance on the inviter's part, a shameful acquiescence on the invitee's. These gatherings *à trois* were as luxurious and uncomfortable as the well-staffed dinner parties, where she went through the ironic motions of scintillating and he repressed his distress and his tiredness and did his dutiful best, at so late an hour, to unbend. The dinner parties were infrequent, mingling an occasional trustee or an even more occasional donor or prospective donor with one or two close friends who could be counted on to help keep the iron ball rolling. With Maude as the unvoiced alibi, no more than a handful of senior faculty—still fewer junior—ever saw the inside of the president's house during the Hutchinses' twenty years' residence.

He would not, of course, complain, beyond lifting his eyes to the hills when a friend asked him, vaguely enough, how things were going, or replying, "You know how things are going." Or if the friend asked, "How are things otherwise?" "There isn't any otherwise." Or, if the friend was close: "None of your business." He exploited his intolerable situation: he could, and did, reject invitations he didn't want to accept by saying, "I'm sorry" without having to say why he was sorry. It was widely and long understood that things were rough at home behind those doors, with marvelous Maude serving as his lightning rod, no less effectively than she served as his lightning. Yielding to her bolts or, sufficiently sharply jolted, hurling one or two back, he did himself and the relationship no good at all. The suspicion that the world had, of an isolated hell behind those doors, proved in the end to have been completely valid. Pastor William James Hutchins and his wife had not brought up their sons to be divorced; and their second son, until he was, could not have believed that a Hutchins ever would be.

None of the yielding could have done any good, and none of it did, however scandalous the lengths to which he carried it. None of those lengths was more scandalous than the one that involved a half-dozen carefully spotted friends who he knew would do anything for him within—or without—reason, and to whom he could go unblushingly. A few months after I went to work in the president's office I discovered, to my fiscal horror, that I had been admitted to this shameful circle. He was willing to employ his silent, shrieking agony not only to duck engagements, not only to generate a generalized sympathy ("poor Bob"), but to get his hands on money to keep his wife "quiet"—as if Maude Hutchins were in want of repeated sedation and solicitousness.

There were probably half a dozen—maybe more—such coconspiratorial victims of the ridiculous keep-Maude-quiet or keep-Maude-busy campaign strategy. Mortimer Adler was one (like the Mayers, the Adlers, too, wound up with a bronze head of the Mrs.) Millionaire Bill Benton was another, whose three children were all headed. Benton was angrily willing to play the game, but his anger overcame his willingness after he was persuaded to commission Maude to do a life-size bronze statue for the garden at his home on Long Island Sound. As Will Munnecke later recalled it— the statue was real and the story too, no doubt—Maude hired the model, made the plaster statue, and had it cast and delivered to the Benton home all within the space of a week, complete with an invoice for $7,500. It was the end of a friendship, between Mrs. Hutchins and Mr. Benton, that had been really warm—but it had kept Maude "quiet," "busy," for a week at a cost of only $7,500.[3]

Tried and truest of the sycophantic friends who served as accomplices to the Hutchinses' domestic melodrama was Mortimer Adler, whose role as public and private associate went all the way back to New Haven, where, on his first visit to the young dean, he was taken up by Maude. By the time the Hutchinses were a year or so ensconced at Chicago—with a costly studio added to the president's house at the president's expense— Adler was ensconced in the law school (having been disensconced from the philosophy department). Though he lived across town on the near North Side, he served as domestic end-man to the Hutchins menage more regularly than any other member of the progressively less charmed circle. Maude had been invited to speak before the ladies of the Friday Club, and she showed them a series of her steel-point anatomical drawings, which characteristically had bodies toting their own heads. She explained straight-faced that her work was "nonnarrative and nonrepresentative." "It is incidental that the human form may be recognized in them," she told the clubwomen, who suspected that their legs were being contemptuously pulled. "The forms you see are not necessarily people." She showed Adler—and, willy-nilly, Hutchins—the drawings on one of those *à trois* evenings and asked him if he could work up any nonnarrative and non-representative texts for them. He could. Some years before he had written a paragraph to illustrate the senseless use of sensible syntax: "We have triangulated with impunity in order that sophistication would neither digest nor slice our conventional drainage. Examples of serious solicitude, cleared away with dishes after dinner, leave some of us unfaithful to the beach and others of us unprepared to skate. You, perhaps, individually have bounced in isolation, careless of benefit derived from saracens, but not wholly too late for the Sunday papers."

The Adler syntactical nonsense was just the ticket. He collaborated with the nonnarrative, nonrepresentative artist in the preparation of a book of her nonsensical drawings with a collection of his nonsensical texts variously entitled "Prayer," "Invective," "History," "Definition," and so on, and Adler's friends Bennett Cerf and Donald Klopfer at Random House published the joint spoof in a volume of 750 copies called *Diagrammatics*. The two producers made appearances on and off the campus in the early 1930s to present and defend their skit, earnestly arguing what Adler called "the significance of form divorced from significant matter in a work of art." After Adler dropped out of the fun, Maude went on with it annually, as she prepared her exorbitant Christmas cards, usually with an extravagant but intelligent and able version of a biblical text, but on at least one occasion with the nude figure of a going-on nubile girl holding a Christmas candle—the model was sensationally reported around town and gown to be the Hutchinses' fourteen-year-old Franja.

Long before the curtain was rung down on the twenty-seven-year run of the Hutchins Follies, one of their friends, the plainspoken wife of a trustee, said, "They're a bore"—something she would not have said of either of the performers singly. They would have been less of a bore if Hutchins had been able to talk—even to the modest extent of saying why he had to make a last-minute change in plans, instead of grimacing, when his interlocutor was simple enough to say, "What's the trouble?" But down, at last, the curtain came, one spring evening in 1947, at the very peak of his multifarious preoccupation with world affairs. He appeared at the door of a close friend who lived just off the campus and said, "May I come in?" The friend might have made a stab at guessing what "the trouble" was; nothing like Hutchins at the door, any door, in the night had ever happened before.

He laid his underarm carrying-case on the living-room table and accepted a chair. He did not, however, accept the invitation to remove his coat. He said (in the same flat tone he used on the platform), "I've left home." The friend—whose wife was present—murmured something intended to sound sympathetic and be unintelligible, and added, "Where are you going?" "Downtown," said Hutchins, who was then working at the Encyclopaedia Britannica on the leave of absence he had taken to see (as he said once, and only once, to a very few individuals) what he could do about his domestic situation. He asked to be allowed to phone for a cab, and left after a silent handshake.

The friend he walked in on that night said later, "At last Bob Hutchins had been caught up with by the things of the sort that make people human. He was human that night, off his demigodly perch—and he could look it, for once. Life, just for a moment or two, had cut him down to size, pulled him down to the level where the rest of us lived."

He took a room in one of the big hotels within walking distance of the Britannica offices and did not return to the President's House to get his things until arrangements had been made for Maude to be out. He said he would never speak to her again—and he never did. The lawyer—there was only one, retained by friends—was more than mildly surprised, even though he was an old friend of the family, when Hutchins declined to argue his wife's high demands. They were enough to strap him the rest of his life; for twenty-seven years he had tried to get himself, not peace and quiet, only enough quiet to do his work. He had used the most insulting and ineffective currency to buy it—giving her whatever she "wanted," whatever, that is, she wanted that could be bought. The last time around, after those twenty-seven years, he did it again; but this time the purchase would be permanent. The uncontested divorce settlement—the formal charge was desertion—awarded Maude $18,000 a year combined alimony, child support, and insurance premiums, but Hutchins was reported to have made an out-of-court contract bringing the total annual transfer to something like $30,000. The $25,000-a-year man was bankrolled by Bill Benton, whose Britannica Hutchins would go on serving, in one role or more (usually more) all his life.

It had not been an amusing marriage, the marriage of those two stunning figures out of F. Scott Fitzgerald. It was not an amusing divorce. It was a calamitous surprise, if not to the two parties or their children, to their friends who found them the kind of bore that would go on until death did them part. It was a calamitous surprise to the two families from the Calvinist parsonage of Brooklyn and the settled world of Oberlin. There were, indeed, no end of marriages made in 1921 that proved to have been made elsewhere than in heaven; but nearly all people stayed married, "whatever."

Maude Hutchins was no helpmeet, and Bob Hutchins was no help. He was hyperbolizing—but not lying—when he said that he never had time to think of anything beyond what he had to do in the next half-hour. He tried to be and do too much, more than a man can try to be and do who has professional standards that do not permit him to shuffle off some, or most, of his work on others. This was a man who felt that he had to have time for every student who wanted to see him—with three exceptions: his daughters Franja, Jo-Jo, and Clarissa. And their mother was unwilling to be the kind of mother his and her mothers (and theirs) had been. The mismating of these two rare birds, so much alike, so colorful of plumage, so piquant of song, may have forced Maude Hutchins to behave shrewishly, but she was none of your ordinary shrews. She was as much of a person as he was, and as much of a woman as he was a man; in some respects, doubtless, more. But his public position was immeasurably higher than hers, and no matter what she achieved, or said, or did, she remained the talented wife of, the brilliant wife of, the artistic wife of, the great man. She could not overcome her resentment of him, or even check it (it grew visibly greater with the years)—resentment of his business, his importance, his independence of her, and the general adulation he had and doubtless enjoyed; the adulation that moved Scott Buchanan to say, "Bob has made homosexuals of us all."

If they were both ridden by the customary devils, and one of the customary devils that rode them both was duty—hers was duty to a hard master, art; and his to a master no harder, the Cause that an Oberlin boy brought to Oberlin with him from the parsonage and carried away to Yale and beyond. The great and terrible factor, the factor that may have held the union together for twenty-seven years instead of seven (or seven months) was the now bent figure of William James Hutchins. He had always counseled Robert against impetuosity; Robert had now to persuade his father that breaking the marriage vow—to which his father had sworn him—was not impetuous. He later insisted that going to his father now was the hardest thing he had ever had to do.

Mother and Father Hutchins survived, as mothers and fathers do, and even then did. (Everybody involved survived, more or less handsomely, as they usually do, and even then did.) Maude Hutchins has survived her ex-husband by many years, and until her old age was writing (and publishing) and sketching; she would not discuss her ex-husband; she said, thirty years later, that "it still hurt too much." Nor would he discuss her or his marriage. The mistakes he made—like those we all make—he would likely make again. His hope was that he would not again be thrown into such hopeless circumstances. Nor was he.

When he left home, his leave-of-absence boss, Bill Benton of the Britannica, instructed the Britannica office manager to furnish him with the brightest and best-looking secretary to be found anywhere. Little Vesta

Sutton Orlick, twenty years his junior, was a head shorter than he—he always called her the little corporal. She was the divorced mother of a small daughter, and very bright and very, very good looking. She was soon promoted to be Hutchins' secretary in his office as chairman of the Britannica board of editors, and a year after his divorce in July of 1948 they were married—by the Reverend William James Hutchins.

Vesta Hutchins was no Maude. Neither she nor her requirements were anything as flamboyant as her predecessor and her predecessor's. She wanted the things that a very busy man could provide—expensively, to be sure, but he was used to that—and provide for a woman who was devoted to him and his work and affected none of her very own. They lived quite privately as he and Maude had done (but without the *à trois* accessory); entertaining little, and leaving parties as invariably early as ever. She was ailing a good deal, but she was much younger than he and survived him busily on their 90-acre estate in the Santa Barbara hills. She wrote no lively novellas, sketched no nude models (or nonnarrative, nonrepresentative figures), sculpted no sculptures to be sold to friends; she didn't need to do much more than travel with him, peripherally participate in his work, and look after the management of the house and garden.

During his twenty-seven-year marriage to Maude, he had never had time for his wife and children. He had never had time, period. But the last twenty-seven years of his twenty-nine-year marriage to Vesta found him differently situated. Once he left the university he was relieved of the intense pressures of the job there and left with the pressures that were within his own power, those that he put on himself. He was a very busy man between 1951 and his death in 1977, but never again as desperately busy as he was in the years at Chicago, never again too busy to pay any attention at all to the kind of life he was living and the kind of trouble that that kind of life entailed for him and others.

Part Seven

A CALL FOR COMMUNITY

36   A Call for Community

Hutchins' sense of the Hiroshima holocaust—and the role he had played in it—was so oppressive that it plunged him headlong into the public affairs of the republic, in effect putting an end to his academic career. Sixty days after Japan's surrender he spoke, at the university chapel, on the atomic bomb versus civilization, predicting that other nations would soon have the bomb and "we shall never be able to appeal to the moral sense of mankind to protect us against it because we used it, and we used it when we did not need to. . . . [The bomb] has produced a world which must live in perpetual fear. And this world is particularly explosive, because it seems destined to be a bipolar world. Only the United States and Russia will be major powers; the other nations will be satellites grouped around them." (This was October 14, 1945.)[1]

If, in the atomic age, the Americans and the Russians refused to sink their national independence in a world state, the outlook would be bleak. But "states do not make communities; communities make states. A state requires authority as well as power, and the authority of a government rests on the common respect and the common conviction of its people. A world state can arise and endure only on the solid foundations of a world community. No such community exists, and, at the present rate of moral progress, none can be created before the world is full of atomic bombs.

"Is the situation, then, altogether hopeless? I think it is not; but the only hope is to increase the rate of moral progress tremendously, to increase it beyond anything we have ever dreamed of, to increase it to an extent which itself, at first glance, may seem hopeless.

"We know that we have a certain amount of time before the world is full of atomic bombs. We probably have not more than five years before some other country has them."[2] And in a speech a few months later:

"When the Russians have the atomic bomb, the position of the United States automatically undergoes a dramatic change. . . . One false step in foreign policy can mean the end, not only of our institutions, but also of civilization. . . . And we can not place our hope on [international] agreements. These agreements are absolutely imperative; but they will simply guarantee, if they are effective, that the next war will end with atomic bombs instead of beginning with them."[3]

Isolationism as a national way of life, he said, was an anachronism in the atomic age. "If we are finally to survive, we must now, as never before in history, act our age." The only way to act our age in the atomic age was to monopolize atomic energy in a world organization. There was no other hope of abolishing war, and mankind's survival required its abolition.[4]

"Let me tell you what we all know. One: There is no defense against the atomic bomb. The only defense is not to be there when it goes off. Two: In a war in which both sides have atomic bombs"—he was now speaking in March, 1947, when the United States still had a monopoly—"the cities of both sides will be destroyed. Three: Since one to ten atomic bombs can reduce any city in the world to ashes, it will not help us much to have more atomic bombs than an enemy country. Four: Superiority in land, sea, and air forces will mean little. The atomic bomb is a weapon directed against civilians. The economy which supports the military can be wiped out before the military can get started. Five: Our monopoly of the atomic bomb can not last more than five years."[5]

So the first desperate item of national business was the campaign for world government. Or, rather, the second. The first was the hurried education of the whole American people—indeed, the people of the whole world—to the acceptance of world community.

"We do not know what education can accomplish, because we have never tried it."[6] "The American people, whatever their professions, do not take education very seriously. And in the past there has been no particular reason why they should. This country was impregnable to enemies from without, and apparently indestructible. It could not be destroyed even by hysterical waste and mass stupidity of the people and its government. Foreign policy, for example, could be the blundering ground of nice old Southern lawyers, and education could be regarded as a means of keeping children off the street."[7]

This pastoral condition was no longer viable, not in the atomic age. "I admit that the Russians are hard to get on with. I do not like their form of government, their philosophy, or their religion."[8] "You may well ask how we can get other people to behave themselves. If our hearts are changed, and those of the Russians are not, we shall merely have the satisfaction of being blown up with changed hearts rather than unchanged ones."⁹ Taken by itself, world government was much too simple a solution for the overriding problems of the atomic age. Its adoption was not enough. The precondition was a change of heart everywhere in the world, to achieve the world community based on "a common stock of ideas and ideals" and upon "the recognition of the common humanity of all human beings."

How to do it? "I should like tentatively to endorse the suggestion of the delegate from Lebanon to the United Nations, who said that the common bond and the common tradition were most clearly revealed in the great works of the human mind and spirit. He suggested that, if all the peoples of the earth unite in the study of these great works, a world community might arise. Plainly the task before us is an educational task. We have to educate everybody, of every age, at home and abroad. And we have five years, more or less, in which to do it."¹⁰

Was he serious? Did he think that he, or anybody, or any catechism or revelation, would or could move the whole human race—more than half of which was illiterate or semiliterate—to "study these great works" by offering "some hope of laying the foundations of a world community"? Or was he, urged by a combination of cosmic necessity with his own compulsion, indulging in transparent polemics? "I do not say that the Great Books program upon which the University of Chicago and the Encyclopaedia Britannica are now embarked is the only answer. . . . I do say that it sounds promising." And to top its promise in a world of three billion people, "I confidently expect to see 15,000,000 Americans studying the great works of the human mind and spirit within five years."¹¹ (Within five years the Great Books adult discussion program across the nation enrolled closer to fifteen thousand than the fifteen million Hutchins had predicted—and the Encyclopaedia Britannica had withdrawn its modest support of it.) He saw hope in the proliferation of radio programs like the university's Round-Table on NBC radio, which with its audience of a million was far and away the country's largest educational broadcast—and which, within five years, would have been eliminated by the network's decision to sell the air time commercially.

These were worthy, and moderately significant, educational ventures, but even if they should be carried to the peoples of the whole earth they would still be only educational ventures, and what was wanted was a moral progress and a change of heart. He had always contended that character cannot be imparted or fortified directly, but only indirectly through the power of the liberal arts to habituate the student to sharp and independent thinking about means and ends. But the influence of the elevated intellect on the unelevated morals was a matter of years of even the best education—and the best education was almost nowhere available (and almost nowhere in America).

He was grasping at straws, and when a friend told him so he said, "Where there is nothing but straws to grasp at, you grasp at straws." He had supposed (or so he said) that the Hutchins Plan would be imitated by universities the country over; it wasn't. He had supposed that colleges the country over would adopt the St. John's nonelective liberal arts curriculum; they didn't. He never gave up inflationary prediction. Twenty-five years later he hailed the announcement of England's Open University scheme—an admirable, but modest, program of adult education—as replacing that country's imperial dreams with "the vision of a community in which every citizen has the opportunity all his life to achieve the maximum development of his highest powers. . . . In the allocation of its financial resources the [British] state has given the highest priority to this commitment."

Exaggerating the impact, present and projected, of the adult discussion program in the great books and the Round-Table of the Air, he saw, he said, no reason to despair of proceeding rapidly in the direction of world community as the precondition of a durable world government, which, without that community, might well collapse into a world civil war. It was, he admitted, very late: "Perhaps nothing can save us. But with the good news of damnation ringing in our ears, we may remember that 'It is not necessary to hope in order to undertake, or to succeed in order to persevere.'"[12] Hutchins would undertake, through his first and only love, education, to achieve the unlikely objective of changing fifteen thousand, or fifteen million, or three billion human hearts; undertake, and persevere.

By the end of 1945 the three nuclear institutes were solidly established and the university relieved of its management of the wartime Argonne National Laboratory established by the government outside Chicago and the giant plutonium production facility at Oak Ridge, Tennessee. Hutchins persuaded his board of trustees to create the post of chancellor of the university for him—that is, to kick him upstairs—and appoint his dean of faculties, Ernest ("Pomp") Colwell, a theologian, as president to take over the day-to-day affairs of the institution. His misbegotten intention was clear: as if he were an interchangeable man, he would henceforth be what most university presidents in fact were, a ceremonial dignitary who could be trotted out on appropriate public occasions. What he told his board was: "The idea of the chancellorship was that, since the University [has] grown to such a size and complexity, its principal officer should be raised above administrative routine so that he might . . . give his time to those matters which [seem] to him most important to its welfare."

He was bone tired of the bootless effort to achieve a basic change in the higher learning, or at least to establish at Chicago a working model for such a change—an effort into which he had poured his life, his unresting energy, and his unresting passion for the past quarter-century. "To think," he told a friend a few years later, as they approached a great university campus where he was lecturing, "that I never again have to work in a place like this." And, on another occasion: "My heart leaps up when I consider that I shall never again have to preside over a meeting of the University of Chicago Senate." He foresaw—it wasn't too difficult—the postwar expansion and concomitant disintegration of the universities. It was not only in the exact sciences, where government grants would determine and dominate the programs; the institution as a whole would undergo a transformation from a cloistered place of quiet intellectual endeavor to a vocationalist forcing bed, providing the kinds of problem-solving, on an ad hoc, hic-et-nunc basis that the achievement of the sustained nuclear chain reaction exemplified: the country had discovered, to its astonishment, that a university was good for something. There would now be relentless pressure, and irresistible funds, for short-term, result-oriented, "crash" undertakings, with fundamental research downgraded in favor of the application of what was already known. Fields would proliferate, and specialization and professionalism be intensified. The decline of the university as the world's one long-term workplace was beginning. Nor was it only the state schools which would soon be recognized as service institutions, providing whatever the public, or any powerful segment of it, thought was needed immediately; the private universities too would expand their facilities and faculties accordingly in the competitive drive for the production of gadgetry and the training of men and women in narrow disciplines instead of their education in the great fields of knowledge. The postwar university was further from Hutchins' vision than it had been when he began his academic career, and would grow even further. He saw himself well out of it, called by his stricken conscience to try his hand at changing the shape of things in the nation at large and in the world. Temporally it was a happy concatenation. He had come to the end of his academic rope with the national preeminence to accord him a respectful hearing on the great issues of the hour, beginning with the greatest of them—the bomb.

He had always had to decline five or ten speaking invitations for every one he accepted. Now he accepted many more than he had previously, especially from organizations and institutions that wanted him to discuss the overall social crisis rather than education. Relieved of his routine obligations to the university, he was out of town, in a given month, as much as half the time (with an additional strain, if any was needed, on his grim domestic situation). In the first five years after the war he averaged five public appearances a month. Many of his performances were broadcast nationally over the radio networks. He spoke before medical schools and churches, chambers of commerce and high schools, library associations, town halls, congressional committees, the National Association of Manufacturers and the liberal National Citizens Political Action Committee, the National Industrial Conference and the radical National Council for the Prevention of War—and the University of Uppsala, in Sweden, and the German National Assembly, at Frankfurt. As always, his fees, ranging from twenty-five (or less) to twenty-five hundred dollars, went to the University of Chicago.

But his main message, always stark, simple, disarmingly straightforward, piling up arguments (or assertions) in solemn series, whose mere weight was convincing, had an almost frantic ring now. Under such lecture titles as "The Atomic Bomb versus Civilization," "We Must Defeat War," "Peace or War with Russia?" and "The Good News of Damnation," he leveled a steady barrage of unremitting fire at his own government as the prime culprit in the continuing crisis and mounting confrontation with the USSR. With its atomic monopoly, the United States had reduced its conventional military power immediately after Hiroshima. Mr. Truman made it clear—his highly respected biographer suggests that he was dangerously underbriefed[13]—that his administration was relying completely on the exclusive American possession of the bomb. On October 8, 1945, according to the official historians of the Atomic Energy Commission, he met informally with reporters and, admitting that the scientific secrets had already spread throughout the world, insisted that the "engineering secrets were something else. The United States would not share them. As a matter of fact, no other country could use them. Only the United States had the combination of industrial capacity and resources necessary to produce the Bomb."[14]

Truman's "underbriefing" turned out to be dangerous indeed. In September of 1949—four years after Hiroshima and a year earlier than Hutchins had predicted—the Soviet Union exploded an atomic bomb. Mr. Truman's atomic monopoly strategy was dead. His response was the massive rearmament of the United States "against the Soviet design for world domination." The defense budget was tripled, and the government, over the moral protest of Robert Oppenheimer and other leading scientists, ordered the work to proceed on the development of the "super"—the hydrogen bomb. By the time the United States had the hydrogen bomb, the Russians had it, and within five years of competitive frenzy on both sides the weapons of Hiroshima and Nagasaki were outmoded.

Back and forth across the country—and across the seas—Hutchins shuttled to speaking engagements, denouncing the Truman policies and proclaiming that "an armaments race in atomic weapons is a race nobody can win. The alternatives before us are peace or suicide. . . . The policy of the United States is based on force . . . confused, contradictory, and incoherent. It is a bad means to a bad end . . . immoral and suicidal . . . a policy adequately described by the historian Tacitus. He said, when force was the policy of the Romans, 'They make a desolation, and they call it peace.'"[15] This was as early on as November 1945 and he stepped up the rhetoric in the months that followed. "The foreign policy of the United States, as announced by Mr. Truman . . . is to have the largest army, navy, and air force in the world and thus ensure peace," he testified before the House Military Affairs Committee. "The policy is the sheerest folly, and it will end in disaster. A few well placed atomic weapons can make junk of all these vast preparations in a few minutes."[16] "A nation which now uses force will perish in the act of using it," he said in a nationally broadcast Modern Forum lecture. "These policies will weaken rather than strengthen the United States. They will involve us in a fruitless armaments race which will waste our substance, divert us from the task of building a better world, deceive us into thinking we are secure when we are not, and inevitably lead to war."[17]

He was ever more widely sought as a speaker, and ever more widely applauded. But he was opposing a spirit in the country which had its own momentum. President Truman had begun whipping up anti-Soviet passions in connection with persuading Congress to accept the Marshall Plan and the Truman Doctrine in Greece and Turkey. The cold war in effect began with Hiroshima, the traditional anticommunism of the country having been galvanized by the American monopoly and the helplessness of a Russia drained of manpower and resources by the Nazi invasion. Hutchins' voice was not the only one heard in the land pleading for accord and the international control of atomic energy, but his was one of the weightiest and angriest. He went on calling for a massive program of domestic social reform: "Everyone knows that the education of negroes is far worse than that for whites. Everyone knows that the amount of education a young American obtains depends upon the income of his parents." But the Cold War was carrying everything before it.

Hutchins served as chancellor of the university for a year, 1945–46, and then applied for (and was granted) a leave of absence for the year 1946–47, assuming the chairmanship of the board of editors of the Encyclopaedia Britannica and moving his seat of operations downtown (but retaining an office and a secretary at the university). The Britannica—that is, his friend Bill Benton—assumed the obligation of his $25,000 salary. He was already a member of the encyclopaedia firm's board of directors and a board member of EB Films, Inc., a thriving venture in classroom documentaries. Now he became chairman of the Britannica board of editors—a post he held for the next twenty-seven years. His formal explanation of the move was the pressing necessity to develop the joint operations of the Britannica and the university—including the great fifty-four-volume set of the Great Books of the Western World. But the formal explanation was for public consumption. In a memorandum to his board on February 12, 1947, he wrote, "My educational interests would lead me, if I return [to the university], to apportion my time in the immediate future about as I have this year." *If I return.* He told a very close friend that he needed a year away "to see if I can't do something about my domestic situation."

He did return to the university in 1948 to remain as chancellor for another three years, during which he withdrew further and further from his elevated post in favor of publicly pleading for action on the national and international crises. If his withdrawal from his university responsibilities was unfortunate, it was at least understandable. In the great showdown with the Burghers of Calais in 1944, culminating in the refusal of his board to come out flat-footed either way, he had realized that he had gone—like things in Kansas City—about as far as he could go. He had won a few battles, some of them, like the establishment of the College, considerable battles. He had not won the war. The war was not going to be won.

His withdrawal was, in at least one respect, not only unfortunate but impermissible. He had mastered his impatience magnificently in fighting with his faculty for twenty years, but there was one issue in which he let his impatience have its way. That was the crumbling of the university neighborhood, a problem that had nothing to do with education but distinctly threatened to destroy the university and to destroy it soon. The war had drawn millions of people into the industrial centers of the country from the hinterland, and especially from the southern hinterland. Blacks (then known as Negroes) from the most backward areas of the country thronged into cities like Chicago, and into Chicago in greater numbers than anywhere else. There were previously unheard-of job opportunities, in unskilled work in particular. Employment at good wages also attracted poorly educated, unskilled or semiskilled white workers, particularly from the South—but the "problem" was the influx of Negroes.

They had long been concentrated on Chicago's South Side, a few miles northwest of the university, which was separated from that concentration by a great park on its western boundary. Another great park on its eastern boundary fronted on Lake Michigan, on whose beach a race riot (so-called) occurred in 1919 when a Negro boy swam into "white" water and was stoned and drowned. Ever since then the university neighborhood of Hyde Park had felt itself threatened by the incursion of Negroes, who had slowly expanded into the immediately neighboring area of Kenwood, north of the campus. Woodlawn, south of the campus and across the broad Midway Plaisance, had long been disintegrating, but it had remained lily-white through the 1920s and the 30s.

The university had never practiced discrimination—at least not formally—on its faculty or in admission to its student body. And its faculty, nearly all of whom resided within a few blocks of the campus, included a high proportion of social liberals. These liberals wanted housing opportunities for the expanding Negro population—but on the whole they were in the consolatory habit of wanting such opportunities to be made available somewhere else. They had not openly protested the university's membership in the local property owners' associations organized by the real estate brokers and designed to prevent Negro ownership or occupancy. In 1920 the Hyde Park Property Owners' Association *Journal* announced that "every colored man who moves into Hyde Park . . . is making war on the white man. Consequently he is not entitled to any consideration. . . . There is nothing in the make-up of the Negro, physically or mentally, which should induce anyone to welcome him as a neighbor." The University of Chicago was a member in good standing of that association, indeed, its leading member.

Just before the war Negroes constituted 3 percent of the population of Hyde Park; ten years later they constituted 38 percent. The university was hemmed in. But the Negroes were hemmed in by another kind of barrier—the "gentleman's agreement" or restrictive covenant among property owners agreeing not to sell or rent to "non-Caucasians." In the immediate postwar years many of the newcomers to the city lost their jobs, and the slum landlords of the once fashionable houses of the area had cut those houses up into one-room apartments, each room housing a family in squalor. The area disintegrated rapidly—very rapidly. Saloons and brothels appeared on the business streets, youth gangs vandalized the neighborhood, and by 1948 Hyde Park had the highest crime rate in Chicago.

The worsening situation had reached the point where neither students nor faculty went out at night except in groups. University buildings were now kept locked in the evening and the campus was floodlit all night, as were the adjacent streets. The university's private force was now the second largest police department in the state of Illinois. Faculty were beginning to leave, regretfully taking jobs at lesser institutions, and undergraduate enrollment was dropping; the dormitories of the undergraduate college were across the Midway, which was a no-man's-land at night and even witnessed daytime robberies, muggings, and rapes. Under the Hutchins scheme, the college, admitting students after their sophomore year in high school, included many sixteen- and fifteen-year-olds, and even a few fourteen-year-olds. The university was a critically unsafe place.

As the 1940s ended, it was clear that something radical had to be done: either to save the university where it was or move it or shut it down. Closing it or moving away would be unprecedented in American education. It was one of the world's great institutions of higher learning. But push was rapidly coming to shove. Closing it was unthinkable; moving it, to the suburbs north or south of the city, to central Illinois, or to the west coast to merge with Stanford, was equally unthinkable. It was a quarter-billion-dollar plant, and financial contributions to its work over a period of seventy years had been considerably greater than that. How would one sell a great collection of Gothic buildings? "There is not much of a market for a secondhand university," said one trustee. But something would have to be done, and done soon, and done on a large scale. It was made-to-order for the Hutchins style.

But he had said and done nothing as the storm gathered. It was not directly an educational problem. He had not seemed greatly interested. But he had—he thought—an idea. The idea was to have the university buy up the whole area, redevelop it, and integrate it racially. He took his idea to sociologist Louis Wirth, an academic opponent who, however, shared his views on civil liberties and civil rights. Wirth conducted a survey to determine feasibility and costs and Hutchins took the survey to his board, adding to his proposal the possibility that they get the university's charter changed so that it would be a public or semipublic institution eligible for public funds. The board was aghast: what Hutchins was talking about was nothing less than socialism—yet again. "Besides," said the chairman of the finance committee, "we can ride it out. We have 98% of the surrounding property tied up by restrictive covenants." Now Hutchins was aghast: "I said that in my opinion the covenants were unenforceable and that they were in any case immoral."

The trustees did not care about the immorality and did not accept his view of the illegality. They refused to budge. "I wrote my moral adviser, my father, and told him that I intended to resign. He let me down: he advised me to stay on for the greater good, and so on. He thought I could work from within. He was wrong." So were the trustees. A few months later the U.S. Supreme Court, in *Shelley v. Kraemer*, decided without a dissenting vote that such covenants were designed to deprive persons of the equal protection of the laws.

"A large part of the rest of my administration," said Hutchins afterward, "was spent trying to do something about the area against the resistance of a board of trustees that would spend no money on it." But nothing was done until after his resignation in 1951. His immediate successors presided over the dismantling of the Hutchins Plan, but they undertook the rehabilitation of the area on a colossal scale. With the pas‹ age of the Federal Housing Act in 1954 and the adoption of slum clearance and urban renewal legislation, government funds at all levels became available. The trustees then appropriated thirty million dollars of the two hundred fifty that went into replacing the surrounding slums with middle-to-upper-class apartments and town houses on a racially integrated basis. Ten years later the fifty-block area was a new neighborhood, 40 percent of whose residents were Black. (They were not, of course, the impoverished blacks who had been there before, but *that* was a problem that Hutchins, even had he been interested in it, couldn't have solved.)

Crime was radically reduced—to the still deplorable level of the city generally—and faculty and students no longer left. The university was saved. But it wasn't Hutchins who saved it. There is no hard evidence that he spent "the rest of my administration" trying to do anything about it—and considerable recollection that he didn't. Economics Professor (and later U.S. Senator) Paul H. Douglas was a fervent admirer of Hutchins' positions on academic and civil liberties. "Hutchins behaved like a thoroughbred"—"the University [under Hutchins] was uninterested in the community around it." As the grand gesture of buying up the area was typical Hutchins, so was his dropping the whole thing after his trustees refused to talk about it. The trustees owned the university. They were the university. Nothing could be done to save the institution from the encroaching disaster if it was not done by them. An apparently petulant, apparently insensitive Hutchins was wrong, almost fatally wrong in terms of the physical survival of the university. He wasn't interested in physical survival. He was interested in educational survival. He was on the right side, but he was content just to be there, and many of his associates then and thereafter believed that he felt that such mundane matters were beneath him. The president's—now the chancellor's—house on the campus was well staffed and well guarded by the campus police. The housing of the faculty was the faculty's problem. The students were old enough to look after themselves; he had long been given to pointing out that in the Middle Ages youngsters of twelve, thirteen, and fourteen traveled alone across Europe to live in the centers of learning. In the last two years of his administration, with no great encouragement (or discouragement) from him, faculty members and students banded together under the leadership of liberal residents of the area to form the organization which spearheaded its ultimate rehabilitation.

For a man who stayed put as long as he stayed put at Chicago, he was singularly interested in the mobility of educational *plants*. Twenty years earlier he had blandly suggested a merger with Northwestern University in suburban Evanston, whither Chicago's undergraduate work would be moved bodily. President Walter Dill Scott of Northwestern, aware of Hutchins' contempt for the kind of institution Northwestern was, stiffly rejected the proposal. On one ceremonial occasion Hutchins said that the University of Chicago would have been a great university the day it opened in 1892 if it had consisted of a tent, and when the university was under attack in the Illinois legislature he suggested that universities in general, in order to be truly free, be conducted in tents which could be folded and moved elsewhere whenever they failed to satisfy the community. By the time he resigned, the University of Chicago had come perilously close to folding its tents; he had been too busy calling for a world community to call very insistently (once his trustees had rebuffed him) for community in one neighborhood of one city, and that neighborhood his very own.

37 A Perennial Adolescent

I was sitting in the sitting room of my modest—but roomy—residence off the campus of the University of Chicago. It was an early June day in 1949. The phone rang. The caller was one of those great men who do not deign to identify themselves when they call. "Is it true," said the caller, "that a Jew will do anything for money?"

"I do not know the method of drawing up an indictment against a whole people," I said. "It is true, however, that this Jew will do anything for money. What is your best offer?"

"You have an unoccupied room in your house," said the caller. "I'm bringing a Nazi physicist and his wife to the university for six months. He needs a room, and his Aryan colleagues won't take him in. Will you?"

"If the price is right."

It was, and a few weeks later there arrived on the Mayer doorstep, without much luggage, the "Nazi physicist," an apple-cheeked man and his tall, handsome wife (the daughter of a Swiss general). The physicist was both renowned and notorious. He was renowned for his 1939 discovery (at twenty-seven) of the nuclear chemistry of solar energy and the publication, in 1948, of his masterful *Theory of Nature*. He was notorious (if only in America) as the wartime associate of the Nobel Prize–winning Werner Heisenberg at the University of Strasbourg. Presumably the brilliant Heisenberg group had been charged by Hitler with developing an atomic bomb. Some of their American colleagues believed they had done their Nazi best and failed for want of the crucial ingredients; some, fewer, believed they had pretended to try but had sabotaged the project.

The Nazi physicist (who wasn't a Nazi, but an anti-Nazi) was Professor Doctor—and soon to be Baron—Carl Friedrich von Weizsäcker. His notoriety did not depend on his wartime work in nuclear physics. It was assured—and, largely, generated—by his being the eldest son of the Baron Ernst von Weizsäcker.

The Baron von Weizsäcker, descendant of a distinguished line of theologians, diplomats, and naval officers, was a career ambassador who elected to remain in Nazi Germany (and accept an honorary generalship in the Hitler SS) as State Secretary in Joachim von Ribbentrop's Foreign Ministry. In spite of the testimony of leading Allied officials and churchmen, he was convicted in 1948 on circumstantial evidence by the two-to-one verdict of an all-American tribunal at Nuremberg. The Norwegian underground hero Bishop Primate Eivand Berggrav characterized him as "one of the noblest men of our generation"—but his official signature appeared on documents ordering the deportation of Jews from France. (He was sentenced to an anomalous seven years in prison, but the US High Commissioner for the Occupation of Germany soon pardoned him.) Like his father, the physicist Carl Friedrich was a diplomatic man. When the anti-Nazi Professor von Laue boldly mentioned the forbidden name of the Jew Albert Einstein in connection with relativity, his friend Weizsäcker suggested that he protect himself by saying that the "Aryans" Lorentz and Poincaré had formulated the theory before Einstein. The fearless von Laue rejected the suggestion—and survived in Germany. But the anti-Nazi Heisenberg did not hesitate to give the "Heil Hitler" greeting, and, like his associate Weizsäcker, to continue to work in Germany throughout the Nazi period in order to try to hold German science together and rebuild it after the war. Largely unsophisticated Americans—including largely unsophisticated American scientists and judges—had a hard time understanding such behavior. They were unaware, on the whole, that the Hitler regime regarded all theoretical physics—which alone could develop the bomb—as contemptibly Jewish.

The University of Chicago physics department refused to accept Weizsäcker as a visiting professor; he was appointed to the university's Committee on Social Thought (which had independent funds raised by Hutchins). At the university he delivered a distinguished series of lectures. Returning to Germany after a successful university tour of the United States—and his residence in the Mayers' back bedroom—he joined with a dozen fellow physicists in refusing to do further nuclear research, even though the German Federal Republic was committed not to develop atomic weapons. In 1957 he accepted a professorship of philosophy at the University of Hamburg, and in 1970 he was invited by the greatest research institution in Germany to establish the Max Planck Institute for the Study of the Preconditions of Human Life in the Modern World. He remained a lifelong associate of Hutchins in the latter's Center for the Study of Democratic Institutions.

Hutchins' invitation to Weizsäcker was part of his one-man mission—yet another iron in the fire—to reintegrate German culture into the life of the postwar world. Immediately after the German surrender in 1945 he had called, and would continue to call, for generous and constructive treatment of the defeated nation and the distinction between its people and its wanton leaders. But he had not waited for the end of the war to begin his missionary work. The German surrender was predictable by the end of 1944, when he wrote to the presidents of Columbia, Harvard, Cornell, and Princeton, and the universities of California and Wisconsin, asking if each of their institutions would undertake, as soon as hostilities ended, to send two faculty members to Germany and accept two German professors. Travel costs and wage supplements for the German visitors would be met by the American hosts. But the American universities declined to participate; the scheme was "premature," though refugee German scholars in America had urged that it be made ready to activate as soon as hostilities ended.

So Chicago went it alone, or rather, Hutchins did, supported by some humanists and social scientists on the faculty and by a few natural scientists. The exchange between Chicago and Frankfurt's Johann Wolfgang Goethe University was set up in 1946, the first of its postwar kind, with the involvement, at the Chicago end, of Arnold Bergstraesser, professor of German cultural history, and Professor G. A. ("Antonio") Borgese, the historian and critic. "The Frankfurt-Chicago arrangement was so successful that I went to Germany to take credit for it."

Invited to address the National Assembly of that country on the centenary of the democratic revolution of 1848, Hutchins spoke solemnly in German, focusing on the role of the universities in the achievement and preservation of self-government. It seemed to him that the political realities of occupied Germany made the outlook for democracy more forbidding now than it had been a century earlier. What was wanted was high moral purpose and hard intellectual work, "and the place for the hard intellectual work which must be done if democracy is to be instituted and to endure is the universities." The present was so grim that one might ask if there was going to be a future. Man's science, his technology, his weapons, and his machines have turned upon him. We are accustomed to thinking of history as a struggle for power: "If that conception is correct, history is about to close, for the struggle for power now leads fatally to war, which can have no end except in annihilation. Half mankind is starving; the other half, not excepting my own country, is afflicted with great fear.

"The totalitarian animal, the man with the machine gun, appeared in the world because of a profound degradation of the ideas of man and the state, of justice and liberty. . . . The questions before us are of this order:

whether there is some way in which modern man will be able to live without becoming daily less and less human; whether it is possible to organize economic life so that the needs of the community take precedence over the profit of individuals; whether it is possible to accommodate the legitimate demands of the society and the imprescriptible rights of the human person. . . . These are intellectual questions. . . . They are not German questions or American questions. They are world questions. The world is now one. . . . Whether we have one good world or one bad one will depend in large part on the leadership that the intellectuals of the world are prepared to exert."[1]

In the 1940s Walter Paepcke, a German-descended industrialist in Chicago, acquired a great deal of land around the village of Aspen, Colorado, with a vague view to establishing a ski area and a still more vague view to establishing a cultural center in the mountains. He had discussed these visions with Hutchins, on whose university board he sat, and in 1948, with the stimulus of the Frankfurt exchange and his efforts to restore Germany to the intellectual world from which it had been isolated by Nazism and the war, Hutchins picked up the possibility of celebrating the bicentennial of Goethe's birth in 1949. Again Bergstraesser and Borgese took the lead and, with another one of Hutchins' blue-ribbon committees headed by that most elder statesman, Herbert Hoover, they organized the three-week Goethe Convocation at Aspen, an event which featured Albert Schweitzer, Thornton Wilder, José Ortega y Gasset, and Hutchins as speakers, and a concert series by the Minneapolis Symphony Orchestra under Dmitri Mitropoulos.[2] The Goethe bicentennial was an international triumph, and it played a considerable role in the restoration of Germanic studies in the United States. On its foundation Paepcke established the cultural center he had had in mind—the subsequently famous and fashionable educational and artistic center known as the Aspen Institute of Humanistic Studies.

With the usual plethora of irons in the fire—too many, said those who accused him of superficiality—Hutchins was doing other things besides restoring Germany to the community of nations. And the other things he was doing had some serious effect on the pro-German entourage he had acquired before, during, and after the war. Most of these people were political and, especially, economic conservatives. He, on the other hand, was growing more radical all the time. Across the land he went, calling for rapprochement with the Soviet Union and denouncing the militarism and rearmament programs at home. But nearly all of his pro-German admirers were violently anti-Soviet and anti-Communist. They could not but see Hutchins as soft—the powerful *Chicago Tribune* was constrained to vituperate him as "a perennial adolescent"—and little by little the allegiance and financial support of his pro-German admirers withered.

Cold war sentiment was already powerful—and growing—within days after Hiroshima. No respectable individual or organ openly proposed an attack on the half-shattered Soviet Union, but the American diplomat and former governor of Pennsylvania, George H. Earle, in a debate with Hutchins in April 1946, urged that "the Congress of the United States and the President immediately appropriate two billions of dollars per year for the development of our atomic bomb. Then to have great fleets of atomic bombers scattered and hidden over a wide area of the United States and Canada, and the Bolshevists given to understand that as reprisal, following the first Russian atomic bomb dropped on us, we can and will wipe out every city, town, and village in Russia." "While we have the atomic bomb," Hutchins replied, "Russia is defenseless and this force is unnecessary. When Russia has the atomic bomb, we shall be defenseless, too, and this force will avail us little." Dragging the skeleton out of the closet, Hutchins concluded: "If we are going to war, we must go *now*. . . . If we are not willing to go to war at once, then threats, intimidations, bomb rattling, and vast displays of assorted military power can result only in feverish attempts by Russia to build up her own military strength, to form a bloc of her own as a counterweight to the Anglo-American bloc. . . . Are we willing to launch a Pearl Harbor attack on Russia now . . . ? We have done everything we could to foster the mass persecution complex with which the Russians are afflicted."[3]

The campaign for universal military training—peacetime conscription—was likewise under way immediately after Hiroshima and even before, ardently supported by President Truman and the generals. Along with other eminent educators, Hutchins attacked it as irrelevant after the atomic bomb was dropped, and went on to denounce it during the debate over the next two years: "Peacetime conscription as a substitute for an intelligent program of education, public health, and economic opportunity is . . . ridiculous . . . a military absurdity. . . . In the next war the greatest handicap a country can have will be large masses of men, half trained by obsolescent officers with obsolete equipment. Professor Einstein has estimated that in the next war two-thirds of the populations involved will be killed. This seems a conservative guess. What the combatants will principally need is not soldiers, expensively trained to fight the war before last, but plumbers, electricians, doctors and nurses. This is what Hiroshima needed."[4] The House Military Affairs Committee, which asked him to testify on the conscription bill, was divided in its enthusiasm when he went on to call the proposal "un-American" and "the most useless of all forms of preparation." He continued, as did several other notables, to speak and write on the issue in a variety of publications and on no end of platforms. A bitterly divided Congress reflected the sentiment of a bitterly divided country and adopted universal military training in 1948.

Just as he had always talked about education no matter what the topic of a lecture was, so now he always talked about world government and the development of a world community to guarantee its acceptance and its survival. Invited by Marquette University to deliver a lecture on the philosophy and theology of St. Thomas Aquinas, he chose to speak on St. Thomas and the World State. "The Catholic tradition...points clearly toward the necessity for world government," he said, working hard at his theme. "In the measure that Catholics have had better grounds than have those whose life was more completely immersed in earthly nations for denying sovereignty to nations and for asserting the existence of an international society, and in the measure that Catholics have had St. Thomas' incomparably lucid analysis of positive law for the establishment, maintenance, and progress of any society, Catholics have, then, always been virtually for world government."[5]

His maximalist position, involving the complete surrender of national sovereignty, never changed, nor did he ever give over arguing for it. Twenty-five years after he first took to the hustings in its behalf, and ten or fifteen years after the world-government movement had lost its whole audience, he said, "The nation state is rapidly becoming an anachronism. No nation can now manage its own economy or protect its own people. Hence it can no longer carry out the only purpose it has had. All problems are now world problems. The nation state is an obstacle to their solution. The industrial system, as the multinational corporation shows, is now at odds with the nation state, which now stands in the way of its expansion over the globe and its claim to roam the world at will free of geographical barriers politically imposed. The industrial system now makes the world state necessary."[6]

Necessary, perhaps; but the sovereign nations and their hostile alliances hardened their nationalist attitudes as the years and the decades passed. The hope waned and the anachronistic nation-state waxed, and Hutchins would live to be a lonely voice in the anarchical jungle alive with nuclear weapons whose possessors—all members of the impotent United Nations—would no longer discuss international control. He would ever thereafter remain the *Chicago Tribune*'s perennial adolescent.

The year 1949 may have been the busiest year of the perennial adolescent's life, fighting, as he was, on an assortment of fronts. One of those fronts was not the University of Chicago, where, returned as chancellor, he maintained a pro forma stance while he continued to be the institution's fundraiser and all-round front man. But all unexpectedly he was dutifully called on, that spring, to stave off another attack on the university by the Illinois legislature—the same sometimes less than august body that had been roundly whipped when it went after the university and Hutchins in the notorious Walgreen affair of 1935. The issue of course was the same; when one of the trustees asked the chancellor, "Are you really teaching Communism in the political science department?" the chancellor said, "We are indeed. And we are teaching cancer in the medical school."

In 1949 things were different from 1935. Roosevelt was gone, Truman's loyalty-security program was in full spate, and our Glorious Ally was the Red Beast again, this time face to face across the boundary in Berlin. Legislative hearings were on in state after state, and their prospects brightened as the climate of the country worsened. They no longer used innocent druggists who might be had on by nineteen-year-old nieces; for their road shows they now had a stable of professional ex-Communists as interrogators, headed by one J. B. Matthews.

The ex-Communists were tough, but they suffered the disadvantage of being out-of-towners. Publisher Victor Watson and the Chicago *Herald-Examiner* were both gone, and their owner, the dying Hearst, had lost a great deal of his nationwide clout. This time around, the Red hunters turned their biggest guns on the State Department and the army, though the universities were still hammered some. When the Illinois legislature, debating a congeries of loyalty-security bills, was harassed by unruly students from the University of Chicago, it voted another investigation of the institution for subversion. Hutchins informed the new committee that "rudeness and redness are not the same"—and challenged it to find an instance of subversion. He went on to advise the inquisitors that "the policy of repression of ideas cannot work and never has worked. The alternative to it is the long, difficult road of education. To this the American people have been committed. It requires patience and tolerance, even in the face of provocation. It requires faith in the principles and practices of democracy, faith that when the citizen understands all forms of government he will prefer democracy and be a better citizen if he is convinced than he would be if he were coerced."[7]

In his *Academic Freedom in Our Time*, the Columbia historian Robert MacIver wrote that Hutchins' "statement and subsequent responses to the 1949 committee constitute perhaps the most signal deliverance of the principles of academic freedom that any political investigating body has ever heard—but it obviously had no influence on the committee."[8] Obviously—yes. But Hutchins was looking beyond the obvious. Here was another occasion to midwife the Socratic learning process, the long, difficult process of education that requires patience and tolerance even in the face of provocation.

But Board Chairman Swift and Attorney Bell (soon to succeed Swift) had grown older and tireder, and Hutchins, at the advanced age of fifty, was older and tireder still. *Déjà vu, déjà dit, déjà entendu.* The 1949 investigation flopped sonorously—the committee issued no report, the legislature refused it further funds, and the Illinois loyalty-security bills did not pass. But it was another hard round, and a wearying one for the champion of academic freedom in his role as educator of legislatures. Laird Bell loved Hutchins and knew him well; he knew that the more bored the president was the likelier it was that he would turn to banter to carry him through a long day or a short evening. Back in 1934 Felix Frankfurter had written Franklin Roosevelt, "I am very glad to infer that you are annexing Bob Hutchins"—the inference was mistaken—"He has many admirable qualities, and not the least among them is that he pursues his social purposes with healthy humor." Bell was worried about the healthy humor in a situation of this kind, but, knowing Hutchins, he knew better than to talk straight to him. Instead he offered to bet him twenty-five dollars that he could not get through the hearings without making a wisecrack. Hutchins took the bet.

J. B. Matthews interrogated him on the Communist associations of the faculty.

Q (by Matthews). Is Dr. Maude Slye on your faculty?

A. She was. Dr. Slye retired many years ago after confining her attention for a considerable number of years exclusively to mice.

Q. Dr. Slye was an Associate Professor Emeritus?

A. She is an Associate Professor Emeritus. She was an Associate Professor. "Emeritus" means retired.

Q. She is retired on pension?

A. Oh, yes.

Q. And still has the prestige of the University associated with her name?

A. No way has yet been discovered of stopping being a Professor Emeritus when you are a retired professor. As a professor Dr. Slye was a distinguished specialist in cancer research.

Q. She was studying cancer when she was studying mice?

A. Correct. She was studying cancer when she was studying mice.

Q. Are you acquainted with the fact that Dr. Slye has had frequent affiliations with so-called Communist-front organizations?

A. I am acquainted with the fact that she has had so-called frequent associations with so-called Communist-front organizations.

Q. Is there not such a thing as indoctrination by example?

A. Of mice?[9]

When the 1949 hearing ended, and the universities of America still stood, Bell demurred at paying off the twenty-five-dollar bet. Hutchins wanted to know why—he thought, he said, that his restraint was a real triumph of avarice over art. Bell said that his reply to Matthews' last question had been a wisecrack. Hutchins proposed that they lay the matter before Political Science Chairman Charley Merriam for arbitration. The two parties to the suit, both being lawyers, elected to represent themselves at bar. The case was heard at the bar of the Shoreland Hotel on the Lake front. Merriam took the matter under advisement then and there, and, as the waiter approached with the check, he handed down his judgment in favor of Hutchins. "What about the last answer to Matthews?" said Bell indignantly.

"What other answer could he have given?" asked Merriam.

Part Eight

THE TEMPER OF THE COUNTRY

38 A Cool Half-Billion

One dark December day in 1950 he asked me to have lunch with him at the Shoreland Hotel near the campus. His invitations always came at the last moment, when he found himself unexpectedly able to get away from it (or them) all. I was one of a half-dozen people in town who were not trying to get something from him or get him to do or stop doing something. He rarely burdened me with administrative matters of a purely academic character, because I neither knew nor cared much about them. We discussed the university's public relations. We discussed the world. And we made an occasional stab at life.

So that December day we discussed the university's public relations, and the world, and life a little. But the discussion took a strange turn. He wanted to know, just, apparently, by the bye, what causes I thought money ought to be spent on and in what priority. On such matters I was as eloquent, and probably as sound (since nobody was sound) as anybody else. But why did a man who needed large amounts of money, and knew what he needed it for, want to know about how to spend money and want to know it from a man who knew how to spend, but not get, small amounts of money?

I didn't find out until we had finished lunch and I made a feint for the check (as I always did, and always lost). Hutchins usually said, "Don't be silly," when I made the feint. This time he said, "Don't be silly. I have four or five hundred million dollars in my jeans—the capital of the Ford Foundation."

"I've never heard of it," said I.

"Nobody has," said he, "but everybody is going to. Paul Hoffman is going to be its director and the Fords have agreed—they wanted Mr. Hoffman that badly—to accept me as associate director."

"And the university?"

"The university will be rid of me and will flourish accordingly."

It seemed that the government was making restive noises about the inactivity of the Fords' family foundation quietly established in 1936 with twenty-five thousand dollars. The restive noises were related to a potential tax of some $321 million on the estate of Henry Ford, who had died in 1947 as principal owner of the privately held Ford Motor Company, the nonvoting 90 percent of whose stock had been transferred to the twenty-five-thousand-dollar foundation. (The estate tax never was collected; the lawyers had done their work well.) The twenty-five thousand had grown, still quietly, to five hundred million, give or take a hundred million; and an immediate outburst of activity was recommended by the Fords' tax lawyers. With its cool half-billion for starters, the foundation was even then the biggest philanthropic institution in the world, "a large body of money," as Dwight Macdonald later described it, "entirely surrounded by people who want some."[1] (The prefigured accumulation of nonvoting stock in the Ford Motor Company would raise the half-billion in time to more than three billion.) Liberal Republican Paul Hoffman had been president of the Studebaker Corporation and administrator of the Marshall Plan. It was widely surmised that he would become secretary of state if Dean Acheson resigned; Hutchins, who had never before been a number-two man, might then become the foundation's director.

The multimillionaire paid the lunch check and I asked him what he and Mr. Hoffman were going to do with their half-billion dollars. "In two years," he said, "we will change the temper of the country." (The temper of the country changed in two years, all right, but it changed for the worse; five hundred million dollars could not do what a howling horde of witch-hunters could do, not even what one ravening senator, Joe McCarthy, could do about the temper of the country. The Ford Foundation was another straw to be grasped; a diamond-studded straw, but a straw.)

Why did he leave the university? Among his gracious public statements: "I suppose that the principal reason I left the University was that I felt it ought to have another chance. I didn't see why, because they made the mistake of selecting a man of 30 to be president of the institution, they should be condemned to go on with him until he reached retiring age. If, having seen what the University would be if it were operated as I thought it should be operated, they preferred to have it some other way, this was certainly a right and even a duty that they had."[2] Among his less gracious public statements, fourteen years later, in his weekly *Los Angeles Times* column: "My observation is that good men become college and university presidents only because they do not know any better. . . . If a man knows what it is like to be a university president and still wants to be one, he is not qualified for the job. He is interested in salary and perquisites, publicity and prestige, and not in education and scholarship. . . . The president of an American college or university . . . must become just another Big Executive. He will be judged, like every other Big Executive, by the state of his balance sheet and public relations. . . . All this was bad enough thirty-five years ago, when I became a university president. It was worse thirteen years ago, when I folded up what was left of my balance sheet and public relations, realizing at last that a university presidency was no place for a man interested in education and scholarship."[3]

He had realized it long before "at last"; he had lamented the barren lot of the administrator, in season and out, during the whole of the twenty-two years he had been one at Chicago. He had compensated himself—until the war left him no time—by teaching the freshman great books honors course with Adler. In twenty-two years he had made hundreds of speeches—and written one scholarly paper, on Edmund Burke. For at least a year before his resignation he had told a few friends that he was determined to get out. And go where, and do what? Where does a fellow go from the top, when he is only fifty years old? Business and industry were out, obviously, and just as obviously was government; he was opposed to Truman's cold (and hot) war policies at home and abroad. (And Truman had no interest in him.) The only possibility that had attracted him, prior to the Ford offer, was a professorship in the university's law school, which he had long since reconstructed in his own image; but he dismissed it, though the law was his scholarly love, on the sound ground that he could not remain as a faculty member without embarrassing his successor. A professorship anywhere else did not attract him at all (nor would the salary have).

Besides the barren grind, there were other reasons advanced for his leaving, some by him, some by others. He went to his father—as he always did—beforehand and William James Hutchins asked him what his principal reason was for getting out. "The trustees, I suppose," said Hutchins, "just having to have lunch with two or three of them two or three times a week. They bore me." "What makes you think," said his father, "that the Ford Foundation trustees will be any different?" To another friend he said, "You'd have to have gone to a thousand faculty meetings to understand. They're like a convention of Nebraska Elks, and I have to face the fact that I appointed most of them." "Twenty-two years is a long time," he said on another occasion. "With the end of the war there seemed to be nothing ahead but real estate problems, labor problems, and government contracts, things that didn't interest me. All that damned"—strong language for him—"Gothic around my neck. I wasn't a great educator, but I was interested in education." In his innocence—a man of fifty-one, twenty-two years a university president—he thought that the Ford Foundation could and would do something about education. The diamond-studded straw.

Among the others who advanced other, less flattering, reasons for his leaving were several trustees, who advanced their reasons privately. One, who would come on the board a year later, and ultimately serve as its chairman, was the advertising magnate Fairfax Cone, whose unenthusiasm about Hutchins matched his unbounded enthusiasm for Hutchins' old enemy (once his old friend), ex-trustee and advertising magnate Albert D. Lasker. "The University was going down hill financially," said Cone afterward. "It couldn't get money; the community wouldn't support it. It had a bad reputation for radicalism, even though the faculty was fundamentally conservative. And Bob had come to the end of his fireworks. He was smart to get out."

There were faculty members, too, who didn't feel much differently, and certainly some few who were glad to see the last of him. One who would never be glad to see the last of him, and who would finally follow him out to the Santa Barbara Center, was Joe Schwab, the William Rainey Harper Distinguished Service Professor of Biology and Education. Schwab was one of the architects of the Hutchins college and a devoted supporter of the Hutchins philosophy of education. Asked, many years later, about his friend's departure from Chicago, Schwab said, "The university had gone into reserves for the fourth successive year when Bob left. It consistently ran a deficit of a million dollars in a fifteen-million-dollar budget, with the comptroller saying that there shouldn't be a deficit greater than half a million. By some sort of alchemy, in which government contracts played an ever greater role, the deficit was made to appear to have disappeared. The school was losing students because of the neighborhood race crisis, which Bob refused to face after the trustees turned down his 'socialist' scheme for buying up the area and desegregating it. It couldn't place its law school graduates in the Chicago firms, which weren't interested in the Hutchins curriculum based on jurisprudence instead of case law. He had long since lost the support of the industrial, business, political, and journalistic communities of the city."[4]

Hutchins himself said nothing to these considerations which were, after all, unvoiced at the time. But he referred to them angrily in later years: "There were two common misstatements at the time I left the University of Chicago. One was that we were running out of money. Absolutely false. We raised more money between 1930 and 1950 than any university except Harvard and Yale—and they had a three-hundred-year head start." A transparent dodge budgetarily, but a genuine testimony to his fund-raising. "The other was that we were running out of students. We weren't trying to enlarge the student body, and our losses were no greater than those of other schools. These charges weren't made openly, so I couldn't answer them. But the trustees knew they were false, and so did the trustees' friends in the faculty."

Entirely apart from the changes he wrought—and tried to wreak—he would be leaving Chicago a much greater institution than he found it, in orthodox terms one of the top three or four universities in the country. And the most fervent of his detractors knew it. So a pervasive mournful-ness overspread the campus the day after he announced his resignation on December 19, 1950. It was all organ tones and lugubrious shades. His own statement, made to a meeting of the council of the faculty senate, assured his colleagues that he had no doubt that the university would continue "on the same level of excellence as had characterized it for the past sixty years," and the council, which contained many of his longest-term oppo-nents, immediately and unanimously adopted the following resolution: "The Council believes it is speaking for the entire academic body of the University of Chicago when it says no greater tragedy could happen to the University than for Mr. Hutchins to persist in his decision to resign as Chancellor." The trustees (whose number also included many of his longest-term opponents) said that "the dynamic and imaginative lead-ership which Mr. Hutchins has given the University of Chicago for the past twenty-one years has kept it clearly in the forefront of the educational world. . . . The trustees of the University accept his resignation with reluc-tance and regret." Never was heard a discouraging word from the camp—the camps—of the enemy among the faculty and the trustees, where the departing hero had been frustrated more often than not.

Nothing but good should be spoken of the resigned.

He would take a leave of absence immediately, remaining on the cam-pus without formal duties. His resignation would take place on June 30, when he would move to Pasadena, California, to the new headquarters of the Ford Foundation in a palatial "cottage" on the grounds of the storied Huntington Hotel. Mrs. Paul Hoffman, who had had enough of Detroit and Washington, wanted to live in California, and thither went the foun-dation's directorate.

For Hutchins it was the abdication of a pulpit, a platform, a podium the likes of which he would never again occupy—the presidency of a great university. He had not (as he told President Roosevelt) been interested in "public life." Or in private, as Maude Hutchins well knew. He had been interested in education, and in changing its character, and in getting support for it. Now, instead of having his hand out for the big money, he would be handing it out in immense wads from the Ford Foundation head-quarters, which he at once denominated Itching Palms. (He said that the nicest thing about philanthropic work was that "you meet so many in-terested people.") He would be leaving behind him dauntless friends and undaunted enemies; he would be leaving behind him a body, too, with whom, remote as he was from them, he felt the closest of all possible affinities: the students who had come to the University of Chicago, so many of them because it was where Hutchins was. A month after the announcement of his resignation he hoisted himself up to the pulpit of the university chapel to deliver his farewell address to the students. The stu-dents were all there; so were a large proportion of the faculty, and many of the trustees and townspeople; the sanctuary was mobbed.

His speech was a patchwork, many sections of it lifted from other speeches and papers. It was as if the occasion was—for the first time—too much for him. He did not know quite what he wanted to talk about, so he talked about a little of everything, beginning with the note he had struck when he first spoke there twenty-two years earlier, and had gone on strik-ing for twenty-two years: "Our mission here on earth is to change our environment, not to adjust ourselves to it. If we became maladjusted in the process, so much the worse for the environment." And for Freud. "If we have to choose between Don Quixote and Sancho Panza, let us by all means choose Don Quixote. The flat conformity of American life and thought, toward which all pressures in this country converge, raises the only doubt one may have about democracy, which is whether it is possible to combine the rule of the majority with that independence of character, conduct, and thought which the progress of any society requires."

Then—this was 1950, mind you—he moved on to a phenomenon that was just then showing the first faint signs of emerging: "The horrid pros-pect that television opens before us, with nobody speaking and nobody reading, suggests that a bleak and torpid epoch may lie ahead, which, if it lasts long enough, will gradually, according to the principles of evolution, produce a population indistinguishable from the lower forms of plant life. Astronomers of the University of Chicago have detected something that looks like moss growing on Mars. I am convinced that Mars was once inhabited by rational beings like ourselves, who had the misfortune, some thousands of years ago, to invent television."

Then—this was 1950, mind you again—he moved on to a situation which the denizens of the world thirty years thereafter might suppose was something new to their own generation: "Our lives are overshadowed by the threat of impending doom. If you were neurotic, I could not blame you. To what extent the threat of impending doom grows out of our ignorance and immorality, and to what extent it grows out of the ignorance and immorality of the Russians, I do not pretend to know. I confess, too, that I have a lifelong hatred of war that perhaps makes it impossible for me to have a rational view of the situation. War has always seemed to me the ultimate wickedness, the ultimate stupidity."

And yet...and yet.... "I am not a pacifist. I would echo the sentiments of Patrick Henry"—perhaps the closest Robert Maynard Hutchins ever came to mouthing a banality—"I grant that when a great power is loose in the world seeking whom it may destroy, it is necessary to prepare to defend our country against it." And yet...and yet. "Yet the goal toward which all history tends is peace." And with the Cold War at its height, and the Korean War even then involving the United States in self-professed representation of the helpless United Nations: "Since it is obvious to the merest simpleton that war must come sooner or later to a world of anarchy, men of good will would hope that their own government would proclaim its desire to transform the United Nations from a loose association of independent states into an organization that could adopt and enforce world law."

There was, he said, "a certain terrifying lightheartedness underlying the talk about war today.... Men in public life are being crucified because they are suspected of trying to keep the peace.... By endless reiteration of the slogan, 'America must be strong' we have been able to put a stop to our mental processes altogether and to forget what strength is. We appear to believe that strength consists of masses of men and machines. I do not deny that they have their role. But surely the essential ingredients of strength are trained intelligence, love of country, the understanding of its ideals, and, above all, a conviction of the justice of our cause. Since men of good will can regard war as conceivable only as a last resort, they must be convinced that all channels of negotiation have been kept open till the last moment."[5] He had (he once said) joined the Oberlin ambulance unit in 1917 because he was a pacifist; since then he had become a patron of peace, and an unhappy practitioner of war.

Just before the close of the address the unhappy practitioner of war interpolated a statement so passing strange as to suggest a positively schizoid attitude in which he condemned himself in terms of his wartime university presidency. The interpolation, in full: "There seems to be something about contemporary civilization that produces a sense of aimlessness. Why do university presidents cheerfully welcome the chance to devote their institutions to military preparations? They are of course patriotic; but in addition I think they feel that education is a boring, confusing, difficult matter that nobody cares very much about anyway, whereas getting ready for war is simple, clear, definite, and respectable. Can it be that modern men have a sense of purpose only if they believe that other men are getting ready to kill them? If this is true, western civilization is surely neurotic, and fatally so."[6]

He had been proud of being an antisentimentalist and an enemy of sentimentalism. But now he was putting an end to his life as an educator, and the educatees were massed before him. He was not a man whose eyes had ever been seen filling with tears. Dry-eyed now, the university president who taught college freshmen said to his collegiate audience: "One of the saddest aspects of my life is that I have not organized it so that I could know the students better. It would be an outrageous presumption on my part to suppose that my presence here has anything to do with yours or that my departure can make the slightest difference to you. . . . Yet, though seldom nourished by the sight of you, and sometimes not even by the thought of you, I have perhaps some right to say farewell to you because you have been the inspiration of my life and have given it such meaning as it has had."[7]

His years there, he said, had witnessed the struggle to create a model university. The struggle had succeeded in part in changing one high school, one college, one graduate school, and one aggregation of professional schools—the University of Chicago's. But a model university in America was necessarily at war with the public. "The fact that popular misconceptions of the nature and purpose of universities originate in the fantastic misconduct of the universities themselves is not consoling. It shows that a model university is needed, but it also suggests the tremendous difficulty of the enterprise upon which a model university embarks and the strength of the tide against which its students have to contend. . . .

"You are getting an education infinitely better than that which my generation, the generation that now rules the world, had open to it. You have had the chance to discern the purposes of human life and human society. Your predecessors in this place, now scattered all over the world, give us some warrant for hoping that as you go out to join them you will bear with you the same spark that they have carried, which, if carefully tended, may yet become the light that shall illumine the world."[8]

So he stepped down, down from the scene of his many successes and his at least equally many failures. Perhaps he should have left five or ten years earlier, reading a lesson from his own wisecrack that a graduate student doesn't know when the party is over. The fireworks had indeed come to an end. His reforms at Chicago would not outlive him, and it would be a few years only when it could no longer be asserted that 75 percent of the texts read in the "Hutchins" college were masterpieces of the intellect and imagination of man. Here, at Chicago, the Boy President had made as much of a mark as it is given an educator to make. The humanistic studies had been given a new, if shortlived, lease on life, even while here, at Chicago, the natural sciences had achieved their terrible apogee in the bomb. Here, too, at Chicago, he and his impossible wife—impossible he and his impossible wife—had gone their impossible way together and, at last, separately; and his children had grown and gone. Now the educator would do his educating by remote control, one might say insidiously. The educator had failed to change the temper of the country in twenty-two years; the straw-grasping philanthropist was going to do it in two.

He was exchanging one kind of exalted privilege for another—the privilege of high-minded mendicancy for the privilege of being bountiful. One of his more acerbic (but not unfriendly) critics said that he was going to try to buy what he hadn't been able to sell.

39 "You and Your Great Big Geraniums"

Paul Hoffman had twenty-seven honorary degrees to Hutchins' twelve. Where Hutchins had spent a mere fifteen million dollars a year as president of the University of Chicago, Hoffman paid out ten billion dollars in his two-and-a-half years as administrator of the Marshall Plan for the relief and reconstruction of postwar Europe. And now he was undertaking to be a kingmaker; in the course of his two-year presidency of the Ford Foundation he spent months at a time on the road in a most unlikely campaign to get the 1952 Republican presidential nomination for a general named Ike Eisenhower.

A moderate—or liberal Republican—he was visibly one of the weightiest men in American public life when he assumed the directorship of the Ford Foundation on January 1, 1951. He was the man the Ford family advisors most wanted for the job and the first and last choice of "Young Henry," the grandson of the founder and head of the company. There was no demurral at his hundred-thousand-dollar salary, a monumental figure in those days. He was a self-made industrial baron. His anti-Communist credentials were more than satisfactory; with Russia's refusal to accept the conditions set by the United States for participation, the Marshall Plan had become, inter alia, America's primary weapon for fighting the burgeoning Communist movements in the ruins of western Europe.

To get the man they were determined to have, Young Henry and his advisors had to accept three conditions. The man they wanted wanted to live in Pasadena, so the foundation had to be moved from Dearborn, Michigan. He was an ardent supporter of the United Nations and UNESCO, a peacemonger in spite of his anticommunism, in a word a bleeding-heart internationalist, while the Fords were just the opposite (except as regards selling cars abroad). And his admiration of Robert

Maynard Hutchins, on whose board he had long sat in Chicago, was and would remain nothing short of fervent. Young Henry knew all he wanted to know about Hutchins, and he accepted this third condition with especially bad and ominous grace.

The three other associate directors—two-and-a-half, actually, since H. Rowan Gaither remained chairman of the air-force-affiliated Rand Corporation and spent only half time at the foundation—were each assigned more or less specific areas of activity. But Hutchins, although he was given control of educational programs, was thought of from the start (certainly by Hoffman) as the first among equals. There was never any question during the two years they were there that the Ford Foundation was Hoffman and Hutchins. In those two years, sixty million dollars were spent, of which more than half, thirty-three million, went into the two great funds that Hutchins got the trustees to approve—the Fund for the Advancement of Education and the Fund for Adult Education. (Hoffman's own international programs got twenty-one million dollars.)

But where Hutchins was luxuriating in staying in the same place for a change, Hoffman was the travelingest of men, spending much of his time in Europe, in Asia, in New York, and in Washington—with way-stops in between to plug Eisenhower as the next president—and was away from Pasadena a great deal more than he was there. The consequence was that nobody was minding the store, and the associate directors each went his own way. It was a circus with three uncoordinated rings and a number of specialty acts in the tanbark. Hoffman was on the road; the trustees were in the east; and the associate directors in Pasadena saw little of each other, each of them on his own reporting to Hoffman when they could catch him. But Hutchins could always catch him, and Hoffman could always catch Hutchins.

The foundation arrangement was unworkable, for reasons both obvious and subtle. Hutchins had never had to work in harness, and the men with whom he was supposed to work in harness now were not at all his cup of tea (nor he theirs). He and Associate Director Chester C. Davis, president of the Federal Reserve Bank of St. Louis, could not possibly have got along; Davis was in charge of budget and administration—Hutchins' own operation at Chicago. Associate Director Milton Katz, who had been deputy director of the Marshall Plan, was in charge of European activities; a Harvard law professor, he and Hutchins disagreed about the nature of law and the nature of everything else intellectual. And the part-time associate director, Gaither, was assigned to supervise activities in the behavioral sciences in which he was inexperienced (and in which Hutchins' experience extended over the best part of a lifetime). In the absence of central control and Hoffman's implicit confidence in Hutchins, dissolution of the directorate was a predictable certainty.

The more subtle reason for predictable dissolution was the Dionysian character of the whole shebang. The directorate knew it was expected to ladle out the money with both hands; the Internal Revenue Act of 1950 raised rough questions about the accumulation of foundation capital, and questions about the Ford Foundation as a tax dodge were being raised in both houses of Congress. What the directorate hadn't known, when it took office, was that both hands were not enough. Nor was a ladle. A battery of steam shovels was wanted. The Ford Motor Company dividends were accruing faster than anyone had imagined they would. While Hoffman was saying, midway through 1951, that the foundation would be appropriating twenty-five million dollars a year, a careful analysis by the *New York Times* put the figure at twice that. And the board of the foundation—with Congress breathing down its neck—called for an expenditure of forty-five million in 1952 "consistent with the principle of due investigation and care to avoid waste." (The directors outdid themselves in 1952, spending fifty-two million.)[1]

Due investigation and avoidance of waste were both impossible; and the amounts disbursed, with the trustees crying "More, more," were exorbitant. If the last remaining American megafortune was being squandered—which is not to say that it was—it was being squandered on the greatest scale in history. Hutchins had always been generous and casual, even (in the view of men like his father) profligate. And he had been investigating education and what he took to be its needs for a quarter-century. After having limped along on a few dollars a year in its first years, the Great Books Foundation got a grant of $826,000 from the Fund for Adult Education and blossomed like the rose, setting up branches across the country. Mortimer Adler's one-man Institute for Philosophical Research—he had left Chicago when Hutchins did—was given $640,000 by the Fund for Advancement of Education to make "a dialectical examination of Western humanistic thought" (which it was still doing thirty years later, without much to show for the investment). Similarly handsome sums were pressed upon other undertakings that were close to Hutchins' heart, including the so-called Fifth Year Program to encourage liberal arts training for teachers and shorten professional training to one year.

The perspicacious Dwight Macdonald, reviewing the early history of the Ford Foundation in the *New Yorker* magazine in 1955, drew a portrait of the big spender from Chicago (and from Oberlin and the Brooklyn parish house): "The modern foundation official should be prudent, judicious, diplomatic, and self-effacing, in all of which qualities Hutchins is singularly lacking. . . . Not only is he a 'controversial' figure of maximum visibility but he also rather obviously enjoys being one. He likes to tread on dignified toes, he rarely produces the soft answer that turneth away wrath, and his formula for troubled waters does not include oil. . . . Clearly [he] was not the foundation type at all, and it is a tribute to Hoffman's salesmanship and to the broadmindedness—and perhaps also to the innocence—of Henry II and his trustees that such a maverick got into the fold even for a while. . . . The trustees were awed by this big-time spender with a big-time vocabulary. But awe is not affection, and as time went on the trustees felt increasingly resentful at having an arrogant highbrow, who made it plain that he found their logic defective by Aristotelian standards, extract from them each year for his educational Funds over half the money at their disposal. 'We felt that that was too big a proportion to be spent on a very special kind of education and that we were in danger of having the bulk of our income committed in advance,' Henry II recalls. 'I guess we gave it to him because he was the fastest talker. But I didn't like the idea of being a rubber stamp for his ideas.'"[2]

Nor did Hutchins' associates in the directorate, with the exception of the deferential Hoffman. And the only good thing the Ford Foundation board could say about Hutchins was that he was willing to spend the money as fast as the tax lawyers wanted it spent. But they were irritated by his high-handed behavior, and their irritation turned against his mentor, Hoffman. The insouciant, the unabashed Hutchins waved their irritation aside. It was increasingly clear to his friends that he realized that he was not going to spend the rest of his life at the Ford Foundation.

But while it lasted. . . . The quintessential Okies, when they gave up on lotus land and headed back to the dustbowl, hung a sign on the back of their jalopy: GOOD BY CALIFORNIA AND YOUR GREAT BIG GERANIUMS. And Samuel Goldwyn, when he visited Paul Hoffman at the Pasadena mansion occupied by the directors—the lower orders were housed in an office building downtown—said, "If you have to give away money, this is a wonderful place to do it." Associate Director Hutchins found time and ironic temper to compose a bit of doggerel to the tune of *Adeste, fidelis*, one stanza of which read:

> How fine a Foundation; we are for peace,
> We live peaceful lives, and we hope wars will cease.
> We've heard mankind's cry, and we've answered the call:
> We're out in Pasadena,
> We're out in Pasadena,
> We're out in Pasadena,
> Away from it all.

There was something supremely Californian about the Ford Foundation and its great big geraniums, and the Rational Animal appeared to be susceptible to its wiles. He and his wife got themselves a richly furnished house in the suburb of San Marino, where the really rich got away from the merely rich in Pasadena, and on his day off the associate director could be seen wearing a Hawaiian sports shirt—he who had never been seen without a sedate bow tie. Over an extended period he flunked the California driver's test two or three times—he had always ridden in taxicabs or livery limousines—and when he passed it he drove around in his Hawaiian sports shirt and a Thunderbird sports car. In a light-hearted exchange with Colonel Lindbergh, he said: "This engagement [for dinner in New York] . . . does not exonerate you and Anne from the responsibility of coming to see us in the Golden West. Since the Ford Foundation moved out here it really is golden. That is why I insist on paying for dinner. I am very rich now."

If the temper of the country was going to be changed in two years, there was no time to be spared getting at it. Or money. Surely there wasn't anything that *that* much money couldn't buy. His freshman students at Chicago would go around the campus chanting the Platonic dictum, "Tyrants have no power." But the Greek rationale did not extend to the powerlessness of money, especially in a nontyrannical democracy dedicated to the proposition that all men are created equally determined to get ahead. Associate Director Hutchins had not forgotten—he never forgot anything—another Platonic dictum to the effect that a man should have only so much gold and silver "as a good man, and only he, can bear and carry." Here was a good man heavily laden. Five hundred million dollars may not have power—but it can try. And it can try the man who has it as assiduously as it tries the man who wants it. For twenty-two years President Hutchins wanted great quantities of money, and now, for two years, Associate Director Hutchins would have it; in this respect his career (except for Cinderella's) was close to unique.

A little money, now, might have a little power, but a little money is sometimes hard to come by. A year after the memorable luncheon at which he picked up the check and informed me that he had a half-million dollars in his jeans, I was in cold and hungry postwar Germany, and I wrote to the associate director of the Ford Foundation to ask him if the foundation could put up $250 for a winter's supply of coal for a group of especially promising students at Göttingen University who, without the coal, could not remain in school. I was writing on behalf of Hutchins' friend, Professor Carl Friedrich von Weizsäcker. "Tell Carl Friedrich," he replied, "that if he would ask for $250,000 we might be able to do something for him."

But I do not know what the Ford Foundation can do about a grant application for $250." (He did raise the $250—but not from the Ford Foundation.)

He had long believed that the American Friends Service Committee— the social welfare arm of the Meeting-House Quakers—might be able to turn a little money into a little power; and in any case it would never know until it had a little money to try. Now, in his new role, he wanted to know if the American Friends Service Committee could do a little something powerful with, say, a million dollars. His inquiry, directed to Mecca (that is, to Philadelphia), went out from there to the Service Committee's regional offices around the country. How much did each of them need and how could they use it? Each of the regional offices asked its regional hirelings how much they needed and how they could use it. Corruptible all, and corrupted (Latter-Day Sinners that they were) by the mere smell of more than a little money, they all submitted their needs to Mecca and Mecca submitted them to the Ford Foundation; all of them but one.

The hireling who did not submit his needs was E. A. ("Red") Schaal, peace secretary of the Service Committee's Middle Atlantic Region. With Red Schaal I had combed and brushed the Middle Atlantic countryside for years, raising money for the AFSC. Red carried the "literature" on and off the day coaches; and though he was old and ill, he would not let a redcap get his hands on one of those ponderous suitcases; hiring people to carry those suitcases (at a dime a suitcase) was not Red's idea of the way to exercise the power of money. When he was asked what part of a million dollars he needed he said he needed none. "I can't," he submitted, "find the people now who want to do the work we're trying to do, and money won't turn them up." "Tell me about Mr. Schaal," said the associate director of the Ford Foundation into whose hands a copy of Red's submission had fallen. So I told him about the time Red and I were coming into a town in West Virginia to do our fan dance and I asked Red how big our constituency was there. "Well," said Red, "when I first came here, twenty years ago, we had three, maybe four supporters, and I reckon we have three, maybe four supporters now. We're holding our own." "He wouldn't," said the associate director, "want to work for the Ford Foundation, would he?" I said I thought he wouldn't; he'd often told me how happy he was where he was and how odd it was to be paid anything at all for being allowed to do the kind of work he was doing. "He is a great man," said the associate director. "An Oberlin boy, you might say," said I. "An *old* Oberlin Boy," said the associate director, jingling his million dollars. (Or being jingled by them.)

He wasn't really being jingled by them, or seduced by California—

except superficially. On the contrary, the lifelong liberal-to-radical in the very first days of his service to the Ford Foundation, once he had his two fat funds established in the field of education, began tooling up for an all-out assault on the country's mounting anti-Communist hysteria. The Truman loyalty-security program of 1947—instituted as a lever to justify rearmament, to "scare the hell out of the American people," as Senator Vandenberg put it to the president—had sown the whirlwind that came to be known later as McCarthyism. (Six years later the ex-president would be subpoenaed to defend himself against the charge that he had appointed a Russian spy to the International Monetary Fund.) The loyalty-security program was followed by an immense rash of legislative and executive moves, beginning with the McCarran Internal Security Act and the resurgence of the House Committee on Un-American Activities, undertaking, at the national, state, and even local levels to unmask the Reds and drive them from both public and private life. This was old stuff to Hutchins; at Chicago he had been able to turn back the witch-hunters in the "Walgreen affair" of 1935 and the Broyles committee hearings of 1949.

And oddly enough the Ford Foundation licensed him—or someone, and no one else was likely to do it—to fight the rising tide of "Americanism." A year-long study by a blue-ribbon committee appointed by the Ford Foundation board in 1948 had produced a very thick Study Report, which the board had adopted and which Young Henry himself had called "one of the most thorough, painstaking, and significant inquiries ever made into the whole broad question of public welfare and human needs."[3] It may have been that Young Henry and his conservative trustees had failed to study the report in critical detail. Of the five program areas outlined, the second ("The Strengthening of Democracy") included under section A a directive to support "the elimination of restrictions on freedom of thought, inquiry, and expression in the United States, and the development of policies and procedures best adapted to protect these rights in the face of persistent international tension."[4]

Section A was Hutchins' meat—and his and Hoffman's eventual undoing at the Ford Foundation and the basis for their subsequent tormented activities as president and chairman of the Ford-financed Fund for the Republic. The colleges and the universities—and the schools—were the prime target of the McCarthyists, as they had always been in periods of domestic stress. "I recognize," said Hutchins in a public speech, "that these are dangerous times and that the state must take precautions against those who would subvert it. I do not suggest that those who want to force conformity upon academic bodies do so from any but the most patriotic motives. I do say that they are misguided. The methods they have chosen can not achieve the results they seek. They will, on the contrary, imperil the liberties we are fighting for, the most important of which are freedom of thought, speech, and association."[5] This was relatively sedate in tone, as befitted a man charged with spending a billionaire's money. Much stronger talk was soon to follow. He attacked loyalty oaths in general as futile and mischievous, and he attacked in particular, as a one-time educator, the notorious oath imposed on the faculty of the University of California. The oath, he said, "originated in the desire of the [state] administration to get money from the legislature. As this genesis suggests, the chief danger to American education is that it will sell its birthright for a mess of pottage. . . . Every time a university . . . makes a concession to public pressure in order to get money, every time it departs from the idea of a university as a center of independent thought, it increases the confusion in the public mind about what a university is. . . . The university should be the symbol of the highest powers and aspirations of mankind. . . . Abandoning vanity and sham, the universities should dedicate themselves to their great symbolic task."[6]

Then he moved in—and moved in frontally—on the hottest and meanest question of the McCarthy era and of many an era before and after: Should a Communist be hired or retained, above all as a teacher? This question outlived Senator Joseph McCarthy and McCarthyism. It was never answered affirmatively by more than a very few persons eminent or obscure. One of those few was, marvelously enough, Senator Robert A. Taft of Ohio, the arch-conservative "Mr. Republican," whose answer was generally forgiven as an aberration of an otherwise sound man. Another was the associate director of the Ford Foundation, whose answer was not so readily forgiven as an aberration but was widely taken (by the trustees of that same foundation, among others) as the predictable position of an aberrative man. His position was clear—clear and costly, in the next few years. But he would never retreat from his first formulation of it:

"Everywhere in the United States, university professors, whether or not they have tenure, are silenced by the general atmosphere of repression that now prevails. . . . When a man becomes a professor, he does not become a second-class citizen, disabled from saying, doing, or joining anything that other citizens may legally say, do, or join. . . . What then are the limitations on the freedom of the faculty? They are the limitations on independent thought. These should be nothing more than the laws of logic and the laws of the country. I would hope that the laws of the country would not seek to control thought. . . . If a professor can think and make his contribution to a center of independent thought, that is all that is required of him. One might wish that he were more agreeable or more conventional;

but he can not be discharged because he fails to measure up to desirable standards in these respects. As long as his political activities are legal, he may engage in them."[7]

He did not then, or thereafter, ask himself what course a university should pursue should the time ever come when the laws of the country themselves would seek to control thought. Communism was—and remained—legal in the United States. "We see that Communism is a subject that is worth thinking about and should be studied in universities. . . . Must we say that Communism can be taught only by those who are opposed to it? Can we permit the appointment of a man who is trying to make us all Communists? If he is a spy or advocating the overthrow of the government by violence, we can not. But convinced and able Marxists on the faculty may be necessary if the conversation about Marxism is to be anything but hysterical and superficial. It may be said that a Marxist can not think and that therefore he is not eligible for membership in a university community according to my definition of it."

Say that the Marxist is a member of the Communist Party, which "is represented as a conspiracy, with everybody in it under iron discipline, which I take to mean that its members and supporters have given up the privilege of independent thought and have surrendered themselves entirely to the Party. If this is so, a member of the Communist Party can not qualify as a member of the university community in any field that is touched by Party policy, tradition, or discipline. . . . The presumption is strong that there are few fields in which a member of the Communist Party can think independently.

"But what if we should find a member of the Communist Party who, in spite of this presumption, did think independently? The fact of membership can not and should not disqualify him from membership in the faculty of a university in view of the additional fact that he does not act as members of the Party are supposed to act. I can not insist too strongly that the primary question in every case is what is this individual man himself, not what are the beliefs and activities of his relatives, associates, and acquaintances. When the life of an individual has been exposed before us for many years, and when he has neither acted nor taught subversively, the doctrine of guilt by association can have slight value. A man who is a bad member of the Communist Party may conceivably be qualified to be a professor, because he has retained his independence; and a good member of the Party may be qualified to be a professor if he retains his independence in the field in which he teaches and conducts his research."

Whether as a university president he "would have had the courage to recommend to our Board the appointment of a Marxist, or a bad member of the Communist Party, or a good member whose field was not affected by the Party line is very dubious indeed. But in the most unlikely event that such persons ever came over my academic horizon, uniquely qualified to conduct teaching and research in their chosen fields, I ought to have had the courage to say that they should be appointed without regard to their political views or associations. The reason why I ought to is that it is of the first importance to insist that the popularity or unpopularity of a man's political views and associations shall not determine whether or not he may be a professor. If we once let go of the Constitution and the laws as marking out the area in which a professor is free to operate as a citizen and of the ability to think independently as establishing the standard he must meet as a scholar, we are lost."[8]

But the much more insidious issue throughout the McCarthy period was fellow-traveling, that is, Communist activity by nonmembers of the Party who joined so-called "front" organizations that in toto or in respect of one matter or another took the Communist position—or more precisely, took a position that the Communists also took. Here the horrifier of his Ford Foundation associates and superiors (always excepting Paul Hoffman) spoke without any trace of the reservations with which he surrounded his analysis of Communist Party membership as a disqualification from teaching: "What I have said of course applies with greater force to those members of university faculties who have joined so-called Communist front organizations. I have never, so far as I know, joined one of these, but the fact that I have to say 'so far as I know' suggests the dangers now involved in joining anything. When a man is asked by a person he trusts to join an organization for stated purposes which he shares, it seems pusillanimous not to accept. Hardly a day passes that I do not feel pusillanimous, because I must now refuse to associate myself with anything without knowing the political views of every other person who is associated or may later become associated with the movement. This is, of course, the most lamentable aspect of the present situation. It is the creeping miasma of intimidation. If one believes, as I do, that the progress of mankind depends on the freest possible expression of diverse points of view, one must feel that we have come to a sort of halting place in American history. The American people, with a revolutionary tradition, a tradition of independence and toleration, now find themselves blocking the revolutionary aspiration of oppressed peoples abroad and declining at home to permit the kind of criticism that has been our glory, and I think our salvation, in the past."[9]

But the American people of the early 1950s, overcome by the creeping miasma of intimidation, had no great enthusiasm for reminders of their revolutionary tradition, still less of the revolutionary aspirations of oppressed peoples abroad whose struggles against a collapsing colonialism were everywhere supported by Communists. These were inflammatory words, at radical variance with the prevailing view of the worldwide Red Menace criers. They were uttered, on several platforms, by the independent man who was invariably, and inescapably, identified with the name of Ford. And the name of Ford was invariably, and inescapably, identified with the largest seller of automobiles in the world.

However assiduously he insisted that he was speaking only for himself, the Ford Foundation official could not possibly, in the prevailing atmosphere of the early 1950s, have been an asset to the sales division of the Ford Motor Company, or to Young Henry, its president and the board chairman of the Ford Foundation. It was impossible to tell Hutchins—everyone concerned knew that—not to talk about education or to make his views known on the condition of education in America in the early 1950s. And that, in addition to shoveling out the money to his two huge funds, was exactly what he was doing when he attacked loyalty oaths for universities and the terror of Red professors that overspread the land.

When he spoke officially for the foundation he was scrupulous—painfully scrupulous—in his avoidance of the controversial. The Free University of Berlin was established in 1948 with a Ford Foundation bequest in the western sector of the divided city. (The ancient University of Berlin was in the Soviet sector.) Willy-nilly it was a Cold War outpost founded and operated with the blessings of the western allies, and as thoroughly exploited by them as was its counterpart in the eastern sector by the Communists. Invited to address the Free University in mid-1952 as the official Ford representative, Hutchins steered studiously clear of his own real concerns and stuck to a succession of homilies about the rational animal and "the republic of learning." Nothing he said in the blandest speech he ever made could have offended the most furious cold warrior. But to be on the safe side he took a passing swipe at Marxism: "A free university . . . repudiates the doctrine that men and their desires are remorselessly moulded by the conditions of production."[10]

But nothing was bland or inoffensive enough to save the Ford Foundation from attack from without and within. With Hoffman's appointment in 1951 the *Chicago Tribune* at once discovered a "Leftist slant" in the organization's being headed by a man who had "given away ten billion dollars to foreign countries." A whole battery of Hearst columnists took up the cry—Walter Winchell, George Sokolsky, Fulton Lewis, Jr. (who would subsequently make a career out of attacking Hutchins in a weekly radio program), and Westbrook Pegler, who characterized Hoffman as "a hoax without rival in the history of mankind" and the Marshall Plan as "the fabulous Roosevelt-Truman overseas squanderbund." A group of rabid reactionaries began selling five-cent pamphlets outside the foundation's New York office, linking the Ford Motor Company with Communism; and it was not long before national officers of the American Legion were on the attack. And then the cry was taken up by the two-fisted patriots in both houses of Congress. An investigation of the Ford Foundation was authorized, the first of several such, all of them with the same ultraconservative bent and all of them dedicated to the public presentation of the testimony of professional ex-Communist informers and other such slavering characters. Its chairman, Congressman Carroll Reece of Tennessee, found at its very outset "important and extensive evidence concerning subversive and un-American propaganda activities of the Ford Foundation. . . . Here is the last of the great American industrial fortunes . . . being used to undermine and subvert our institutions."[11]

Complaints from Ford dealers across the country began flooding the Ford Motor Company's headquarters, together with that most formidable of all commercial terrors: the threat of a boycott of Ford products, purposively engendered by the foundation's enemies. Dealers, customers, and cranks, inspired by the Hearst columnists and the Carroll Reeces, indignantly wrote to Young Henry: Why was tax-exempt American money being handed out to Communists and foreigners in Communist (a McCarthy-era synonym for foreign) countries? The Ford dealers had a particular grievance: the recipients of the Ford largesse abroad were not, and were not likely to be, Ford customers. True, the talk of boycott, though it turned shrill and voluminous, was not reflected in a decline of Ford sales—and the company's rising dividends enriched the Hoffman-Hutchins enterprise faster than ever.

The international operations of the foundation were Hoffman's own bailiwick, and, while he neither repudiated the Cold War nor left off condemning Communism, he continued to appear in the suspect guise of a man of peace: "The world can't go on indefinitely this way. You are either going to have a war or peace, and I think we all want peace." He commissioned John J. McCloy (who had just resigned as US High Commissioner for Germany) and elder statesman Grenville Clark to spend whatever they needed to determine the "conditions" for establishing and maintaining world peace. This simplistic undertaking produced nothing but a long report by Clark proposing revisions of the United Nations charter in the direction of world law. (Nothing ever came of that, either.)

Hutchins muffled his skepticism of the United Nations as a talking club whose talk revealed its toothlessness, and Hoffman persuaded his trustees to make an interim grant of $1.9 million to the UN's hard-pressed High Commission for Refugees (none of whom was likely to buy a Ford). Young Henry certainly reflected the sentiments of many (perhaps of most) Americans; he was simply antagonistic to something that was brand-new on the American scene, something Americans had not ever had occasion to consider: their country's involvement (except in war) with other countries and the destinies of faraway peoples. It was called, pejoratively, globalism, and it was exemplified by the United Nations. When Hutchins reported on the grant to the Refugees Commission, Ford said, "I don't like the U.N. I'm against it. I think the U.S. should get out of the U.N. and the U.N."—this was a bromide of the moment—"get out of the U.S."

40   The Eye of the Storm

Young Henry was beginning to wonder why the Ford Foundation wasn't doing anything much to support the system—capitalism—that had made it possible. Most of its activities seemed to involve the direct or indirect support of what his closest associates called socialism, or communism (or bolshevism). And none of them was clearly directed to the maintenance of the free enterprise system, in spite of Hoffman's and Hutchins' high-minded insistence, on stage and off, that their every undertaking involved fortification of that system. Young Henry was growing visibly unhappier as the second year of the Hoffman regime proceeded. "I told Henry before I took the job," said Hoffman afterward, "that I'm a militant and maybe he didn't really want me. I told him that I wanted to experiment, to change things, and that change always means trouble. But every time we got a dozen letters objecting to something we'd done—a radio show or an overseas program or whatnot—I'd have to spend hours reassuring the board. I got tired of wasting time that way. I felt I'd done a first-rate job and if, after two years, the trustees didn't agree, I didn't want to have to keep selling them." [1]

Young Henry wasn't being sold: "I couldn't see how the Foundation could go on the way Paul was running it without falling apart at the seams," he said later. "I first got an idea of what was happening when Paul took four months off in the spring of 1952 to campaign for Eisenhower's nomination. We didn't object to that . . . and anyway I was for Eisenhower myself. But during those months I took over some of the administration for the first time—spent one week every month in Pasadena. I found there was no coordination—no contact, even—among the four associate directors. Each one was running his own show, all by himself. . . . Later I met some trustees at Hot Springs and told them about conditions in Pasadena.

We agreed that the Foundation had to be operated on a businesslike basis."[2]

On February 1, 1953, the *New York Times* quoted Hoffman as saying, "We have got another couple of years' work ahead of us . . . before we can say that we are really well organized." On February 3 he conferred privately with President Eisenhower about assignments he might take for the government. On February 4 he resigned as president and director of the Ford Foundation. (The decision to fire him had been made at a board meeting in New York at the end of January.) The announcement of his departure stated that the trustees having decided to transfer the headquarters of the fund from Pasadena to New York, and Mr. Hoffman having expressed the desire to remain in Pasadena, "he has therefore asked to resign as President. . . . This resignation the trustees have reluctantly accepted."

The day after Hoffman's resignation the appointment of part-time Associate Director Gaither as president of the foundation was announced. From that time forward, through a succession of administrations, the Ford Foundation labored mightily to get rid of money, but the money was spent, on the whole, on safe and sane enterprises that finally identified it indistinguishably with the other two respectable, and respectably big, foundations—Rockefeller and Carnegie. How, in the end, could it have been otherwise and men like Hoffman and Hutchins survive? A half-billion—a billion, three billion—dollars soon or late finds its way into the right hands. By 1966 an intrepid investigator of foundations analyzed the credentials of the Ford trustees and concluded that "with one probable exception there is not a non-Establishment man"—they were all men— "among them."[3] Speaking many years afterward of his lifelong employment by boards of trustees, Hutchins said to a younger associate, "Don't ever work for people you don't respect on the grounds that you can 'handle' them."

Young Henry, growing no more radical with the years, went on complaining about the foundation's policies, with some justification from his point of view, during the short presidential tenure of the moderately liberal McGeorge Bundy. Ford ultimately resigned from the board—in 1976— unreconciled even to its new cautious activities under increasingly cautious regimes. "I'm not playing the role of the hardheaded tycoon who thinks all philanthropoids are Socialists and all university professors are Communists," he said, "I'm just suggesting to the trustees and the staff that the system that makes the Foundation possible very probably is worth preserving."[4]

Hoffman's departure was promptly followed by the resignation of two of his hand-picked associate directors—Chester Davis and Milton Katz. It was not followed by the resignation of Associate Director Hutchins. Hutchins went on sitting in his now largely deserted office—and drawing his salary—in the Pasadena outpost for more than a year. Visitors found him busy with one thing or another connected with the foundation and with the Fund for the Advancement of Education (whose president, Clarence H. Faust, had been dean of the Hutchins college at Chicago). But he was off in a corner, for the first time in his professional life; the foundation was being run from New York. The surviving associate director told a visitor, "I'm the associate who doesn't associate with anybody and the director who doesn't direct anything." It was the strangest of interludes and one in which his independent activity was also minimal; in the sixteen months in which he sat solitarily in Pasadena he made fewer public appearances of any kind—thirty-two in all—than he had ever made in a comparable period; and his public addresses were on the whole confined to education.

The two years had passed 1951 and 1952, in which Hutchins and his colleagues were "going to change the temper of the country," and by the beginning of 1953 McCarthyism had America by the throat. Loyalty-security legislation and executive orders cascaded from the White House, the state capitals, and even the city halls. Taking over as president of the bedeviled United States in 1953, General Eisenhower extended the Truman loyalty programs to provide for dismissal from government service of a person who was deemed even likely to be treasonable—without any clear definition of likelihood. The separate states tumbled over one another to follow suit, requiring oaths disclaiming communism from public school teachers, professors, and other state employees, and setting up investigating units in parallel with the congressional committees that toured the country with their troupes of informers, whose unsubstantiated testimony was driving thousands of liberals and intellectuals to the wall.

Senator Joe McCarthy, enjoying congressional immunity, swore to root out of the national life the miscreants who had sold the country to the Reds. He led the pack in playing the new numbers game, claiming variously that the State Department was "thoroughly infested with Communists" variously said to number—the figure differed from speech to speech— anywhere from fifty to two hundred fifty. (He never identified one.) The other executive agencies staffed by what he called the Commiecrats were similarly pilloried. A kind of cold pogrom of federal workers ensued. A special counsel to the president announced in midyear that 1,456 subversives had been kicked out of the government since General Eisenhower took office, and Vice-president Nixon said: "We're kicking the Communists and fellow travelers and security risks out of the Government, not by the hundreds, but by the thousands."[5] The ultimate toll announced by Eisenhower's attorney general was 8,008. "In case after case, government employees were faced with vague and often irrelevant charges; were forced to hire attorneys while suspended without pay, for weeks and even months; were denied access to evidence used against them; were denied the opportunity to cross-examine anonymous informers; and were denied any right of appeal. Grounds for suspension and discharge might be a slightly unorthodox comment, a joke, a rumor about homosexuality—might be anything read or said in one's entire lifetime that could be found objectionable in the effort to 'defend national security.'"[6] A negro employee was charged with "left-wing" leanings when he said he would "rather be a second-class citizen in Mississippi than a first-class citizen in Russia." A postal worker was truthfully charged with having a copy of *Das Kapital* in his home (it had been recommended reading in a college course years before). The new chairman of the House Un-American Activities Committee, Harold Velde, denounced "the influence of Eleanor Roosevelt in the promotion of Communism, of immorality and indecency among so-called minority groups."[7] Senator McCarthy characterized General George C. Marshall as a member of "a conspiracy so immense, an infamy so black, as to dwarf any in the history of man."[8]

The great Red hunt was a first-class ticket—and the only ticket—to political preferment. Candidates and applicants, whatever else they did, had to curse communism and Communists from every platform. Senator Vandenberg's rationale for rearmament—to "scare the hell out of the American people"—was a howling success. The distinguished French editor Claude Bourdet, after a lecture tour of the country, said: "You can say anything you want to in America about anything, as long as you begin by saying, 'I hate Communism.'" The spectre that Marx and Engels saw haunting Europe a century before was haunting America now, and the vigilantes in and out of office were riding high and wide as the shotgun investigations proliferated. McCarthy's denunciation of the Democrats for their "twenty years of treason" put the Republicans into power in 1952, nationally and locally. "Jumping Joe" had the party in his pocket; John Foster Dulles was friendly to him, "Mr. Republican" Robert A. Taft praised his "fight for America," and he appeared on the networks as the party's climax speaker in the presidential campaign. Respectable Republicans fell silent while eminent old and new New Dealers were shot down and out of public life. The Democrats, on the defensive, were reduced to trying to outdo their opponents: "I," said President Truman, after the conviction of Alger Hiss, "put my Communists in jail"—whereas the McCarthyites only "exposed" theirs.

But denunciation as often as not had the effect of jail. These were the years of psychological terrorism and torture that destroyed the careers and even the lives of tens of thousands of sympathizers with causes, "bleeding hearts" who had pushed doorbells, distributed leaflets, joined committees, organized meetings and demonstrations in behalf of the downtrodden, the dispossessed, the exiled, the rebels, the suspect. Pacifists religious and secular were caught up in the torrent; "peace" was a dirty word. Critics of the public policy of increased armaments—and of the unwinnable Korean war then in progress—were ruined. Distinguished academics like Owen Lattimore, Jr., of Johns Hopkins (McCarthy called him "the top Soviet espionage agent") were driven out of public service for having "lost China" to the Communists; and physicist Robert Oppenheimer, the developer of the atomic bomb at Los Alamos, lost his security clearance because he opposed the Truman program to develop the bigger and better H-bomb.

There were Communists in America—a handful—and Communist sympathizers. There were a few traitors, spies, and agents, and more than a few dupes. And there were thousands of nonconspiratorial people who still saw in the Russian revolution the hope, if a fading hope, of building a new world. (It was, after all, only a few years since the democratic leaders of the world were supporting the Soviet Union in its mortal struggle against Nazi Germany, and many Americans who could not accept the disenchantment of that country's Stalinist horrors believed that mankind's was a black-and-white choice between communism and fascism.) And there were more thousands of Americans who adhered, however halfheartedly, or less, to the Russian experiment, with all its terror and travail, as a possible alternative to the bootlessness of the world wars between great capitalist blocs of imperial powers. (Many of these fellow-travelers, so-called, had got off after one or two stops—which redemptive defection did not, however, save them from the trackers-down of Red devils.)

But there was no Communist movement in the United States, and there never had been. The American Communists and their sympathizers—or the sympathizers with causes the Communists also supported—were with the rarest of exceptions what the witch-hunters called eggheads, members of that broadly definable middle-class intelligentsia who generally constituted the backbone of all liberal and radical causes. They were generally college and university graduates or students, teachers, or figures in the entertainment and artistic worlds. The miasma of intimidation paralyzed campus activists, and the boycott and blacklisting of public performers and their works was effectively urged by broadcasters and leafleteers. The witch-hunt addressed itself to the crudest and most regressive impulses in the country. It was blatantly anti-intellectual and anti-aesthetic. Latent anti-Semitism flourished just beneath the surface. (The *Williams Intelligence Summary* of Los Angeles asked its readers to dig up evidence that the villainous Robert M. Hutchins was a Jew.)

The witch-hunters had it both ways: either there were millions of hidden Communists to be hauled out of the closet or, if there were in fact only a few abroad in the land, it had to be remembered that the Bolsheviks who staged the revolution in Russia had numbered only a few thousand. Americans were not notably well schooled in modern—or ancient—history. They thought they knew that Russians (and most other peoples) were somehow backward and inconsequentially unfortunate not to be Americans; they neither knew nor cared that the social conditions of much of Europe and most of the rest of the world were conducive to the acceptance of social revolution. What they knew from their everyday experience— until they had the hell scared out of them—was that theirs was not the soil in which revolution grew. The call to revolution, even the genteel call of the doctrinaire Socialists, fell on deaf ears in the land of entrepreneurial opportunity. The American "workers of the world" were united, all right; they were united in their indifference to communism (and to ideology in general; they had a politics, denominated Republican or Democrat, but no clear political philosophy).

Still less did they have an economic philosophy. What they had was an unexamined economic practice. Except for a few of the immigrants from central and eastern Europe, they had no acquaintance, near or remote, with Marxism as a doctrine or an analysis of human nature and human society, and none whatever with a living Marxist of any variety. They had all heard rabid accounts of Soviet Russia, and they had all heard of the bugbear Communist, Bolshevik, or Anarchist with, as Alfred Emanuel Smith put it, "wire whiskers and a bomb in each hand."

This mortally dangerous isolation from the most significant historical reality of the age was not confined to a mere majority of the American people; one way or another it embraced almost all of them. In 1954 the Fund for the Republic financed "the most expensive survey of public opinion ever made," a $125,000 poll of the country's attitudes toward communism directed by the American Institute of Public Opinion and the University of Chicago's National Opinion Research Center, under the general supervision of Dr. Samuel Stouffer, director of the Harvard University Laboratory of Social Relations. The survey revealed that, although less than 1 percent of the American people were more concerned about communism than they were about personal and domestic issues, 77 percent would revoke a Communist's citizenship (and 51 percent would jail him); 73 percent thought that "suspicious" behavior of neighbors should be reported to the FBI; and 64 percent approved of the wiretapping of suspects. Ninety-four percent would refuse to let an atheist teach in a college—and 68 percent would deny such employment even to a Socialist. Nor was the general public alone endemically infected with the hysteria; even 50 percent of the nation's attorneys said they considered the invocation of the Fifth Amendment an indication of guilt.[9]

During General Eisenhower's presidency the Madison, Wisconsin, *Capitol Times* asked, "What is a Communist?" of the typical man (and woman) in the street. One housewife replied: "I really don't know what a Communist is. I think they should throw them out of the White House." Since there were so few known—or unknown—Communists in the country and no American was likely to know one *as a Communist*, the anti-Communist crusade was necessarily fueled by suspicion of the most vagrant kind. Ten percent of the Stouffer interviewees were suspicious of one or another person of their acquaintance: "I saw a map of Russia on a wall in his home." "He had a foreign camera and took many pictures of New York bridges." "He was always talking about world peace." "He didn't believe in Christ, heaven or hell." "My husband's brother drinks and acts common-like. Sometimes I kind of think he is a Communist."[10] These were the meat on which the McCarthyites gorged.

College graduates were as ignorant of Marxism as were high school dropouts. They were unaware of the implications for America of the "Marxist-Leninist" address to the industrial proletariat—the people without property and with nothing to sell but their labor. Most Americans had property—something to lose besides their chains—and those who didn't believed that they would, any day now. Men who lost their jobs in hard times did not *think* they would get another—they *knew* they would (and they usually did). There was plenty of starvation in the richest of all great lands, but even the starving were incapable of seeing themselves as the Marxists' prisoners of starvation. The closest thing to a proletarian in America was the Negro—but even he, armored by the hope of a better life both hereafter and here, was impervious to the siren songs of the revolutionaries. The Negroes had been unreachable even during the Great Depression of the 1930s, when a majority of them were out of work.

But the reality of the actual social fabric in America did not impinge on the fantasy of the supposedly Red-infested country—or, of course, on the strategy of the exploiters of that fantasy. There was a new reality threatening as McCarthyism in its myriad manifestations seemed to be achieving undreamed-of proportions, as the dreadful year of 1953 went forward and Robert M. Hutchins, the exponent of free disputation and free dissent seemed to be sitting it out among the great big geraniums of Pasadena. The threatening reality was the collapse altogether of the spirit of individual independence, of forthrightness, and, most fragile of all, of toleration in the happy American fabric. Solemn people, and not just hysterics, began talking about fascism and whether "it" could happen here; Huey Long was quoted as saying that if fascism ever came to the United States it would be called Americanism.

Ever since he had come to the Ford Foundation and encountered its board of trustees, Hutchins had pondered the language of that section A of the Second Program Area of the Study Report that those trustees had adopted at the end of 1949: "The Foundation should support activities directed toward... the elimination of restrictions on freedom of thought, inquiry, and expression." Section A appeared to have fallen into the direct jurisdiction of none of the associate directors, and nothing of any significance had been undertaken to implement it as the loyalty-security programs and investigations mounted in Washington and swept across the country. But in August 1951 Hutchins submitted a two-page proposal for a Fund for Democratic Freedoms, which would deal "almost wholly with unpalatable causes." The first thing such a fund would do—he later proposed The Fund for the Republic as its name—would be to make "continuing studies and reports on the ever-new and current dangers which threaten the unalienable rights of men in a democratic society." Nothing too hopelessly unpalatable there. But its second function was something else again. To be established by the Ford Foundation with a distinguished board of directors, the Fund would have the authority to defend individuals and groups directly and "provide backing" for scientists and teachers embroiled with problems of scientific and academic freedom.[11] It would be an activist agency dealing with actual cases and offer financial assistance to defendants. It would, in a word, function as no such philanthropy had ever functioned before.

The proposal moved slowly, but, surprisingly enough, it moved. The other senior officers of the foundation joined in the recommendation to the board, saying that "none of the tasks before the Foundation is more critical than this; it is timely for the Foundation to take it." Neither Young Henry nor his board could say later that they had bought a pig in a poke— however much they might have liked to. They may have been lulled by the fact that the officers of the foundation proposed that each member of the board of the new Fund would have to be approved unanimously by the board of the foundation—a provision that did in fact produce a "representative" (that is, a careful) group of trustees. They may have been reassured by the provision that the new Fund, unlike the other foundation spin-offs, was to be wholly independent of the foundation, so that its activities could not jeopardize the foundation's tax exemption. (Hutchins would subsequently refer to it as "a wholly disowned subsidiary of the Ford Foundation.") They may have been further lulled by the provision that the capital of the new Fund, a modest fifteen million dollars, would revert to the foundation if the Fund should ever lose its tax exemption (which it had yet to obtain). They may have been emboldened by a disarming memorandum submitted by W.H. "Ping" Ferry, the wealthy young Detroiter who had been Young Henry's speechwriter, was now public relations adviser to the foundation, and was destined to be the vice-president of the new Fund. Ferry's memorandum called for "bold experimentation" by the Fund and added: "Such a policy is not in conflict with the real interest of the Ford Motor Company, although it may sometimes prove irritating to some of its officials, and may embarrass, temporarily, members of the Ford family. In the long run it will bring more credit to the Ford name than the easy and innocuous course of making impressive contributions to established activities or undertaking programs that can not arouse criticism or opposition. Here it should be remembered that the reputation of the Ford Motor Company largely centers around Henry Ford's lifelong preoccupation with experimentation and pioneering ventures."[12]

It wasn't until December 1952 that the Foundation board brought the Fund for the Republic into corporate existence, after a monumental exchange of memoranda generally directed to hedging it about with large generalities which would antagonize nobody. But among those memoranda was a steady succession from Hutchins in Pasadena pushing for speedy action on the whole front of burning political issues. "The Fund" he wrote, "should feel free to attack the problem of the freedom of the press; of migrant workers; of the immigration laws and the McCarran [Internal Security] Act; of loyalty investigations; of the House Un-American Activities Committee; of conscientious objectors; of academic freedom and teachers' oaths; of racial and religious discrimination in all its manifestations, from lynching to inequality of educational opportunity; of disfranchisement; of dishonesty in government; of the liberties guaranteed by the first and fourteenth amendments; of the administration of justice."[13] With a grimace of annoyance by his fellow associate directors at the foundation—this was before Hoffman's resignation—Hutchins placed the development of the Fund for the Republic under his own administrative jurisdiction.

Hoffman, resigning as president of the foundation, was named board chairman of the new Fund; with whatever reservations the foundation's board members might have had about his liberalism (and about his devotion to Hutchins), the appointment took the public relations sting out of Hoffman's separation from the foundation—and he was, after all, still an Eisenhower Republican. Casting about for a president of the Fund, the foundation trustees lit upon another Eisenhower Republican, this one, however, a much more reliably moderate man than Hoffman: Congressman Clifford Case of New Jersey, who resigned his seat in the House to take the job. In foundation circles it was thought, or, at least, hoped, that the selection of a respectable member would relieve the foundation (and ultimately the Fund) of some of the heat that was galvanizing congressional investigations into both the fiscal and the political policies of the foundation and its offspring. But the *New York Times* reported that "a decision by the Ford Foundation to grant $15,000,000 to inquire into the methods of Congressional investigations into Communist infiltrations and civil rights appeared to rankle a large section of the House."[14]

From its inception the Fund was pitted against powerful forces in Congress, and against the congressional courtesy that at times such as these tended to unite its members. Shortly after Hoffman became its chairman, the board of the Fund approved a staff prospectus that contemplated, inter alia, "a study of the activities of the House Un-American Activities Committee, the Senate Internal Security Committee, and other Congressional investigating committees." And its very first allocation of funds was a grant of fifty thousand dollars to the American Bar Association's Special Committee on Individual Rights as Affected by National Security. The ABA's request for the grant had been made to Hutchins prior to the incorporation of the Fund, and it proposed an examination of "the extent to which Congress should place any limitations upon the scope of its investigations or should regulate their procedures so as to protect the rights of individuals by providing some of the safeguards of due process at trials."

Just before Case's resignation from Congress to take the Fund presidency, the House had authorized a new round of Red hearings under Congressman Carroll Reece of Tennessee, who told his colleagues: "There can be no question that Hutchins is behind this new Ford Foundation project, for he has consistently expressed his concern for the civil liberties of Communists. Since we know Hutchins' attitude toward communism and we know that his conception of civil liberties is similar to that of the Communists, we can be sure that the new Ford Foundation project will aid the Communist conspiracy and will try to discredit all those who fight it." Appealing—successfully—for a second investigation of the Ford Foundation after Hoffman's replacement by Gaither, Reece said, "Gaither is a mere figurehead and Hutchins is still running the Foundation. Gaither has accepted the presidency only for a year, and thus Hutchins may yet become the formal head of the organization."[15]

No sooner was the Fund incorporated and Hoffman named its board chairman, than he received a letter from Senator McCarthy: "I understand that you have just been elected President of a new foundation. . . . I would appreciate it if you would . . . advise when you can appear in Washington without too much inconvenience." Hoffman detested McCarthy, who had engineered the brutal defeat of his (and Hutchins') close friend Bill Benton for reelection to the United States Senate from Connecticut in the 1952 election. With exemplary courage the one-time ad man had risen, alone, on the floor of the Senate on August 6, 1951, and, waiving his congressional immunity, delivered an all-out attack on McCarthy and introduced a one-man resolution to expel him from the chamber.

But Hoffman was careful to reply courteously to McCarthy's request that he appear in Washington, informing him that he would be glad to do so but would be out of the country on a trip he was undertaking for the Studebaker Corporation. McCarthy then asked for a list of the personnel of the Fund for the Republic, which Hoffman submitted.[16] McCarthy later issued a press release to the effect that the fund's "principal objective is to torpedo any effective security program." Meanwhile Hoffman was solemnly assuring Eisenhower's vice-president, Richard M. Nixon, that the Fund would be making a fundamental study of "the extent and nature of the internal communist menace and its effect on our community and institutions."

Though the American Legion news letter, *Firing Line*, referred to the Fund as "a huge slush fund for a full-scale war on all organizations and individuals who have ever exposed and fought Communists," the Fund during the year and more of the Case presidency did very little besides obtain its tax exemption and its terminal grant of fifteen million dollars from the Ford Foundation. Its internal memoranda were on the whole temperate enough to mollify anyone short of the most fanatical Red baiters; it had issued no printed matter; it had issued two colorless press releases; and it had made cash grants to four tax-exempt recipients (largely in the respectable area of race relations). The most conservative of its board members had no fault to find with its program, which was heavily devoted to research and study projects such as a long-term history of American Communism. But there was sufficient resentment arising from below—and from Hutchins in Pasadena—so that in early 1954, when Case offered to leave (and go on to be a mildly liberal senator from New Jersey), his resignation was promptly accepted.

Thomas C. Reeves, author of an exhaustive history of the Fund, recounted Hutchins' situation at the Ford Foundation after Hoffman's resignation: "The associate director sat in the rump office in Pasadena, looked upon by many insiders as an unnecessary vestige of turbulent times, an overly outspoken crusader whose retention was due solely to the corporation's unwillingness to invite controversy. No one within the Foundation offered any positive suggestions about the future of the fifty-four-year-old administrator, and Hutchins himself seemed unready to seek other employment voluntarily. His advice was sought on several occasions, but he provoked ill will by insisting repeatedly that the Foundation had higher responsibilities than it currently recognized, and should be much more than a pliant device of a recreant donor. The already strained relationship between Henry Ford and Hutchins became increasingly poor as months passed. By the end of 1953 the educator's presence was becoming intolerable."[17]

He continued to waft memoranda to New York deploring the Fund's quietism and urging an activist program against the extremists in and out of the government. The trouble was that he was still an associate director of the Ford Foundation, and the Fund for the Republic was a wholly independent organization. The nexus, of course, was Board Chairman Hoffman of the Fund. Board Chairman Hoffman was out of town—town being New York now, instead of Pasadena—more than he was in. But he shared Hutchins' impatience for aggressive action against the high tide of McCarthyism—and he still had his unabated enthusiasm for Hutchins and Hutchins' aggressive views and aggressive tactics.

With Clifford Case's resignation pending, a search for a new president of the fund went forward on several fronts. Hutchins participated, though he had no corporate right to do so. He spent three hours in Sacramento with the Republican governor of California, Earl Warren. Governor Warren was interested in the Fund, but he told Hutchins that he would be unavailable as a presidential candidate since it appeared that he was going to be offered another post. (As indeed he was, almost immediately thereafter: the chief justiceship of the US Supreme Court). Manufacturer William Joyce and the pollster Elmo Roper, both of whom Hutchins had suggested as board members when the fund was established, put Hutchins' name forward after "some exchange with trustees of the Ford Foundation. . . . They were not wild about the idea," said Joyce, "but there was no vote." Fund Chairman Hoffman was unreservedly enthusiastic, and though there was some opposition in the Fund's board, a majority was receptive—if a little worried. His presidency was announced on May 25, 1954, during the uproar of the Army-McCarthy hearings.

The Fund's trustees had a little to be worried about. Hutchins' acceptance of the offer with, he told the board, "willingness and pleasure," meant that the Fund for the Republic would ride right into the eye of the storm. He had made his position plain: the fundamental freedoms of the American republic were under remorseless and relentless attack by powerful politicians, who scrupled at nothing in their exploitation of the popular panic engendered by the Truman/Eisenhower cold war policies in conjunction with the traditional American dread of bolshevism. (Perhaps one in a million Americans actually knew a real, live Communist.) Robert Maynard Hutchins' reputation as a trouble-maker—as if there would be no trouble were it not for him—went back to his assumption of the presidency of the University of Chicago. The decades had not tempered him; quite the opposite. He had never had to look for trouble; he had been drawn inexorably to where trouble was. Between February of 1953, when he was stranded in Pasadena, and May of 1954 he had been making portentous and premonitory rumbles and it wasn't like him to confine himself to memoranda. By way of underscoring his intentions, if they needed underscoring, he at once asked W. H. "Ping" Ferry—who was, if anything, more radical than Hutchins—to serve as vice-president of the fund. The job would mean a considerable financial sacrifice for the forty-one-year-old Ford public relations man, but he accepted without hesitation.

On taking his new post, Hutchins resigned from the Ford Foundation; so much for the half-billion dollars that were going to change the temper of the country in two years; so much for the diamond-studded straw he'd grasped at. Now he had fifteen million dollars—peanuts, in Ford terms—but he was expected to get rid of it in five years and go out of business—if, in the meanwhile, the witch-hunters in Washington did not succeed in persuading the IRS to withdraw the fund's tax exemption. In his *Never Complain, Never Explain: The Story of Henry Ford II*, Victor Lasky wrote, "The Hutchins appointment was not exactly greeted with joy by either Henry or his fellow trustees at the Foundation, one of whom said, 'This means trouble.'"[18]

41 All over Mud

Mrs. Mary Knowles did not appear to be redoubtable, but she was; more redoubtable, in the end, than the United States Congress, the Federal Bureau of Investigation, the American Legion, and the most redoubtable representatives of the American press. When she was hired in 1954 by the Plymouth Monthly Meeting of the Religious Society of Friends, she had been a professional librarian for twenty-five years. She was hired as librarian of the meeting's William Jeanes Memorial Library, just outside Philadelphia.

She had lost her library job in Massachusetts the year before when she refused to answer questions before the Internal Security Subcommittee of the US Senate. From 1945 to 1947 she had worked as a secretary at the radical Samuel Adams School in Boston—the school was on the attorney general's list of "subversive organizations"—and an FBI undercover agent said she had been a Communist then. When it hired her, the small meeting minuted its unanimous feeling "that we should be motivated by our Quaker principles and any compromise at this time would be wholly incompatible with our basic faith." It knew all about Mary Knowles's political beliefs and associations, including her religious pacifism. (She did not in the least mind telling people about them—but she would not reveal them under duress.)

Refusing to cooperate with the Senate subcommittee before she left Boston for Philadelphia, she said: "In the first place I have committed no crime, nor am I facing criminal prosecution. . . . In the second place . . . recourse to the First Amendment could very easily lead to a contempt of court citation. . . . In the third place, if, under compulsion, I testified concerning my religion and politics, but refused to answer questions about others, I would also be held in contempt of court. . . . Fourth, if I refused to answer questions on moral or ethical grounds without invoking the Fifth Amendment, I would also be held in contempt of court."[1]

She pointed out that the issue was strictly one of constitutional rights, and that no question had been raised as to her professional qualifications. Shortly before she was hired by the Quakers she declined to take the Pennsylvania loyalty (more precisely, non-disloyalty) oath, thereby rendering herself unemployable by any state or local agency of any kind. With her respectful refusal she enclosed a signed statement: "I believe firmly in the United States of America and in the documents upon which it is founded—the Declaration of Independence and the Constitution of the United States, and do support, obey, and defend them. I do also support the Constitution of the State of Pennsylvania. . . . Since leaving the Samuel Adams School, I have had no connection formal or otherwise with any so-called leftwing or 'subversive' organization." On her own initiative she submitted a notarized statement to the Plymouth meeting on entering its employ: "Mary Knowles, being duly sworn according to law, deposes and says that she is not a Communist or a member of any subversive organization."[2]

But her refusal to take the state loyalty oath was generally known, and city officials publicly challenged her having been hired. The boards of commissioners of two townships and the local Community Chest promptly canceled gifts to the library, and local school boards refused to continue sending children to classes there. The Valley Forge chapter of the Daughters of the American Revolution "wholeheartedly" applauded these actions, as did the local American Legion post. The area's Alerted Americans Group, one of dozens of such extremist organizations that had recently come to life all across the country, demanded in their monthly newsletter the dismissal of the librarian: "No Security Risk should be employed in a sensitive post of honor and esteem where she is in a position to harm the community. Mrs. Knowles' controversial beliefs and unpatriotic behavior have already disturbed the peace, set a bad example for our young people and caused widespread suspicion and criticism of the whole Friends Meeting. The Communists started all this furor and screaming about 'academic freedom' and 'civil liberties.'"[3]

The pressure on the Friends Meeting was mounting, but the Meeting continued to reaffirm its support of the librarian. The Alerted Americans claimed to have twenty-two members of the Meeting among their supporters, and a petition was presented to the Meeting's library committee containing sixty signatures of adult members (only thirteen of whom regularly attended worship; twenty-nine had not attended in twenty years).

The meeting was resisting the local clamor staunchly, and its library committee issued a public statement of its position:

Should an accusation of association with the Communist Party eight years ago be disqualification for employment? We think it should not. . . .

Is it a disqualification for employment if a loyalty oath is declined? . . . As Friends we have not, and shall not, require an oath [of Mary Knowles], believing that truth is no stronger under oath.

Should a plea of the Fifth Amendment give rise to unfavorable inferences? We think not. The right to be silent (Fifth Amendment) is equal to the right of freedom of speech, free press, and freedom of religion (First Amendment). These rights must be respected for all persons or they are endangered for each of us.

Finally it is suggested that one who does not cooperate with a Congressional Committee should be penalized by exclusion from employment in his chosen field. But when silence is the exercise of a constitutional right, to penalize that silence would jeopardize that constitutional right.[4]

The Mary Knowles case might well have ended at that point. But instead of ending, it blew up into a national *cause célèbre* that continued for another two years. It blew up because Hutchins of the Fund for the Republic happened to hear about it just after the Fund's directors, in May of 1955, appointed a Committee on Special Awards consisting of three distinguished members: Mrs. Eleanor B. Stevenson, the wife of the president of Oberlin College; President Albert Linton of the Provident Mutual Life Insurance Company of Philadelphia; and Robert E. Sherwood, the eminent dramatist and adviser of the late Franklin D. Roosevelt. The committee was authorized to disburse $100,000 "in honoring and rewarding the conduct of men, organizations, and institutions that exemplify the liberties this Fund was established to support." After hearing a report by President Hutchins the board of the Fund unanimously made its first Special Award of five thousand dollars to the Plymouth Monthly Meeting of the Religious Society of Friends "in recognition of its forthright stand in defense of individual freedom." In his announcement to the press Hutchins said that the award was for "courageous and effective defense of democratic principles" in the face of organized attack. "I hope," he said, "that Plymouth Monthly Meeting's example will be followed elsewhere in America, particularly when our libraries—which seem to be a special target of self-appointed censors and amateur loyalty experts—are involved."[5]

Ten days later Chairman Carroll Reece of the House of Representatives subcommittee to investigate foundations took the floor to deliver a tirade against the fund's award to the Plymouth Meeting, and a few days later Mary Knowles was subpoenaed by the Senate Subcommittee on Internal Security.

Now the attack on the fund went into high gear among the congressional committees, veterans' organizations, and extremist groups the country over—and major sections of both the printed and electronic press. The pace was set by the Hearst papers, which added two more right-wing commentators, Victor Riesel and George Sokolsky, to the assault by the syndicated columnist Fulton Lewis, Jr., with his daily broadcast over 214 radio and 50 television stations (his radio audience alone numbered sixteen million). In the course of the ensuing year Lewis devoted no fewer than sixty commentaries on the air to the horrors of the Fund for the Republic and its president: "So continues the case of Mrs. Mary Knowles, the Fifth Amendment librarian, whose case was considered by Dr. Hutchins and Mr. "Ping" Ferry to be worthy of five thousand dollars of money which is supposed to be spent in the general public interest and welfare. The question is whether you agree that this falls in that category."[6] Broadcast after broadcast by Lewis ended in this provocative fashion: Do you agree? Where do *you* stand? What do *you* say? Untold thousands of his listeners and readers stood up and said, proceeding to their American Legion posts, churches, school and library boards, and, above all, to their congressmen and senators. Congressman Reece's subcommittee having already issued a 432-page report condemning the foundations generally for promoting socialism, subversion, and "moral relativity," wanted them closely supervised by the federal government. Two dissenting members of the subcommittee called the report "barbaric," and, in a speech before the National Press Club, with the subcommittee chairman in the audience (as well as fund supporters Felix Frankfurter and Justice William O. Douglas), Hutchins lit into the Reece report in one of the most violent outbursts of his life:

"I can not regard the Reece committee as having more than symbolic or symptomatic importance. Its wild and squalid presentation affords a picture of the state of our culture that is most depressing. Its aims and methods are another example of the exploitation of public concern about Communism and subversion to further political ambition and to work off political grudges. . . . We may as well state it plainly: the Reece investigation in its inception and execution was a fraud."[7]

It was the first time a tax-exempt organization had ever launched a head-on challenge to a congressional agency. The congressional (and noncongressional) attack on Mary Knowles continued to mount, a transparent cover for the attack on the Fund for the Republic. In time the Plymouth Friends Meeting began to waver, in spite of the fact that Philadelphia Yearly Meeting, representing ninety-three monthly meetings (and jokingly known among Quakers as "the Vatican"), had unanimously supported the

Plymouth Meeting's hiring of Mrs. Knowles. Ultimately the Plymouth Meeting decided to keep Mrs. Knowles on by a slim majority of thirty-four to thirty, one of its members breaking out in agonized exclamation: "If we could get rid of the $5,000 Fund for the Republic money, I think maybe we all would fall on each other's necks and say, 'Let's forget it all and let the woman stay.' But it is the $5,000 that holds everything up because everybody says, 'What did you ever do to get a Communist $5,000? Everybody is stigmatized. Are you all Communists?' "

In one House Un-American Activities Committee (HUAC) hearing on the activities of the fund, its chairman, Congressman Francis Walter said: "The committee wishes to know more about the factors which prompted the Fund for the Republic to consider the retention of *a Communist*, a defense of 'democratic principles' worth $5,000 of its tax-exempt money. . . . The Communists and their dupes will undoubtedly try to distort our inquiry into appearing as an interference with the great freedom of religion. . . . Our sole concern is with the dubious ventures of the Fund for the Republic."[8] At the conclusion of the HUAC hearing the Plymouth Meeting's library committee, still standing pat, said, "A Committee of Congress has just spent virtually a whole day ventilating the unhappy internal affairs of a small religious group, Plymouth Monthly Meeting of the Religious Society of Friends. Not a single fact has been developed that was not known before."

In January of 1957—more than three years after she had been hired by Plymouth Meeting—Mary Knowles was convicted in federal court on fifty-two counts of contempt of Congress. (One of the fifty-two citations was made by a *unanimous* vote of the Senate when she refused to answer questions at a hearing of its Internal Security Subcommittee.) She was sentenced to 120 days in jail and a five-hundred-dollar fine—the heaviest sentence ever given a woman for contempt. The rightist press rejoiced, and Congressman Gordon Scherer promised that the HUAC investigation of the Fund for the Republic "was barely started." Reflecting the mounting resistance to the witch-hunt, he said: "It is time that some people . . . join with us in chasing the criminal instead of always attacking the policeman." Pointing to the conviction of Mrs. Knowles, he asked inquirers if they thought that the five-thousand-dollar award in honor of the convict should be tax-exempt.[9]

Three-and-a-half years later, on June 19, 1960, almost seven years after she was hired by Plymouth Meeting, and five years after the Meeting received the Fund's award, Mary Knowles's conviction was reversed by the United States Circuit Court of Appeals. The McCarthy terror had long since come to an end, and there was no comment by so many as one of her persecutors or the opponents of the Fund for the Republic.

The insult of the fund's defiance of Congress and the patriots was compounded by the injury it was able to do with its fifteen million dollars. "This is the first time," said Hutchins, "that an organization dedicated to civil liberties has had any money." It takes (or in those days took) a long time to get rid of fifteen million dollars. In the first three years of its existence the Fund for the Republic had managed to unload only five-and-a-half million, in spite of its lavish outlay for administrative purposes (a bloated 35 percent of its total expenditures).

Some 95 percent of the Fund's grants were unexceptionable, except by the most rabid of the rightist extremists; when it announced that its largest cumulative expenditure during the first three years of its history had been in race relations, Fulton Lewis, Jr., informed his radio audience that this effort "follows the standard Communist tactic of arousing racial strife and friction as a means of inflating trouble and disharmony on which to play for their own Communist advantage." The largest single appropriation of the fund was $550,000 for a massive study of Communism in the United States, under the general aegis of the conservative Professor Clinton Rossiter of Cornell. The project, said the fund's Board Chairman Hoffman, "was not organized solely to oppose Communism; it was organized to study and disclose the facts about all threats to civil liberties, including Communism."

Bent on studying and disclosing the facts, the scholarly staff of the Rossiter project retained the services—for a few weeks, at seventy-five dollars a week—of Earl Browder, the American Communist Party leader. Browder, under federal indictment for perjury, was a "source of information and raw material . . . commenting on events in which he took a leading part." This conventional research procedure set all the jingoist bells jingling. Out in front was Fulton Lewis, Jr., who characterized Rossiter with blasé abandon as "an extreme liberal." This, said Lewis, was the way the Fund spent their fifteen million dollars of tax-free money, and what did his audience think about *that?* The Hearst papers found it an "offense to any decent and honest sense of propriety for [a man like Browder] to have any part in the preparation of the reference books and texts from which American children may shape their political and economic philosophies." The Scripps-Howard chain was equally strident, with headlines like FORD FUND PROJECT HIRES EX-RED BOSS BROWDER. To the repeated, nay, the continuing distress of Young Henry and his associates, many newspapers ran variants of FORD FOUNDATION PAYS BROWDER AS RED HISTORY AID.

Many of the country's most highly respected newspapers defended the fund, including the *New York Times*, the *Christian Science Monitor*, the *Atlanta Constitution*, the *St. Louis Post-Dispatch*, and the *San Francisco Chronicle*. But the press as a whole bayed with the hounds. "We are trying," said Hutchins, pouring a soupçon of oil on the fire, "to save the Republic. We can expect few cheers from those we are saving it from."

It was such trivialities as the "hiring" of Browder at seventy-five dollars a week and the minuscule award of five thousand dollars to the Plymouth Friends Meeting that riled up the animals, and kept them riled, while the allocations of the fund in noncontroversial areas went unremarked. Stanford's conservative trustees were peppered, and then pilloried, because the university's staid school of law accepted a $25,000 award to finance an analysis of the testimony of witnesses in proceedings relative to communism. Attacking the Stanford grant, radio network commentator Paul Harvey said: "Russia will never have to take us into a shooting match if she can poison us while we sleep. It is time to destroy the tax-exempt status of these outfits"—the Fund, or Stanford, or both?—"that manufacture the poison."[10]

A month after Hutchins' assumption of the presidency of the Fund in May of 1954, the board of the previously almost dormant organization approved the establishment of a commission to examine the country's loyalty-security programs, approved a study of right-wing extremist groups, approved a grant to the American Friends Service Committee to support four projects of its community relations program, approved a grant to expand the work of the Common Council for American Unity in protecting and publicizing the rights of illegal aliens, and approved a grant to the Catholic Interracial Council. The president promised the board that at its next meeting the officers would propose a study of fear in education, a study of the uses of the mass media, an investigation into blacklisting in private industry, the support of experimental community-level activities, and a program to increase public awareness of civil liberties and civil rights by means of awards, essay contests, and television.

The pace of the Fund's activity escalated with the escalation of the domestic political crisis. Board meetings ran as long as seven hours a day for two days running. A typical progress report, submitted in November 1955: In intergroup relations, a chairman of the Fund's Indian Commission had been named; the American Friends Service Committee and the Catholic Interracial Council were expanding their work on racial tensions; the Southern Regional Council, financed by the Fund, now had full-time staff members in every southern state; the Fund's Commission on Race and Housing now had a research staff of sixteen, with studies planned at major universities; with Fund support, the Public Education Association had completed its study of racial discrimination in the New York City public schools; the American Heritage Council's Fund-subsidized discussion materials were being used by sixty to seventy American Legion posts in Illinois (in spite of condemnation by the Illinois Department of the Legion); recordings of the Classics of Freedom were well under way; a fund-sponsored Freedom Agenda conference reported the distribution of great quantities of fund-provided literature, with the support of many national organizations, including the AMVETS, the American Jewish Congress, the Campfire Girls, the YWCA, the YMCA, and the League of Women Voters. And on, and on.

With the Fund under unremitting fire from every direction, its board members were scrupulous in their labors. More than scrupulous, they were an edgy group of eminent men and women with close ties to many of the most select segments of the established order. They were a strong, and strongly convinced, group and, with a few exceptions, courageous under attack. (True, most of them had been hand-picked by Hutchins when he was still at the Ford Foundation and the Fund was established.) But, unlike Hutchins of Chicago, very few of them had had the experience of being publicly savaged day after day. The lid finally blew off the board when the vice-president of the Fund, "Ping" Ferry, audaciously hired (as a temporary publicity man) a former Communist who, invoking the Fifth Amendment, refused to tell a congressional committee whether he had been a Party member. The public storm was immense, the headlines bigger and blacker than ever, the agonies of congressmen, commentators, and right-wing crusaders unappeasable. Hadn't the McCarran Internal Security Act, the Communist Control Act, and an 84-0 Senate roll call denominated communism an international conspiracy directed at the overthrow of the US government and the seizure of the country and its institutions? Forgotten was the fact that the Party was still legal in America—forgotten except by the last-ditch fighters for the legal rights of every American. But the board of the Fund for the Republic was badly shaken by the most furious outcry it had yet been subjected to. One member, a partner of the most powerful law firm in New York, resigned; and the subsequent resignations of two or three others, including Dean Erwin Griswold of the Harvard Law School, were plainly influenced by the incident. (Thirty-five thousand copies of Griswold's classic defense of the Fifth Amendment had been distributed by the Fund, which sent out a mere thousand copies of an attack on the Fifth Amendment by a Notre Dame professor of law—and the Fund was then attacked by the *National Review* and other conservative agencies for the discrepancy of the distribution.)

Hutchins' most serious difficulties with his board dated from that hulla-baloo and the theoretical question of hiring an actual Communist. On this point he stood pat, arguing against most of the trustees that neither past nor present association with a legal organization justified exclusion from employment. In the election of fund officers in January 1955, Hutchins, who had offered to step down, was retained by an undisclosed vote; but no less than a strong minority of the trustees continued to grumble, with out-breaks of real acrimony at board meetings and a pervasive atmosphere of general uneasiness about some of the uncompromising attitudes of Vice-president Ferry (who had Hutchins' backing). Even Paul Hoffman found himself faltering in the face of the continuous unremitting siege of the Fund by the McCarthyites. In a widely circulated letter to Young Henry, who had been goaded into a public denunciation of the fund, the embat-tled and embarrassed board chairman felt called upon to profess his (and the Fund's) ardent anticommunism. The Kremlin, he said, "is in deadly earnest about communizing the world." The Fund, he wanted to assure Ford (and the trustees of the Ford Foundation, who received copies of his letter), stood in the patriotic middle, admired by neither the far right nor the far left.[11]

Now Hutchins understood his father's question when he left Chicago for the Ford Foundation: What ever made him think that one board—even one in whose selection he had a voice—would be easier to deal with than another?

But the Fund's basic program was beginning to pick up support from some unexpected quarters. By the spring of 1956 the great Red scare was palpably beginning to fade, its proponents increasingly frustrated by the Fund's continued expansion of its programs and its refusal (at least in public) to be cowed. Former Senator Harry P. Cain, a member of the Sub-versive Activities Control Board, after a discussion with Eisenhower, announced that the president intended "to protect the individual against any unreasonable encroachment on his movements, speech, and mind." The Republican Party—and Ike as its figurehead—had reaped consider-able profit from the witch-hunting, and the president himself had beefed up the loyalty-security programs and had tolerated the defamation of men like General Marshall as Communists or Communist sympathizers. Now, in early July, he nominated the US delegates to the United Nations, includ-ing his friend Paul Hoffman. The enemies of the Fund were enraged. McCarthy, whose star had been sinking since his attack on the army as Communist-infiltrated, told the Senate that an article the Fund's board chairman had written was "either the irresponsible twaddle of a halfwit, or the calculated propagation of the approved Communist Party line." But the liberal majority of the Warren Court had at last swung into action. In one case after another it invalidated state sedition and antisubversive statutes, held that New York could not designate a teacher as disloyal and dismissable solely on the ground that he had invoked the Fifth Amendment before a congressional committee, and (by a six-to-three majority) struck down the application of the Eisenhower security procedures to federal employees in "sensitive" positions. The radical right, in Congress and out, turned its guns on the Court now; billboards appeared, reading IMPEACH EARL WARREN.

Then the fund launched its blockbuster, a one-hundred-twenty-seven-thousand-dollar report, in two large volumes, on the widespread, but hitherto undocumented, practice of blacklisting in industry, with special emphasis on the movies and television. Actors and writers by the hundred had lost their jobs as Reds, no matter how slightly they had deviated from the McCarthyite code of loyalty—or had been alleged to deviate by faceless informants. They had lost their jobs and been denied further employment anywhere in the entertainment world, whose bosses (and whose sponsors in television) were terrified of the kind of popular sentiment that made itself known at the gate. To be reinstated, the blacklist victims had to be "cleared" by hitherto unidentified patriotic experts, including columnists, commentators, advertising executives, and officials of right-wing organizations such as the American Legion's Americanism Commission, as well as by staff members of HUAC (before whom the unemployable penitent could struggle for restoration by confessing and implicating others). The report was a grim and unanswerable indictment of the process by which workers of liberal or radical social views were destroyed. It named celebrated names in the entertainment world, and the publicity attending its publication was enormous. The national commander of the American Legion called the revelations ridiculous and added that Hutchins' mind "seems to be impervious to any understanding of the Communist menace."

The fund's study of blacklisting had been directed by John Cogley, executive editor of the liberal Catholic weekly *Commonweal* and the former editor of *Today*, the national Catholic student magazine. Cogley was as fearless as he was gifted, and when he was subpoenaed by HUAC to be interrogated on the study, he said: "The question is, Should a man be summoned before his elected representatives to defend or explain a book he has written or divulge the confidential sources of his information?"[12] (Hutchins called the subpoena "an unprecedented invasion of thought and expression in the United States.") Under intensive interrogation by the committee, Cogley blandly declined to divulge those sources. Hour after hour on the stand Cogley kept his temper and regretfully refused to answer questions about his associates. He invoked neither the First nor the Fifth Amendment. The hearing went on for six days—and collapsed. The committee did not ask Congress for a contempt citation—a sign of the changing times.

But there was one center of hostility to the fund whose efforts did not abate, and that was the anti-Communist left. Willy-nilly, though they attacked McCarthyism in passing, they augmented it with their own sophisticated anticommunism. Still, the McCarthy right never embraced them, for they, too, for all their present protestations, were, or had been, dangerous radicals themselves. Some of them had been Communists— Whittaker Chambers, among others—and many of them had been Marxists, including their principal spokesman, Professor Sidney Hook, the longtime chairman of the Department of Philosophy at New York University and an equally longtime opponent of Hutchins' educational views. (And an ardent disciple of Hutchins' philosophical opponent, John Dewey.) Most of them had been sympathetic with the original aims of the Russian revolution. Most of them had been vigorous critics of capitalism and the American social order. Their current hatred of communism was understandable; as there is nothing like the fervor of the convert, so there is nothing like the fury of the apostate.

In some sense these were the most formidable of the fund's—and Hutchins'—enemies. They were not yahoo fanatics or low politicians and still lower journalists milking the public hysteria. They were intellectuals in the universities and in arts and letters and were well known. They were in Hutchins' own league. They spoke his language. They included some of his friends and associates in the domestic battles on the social issues, the Socialist leader Norman Thomas, for instance. Their antagonism was much more painful than that of the far right; painful and, in the literary-intellectual elite, more telling. ("When it came to close argument, Hook was unbeatable," said one of the most perceptive of his contemporaries. "He was the most devastating logician the world would ever see. . . humorless, but never petty; obstinate, but not malicious; domineering, but not self-centered.")[13] In their view Hutchins simply did not understand the nature of communism. These opponents on the left, most of them activist veterans of one or another of the 57 varieties of splintered socialism or communism, were nearly all of them philosophical pragmatists and relativist critics of his educational views. They saw him, not as a traitor (as the right did), but as a simpleton. With his Great Books fixation and his supposed denigration of facts in favor of theory, they took it that all he knew about communism he had learned by reading the classical utopians. He probably knew something about Marx's theory of surplus value, but to know Marx and what communism was supposed to be was to know nothing about communism in the middle of the twentieth century. Communism under Stalin was not a mere intellectual, or even a political, heresy. It was a worldwide criminal conspiracy.

"The most notable of [Hutchins'] confusions," said Hook, "is his apparently incorrigible belief that efforts to bar members of the Communist conspiracy from positions of trust in Government and society must necessarily lead to the abandonment of the Bill of Rights.... We are accustomed to the unedifying spectacle of the professional patrioteer who, whenever he is attacked, wraps himself in the flag and denounces his critics for being un-American. It is no more edifying to watch Hutchins, under fire for foolish and extreme statements, wrap himself in the Bill of Rights and, instead of replying to responsible criticism, imply that all his critics are enemies of freedom.... We have to worry about...extremists on the Right.... We have to worry about establishing an intelligent security system.... We have to worry about the growing strength of the Communist world. We have to worry about soapy-minded liberals...about irresponsible exaggerations like those of Hutchins."[14]

The position of Hook and his friends was clear. Participants in the Communist movement, whether or not they were Party members, were not to be granted the constitutional protection afforded other Americans. Such persons—above all, members of the Party—had to be excluded from government and, in particular, from the academic community; and they should be disqualified from functioning as scholars and teachers. The traditional liberal axiom doggedly maintained by Hutchins had to go— the axiom that an individual's competence alone should determine his employability, not his membership in an organization. There was such a thing—which Hutchins rejected—as guilt by association, inasmuch as a person who associated himself directly or indirectly with the Communist conspiracy could be assumed to know what he was doing. Under these desperate circumstances, employment in any position of responsibility or influence, such as a teacher's, had to be denied to a person who invoked the Fifth Amendment. The radical left admitted that communism might not be a danger *to* America—but it was a danger *in* America, with its network of espionage agents, disguised "fronts," and infiltrators of democratic organizations and societies. McCarthyism was guilty of "flagrant injustices"—though its influence was exaggerated by Hutchins—but communism was worse, because it was "masked and insidious."

These anti-Communist leftists were loosely organized, together with a few conservatives, in a group called the American Committee for Cultural Freedom. Like the most rabid of the rightists, the ACCF was given to such antics as labeling organizations Communist fronts without advancing any evidence whatever to support its charges. Like Hutchins *and* the Communists, the radical left had no mass base at all; but its genteel extremism served as a marginal force behind the only people who did have a mass base in the country—the McCarthyites. They were *professors*, whom the congressmen and the columnists could quote. The committee had had a long and unhappy relationship with the Fund, possibly stemming in part from the fund's consistent rejection of its applications for grants. It finally launched an implacable barrage with the publication of the fund-financed bibliography of the Communist problem in the United States, prepared by a committee of highly respected scholars. The project had been authorized before Hutchins became president of the Fund, and the Fund had nothing to do with its contents. Its publication was generally praised, but among its thousands of bibliographical citations there was a handful of serious omissions, including important works by Arthur Koestler, Bertram Wolfe, Max Eastman, Norman Thomas, Joseph Wood Krutch, and Angelica Balabanoff, first secretary of the Communist International—works which were highly critical of the rise of Stalinism and its betrayal of the Communist ideal. The Committee for Cultural Freedom was right on target: the omissions were not only significant in themselves, but they were conceivably suspect as reflecting a bias against anticommunism by the editors. The editors acknowledged "mistakes" and undertook a revision. The public was, of course, uninterested in such an astral controversy; but the right wing, with the Hearst columnists and commentators again at the head of the pack, seized the occasion for another assault. Fulton Lewis, Jr., told his national radio audience that here was one more piece of incontrovertible evidence of Robert Hutchins' blatant opposition to anticommunism. What Hutchins was, was an *anti-anti-Communist*.

42   Is Anybody Listening? (1)

Under relentless pressure from right-wing quarters—official and un-official—the Treasury Department let it be known that it was actively reviewing the Fund for the Republic's tax exemption, to determine whether the statutory requirements were being met. Chairman Francis E. Walter of the House Un-American Activities Committee, announcing a new investigation, said, "We're not going into the Fund for the Republic. We're going into Dr. Hutchins."[1] And several members of Dr. Hutchins' board were articulately unhappy over the fund's having hired a "Fifth Amendment Communist." Board member Griswold refused to accept any further compensation for his service, and finally resigned. Hutchins, according to board member Elmo Roper, came "close" to being removed as president.[2]

It was November of 1955, a year and a half after Hutchins assumed the fund's presidency. It was a bad month. It turned out to be the worst month of his career.

It began with his submitting to an inquisitorial press conference on November 7 with twenty reporters, columnists, and commentators, an outspoken majority of whom were openly hostile. Hutchins made an effort to talk about the fund's work as a whole and its overall support of agencies and institutions engaged in the front-line support of democracy and the democratic faith. His calumniators turned his recital aside and zeroed in on the question that now constituted the basis of every attack on him: Would he hire a Communist? A former Communist? A man who invoked the Fifth Amendment in refusing to tell Congress whether or not he was, or had been, a Communist? The weary interviewee made a cursory stab at answering the bear-baiters: His position had been clear since he stated it a quarter-century before. It seemed to him "stultifying to say that never under any conditions should any Communist be hired for any job." It was unconstitutional to penalize a man for belonging or having belonged, or for refusing to say whether or not he belonged or had belonged, to a legal organization. "It is also unchristian. In the absence of a showing that a man is a conspirator or a spy it seems inhuman to deprive him of a chance to earn a living in a position that he is competent to fill and in which he can do no damage." Dr. Hutchins might have expounded upon this essentially conservative viewpoint with grace and wit; he might have softened his position during the press conference with a fashionable tirade against the Communist conspiracy; he might have alluded to his war record or to the pertinent fact that he had never employed a Communist for any position with which he was connected. But faced with the hostile and suspicious questions shooting out from behind the hot, glaring lights, he was able to repeat only briefly and haltingly his lifelong enmity toward limitations upon independent thought, and contend that under the proper conditions the employment of a Communist was justifiable. What made the news the next day was simply: "I wouldn't hesitate to hire a Communist for a job he was qualified to do provided I was in a position to see he did it."[3] What made headlines the next day was one or another variant, all over the country, in antagonistic, friendly, and neutral newspapers, of HUTCHINS SAYS HIRE REDS. HUTCHINS SAYS HIRE REDS.

All hands—Hutchins included—agreed that the press conference had been a disaster. The historian, Walter Millis, who attended it as a fund consultant, said later, "Bob was just too intellectually arrogant to submit to the pounding they gave him. We all thought...that the whole thing was a dreadful show."[4] His media enemies had discovered his Achilles' heel: He was not, as he himself said afterward, a very good cross-examinee. He was an excellent debater; he could devastate an opponent who played by the same serious rules he did. But he wasn't a street fighter. A man of pride *and* ego (and, by his own account, vanity), he was accustomed to respect—respect for himself and his position and the institution he represented. His academic opponents admired many of his views; none of them considered him a fool or a rogue. But the McCarthyites, in and out of the press, in and out of Congress or the patriotic organizations, had no regard for him or his works or his connections or his status. Whether they were hysterical or villainous or, as in the case of some of the press people, simply on the hunt for a kill, they did not defer to him in the least.

Two weeks later he was subjected to something worse than the press conference. He agreed to face a battery of four interrogators on the nationwide television and radio program, "Meet the Press." For thirty minutes under the kliegs he was subjected to the hammering of openly unfriendly journalists who kept at him with trip-hammer ferocity on the question: Would he hire a Communist? The inquisitors had learned a lesson from the press conference: Keep at him on this one point, and don't let him shift ground and talk either in elegant generalities or in terms of the Fund's actual program and its achievements. As the painful program wore on, the malicious focus of the questions caused him "to bristle with anger and become evasive, cold, and spiritless. Even though a team of public-relations men had coached him before the program"—for the first time in his life—"the insolent character of the interrogation shattered his usual imperturbability and incapacitated his celebrated rhetorical brilliance."[5] His answers were unhelpful. "There are," he said, without amplification, "many gradients of membership in the Communist Party," a point of fact on which he was uninformed (and in which he was uninterested). The members of the panel were familiar with his views on the Fifth Amendment, but they kept quizzing him on them, and he finally said, as uncooperatively as he could, "The Fifth Amendment is part of the Bill of Rights"—the kind of cryptic statement that would have meant more to a university audience, even to a congressional committee, than it possibly could to a nationwide audience on TV and radio.

The recorded script of the show contained many passages like this:

Fredrick Woltman of the New York *World-Telegram and Sun*: Dr. Hutchins, as a matter of fact you said a few weeks ago in New York that you would not hesitate to hire a present member of the Communist Party to work for the Fund, did you not?

Hutchins: The Fund for the Republic is committed to the proposition that Communism...

Woltman: Will you answer the question?

Hutchins: I'm going to. The Fund for the Republic is committed to the proposition that Communism is a menace. The Fund for the Republic is also committed to individual liberty and individual rights. The Fund has condemned boycotting and blacklisting; it has insisted on due process and the equal protection of the laws. It has condemned guilt by association. The principle is that the individual stands on his own merits.

Woltman: Now, would you mind answering the question?

Hutchins: This is a principle that was enunciated very often by the late Senator Robert A. Taft, therefore, what I was simply trying to do when I answered the question to which you refer was to dramatize the proposition that the individual must be judged on his individual merits.

Woltman: Would you also hire a Nazi or a Fascist or a Ku-Klux-Klanner?

Hutchins: This question is a real flying saucer; so was the other one.

Woltman: Well, you didn't answer it.

Hutchins: I beg your pardon, I did.

Woltman: You would also hire a Nazi . . .

Hutchins: No, I didn't say I would.

Woltman: I am sorry, I thought you said you would hire a Communist.

Hutchins: No, I said the great question always is what is the individual in himself. This is the American principle, therefore the question cannot be answered . . .

Woltman: Well, would you still say whether you would knowingly hire a member of the Communist Party?

Hutchins: This question cannot be answered in those terms.

Woltman: You were quoted in many newspapers throughout the country several weeks ago and made no denial.

Hutchins: I saw that.

Woltman: Do you deny you said that?

Hutchins: I do not regard the headlines as an accurate description either of what I said or what I had in mind.

Woltman: And you made no challenge whatsoever of the New York *Times* and the New York *Herald Tribune*, press associations, *World-Telegram and Sun*?

Hutchins: If I were to involve myself in commenting on all newspaper reports, I would have a great deal to do.

Woltman: Well, I heard you say it, for one.[6]

His performance astonished his friends, none of whom had ever before seen him so completely unstrung. Newspaper editor Harry Ashmore, of the Fund's board, saw some University of Chicago colleagues in tears when the broadcast ended. A Fund board member, Roger Lapham, a former mayor of San Francisco, thought that his performance had done their cause more harm than good, and Mrs. Lapham said, "Had I not known you and your very sincere belief in what you feel the Fund for the Republic can accomplish, there would have been no doubt in my mind but that it was a high-sounding name for a Communist front organization." The enemy gloated. Fulton Lewis, Jr., hoped his listeners had tuned in to the program: "It was about as clear a lesson on the subject of Mr. Hutchins and the Fund for the Republic as you would ever find. He proved everything that has been said about him . . . a sort of incredible sort of total suicide, the explosion of a myth about a man."[7]

Hutchins told his friends that before the program he had taken a medication that had affected him—a story that the fund chronicler Thomas C. Reeves says "was met with much skepticism." Perhaps the most dismal item of all—in the light of Hutchins' house motto of the Fund, "Feel Free"—was the refusal of requests for transcripts of the program.

Two weeks later, his aplomb restored, he and Fund consultant Paul Jacobs met with Sidney Hook and a group representing the American Committee for Cultural Freedom, with a view to clarifying their differences. The discussion was hot, but it was not abusive; the atmosphere was reminiscent of a controversial meeting of the University of Chicago Senate. The committee's representatives proved, however, to be interested in the same primitive issue that engrossed the wild men of the press, Congress, and the patriotic societies. Jacobs recounts that "Hook got down to cases by vigorously attacking what he believed to be three incorrect positions held by Hutchins on the Communist question: a refusal to concede that some guilt could be attributed through association; a willingness to employ subversives in government posts; and the employment of Communists in institutions such as the university or the Fund itself. Hutchins defended his view just as vigorously, pointing out that he had always opposed Communism as a system, but that he distinguished between that opposition and a blanket refusal to hire Communists. He pointed out that he believed it necessary to emphasize publicly the necessity of judging each case of a Communist individually because of the possibility, even though it might have been a very limited one, that an individual Communist might be worthy of employment."[8]

It ended (said Jacobs) amiably; but it had got nowhere, both parties holding their ground irreconcilably. The radicals, ex-radicals, Marxists, and ex-Marxists of the ACCF had the weight of disenchanting experience on their side; many of them were specialists in Communist infiltration of professional, cultural, and political activities in New York City, which was unknown territory to Hutchins. He could not begin to gainsay their experience. But in principle—principle was the rub—he was dead right and they (and all his enemies at every level) were dead wrong. The Constitution guaranteed the equal protection of the laws to every American citizen, no matter how obnoxious he or his words or acts might be, even to every convicted American. Hutchins was indeed arrogant, as so lonely an advocate could hardly help being; he stood on the ancient Roman ground, *Fiat justitia, ruat coelum*, "Let justice be done though the heavens fall." His opponents—literate, illiterate, honest, dishonest, sane, mad—disagreed: The American heavens of national security might not be jeopardized for the sake of justice to an individual suspected of conspiring to pull them down. Hutchins: There were adequate statutory procedures for protecting the country against treason and espionage. Hook et al.: Hutchins was ignoring the proven cases of traitors who had successfully circumvented those procedures. Hutchins: A very few cases, in no way justifying throwing the Constitution out the window. Hook: One such case might well be enough to destroy the republic. Hutchins: Let justice be done. . . .

Through the ravaging years of the McCarthyite locust he stood lonelier and lonelier in a public position of power, as perpetrators and exploiters of the Red scare kept their fire turned on him. He was their most eligible target, an egghead throwing tax-exempt millions to the country's enemies. Years afterward it was revealed that the enemy of the country's enemies, J. Edgar Hoover himself, had tried and failed to destroy the profligate egghead. On January 7, 1976, the syndicated Washington columnist Jack Anderson wrote: "The Fund for the Republic conducted a scholarly study of domestic communism, which concluded the FBI was overblowing its importance. This inflamed Hoover, who ordered an all-out investigation of both the Fund and its head, Dr. Robert Maynard Hutchins. The FBI chief directed his subordinates to prepare a monograph ripping Hutchins to pieces. They became so impressed with Hutchins from their research, however, that they produced a mild monograph. Down came instructions to rewrite the piece, making it suitably derogatory, on pain of being censured. The second, more vicious monograph was leaked to the press."

Hoover got no further, but Young Henry was still being heard from. In public response to a public inquiry by Fulton Lewis, Jr., he charged "the fund" with "poor judgment." ("At least," said Hutchins, sotto voce, but loudly enough to reach Young Henry's burning ears, "we didn't invent the Edsel.") Even Paul Hoffman faltered under the frenzy that followed the awful "Meet the Press" broadcast. In a reply to a friend who wrote him after that fiasco, he said: "I share your disappointment that Mr. Hutchins did not give an unqualified 'no' to the question of whether he would employ a communist. If I had been asked that question, I would have so answered. I would have made this reply despite that fact that there are probably some intelligent people who are intellectually committed to communism and who conceivably might be employable. Whether this is what Mr. Hutchins had in mind, I do not know. I do know that he is a *totally* honest person and a purist. There are times that I wish he were a weak-kneed compromiser like myself."⁹

Again and again he told nonresponsive audiences, "I am against Communism," and insisted that the Fund's mission was to fight it by preserving our liberties in the process of exposing the Reds' machinations. The first statement ever made by the board of the Fund read, "The major factor affecting civil liberties today, in our opinion, is the menace of Communism and Communist influence in this country." Far from ever repudiating that statement and asserting his belief that McCarthyism was a greater menace to American liberties than communism, he continued to quote it defensively during the next three years.

But in maintaining that a Communist had every right that every other American had, including the right to be judged as an individual applicant for a job, Robert Maynard Hutchins was more "totally" honest than any similarly situated American of his time, a time of terrible panic sweeping every section of the country and every segment of society to a degree that a generation later, even during the belligerent years of the Reagan 1980s, was an unbelievable bad dream.

By the spring of 1957 the McCarthyite madness was palpably subsiding. In some part it was simply burning itself out, leaving untold wreckage behind it. The tiny US Communist Party, so long hounded and harried, together with its fellow-travelers was pretty well shattered by the Soviet invasion of Hungary and Khrushchev's denunciation of Stalin in 1956. At home a former chairman of HUAC had gone to prison for financial crimes, and its principal paid informer against the Reds had tripped himself up and finally confessed that he had been paid to testify falsely—with Senator McCarthy's knowledge—against 244 persons "charged" with communism before congressional hearings. (He added that he was not the only government informer who had so lied.)[10] The congressional committee had pretty well outworn their road-show welcome around the country and were under attack from many influential quarters, including the Supreme Court. The Court's belated decision in behalf of civil liberties had heartened the lower federal bench in undercutting passport restrictions, loyalty oaths, and denial of free speech; and state courts were following suit and reversing local loyalty-security legislation. After facing up to the charges of the Wisconsin senator, the army had relaxed its own loyalty-security measures to a modest degree. And in May of 1957, Joe McCarthy, long since condemned by a vote of his fellow senators, was dead. (But his soul would go marching on; documentation obtained under the Freedom of Information Act revealed that in the decade 1967–76, 5,145 secret informers had been reporting to the FBI on hundreds of community, political, and social reform groups, and in 1983 the Supreme Court upheld the award of massive damages to Chicago civil-liberties lawyer Elmer Gertz, who had been called a Communist by the patrioteering John Birch Society.)

Mirabile dictu, there were even signs, in the last years of the 1950s, of softening on the part of the anti-Communist left (though twenty years later Sidney Hook would still be demanding withdrawal of tax exemption from the Fund's Center for the Study of Democratic Institutions as "a propaganda center . . . which never publishes anything in the interests of public discussion favorable to American foreign policy.")[11] The "Deweyite" publication *School and Society* published a marveling article, "Robert M. Hutchins—Crusading Metaphysician," in which it asked, "What is one to think when the Progressives' favorite dragon abruptly transforms himself into St. George?" What one was to think, the author said, was, "Dragon he may have seemed, but chameleon he has never been." The progressive educators' most implacable and influential enemy had always fought for the university as an untouchable center of independent thought as the foundation of "the argument against restrictions on freedom, against loyalty oaths, against local and federal interference in the life of the school." His having dared to call down on his head the wrath of the McCarthyites "has evoked the awed admiration of liberals throughout the country. There are numerous friendly voices now being raised on behalf of the liberal arts and in opposition to vocationalism, and the other *bêtes noires* of Dr. Hutchins' apocalypse. . . . It is supremely ironic that a man who has scorned the experiential test for what is important should now be judged important by the consequences of his work in actual life."[12]

Had the three-year fight been worth the candle? Had the Fund for the Republic contributed anything significant to the repulse of McCarthyism? It was hard to say; hard, but not impossible. It had spent more than ten million dollars in those three years, and some three-fourths of its allocations above expenses had been direct grants to secular and sacred agencies engaged in the struggle to preserve and increase the national understanding and acceptance of civil liberties and civil rights. Its grants to church and civic organization in the field of race kept many of those organizations alive in the 1950s and provided the facilities for their expansion on a large scale; the immense financial appropriations to such starveling agencies, coming on the heels of the Supreme Court's school decision in *Brown v. Board of Education*, constituted the single most significant contribution to equality of racial opportunity between the Emancipation and the civil rights legislation of the 1960s.

Beyond the direct allocations of those millions there were the Fund's own publications, the publications it sponsored, and the publications it distributed. These items numbered in the millions of copies over the three years of Hutchins' presidency. The Fund was, apart from the government, by all odds the country's largest noncommercial mailer. It subsidized the distribution not only of its own publications but those of other agencies and institutions that addressed themselves to the Fund's libertarian purposes. The Rossiter team's study of the history of American communism ran to fifteen volumes. (Somebody said, "One volume for each member of the Communist Party.") It was praised more widely than it was prized; commercially it would have been a colossal flop.

Millions of dollars went for the dissemination of literature which the fund's own studies indicated was not widely read. Millions of dollars went into millions of waste baskets. Their materials ignored by much of the periodical press, they were driven to a variety of demeaning stratagems to get a hearing in respectable circles. One of these demeaning stratagems came to light long afterward. In the May 1968 issue of *Harper's*, John Fischer, the magazine's editor, reflected at length on what he called "The Perils of Publishing"; the article was subtitled "How to Tell When You Are Being Corrupted." He reported that advertisers had tried it now and again, authors once in a while, and always pressure groups of one sort or another. The threat was blackmail. The magazine would publish what the blackmailer wanted published, or refrain from publishing what the black-mailer didn't want published—or else the magazine would one way or another be booby-trapped. But "the trickiest booby-trap in the editor's path is the Temptation of Good Causes. His friends, eminent citizens, and his own conscience exhort him without respite to give more of his space (always pitiably limited) to the promotion of some worthy cause. . . . In this heady state of mind he is all too likely to forget that worthy causes seldom make interesting copy—and that a publication which harps on one subject too often is sure to sound like a stuck phonograph record."

Only once in his long experience, Fischer went on, were these seductions accompanied by hard cash. "It was proffered by—of all people—Dr. Robert Hutchins, perennial guardian of the public morality. At the time he was head of the Fund for the Republic, devoted to furthering the ideals of a democratic society. He proposed that the Fund should take over each month a section of *Harper's*—say thirty-two pages—and fill them with articles of its own production. In return it would pay *Harper's* $500,000 the first year, and if the results were satisfactory the arrangement might be continued.

"Did Dr. Hutchins mean that he would like to buy thirty-two pages of advertising space each month? No, no, that wasn't the idea. The space to be filled by the Fund would not be labeled as advertising. In fact, the name of the Fund would not appear at all. The articles it provided would seem to be a normal part of the magazine, so the readers need never know that they had not been developed by the regular editors. The impact, he suggested flatteringly, might be greater that way.

"As I remember it, I assured Dr. Hutchins that I was in favor of both ideals and a democratic society, and probably would agree heartily with the most of the causes he wanted to promote. But, I added, the primary responsibility of all editors was to their readers. In good conscience, therefore, an editor could not surrender control over the editorial content of his publication, even for the best-intentioned of purposes. Neither could he offer the readers somebody else's product under the guise of his own."

What Hutchins had run, during those three years at the Fund, was a cash register, a mail room, and a public relations effort. Into that effort, the lowest of all the low enterprises in his lexicon, had gone a great deal of the extravagant 35 percent of the Fund's outlay devoted to administrative costs. He had been demeaned on every hand, and had demeaned himself, to get a hearing. He had indeed "tried to buy what he couldn't sell," and buy it with cash. He knew better than to go to his friend Fischer at *Harper's* with an indecent proposal, but he did not know how to get publicity any other way; he had never had to know. Publicity had always attached itself to him, and editors had always sought him out, not he them.

He had sacrificed something of himself, something vital, on the altar of the American Bill of Rights: his lifelong independence of public opinion in the practice of his profession. And it showed. It showed in his frantic behavior as he tried, for three unrewarded years, to get the American people to listen to him and to heed his clarion call. It showed in his collapse at the press conference and on the "Meet the Press" program. He had never before failed on the platform; he had always before succeeded. He had never before been humiliated in public; he had always emerged from an encounter a cubit or two taller than he had entered it. The sacrifice showed in his appearance. He face was lined now, in his middle fifties, his hair greying. True, he had said that at the university he had been frustrated and furious; but being frustrated and furious is not as desponding as being rattled and impotent.

The Fund for the Republic was an eminently assailable institution. The university was unassailable. Whoever attacked it—like the Illinois legislators in the Walgreen affair—did so at their peril, not at its. At Chicago he had been in control, he had carried the fight to his opponents. There was image there, in the tower, as there was here in the mud; but the image there reflected a reality that was noble at least in concept and to a considerable extent in practice. In those three years of the Fund Hutchins had made the monumentally depressing discovery that there was a world in which image was the only reality, and the image he "projected" was that of a disdainful, contemptuous man who thought he could get away with being disdainful and contemptuous because he had talked a foolish (and now rueful) billionaire out of some of his money.

Here, in the bull pit, his opponents, not he, determined the conditions of discourse and even the setting. Hectoring, vilifying, slandering at will, they were able to drive him from his command post and force him to fight a battle of movement, a losing battle for a yard of ground in the form of an inch of newspaper space or a minute of prime TV time. They were, on the whole—Joe McCarthy was only the most notorious of them—the most unconscionable of men with an insatiable hunger for preferment, men without so much as a peripheral concern with principle.

Hutchins was no match for these masters who scrupled at nothing. They were impervious to the magnetic man's magnetism. They were a world away from the worlds he had known, the worlds of the parsonage and the Cause at Oberlin, of the rational animal and the liberal arts and the great books at Chicago, of the antiwar speeches in the great university chapel or in the President's House with the radio network people tiptoeing around him. Franklin D. Roosevelt had offered him the posts that would likely have led to the vice-presidency and the presidency, and he had replied flatly (albeit courteously), "I am not interested in public life." For the past three years he had been forced to be interested in nothing else and, what was more, in its cruelest conditions—behind him his cautious worried board, before him the men of a desperate age who seemed bent on demonstrating that men generally may be counted on to be rascals or rabbits.

The fund had contributed some ten million dollars' worth of facts, an encyclopaedia with no discernible pattern or design. "What good are the facts," Hutchins told the *Washington Post*, "if you don't know what to make of them?" The Fund had commissioned exhaustive studies of every aspect of civil liberties and civil rights. Its approach had been confined to presenting the case—the facts—to the public, and stopping there. "We assumed that the state of the public mind was lack of knowledge about the facts, and after the public were only informed about the facts, the state of the public mind would change. We were disturbed, and we thought they would be too." Now he saw this approach as "naive."[13]

Ten million dollars, and it seemed that nobody much had been listening. The Fund for the Republic had invested heavily, not just in money, but in reputation, in the spectacular Cogley report on blacklisting in the entertainment industry. The factual revelations were—or should have been—devastating. But the country generally ignored it, and Hutchins admitted his disappointment at its reception. What had been wrong with it? Nothing, nothing at all; except, as President George N. Shuster of Hunter College said, it had done nothing to solve "the intellectual problems." (Shuster was vice-chairman of the fund's board.) Monsignor Francis J. Lally, another board member, complained that the report had opened upon the real problems without actually coming to grips with them. Looking back at it, John Cogley said, "When we got through, it was very clear that the basic issues simply were not discussed and people such as myself did not know how to discuss them. . . . I think the feeling at the Fund was that enough fire alarms had been answered."[14]

The basic issues. Robert Maynard Hutchins had deplored the grubbing for undigested facts as the curse of university research. Now for three rough-and-tumble years in the mud he had operated a great undigested-fact factory. Here was a badly battered and blackened man who had, apparently, been fighting the right fight in the wrong way. The fund had not been a failure. But it had failed to do what he'd said the new Ford Foundation was going to do: change the temper of the country. It had been yet another straw for a man to grasp.

On May 16, 1956, the board of the fund received a sort of distant early warning in the form of an eleven-page memorandum from President Hutchins—its length was itself premonitory—proposing that a committee be established "to advise the Board of Directors on the desirability, feasibility, program, organization, financing, location, and personnel of an institute or council for the study of the theory and practice of freedom." The new body should have a five-year existence and be authorized to spend no less than a million dollars and no more than the five million or so remaining of the fifteen-million terminal grant from the Ford Foundation. The present program of the Fund had been "on the whole" successful and in some form should be continued. But it was clear (he went on) that very little had been done "to relate one study to another or to relate any studies to the clarification of important ideas." A succession of "commentaries on current events" had been produced, which were not very significant.

What was wanted, he suggested, was what he had long crusaded for in the higher learning: the integration of thought on the most serious of social subjects, with the kind of material the fund had thus far assembled to serve as illustration and confirmation. What was wanted was an institute or council "to promote coherence and intelligibility in the program of the Fund, to relate every study to every other, to be sure that efforts in public education were enlightening rather than confusing, to enable the Board to function with confidence even though it could not afford the time for protracted philosophical discussion, to permit the Officers to proceed with confidence in the absence of clear agreement on fundamental principles in the Board, to give the studies sponsored by the Fund permanence and universality, to develop a basis of common conviction in the West, and to show a pluralistic society how it can reach unanimous devotion to justice and freedom."

It was a large order, its unaccustomed prolixity indicating that its author had simply sat himself down and written it. But what it proposed was readily recognizable: an ascent from the mud to the tower. Robert Maynard Hutchins wanted to convert the Fund for the Republic from a badly buffeted agency engaged in the dissemination of money and unevaluated raw materials in the great field of freedom, into something resembling the institution he had spent the most productive years of his life trying to achieve at Chicago: a center for the clarification of principles (including "first principles") and the coordination of human knowledge with the transcendent aim of breaking the barrier of man's thinking. What he wanted might have been said to be a think tank, or, if you will, a university.

Part Nine

THE WESTERN SLOPE

43   Basic Issues

Hutchins was not only battered and blackened; he was bored—bored with ladling out facts and money. Fighting McCarthy and McCarthyism had been exciting—too exciting sometimes—and all hands agreed that the expenditure of some ten million dollars to demolish the Wisconsin senator and his allies had been an exemplary contribution to the general welfare. But it, too, in its own tawdry way, had been a bore. There had always been McCarthys to tear the country to pieces. There always would be (and the next one, or the one after that, might not make the senator's fatal mistake of attacking the army). The cure of McCarthyism on something more than an ad hoc basis was to discover its causes in a democratic society and see if anything could be done about them. That was something that neither the Fund for the Republic nor any other institution had tried to do.

The "institute or council" Hutchins proposed to the Fund's board in 1956 he came to call, as discussion proceeded, the Institute for the Study of the Theory and Practice of Freedom. In his long memorandum to his board he said that "the Institute would be something like a university, except that it would be limited to the study of freedom, it would do no classroom teaching, it would not confer degrees, and it would not require them of its members. They would do some research, but they would be primarily involved in seminars, conferences, discussions, and debates."[1] In other words, it would *not* be something like a university. But neither would it duplicate the Institute of Advanced Studies at Princeton, or All Souls College at Oxford, or the Ford-financed Center for the Behavioral Sciences at Palo Alto (headed by Hutchins' old friend and former Chicago dean, Ralph Tyler). These were places where scholars pursued their individual interests, free from the demands of their colleagues or students. The Hutchins conception was exactly the opposite. At Hutchins' institute "the greatest minds of our time in all fields . . . would be committed to devote part of their time to work on a common problem. . . . The essence of the enterprise would be intellectual cooperation."[2]

He had once defined a university as a community of scholars. This (he said now) was an exaggeration; he was talking about a *true* university, and on that definition there was not a true university in America—or anywhere else. Professors were isolated workers, unacquainted outside their departments and often unacquainted within them. The "corporate intellectual purpose" of the Hutchins institute would command the cooperation of every man or woman who worked under its auspices.

One approach to the work of the institute might be to ask "whether the Bill of Rights meets the needs of the citizens of a huge, industrial, Twentieth Century democracy as well as it served those of the citizens of thirteen small agricultural states one hundred sixty-five years ago." How did the Constitution apply to institutions and situations that the fathers could not have imagined? Jefferson said that there were four reasons why the American republic was going to succeed. First, we weren't going to live in cities. Second, we were all going to be self-employed. Third, we were all going to participate in local government. And fourth, we were all going to be so well educated that we could cope with any problems that confronted us. "Jefferson's ideals are valid. But how do they maintain their vitality when the facts to which they were applied have been entirely altered? We hide behind a cliché curtain, a veil of slogans and illusions that separate us from reality. We go right on talking as though we were still in the Eighteenth Century. But the facts are quite different."[3] The political party system, the corporation, the mass media, the church-state relationship, the trade union, the welfare state, war and militarism, technology, world organization—none of these institutions in their present form was known at the time the Constitution was adopted.

There were thousands of individual thinkers—not all of them in universities—who were grappling with one or another of the questions raised by one or another of the new institutions and conditions, but they were working solitarily. For twenty years Hutchins had tried in vain to transform the University of Chicago into a scholarly community. He had dreamed of creating something like a world university ever since, at the end of the 1930s, he realized that he would never be able to establish one at Chicago. The dream had certain constants: it would be composed of polymaths, men and women who were able to function in a variety of fields—humanistic scientists, mathematical philosophers. They would agree, at the outset of their joint labors, on what they considered the most important social problems confronting the world, on the basic issues, and would pursue their investigation of those issues together. At least several months a year, they would have no diversionary activities or interests. And they would undertake their investigations on a lifelong basis.

This democrat of democrats was in the final analysis a genuine elitist who wanted to establish a kind of Lords Spiritual to lead the country and the world out of the intellectual wilderness. They would not govern. They would not make political decisions. They would not be concerned with popular acceptance. They would, in due season, clarify the great problems of the race in interrelated terms and democratically (and lordlily) submit their clarification to their fellow men. Hutchins had known a few such polymaths—there were not many—and had succeeded in having a few at Chicago from time to time, men like Scott Buchanan, Leo Szilard, Jacques Maritain. But he knew of other such rare birds, in America and in Europe. Now he wanted to round them up and sound them out.

The spring of 1953 was the time to do it. Still an associate director of the Ford Foundation, he had succeeded in getting the foundation to establish the Fund for the Republic (in New York, where the foundation itself was now located) and he was sitting it out alone in Pasadena, his Ford days numbered. (Paul Hoffman had already gone.) During the preceding year and a half he had occasionally spoken to his Ford colleagues about his idea, but they had not encouraged him to pursue it. So, still with foundation money to meet his expenses, he invited a group of leading American scholars and nonscholars to meet with him in Princeton and a group of eminent Europeans to meet with him in London. The Princeton gathering included Etienne Gilson, Charles Malik, Jacques Maritain, Robert Oppenheimer, Paul Tillich, Owen J. Roberts, Paul Mellon, Walter Lippmann, and Barry Bingham. The European personnel of the London conference was even more stellar; it included Isaiah Berlin, Niels Bohr, Werner Heisenberg, Sir Arthur Keith, Sir Richard Livingstone, José Ortega y Gasset, Michael Polanyi, and R. H. Tawney.

Satisfied that the Ford Foundation would not be interested, Hutchins had turned to his multimillionaire friend and associate Bill Benton, with a long memorandum that ended, "This is an attempt to start an effort unparalleled and unprecedented in the contemporary world. It is important to proceed slowly and tentatively, free from pressure for 'results.' For an institution that might revitalize education, the universities, research, and the effort to solve the most important practical problems of our time, I think $10,000,000 over ten years is not excessive."[4]

The idea of an Academy—as he now called it, with Plato's classic circle in mind, "an Athens for our time"—developed because of "the widespread concern about the disintegration of the intellectual world, which results from specialism, nationalism, and philosophical diversity." The universities used to set the intellectual tone of the world and clarify the concepts on which civilization was based. This was done by discussion among people who understood each other. The present-day university is "a collection of non-communicating specialists who do not understand the implication of what they are doing." What was needed was "some group or institution that can try to do for our own time what the universities used to do: to formulate, state, clarify, and advance the ideas that underlie or should underlie our civilization. This is not being done anywhere by anybody now."

The way to begin, he told Benton, was to bring together "a relatively small group of senior men...have them decide on the problem with which they want to start, assign writing jobs to each of them, and circulate the results among them." They would then meet to collate and clarify their thinking and repeat the process until they were satisfied that maximum agreement and clarity had been achieved. The results would then be published. At this stage they would have been required to spend no less than one-fourth of their time in the work, with research and clerical assistance. Their meetings might last a month or more, but they would not be required to give up their present posts or move to a common center. Ultimately, however, "we should decide which members we want to join a residential group. I think that they should be together for at least six months of the year. I am certain that face-to-face discussion is necessary for complete understanding and real progress." The Academy should be in close touch with individuals and groups, inside and outside the universities, that were working in the same direction.[5]

Asking Benton for a million dollars a year for ten years, he was strangely cryptic in his report of the Princeton and London conferences. In addition to listing the names of the conferees he said only, "The conferences endorsed the idea of the Academy." Nowhere did he indicate what the conferees thought in detail or, what was much more important, how the great men reacted to the possibility that they might be invited to join his academy. Many years afterward he told a friend, "I think I might have got half of them." This additional cryptic assertion was not very convincing, but it was never put to the test because Bill Benton showed no more interest in putting up the ten million dollars than the new officers of the Ford Foundation did.

Might he have got half, or one-fourth of the famous conferees? They were all middle-aged or older. They all held positions of lifetime renown and security. They had no great interest in moving themselves and their families to another country or even to another town. Hutchins said that the Academy could be located "anywhere in the world." But the long-term interests and close associations of the prospective Academicians were where they lived, or nearby. They took trips to meetings and conferences—but not for a month at a time. And they certainly had no notion of ultimately being together in a residential center at least six months of the year. No doubt they endorsed the idea of the Academy —without actually indicating whether they might be available for membership.

There was something else fatally wrong with the proposal he put before the great men of America and Europe. And that something else, which was central to the proposal, would plague his Center for the Study of Democratic Institutions years afterward. The heart of the Academy (and later of the center) was to be its cooperative character. Its members would work together to produce common—not, in the end, individual—findings and documents. This was something that in all probability none of them had ever done or contemplated doing—or, just as likely, even believed possible. They did not think of thinking as an orchestral affair, nor did they readily think of great results in any field that had been achieved by a group of men and women. Seminal thinking throughout history had been done by solitary individuals, even when—the Declaration of Independence, for instance—it bore several signatures. In the sciences there had been occasional, if only occasional, triumphs of collaboration between two individuals, men, but not in the arts or the humanities, least of all in philosophy. And what Hutchins was talking about was essentially political philosophy.

As an educator he had touted what he called the civilization of the dialogue and deplored the lecture method of the universities and the isolated conditions under which scholars did their work. He was an ardent interdisciplinarian. But nearly all of his conferees in Princeton and London had made their mark in solitary thought. They weren't team members, and their committee memberships were incidental to their individual preoccupations. Many of them shared Hutchins' enthusiasm for dialogue as an instrument of education through to the bachelor's degree, and for its continuance, as their work permitted, beyond that. But it simply wasn't likely that in midcareer men of their sort would respond to an invitation to do "some research, but be primarily involved in seminars, conferences, discussions, and debates." Whether or not they were active as university professors, they were nearly all of them intellectual loners. Hutchins had a penchant and a talent for assembling eminent thinkers for ad hoc endeavors like the Freedom of the Press Commission and the Committee to Frame a World Constitution. But the Academy was no ad hoc affair.

Some of the members of his board were interested in his basic-issues proposal, even to the point of eventually accepting it, in one form or another, as "a major effort" for the rest of the life of the Fund. Some were willing—and a few were more than willing—to see the Fund shift its focus to what would certainly be a less controversial level than the one on which it had been operating. And some objected to change in the Fund's direction. Clearly what Hutchins had in mind was the curtailment, or even the termination, of its grants to secular and religious agencies for civil liberties and civil rights work, grants that had averaged a total of some $750,000 a year. In the course of board discussions following his proposal, Hutchins suggested cancellation of unexpended appropriations and a series of terminal grants that would leave the Fund with, he thought, as much as seven million dollars to undertake the new program.

The board required many months of persuasion to accept the basic-issues proposal, shorn of the institute or Academy aspects. Its members understood philanthropy, and their experience with the fund had instructed them on the struggle for civil liberties and civil rights. But basic issues? "Perhaps I'm not educated enough to deal in the abstract along the lines Bob seems to enjoy," board member Roger Lapham wrote to Paul Hoffman. "When I consider this proposal to study the theory and practice of freedom I'm reminded of what I believe Thomas Huxley said about philosophy: 'Philosophy is a hunt in a dark room of an empty house at midnight for a black cat that isn't there.'"[6] In the ensuing months Hutchins pushed his proposal relentlessly, while the board hung back. Some members thought it might be tried on a one-year basis; rather than doing that, Hutchins said he'd prefer not to try it at all. But the board dug in its heels, and a disappointed Hutchins accepted its decision in May of 1957 to "concentrate" on the basic issues for a period of a year.

The new direction alienated board members who had previously disagreed with Hutchins, to the point that five of them resigned within a year or so of its announcement, leaving only eight of the original fifteen members of a board that now numbered twenty. Two of the fund's five officers quit—the vice-president and treasurer, David F. Freeman, and the secretary, Adam Yarmolinsky. They felt that the new approach would mean abandonment of the many worthwhile projects the Fund had sustained in the past and that it was contrary to good foundation procedure and competitive with, perhaps a duplication of, academic work. They wanted the money spent and the Fund disbanded within five years—something Hutchins had no intention of doing. They had gone directly to the board with their complaint, and Yarmolinsky said later: "We were not challenging his authority, but Hutchins was outraged by what he considered insubordination." (Hutchins told Vice-president Frank Kelly that the officers should have brought their complaints to him, not to the board.)[7]

He forged ahead undaunted. With a minuscule financial allocation by the board, he appointed another of his blue-ribbon committees as consultants on the basic issues program. They were A. A. Berle, professor of corporation law at Columbia University; Scott Buchanan, former dean of St. John's College at Annapolis; political scientist Eugene Burdick of the University of California; Eric Goldman, professor of history at Princeton; labor expert Clark Kerr, chancellor of the University of California; Henry R. Luce, editor and publisher of *Time*, *Life*, and *Fortune*; theologian John Courtney Murray, SJ, of Woodstock College in Maryland; President Reinhold Niebuhr of Union Theological Seminary; Isador Rabi, Nobel Prize–winning physicist and chairman of the General Advisory Committee of the Atomic Energy Commission; and anthropologist Robert Redfield of the University of Chicago. On their behalf Hutchins presented to the May 1957 meeting of his board a list of six study projects in the field of freedom. The first and second of them were approved, with an allocation of funds: one on the corporation, with an introductory paper by Berle; and one on the relation of individual liberty and the common defense, with an introduction by military historian Walter Millis. The third project, "The Individual and the Trade Union," raised questions on individual rights in collective bargaining, national strikes affecting the public interest, and community-union clashes. A fourth, "Religious Institutions in a Democratic Society," considered organized religious pressure groups, the question of released classroom time for religion in the public schools, and the influence of ecclesiastical directives on legislators and voting blocs. The fifth and sixth projects dealt with censorship problems arising from mass communications media and voluntary pressure-group associations and their importance to individual livelihoods. By the end of the year the board, with considerable deliberation and no little grumbling, had accepted and funded (at $100,000 apiece) all six of the consultants' projects.

"The purpose of the enterprise," Hutchins told them, "is to determine the essential requirements of a free society in the contemporary world. . . . It would be pretentious to suppose that a group many times as intelligent as this, with many times the money that the Fund has left, could solve the problem of how to maintain a free society in an industrialized, polarized world. . . . But it should be possible to straighten out the issues, to show what the questions are, and to offer some preliminary answers that might be debated in the country."[8]

With the assistance of the consultants, advisory committees of distinguished academics and nonacademics were invited (and paid) to cooperate in the six projects. The members of the fund's staff were assigned to serve as liaison persons for each study. In the course of the following year the fund's other programs and philanthropies were wound down, and a battery of papers was prepared and disseminated on each project for discussion in schools, colleges, and adult education groups. Several large commercial institutions, among them the General Electric Company, included the papers in their executive training programs. Altogether a total of eighty publications with a distribution of two million copies came out of the basic-issues program between 1957 and 1959.

Congressman Walter of the House Un-American Activities Committee, the American Legion, and Fulton Lewis, Jr., were still demanding that the Treasury Department revoke the fund's tax exemption on the ground that it was a propaganda and not an educational agency; but the secretary of the treasury gave Board Chairman Hoffman "grave assurances that he had no intention of embarrassing in any way the Fund's distinguished board."[9] Public reception of the basic-issues program was overwhelmingly favorable. "The Fund," said the *New York Times* editorially, "has been spending its money by and large in some exceedingly useful directions despite ill-informed and often irresponsible criticism that has been directed against it. In so doing, the Fund has helped strengthen American democracy, and the new study . . . gives every indication of being a major contribution to this end."[10]

At the May 1958 meeting of the board, Hutchins reported: "I think we are now entitled to say that the program, in spite of imperfections and uncertainties in it, is soundly conceived and will be successfully carried out. Even if it succeeds beyond our hopes, it will not solve all the problems—or even clarify all the issues—that plague our society. But it is already an important educational force, and there is every sign that it will continue to be so. I therefore suggest that the board make a three-year commitment to it."[11] He urged the directors to commit the Fund's remaining assets to the new program. They finally yielded after getting his reassurance that they would have the power to approve "purposes, projects, and personnel." The vote was unanimous to use four million dollars to finance the basic issues program for three years, with the remaining one million dollars to be used for other projects.

One of the imperfections and uncertainties of the new program was the work of the ten consultants. Three or four of them were seriously ill at one time or another. Robert Redfield, the Chicago dean and Hutchins confidant, died in October of 1958. Luce was rarely available, and Kerr became president of the University of California. One of the consultants resigned in disagreement with his colleagues. (Hutchins persuaded his old friend Justice William O. Douglas to join the group, but Douglas attended only one meeting.) Meetings were supposed to be weekends at six-week intervals, but they were sometimes canceled because of the inability of members to attend. Altogether the consultants met twelve times for a total of thirty days. "Their conversations, bound in blue, were placed in storage," wrote Fund historian Thomas C. Reeves.[12] Mortimer Adler read the transcript of one session and wrote Hutchins, "Collectively, the result is almost zero. There is almost no evidence that any member of the group learned anything from anything said by anyone else."[13] Hutchins replied, "I don't say that they will do better. I say only that their inadequacy in the past does not prove that they will be inadequate in the future."

But they were. Attendance at their meetings fell to as low as five, and the discussion was habitually inconsequential, as Adler suggested. Scott Buchanan confessed to "a kind of despair for the Consultants and their projects."[14] Hutchins insisted that there had been the "gradual clarification of some basic issues," but nobody agreed with him. Finally he was forced to report to the board, in the spring of 1959, that "on the basis of our experience it is clear that though part-time men can be effective critics they can not be relied upon to develop and guide a program in this vast and complicated field. They are under too many different pressures. The more famous they are, the greater the pressures."[15]

The famous consultants did not actually disband; they faded away as a formal body—and with them the advisory committees and six basic-issues projects, though perceptive papers were produced on one or another of the projects during the life of the consultants, several of whom continued (on and off) their association with the Fund in its next incarnation as the Center for the Study of Democratic Institutions. The unhappy history of the Consultants—with a capital C—paralleled Hutchins' many efforts to draw upon men and women (usually men) of nationwide or worldwide eminence to serve on working committees—or, more precisely, to lend their names to them and attend occasional meetings. It was something he himself had been scrupulous never to do; he never joined a committee he had no time for.

He had never given over the idea of the resident Academy he had urged on Benton five years before. He "made it clear to me and the other officers," Frank Kelly said later, "that he still had in his mind the idea of establishing a center where the Consultants—or others of their caliber— could give their whole time to the program for the years ahead. With the board's support, he hoped that such a center could be formed on a lasting basis. He hoped that the center would be located in Santa Barbara." He canceled the June 1958 meeting of the consultants and asked them instead to participate in a five-day meeting at the end of July—in Santa Barbara. "Santa Barbara," he wrote them, "is beautiful in the summer." "The principal results," said Kelly, "seemed to be enthusiasm for the beauty of Santa Barbara and encouragement for Hutchins to establish the Fund's headquarters there."

In 1954 the Hutchinses had had to move to New York when he took over the presidency of the Fund for the Republic. He didn't like New York (or Chicago) and never had. They took a spacious apartment in Manhattan. When the apartment was burglarized, they moved to a no less spacious house in Darien, Connecticut. But he didn't like being a commuter, either. The Fund occupied a—spacious—penthouse on the fifty-fifth floor of a midtown building, and he didn't like that. It was suitable as the headquarters of a philanthropic agency, much less so for a contemplative organization committed to the study of the basic issues in the field of freedom.

The Fund's board was to meet May 20, 1959, and the members received a memorandum from Hutchins two weeks before the meeting. After informing them that 1,200,000 copies of fifty-four Fund publications (including kinescopes and audiotapes) had already been distributed in the basic-issues program, he said, "Apparently many people have become aware of the crisis through which democratic institutions are passing and hope that some sustained attempt can be made to promote understanding of it. The Fund is the only organization dedicated to this task." Then, as if incidentally, he added, "We should look forward to a residential center, composed of men who will devote their whole time to the program for considerable periods. Men who are interested and qualified, but who can not look upon their connection with the program as a primary obligation, should be regarded as critics and should not be expected to initiate or direct the work. Some of the consultants could devote themselves to the program, others couldn't: If the Board does not object, I propose to effect a differentiation in the roles of the two groups.

"The full-time group should move out of New York City at the earliest opportunity. Our lease expires next April and could not be renewed at any price. I think that well before that date we should establish a residential center elsewhere."[16] It was clear to most of his board members that by "elsewhere" he meant Santa Barbara. He had bought twenty-six acres in the hills above the plush suburb of Montecito there, with a small house. He intended to build a home to spend the rest of his life in.

Surprisingly, perhaps, given his Calvinist antecedents, he wanted to be a Californian. And when he became one he became a Californian for fair, in a Hawaiian sports shirt driving a Thunderbird. And by the spring of 1959 he was sure of getting what he wanted from a board pruned of its dissenters and completed now with lukewarm to ardent admirers. He did not have to threaten to resign in order to get his way. He got his way by unanimous vote.

Wealthy Los Angeles friends were willing to put up $100,000 to transport the Fund's staff west and provide severance pay for those few employees who were unwilling to leave New York. And a Santa Barbaran of his acquaintance knew of a forty-two acre estate looking over the city, that would be available for $250,000. Board member William Joyce of Santa Barbara thought it was a first-class investment. So did the eccentric—that is, radical—multimillionaire Cyrus Eaton of Cleveland (who offered to buy it and let the Fund use it). The board voted unanimously to purchase it and agreed to call it the Center for the Study of Democratic Institutions, serving as the actual working arm of the Fund for the Republic.

That was the spring of 1959. Less than a year earlier the Fund had announced its probable demise in 1961, in the hope of attracting foundation support. There was now about four million dollars left. Hutchins told the board meeting that voted for Santa Barbara, "At the present rate of income and expenditure the money the Fund has will last about three years more. It is unlikely that the need for the work the Fund is doing will have disappeared by 1963. Nor is it probable that some other agency will take over the Fund's responsibilities if it goes out of business. I suggest that the Board begin to plan now to obtain funds to maintain a Center for the Study of Democratic Institutions for an indefinite period."[17]

Plan now to obtain funds . . . for an indefinite period. In just this offhandedly grand manner—typically Hutchins—he made it clear that the Fund for the Republic was to become the Center in Santa Barbara and occupy him the rest of his life. His board didn't balk. It didn't even blink. It was he who should have blinked, and perhaps, balked. The board of the Fund was not a money-raising board. It was a money-spending board, or rather, a money-allocating adjunct of a money-spending president. Now, at sixty, Hutchins was taking on the administration of a new project and resuming the oratorical task. Ever since Yale he'd wanted—or thought he wanted—to do some serious and sustained thinking. He thought that at last he was going to. Calm Santa Barbara was just the place to do it. True, the new Center was a heady challenge, but it was a small operation and after a while would pretty much take care of itself.

He was wrong, of course. He would spend the next nineteen years—the rest of his life—doing what he had always found himself doing: raising money and administering, or trying to; with middling, and diminishing, success.

44   El Parthenon

In a time Apocalyptic
On the mountain Eucalyptic
Full of thought Acropolyptic
Stands the Hutchins Hutch.

In this intellectual Attic
Institutions Democratic
Are studied by the Mode Socratic
With the Midas Touch.
—Kenneth Boulding

Said an associate of the business-and-industry-connected Stanford Research Institute: "Don't call us a think tank—we've got more to do than
think. We produce. I'll tell you what a think tank is—it's that place down
in Santa Barbara. Those guys are paid to think. That's all they have to do:
think." The thinking was done in an expensively remodeled (and, of
course, spacious) mansion of Greco-Hispanic pretensions—Hutchins
called it El Parthenon—atop a hill on the edge of Santa Barbara's suburb
of Montecito. The old one-storied structure stood pompously at the vista
end of a long curving driveway. Inside the great front doors was a great
marbled lobby. Offices ran down the sides. Across the back of the building
was the great conference room overlooking the rear terrace above the
gigantic swimming pool, and the city of Santa Barbara, and the ocean in
the distance. The conference room, the heart of the operation, the reason
for the Center's being, the scene of a thousand dialogues, was dominated
by the great rectangle of baize-covered tables laden with microphones connected to a soundproof recording studio.

Everything, including the intentions, was great. Of the many hyperboles that came cascading down Eucalyptus Hill from the Center, perhaps the most hyperbolic was Fellow Harvey Wheeler's regarding the conference table: "It seems," he wrote, "to have led me to visualize the Center dialogue as a vast, immortal, computerized memory bank—a kind of contemporary electronic variant of the ancient notion of the logos (speech, word, reason). In my imagination I pictured our private electronic logos as hovering unseen about twenty feet above our conference table, a 'brooding omnipresence,' so to speak."[1]

Hutchins' dry-land luxury liner was berthed about as far from madding midtown Manhattan as it was possible to get. Santa Barbara, California, had long been the destination of New Yorkers and their eastern likes who wanted to retire away from it all, for good and all, in the decades that preceded Palm Springs. It was quiet, conservative Republican California, a begonia-bursting bastion, in the 1950s, of the John Birch Society. The influential publisher of the local newspaper, Tom M. Storke, for all his conservatism, saw the advent of the Center as a cultural blessing for the town. But it was remote from the areas of the country where the great public decisions were made, remote even from Los Angeles, ninety miles to the south. Its location mystified easterners who said, not "What are they doing there?" but "What are they doing *out there?*" The weather was ideal; the climate wasn't. It was far from being a satisfactory locale from which to try to influence opinion in high or far places. It was a far jaunt for most of the eminences invited to participate in the Center's programs; their bases were two to three thousand miles eastward, or in Europe.

Having failed to get a commitment from any of the great men he sought as permanent residents, Hutchins settled for bringing out with him the principal members of the fund's New York staff and installing them as Fellows of the Center. In theory they were to serve as research factotums for the likes of the capital-C Consultants, but the Consultants gradually fell away, some of them appearing at the Center for an occasional discussion or presentation of a paper, and some of them not at all. Their chairs were filled, in the main, by the New York Fellows, who were primarily journalists, publicists, and junior administrators and whose work had been so effective in the crusading-cum-philanthropic programs of the Fund for the Republic. They were none of them possessed of scholarly distinction, none of them original thinkers. Publicist "Ping" Ferry, demurring at coming along, said flatly, "I don't have a first-rate mind"—but in the end he came along as one of the Center's two vice-presidents.[2] The other was a former war correspondent and speechwriter for President Truman, Frank K. Kelly. Subsequently brought on as a vice-president (and, for a period, president) was Harry Ashmore, editor of the Pulitzer Prize–winning Little Rock, Arkansas, *Gazette* and a front fighter in the struggle for civil rights in the South. Hallock Hoffman (son of Paul) served as coordinator of studies, having previously managed a regional office of the American Friends Service Committee in Pasadena. John Cogley had been religious editor of the *New York Times* before coming to the fund and the Center. Overseeing Center dialogues, and ultimately editing the *Center Magazine*, was Donald McDonald, who left the journalism deanship at Marquette University. Director of development, John L. Perry, was a Florida newspaper reporter who had been deputy to a Commerce Department undersecretary. And Edward Reed, director of Center publications, had been editor of *Theatre Arts* magazine.

Hutchins' selection of these men and their likes set the day-to-day pattern of center discussions in the absence of the great men, who came out on special occasions. The center never recovered from the wholesale importation of the team, or troupe, from the east. They were, to be sure, articulate; whatever else it did, the dialogue didn't sag. But neither did it leap to the heights, nor plumb the depths, that Hutchins either anticipated or somehow hoped it would. Over the next ten years there were a few academics who became attached as Fellows: Wheeler, a political scientist; Rexford Guy Tugwell, the one-time Chicago economist and Roosevelt Brain Truster; John Wilkinson and William Gorman, young philosophers; Stanley Sheinbaum, a young economist; sociologist John Seeley; none of them, however, of the caliber that Hutchins had originally tried to get. An ailing Scott Buchanan—who was of that caliber—came out for a few years preceding his death, as did his St. John's associate, historian Stringfellow Barr. Another of the Fellows was Elizabeth Mann Borgese, nonacademic daughter of Thomas Mann and widow of Hutchins' old associate, G.A. Borgese. Nobel Prize–winning chemist and peace activist Linus Pauling and the controversial Episcopal bishop James A. Pike accepted fellowships but were more often than not away.

The dialogue, Hutchins maintained, was the reason for the Center and its end product. This pedagogic procedure had been a successful technique in the undergraduate program at Chicago with Adler, and a popular alternative to the lecture method. It had considerable vogue around the country with self-selected adults. But it had not been tried, in modern times, with a group of supposedly sophisticated intellectual peers. As a teaching device it defied very close inspection. It was, at best, a roundabout way of getting at the truth. At worst, it was a kind of fencing match in which reasoning was attenuated to the point of fatuity.

Dialogue is likely as not to be a verbal ramble—one of its friends called the Center the La Scala of the bull session—or a more or less serious gamesmanship enterprise in doing down an opponent. As an earnest inquiry into a serious problem, a cooperative search, it is better suited to learning than to teaching. The participants in the Center discussions were supposed to be learners, but the Center itself was trying to reach the public with its transcripts, tapes, and publications and persuade the public to consider basic issues—that is, it was trying to teach by example. Good dialogue is, however, by definition inconclusive. "The questions that can be answered are not worth asking," said Scott Buchanan. The dialogue at the Center was intended to clarify problems, not present solutions; so its general appeal was limited, its output unsatisfying to the great audience, which would rather be taught (or told) than participate in the pain of trying to advance knowledge.

Over the years the Center achieved a respectable degree of popularity among professional intellectuals—the *Center Magazine*, established in 1967, reached a circulation, at its peak, of 100,000, nearly all of it in the colleges and universities—but it never reached the general public. Whatever general influence it may have had was indirect and immeasurable. Neither, of course, do the lucubrations of a university have an audience outside the academic world; but a university, unlike the Center, has no such explicit purpose as the Center's to bring its work to the public at large.

The dialogue in Santa Barbara was further handicapped by the disposition of its moderator. Sitting at the head of the conference table Hutchins would light and relight one of his pipes and then settle for a cigarette, on the whole maintaining a seemingly attentive silence. He never directed the discussion beyond recording the names of those who indicated a desire to talk and then calling on them in succession. He rarely contributed to the conversation, beyond occasionally asking a question that suggested that he was following it closely. And he was following it closely, or closely enough, in the way he followed all conversations while his mind was elsewhere. He did not pursue the answers to the occasional questions he asked. He was unfailingly polite, too polite to indicate that he was bored; but after several years of the Center he told a friend one day, "We have had two hundred visiting speakers this past year, and I don't want to have to listen to any of them again."

The visiting speakers or conferees were mostly academics who had a paper they wanted to read—or a paper plus an inclination to get out of the winter weather of the north (or just the inclination). They were mostly proposed by a friend or ex-colleague at the Center; the Fellows had an almost unfailing tendency to go along with one another's recommendations. This practice itself was enough to demoralize Hutchins' vision of the dialogue. Instead of having some sort of discernible organization, the program was a miscellany and, as such, an open invitation to visitors and residents alike to bring to the table any topic they chose and to digress freely during the course of a given discussion, which sometimes sank, unchecked by Hutchins, to nitpicking and bickering far from the subject at hand. For all its flow of papers read by visitors and residents, the work of the Center had no coherence.

Hutchins called the Fellows to the conference table by ringing an old school bell three or four mornings a week—occasionally five—at 11 A.M. The twenty to twenty-five persons assembled as often as not included whoever happened to be on the premises, invited or uninvited. Staff members, local and visiting financial contributors, guests, and friends of guests might take chairs at the table instead of along the wall at the back. Having instituted the fund-raising category of Founding Members, at a thousand dollars a year apiece, Hutchins was helpless, and his colleagues knew it, to move such members away from the table or exclude them from the discussion; or, if not helpless, too polite; or, if not too polite, too downhearted.

The photocopying facilities in the converted garage on the grounds never stopped running. A paper to be discussed was distributed in advance, to be studied before the school bell rang. The author of the paper—resident or invited visitor—presented a short précis of it, which sometimes turned out to be a very long précis. Then the meeting was opened for discussion. Sometimes the author was quizzed, and sometimes in the course of his elucidation a meaningful exchange ensued. But often the discussion went off on its own around the table. At 12:30 Hutchins adjourned the meeting for lunch, and usually for the rest of the day. Fellows, staff, and visitors partook of a generally tasty $1.50 buffet lunch, with wine, and small groups ate on the terrace outside the conference room or at the table. Hutchins rarely missed a conference-table meeting, but he was often in town having lunch at the Biltmore with a prospective supporter. "Out there" he traveled less frequently than he had at Chicago, and he accepted (and received) progressively fewer speaking invitations. He no longer wrote articles except in the *Center Magazine*, where he tackled constitutional issues and generally supported the Warren Court's doctrine of judicial activism. In 1963 he undertook to write a syndicated weekly column for the *Los Angeles Times*. It ran in some thirty newspapers of modest circulation and dealt crisply and controversially with social issues and with education. It did not make a great splash, however, and after two years the *Times* readily agreed to his dropping it.

Leisurely-pleasurely Santa Barbara took its toll of the Center early. The boss was the first to arrive—the early riser. The other Fellows trickled in around nine or nine-thirty. They went through their mail or finished reading the Center's daily bible: the *New York Times* delivered by air. Sometimes they also got through the paper to be discussed at eleven. Sometimes they didn't. And after a reasonably hearty luncheon, complete with a glass, maybe two, of wine, they drifted back to their offices, sometimes taking a constitutional first; got their mail out; got in an hour's work or so; and tooled down the great driveway in the direction of home not too much later than four o'clock (Hutchins and two or three others excepted).

What were they doing *out there*? They were pushing their assorted Center projects forward, rounding up scholars by mail and phone to prepare papers or commentaries on papers, and planning two- or three-day conferences with a given visitor. But most of them had work of their own to be done; some of them were engaged on books. For these, the eleven o'clock meeting was something that interfered with their work. It was something they were none of them accustomed to. The morning was the best time to write, for most of them. Several of them—perhaps most of them— resented the interruption. It shot the day. But they were unfailingly faithful in their attendance: the dialogue was the Center's reason for being. It was sacred—to Hutchins. Hutchins was the Center's center.

But for all his longtime talk about a community of scholars, the "consecrated community" that the university should have been and wasn't, he was not himself a communitarian; and neither were the rest of the Fellows. Like university professors—and poets and painters (and people generally?)—the Fellows and staff members, and certainly the visiting conferees, were private persons living private lives and emerging from their studies and their libraries and offices only for social or professional occasions. Some of them, and many of the invited visitors, were prima donnas who actually resented that school bell. The Fellows got themselves houses all over town, without any suggestion by Hutchins or anyone else that they might live within communal distance of one another or build themselves houses on the handsome Center-owned acreage. There was no community, consecrated or not, on Eucalyptus Hill.

It would certainly have taken nothing less than the spirit of community to hold the Center together in the face of the forces that pulled it apart from the first. Like other people who are thrown together too closely, the Fellows eventually got on one another's nerves. All of them knew what each of them was going to say at the conference table as soon as he began talking. (Plato's dialogists did not meet every day at 11 A.M.) At best the Fellows, and participating staffers, and frequent visitors, came to bore one another; at worst, to annoy. They were every one of them forceful personalities. Several of them were a pleasure to listen to—but not all of them every day. Animosities fed on boredom and annoyance, on the repetition of pet sentiments and even of pet expressions. And there was no objective force to restrain those animosities.

In commerce and industry the objective force exists pretty much up and down the line: the sales charts. In the arts and pure sciences, especially in the humanistic arts and sciences, the objective control of the sales charts is missing. And in Santa Barbara personality clashes and cliques were not only inevitable but inveterate. It was all predictable—the jealousy, the contempt, the scorn, under ordinary conditions masked but still understood around the table, under trying conditions flaring into the open. A strong leader could have exerted control at least over the manifestations of tension and distress; but Hutchins refused to be a strong leader.

Ten years after the Center was established in 1959 the tension and distress would finally break out into the open—even into open court—and on one of those wretched occasions Hutchins would shake his head sadly and say, "And I appointed them all." But for those ten years, until he reorganized the institution (and thereafter), the fires would smoulder and occasionally erupt. The Center group had come to Santa Barbara far, far from home. Its members were unacquainted locally—unacquainted with, and a little contemptuous of, the faculty of the burgeoning local branch of the University of California. They were thrown into each other's arms socially—these same men who were thrown into each other's arms professionally every day. They were stuck with each other in an intolerable degree of proximity.

The time would come when Robert Maynard Hutchins, the lifelong promoter of the dialogue, would confess that "the right formula for the dialogue hasn't yet been found." But by that time he would be in his seventies.

45 The Only Saloon in Town

Along with the usual complement of interlopers, the Fellows were engaged (as they so often were) in a less than immortal dialogue on one immortal topic or another when a secretary entered the conference room and handed Hutchins a note. He looked at it, indulged himself in the unusual antic of rapping on his waterglass with a spoon, and said, "President Kennedy has just been assassinated in Dallas," and then signaled the resumption of the discussion.

"He should have adjourned the discussion then and there," said one of the philosophical Fellows a week later. They were gathered around the luncheon table. (Hutchins was absent). "But," said one, "the dialogue was important, wasn't it?" "As important as the assassination of a President?" asked another.

"I should have supposed so, to a company of philosophers."

"Nonsense," said a third.

"His behavior was unspeakable," said a fourth.

"Did you all find it unspeakable?" (Three of the eleven Fellows present that day had found it unspeakable; they had got up and left the room immediately after Hutchins' announcement, and one of them had been crying before he reached the door.)

There was an unencouraging silence, and then one of the younger Fellows said, "I suppose he did the right thing. But it seemed somehow— incongruous. It still does. Maybe it won't a year from now."

The silence was a little stiff now. One of the Fellows got up and studied his watch and said, "Back to work." Others got up, and the group dissolved. One was left with senior Fellow Scott Buchanan, who had said nothing. The two were old friends. "It's the bathos," said the friend, "everywhere. Even here."

"I know," said Buchanan, "but you're in the wrong. So is Hutchins. You think that ritual is infantile. You want society to be above it, to be 'adult.' But it isn't adult to be above ritual. It's angelic, but it isn't adult. Ritual and ritual alone holds society together."

"Primitive society," said the other.

"All societies are primitive," said Buchanan.

The dialogue, then, was more sacred than ritual, even if, as it happened that November 22, 1963, the dialogue wasn't very good. "It's not a very good center, but it's the only one there is," Hutchins had said. Salty Vice-president W. H. "Ping" Ferry put it more pithily: "It's the only saloon in town." And it was. Its four-to-five-times-a-week dialogue sessions had no counterpart anywhere. Nobody anywhere else was trying to do what Hutchins was—however unsuccessfully—trying to do. The Center, said Hutchins in his presidential report in 1968, "receives no money from government and none from large foundations or corporations. It is not a think tank . . . neither is it a refuge for scholars who want to get away from it all to do their research and write their books. It is an organized group, rather than a collection of individuals. It is an organization of men who are free of any obligation except to join in the effort to understand the subjects they have selected to study. It is a community, and, since its members are trying to think together, it may be called, at least in potentiality, an intellectual community." But he added by way of understatement, "This description may be a little high-flown."

It was more than a little high-flown. Less than a year later, in February 1969, he was telling his friend and vice-president, Frank Kelly, "I'm going to quit. I can't see any way of making the place what it should be."[1] The trouble was only in part that the Fellows were not up to the idea of the dialogue, and only in part due to the nature of the dialogue itself. The trouble was also in the ridiculous grandiosity of the program, which persistently bit off more than any program of investigation could possibly chew. In November of 1968 its then dean, John Seeley, presented to the board of directors what he called the Center Program of Studies and Projects adopted by the Fellows (including Fellow Hutchins). A study was defined as a topic deserving long and deep examination; a project was defined as a matter requiring "brief attention."

The studies already under way were "constitutionalization of the world . . . constitutionalization of the United States . . . constitutionalization of science and technology . . . constitutionalization of criminal justice administration . . . organization theory . . . and the civilization of the dialogue." Studies "preliminarily or well defined and in development" included "federalism . . . policing and policy . . . national service . . . corporate development . . . potentials of the United States Constitution . . . the school (and education) . . . and the professions."[2] (Fellow Edward Engberg, directing the study of the professions, resigned from the Center in the spring of 1969, informing Hutchins that the dialogue was "a shambles.")[3] Studies of religious institutions and the city were "not yet adequately defined but definitely to be explored." Projects on youth, the law of the sea, Africa, and dissent were to be "further defined and adopted only if definition is adequate and resources permit."

Said Seeley, "We have failed so far to develop a unifying view and statement as to what holds together each of the studies adopted severally, even though they were adopted on good grounds after lengthy reflection. We trust to coming experience to reveal the unity, and permit a statement of its nature. I look to this next year for some fruition from all this labor, and a happy issue out of some of our afflictions." Dean Seeley's report included the names of dozens of subjects and the assertion that more than a hundred papers had been read at the Center during a six-month period.

The board congratulated Seeley on his development of the program, and Hutchins did not express dissatisfaction with this megalomaniacal assortment of studies and projects. The program was expected to consume the energies of the Center for "several years ahead, subject only to alteration upon sufficiently weighty new considerations," said the dean. The weekly meeting of the Fellows, consultants in residence, and administrative and publications personnel had "ordered and routinized and settled a great many matters in a manner more satisfactory than heretofore. It has also served to draw together and strengthen the Fellowship, while at the same time better, more readily, and more surely coordinating the Center as a whole. It marks a true, good, and important advance into Collegiality."[4]

Within the year of all this rampant prose and poesy seven members of the fellowship—including Hutchins—would vote to fire the dean and several other Fellows and staff members with him, and to reorganize the Center. There was, however, nobody to fire Hutchins, who had so recently appeared to place much confidence in the dean; or the board of directors, who had been reported as having been impressed by the dean's Program of Studies and Projects. Nor was there anyone to fire the whole fellowship for its formulation and promulgation of an indigestible concoction of just about all the things in general that could possibly occur to the vagrant mind of man.

46   Is Anybody Listening? (2)

The papers kept pouring forth from the photocopying machines and the printers, along with the audiotapes on which the dialogues were voluminously recorded. But general publicity languished, in spite of the capable drumfire of public relations handouts produced by former newspaperman Frank Kelly. Aside from the attacks and threats by the John Birchers—the ex-New Yorkers at the Center were used to that—the City of Santa Barbara wasn't interested in the machinations atop Eucalyptus Hill, nor was the country as a whole. It was hard to get any notice at all; with Watts, Detroit, and Newark burning and national leaders being assassinated, people didn't care all that much about, say, the constitutionalization of science and technology or long-term trends and futurological speculations. There was just too much of it—some seven million copies of papers, tapes, magazines, leaflets, booklets distributed on an often random scale over the first ten years on the hilltop. (Between two and three thousand educational institutions, high schools, colleges, and universities, subscribed to the tapes of the Center dialogues.)

The octogenarian Rex Tugwell worked for several years drafting a proposed new Constitution for the United States. His fellow Fellows weren't much interested in the undertaking, and it very rarely figured in the discussions around the conference table. (And when Tugwell participated, which wasn't seldom, his observations were likely to be casual and peripheral.) When his finished Constitution was unveiled, in something like its thirty-fifth draft, it made a considerable one-day splash in the *New York Times*; in the rest of the country it sank like a stone, and like a stone, never rose. It was that way with a great deal of the Center's output, more often than not.

After all, a university doesn't get much notice unless it is the scene of a student riot or a sports event or its biologists produce a sure cure or its physicists a sure kill. And a university has an ancient name and ancient ceremonials, great public status, and a great many alumni. And both public and alumni think they know what a university is for and what it does. The Center had none of these redeeming and beguiling features. It sponsored what it called convocations, both at the Santa Barbara center and across the country, to nourish its supporters and attract new ones; many of these symposiums featured the all-star names which Hutchins was able to attract to an ad hoc event, especially with the payment of always generous fees and travel expenses. And still the public notice was minimal.

Of all the multifarious conferences and convocations it set up at home and abroad—in Mexico City, Athens, Malta, Geneva—the most spectacular were the *Pacem in Terris* meetings, the name taken from Pope John XXIII's famous encyclical. These were all-out extravaganzas staged on an amazingly grand scale for so small—and financially hard-pressed—an institution as the Center. They signaled the transition of the Center's focus from national to international affairs. The first was held in New York in February of 1965, with two thousand people in attendance. Its announced purpose was "an attempt to see whether the understanding and interchange advocated by Pope John XXIII is possible." It drew scholars and statesmen from all over the world as participants, and its drama was intensified by President Johnson's order for the continuous bombing of North Vietnam, put into effect three days before the convocation opened. The president declined an invitation to speak, but he sent the newly elected Vice-President Humphrey, together with a message saying that he had "no doubt that such discussion, under private auspices, of the problems of peace will provide a major contribution to the greatest single problem of our time."[1] Other United States representatives were senators George McGovern and Eugene McCarthy, Chief Justice Earl Warren, and Adlai Stevenson, head of the American delegation to the United Nations. Non-governmental celebrities included George Kennan, former ambassador to the USSR; the philosopher Paul Tillich; the Nobel laureate Linus Pauling; and Henry R. Luce, the publisher of *Time, Life,* and *Fortune.* Foreign participants were Abba Eban, deputy prime minister of Israel; U Thant, secretary general of the United Nations; N.N. Inozemtsev, deputy chief editor of *Pravda*; Yevgeni Zhukov of the Soviet Academy of Sciences; and the philosopher Adam Schaff, a member of the Polish Communist Party's central committee. Hutchins presided over the principal sessions.

In terms of national—and international—coverage, the three-day *Pacem in Terris* was a resounding success, bringing the Center greater attention than all its previous efforts together. *Life* magazine called it "an extraordinary assemblage of the world's movers and shakers. . . . The speeches and seminars, recorded for distribution to 90 U.S. educational TV and 125 radio stations, are only a beginning. But it is a beginning that holds promise for new departures in world statecraft."[2] The guest list (said *Life*) would have done credit to a United Nations charter gathering. The prestigious panel members explored every aspect of a durable world peace and the obstacles to it.

No sooner had the echoes of *Pacem in Terris* died down than Hutchins and Harry Ashmore—soon to be appointed executive vice-president of the Center—began planning a replay, this time in Geneva in May of 1967, specifically designed to "see what private peace-making could accomplish in regard to the war in Vietnam." Here the gathering was much smaller, with some three hundred in attendance, but more highly flavored internationally, with participants from seventy countries. The official attitude of the U.S. government was cold this time. The second *Pacem in Terris* coincided with a mighty escalation of the war in Vietnam; President Johnson and his entourage were in no mood to help provide "a major contribution to the greatest single problem of our time." Not only did the United States and the Soviet Union send no delegations—Senator William Fulbright participated unofficially—but China also declined the invitation. When North Vietnam decided not to attend, the Center, bent on evenhandedness, declined to let the South Vietnamese speak. And most of the Arab delegations, with the onset of the Israel-Arab war, simply melted away. The coolness around the world was reflected in the press, which gave the second *Pacem* almost no attention, even though it marked the first high-level and fruitful contact between the two Germanys.[3]

Two more *Pacem* convocations were held. One took place in October of 1973 in Washington, attended by three thousand people, who heard Henry Kissinger and William Fulbright in a knock-down, drag-out debate on American foreign policy. The concluding *Pacem in Terris IV* in Washington in December of 1975, was attended by two thousand people. The four conferences, while they produced both notice and income, also produced additional dissatisfaction among the Fellows of the Center, many of whom felt that the Hutchins-Ashmore impresario ventures, successful as they were, were diverting the Center from its appointed task: the dialogue. There was nothing resembling real dialogue—panel discussions and debates had long since become commonplace—at the convocations. Any public policy institution could have staged them. The attention and energy they consumed in Santa Barbara left the very idea of the dialogue dangling in midair while the "communications" program flourished. The cleavage widened on Eucalyptus Hill between the administrators and journalists typified by Ashmore, on the one hand, and the scholars and academics, typified by Harvey Wheeler, on the other. The relations between these two grew progressively strained and eventually emerged as head-on conflict.

There was further dissatisfaction in the fellowship over the financing of the *Pacem* convocations. The money for them—they were all done in the sumptuous Hutchins manner—came to something approaching a million dollars apiece. Hutchins was able to assure his critics, both among the Fellows and the board members, that their cost was met by fund-raising separate from that for the Center budget, and that no considerable amount of money was raised for them that might otherwise have gone into regular expenditures. But it was still a lot of money for a small institution that was spending, in its regular outgo, some $1.5 million a year and habitually running a relatively colossal million-dollar deficit.

The Center's informal motto was "Feel Free," and the Fellows, including the laissez-faire Hutchins, felt free with money. Salaries compared favorably with the highest paid in the universities; Hutchins was paid $68,000 a year, and the senior Fellows ranged up to $40,000. It was doubtful if many of the Fellows would have been paid that much anywhere else. (On the other hand they *had* cast their lot with an unendowed institution of dubious longevity.) The long-distance telephone bills were staggering and travel expenses phenomenal.

A few board members grumbled, but none of them wanted to suggest that Bob cut down; the Hutchins style had always been lavish. The financial situation was perennially acute, and if it had not been for one man, Chester Carlson, the inventor of Xerox, it would have been fatal; over the years Carlson provided ten million of the twenty-four million dollars the Center grossed between 1959 and 1978. It was an awful lot of money in its time, no matter where it came from.

Where it came from was something else. Some of it was produced by the sale of high-priced seats for the mass-attended *Pacem* conferences; and the Center membership fee of ten to fifteen dollars, paid by up to 100,000 members, grossed another million or more. But some of the Center's funds were extracted from more questionable, and even shadier, sources, especially in connection with the limited attendance at *Pacem II* in Geneva. The sum of $100,000 was contributed by the Albert Parvin Foundation, established with Las Vegas money by an otherwise little-known American whose business dealings with big-time mobsters was a matter of public record. Most of the rest of the almost one-million-dollar outlay for Geneva was provided by, of all people, Bernard Cornfeld—the man who, before his collapse and takeover by the plunger Robert Vesco, from his Swiss base sold stock through his paper empire of Investors Overseas Services to naive Europeans, who were approached by his salesmen with the question: "Do you sincerely want to be rich?" Cornfeld's man Jimmy Roosevelt, the president of IOS, was, at Cornfeld's suggestion to Hutchins and Ashmore, appointed secretary general of *Pacem II*, and the convocation was roundly and embarrassingly plastered with propaganda for the gigantic bucket-shop balloon which was about to burst.[4]

Hutchins, it will be remembered, had a small sign which he liked to display on his desk at the University of Chicago, which read: "We Wash Money." And wash money he did, as does every head of an institution which maintains itself by begging. (One of Hutchins' fellow directors of the Albert Parvin Foundation was the president of Princeton.)[5] But money, needing washing or no, can be powerfully hard to come by, and it was during most of the Center's history. The reason it was hard was only in small part that people with (or without) money did not understand what the Center was or what it was doing; that can be said, in considerable measure, of a university too. In larger part the Center's generally desperate history was due to the inability, or unwillingness, of its board members to get out and get it—or stay in and give it.

As the first *Pacem in Terris* convocation approached, the financial straits of the Center were dire in the extreme. One of the board members proposed a fund-raising dinner in New York in honor of Hutchins, and his fellow directors were enthusiastic; except for Hutchins, who demurred strongly, saying that he did not want his friends to be asked for money on his account. But the directors overcame his objection by pointing out what he already knew, that the Center might have to close otherwise. He yielded unhappily. The dinner was given the evening the convocation ended, with pollster Elmo Roper as chairman; Bill Benton, Henry Luce, Norman Cousins (of the *Saturday Review*), and Morris Levinson of the Center board as cochairmen; and Ralph Bunche, Paul Hoffman, and Adlai Stevenson as honorary chairmen. Hutchins sat squirming while his praises rang and the professional fund-raisers counted the gifts and pledges, which came to a staggering $1.4 million. "Moved by that outpouring of affection and the substantial evidence of support for his intellectual enterprise," Frank Kelly wrote, "Hutchins found it difficult to speak that night. He was on the verge of weeping."[6] It was on that occasion that he responded to the toasts by saying, "If I'm such a great man, why haven't I been able to quit smoking?"

The Center had exhausted its four million dollars, and on several occasions the board agreed to undertake an endowment drive. But the drive was never undertaken. There were some rich men and women on the board, including some millionaires; but there were no Rockefellers, and this was no University of Chicago. The lethargy of the Center board—largely men and women of Hutchins' own selection—was a bitter disappointment to him as long as he lived.

How long would he live? The Center for the Study of Democratic Institutions was the lengthened shadow of Robert Maynard Hutchins. Donors to the University of Chicago had been donors to a great university; donors to the Center had been donors to a *Hutchins* undertaking. The board members were many of them willing to support the Center on an ad hoc basis, to see it through its recurrent crises; some of them were willing to go outside and ask for money for a then-and-there need. Long-term endowment was something else altogether. It aroused no enthusiasm inside or outside the board. The irony lay in the fact that it *was* Hutchins' Center and no one could say how long it would remain so.

He was a very tired man. He had been tired when he established the institution at the age of sixty. Within five years he was urging his closest associates on the board to search for his successor. Within ten years he underwent major coronary surgery, and from then on he was an extremely tired man and ever more urgent in his desire to lay the burden down. A few years later he quit asking and urging, and simply informed the board that he had to get out. A successor was finally found—a series of short-term successors. But these successors were successors to the office, not to the man. There could be no successor to Hutchins, and the people who might have asked other people for long-term money all knew it. It was not immodest for him to know it too. It was not immodest for him to know that he himself was the reason the endowment was never established.

47 The Refounding Father

As big-name conferences and convocations flourished and dialogue faltered, bickering and backbiting became the order of the day at El Parthenon. The animosities between individuals and cliques in the fellowship grew apace. Nineteen sixty-eight saw the death of Scott Buchanan, whom Hutchins had tried to persuade to serve as the Center's first dean. The bickering went on. Hutchins knew he had made a mistake in bringing the New York staffers to California and establishing them as Fellows of a philosophical center, but he didn't know what to do about it now. He saw only one way to avoid an open explosion, and that was to reorganize the enterprise.

By the spring of 1969 the talk of "constitutionalizing" the Center had been going on for almost a year, with no discernible progress. The structure was intolerable. Hutchins was the chief executive officer, and the other officers and staff members all played up to him. Ashmore had his ear, and Ashmore was not popular in the fellowship. Harvey Wheeler carried considerable weight, but divisively; "Mr. Wheeler," Hutchins told a friend, "has something of a conspiratorial nature." There were conspiracies swirling around the man who had meant to establish a consecrated community. This one was neither consecrated nor communal. And the constitutionalizing process—whatever that pomposity may have meant—was getting nowhere.

"I'd led a sheltered life," said Ashmore the nonacademic, "until I got mixed with academics. . . . The kind of politicking that goes on in the academic community is far more virulent than goes on in city hall or the state legislature. . . . What you have is a kind of ruthlessness in jockeying for position. It's probably not much worse than a run-of-the-mill bureaucrat or journalist on a big newspaper fighting for preference or advancement. But the difference between [that and] what happens here—and in any university community—is that all the jockeying and struggling and climbing over people is coupled with protests of utter morality."[1] More and more people crowded around the conference table, and more and more often the political activists among the Fellows were busy about social issues elsewhere. Something radical was crying to be done.

Even then it is questionable whether the extremely weary Hutchins would have done anything drastic. What finally moved him to action—though he still managed to avoid firing anyone himself—was the last of Chester Carlson's bequests, amounting, as part of his residual estate in 1968, to almost five million dollars in Xerox stock. For the first time since the original Ford grant had run out, something could be done at the Center with a perspective of more than a few months at a time. Hutchins asked a committee of five of the Fellows to advise him about the reconstituting of the operation. One of the five, John Cogley, suggested a procedure that was generally acceptable. The fellowship would be dissolved and Hutchins would appoint himself a senior Fellow and select another from the group. These two would select a third, and so on, until a majority could no longer be mustered. Hutchins selected the controversial Wheeler, and the two of them spent a week on the long-distance telephone—largely to Europe—inviting the usual great men to come to the Center for nine months a year at $25,000. (Tugwell later said that Hutchins had indicated to him that he hoped that the reconstituted Center would consist of "the most distinguished people to be found anywhere in the world.") The telephonic invitation to the most distinguished people in the world was uniformly rejected, and Hutchins was face to face at last with the fact that he could not get anything like the world university of his dreams.[2]

Then he and Wheeler chose the elderly Tugwell; while the three men deliberated Ashmore suggested that he and Cogley be named ex officio, and they were both named full senior Fellows. The five elected John Wilkinson, and the six elected Elizabeth Mann Borgese. There the majority vote failed for the remaining Fellows—Ferry, Seeley, Pike, Barr, Gorman, Hallock Hoffman, and Pauling. The part-time paid consultants were dismissed en masse and told that they would be hired on an ad hoc basis.

The election, and rejection, came as almost as great a shock to the electors as it did to the rejectees. The perfervid Ferry, a vice-president from the start, had lost favor around the table (from which he was frequently absent) and with Hutchins, whom his extreme public statements had often embarrassed. Seeley had been the dean in whom Hutchins was supposed to have placed great confidence. Hoffman, like Ferry, had come from the Fund for the Republic. The rambunctious Bishop Pike, like Linus Pauling, had been a frequent absentee; but the aging "Winkie" Barr was an intimate friend of Hutchins.

Some of those who were told to move on—with generous severance pay—took the pink slip very badly, above all Ferry, who, along with Hoffman and Seeley, represented a strong political activist segment of the fellowship. Looking back on the purge, Ashmore suggested that there was more to the selection process than scholarly work. "The divisions within the group had become evident," he said. "I think they were in part spurious, but you had the classic political radical view represented by Ferry. Then you had this hippy-radical thing represented by Hallock Hoffman and Seeley. And then you had me as the old, square liberal."[3] The rejectees had not all been activists, nor the acceptees all nonactivists, but it was true that the political activists on the whole had skimped their work at the Center in favor of other activities. The other rejectees—Kelly, McDonald, Reed, and Sheinbaum—were asked to continue what they were doing, but as non-Fellows they were excluded (along with all the droppers-in) from the dialogue at the conference table.

Ferry had received his unexpected notice while he was on holiday in Scotland. Returning to Santa Barbara, he informed Hutchins that his dismissal "shattered" him. He had been vice-president of the Fund before the Center was established and had anticipated spending the rest of his working life on Eucalyptus Hill. Having to face a man he was firing, Hutchins retreated behind the supposed new fact of life that, with the refounding of the Center, he was merely one of seven equals and could only take up Ferry's case with the other six. Ferry's unhappiness was unassuaged. Hutchins had been one of his closest friends (as he had been one of Hutchins'). He had assumed he had lifetime tenure—though the notion that there could be tenure in an unendowed institution was more than a little far-fetched. True, he had been absent from Santa Barbara at least a third of the time on speaking trips, and his designation as the Center's vice-president when he made his unfailingly radical public proposals—such as unilateral disarmament—had, he knew, distressed many members of the board. But he had acted on the informal motto of the Center, "Feel Free." He thought his removal should be reversed.[4]

When Hutchins reported to him that the new fellowship could find no place for him,[5] Ferry's grief turned to fury. He rejected the offer of a $100,000 settlement and filed suit against the Fund for the Republic, as parent body of the Center, for general damages of $263,000 and exemplary damages of $400,000, accusing Hutchins and Ashmore, as chief officers of the fund, of having acted with malice toward him. Hutchins and the other surviving Fellows were subpoenaed and required to give extended depositions defending their action in dropping him. After two years of legal harassment of the Center and its board, Ferry accepted the Center's original offer of $100,000 as a settlement and left Santa Barbara to continue the fruitful life of social activism in the east.[6] He and Hutchins had no further contact. Hoffman, who had also been with the fund since the beginning, amiably settled for two years' severance pay, as (less amiably) did Seeley.

The first action of the refounded Center, in the summer of 1969, was to invite a dozen prominent men from Britain, France, Argentina, and American universities to a week's discussion in Santa Barbara to help "complete the transformation of the Center into an intellectual community in which the disciplines are forced to come to terms with one another and in which some of the best minds of our time may work together to bring reason to bear on human affairs. This would be a true university." Hutchins added, in his memorandum to the conference participants and his board: "They would also be free to decide whether or not they wanted students. The seven senior fellows now in residence believe that young people should be admitted as assistants or junior partners. . . . The members should regard themselves as professors in a world university, free to study and discuss whatever seemed to them worthy of their attention."[7]

Following the meeting the seven self-established Fellows announced the appointment of twelve associates, and Hutchins said, "As the first ten years of the Center draw to a close, as one era ends and another begins, I look back with some satisfaction to the successful attempt to found a center of independent thought and criticism, to learn how to gain comprehension through dialogue, to clarify the basic issues—and some burning ones—and widen the circles of discussion about them."[8] Of the dozen men who attended the post-refounding conference, several agreed to write papers for dialogue sessions and to attend center discussions "as often as possible." Five of them accepted appointments as associates, but only one of the five would ultimately become a fellow of the Center: Alexander Comfort of England, the respected gerontologist whose pop book *The Joy of Sex* would become one of the all-time nonfiction best sellers—and who would figure spectacularly in the last years of Hutchins' career.

The reorganization produced a small flurry of attention in the nation's press, much of it emphasizing the fact that Hutchins had been elected the Center's board chairman (in place of Justice William O. Douglas, who had resigned) as a likely prelude to his retirement. Vice-president Ashmore took his place pro tem as president.

The country was still asking—when it thought about the Center at all— What are they doing out there? They were going on with the dialogue and the conferences and the production and distribution of great quantities of publications. A few months after the refounding, the Center published a collection of statements by senators Edward Kennedy, William Fulbright, Mark Hatfield, and John Sherman Cooper, sensationally advocating an end to the American refusal to recognize Communist China—yet another of the "distant early warnings" of things to come that had emanated from the Center. The publication of *Asian Dilemma: United States, Japan, and China* provoked a new round of attacks from the right, with Congressman Charles Teague of California reiterating his demand for an investigation by the IRS and saying that "the staff is extremely oriented toward the left and is more interested in developing and disseminating extremely liberal propaganda than it is in true education.⁹ Once more the board of directors, approving the reorganization, undertook (or, more precisely, agreed to undertake) a search for endowment of the institution.

But with the state of the nation what it was in 1969, what the Center was doing out there seemed to be more remote from reality than ever. Two years earlier the Center invited a group of student leaders from across the country to join the senior Fellows in a three-day conference—which turned out to be a farce, with the representatives of the waterbed generation calling for revolution and the aging denizens of Eucalyptus Hill demanding in vain that the young come up with a theory of human society. (One of the young red-hots said afterward that the Center conference had been "like going to grandfather's.") After the reorganization of 1969 a handful of junior fellows was installed around the table, but that experiment petered out and it was clear that the Fellows envisioned no generational succession to themselves.

Did Hutchins suppose that the refounding of the Center was something more than a holding operation, with seven persons participating who had already been at the conference table for ten years? Were they (himself included) "some of the best minds of our time," who would constitute the core of a world university? Not likely; he knew them (and himself) too well for that. Or was he going through an old man's motions, protesting ever more urgently that he wanted to lay the burden down? He was a manful man and, as he had always been, a dutiful one. Somebody would have to be found soon, very soon, to take his place. Until then he would have to carry on (or go through the motions of carrying on?). He had said so often that it is not necessary to hope in order to undertake, nor to succeed in order to persevere; what was there to do but to persevere, even anew to undertake, to do what he had always done?

48   The Sinking Ship

He'd been saying it for years: "Welcome aboard the sinking ship," by way of greeting each new arrival at the portals of El Parthenon. And the ship had all the while been sinking. Had the five-million-dollar bequest by Chester Carlson in 1968 been set aside as the "nut" in an endowment drive, the story might have been different. But probably not. With the Carlson money (and more) gone by 1972, the tired, ailing Hutchins offered to tour the country to try to raise money if the board would open doors for him, and the board had not responded. Now, in March of 1973, one of the board members, Arnold Grant, proposed a Robert Hutchins Endowment of five million dollars—half of it to be put up by the board; again, no takers.

And the operation continued to run a deficit of a million dollars a year—and sometimes more. At the critical board meeting in March, Norton Ginsburg, a University of Chicago geographer on leave as the Center's dean, announced a radical change in Center policy: it would surrender its independence of financing by the government, the great corporations, and the great foundations, and would actively solicit support from all possible sources. Two senior Fellows had been added to the original "new" seven: Ginsburg and Lord Ritchie-Calder of the University of Edinburgh. It was financially impossible to add any more—at a total cost of something like fifty thousand dollars a year apiece—but it was possible to make an exception in the case of Dr. Alexander Comfort, "probably the world's most distinguished gerontologist," director of research in gerontology at University College, London. Dr. Comfort could be got—Dean Ginsburg didn't say how—at no additional cost to the Center.

There was some small murmur of board concern at the appointment of the now famous (or, as you will, notorious) compiler of the best-selling *Joy of Sex,* but the murmur subsided with the unanimous expression of board policy to let the administration be the judge of its own appointments—finances permitting. How would finances permit the appointment of a $28,000-a-year Fellow who would cost the Center nothing? The board heard the dean say of Comfort, "His humanistic inclinations and talents will help provide that kind of interdisciplinary bridge which is so characteristic of the Senior Fellows already in residence"[1]—heard the dean and refrained from asking where the $28,000 would come from.

The financing of the Comfort appointment was a mystery that neither the board nor the Fellows showed any disposition whatever to solve. The reason could only have been that it was an open secret. The administration of the Center—headed by Hutchins—had made a deal with the great gerontological author of the famous sex book. Comfort would turn over his American dollar royalties to the Center and the Center would pay him his salary—and Her Majesty's Inland Revenue Service would whistle in vain for income tax on those dollar earnings. The universal silence of both board and officers on the source of Dr. Comfort's salary could only mean that the board and Fellows had learned of the deal by highly informal word of mouth. Was it legal? Presumably. Was it, though legal, just the least bit shady—shady enough to explain the general reluctance to discuss it? Was Hutchins washing money again?

There seemed to be no way to staunch the financial outgo, in spite of the board's reluctance to come face to face with the perpetual crisis. The money went largely for salaries and travel expenses—and the continuous import of expensive performers carelessly invited from all over the world. It was a coup to get the Nobel Prize–winning economist Gunnar Myrdal and his distinguished wife Alva from Sweden as visiting Fellows for six months; but their visit cost close to $100,000, and neither of the Myrdals was overwhelmed by the experience. "The subjects of conversation are spread quite thinly," Mrs. Myrdal told the *New York Times*, "so there's a diffusion of energies." "It's not my method," said Mr. Myrdal. "I've always learned more from individual talks, not from conferences."[2] "I'm very disappointed with the dialogue. It's too inbred—incestuous," said Visiting Fellow Alexander King.[3] (King had been director of the Organization for Economic Cooperation and Development in Paris.) Comments like these in the *New York Times*—the newspaper most widely read by potential donors to the Center—didn't help raise money.

The press on the whole was scornful of the Center and always had been, except for its notices of the spectacular events like *Pacem in Terris*. The *Times* story that quoted the Myrdals and King informed its readers that "the Center is running out of money" and quoted the various senior

Fellows gloomily. Pointing to Hutchins' illnesses, John Wilkinson said that the Center had been marking time, "drifting." Elizabeth Borgese was quoted to the effect that "the group is pretty polarized" between those who were trying to do something and those "who feel they have to be cynical." Newcomer Alex Comfort said of the dialogue, "We try to squeeze each lemon, but some have very little in them but pips."

Over the years the brickbats had wafted in from both the right and the left. The *Wall Street Journal*, characterizing the tottering Center as "a richly endowed organization," castigated "the hubris of its proclamations and an overlay of certitude that its prescriptions are unassailable. The sum total of its preachments amount to little more than demands for greater government regulation of human activity." On the more sober-sided left, the radical author Marcus Raskin, conceding that the Center had done some good work, found it a failure in four distinct areas: it had succeeded over the years in isolating itself from the young; it looked at society institutionally, denying that some of our institutions might not be worth saving; it had turned away from putting ideas into actual practice and existed in a world composed only of ideas; it had overemphasized dialogue and dialogical thought without analyzing the actual situations as they existed in the United States and the world—it had talked itself away from reality. A good deal of the criticism was savage. In the *Saturday Evening Post*, Joan Didion and John Gregory Dunne wrote: "The Center is supported on the same principle as a vanity press. People who are in a position to contribute large sums of money are encouraged to participate in clarifying the basic issues. Dinah Shore, a Founding Member, is invited up to discuss civil rights with Bayard Rustin. Steve Allen talks over 'Ideology and Intervention' with Senator Fulbright and Arnold Toynbee. Kirk Douglas, a Founding Member, speaks his piece on 'The Arts in a Democratic Society.' Paul Newman, in the role of 'concerned citizen,' is on hand to discuss 'The University in America' with Dr. Hutchins, Supreme Court Justice Douglas, Arnold Grant, Rosemary Park, and another 'concerned citizen,' Jack Lemmon. Everyone goes home flattered, and the Center prevails. Well, why not?"[4]

But by the spring of 1973 the Center could by no stretch of the imagination be said to be prevailing. Membership at fifteen dollars a head was down from 100,000 to 75,000 and still falling. The financial situation was desperate, with a projected deficit of $925,000 for 1973–74. And Hutchins informed the board that he simply had to quit within the next year; he was no longer just asking that an effort be made to find a successor. His energy was failing now, and more than ever he allowed his six fellow Fellows to feel free with the program. Ashmore said that "the centrifugal effect of the specialized interests of the Fellows has increasingly debilitated the dialogue. . . . The dialogue is perishing as we seem to be moving steadily in the direction of a conference center which serves as a kind of administrative hub for a variety of unrelated programs." Taking note of the heterogeneity of the program, Dean Ginsburg found that "most of the topics presented can be related to the major thematic interests of the Center," but he admitted that the topics to which some of the invitees addressed themselves "may not fit the broad themes that characterize the Center's program as closely as in other cases." In fact the topics ranged all over the lot in pell-mell fashion. In November and December of 1973 there was a succession of six major meetings, on "Global Science Policy," "Energy Policies and the International System," "Legal, Political, Social, and Economic Aspects of Climate and Weather Modifications," "The Criminal Justice System: Barriers to Reform," "The Public Interest in Education," and "The Constitutional Implications of Watergate."[5] The first of these conferences alone brought scientists from the Soviet Union, Sweden, France, Britain, the United States, and the United Nations—at enormous expense.

On October 8, 1973, a search committee of the board recommended the election of President Malcolm Moos of the University of Minnesota as Hutchins' successor. The job had been turned down by President Kingman Brewster of Yale and John Kenneth Galbraith of Harvard, and one or two other possible candidates had indicated that they were not interested. When Moos took over, Hutchins said to him, "I bequeath to you the Robert Maynard Hutchins Memorial Deficit." It was a wonder that any sound man could be found to accept the post, to suppose that money which could not be got for a Hutchins Center with Hutchins could be got for one without him. But Moos had a reputation in the academic world as an able fund raiser. He had been a speech writer for President Eisenhower. (He wrote the memorable farewell address in which Ike warned his countrymen against the military-industrial complex.) He had been a consultant to the Rockefeller philanthropies and the Ford Foundation, and he had raised a good deal of money from private sources during his tenure at Minnesota. His reputation as an effective administrator was much weaker, and his Minnesota board was willing to see him go. Still, the hard-pressed Center directors found him highly qualified and—with Hutchins' concurrence—unanimously voted to invite him to take over.

Hutchins was determined that Moos should have a free hand, and when the board offered him a year's leave with pay he accepted the offer for six months. He and Mrs. Hutchins planned to travel—his own thought was simply to stay out of town—but she developed a serious heart complaint and they decided they had to remain in Santa Barbara. Moos was to take office on June 1, 1974, and Hutchins had agreed to run the Center during the eight-month interval following the election. By the time he actually took office, Moos's fate was largely decided: he would soon be out, certainly if he failed to raise a great deal of money.

He failed to raise money, and his relations with other Fellows of the Center disintegrated immediately after his selection. Frank Kelly, who witnessed the developments from inside as a vice-president, wrote afterward: "Hutchins and Ashmore were striving to make sure—as far as they could—that the election of Malcolm Moos as the Center's chairman would not mean an accession to power by Harvey Wheeler."[6] Moos and Wheeler had been friends at Johns Hopkins, and Wheeler had been proposing Moos for the chairmanship of the Center for several years. Hutchins was worried about Wheeler's influence under a Moos presidency.

Hutchins' concern reached into the board, dividing it so sharply that right up until Moos took office there was some question as to whether the invitation should not be withdrawn. But Hutchins' go-ahead was decisive, and the inheritor of the Robert Maynard Hutchins Memorial Deficit moved in. Within ten stormy months he was moved out, on what amounted to a divided board vote of no confidence. The ostensible occasion for this vote was a disagreement between Moos and Frances McAllister, a strong-minded (and strong-willed) board member who mistrusted Wheeler and mistrusted Moos's plan to reshape the Center into what Wheeler called a communiversity, which would consist largely of several occupants of named chairs and a limited number of graduate students. (Moos wanted Wheeler in charge of the project.)

In the course of his short tenure Moos missed more gatherings around the conference table than he had attended; and Mrs. McAllister, and the board majority that sided with her, felt that the vaguely projected new communiversity would downplay the dialogue or do away with it altogether. Hutchins himself declined to participate in the welling conflict, but his sentiments were well known; and when the time came to oust the luckless Moos, Hutchins did not object.

At an emergency board meeting in the late fall of 1974, Moos had been instructed to reduce expenditures radically. Moos then cut the Center's budget by dismissing secretaries, file clerks, and mail-room employees with severance pay. He closed the Washington and Los Angeles offices. He asked Fellows to hold down their outlay—and, wonder of wonders, to refrain from organizing conferences.[7]

This last was, in effect, the end of the Center as it had been for many years, during which it had capitalized on Hutchins' proclivity and ability to get eminent personages to accept invitations to speak or join commit-

496 / *The Western Slope*

tees. Though the galaxy of notables—and celebrities, as distinguished from notables—invited for short conferences, symposiums, or convocations did not provide the continuity that dialogue demands, though, indeed, it actually frustrated that continuity, nonetheless, the Center had assembled, on one occasion or another, the most diversified list of eminently serious personages of the era, among others Barzun, Bronowski, Brown, Burger, Burns, Buckley, Carter, Chavez, Clark, Commoner, Day, Douglas, Doxiados, Ehrlich, Ervin, Galbraith, Goldberg, Goldstücker, Huxley, Illich, Jensen, de Jouvenal, Kennan, Kennedy, King, Kissinger, Lippmann, McLuhan, Marcuse, Marshall, Mondale, Myrdal, Niemöller, Palme, Pauling, Reuther, Rustin, Salk, Skinner, Spaak, Spender, Stevenson, U Thant, Tillich, Toynbee, Warren. No other organizaton had ever attracted so stellar a company to its program or was ever likely to.

With the departure of Moos—who took with him $75,000 in severance pay—the disintegration of the Center was all but complete. But the mansion remained atop Eucalyptus Hill. The Fellows—now ten in number—remained in the mansion. And a couple of miles away, in the hills above the city, and in a small, but spacious enough, and lavish enough, house that the Hutchinses had built when their earlier home was destroyed by fire in 1964, there remained Bob Hutchins, who was now, in 1975, seventy-six years old and the survivor of surgery performed by an eminent physician, who said to him, "Don't worry—I'll have you back on the tennis courts in six weeks," to which Hutchins replied, "In that case the operation's off."

Two of the trustees who were Chicagoans offered to put up a total of $200,000 for each of two years if the Center was willing to move all or part of its program to Chicago and retain the part-time services of the myriad scholars in that area. Hutchins undertook to check out the possibilities there and did so, returning with a positive report on the project, which would be headed by his old social science dean, Ralph Tyler. (Tyler would become a Center vice-president.) The Chicago program actually went into effect and ran until Hutchins' death—but neither he nor the other Fellows were interested in moving to Chicago. There were talks with the administrations of the University of California at Santa Barbara and at San Diego about possible affiliation. There was talk about opening part-time centers, à la Chicago, at Boston, at Palm Beach. . . . There was talk.

There was talk, but there was almost no money at all. There was, in point of fact, no money at all except for the fortune El Parthenon would bring on the block and some tag ends of funds here and there—not enough to do anything very much. And at last nothing very much was contemplated.

One of his admirers once said, "I don't envy the fellow who succeeds Hutchins, but I envy the fellow who succeeds the fellow who does." The fellow who succeeded the fellow who succeeded Hutchins was Hutchins. On May 10, 1975, he came down from the Santa Barbara hills in his silver Jaguar to reassume the presidency. He was still the first man at the office in the morning and just about the last to leave at 5 P.M. He seemed somehow to be reenergized, though he was now pale, drawn, and a little stooped. He had grown old. When Scott Buchanan died in 1968 he had written a mutual friend: "Scott was not very cheerful or very comfortable during the last three years of his life. He kept on working, but I had the impression that he was rather tired of it all. How could he fail to be? He was an intelligent man." Now Hutchins was about to bury his oldest personal friend, Thornton Wilder; and his oldest academic friend, Bill Douglas, had become incapacitated and retired from the Court. It was a lonely man—he himself—who welcomed him aboard the sinking ship on Eucalyptus Hill. It took more energy than he had, to do what had to be done; but he found the dogged energy to do it. The exigencies of the moment left him—and his board—almost no room at all for maneuver. But maneuver they did. They had to.

The Fellows were all dismissed, except for a grand total of two. The staff was cut to a couple of dozen, to handle administration, membership, publications, and the bare minimum of secretarial work. Hutchins hired as the Center's program director a young history professor from the University of California at Santa Barbara, and he not only planned a program of assorted conferences, but executed it, with inexpensive invitees from the neighborhood. Of the eleven regular participants in the dialogue, four received no compensation at all, four got nominal fees, and three, including Hutchins (who had cut his own salary in half), were full-time administrative or editorial employees. (Visitors pronounced the dialogue no worse than it had ever been—and no better.) A new skinflint Hutchins informed the board that the Center was now paying a maximum of $250 for papers read, and nothing except travel expenses to the nearby, non-paper-reading participants. An incredulous press was told that the Center was planning to expand—while the incredulous press proclaimed that it was going to close.

It couldn't close.

The reason it couldn't close, and couldn't leave Santa Barbara, was the money Hutchins had washed when Dr. Alexander Comfort of *The Joy of Sex* joined the Center fellowship.

Dr. Comfort had a written contract with the Center—no one else did—and was determined to stand up at the bar of justice and see that contract honored. The Center that was going to be compelled to honor its contract with Dr. Comfort now consisted, apart from its vestigial support staff, of the gerontologist Alexander Comfort and the aged Robert Maynard Hutchins, and these two men stood face to face and alone in the arena. Comfort versus Hutchins was just about all that was left of the Center for the Study of Democratic Institutions.

49   A Shabby Pact

While the Comfort affair was heating up, Hutchins and Board Chairman Jubal E. Parten clashed mortally over what Parten called "a breach of trust." The same meeting of the board which dismissed the Fellows and returned Hutchins to the presidency had directed the president to put El Parthenon in trust to guarantee severance pay of one month's salary for each year of every employee's service.[1] Hutchins then informed Parten of an offer to lend the Center 60 percent of the appraised value of the property and explained that the establishment of the trust awaited an appraisal. Parten rightly observed that appraisal had nothing to do with establishing the trust and informed Hutchins of his stern objection to encumbering the property with a mortgage, in view of the board's resolution. (The value of the real estate was around $685,000, and the cash severance pay to employees was some $340,000.)

The two men were at loggerheads. Hutchins was insistent on mortgaging the property and equally insistent that the money was not needed for current expenses—the Center was "in the black" as a result of several substantial gifts from directors (including Parten) for its re-refounding. Parten was sure that Hutchins did not want to move the Center from its magnificent hilltop. Hutchins, insisting that he was not so insisting, nevertheless went on calling for the mortgage. Parten wrote, "It seems to me that the cost of occupancy is approximately $100,000 per year. . . . I feel sure that we could get suitable quarters in downtown Santa Barbara for a small fraction of this cost."[2]

The conflict was actually the culmination of a series of disagreements between the two friends over the issues surrounding the advent and departure of Malcolm Moos. This time neither Parten nor Hutchins would yield, and Parten, knowing that a majority of the board would string along with

Hutchins, finally resigned—painfully reminding Hutchins that he, Parten, was the last remaining member of the original board of the Fund for the Republic appointed by the Ford Foundation in 1952. The two men had never been intimate, but they had worked together for forty years. Parten, a Texas oil man, had been on the board of the University of Texas when that institution and the University of Chicago jointly established the McDonald Observatory in Texas as a counterpart to Chicago's Yerkes Observatory in Wisconsin. As a board member of the Fund and the Center, Parten had always been an exceptionally staunch and generous supporter of Hutchins both publicly and privately.[3]

On July 24, 1975, Alexander Comfort filed a suit in the US District Court in Los Angeles, alleging that the action of the board on May 10 constituted "a dissolution of the Center...and a declaration of...insolvency." He wanted restitution of royalties totaling $93,320 from *The Joy of Sex* that had been given the Center under his contract with it, plus $60,000 in severance pay, plus $250,000 of exemplary or punitive damages on the ground that the Center had acted with malice and wanton disregard of his rights. The Fund for the Republic, as the corporate parent of the Center, denied all these charges and claims and on September 5 filed a countersuit, alleging that Comfort without consent of the fund wrote a work entitled *More Joy* (on the same subject as *The Joy of Sex*) which "competes with and injuriously affects the sale of 'The Joy of Sex.'" The Fund claimed that Comfort had written the second book while he was a senior Fellow of the Center, using the Center's facilities and staff. The loss to the Fund because of *More Joy*'s publication was estimated in excess of $250,000. The Fund wanted $2 million in "exemplary or punitive damages" on this charge ("malice," etc.), and another $2 million in "exemplary or punitive damages" for loss to the reputation of the Center in the alleged amount of $780,000.[4]

The case bade fair—or fairly fair—to be another Trial of the Century, involving, as was supposed, the two sure elements of a histrionic event: money and sex. It proved, in the event, to be essentially a contest of bookkeepers. But it did reveal the nature of the agreement between Comfort and the Center and—to Hutchins—the further shameful fact that the contract had never come before the board. In addition, the trial of the two suits "revealed" what everyone already knew: that the scheme to bilk the British government of taxes was based on the pretense that *The Joy of Sex* had been written in the United States.

The trial also brought to light evidence of low shenanigans by Center personnel during the struggle to oust Moos. Questioning Comfort, a lawyer for the Center said, "You are quoted as saying, 'We've had spying, back-knifing, paper stealing, and Watergating. . . .' To what were you referring. . .?" Comfort replied: "Senior Fellows and others certainly listened at each other's doors and interfered with each other's correspondence. Mr. Ashmore's going around behind Mr. Moos sabotaging his fundraising efforts is what I would describe as back-knifing. Papers were stolen from Mr. Moos's desk and were returned to him with impertinent remarks by Mrs. McAllister."[5] Ex-Fellow Harvey Wheeler supported Comfort's contention that for all practical purposes the Center had been dissolved, and one of the directors testified that a look at the balance sheet was enough to show that the institution was on the way to insolvency.

Having listened at great length to the charges and countercharges in the suits before him and to the allegations by each of the parties of scurrilous conduct by the other, Judge David W. Williams of the U.S. District Court in Los Angeles handed down his evenhanded decision on November 22, 1976. Ordering the Center to return to Comfort all royalties it had received since May 10, 1975, the court said: "Implicit in both parties' understanding of what led to the unholy contract was knowledge that Comfort wanted Eucalyptus Hill as a change of scene from the many years he had spent on the faculty at University College, London, where he had tenure; that he cherished a fuller participation in the Center's dialogues; that he wanted to do the type of research that Eucalyptus Hill encouraged; that he wanted to contribute to the prestigious *Center Magazine.* . . . In this respect the Center must be held to have dissolved itself on May 10, 1975, within the meaning that term is used in . . . the book contract. . . .

"In his spare time from his duties as a professor in a London college, Dr. Alexander Comfort wrote what proved to be a popular book which he titled *The Joy of Sex.* . . . After signing the publishing contract Comfort realized that his gathering wealth from royalties was going to be substantially taken from him in English taxes and he contrived a scheme to salvage those funds. He would find an American nonprofit organization that would claim that it had contractual rights to the copyright of *Joy* and together they would direct the flow of the money in American dollars rather than English pounds to an American organization. It would then share these royalties with Comfort, who planned to become a resident of this country. Then only the lower American taxes would be due on the author's portion."

Comfort had participated in Center conferences and had impressed Hutchins, who wanted him to join the Center as a Senior Fellow. "Comfort resisted these invitations until he became enmeshed in tax problems surrounding his book, and then he realized that the Center might be exactly the type of nonprofit American organization that his English tax counsel had told him could be used as a conduit to funnel *Joy*'s royalties to America and away from the British tax collector. . . . He solicited a formal invitation from Hutchins to join the Center staff and was given a letter employment contract at $28,000 per year plus unspecified severance pay upon termination.

"Comfort then proposed the book contract to his new colleagues. . . . He proposed to assign the copyright of *Joy* to the Center so it could collect the royalties from [the British publisher]; then the Center would remit 80% of the money to [Comfort] and retain 20% to itself. The men on Eucalyptus Hill were uncomfortable with Comfort's scheme but the thought of adding him to the staff plus having him effectively pay his own salary, was tempting. The shabby pact was one in which Comfort untruthfully represented that he had written *Joy* in the United States and under the auspices of the Center while using its facilities; the Center winked at the fraud.

"At the trial, by the use of evasive testimony and feigned legal ignorance, Comfort would have the Court believe that he joined the Senior Fellows only because he felt that they were a self-perpetuating, independent, intellectual group who could not be fired."[6] Judge Williams concluded that there was no merit to Comfort's allegation of fraud and he was entitled to no punitive damages. Since Comfort had voluntarily ended his work at the Center and rejected the offer to continue him as a senior Fellow, the Court held that he was not entitled to severance pay or other benefits. But he was held to be the prevailing party on the contract agreement and was therefore entitled to recover reasonable attorneys' fees from the Fund for the Republic.

Neither of the two parties to the shabby pact was disposed to appeal the ruling. They were both well out of it, though the fund had previously refused Comfort's offer to negotiate a settlement out of court. Hutchins declined to make a statement on the verdict, and his few remaining colleagues at the Center would ever thereafter recall that he did not appear in his office the following day—and did not give his secretary a reason for not appearing.

50 As on a Darkling Plain

Time will corrupt you. Your friends, your wives or husbands, your business or professional associates will corrupt you; your social, political, and financial ambitions will corrupt you. The worst thing about life is that it is demoralizing. . . . So I am worried about your morals. . . . Believe me, you are closer to the truth now than you ever will be again.

In what turned out to be his last full report to his directors, Hutchins wrote extravagantly—as he so often did of the Center (and as he never had at Chicago): "The Center has maintained its program in Santa Barbara, started a new one in Chicago, covered its severance obligations, reduced its expenditures by approximately two thirds. . . . I think there will not be any argument about the desirability, even the necessity, of the work the Center is doing. That the Center has been able to withstand the trials of the last two years is a tribute to the power of the ideas on which it is founded."[1] But the founder had not withstood the trials so well. He was perceptibly deteriorating.

Still erect and ostensibly attentive, he was no longer jaunty or razor-sharp responsive. He was aging day by day. Early one morning one of his colleagues, arriving for work, found him sitting on a sofa in the lobby instead of in his office; he said he was resting, and he was. One friend asked him how he was one day, and he replied with what may have been the only cliché of his life: "I'm falling apart like the one-hoss shay." When another friend asked him how he was feeling, he cocked an ironic eyebrow and quoted the words of the Earl of Rochester on the end of the philosopher: "Huddled in dirt the reasoning engine lies, who was so proud, so witty, and so wise."

Apart from migraine headaches his health had been good until his early seventies. Then in succession he underwent open-heart surgery and a radical bladder operation that left him equipped (as he put it) with outdoor plumbing. In March of 1977—two months after his seventy-eighth birthday—he was taken to the Cottage Hospital in Santa Barbara with a kidney infection. For six weeks he lay in the intensive care unit, semicomatose much of the time. There was a period of "guarded optimism," and he underwent physical therapy. Then there was a relapse. On the night of May 14 he died of uremic poisoning.

He was buried in a view lot in Santa Barbara's finest cemetery, and an Episcopal priest officiated. There were memorial services at the Center and in the Rockefeller Chapel of the University of Chicago.

El Parthenon was sold, and, after severance payments were made, what was left was ultimately transferred to the University of California at Santa Barbara, where it was modestly housed as the Robert Maynard Hutchins Center for the Study of Democratic Institutions—a successful conference center under a succession of presidencies of the men who succeeded the man who succeeded the man who succeeded Hutchins.

In the hospital he had seen almost nobody except his wife. What was probably his final word was addressed to Vesta Hutchins when she asked him how he was. Urbane to the last, he said, "Bored." Esther Donnelly, his secretary, asked him if he wanted reading material in bed. For the only time in his life he didn't. On his sixty-fifth birthday an interviewer had asked him for the meaning of life in one word, and Hutchins had said, "Learning." ("Generally people say 'Loving,'" said the interviewer.)

He was through learning—at least from books.

And through teaching from books. His two last writings were published in the weeks before his death in the Center's occasional periodical *World Issues* and the *Center Magazine*.[2] There was only one solution to the world's problems, he said in "Why We Need World Law," and that solution began at home: "We have to stop throwing our weight around. We have to stop talking about being the most powerful nation on earth. We have to think of the nurture of human life everywhere, otherwise we return to Matthew Arnold's *Dover Beach*, written a hundred years ago:

> The world which seems
> To lie before us like a land of dreams,
> So various, so beautiful, so new,
> Hath neither joy, nor love, nor light,
> Nor certitude, nor peace, nor help for pain;
> And we are here, as on a darkling plain
> Swept with confused alarms of struggle and flight,
> Where ignorant armies clash by night.[3]

The law had been the third love of his life. The university had been the second, and in "The Intellectual Community" he now returned to it. "A university," he wrote, "is or ought to be an intellectual community. . . . An intellectual community is one in which everybody does better intellectual work because he belongs to a community of intellectual workers. An intellectual community can not be formed of people who can not or will not think, who will not think about anything in which other members of the community are interested. Work that does not require intellectual effort and workers that will not engage in a common intellectual effort have no place in a university. A common language, a common stock of ideas, and a common aim are the prerequisites of an intellectual community."[4]

But his first love was Oberlin, and as his life closed he found himself recalling that "the most important word in the Oberlin vocabulary was 'ought.' . . . I have often asked myself in recent years a question I am unable to answer. The question is, what happened to the virtues? The virtues used to be good habits, moral and intellectual. Both kinds were said to have a place in education at all levels. The argument was not about whether, but about where, when, and how they should be inculcated. I never heard it argued that education had nothing to do with morality. The Oberlin view was almost exactly the reverse. . . .

"The intellectual virtues can be taught. A teacher can impart the habit of geometry or any other body of knowledge. Whether the moral virtues can be taught remains a disputed question. They are formed by acts. The virtue of punctuality, if it is one, is formed by being on time. . . . The atmosphere of an educational institution should be conducive to the formation of the moral virtues. And since these virtues and their opposing vices are formed early in life, the emphasis on moral aims, however achieved, should be conspicuous in the early stages of education.

"Or at least so it would seem. And if it should seem so, the question recurs: What happened to the virtues? We must assume that their disappearance from educational discussion is the result of the disappearance of our belief in them. Value-free social science, value-free science—everything valuable is now value-free. Watergate shows that politics has become the pursuit of power. The whole operation of society shows that we expect to get along without good people. People who would have been regarded as good sixty years ago would now be regarded as merely dull, perhaps even stupid, because they did not understand that the virtues are outmoded.

"There have always been bad people. But until Machiavelli, at least, there was thought to be some standard, other than their 'success' in life, by which they could be judged. . . .

"Nowadays you can't say a man is wicked. He may be maladjusted, or sick, but not bad. Of course there are many sick and maladjusted people. Every effort must be made to cure them or straighten them out. Moreover, we know now that traditional methods of achieving these objects, such as confining them in mental institutions or prisons, are, as the saying goes 'counter-productive.' We know, too, that the evidence for the bad effects of a bad environment, particularly in the earliest years, is overwhelming. Since individuals are not to be blamed for their environment, particularly in the earliest years, how can we distinguish between good and bad men, with any connotation of praise or blame? How can we distinguish between good and bad acts?

". . . The Greek idea was that the city educates the man. And the greatest Greeks thought of themselves as participating in that educational function. . . . The interpenetration of the political community and the intellectual community gave the Greeks that mastery of the whole, that grasp of principle, those critical standards, that comprehension, in short, which has extended their influence through thousands of years. Unless our political and intellectual communities can achieve similar vitality we can not hope to approach a similar educational ideal."[5]

On reading that article, his friend Clifton Fadiman wrote him that the "techno-state" did away with the necessity of distinguishing good and bad and the necessity to understand anything. Hutchins managed to reply:

"Perhaps I overrate the power of reason, the resilience of the spirit, and what Aristotle declared in the opening sentence of the *Metaphysics*—the fact that all men by nature desire to know. But these are impressive human credentials, and it is not at all clear to me that the techno-state, as you have described it, is indomitable.

"You and I have lived long enough and read enough books to know that every generation tends to think that its age is at the crossroads, that the survival of mankind is at stake. Ours may indeed be such an age. The techno-state is in fact a powerful force. The techno-culture may threaten to sweep all before it. But if that is true, all the more reason to rally human resources, summon the best in man, and try to create those intellectual communities which will subordinate technology to higher purposes.

". . . I had not realized how optimistic I am."

On his office bookshelves he had cleared a space for an informal photograph of Scott Buchanan and a small metal sculpture of Sisyphus eternally rolling that stone up that hill.

I am inclined to string along with the proposition enunciated by William the Silent (or was it Charles the Bold?) that it is not necessary to hope in order to undertake, nor to succeed in order to persevere.

Epilogue

No man need bother writing his friend's biography—or his enemy's. It will be a bad biography for the main and simple reason (as Penrod would say) that no man is a judge in his own cause (as Aristotle would say).

Both the biographer and the biographee may come off miserably, and one of them must. For men appear better to their friends and worse to their enemies than a man could possibly be, and the author ineluctably accents the wonders of the friend, the warts of the enemy. The closer he approaches his subject, the closer he approaches himself. The instinct for the jugular—to attack or defend it—is nothing to the instinct for the ego.

In the instant case the biographer assures himself that the difficulty is not all that insuperable. Loving his neighbor as himself, he sees himself in his neighbor; and knowing himself for a sinner, he knows his neighbor likewise. You don't have to know a man "intimately"—a close-mouthed man—to know him intimately; thirty or forty years of close-mouthed association will do it. And what you come to know is especially gratifying when what you come to know is a celebrated man and, especially, a celebrated man who sits gray-eyed in judgment on you. Why, *he* is no better, or not all that much better, than I am—a poor consolation, but mine own. Thus the instant biographee, that gray-eyed celebrity, is, at (or near) bottom, bad. . . . If only you knew him as I did. . . .

One of Hutchins' bosom friends liked (and badly needed) to refer to him (out of his presence, of course) as Old Clayfoot. (He was careful to attribute the appellation to another close friend—lest, like everything else, it got back to the subject.) Old Clayfoot he was, Young Clayfoot he had been. The view that Machiavelli wound up with (and Calvin began with)—namely, that men are bad—seems to have some persistent validity. If men are bad, and Hutchins was a man, it follows, as the conclusion from

507

the premises major and minor, that he was a bad man even though he himself said he was.

Demigodliness is not the same as goodliness, and the demigods get no credit for having got that way. Bob Hutchins was not the very best man I have known, not by a long shot (nor yet the very worst, by a longer shot still). But he was the only great man I knew both well and long. I knew him well enough and long enough to know that he was a great man who wanted to be good—and got greater. But not as great as he would have got had such goodness as he had had permitted him (as we say these days) to stroke the right people. Oberlin—Oberlin and morning prayer, Oberlin and the picture on the piano, Oberlin and the martyr's arch, Oberlin and the code of morals—Oberlin pulled him down every time he came within sight of the summit of the kingdoms of this world, the summit that so many people who didn't know Oberlin said he'd achieve in an easy lope.

The best that I can say for him, and I say it now, is that he was of all the men I have known, the most penetrating and the most perceptive and, of all the men I have known, the best polemicist (far and away), the best memoried and the best mannered, the most implacably driven and the most implacably dogged, the most gluttonous for punishment, and, withal, the most engaging and the boonest of long-term companions. That these qualities one and all are only relatively creditable, I know. I know, too, that they do not, all of them together, add up to a man's being any good. But they were the only qualities he had in cornucopic quantity, and in a man who never had time to lift his head from the fleshpots or bow it in meditation the combination was perhaps unexampled.

Well (as Gertrude Stein would say). Or (as John Emerich Edward Dalberg, Lord Acton, did in fact say, if only people would hear him out to the end), "Power tends to corrupt and absolute power corrupts absolutely. Great men are almost always bad men."

It must be difficult to be both preeminently preeminent and preeminently good. It may actually be more difficult to be good than great. And it must be herculean to be any good at all when greatness is the evident consequence of being inordinately tall and handsome and inordinately glib and of having an inordinate father, who, while you were still impressionable, got you up early in the morning and transported you to Oberlin.

It would seem to follow, if nothing but good should be spoken of the dead, that all their evil should be spoken of the living, since men are pretty generally a nice balance of the two and, under the *nil nisi bonum* rule, the balance has got to be struck sooner rather than later.

Well. Here was a man who spoke all his evil of himself.

About the Author

Milton Mayer (1906–1986); educator, journalist, editor, author; native of Chicago, educated in its public schools and precincts, and at the University of Chicago. He was a writer for the Associated Press, Chicago *Post*, and Chicago *American*. For such periodicals as *Harper's, Forum, Saturday Evening Post, Commonweal, Reporter, Christian Century, The Progressive*, he wrote probing essays on education, religion, and public affairs. In politics he was independent; in religion a Jewish member of the Society of Friends (Quakers).

At the University of Chicago he was aide to the president; moderator for Chicago's *Round-Table of the Air*; tutor for the Committee on Social Thought; and assistant professor of classics. He became academic director for the Great Books Foundation; a contributing editor at *Encyclopaedia Britannica, Negro Digest*, and *The Progressive*. He lectured abroad for the American Friends Service Committee; directed "Voices of Europe," for Educational Broadcasters, Ford Foundation; and served as consultant to the National Institute of Public Affairs, the Christian Peace Conference, the Council on International Education, and the Center for the Study of Democratic Institutions.

He held visiting professorships at William Penn, Western Reserve, the universities of Frankfurt and Paris, the Comenius Theological Faculty (Prague), and the Max Planck Institute (Germany). He was professor of English at the University of Massachusetts (Amherst); held similar posts at Hampshire and Windham colleges; was Regents Lecturer, University of California; and Bingham Professor of Humanities, University of Louisville.

His many books, monographs, essays (often controversial) explore moral and social issues in a style of zestful hyperbole tempered with irony, insight, and uncommon wit. Pastor Martin Niemöller called him "an eminent and remarkable analyst of enduring influence."

His honors included the George Polk and Benjamin Franklin prizes for writing; the Ralph Atkinson Award (ACLU); Communicator of the Year (University of Chicago); National Endowment for the Humanities Fellowship; Litt. D., Windham College. Selections from his writing have appeared in foreign translation, and in various collections of best articles.

His association with Robert Maynard Hutchins extended over many years: from early days at Chicago, to their involvement with Great Books, adult education, and the Britannica, to the Ford Foundation, down to final years at the Center in Santa Barbara. Differing much, they shared much. Their friendship was rare for its mutual wit, candor, and understanding.

JHH

A Note on the Text

For over a decade, between other writing and teaching assignments, Milton Mayer worked intermittently on a memoir of his friend and associate Robert Maynard Hutchins. He had his subject's full cooperation and approval for the use of documents published and unpublished. By 1983 he had amassed over twelve hundred pages of rough copy. These Mayer set about to shape and revise with editorial help. By 1985 he had a draft of some nine hundred typescript pages. In spite of serious illness, the remaining year of his life was devoted to additional cuts and revisions that he did not live to complete.

At the time of his death in April 1986, Mayer left his memoir in a form close to what is offered here. The editor, who had been working closely with him on the manuscript, has endeavored with Mrs. Mayer's help to complete the necessary reductions essential to bring the book to press. He has added nothing other than grammatical linkages required for coherence or continuity, and has striven to keep intact Mayer's style and liveliness.

Because he was a participant in many events, and a keen observer of countless more, Mayer is a valuable primary source of information about Hutchins. His authority is frequently personal: his witness to events early and late; his knowledge based on long friendship; his acquaintance with many in the Hutchins circles; not least his ear for talk, whether by Hutchins or those around Hutchins. He had a retentive memory, and a good writer's sense for scene and drama. The Chicago background, from precinct and police court to City Hall and college campus, Mayer knew thoroughly; he was native to it. The Hutchins foreground he saw and heard close up. Mayer conveys, with vivid immediacy, the Hutchins voice and verbal style, the cut of his manner, the different kinds of excitement Hutchins could generate, and a sense of how it felt (early and late) to be within the radius of that powerful presence.

The effect is a counterpoint of views: Hutchins as he appeared to various others, Mayer's perception of his friend, and Hutchins' own view of himself. The combination allows Mayer to be as critical of the man he admired as the man himself was. The composite portrait becomes complicated in a fascinating way, and we see Hutchins at crucial phases in the development of his private-become-public persona.

In the working draft left at his death, Mayer kept the formal paraphernalia of scholarship to the severest minimum, seeking to incorporate necessary citations unobtrusively, even casually, into the text. At the request of the University of California Press, the editor has provided somewhat more detailed documentation in the notes that follow. These notes, where possible, identify the specific sources Mayer drew upon when quoting Hutchins or others, and clarify dates that Mayer omitted or left ambiguous. The information has been taken from Mayer's extensive notes and files, and from marked and annotated volumes and off-prints, transcripts, and periodicals in his library. For quotations left undocumented the reader must assume the authority of Mayer's reconstruction from notes or memory, and my failure to locate a published version or other form of record.

On subjects he thought important, Hutchins repeated the same views many times, in many places, and in similar if not always identical words. (In Mayer's laconic phrase Hutchins gave "eleven speeches eleven hundred times.") Except for a few selected instances, there is no cross-reference between occasions on which Hutchins addressed the same or closely related subjects, nor any effort to cite Mayer's previous use of part of the material he presents here.

Mayer's only recorded interviews with Hutchins were held at the Center for the Study of Democratic Institutions at Santa Barbara, October 2–4, 1973 (transcripts are in Mayer's files). Extensive conversations with Hutchins were held, Mayer said, "throughout 1969 and 1970." Of these, there is no summary or list. Mayer's earliest interviews with Hutchins, dating back to the 1930s, became the basis for articles about Hutchins, Chicago, and American education, such as "Rapidly Aging Young Man" for *Forum and Century* in 1933, and "Hutchins of Chicago," published in two parts, for *Harper's* in 1939.

The major repository for the Hutchins papers is the Joseph Regenstein Library at the University of Chicago. These records contain the originals of most of the Hutchins references cited in this book. The Regenstein Library, Department of Collections, has also been designated as the repository for the papers of Milton Mayer. These will include all of the materials—notes, transcripts, letters, photocopies, documents, and drafts—Mayer accumulated in writing this volume.

The Hutchins Library at Berea College, and the Oberlin College Library, hold Hutchins family records, correspondence, and photographs. The Hutchins papers at Yale are held at the Law School Library, the University Library, and the Beinecke Rare Book and Manuscript Library. Archives of the Fund for the Republic are in the Mudd Library at Princeton University. Archives of the Center for the Study of Democratic Institutions are deposited with the library of the University of California at Santa Barbara.

The many Hutchins friends, family, and colleagues Mayer consulted, and the names of others who helped him with this book, are entered in the list of acknowledgments that Milton Mayer carefully prepared before his death.

The editor wishes to thank George Anastaplo of Loyola University (Chicago) for help with photographs and elusive citations; William J. McClung, Editorial Director of the University of California Press for his thoughtful guidance; editors Douglas Abrams Arava, Mark Pentecost, and copyeditor Tony Hicks of the Press for their care and vigilance; and especially Professor Richard Haven, a former fellow editor on the *Massachusetts Review* and my colleague at the University of Massachusetts (Amherst), for his counsel and generous hours of assistance during what he had expected would be vacation time.

John H. Hicks

Notes

PROLOGUE: HIRED HAND

1. "To the Graduating Class, 1935," published in R. M. Hutchins, *No Friendly Voice* (Chicago: University of Chicago Press, 1936), pp. 1–4.
2. Hutchins, Radio address, April 18, 1935, broadcast by the National Broadcasting Company under the auspices of the National Congress of Parents and Teachers; published in *No Friendly Voice*, pp. 5–11.

CHAPTER 1   THE END OF AN EREA

1. Hutchins' account of this is given in "Conversation with Eric Sevareid," transcript of CBS television broadcast, August 31, 1975, p. 8.

CHAPTER 2   THE WAY IT MAYBE WAS

1. Hutchins, "The Sentimental Alumnus" (Oberlin College commencement address, June 4, 1934), published in *No Friendly Voice*, pp. 87–94.
2. Hutchins, interview with Frank K. Kelly, "Trees Grew in Brooklyn," *Center Magazine*, November 1968, p. 17.
3. Hutchins, interview with the author, Center for the Study of Democratic Institutions, Santa Barbara, October 3 and 4, 1973, tape 4, transcript p. 19.
4. Hutchins, "The Autobiography of an Uneducated Man," in *Education for Freedom* (Baton Rouge: Louisiana State University Press, 1943), p. 1.
5. Ibid.
6. Nathaniel Howard, "Further Particulars of the Great Oberlin Auto Heist," *The Cleveland Plain Dealer*, August 4, 1977.

7. William G. Hutchins, letter to the author, September 17, 1972.

8. Ibid.

9. William G. Hutchins, letter to the author, November 5, 1972.

10. R.M. Hutchins, interview with the author, 1973, tape 4, transcript p. 10.

11. Cf. Hutchins, testimony before the Broyles Commission, Illinois state legislature, April 1949; "The Freedom of the University" (Speech to the Parents Association, University of Chicago Laboratory School, November 1, 1950); "Academic Freedom," in *Freedom, Education and the Fund* (New York: Meridian Books, 1956), pp. 38–40; "Education and Independent Thought," in ibid., pp. 158–59.

12. Hutchins, introduction to *Freedom, Education and the Fund*, p. 14.

13. Ibid.

14. Ibid., p. 15.

15. Ibid.

16. Hutchins, interview with Kelly, p. 17.

17. Hutchins, "Sentimental Alumnus," p. 90.

18. "Sound Portrait of Robert Maynard Hutchins," radio broadcast with Paul Newman, July 17, 1969, transcript p. 4.

19. Hutchins, "Autobiography of an Uneducated Man," p. 2.

20. Ibid., p. 3.

21. Ibid.

22. Ibid.

23. Ibid.

24. Hutchins, "Sentimental Alumnus," p. 87.

25. Ibid., p. 88.

26. Thornton Wilder, conversation with the author, New Haven, Connecticut, 1974.

CHAPTER 3 FALLEN AWAY

1. Hutchins, interview with the author, 1973, tape 4, transcript p. 34.

2. Ibid., p. 27.

3. William G. Hutchins, "Prize Code of Morals for Children," *American Magazine*, April 7, 1918, pp. 26–27.

4. Cf. R.M. Hutchins, "Sentimental Alumnus," p. 93; "Morals and Higher Education," University of Chicago Round-Table no. 16, January 15, 1950; "Morals, Religion, and Higher Education" (Bedell Lecture, Kenyon College, October 4, 1948), Hutchins, interview with the author, 1973, tape 3, transcript p. 20.

5. Thornton Wilder, *Theophilus North* (New York: Harper and Row, 1973), p. 2.

CHAPTER 4 THE VERB "TO SOLDIER"

1. Hutchins, "Autobiography of an Uneducated Man," pp. 4–5.
2. William G. Hutchins, letter to the author, September 17, 1972.
3. R.M. Hutchins, interview with Kelly, p. 18.
4. Hutchins, "Autobiography of an Uneducated Man," p. 5.
5. "Sound Portrait of Robert Maynard Hutchins," transcript p. 5.
6. Hutchins, interview with Kelly, p. 17.

CHAPTER 5 THE YALE MAN

1. Sidney Hyman, *The Lives of William Benton* (Chicago: University of Chicago Press, 1969), p. 48.
2. Ibid., p. 68.
3. William G. Hutchins, letter to the author, November 5, 1972; and conversation with the author, Black Mountain, North Carolina, May 1981.
4. Hyman, *Benton*, p. 51.
5. "Sound portrait of Robert Maynard Hutchins," transcript p. 24.
6. R.M. Hutchins, "Working Your Way through College," (Draft typescript prepared for the editors of *Liberty Magazine*, November 25, 1940).
7. Ibid.
8. Ibid. Cf. Hutchins, speech to Wolf's head, Yale senior honor society, January 1923.
9. Hutchins, "The Education We Need" (speech at the installation of the new president of the University of Illinois, May 16, 1947), published as Human Events Pamphlet no. 22 (Chicago: Henry Regnery, 1947), p. 7.
10. Hutchins, "Autobiography of an Uneducated Man," p. 8.
11. Ibid., pp. 7–8.
12. Hyman, *Benton*, p. 68.
13. Hutchins, Class Day speech, Yale University, 1921.
14. Hutchins, interview with the author, 1973, tape 4, transcript p. 13.
15. Hyman, *Benton*, p. 68.
16. Cf. Hutchins, interview with the author, 1973, tape 4, transcript p. 19.

CHAPTER 6 A FELLOW HAS TO DO SOMETHING

1. See Hutchins, interview with Kelly, p. 18.
2. Hutchins, "Autobiography of an Uneducated Man," pp. 9–10.
3. Reported by William G. Hutchins in a letter to the author, September 17, 1972.

CHAPTER 7   A BLOW ON THE HEAD

1. Hutchins, "Get Ready for Anything: A Conversation with Clifton Fadiman," *Center Report* 8 (June 1975): 20.

2. Ibid., p. 21.

3. Hutchins, "Autobiography of an Uneducated Man," p. 10.

4. Hutchins often expressed himself on this subject. See, e.g., "The Bar and Legal Education" (Speech to the American Bar Association, September 29, 1937).

5. Hutchins, "The Autobiography of an Ex–Law Student," in *No Friendly Voice*, pp. 45–46.

6. See Hutchins, "The Bar and Legal Education."

7. Hutchins, "The Political Community: The Black Country" (Address to the Fund for the Republic dinner in honor of Justice Hugo Black, June 1, 1961).

8. Hutchins, remarks delivered at the dedication of the new Graduate Studies and Research Center, California State University at Long Beach, published under the title "All Our Institutions Are in Disarray," *Center Report* 7 (December 1974); see pp. 20–21.

9. Hutchins, "Political Community."

10. Hutchins, "Autobiography of an Uneducated Man," pp. 11–12.

CHAPTER 8   ANYONE OVER THIRTY

1. Hutchins, address delivered at the Sixth Annual Dinner of the ALI, published in *American Law Institute Proceedings* 6 (July 1927 – June 1928): 592–602.

2. Ibid.

3. This conviction is one Hutchins expressed early and late: as early as the 1920s, when he was a law school lecturer and dean; and as late as 1974, when the quotation appears in "All Our Institutions Are in Disarray," p. 20.

4. Another wording of the same idea is provided in "Toward a World Community," the address Hutchins gave for the Jane Addams centennial, Simmons College, November 22, 1960.

5. Ibid.

6. Hutchins, "Connecticut and the Yale Law School" (Speech delivered at Waterbury, Connecticut, April 20, 1928).

7. Hutchins, "Autobiography of an Ex–Law Student," pp. 48–49.

8. Ibid., p. 47.

9. Hutchins, "The New Atlantis" (Berea College commencement address, June 1, 1931; Convocation Address, University of Chicago, June 16, 1931), published at Chicago in *The University Record* 17 (July 1931).

10. Ibid.

11. Hutchins, "Autobiography of an Ex–Law Student," p. 50.

12. William O. Douglas, *Go East, Young Man—The Early Years* (New York: Random House, 1974), p. 166.

13. Ibid., p. 163.

14. Ibid., p. 165.

15. Ibid.

16. Hutchins, "Experiments in Legal Education at Yale" (Address delivered to the Association of American Law Schools, Chicago, Illinois, December 28, 1928).

17. Hutchins, address delivered at the Yale Law School Alumni luncheon, June 1928.

18. Douglas, *Go East, Young Man*, p. 170.

19. Ibid., p. 182.

CHAPTER 9   7:00 A.M.

1. Hutchins, interview with Donald McDonald, Columbia University Oral History Project, November 1967, parts 1 and 2, transcript pp. 1–2.

2. Ibid., pp. 2–4.

3. Hutchins, interview with Kelly, pp. 19–20.

4. Hutchins, interview with McDonald, transcript pp. 6–7.

5. Ibid., p. 5. Also Hutchins' speech at Dedication of the University's Laird Bell Quadrangle, October 12, 1966, describes this embarrassment at more length.

6. Winthrop S. Dakin, letter to the author, May 23, 1976.

7. Hutchins, 155th Convocation address, University of Chicago, June 11, 1929.

8. *Inaugural Address of Robert Maynard Hutchins, Fifth President of the University of Chicago*, November 19, 1929, p. 13.

9. Quoted in "Splendor Marks Induction of Dr. Hutchins," *Chicago Tribune*, November 19, 1929.

CHAPTER 10   OF CAWSE IT'S IMPAWTANT

1. Felix Frankfurter, letter to Hutchins, January 4, 1933.

2. Hutchins, letter to Frankfurter, April 4, 1933.

3. Frankfurter, letter to Hutchins, April 15, 1933.

4. University Senate vote, October 22, 1930. See *The Idea and Practice of General Education: An Account of the College of the University of Chicago* (Chicago University Press, 1950), pp. 49–50. Also Hutchins, interview with McDonald, transcript p. 21.

5. The College faculty adopted the new program (widely referred to as the New Plan) March 5, 1931. *Idea and Practice of General Education*, pp. 50–51.

6. Ibid., p. 53.
7. Ibid., pp. 51–52, 56.
8. See also George W. Dell, "Robert Hutchins' Philosophy of General Education and the College at the University of Chicago," *Journal of General Education* 30 (Spring 1978): 45–58.
9. Hutchins, *The Higher Learning in America* (New Haven: Yale University Press, 1936), p. 85.

CHAPTER 11   MERT

1. Mortimer Adler, *Philosopher at Large* (New York: Macmillan, 1977), pp. 109–11.
2. Gertrude Stein, *Everybody's Autobiography* (New York: Random House, 1937), pp. 205–7.

CHAPTER 12   THE BLUE SKY

1. John U. Nef, *The Search for Meaning: The Autobiography of a Non-Conformist* (Washington: Public Affairs Press, 1973), p. 125.
2. Dodd's view of their disagreement appears in William E. Dodd, *Ambassador Dodd's Diary*, ed. William E. Dodd, Jr., and Martha Dodd (New York: Harcourt, Brace, 1941), pp. 96, 335–36.
3. Ibid., p. 337.
4. Adler, *Philosopher at Large*, p. 49.
5. Hutchins, letter to Felix Frankfurter, n.d.
6. Richard McKeon, "The Battle of the Books," in *The Knowledge Most Worth Having*, ed. Wayne C. Booth (Chicago: University of Chicago Press, 1967), p. 192.
7. Irene Tufts Mead, interview with Lloyd E. Stein, reported in "Hutchins of Chicago: Philosopher-Administrator," (Doctoral dissertation, University of Massachusetts, Amherst, 1971), pp. 99 ff.
8. Adler's summary of this period appears in *Philosopher at Large*, pp. 127–34, 145–48.

CHAPTER 13   THE END OF EVERYTHING

1. Hutchins, "The Y.M.C.A." (Speech to the Employed Officers Association of the YMCA, College Camp, Lake Geneva, Wisconsin, June 9, 1933), published in *No Friendly Voice*; see pp. 132–33, 134–35.
2. Hutchins, introduction, to *Freedom, Education and the Fund*, p. 18.
3. "Sound Portrait of Robert Maynard Hutchins," transcript pp. 21–23; Hutchins, interview with Kelly, p. 20.
4. Hutchins, letter to Harold H. Swift, July 18, 1936.

CHAPTER 14   THE UNKINDEST CUT

1. Hutchins, "Y.M.C.A.," p. 135.
2. John Gunther, *Taken at the Flood: The Story of Albert D. Lasker* (New York: Harper and Brothers, 1960), p. 225.
3. Hutchins, "Gate Receipts and Glory," *Saturday Evening Post*, December 3, 1938, p. 23.
4. Hutchins, "Football and College Life" (Address to undergraduates, Mandel Hall, University of Chicago, January 12, 1940).

CHAPTER 15   THE RED ROOM

1. An earlier version of this chapter appeared as an article in *The Massachusetts Review* 16, no. 3 (Summer 1975): 520–50.
2. Hutchins, "The Tenure of Professors" (Address delivered to the annual meeting of the American Association of University Professors, November 27, 1931).
3. Franklin D. Roosevelt, letter to Hutchins, July 1, 1935.
4. Harold L. Ickes, *The First Thousand Days: 1933–1936*, vol. 1 of *The Secret Diary of Harold L. Ickes* (New York: Simon and Schuster, 1935), p. 376.
5. Hutchins, "What It Means to Go to College," CBS radio address, October 2, 1935, *No Friendly Voice*, p. 22.

CHAPTER 16   CEASE-FIRE

1. *Idea and Practice of General Education*, p. 54.
2. Hutchins, interview with McDonald, transcript pp. 79–80.
3. Scott Buchanan, "A Crisis in Liberal Education," *Amherst Graduate's Quarterly* 27 (February 1938): 117.

CHAPTER 17   LIKE A PRESIDENT SHOULD

1. Hutchins, "Reply to Professor Whitehead," *Atlantic Monthly*, November 1936, pp. 582–88.
2. Hutchins, letter to Richard McKeon, September 8, 1936.
3. E.g., Hutchins, "The Atomic Bomb versus Civilization" (chapel sermon, University of Chicago, October 14, 1945), published as Human Events Pamphlet no. 1 (Chicago: Human Events, 1945); "How to Blunder into War with Russia" (Lecture to Modern Forum, Inc., Los Angeles, March 25, 1946), later published in *Western World*, March 1959, pp. 12–15; "Science, Technology, and Political Community" (Speech at University of California Extension at Los Angeles, June 30, 1960); also "Science and Politics" (Speech at a dinner for the Twelfth Region U.S. Government Civil Service Commission, Santa Barbara, January 23, 1962).

4. Hutchins, "How to Blunder into War with Russia," p. 12.

5. Hutchins, "Autobiography of an Uneducated Man."

6. The letters quoted here are from a collection entitled "The Voluptuous Paragraph: A Critical Study of the Correspondence of Robert Maynard Hutchins," prepared by "an Admirer," June 30, 1948.

7. Hutchins, letter to Felix Frankfurter, April 4, 1933. Hutchins to William O. Douglas, June 5, 1956. Hutchins to Adlai Stevenson, January 13, 1937. Hutchins to Edward H. Levi, February 15, 1968. Hutchins to Henry R. Luce, December 6, 1949.

8. Hutchins, "Education at War," in *Education for Freedom*, p. 90.

9. Hutchins, "What Kind of World," typescript for Los Angeles Times Syndicate, September 1, 1963.

10. Hutchins, "Back to Galen," in *No Friendly Voice*, p. 51.

CHAPTER 18   THE BAD MAN TRICK

1. Hutchins, speech given at Aspen Institute for Humanistic Studies, Aspen, Colorado, July 5, 1969.

2. Hutchins, interview with Kelly, p. 21.

3. Hutchins, response at a dinner in his honor, New York, February 20, 1965.

4. Hutchins, "What Kind of World," typescript for Los Angeles Times Syndicate, November 8, 1969.

5. Hutchins, interview with the author, 1973, tape 4, transcript p. 20.

6. Hutchins, interview with Kelly, p. 20.

7. Ibid., p. 22.

8. Hutchins, "Materialism and Its Consequences," in *Education for Freedom*, p. 46.

9. Hutchins, "A Democratic Platform" (Speech to the Young Democratic Clubs, Chicago, June 27, 1932).

10. Hutchins, interview with the author, 1973, tape Z-32, transcript p. 15.

11. Harold L. Ickes, *The Inside Struggle, 1936–1939*, vol. 2 of *The Secret Diary of Harold L. Ickes*, p. 384.

12. Hutchins, conversation with Eric Sevareid, CBS television broadcast, August 31, 1975, transcript p. 14.

13. Ibid., p. 15.

CHAPTER 19   SOMETHING FOR POOR BOB

1. Hutchins, interview with Kelly, p. 21.

2. *Harper's Magazine*, November 1938, pp. 561–71.

3. Milton Mayer, "The Case against the Jew," *Saturday Evening Post*, March 28, 1942, pp. 18–19.

CHAPTER 20 ONWARD AS TO WAR

1. Harold L. Ickes, *The Lowering Clouds, 1939–1941*, vol. 3 of *The Secret Diary of Harold L. Ickes*, pp. 256–59.

2. *New York Herald Tribune*, October 9, 1944.

3. Hyman, *Benton*, p. 138.

4. Alexander Woollcott, "Town Crier," broadcast 1944.

5. Hyman, *Benton*, pp. 230–31.

6. Hutchins, "What Shall We Defend?" reprinted in *Vital Speeches of the Day* 6 (July 1, 1940): 547–49.

7. Hutchins, "Higher Education and National Defense" (Speech to the Chicago Association of Commerce, January 29, 1941).

8. Harry Hopkins, letter to his brother, Emory Hopkins. Quoted in Robert Sherwood, *Roosevelt and Hopkins: An Intimate Portrait* (New York: Harper and Brothers, 1948), pp. 123–24.

9. Hutchins, "Democracy, Defense, and War" (Edward Douglas White lecture, Louisiana State University, April 25, 1941), printed as "Education at War" in *Education for Freedom.*

10. Quoted in Hyman, *Benton*, p. 239.

11. Ickes, *Lowering Clouds*, p. 472.

12. John Gunther Papers, box XXV, F. 14, Regenstein Library, University of Chicago.

13. Hutchins, letter to Philip Jessup, April 22, 1941.

14. Wayne S. Cole, *America First: The Battle against Intervention, 1940–41* (Madison: University of Wisconsin Press, 1953), p. 174.

15. Chester Bowles, letter to Hutchins, June 16, 1941.

16. Joseph L. Jaffe, Jr., "Isolation and Neutrality in Academe, 1938–1941" (Doctoral dissertation, Department of History, Case Western Reserve University, 1979), p. 31.

17. Hutchins, letter to Charles Lindbergh, April 14, 1952.

18. Clarence B. Randall, letter to Hutchins, March 31, 1941.

19. Hutchins, letter to Clarence B. Randall, April 2, 1941.

20. Richard H. Goldstone, *Thornton Wilder* (New York: Saturday Review Press, 1975), pp. 140–41.

21. Hutchins, speech at memorial service for Thornton Wilder, New Haven, Connecticut, January 18, 1976.

22. John Gunther, *Taken at the Flood: The Story of Albert D. Lasker* (New York: Harper, 1960), pp. 181–82.

23. Ibid., pp. 265–66. [Editor's note: To this information, Gunther adds the following sentences (that Mayer omits to include or to mention): "But this had not been Mayer's title. He had called the article 'The Wondering Jew' and the *Post*, without his knowledge or consent, changed it to 'The Case Against the Jew.' But Lasker would not be mollified" (p. 266). Whether or not this is correct about the titles, or as to what presumably Lasker was told, Mayer apparently refrained from public comment or dis-

claimer, and stoically assumed, then and thereafter, the consequences of the printed (and eventually reprinted) title appearing over his name. From among Mayer's papers, drafts, notes, marginalia, or surviving associates, I discover no evidence to confirm (or deny) the version Gunther gives in his biography of Albert Lasker.

But many years later—in a speech at Chicago in 1967 to receive the University's "Communicator of the Year" award—Mayer said this about this controversial article and its title: "My thesis was the well-worn platitude that Gentiles are no good and nobody should imitate them. I was, in a word, making out a case for the Jew. The title I used was 'The Case Against the Jew.'" Mayer, "The Remote Possibility of Communication," *University of Chicago Magazine* (November 1967), p. 21.]

24. Hutchins, letter to Thornton Wilder, February 22, 1941.

25. Hutchins, "America and the War," NBC radio address, January 23, 1941, printed in the *University of Chicago Magazine* (February 1941), p. 7.

26. Ibid.

27. Hutchins, "Democracy, Defense, and War" (Edward Douglas White Lecture, Louisiana State University, April 25, 1941); "Education and the Defense of Democracy" (Loyola University [Chicago] Convocation, May 13, 1941).

28. Hutchins, "Political Community."

29. Hutchins, "Proposition Is Peace."

30. Hutchins, "America and the War," p. 5.

31. Hutchins, "Proposition Is Peace."

CHAPTER 21   A WAR PLANT

1. Hutchins, "The University at War" (Speech given at the trustee-faculty dinner, South Shore Country Club, January 7, 1942), published in the *University of Chicago Magazine*, January 1942, pp. 1–7.

2. Ibid., p. 1.

3. Ibid., p. 3.

4. Ibid.

5. Hutchins, interview with McDonald, transcript pp. 128–31.

6. Hutchins, "How to Save the Colleges" (Dinner speech, May 26, 1942), published in *Education for Freedom*, pp. 65–79. The quotations are from pp. 65–67, 69–70.

7. Hutchins, Western Union cable to Chancellor O.C. Carmichael, Vanderbilt University, February 8, 1942.

8. January 19, 1943.

9. November 13, 1942.

10. Hutchins, "Education at the University" (Address given at the trustee-faculty dinner, South Shore Country Club, January 12, 1944.

11. Hutchins, "University at War," p. 1.

12. Hutchins, letter to Malcolm Sharp, January 19, 1943.

13. Hutchins, typed draft of column for the *Los Angeles Times* (among Mayer's papers).

14. "University at War," p. 7.

15. Hutchins, "Blueprint for Wartime Education," *Saturday Evening Post*, August 15, 1942, p. 17.

CHAPTER 22   UNHAPPY WARRIOR

1. Wilbur C. Munnecke, letter to the author, July 2, 1981.

2. Hutchins, "Democracy and the War" (University Chapel sermon, April 12, 1942).

3. Hutchins, "The Press and Education" (Address to the American Society of Newspaper Editors, Washington, DC, April 18, 1930).

4. Hutchins, remarks to the National Society of Newspaper Editors, Washington, DC, April 21, 1955, published in *Freedom, Education, and the Fund*, pp. 56–67; the quotation is from p. 58.

5. Hutchins, speech to the National Conference of Editorial Writers, Louisville, Kentucky, November 19, 1948, published in *Freedom, Education, and the Fund*, pp. 46–56.

6. *Time*, March 31, 1947, pp. 67–68. *Fortune*, April 1947, pp. 2–5; see also supplement of same date, pp. 1–21.

7. *The Knickerbocker News*. See Hutchins, *Freedom, Education, and the Fund*, pp. 47–48.

CHAPTER 23   THE GOOD NEWS OF DAMNATION

1. Diary entry for July 25, 1945, in *Off the Record: The Private Papers of Harry S. Truman*, ed. Robert S. Ferrell (New York: Harper and Row, 1980), pp. 55–56.

2. Hutchins, "Atomic Force: Its Meaning for Mankind," University of Chicago Round-Table of the Air, NBC broadcast, August 12, 1945, transcript p. 12.

3. Quoted in *The New Yorker*, March 17, 1973, p. 89.

4. Hutchins, "V-E Day" (Address delivered at the Special Assembly, University Chapel, May 8, 1945).

5. As president of the Committee to Frame a World Constitution, organized in 1946, Hutchins expressed his views in a forty-page lead article entitled "1950," published in the first issue of *Common Cause* (June 30, 1947), a monthly report published by the committee; see the *New York Times*, June 29, 1947. In the last year of his life Hutchins published "Why We Need World Law," *World Issues*, December 1976 / January 1977.

6. Hutchins, "1950."

7. Hutchins, "The New Realism" (University of Chicago convocation address, June 15, 1945).

8. Hutchins, "Atomic Force," transcript pp. 7, 9, 12.

9. Stanley Blumberg and Gwinn Owens, *Energy and Conflict: The Life and Times of Edward Teller* (New York: G.P. Putnam, 1976), pp. 154–57.

10. Ibid. See also James F. Byrnes, *All in a Lifetime* (New York: Harper, 1958), p. 284.

11. See, e.g., Hutchins, "Atomic Bomb versus Civilization"; "Peace and the Atom Bomb," University of Chicago Round-Table of the Air, NBC broadcast, November 11, 1945; "Government Control of Atomic Energy," Hutchins' testimony to the Special Committee on Atomic Energy, US Senate, Washington, DC, January 25, 1946.

12. Ernest Borek, "Cheating in Science," *New York Times*, January 22, 1975.

13. Hutchins, interview with McDonald, transcript pp. 98–99.

14. John Gunther, *Chicago Revisited* (Chicago: University of Chicago Press, 1967).

15. Major General L.R. Groves, letter to Hutchins, September 15, 1945. [Editor's note: Groves's letter was intimidating, but it did not quite flatly ask for a cancellation of the conference. Groves did insist, however, that all conferees be given copies of security regulations.]

16. Hutchins, letter to Major General L.R. Groves, September 17, 1945.

17. This was a debating strategy Hutchins consistently repeated to expose the logical consequences of certain Cold War zealotry. It is repeated, for example, in "What Should Be Our Policy Toward Russia?" Town Meeting of the Air, New York City, April 25, 1946, published in *Town Meeting* 11, no. 52; see pp. 8, 10.

18. Hutchins, press conference, August 9, 1945 (Statement issued by University of Chicago office of press relations).

19. Dixon Wector, "Can Metaphysics Survive?" *Saturday Review of Literature*, April 10, 1948, p. 7.

20. Hutchins, letter to Colonel Charles Lindbergh, December 20, 1945.

21. Hutchins, press conference, August 9, 1945, quoted from the *Chicago Sun*, August 10, 1945.

CHAPTER 24   THE GUILTY FLEE WHERE NONE PURSUE

1. As for the utility of science in confrontation with problems of human life—on June 3, 1966, the Dow Chemical Company issued this statement: "Our position on the manufacture of napalm is that we are a supplier of goods to the Defense Department and not a policy-maker. Simple good citizenship requires that we supply our government and our military

with those goods which they feel they need whenever we have the technology and capability and have been chosen by the government as the supplier." Quoted in Robert I. Heilbroner, *In the Name of Profit* (New York: Doubleday, 1972), p. 142.

2. Hutchins, "How to Blunder into War with Russia."

3. Hutchins in "Atomic Force."

CHAPTER 25   ONE WORLD OR NONE

1. Hutchins in "Atomic Force."

2. Hutchins, "Atomic Bomb versus Civilization," p. 11.

3. G. A. Borgese, *A Proposition to History* (Chicago: Committee to Frame a World Constitution, 1948). Borgese, *Foundations of the World Republic* (Chicago: University of Chicago Press, 1953).

4. "The Problem of World Government," University of Chicago Round-Table of the Air, NBC broadcast, April 4, 1948.

5. Hutchins, Atomic Bomb versus Civilization," pp. 11–12.

CHAPTER 26   "WE'RE ONLY SCIENTISTS"

1. Bernard M. Loomer, "An Atomic Energy Proposal," *University of Chicago Magazine*, Autumn 1979, p. 21.

2. Ibid., p. 23.

3. Ibid., p. 24.

4. Ibid., p. 26.

CHAPTER 27   THE GREAT BOOKS INDUSTRY

1. Hutchins, "The Basis of Education," in *The Conflict in Education in a Democratic Society* (New York: Harper, 1953), pp. 75–76.

2. Hutchins, "Where Do We Go from Here in Education?" (address to the Economic Club of Detroit, May 12, 1947).

3. Hutchins, "The Education We Need," p. 9.

4. Hutchins, "Where Do We Go from Here in Education?"

5. Ibid.

CHAPTER 28   AD MAN

1. Hutchins, letter to William Benton, February 11, 1937.

2. Hyman, *Benton*, pp. 556–57.

3. Harvey Einbinder, *The Myth of the Britannica* (New York: Grove Press, 1964).

4. *In the Matter of Encyclopaedia Britannica, Inc.*, 59 F.T.C. 24 (1961).

5. Adler, *Philosopher at Large*, p. 259.

6. Hutchins, introduction to *Education For Freedom*, University of Chicago Round-Table of the Air radio discussion, NBC, March 21, 1943, p. 1.

CHAPTER 29   "EAT, SHIRLEY"

1. Quoted in Don Sider, "The Midway and the Potomac," *University of Chicago Magazine*, Summer 1976, p. 13.
2. Stein, *Everybody's Autobiography*, pp. 212–13.
3. Hutchins, interview with Kelly, pp. 21–22. See also interview with McDonald, transcript pp. 88–90.
4. Daniel Bell, *The Reforming of General Education* (New York: Columbia University Press, 1966), p. 32.

CHAPTER 30   DISTURBING THE WAR

1. *Newsweek*, June 20, 1938, p. 18.
2. Hutchins, memorandum to the board of trustees, July 18, 1942.

CHAPTER 31   THE CANNON

1. Victor Hugo, *Ninety-Three* (Edinburgh: John Grant, 1903) 1:54–59.
2. Hutchins, speech given at the trustee-faculty dinner, South Shore Country Club, January 12, 1944, published in the *University of Chicago Magazine*, April 1944.

CHAPTER 32   BROOKS BROTHERS BOLSHEVIK

1. Hutchins, interview with McDonald, transcript pp. 76–78.
2. Hutchins, speech given in Chicago, June 27, 1932.
3. Hutchins, interview with McDonald, transcript pp. 115–20.
4. "Surplus value is the difference between the price paid for a product and the price paid labor for its manufacture." William L. Reese, *Dictionary of Philosophy and Religion* (Atlantic Highlands, N.J.: Humanities Press, 1980).

CHAPTER 33   SHOWDOWN

1. Hutchins, luncheon speech to the American Association of University Professors, Evanston, Illinois, February 14, 1944.
2. *Chicago Daily News*, March 2, 1944.
3. Letter to President R. M. Hutchins, February 28, 1944, signed by six faculty members: Jacob Viner, R. S. Crane, Sewall Wright, A. O. Craven, E. J. Kraus, and Frank H. Knight.

4. Hutchins, letter to the six faculty members, March 2, 1944.

5. Letter from the six faculty members to Hutchins, March 18, 1944.

6. Hutchins, letter to the six faculty members, March 25, 1944.

7. "Memorial to the Board of Trustees on the State of the University," resolution adopted by the university senate, May 22, 1944. The text of the memorial, the reply of the board of trustees through its chairman, and the statement made by President Hutchins after the board had taken its action, appear in the *University of Chicago Magazine*, June 1944, pp. 5–9, 11.

8. Board of Trustees, Harold H. Swift, chairman, "To the Senate," ibid., pp. 8–9.

9. "Statement by the Chairman of the Board of Trustees," ibid., p. 9.

10. "Statement by the President after the Board of Trustees' Meeting," ibid., pp. 9, 11.

11. Hutchins, "Personal Aspects" (Memorandum to Harold H. Swift, for distribution to the Board of Trustees Committee on Instruction and Research, May 31, 1944).

12. Hutchins, "The Organization and Purpose of the University" (Address to the students and faculty, Rockefeller Chapel, University of Chicago July 20, 1944).

CHAPTER 34   DENOUEMENT

1. Hutchins, "The Administrator" (University of Chicago lecture, April 23, 1946), revised for *Freedom, Education, and the Fund*, pp. 167–185.

2. Hutchins, letter to Laird Bell, December 1, 1944.

3. Writing in the *University of Chicago Magazine*, (Winter 1985), pp. 37–38, Donald N. Levine, dean of the College, said: "No sooner did Hutchins leave the University than the key elements of the colleges that had taken shape under his leadership began to wither away. Without the protection he afforded them, one by one, most of the great staff-taught general education courses that developed during his tenure were dissolved. The independent Board of Examiners was disbanded. The comprehensive examinations as a substitute for course credits disappeared. The custom of carefully constructed course syllabi vanished. The notion of sequential work in the disciplines faded away. And the lynch-pin . . . which Hutchins cherished so much—the awarding of the B.A. after a program of general education co-extensive with the old junior college—was pulled out."

4. Quincy Wright, "What Is a University?" *Bulletin of the Association of University Professors* 30, no. 2 (Summer 1944), p. 175.

5. Harry Woodburn Chase, "Hutchins' Higher Learning Grounded," *The American Scholar*, June 1937, pp. 236–44.

6. John Dewey, "Challenge to Liberal Thought," *Fortune*, August 1944, pp. 154–57.

7. Hutchins, interview with McDonald, transcript pp. 130–31.
8. Ibid., pp. 131–32.
9. Ibid., pp. 17–18.
10. Hutchins, "The Administrator," p. 175.
11. Hutchins, "The Administrator Reconsidered" (Address to American College of Hospital Administrators, Atlantic City, NJ, September 19, 1955), revised for *Freedom, Education, and the Fund*, pp. 185–196; the quotation is from pp. 187–88.

CHAPTER 35   DENOUEMENT (2): MAUDE

1. Paul Jacobs, memorandum to the author, May 28, 1969.
2. Maude Phelps McVeigh Hutchins, *A Diary of Love* (Westport, Conn.: Greenwood Press, 1950).
3. Wilbur C. Munnecke, letter to the author, April 16, 1981.

CHAPTER 36   A CALL FOR COMMUNITY

1. Hutchins, "Atomic Bomb versus Civilization," p. 9.
2. Ibid., p. 10.
3. Hutchins, "Atomic Energy: Peace or War with Russia," CBS Radio Address, March 5, 1946.
4. Ibid.
5. Hutchins, "The Good News of Damnation" (Speech at St. Louis, Missouri, March 4, 1947), published in the *University of Chicago Magazine*, April 1947, pp. 5–8.
6. Hutchins, "How to Blunder into War with Russia," p. 15.
7. Hutchins, "Where Do We Go from Here in Education?"
8. Hutchins, "How to Blunder into War with Russia," p. 15.
9. Hutchins, "Good News of Damnation," p. 7.
10. Ibid.
11. Ibid.
12. Ibid.
13. "Truman seldom was briefed on developing nuclear strategy and had only a cursory knowledge." Robert J. Donovan, *Tumultuous Years: The Presidency of Harry S. Truman, 1949–1953* (New York: Norton, 1982), p. 100.
14. Richard G. Hewlitt and Oscar E. Anderson, Jr., *The New World, 1939–1946: A History of the United States Atomic Energy Commission* (University Park: Pennsylvania State University Press, 1962) 1:455–56.
15. Hutchins, "Peace and the Atom Bomb." pp. 7, 8, 11.
16. Hutchins, testimony before the House of Representatives Military Affairs Committee, Washington, DC, February 18, 1946, published in *Presbyterian Tribune*, April, 1946, pp. 13–14.
17. Hutchins, "How to Blunder into War with Russia," p. 15.

CHAPTER 37 A PERENNIAL ADOLESCENT

1. Hutchins, "The Task for Intellectuals and the Need for World Government," (Address to German National Assembly, Frankfurt, Germany, May 18, 1948).

2. At the Aspen Convocation Hutchins gave an address entitled "Goethe and the Unity of Mankind," July 13, 1949.

3. Hutchins, "What Should Be Our Attitude Toward Russia?" Town Meeting of Air broadcast, New York, April 25, 1946.

4. Hutchins, "How to Blunder into War with Russia," p. 14.

5. Hutchins, "St. Thomas and the World State" (Lecture delivered at Marquette University, March 6, 1949), printed in Hutchins, *Saint Thomas and the World State* (Milwaukee: Marquette University Press, 1949).

6. Hutchins, "An American Road to a World Society" (Address given at Santa Barbara, California); highlights from this talk appear in "Why We Need World Law," *World Issues* 1 (December 1976 / January 1977): 29–30. Cf. Hutchins, "1950."

7. Hutchins, testimony to the Illinois Seditious Activities Investigation Commission, published in the commission's *Special Report* (1949), p. 21.

8. Robert MacIver, *Academic Freedom in Our Time* (New York: Columbia University Press, 1955), p. 35.

9. Illinois Seditious Activities Investigation Commission, *Report of Proceedings* (1949), quoted in Robert Lasch, "Two Intrepid Colleges," *The Reporter*, June 21, 1949, p. 23.

CHAPTER 38 A COOL HALF-BILLION

1. Dwight Macdonald, *The Ford Foundation: The Men and the Millions* (New York: Reynal and Co., 1959), p. 1.

2. Hutchins, interview with McDonald, transcript p. 127.

3. Hutchins, typescript for the *Los Angeles Times*, November 8, 1964. Cf. Hutchins, interview with McDonald, transcript pp. 67–68.

4. Joseph Schwab, undated conversation with the author.

5. Hutchins, farewell address, University of Chicago, February 2, 1951, published with some revision as "A Message to the Young Generation," in *Freedom, Education, and the Fund*, pp. 75–80.

6. Ibid., p. 80.

7. This passage is omitted in this published version of the address, but it appears in the reprint of the speech for the university's *Tower Topics* (March 1951).

8. *Freedom, Education, and the Fund*, p. 80.

CHAPTER 39 "YOU AND YOUR GREAT BIG GERANIUMS"

1. Thomas C. Reeves, *Freedom and the Foundation: The Fund for the Republic in the Era of McCarthyism* (New York: Alfred A. Knopf, 1969), pp. 13–14.

2. Dwight Macdonald, "Profile," *New Yorker*, December 17, 1955. See also Macdonald, *Ford Foundation*, p. 153.

3. Quoted in Reeves, *Freedom and the Foundation*, pp. 5–6.

4. Ibid.

5. Hutchins, "Education and Independent Thought" (Speech given at Santa Monica, California, Town Hall, February 20, 1952), published in *Freedom, Education, and the Fund*, pp. 152–66; the quotation is from p. 161. Cf. Hutchins, "Can We Preserve Freedom and Achieve Security?" (Hillman Lecture, Sidney Hillman Foundation, Harvard University, February 16, 1951).

6. Hutchins, "Education and Independent Thought," pp. 165–66.

7. Ibid., pp. 156–57.

8. Ibid., pp. 157–59.

9. Ibid., pp. 159–60.

10. Hutchins, "The Civilization of the Dialogue" (Speech given at the Free University of Berlin, August 6, 1951).

11. The congressional investigation of tax-exempt foundations, under the direction of Representative Brazilla Carroll Reece of Tennessee, was authorized in the 83d Congress, 1st Session, 1953. The 432-page Reece Report was published in late December 1954. See Reeves, *Freedom and the Foundation*, pp. 56, 78–79, 102–4, 107–9.

CHAPTER 40 THE EYE OF THE STORM

1. Quoted in MacDonald, "Profile," p. 53.

2. Quoted in ibid., p. 54.

3. Philip M. Stern, "An Open Letter to the Ford Foundation," *Harper's Magazine* January 1966, p. 85.

4. Quoted in Victor Lasky, *Never Complain, Never Explain: The Story of Henry Ford II* (New York: Marek, 1981), p. 205.

5. Quoted in Reeves, *Freedom and the Foundation*, pp. 80–81. Much of the documentary material in this chapter, and the next, is from Professor Reeves' book.

6. Reeves, *Freedom and the Foundation*, pp. 133–34.

7. Quoted in ibid., p. 63.

8. Quoted in ibid., p. 25.

9. Ibid., pp. 98–99.

10. Quoted in ibid., p. 99.

11. Ibid., p. 13.

12. W. H. Ferry, memorandum, September 11, 1951, quoted in Reeves, *Freedom and the Foundation*, p. 24.

13. Hutchins, memorandum, October 15, 1951, quoted in Reeves, *Freedom and the Foundation*, p. 31.

14. *New York Times*, July 28, 1953.

15. Quoted in Reeves, *Freedom and the Foundation*, p. 56.

16. Ibid., pp. 51–52, 307n.

17. Ibid., p. 73.

18. Lasky, *Never Complain*, p. 198.

CHAPTER 41   ALL OVER MUD

1. Quoted in Reeves, *Freedom and the Foundation*, p. 118.

2. Ibid., pp. 119–21.

3. Quoted in ibid., p. 121.

4. Ibid., p. 122.

5. Quoted in ibid., p. 123.

6. Quoted in ibid., p. 142.

7. Hutchins, speech to the National Press Club, Washington, DC, January 26, 1955, published under the title "The Fund, Foundations and the Reece Committee," in *Freedom, Education, and the Fund*, pp. 201–12.

8. Quoted in Reeves, *Freedom and the Foundation*, p. 227.

9. Ibid., p. 253.

10. Paul Harvey, ABC network broadcast, August 28, 1955, quoted in Reeves, *Freedom and the Foundation*, p. 131.

11. Reeves, *Freedom and the Foundation*, p. 191.

12. John Cogley, Fund for the Republic press release, June 28, 1956.

13. Alfred Kazin, *Starting Out in the Thirties* (New York: Vintage Books, 1980), pp. 71–73.

14. Sidney Hook, *The New Leader*, March 19, 1956, p. 28.

CHAPTER 42   IS ANYBODY LISTENING? (1)

1. Quoted in Reeves, *Freedom and the Foundation*, p. 189.

2. Ibid., p. 184.

3. Quoted in ibid., p. 162. Hutchins' views on this subject are explained in detail in a speech he gave three-and-a-half years earlier at Santa Monica, California, February 20, 1952, published as "Education and Independent Thought" in *Freedom, Education, and the Fund*; see pp. 157–59, 161. See also Hutchins, *Education for Freedom*, pp. 22–23, 41–42.

4. Quoted in Reeves, *Freedom and the Foundation*, p. 161.

5. Ibid., p. 172.

6. "Meet the Press," radio and television broadcast, November 20,

1955, reprinted in the *National Review*, December 7, 1955, p. 7. The panelists were Lawrence Spivack, moderator; James McConnaughy, Jr., of *Time*; Frederick Woltman of the *New York World Telegram and Sun*; and May Craig of the Portland, Maine, *Press Herald*.

7. From the text of the broadcast by Fulton Lewis, Jr., over WOR and MBS Network, November 21, 1955, prepared for the Fund for the Republic by Radio Reports, Inc.

8. Paul Jacobs, *Is Curley Jewish?* (New York: Athenaeum, 1965), p. 223.

9. Paul Hoffman, letter to Mrs. Roger D. Lapham, November 23, 1955, quoted in Reeves, *Freedom and the Foundation*, p. 173.

10. Reeves, *Freedom and the Foundation*, p. 117.

11. *Los Angeles Times*, April 11, 1974.

12. Maxine Green, "Robert M. Hutchins—Crusading Metaphysician," *School and Society*, May 12, 1956, pp. 162–66.

13. *Washington Post*, December 29, 1957.

14. Ibid.

CHAPTER 43   BASIC ISSUES

1. Hutchins, memorandum to the board of trustees, April 18, 1956, quoted in Frank K. Kelly, *Court of Reason: Robert Hutchins and the Fund for the Republic* (New York: Free Press, 1981), p. 118.

2. Hutchins, letter to William Benton, June 8, 1953.

3. Hutchins, memorandum to the board of trustees, May 4, 1956, quoted in Kelly, *Court of Reason*, p. 120.

4. Hutchins to Benton, June 8, 1953.

5. Ibid.

6. Roger Lapham, letter to Paul Hoffman, October 26, 1956, quoted in Reeves, *Freedom and the Foundation*, p. 247.

7. Kelly, *Court of Reason*, p. 129.

8. Quoted in Reeves, *Freedom and the Foundation*, p. 263.

9. Ibid., p. 271.

10. *New York Times*, July 19, 1957.

11. Quoted in Kelly, *Court of Reason*, p. 162.

12. Reeves, *Freedom and the Foundation*, p. 275.

13. Quoted in ibid., 273.

14. Hutchins, letter to Adler, October 14, 1957. Quoted in Reeves, *Freedom and the Foundation*, p. 273.

15. Quoted in ibid., p. 275.

16. Hutchins, memorandum to the board of trustees, May 7, 1959, quoted in Kelly, *Court of Reason*, p. 169.

17. Quoted in ibid., p. 170.

CHAPTER 44   EL PARTHENON

1. Quoted in James Real, "Meanwhile, Back on Mount Olympus," *West*, October 5, 1969.
2. Kelly, *Court of Reason*, pp. 359, 361.

CHAPTER 45   THE ONLY SALOON IN TOWN

1. Quoted in Kelly, *Court of Reason*, pp. 348–49.
2. Quoted in ibid., p. 340–41.
3. Ibid., p. 367.
4. Quoted in ibid., p. 341.

CHAPTER 46   IS ANYBODY LISTENING? (2)

1. Quoted in Kelly, *Court of Reason*, p. 256.
2. John K. Jessup, "Search for Something More than a Community of Fear," *Life*, March 5, 1965, pp. 34–36.
3. Kelly, *Court of Reason*, pp. 282–83, 293, 297–99.
4. Ibid., p. 304.
5. Ibid., p. 203.
6. Ibid., p. 271.

CHAPTER 47   THE REFOUNDING FATHER

1. Quoted in Real, "Meanwhile, Back on Mount Olympus."
2. Kelly, *Court of Reason*, pp. 342–44, 350–52, 357.
3. Quoted in Real, "Meanwhile, Back on Mount Olympus."
4. Kelly, *Court of Reason*, pp. 361–62.
5. Hutchins, letter to Ferry, June 4, 1969.
6. Kelly, *Court of Reason*, pp. 363, 378, 445, 455.
7. Quoted in ibid., pp. 371–72.
8. Quoted in ibid., p. 373.
9. Quoted in ibid., p. 376.

CHAPTER 48   THE SINKING SHIP

1. Quoted in Kelly, *Court of Reason*, p. 493.
2. *New York Times*, June 8, 1974.
3. Ibid.
4. Joan Didion and John Gregory Dunne, "California Dreaming," *Saturday Evening Post*, October 21, 1967, p. 26.
5. Kelly, *Court of Reason*, pp. 490–91, 519.
6. Ibid., pp. 508–9.
7. Ibid., p. 558.

CHAPTER 49 A SHABBY PACT

1. Kelly, *Court of Reason*, pp. 602, 614.
2. Quoted in ibid., pp. 612–14.
3. Ibid., pp. 615–16.
4. Ibid., pp. 611–12.
5. From a transcript of Dr. Comfort's deposition, quoted in ibid., p. 628.
6. Quoted in Kelly, *Court of Reason*, p. 636–37.

CHAPTER 50 AS ON A DARKLING PLAIN

1. Hutchins, report for a meeting of the directors in Chicago, April 13, 1976, quoted in Kelly, *Court of Reason*, p. 634.
2. Hutchins, "Why We Need World Law," *World Issues*, December 1976 / January 1977, pp. 29–30; "The Intellectual Community," *Center Magazine*, January-February 1977, pp. 2–9.
3. Hutchins, "Why We Need World Law," p. 30.
4. Hutchins, "Intellectual Community," p. 3.
5. Ibid., pp. 8–9.

Index

Hutchins, Robert Maynard (*continued*)
350, 402; self-appraisal, 1, 20, 21,
23, 29–30, 31–32, 41–43, 44, 57,
77–78, 86, 173, 190, 191, 195,
199, 202, 273, 274, 276, 325,
354–56, 358–59, 361, 396–97,
398–99, 402, 478, 504; tempera-
ment, 139–40, 141, 178–81, 193,
195, 241, 406–7; tragic figure, xi,
452, 453, 454, 502, 506, 507, 508;
wit, xi, 7, 17, 40, 123, 128, 137,
140–41, 178, 179, 181, 182, 183,
185, 188, 199, 204, 205, 339, 361,
389, 390–91, 400; work habits,
49, 84, 85, 89, 253–54, 362, 365–
66, 367, 485, 491, 497; as writer,
182, 183–89
— public life: considered for U.S.
Court of Appeals, 59, 65; considered for U.S. Supreme Court,
222–23; declines Roosevelt's
offers, 94–95, 196; seeks Vice-
Presidential nomination, 209–13,
215, 222; speaks to nation on
issues of the day, 236–37, 269,
272, 277, 371, 375–76; as public
trustee of New York Stock Exchange, 196
— social and political views: on atomic energy, international control
of, 267–68, 272–73, 283, 285–
86, 372–73, 376–77; civil liberties, defense of, 410–13, 424–25,
429, 432, 433, 435, 436–37, 439
(*see also under* Administrator:
academic freedom, defense of); on
democracy, 5, 230–31, 328, 400,
410–11; on discrimination, racial/
religious/social, 227, 252–53, 275,
312–15, 379, 383–84; Germany,
postwar reconstruction of, 261–
63, 385; on hiring a Communist to
teach, xii–xiii, 19, 411–13, 438,
443, 445, 447, 448; military conscription in peace time, folly of,
387; national strength, conception
of, 400–401; non-interventionism,

pre-Pearl Harbor, 2, 113, 213,
217, 218, 221, 225–26, 230, 274;
on pacifism, 274–76; on the press,
responsibilities of, 255–57; "the
questions before us," 336, 385–86;
on Russia, relations with, 371–72,
373, 376, 386–87; on science and
technology, effects and limits of,
183, 272–73, 385, 403, 506; on
socialism, 335–36; social legislation and renewal of social order,
need for, 2, 135, 193–96, 252,
253, 261–62, 264, 328, 331, 335–
36; war and peace, xiii, 376–77,
401, 402; world community, 260–
64, 278, 280–81, 371, 372, 374,
382–83, 504
Hutchins, Vesta Sutton Orlick (second
wife), 366–67, 504
Hutchins, William Grosvenor
(brother), 15, 17
Hutchins, William James (father), 11,
13, 14, 25–28, 29, 35, 41, 86, 93,
206, 362, 365, 366, 367, 380, 397
Huxley, Aldous, 18, 496
Huxley, Thomas, 464

Ickes, Harold, 18, 164, 196, 209–10,
212–13, 217–18, 222, 223, 226
Ickes, Jane, 209, 227
Innes, Harold A., 279
Insull, Samuel, 21, 129, 132–33
Inozemtsev, N. N., 481
Institutes of Nuclear Studies (Uni-
versity of Chicago), 269, 270–71,
272–73
Internal Security Subcommittee, U.S.
Senate, 430

Jacobs, Paul, 359, 447
Jerger, Wilbur, 308
Jessup, Philip K., 218, 220
John XXIII (Pope), 481
Johnson, Lyndon, 481, 482
Jones, Howard Mumford, 160
Joyce, William, 298, 428, 469
Jung, Harry A., 157, 159